OBJECT-ORIENTED SOFTWARE DESIGN AND CONSTRUCTION WITH JAVA

Dennis Kafura

Department of Computer Science
Virginia Tech
Blacksburg, VA

An Alan R. Apt Book

Prentice Hall
Upper Saddle River, NJ 07458

Library of Congress Cataloging-in-Publication Data

Kafura, Dennis.

Object-Oriented Software Design and Construction with Java / Dennis Kafura

p. cm

ISBN 0-13-011264-x

1. Object-oriented programming (Computer Science) 2. Java (Computer program language) 3. Computer software--Development. I. Title

QA76.64. K35 2000

005.13'3--dc21 99-088967

Vice President and Editorial Director: *Marcia Horton*
Publisher: *Alan Apt*
Project Manager: *Ana Anias Terry*
Editorial assistant: *Toni Holm*
Executive managing editor: *Vince O'Brien*
Managing editor: *David A. George*
Vice President of production and manufacturing: *David W. Riccardi*
Editorial supervision/Page composition: *Scott Disanno*
Cover director: *Heather Scott*
Cover: *John Christiana*
Marketing manager: *Danny Hoyt*
Manufacturing buyer: *Pat Brown*

Printed in the United States of America

10 9 8 7 6 5 4 3 2 1

ISBN 0-13-011244-X

Prentice-Hall International (UK) Limited, *London*
Prentice-Hall of Australia Pty. Limited, *Sydney*
Prentice-Hall Canada, Inc., *Toronto*
Prentice-Hall Hispanoamericana, S.A., *Mexico*
Prentice-Hall of India Private Limited, *New Delhi*
Prentice-Hall of Japan, Inc., *Tokyo*
Prentice-Hall (Singapore) Pte., Ltd., *Singapore*
Editora Prentice-Hall do Brazil, Ltda., *Rio de Janeiro*

Audience

This book is intended for undergraduate students. It is assumed that the reader has had a single preceding programming course. Students at Virginia Tech have used drafts of this book in a first semester sophomore year course. In particular, only an understanding of basic data structures (e.g., linked lists, stacks) is needed, and that only in the second half of the course. A specific course on data structures is not required.

This book focuses on the object-oriented programming aspects of Java. It is assumed that the syntax of the basic programming constructs (decisions, iterations, etc.) are known, or at least learned independently of this book. Since Java borrows much of its syntax from the "C" language, a basic familiarity with these programming constructs in "C" is adequate. Only a basic familiarity with "C" is required; it is not necessary to be an expert in this language. A person competent in a statically typed procedural language other than "C" should be able to understand most of what is contained in the book. Doing the programming exercises, of course, requires at least a minimal proficiency with the basic programming constructs of Java.

The motivating examples and programming exercises do not assume familiarity with concepts or intuitions derived from experiences that would normally only occur during the junior or senior years of study. The problems are drawn from common graphical user interface (GUI) systems and from a model of a very simple ecological system. Anyone who has used a GUI-based document preparation systems, spreadsheet, drawing tool, or the like, has the necessary context for the user interface examples and problems. No special background is required for the ecological simulation.

Intent

The most important intent is to support a person's study of object-oriented programming in Java. While only the Java language is described, the object-oriented concepts on which Java is based are realized in numerous other object-oriented programming languages including C++, Smalltalk, and Eiffel. The initial chapter describes the broad concepts of object-oriented programming without specific reference to Java. The broader object-oriented context is also reflected by the use of terms from different languages and analysis methods. For example, the terms "member function," "method," "operation," and "action" are used interchangeably. While distinctions can be drawn between these terms, the distinctions are not real differences for beginning students of object-oriented programming.

An important secondary intent is to raise the student's level of programming competence by emphasizing:

reuse

The value of software reuse is conveyed by initial and pervasive reuse of software in the presentation, exercises, and projects. In fact, few exercise calls for the development of a program "from scratch." Almost all exercises use a provided set of classes and, later, an extensive class library from the Java distribution.

tools/techniques

The tools and techniques needed to develop systems are presented in addition to the language features. Knowing the language and writing the code is only half (sometimes much less than half) of what is required to build a real system. Developers must also cope with testing, debugging, and documenta-tion. While these are ideas are often covered in a senior-level software engineering course, the foundations for that more advanced study are established here.

GUI library

Through the exercises and projects students learn object-oriented techniques for building GUI-based systems. The techniques and, later, the Java Swing toolkit, are intended to become a part of the student's repertoire, being used in programming projects in subsequent courses. This knowledge can be easily transferred to other similar class libraries.

event-driven systems

Exposure is given to event-driven systems. Beginning programming courses typically deal with problems where the program being written is totally in control at run-time. However, in event-driven systems (like user interfaces, interactive applications, operating systems, command and control systems) the program is not in total control. Instead, the program reacts to (is driven by) external events. Seeing event-driven systems broadens the student's experience and perspective, and provides a source of intuitions useful in later courses on operating systems, computer architecture, networking, and similar courses that involve asynchronous events.

Pedagogy

Applets and On-Line Questions

http://www.prenhall.com/kafura

The web site that accompanies this text contain both interactive questions and Java applets. These additions enhance the quality of the conceptual material through:

animation

Applets provide a visual representation that is often better able to communicate a concept than a static figure, a series of static (before/after) figures, or simply a written description. This is particularly true for concepts that are inherently involved with change or action. The "picture" that a teacher has in their own head is better conveyed to a learner in this graphical and animated form.

interaction

Applets that have active elements (buttons, menus, etc.) allow the learner to gain experience with a concept in a way that allows the learner to have control of the experience. In particular, applets of this form are valuable in giving experience with constructive, programming concepts without having to be concerned with the syntax and other non-essential issues.

feedback

Simple multiple-choice in-line tests can allow the learner to gain a measure of their understanding and develop a sense of confidence. This means is more efficient and less loaded with psychological baggage than in-class quizzes or exams.

Beyond their ability to better convey certain concepts, the on-line questions and applets help to create an engaging learning environment.

The *jake* Environment

The software that accompanies the text contains a simple, visual programming environment named *jake*. The *jake* environment contains icons that provide a visual depiction of a set of classes that are used in examples and exercises in the text. Objects of these classes can be created either by direct manipulation of the icons or by programs using the library provided with *jake*. Associations formed between objects are represented by a line drawn between the corresponding icons. The *jake* environment is described in the text as are all of the classes with which it operates.

Mastery Exercises

Almost all sections are immediately followed by a set of exercises. Each exercise is designed to be completed in a short amount of time. In an ideal case, at least some of the exercises for a section should be done before proceeding to the next section. More realistically, students and instructors are encouraged to arrange deadlines that support the practice of completing as many as possible of the exercises in each set in a timely manner. The exercises are designed to instill mastery through practice. In this sense the exercises are primarily an aid to learning and not a tool for evaluation and grading. The exercises are important. Each exercise is focused on a single, new idea. A student who understands the concepts in a section, pays little penalty in time to complete exercises for that section. A student who has some misunderstandings (or who simply learns best by working with the concept in practice) benefits from the task of working through the exercises.

Continuing Theme Examples

Two recurring examples are used throughout the book that focus on the themes of graphical user interfaces and ecological simulation. The continuity of the examples allows a more complete solution to a problem to be developed as new concepts and techniques are introduced. The examples are also more complete, substantial, and coherent a collection of unrelated trivial examples. The examples and problems are designed to be engaging and to strengthen the relationship between the "objects" in the program and their "real world" counterparts. For example, the first programming exercises involve the display of a window on the screen or the simulation of a simple predator in a simulated ecology. Subsequent early exercises involve moving and resizing the window and introducing prey to form a predator—prey model. In approximately three weeks the student is building simple systems that involve buttons, timed events, and text displays in the graphical user interface domain, and more complicated scenarios in the ecological simulation. Problems of this kind are more engaging of a student's interest than the more common objects like Date, String, Address, etc. In addition, the ability to see visually how the window moves on the screen in direct response to applying the moveTo method in the class from which the window was created, strengthens the notion that an objects models directly its real world counterpart.

UML and Swing

As new object-oriented structures are introduced, the corresponding representation in the Unified Modeling Language (UML) is given. Since UML is a large and complex language, only its basic features are described and used in the text. Included are UML diagrams for classes, objects, associations, aggregations, interfaces, sequences, state transitions, and inheritance. This set forms the core of UML and is sufficient to allow students to describe reasonably complex systems.

The text includes an introduction to the latest Swing library that was introduced with the Java 1.2 release. Since Swing is a rich and complex library, only the basics of the Swing components are presented. The presented components are sufficient to construct a wide range of interesting user interfaces. The presentation lays the foundation for further study of Swing in book devoted exclusively to this purpose. A pair of simple applications, one for a simple graphical drawing tool and one for a simple text editing tool, are used to illustrate the basic user interface control provided in Swing. Extensions of these two tools are used as the source of numerous programming exercises.

Unique Organization

The material is organized in two related ways: by concept and by role. The conceptual organization as given in the first chapter is based on four concepts that underlay object-oriented programming languages: abstraction, separation, composition and generalization. The first chapter allows all of these concepts to be understood at a very high level before proceeding with any of the detailed material in Java. However, it is also possible (and usually preferable) to interleave a study of the concepts with a study of how they concepts are realized in Java and how they are put to use to build systems.

The second organization is a progression of the various roles assumed by a programmer in writing software. The roles are:

user of a single existing class

In this presentation the single class represents a graphical user interface window or the predator. Many important concepts can be presented naturally within this simple and intuitive context (e.g., overloaded methods, constructors, scope, static vs. dynamic objects). Note that from the first sentence the importance of classes and objects is stressed.

user of multiple existing classes

Composition is seen as a way to build systems by combining together interacting objects. At this point the student builds several small time-driven systems with button and text interactions or simulations involving predators and prey.

implementor of a single class

It is only at this stage that the internal structure of a class is revealed. It is emphasized here that the role of an implementor involves more than coding, it also involves design, documentation, debugging, and incremental testing and development.

implementor of multiple related classes

The chapter about this role introduces inheritance as a mechanism for sharing implementation and/or interfaces among a set of related classes.

This organization allows the language features to be presented in rational and coherent manner. Each chapter focuses on what the student needs to learn in order to fulfill that role.

Acknowledgments

A number of people have contributed to the development of this book. Much of the work in writing the on-line test questions and answers was done by Mr. Michael Gussett. Several graduate teaching assistants contributed to the book through their interactions during the teaching of the class for which this book was targeted. Two graduate students helped with the initial development of the applets, Sadanand Sahasrabudhe and Srinivas Gaddam, that were later extended by Ketan Shah. Philip Isenhour made a major contribution to converting the code examples to be compatible with Java 2. Tom Plunkett has used the on-line development version of this book in teaching several courses at Virginia Tech's Northern Virginia Center. THANKS TO ALL!

Many individuals in the Prentice-Hall organization were also of great help and encouragement including Alan Apt, Ana Terry, Scott Disanno, and Toni Holm.

Software

The complete code for the examples used in the book is available. In addition, a simplified execution environment, named *jake*, is provided for early programming of graphical user interface exercises. This environment allows simple but interesting interfaces to be constructed without having to be concerned with all of the underlying and distracting detail. The environment also provides for graphical representation of object created by the program and direct manipulation of these objects.

Comments

Comments, helpful suggestions and criticism are welcomed. Send email to kafura@cs.vt.edu or by postal mail at:

Department of Computer Science
Virginia Tech
Blacksburg, VA 24061

Dennis Kafura
Blacksburg, Virginia

CONTENTS

CHAPTER 1

Basic Concepts

1.1 Introduction

1.1.1 Object-Oriented Strategies

Object-oriented programming embodies in software structures a number of powerful design strategies that are based on practical and proven software engineering techniques. By incorporating support for these strategies in software structures, object-oriented programming enables the manageable construction of more complex systems of software than was previously possible. The nature of these software structures has been shaped by decades of software engineering experience. The basic design strategies that are embodied in object-oriented programming are presented in Table 1.1. The design strategies evolved as techniques for dealing with complex natural and man-made systems. Because these strategies are so fundamental, they are encountered in other contexts and in other programming language forms. What is stressed here is the relationship of these strategies to the design and construction of object-oriented software. These strategies are widely supported by existing object-oriented languages, though different languages may present them indifferent ways and some languages may support other variations of each one. For example, some object-oriented languages have additional ways of supporting generalization.

The design strategies in object-oriented programming are effective for constructing software models of entities in the problem domain. In fact, some have argued that software design is largely about constructing a software model of the "real world" where each "real" entity is represented in the program by a corresponding software object; the software object simulates the actions and conditions of its real-world counterpart. The "programming as modeling" philosophy is most evident in three-dimensional virtual environments where the visual and auditory characteristics of the real world are simulated within the virtual world.

Table 1.1 Design Strategies Embodied in Object-Oriented Programming

Design strategy	Definition
Abstraction	Simplifying to its essentials the description of a real-world entity
Separation	Treating independently "what" an entity does from "how" it does it
Composition	Building complex "whole" systems by assembling simpler "parts" in one of two basic ways: •association •aggregation
Generalization	Identifying common elements among different entities in one of four ways: •hierarchy •genericity •polymorphism •patterns

1.1.2 Design Strategy Definition

A Plan of Study

The study of a body of material depends on the learning style of the individual and is often iterative in progression. Some people learn more efficiently by understanding the overall concepts first before proceeding to more concrete details. Other people learn more efficiently by intermixing abstract concepts and concrete examples. Regardless of the preference for a breadth-first approach or a depth-first approach, there are necessarily some ideas that must be learned before others because the ideas build on each other and are not independent. In both styles, a single reading is usually not sufficient. Backtracking and revisiting earlier concepts often enriches understanding and allows the formation of deeper insights.

The overall structure of the material presented here is shown in Figure 1.1. The design strategies are shown on the left side of the figure. It is possible to read about these design strategies top-to-bottom and obtain a broad overview of object-oriented concepts and ideas. At any point it is also possible to follow one of the arrows to the right. Following an arrow in this direction leads to a more concrete presentation of the concept and its eventual description in Java. There are six major milestones shown in the overall guide. Each milestone falls into one of three roles that are shown at the bottom of the figure. Each milestone is associated with a major design concept and represents a significant step forward in the practical skill of developing object-oriented software systems. The milestones, however, are ordered. It is not possible to proceed to a later one (one lower and

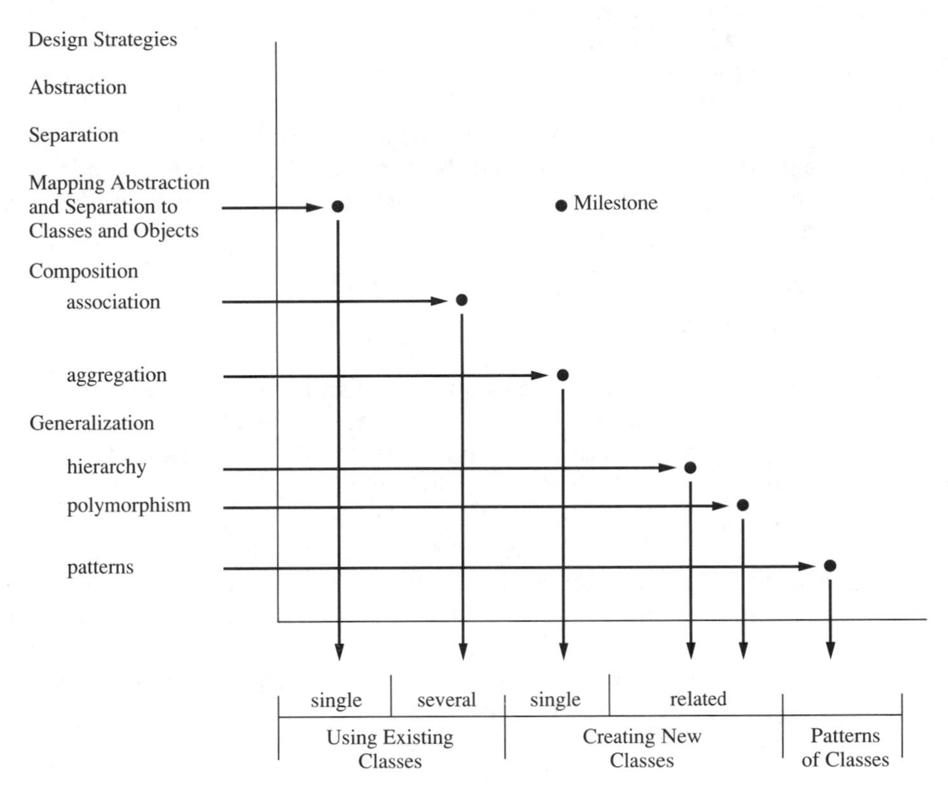

Figure 1.1 Guide to Material

more to the right in the figure) before all of the earlier ones (ones higher and to the left) have been completed.

The milestones form a progression of roles as shown along the bottom of Figure 1.1. The simplest role is that of a programmer using a single class or several classes that has already been developed. Simple, but interesting systems will be constructed in this first role. Initially, a single class will be used to explore and master basic issues of creating and manipulating objects. Several more classes are then added, allowing the construction of simple systems of interacting objects. Learning how to use existing classes to create and manipulate objects is the first step in learning about object-oriented programming. This first role is important, not only because it establishes the foundation for the basic concepts of object-oriented programming, but also because this is the preferred role in developing real systems. As a user, you are able to benefit from the hard work already done by the designers and implementors of existing classes. The ability to use existing classes is one of the major benefits of software reuse in general and object-oriented programming in particular. The second role is that of a developer creating one or more new classes. Initially, each class captures an independent abstraction. More difficult, but more powerful, is the development of collections of related classes using one of the forms of generalization. These first two roles will be extensively used. The third role involves pattern-general organizations of classes and objects that have proven useful in solving commonly occurring design problems. This role will be explored, but only minimally. Mastery of the use of patterns requires considerable experience in building systems in one or more application domains.

1.1.3 Examples

Throughout the book, design concepts and programming constructs are illustrated by continuing examples from two independent problem domains. One set of examples is based on graphical user interfaces (GUIs). The examples in this domain illustrate how object-oriented features of Java and the design strategies are applied in using a set of predefined GUI classes to build increasingly more complicated interfaces for small applications. The second set of examples is based on simulating a simple ecological environment. These examples use simple text output. Two independent sets of examples are used to give different examples of each concept and to allow a more varied choice of programming exercises. The examples continue from section to section and chapter to chapter so that their progressive development can be seen as more design strategies and Java features are presented. In some cases, an earlier design is revised to take advantage of a newly introduced strategy or feature.

1.1.4 The UML Design Notation

The ability to *design* an object-oriented system is simultaneously the most important skill for a software developer to possess and the most elusive to learn. Design skill is important because a system's design determines to what extent the system realizes most of the crucial software-engineering principles such as separation, encapsulation, and information hiding and key design goals such as abstraction and generalization. The skill of good object-oriented design is elusive because, like all design activities, it cannot be reduced to a mechanical process. Good designers bring to their task both native ability that emerges as insight and inspiration and experience gained through practicing the art of object-oriented design on numerous software projects. Although insight, inspiration, and experience cannot be articulated, the heuristic rules and guidelines that characterize a good design may be elicited for study.

Designing an object-oriented system is aided by a semi-formal, high-level, graphical representation of classes, objects, and their relationships. The graphical nature of the representation allows easy visualization of the structural aspects of the system. The design is represented at a high level in that only the essential elements of the design are present independent of lexical details or the specifics of the implementation. Design representations are useful in that they externalize a designer's ideas so that they maybe subject to analysis, evaluation, and comparison with alternative designs, act as a blueprint for those implementing the design, and document the final design for those performing later maintenance and extension.

There are three specific uses for a high-level, graphical design representation. First, the representation provides a language that quickly describes an idea being considered by a single designer or a design team. Because it can be quickly drawn and easily modified, the representation aids in thinking about the design and encourages exploring design alternatives. Second, the representation is a means of documenting a design. The design document serves as a guideline for the implementor and, later, for those who will modify and maintain the system. The graphical and high-level nature of the representation are useful as a documentation device because only the essential structural elements are described, more detailed information is left to the code and other documentation. Third, once represented, the design may itself be the object of reuse. Commonly occurring design solutions may be identified, documented, and collected for use in situations other than the ones in which they were initially encountered. Students of object-oriented design should study the artifacts (designs) produced by good designers in much the same way that art students study the great masters, architecture students study famous structures and buildings, and writing students study the classics in literature. For students of object-oriented design, the notion of a design pattern has recently emerged and allows great (or at least commonly needed and fundamental) designs to be studied.

The Unified Modeling Language (UML) is used throughout the book to visually depict object-oriented designs. UML is a well-known graphical notation for representing the components and organization of an object-oriented system. As new Java language features are introduced throughout the book, the corresponding UML notation is presented. UML is a rich visual language, more comprehensive than is required for the purposes of this book. Thus, only a core subset of the UML notation is described here. There are many other books that describe the full UML notation.

1.1.5 General Organization

The material in this book is generally divided into two parts. The first part of the book, encompassing Chapters 1 to 6, focuses on object-oriented programming concepts and Java as an object-oriented programming language. These chapters are organized as shown in Figure 1.1. Chapter 1 briefly describes the design strategies that are listed on the vertical axis in Figure 1.1 and summarized in Table 1.1. Chapters 2 through 6 follow the progressive steps shown on the horizontal axis in Figure 1.1. Chapter 2 uses a single existing class to introduce the basic concepts of classes and objects. Several existing classes are used in Chapter 3 to show how small systems of objects can be built. Implementing a new class is described in Chapter 4. Chapter 5 presents concepts and techniques for designing, debugging, and documenting new classes. Chapter 6 explains how related classes can be organized in a way that allows them to be more easily understood, implemented, and extended using object-oriented inheritance. Design strategies for class hierarchies created by inheritance and design patterns are also described in Chapter 6.

The second part of the book contains material about advanced features of Java that are not inherently part of its object orientation but are contained in libraries that accompany the Java distribution. These topics are included because they are fundamental to working in the Java environment for anything beyond simple demonstration examples. In fact, when people talk about "Java" they often are referring to the utilities provided by the libraries and not by the basic language itself. The tools, features, and libraries presented in this book are organized as follows:

- The User Interfaces (Chapter 7): The classes, interfaces, and conventions for building graphical user interfaces Java using the new library introduced with the Java 1.2 release.
- I/O (Chapter 8): The facilities defined in Java for transferring data to standard devices and files. These facilities allow for the handling of data in a text format, binary format, and object format.
- Threads (Chapter 9): The mechanisms in Java for concurrent programming. This material shows how to create and synchronize independent, asynchronous activities.

Because Java and its libraries are something of a moving target, the material presented here conforms to the Java 2 release. Every effort has been made to use those features of Java and the libraries that are more central and less subject to change.

Lets get to it!

Exercises

1. Search the World Wide Web to find references to different object-oriented languages. How many can you find? Can you recognize in their descriptions any of the basic strategies identified above?
2. Search the World Wide Web to find locations of other courses on object-oriented programming. What topics do these courses have in common? Save these links for reference during your study.

3. Look at the Free On-LineDictionary of Computing. Find the definitions of the terms:
   Abstraction
   Aggregation
   Encapsulation
   Hierarchy
   Genericity
   Polymorphism
   Save this link for future reference.

4. Look at the Java Virtual Library. Browse this library for ten minutes and report on three interesting things that you found. Keep this link for reference.

1.2 Abstraction

Abstraction is a design technique that focuses on the essential aspects of an entity and ignores or conceals less important or non-essential aspects. Abstraction is an important tool for simplifying a complex phenomenon to a level where analysis, experimentation, or understanding can take place. For example, in attempting to understand the mechanics of the solar system, early mathematicians and astronomers applied abstraction to a "planet," treating the planet as a body all of whose mass is concentrated at a single point. Such an abstraction ignores a wealth of details about each planet—its actual diameter, its atmospheric content, its average temperature, and so on. However, these details are not relevant to understanding and modeling the basic orbital mechanics of the solar system.

In software, abstraction is concerned with both the "attributes" and "behavior" of entities. Attributes refer to the properties or characteristics associated with an entity whereas behavior refers to the set of actions that the entity can perform. In a software object, attributes are represented by data that is associated with the object. For a sales tracking system, relevant attributes of a salesperson (see Figure 1.2) might be: name, number of vehicles sold, value of vehicles sold, list of customers, commission rate, total commissions. An action of the object corresponds to an operation or function associated with the object. Actions for a "salesperson" might include "sellCar," "reportIncome," and "increaseCommisionRate."

Abstraction is vital to creating tractable software objects because the real-world objects are far too complex to be captured in complete detail. Consider the simple "salesperson" object referred to above. A real "salesperson" has an identity, a family genealogy, a medical history, a genetic profile, a credit record, a set

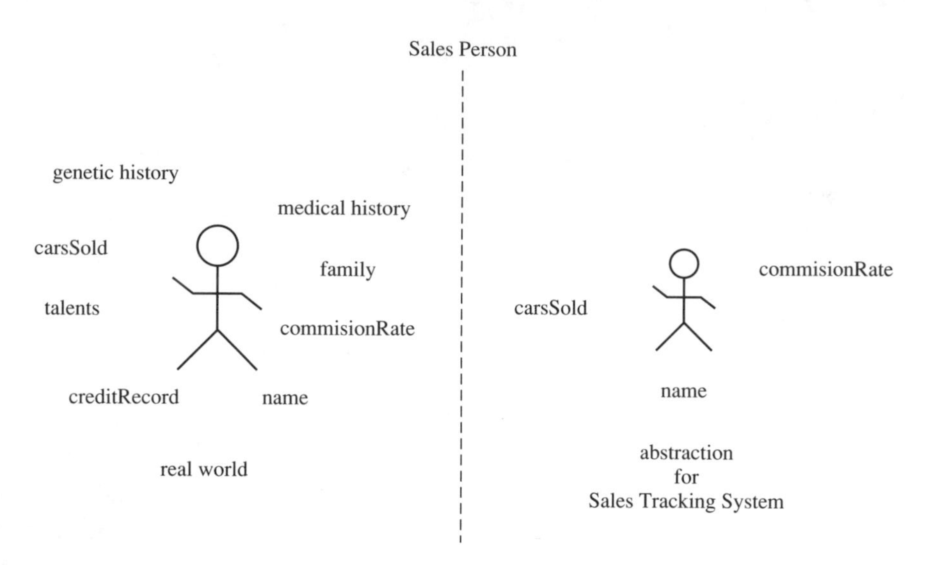

Figure 1.2 Abstraction of a SalesPerson

of talents, and many more. Similarly there is a rich set of actions of which the salesperson is capable (sellCar, answerPhone, buyHouse, haveChild, getSick, increaseCreditLimit, payBills, etc.). Trying to capture even a small part of this enormous detail in a software object is pointless. It is important to capture only those aspects of a "salesperson" that are relevant to the development of a particular system (e.g., the sales tracking system).

The objects in an object-oriented system are often intended to correspond directly to entities in the "real world." Objects such as "salesperson" and "automobiles" that might occur in an automobile dealership tracking system correspond to the actual people on the staff of the dealership and the actual cars owned and sold by the dealership. The correspondence between the software objects and the real-world entity that they represent is often so direct and real that computer-based theft or fraud often involves tampering with the software objects that are trusted by others to correspond to real-world artifacts. This sense of correspondence is also expressed as the "program" being a "simulation" or "model" of the real-world, changes in one being reflected in the other. A "good" program is one that models or simulates accurately what is happening in the real-world.

Figure 1.2 can be manipulated to illustrate the concept of abstraction for a SalesPerson. The blue portion of the figure represents the real-world person, while the yellow portion represents an abstraction, acting as a filter that makes visible only those aspects of the real-world entity that are relevant to the abstraction being formed. Move the yellow filter around in the figure to see what attributes of the real-world entity are relevant.

The examples above motivate the following definition of abstraction:

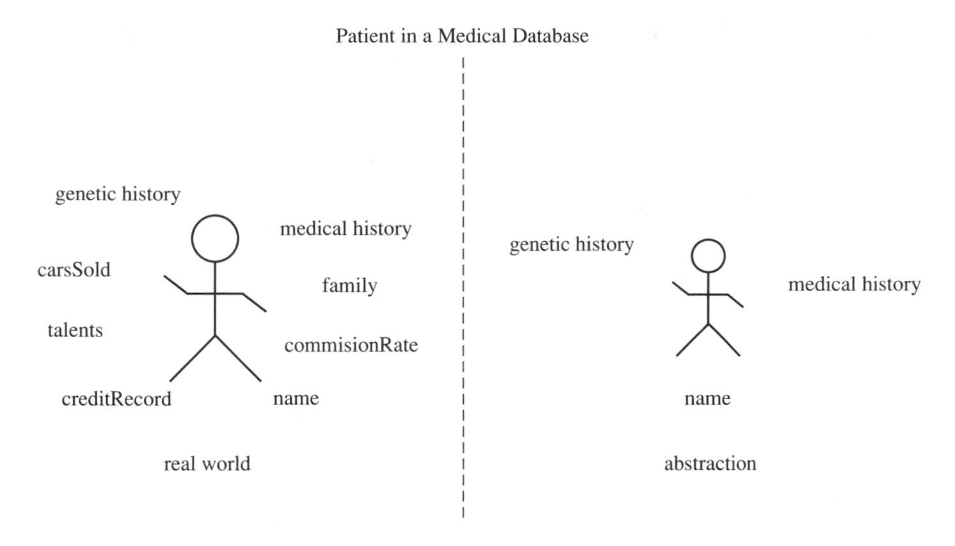

Figure 1.3 Abstraction of a Patient in a Medical Database

abstraction: a named collection of attributes and behavior relevant to modeling a given entity for some particular purpose.

A single entity may have many valid abstractions. While the genetic profile of a salesperson is not relevant to a sales tracking system, it may be relevant to a medical database system. This alternative abstraction is shown in Figure 1.3. Correspondingly, the medical database system developer would not consider the number of vehicles sold to be a relevant aspect. The name of the abstraction is useful to distinguish among different abstractions for the same entity and among abstractions for different entities. A critical part of object-oriented design is deciding which attributes and behavior to include in a given abstraction.

Figure 1.3 can be manipulated to illustrate the concept of abstraction for a patient in a medical database. The blue portion of the figure represents the "real world" person. The yellow portion of the figure represents an abstraction as a filter that makes visible only those aspects of the real-world entity that are relevant to the abstraction of this person from the point of view of a medical database application. Move the yellow filter around in the figure to see what attributes of the real-world entity are relevant.

1.2.1 Properties of a Good Abstraction

Although there may be many abstractions of the same entity, each abstraction should have certain properties that distinguish it as a "good" abstraction. These desirable properties are:

Well named: The nature of an abstraction is conveyed by the name given to that abstraction. An abstraction is well named if the meanings, intuitions, impressions, and expectations implied by a name accurately reflect the nature of the abstraction. Whether a name is meaningful depends on the community of people who will use the abstraction. In some cases the name might be a technical term in an application domain that communicates an abstraction perfectly to the group of people in that application area but may mean little to a non-technical group. In other cases, abstractions for widely known entities (e.g., "Automobile" or "Zip Code") may have names recognizable to a general population. Ambiguous names (i.e., those with multiple interpretations possible) should be avoided.

Coherent: The abstraction should contain a related set of attributes and behavior that make sense from the viewpoint of the modeler. The attributes and behavior have to be what is needed and expected in a given setting. For example, defining a Sales Person abstraction that consists of the attributes "commisionRate," "family," and "talents" is not a coherent abstraction because it does not make sense from the viewpoint of a designer building a sales tracking system.

Accurate: The abstraction should contain only attributes or behavior that are a part of the entity being modeled. The abstraction should not be endowed with "powers and abilities" far beyond those of the actual entity. Although this principle is usually observed, there are special circumstances where this principle may be relaxed. For example, in a virtual environment it may be possible to "walk through the walls" in a scene. Such behavior clearly violates the behavior of real walls.

Minimal: The abstraction should not contain extraneous attributes or behavior for the purpose for which it is defined. For example, adding a mail Addressor telephoneNumber attribute to the SalesPerson abstraction would be extraneous if these additional attributes were not required for the sales tracking system.

Complete: The abstraction should contain all of the attributes and behavior necessary to manipulate the abstraction for its intended purpose. Assuming that the sales tracking system needed to know the commisionRate for each SalesPerson, an abstraction that did not include this attribute would not be complete.

These properties are clearly subjective and qualitative in nature. This fact implies that the ability to form good abstractions requires good judgment and the benefit of practice and experience.

Exercises

1. Define plausible abstractions for an "automobile" from the point of view of:
   - the manufacturer,
   - the owner,
   - the governmental agency that licenses vehicles.
2. Define plausible abstraction for a "book" from the point of view of:
   - a reader,
   - a publisher,
   - a bookstore.
3. Define plausible abstractions for an "airplane flight" from the point of view of:
   - a travel agent,
   - an airline company,
   - a passenger,
   - an airport.
4. Evaluate your "automobile" abstractions against the four properties of good abstractions.
5. Evaluate your "book" abstractions against the four properties of good abstractions.
6. Evaluate your "airplane flight" abstractions against the four properties of good abstractions.
7. Identify a common, real-world entity and at least three different points of view that would lead to different abstractions of that entity.

1.3 Separation

Separation refers to distinguishing between a system's observable behavior and the means or mechanism by which this behavior is achieved. This is often described as separating "what" is to be done from "how" it is to be done. These and other pair of terms that reflect the idea of separation are shown in Table 1.2. Separation is also often expressed as drawing a boundary between the external,

Table 1–2 Pairs of Terms Reflecting Separation

What	How
Goals	Plans
Policy	Mechanism
Product	Process
Interface, specification, requirement	Implementation
Ends	Means

visible aspects of a system, the "what" part of the system, and the system's internal, hidden machinery, the "how" part of the system. Drawing such a boundary is useful both to those developing the system as well as to those using the system.

Separation is a powerful aid for developing complex systems because it allows the development activities to be organized into two distinct levels, often characterized as the design level and the implementation level. At the design level, the system's behavior can be stated, discussed, evaluated, communicated, and related to the behavior of other systems without concern for how the behavior is achieved. The activities at this level are simplified because the details of achieving the behavior are set aside. The implementation level focuses on how to achieve desired behavior. Because the system's behavior is fixed by the design, the activities at this level are concentrated on specifying the operational details and evaluating trade-offs among different ways of manifesting the behavior. The two levels have different measures of quality. The design level is evaluated in terms of the utility of the system and how well it matches the user's requirements, whereas the implementation level is evaluated in terms such as efficiency and maintainability.

Separation helps a user work with a complex system because the system's effects are often simpler to understand than the means needed to achieve the effect. For example, it is easier to know that "this button justifies the highlighted text in a document" than it is to understand the algorithmic details of how the words in the text are rearranged to align the margins so that distracting vertical runs of white space are avoided. Programmers are also familiar with this aspect of separation, as it is present in all manuals and documentation. For example, a typical description of the command `read(f, buffer, nbytes)` is that the command transfers `nbytes` of data from file `f` to the specified `buffer`. The mechanism required to achieve this effect involves the disk hardware, software device drivers, the file system, the disk block management code, and run-time I/O library routines, none of which need be mentioned in the description of the `read` command.

Separation is reflected in the designed structure and operational use of many machines and organizations that we encounter in day-to-day life. Consider, for example, a television. From a development perspective it is useful to separate the television's external controls from its internal electronic components. The external controls are related to the television's effect: when should it produce its images, from what channel is the signal drawn, at what volume is the sound generated, and so on. There are numerous issues about these external controls such as where they are located, whether they are labeled by icons or words, are they operated by remote control, and so on. The internal electronic components react to the control and produce the required visual effect. The engineers who implement the internal components face many decisions on the arrangement of the circuits, the power supply required, the heat generated, and so on. From a user's perspective, only the television's external controls need to be understood. The separation conceals the internal electronic machinery from the user and allows the user to operate the television without concern for how the electronic components function. The television's outer shell or box is a physical manifestation of the separation.

A well-established use of separation in software artifacts is the separation of an interface from an implementation of that interface. In the context of software system, an interface is defined as:

software interface: the external, visible aspects of a software artifact by which the behavior of the artifact is elicited.

This definition captures the notion that the interface is the means by which the software artifact is manipulated from the outside. For a programmer using the artifact as part of a system, the artifact's software interface is the external aspect that must be understood to use the software artifact. The terms "software interface" and "interface" will often be used interchangeably. There is some possibility of confusion, however, because Java has a specific programming construct that also uses the term "interface," which will be seen later. Which meaning is intended should be clear from context; more specific terms will be used when necessary for clarity.

Behind the visible interface is the implementation. The implementation carries out the work promised by the interface. Specifically for a software context, the implementation is defined as:

software implementation: the programmed mechanism that realizes the behavior implied by an interface.

The implementation is viewed as the hidden, internal aspect of the software that is important only to the implementor. An implementation is said to *satisfy* an interface if the behavior specified by the interface is provided by the implementation.

The concept of separation as it is used in a software context can then be defined as:

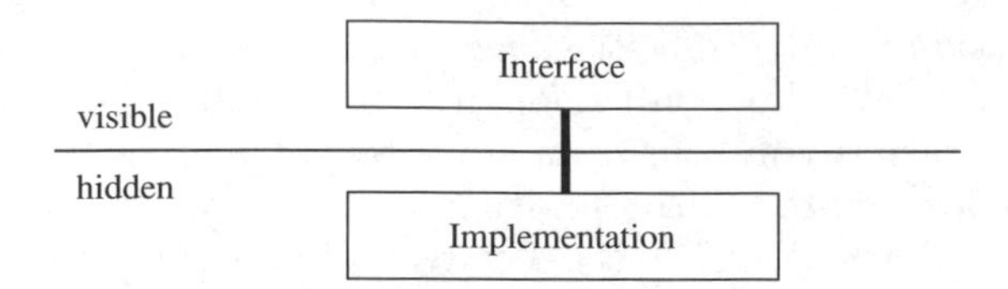

Figure 1.4 Separation of Interface from Implementation

separation: in software systems, the independent specification of a software interface and one or more software implementations of that interface.

The interface-implementation separation is suggested by Figure 1.4. Separation is often viewed as establishing a "contract" between a software artifact and the code using that artifact. The artifact's interface represents the terms of the contract. The contract is a guarantee to the using code that the implementation will provide the promised behavior. The contract is also a guarantee to the implementation that it is required to provide only that behavior advertised in the interface. The contract may also be viewed from the perspective of the people developing the system. In this case, the contract is an understanding between the developer programming the implementation of a software artifact and the developer using the artifact through its interface. Problems in developing software systems often arise because the contract between the developers is not understood the same way by both parties or because the original contract was later found to be insufficient.

Separation is evident in software systems in several different ways. Manual pages for libraries describe only the interface properties of individual operations without describing how any of the operations are implemented. A complex layer of software (e.g., a windowing system or a networking environment) may be described by an Application Programmer's Interface (API). The API defines what data structures and facilities are available for use by the application programmer without defining how the structure and facilities are implemented. Another example is software standard. A standard is a commonly accepted definition of a service (e.g., the TCP/IP communication protocols standard). Such a standard defines the external behavior that a compliant system must exhibit but leaves the implementor free to decide how to implement that behavior.

Separation provides flexibility in developing a system because different implementations may satisfy the same interface. The several implementations may differ in time or space efficiency, purchase price, maintainability, documentation quality, reliability, or other non-functional characteristics. If separation is fully observed, one implementation for a given interface can be replaced by a different implementation of that interface without altering the overall operation of the larger system of which it is a part. The ability to associate different imple-

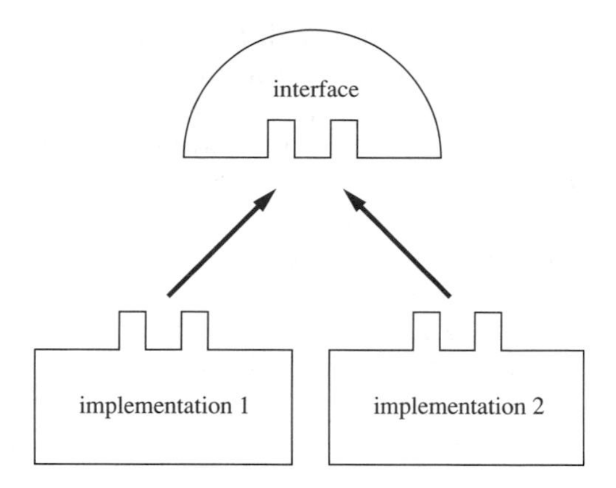

Figure 1.5 Interchangeability of Implementations

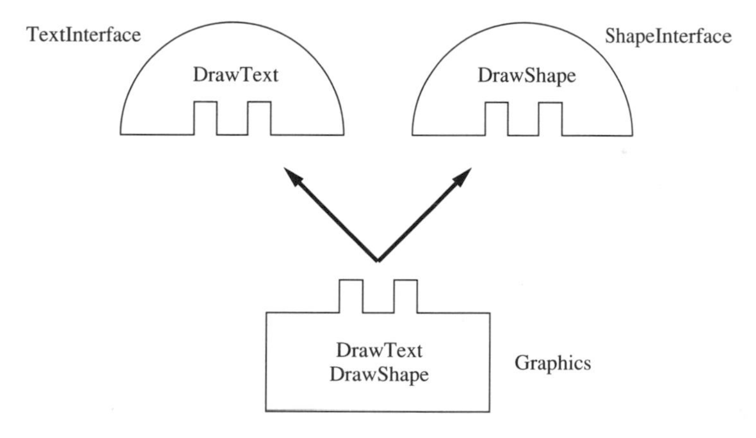

Figure 1.6 Interchangeability of Implementations

mentations with the same interface is shown in Figure 1.5. Two different interchangeable implementations of the same interface are said to be "plug compatible"; unplug the current implementation and plug in its replacement. Certainly many non-software products take advantage of this interchangeability: tires on a car, speakers on a stereo, and monitors on a computer.

Through separation a single implementation can satisfy simultaneously several interfaces. In such a case, the implementation contains the union of all of the methods required by each of the interfaces (and possibly additional methods that are not used by any of the current interfaces). Figure 1.6 shows a single implementation, named Graphics, that contains two methods, DrawText and DrawShape. Two interfaces are also shown: TextInterface that defines only a DrawText method, and ShapeInterface that defines only a DrawShape method. Clearly the Graphics implementation satisfies both of these interfaces. As shown in the figure, each interface provides a different view of the implementation. Each view may expose only a subset of the implementation's full capabilities. Such a restricted view is useful in isolating those capabilities that are required in a given situation or by a specific part of the system. Isolating the most limited set of capabilities needed makes it possible to replace a more capable implementation (e.g., Graphics) that may contains unneeded operations (e.g., DrawShape) by a smaller implementation that contains only those methods defined in the more limited interface. For example, suppose that a part of the system needed only the methods defined in the TextInterface. This need could be satisfied by a more limited class that implements only the TextInterface and not the ShapeInterface. Because it is more specific, the smaller implementation may be more efficient in execution time, need less memory, be easier to maintain, or be more portable across different platforms.

Figure 1.6 illustrates the idea of one implementation (Graphics) being able to satisfy two different implementations.

Exercises

1. Explain how separation is used in the following commonly occurring, real-world entities:
    - A telephone
    - A package or postal delivery service
    - A stereo or television
    - A restaurant
2. Explain how separation is used in the following software entities:
    - An operating system
    - A web browser
    - A text editor
    - A compiler
3. Look at the documentation for your computer system and identify three instances of separation. For each instance, hypothesize several aspects of the implementation that are hidden by the separation.

1.4 Classes, Objects, and Abstract

Software development centers on rendering abstractions in a form that allows them to be manipulated within a software system. An abstraction was described

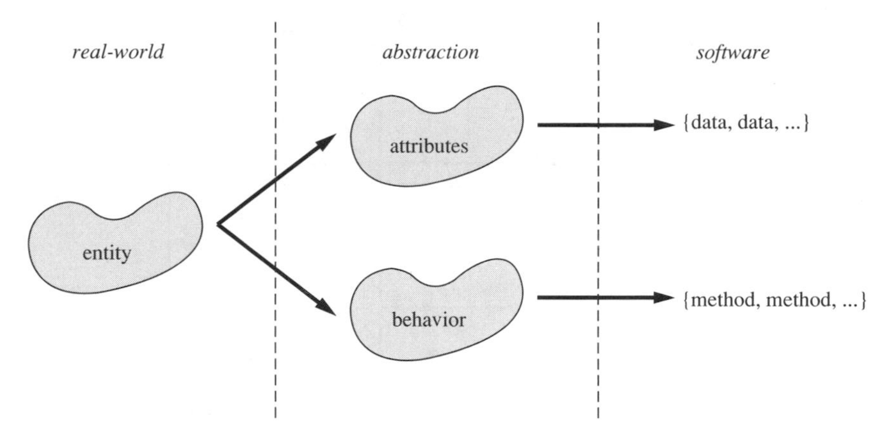

Figure 1.7 Mapping Abstractions to Software

as a collection of attributes and a behavior. As shown in Figure 1.7, the attributes of an abstraction are mapped to a set of data (variables, array, lists, complex data structures, etc.) and the behavior of an abstraction is mapped to a set of methods (also known as operations, functions, actions). The rendering of abstractions in software has always been the implicit goal of programming, though it may have been overshadowed by more mechanical considerations. What object-oriented programming brings to the task of capturing abstractions in software are more sophisticated structures, namely ***classes, objects***, and ***interfaces***, for representing abstractions. These new software structures permit abstractions to be represented more easily, more directly, and more explicitly.

1.4.1 Class

A class defines the specific structure of a given abstraction (what data it has, what methods it has, how its methods are implemented). The class has a unique name that conveys the meaning of the abstraction that it represents. The term "class" is used to suggest that it represents all the members of a given group (or class). For example, a SalesPerson class might represent all individuals in the group of "people selling cars at an automobile dealership." An object represents a specific member of this group.

Separation of interface from implementation is used to divide the class into two parts, commonly referred to as the *private* part and the *public* part. The data and methods are mapped to these two parts of the class as shown in Figure 1.8. This separation of private data and code from the visible names of methods is motivated by long years of software engineering experience showing that it is important to protect the data against unexpected, unwanted, and erroneous access from other parts of the software that is manipulating the object. The separation also serves to hide the algorithm used to perform a method.

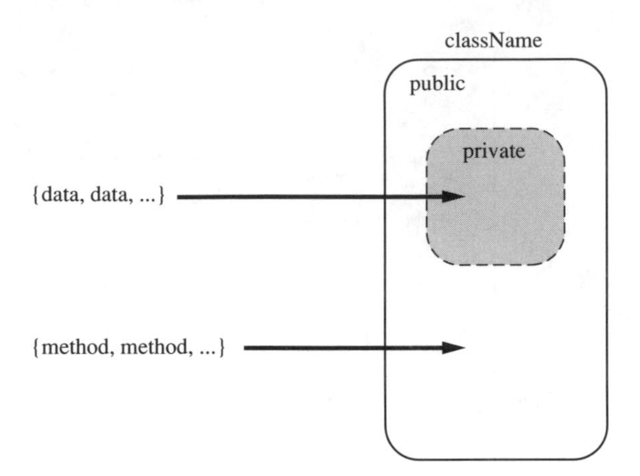

Figure 1.8 The General Structure of a Class

The relationship of a class to abstraction and separation is reflected in the following definition:

class: a named software representation for an abstraction that separates the implementation of the representation from the interface of the representation.

The obvious similarity in the definitions of the terms "abstraction" and "class" underscores how explicitly and directly a class is meant to model a real-world entity.

It is interesting to note that there are object-oriented languages that do not have classes but use other techniques to achieve a similar effect. Languages, like Java, C++, and others that have a class concept are referred to as "class-based languages."

1.4.2 Object

Although a class defines the structure of an entire collection of similar things (e.g., anyone who is a SalesPerson), an object represents a specific instance of that class (e.g., the sales person whose name is "John Smith," who has a commission rate of 15 percent, etc.). The class definition allows the common structure to be defined once and reused when creating new objects that need the structure defined by the class. An object's properties are exactly those described by the class from which it was created.

The key aspects of the object structure, as shown in Figure 1.9, mirrors the structure of the class from which it was created. As with a class, the two main parts of an object are its:

implementation: the data and the implementation of the methods that are hidden inside of the object, and

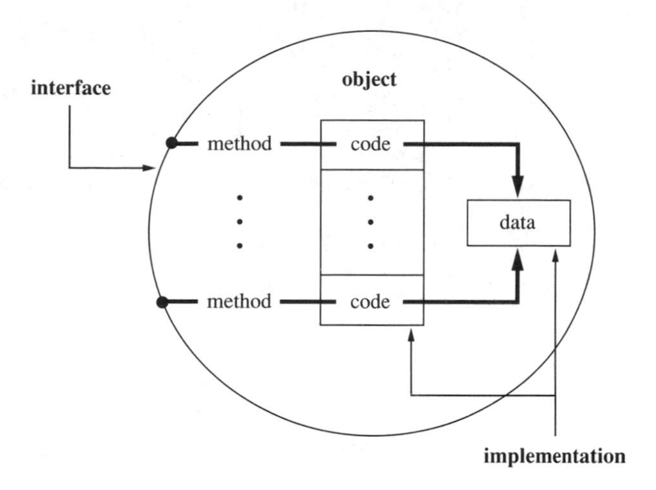

Figure 1.9 The General Structure of an Object

interface: the collection of all methods that are visible outside of the object.

In the figure below, the methods that can be invoked from outside the object are shown as small dark circles on the border of the object's boundary. The code that implements the methods is part of the object's implementation and is hidden inside the object. The term "encapsulation" is often used to describe the hiding of the object's implementation details. It is common to read that "an object encapsulates its data." Encapsulation is defined as:

encapsulation: in object-oriented programming, the restriction of access to data within an object to only those methods defined by the object's class.

The notion of encapsulation is fundamental to an understanding of objects and object-oriented programming.

1.4.3 Mapping an Abstraction to a Class

Figure 1.9 interactively illustrates how a class is a software structure capable of representing an abstraction. The left part of the figure is the same as that used earlier to illustrate how abstraction is a process of simplification. Once an abstraction has been created using the controls on the left side, a class can be formed using the controls on the right side of the figure. The "Define Attributes" and "Define Behaviors" buttons show how the attributes and the behaviors of the abstraction are mapped to the private and public parts of a class, respectively. The "Encapsulate" button shows the logical effect of encapsulating the private parts of a class definition. The private part of the class definition is blacked out

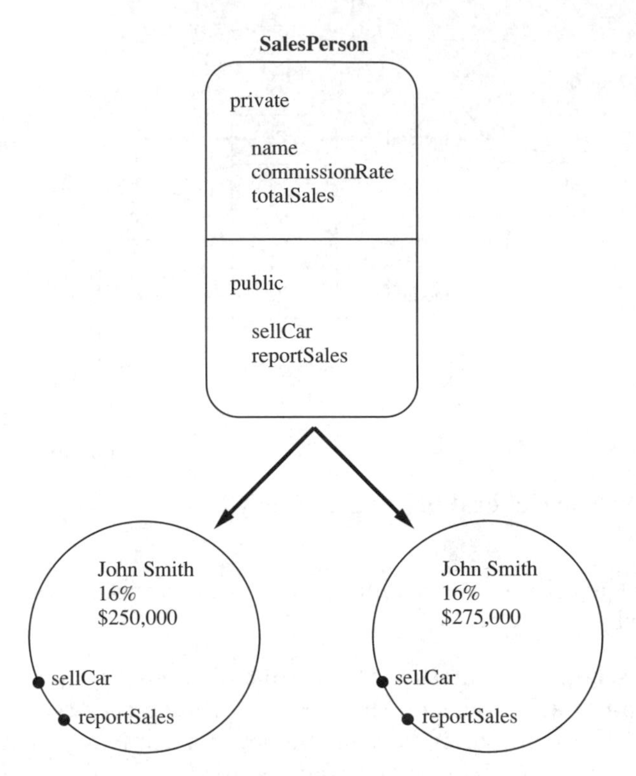

Figure 1.10 Multiple Instances of a Class

to suggest that the private elements of the class cannot be seen outside of the class. The "Decapsulate" button re-exposes the private elements. The "Reset" button returns the class definition area to its original condition.

The term "instantiation" is used to describe the act of creating an object from a class and the object is called an "instance" of the class. Numerous instantiations can be made of a given class, each yielding a distinct object. This leads to definition of an object as:

object: a distinct instance of a given class that encapsulates its implementation details and is structurally identical to all other instances of that class.

This definition highlights the fact that all objects that are instances of a given class are structurally identical: they have the same arrangement of data and can respond to the same set of method invocations. However, as shown in Figure 1.10, each object may, and usually does, have different values for its data. The data values of an object represent its current state. In the figure there are two instances of the SalesPerson class. Both objects encapsulate the same type of data (name, commissionRate, and totalSales). The two objects currently have different values for the name and totalSales data but they currently have the same value for the commissionRate data. Both objects have two methods that can be invoked: sellCar and reportSales.

1.4.4 Creating Objects from a Class

The relationship between a class and the objects that can be created using the class is often likened to that of a factory and the things produced by that factory. An automobile factory produces automobiles in the same way that an Automobile class can be used to create Automobile objects. Also, an Automobile class can produce only Automobile objects just as an automobile factory can produce only automobiles, not vacuum cleaners or rocket ships.

Classes and objects are often discussed by developers in life-like, personal, anthropomorphic terms. A developer might say that "The class should not be responsible for that." or "I expect the object to reply to inquiries about its current state." The developer may even assume the identity of the object to better understand the role of the object in a system's design. In this mode, a developer may ask "What is expected of me?" "How will I be able to do that?", or "Why do you want to know that about me?" Questions such as these often lead a developer to a better intuitive understanding of an objects and its relation to other objects. The personification of objects reflects the correspondence developers see between the real world entity and its the abstraction, on one hand, and the classes and objects that are their software counterparts, on the other. This view also reflects the autonomy and encapsulation assigned by designers to objects and classes.

A simple and popular design technique is intuitively related to the anthropomorphic view of objects. This technique focuses on identifying for each object (or class of objects) its *responsibilities* and its *collaborators*. An object's (or class's) responsibilities are those properties or duties the object (or class) is obligated to maintain or perform. An object's (or class's) collaborators are those other objects (or classes) with which the given object (or class) must interact to perform its responsibilities. The terms "responsibilities" and "collaborators" reflect the anthropomorphic view of objects.

1.4.5 Abstract Interfaces

The advantages of separation are only partially realized by the class structure. In a class, separation achieves a simplifying effect because the developer using the class only needs to understand the class's interface and not the class's implementation. However, because a class binds the interface of the class to the class's single implementation, a class can have neither interchangeable implementations nor can a class satisfy several interfaces. Because these later advantages of separation are useful in building sophisticated software systems, a structure in addition to a class is needed.

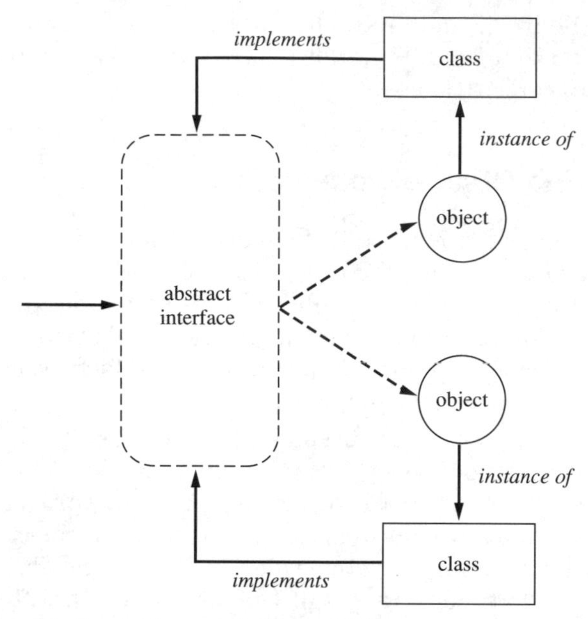

Figure 1.11 Interchangeability of Objects Using an Interface

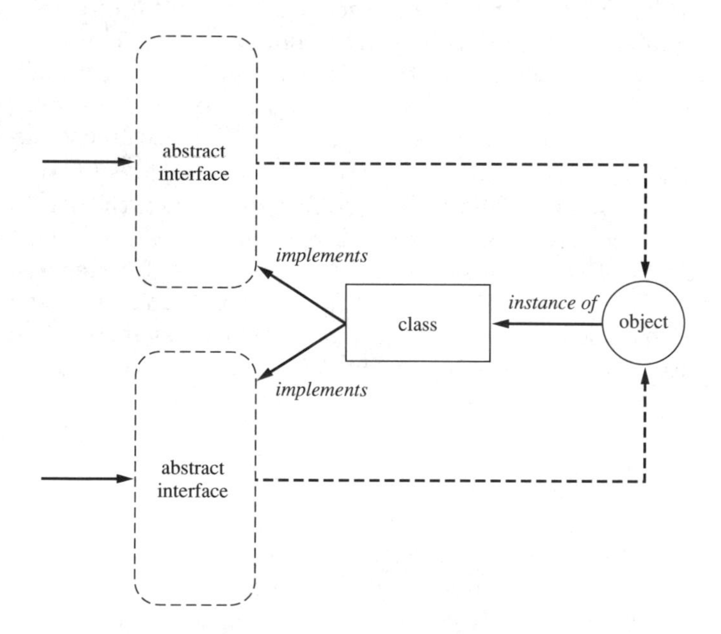

Figure 1.12 Manipulating an Object via Different Interfaces

An abstract interface is a programming structure that realizes more completely than does a class the advantages of separation. Similar to a class, an abstract interface captures the behavior of some abstraction by defining a collection of methods. Unlike a class, the abstract interface does not provide an implementation of the behavior; the implementation is provided by any class that defines and implements the behavior specified by the abstract interface. These properties of an abstract interface lead to the following definition:

> **abstract interface:** a named software representation for an abstraction's behavior that is intended to be implemented by one or more classes.

Notice that an abstract interface captures the behavior of an abstraction and not is attributes. Because an interface contains no implementation it has no hidden, private section; all of the methods in an interface are public, visible methods.

An abstract interface can be used to manipulate objects. As shown in Figure 1.11, the object must be an instance of a class that implements the abstract interface. The term "implements" means that the behavior defined by the abstract interface is a subset (or the same as) the behavior defined and implemented by the class. This arrangement is type-safe because any method defined in the abstract interface is guaranteed to be implemented by the object. This type-safety can be checked at compile-time.

An abstract interface achieves the full advantages of separation. First, as shown in Figure 1.11, interchangeability is achieved because several classes can implement the same abstract interface. The objects of these classes can be manipulated through the same, single abstract interface. It is even possible, and often the case, that a single abstract interface will be bound to objects of different classes at different times during the program's execution. Notice that the manipulator of the object does not need to know the class of the object—only the abstract interface need be known by the manipulator. Second, as shown in Figure 1.12, a single class can implement multiple abstract interfaces. It is only required that the class implement all of the methods defined in each abstract interface. In this way an object of a class can be accessed via different interfaces. Here again, the manipulator of the object only needs to know the abstract interface and not the actual class of the object being manipulated.

Exercises

1. Answer True or False to each of the following statements:
   - **a.** Many objects can be created from the same class.
   - **b.** A single object may belong to several classes.
   - **c.** Two objects of the same class must have the same data and methods.
   - **d.** Two objects of the same class must have the same values for their data.

   e. The data of a class is typically in the public part because it is a known attribute of the entity being modeled.

2. Define relevant attributes and behavior for each of the following entities:
   a. A telephone
   b. A calculator
   c. An automobile
   d. A patient in a hospital
   e. A vending machine

3. For each of the entities in the previous question, show the general organization (the name, public part, and private part) of a class.

1.5 Composition

1.5.1 Concept of Composition

Composition deals with a single, complex system as an organization of more numerous but simpler systems. Composition is often used to study and explain complex human organizations (the government is divided into three major branches), complex biological systems (a human being consists of a respiratory system, a circulatory system, an immune system, a nervous systems, a skeletal system, etc.), complex machines (an aircraft consists of a propulsion system, a control system, a navigation system, etc), and complex programs (an operating systems consists of a user interface, a file system, a network system, a memory management system, etc). With composition it is important to understand both the individual (simpler) parts and the relationships or collaborations among them.

As a constructive activity, composition refers to the assembly of interacting parts to form a whole. The part-whole relationship is a fundamental one in object-oriented programming. One of the major goals of object-oriented programming, software reuse, is accomplished by composing existing objects (the parts) in new and different ways to form new or objects or systems (the whole). Composition might be viewed as the "lego" approach to software development—using standardized, specialized parts to construct a wide range of interesting artifacts.

Composition can be defined as:

composition: an organized collection of components interacting to achieve a coherent, common behavior

The "part-whole" relationship is often expressed as a "has-a" relationship. For example, in referring to the relationship between an automobile and the automobile's windshield, the statement "the automobile has a windshield" suggests why the term "has-a" is used to describe part-whole compositions.

There are two forms of composition named *association* (also acquaintance) and *aggregation* (also containment). These two forms of composition are similar in that they are both part-whole constructions. What distinguishes aggregation from association is the visibility of the parts. In an aggregation only the whole is visible and accessible. In an association the interacting parts are externally visible and, in fact, may be shared between different compositions. A soda machine is an example of aggregation. The machine is a whole composed of several internal parts (a cooling system, a coin acceptor, a change maker, a soda supply). These internal parts are not visible or accessible to the normal user of the soda machine. A computer workstation is an example of composition using association. The workstation consists of a keyboard, a mouse, a monitor, a printer, a modem, and a processor. Each of these interacting parts are visible to the user and can be directly manipulated by the user.

In some cases the more generic term "composition" will be used in favor of the more precise terms "association" or "aggregation." This occurs when the statement applies to both forms, when the difference between the two forms is much less important than the general idea of forming a whole from parts, or when the precise form of composition can be inferred from context.

Both forms of composition are useful. Aggregation offers greater security because its structure is usually defined in advance and cannot be altered at run-time. The implementor of the aggregation is secure in the knowledge that the integrity of the aggregation and its proper functioning cannot be adversely affected by direct interference with its internal mechanisms. Association offers greater flexibility because the relationships among the visible parts can be redefined at run-time. An association can, therefore, be made to adapt to changing conditions in its execution environment by replacing one or more of its components. Interesting design decisions can revolve around which form of composition to use, balancing a need for security against a need for greater flexibility at run-time.

The two forms of composition are frequently used together and in combinations. The computer workstation was given as an example of an association among a mouse, keyboard, processor, modem, and monitor. However, as shown in Figure 1.13, the processor of the computer workstation is itself an aggregation that consists of hidden parts including a CPU (processor chip), memory, and a disk. More detailed examination of the processor chip would show it to be an association of smaller elements some of which might be other associations or aggregations of parts. Objects may also exhibit a complex structure formed by layers of associations and aggregations. The subsections below on association and aggregation will give examples of such structures.

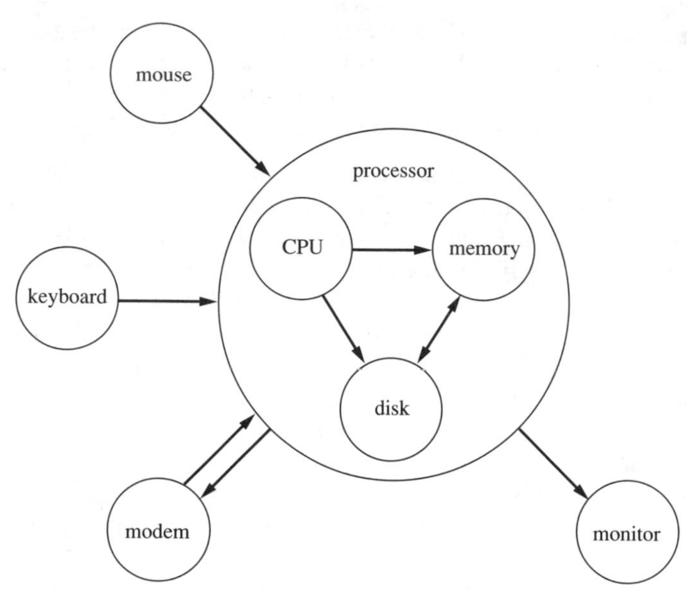

Figure 1.13 Association and Aggregation

1.5.2 Composition Using Association

Association is a part-whole organization in which the "whole" is exactly defined by the "parts" and the relationships among the parts. The parts of the composition maintain their identity, their external visibility, and their autonomy in the composition. The parts are often viewed as peers, collaborators or acquaintances, such terms reflecting the primacy of the parts in the part-whole composition. In some sense, the whole is the sum of its parts. This leads to the following definition of association.

association: a composition of independently constructed and externally visible parts.

The organization of a computer workstation, depicted in Figure 1.14, is a typical example of a real-world association. Each of the parts shown in this figure is externally visible and can be manipulated in its own right. The notion of "computer workstation" refers to the particular assembly of these parts in a way that gives rise to the functionality expected of a computer workstation. The expectations of a computer workstation would not be met by an assembly of fewer parts (i.e., no monitor), extraneous parts (i.e., two keyboards), or the correct parts associated differently (i.e., the mouse connected to the modem).

An association among software objects is created when an object contains references to other objects. An example of an association among objects is shown in

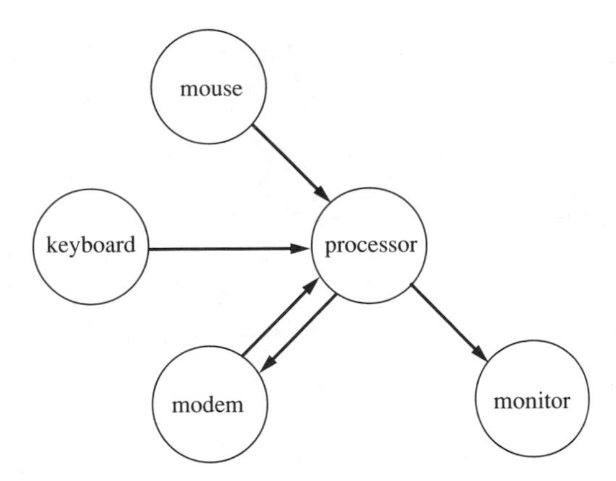

Figure 1.14 A Real-World Association

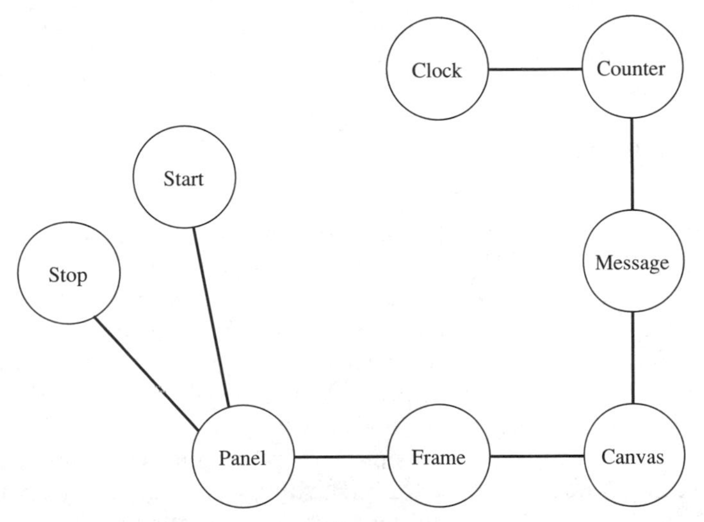

Figure 1.15 An Association of Objects

Figure 1.15. This association creates a simple one-second timer that is displayed in a graphical user interface window and that is controlled by "Start" and "Stop" buttons. The Clock object is responsible for determining the end of each one-second interval of time. At the end of each such interval the Clock object invokes an operation on the Counter object to increment its interval value. Incrementing its value causes the Counter object to send a string representation of its value to the Message object. The Message object is responsible for displaying its current value in a drawable Canvas object. The Canvas is responsible for maintaining the consistency between the images or text drawn in the Canvas and what is displayed in the Canvas's portion of the user interface. In addition to providing an area on the

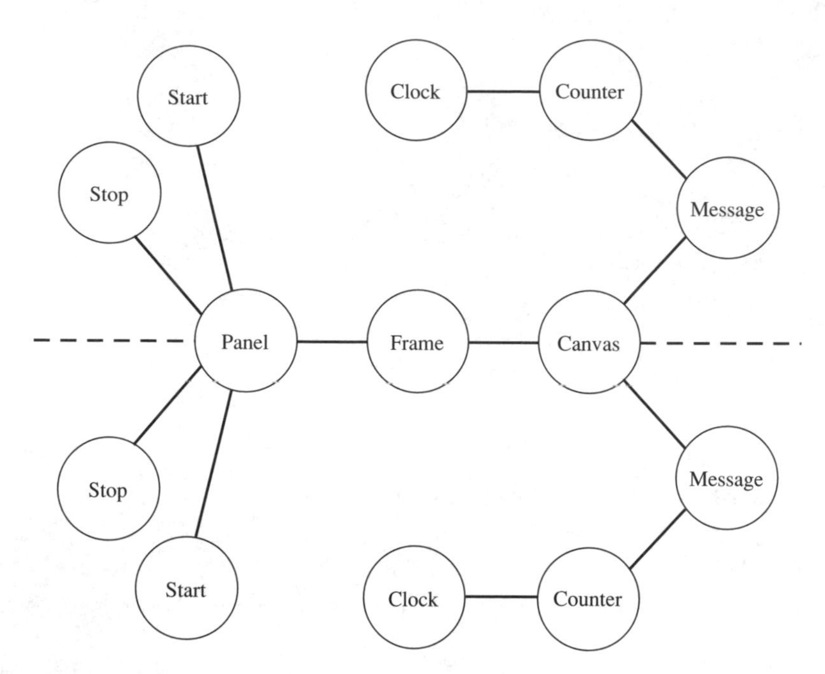

Figure 1.16 Shared Objects in an Association

user's display for the Canvas, the Frame also provides an area for a Panel object to display the "Start" and "Stop" button controls that it manages.

One advantage of an association is that the parts may be shared between different compositions. This is easily accomplished by having the same object be connected to (referred to) from two objects, each of which is in a different composition. Using the computer workstation example mentioned above, it is possible to have a single printer shared between two different workstations. In the one-second timer example, it is possible to have multiple timers displayed in the same window through a shared Frame object. A shared Frame object is shown in Figure 1.16. The dashed line indicates the logical partition between the two distinct one-second timers that are displayed in the same (shared) user interface window (Frame).

A second advantage of an association is that the parts in an association can be dynamically changed. This can be accomplished simply by having a member in the composition connect to (point to) a different object. This change is dynamic in that it can be done at run-time. Again using the computer workstation example, it is possible to change the keyboard or mouse or to change the printer connected to the system. In the one second timer example, it is possible to replace the one second clock by a faster clock allowing more accurate timings to be made.

1.5.3 Composition Using Aggregation

Aggregation is a *composition* in which the "whole" subsumes and conceals its constituent "parts." This relationship is suggested by Figure 1.17. In contrast to an association, the parts are not visible externally. They do not have an identity as far as a user of the composition is concerned, and they do not possess autonomy to the same degree as parts of an association. The "whole" is the single visible entity. This suggests the following definition.

aggregation: a *composition* that encapsulates (hides) the parts of the composition.

Figure 1.17 shows the general model of an object defined by aggregation. The outer objects contain inner (encapsulated) sub-objects, which themselves may have hidden internal objects.

Composition using aggregation occurs in many familiar natural and man-made systems. Table 1.3 shows how several familiar systems can be mapped to the general structure of an aggregation shown in Figure 1.17. Notice that the sub-objects and the sub-sub-objects are generally considered to be internal components of the object.

An aggregation of objects is created when one object (the "whole") contains in its encapsulated data one or more other objects (the "parts"). The simple one-second timer created above using association can also be implemented via aggre-

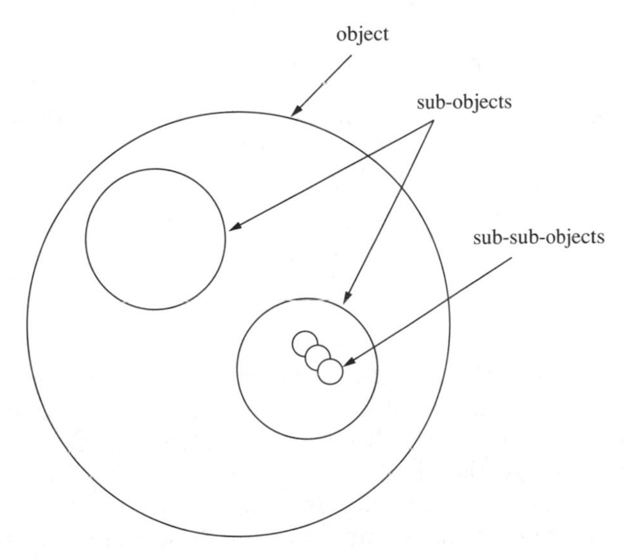

Figure 1.17 Composition via Aggregation

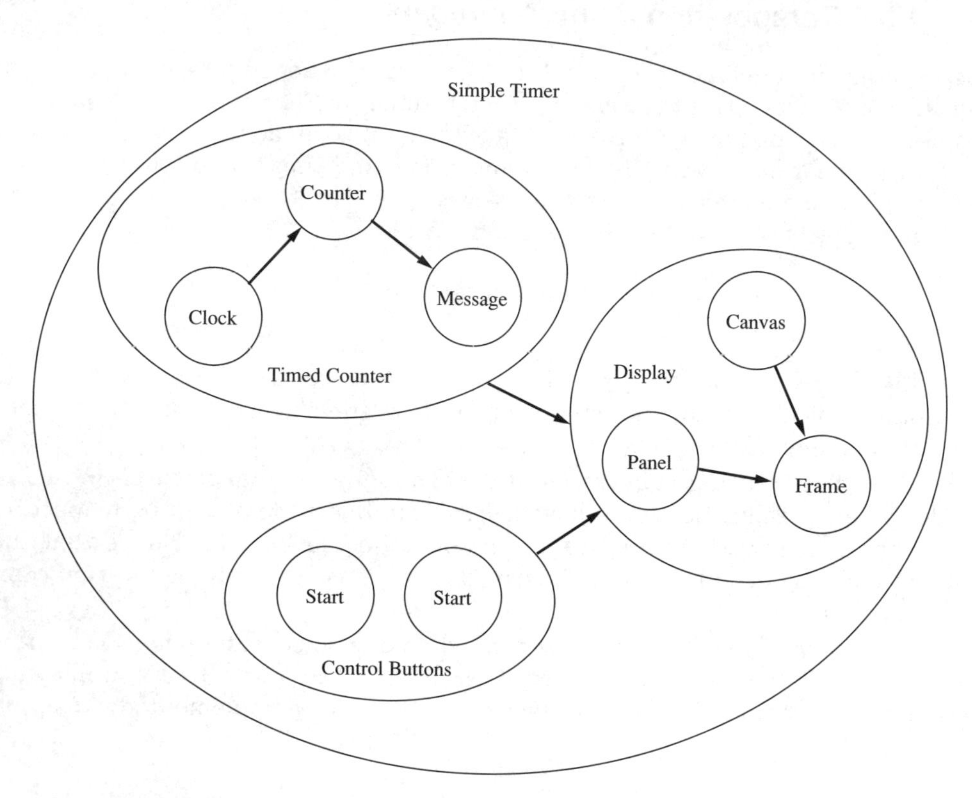

Figure 1.18 Composition via Aggregation

Table 1.3 Examples of Common Aggregations

Object	Sub-Object	Sub-Sub-Object
Automobile	Engine	Pistons
Computer	Mother board	Processor chip
Molecules	Atoms	Quarks

gation as shown in Figure 1.18. In this figure the basic objects that form the timer (Clock, Counter, Message, Frame, Canvas, Panel, Start, and Stop) are contained within other objects (TimedCounter, Display, and ControlButtons) that are, in turn, contained in the single encapsulating object, SimpleTimer. Notice that from the outside, only the SimpleTimer is visible; all other objects are concealed within the encapsulating boundary of the SimpleTimer object.

The first advantage of aggregation is that the outer object may be used without much, if any, concern for the operation, or even the existence, of the internal sub-objects. When driving a car we are rarely concerned about the thousands of parts that are composed together to realize the car. The ability to ignore the finer structure of an object greatly simplifies the task of understanding how a system works or building a system that works in a particular way. The second advantage of aggregation is that internal parts may be changed without affecting the user's view of the external whole. The internal structure of the parts may be completely changed or only individual parts may be replaced. Improvement in efficiency, reliability, or cost may motivate the replacement of parts.

Exercises

1. Consider a merchandising company that accepts phone orders and relays the orders to a warehouse where the merchandise is packaged and shipped via package delivery service. Draw a diagram showing the associations and/or aggregations in this system.
2. Consider a home entertainment system with a satellite dish, a television, and a remote control. Draw a diagram showing the associations and/or aggregations in this system.
3. Consider an air traffic control system with radars, controllers, runways, and aircraft. Draw a diagram showing the associations and/or aggregations in this system.

1.6 Generalization

Generalization identifies commonalities among a set of entities. The commonality may be of attributes, behavior, or both. For example, a statement such as "All GUI windows have a title" expresses a common attribute among all entities that are considered windows in a graphical user interface. Similarly, the statement, "All GUI windows can be resized" expresses a common behavior that all windows provide. Generalizations are usually easy to recognize as they contain words such as "all" and "every."

Generalization may be defined as:

generalization: the identification, and possible organization, of common properties of abstractions.

This definition shows that generalization is not abstraction, although the two are often confused. Abstraction aims at simplifying the description of an entity, whereas generalization looks for common properties among these abstractions.

Generalizations are clearly important and prevalent in many disciplines of study. In science and mathematics, for example, the statements of "laws" and "theorems" are often generalizations. They state some property that holds over a group of things; the more powerful the generalization, the more things to which the generalization applies. The search for the basic forms of matter represents the physicists' quest for a generalization that applies to everything in the physical universe. The biologist's use of generalization is reflected in the organization of plants and animals into the taxonomy whose divisions are kingdom, phylum, class, order, and so on.

Generalizations are equally important to software. Much of the effort in building software systems is to allow parts of the system to operate in the most general way possible. In some cases this might mean designing the system so that it can handle any *number* of things of the same kind. For example, the system might be expected to process any number of lines of input. In other cases the major design problem is how to handle things of *different* kinds or types. For example, the system might be expect to process input that comes from files of different formats or from both local as well as remote locations. An approach to solving some of these problems is to be able to capture more completely in software the idea of generalization.

One of the three forms of generalization is *hierarchy*. In the case of hierarchy, the commonalities are organized into a tree structured form. At the root of any subtree are found all the attributes and behavior common to all of the descendents of that root. This particular kind of tree structure is referred to as a generalization/specialization hierarchy because the root provides more general properties shared by all its descendents whereas the descendents typically add specializing properties that make them distinct among their siblings and their siblings' descendents.

The second form of generalization is *polymorphism*. Polymorphism captures commonality in algorithms. An algorithm may have a nested if-then-else (or case statement) logic that tests for the exact type of an object which it is manipulating. the algorithm performs some operations on the object based on the exact type of the object. However, in many algorithm the operations to be performed are the same, only the type of the object on which they are performed varies. Polymorphism allows this nested logic (or case statement) to be collapsed to a single case in which the different object types are treated in a uniform manner. Through a mechanism called *dynamic binding*, the algorithm allows the object to determine which of its operations to perform in response to the algorithms invocation. Thus, the algorithm need not know the exact type of the object. The algorithm only needs to know that the object can respond to the invocation in an appropriate manner.

The third form of generalization is *patterns*. A pattern expresses a general solution (the key components and relationships) to a commonly occurring design problem. The attributes and behavior of the individual components are only partially defined to allow the pattern to be interpreted and applied to a wide range of situations. For example, a "wheeled vehicle" pattern might be defined in terms of the components "wheel," "axle," "frame," "body" and "power source." The pattern would also show how these components would be arranged in relation to each other (e.g., the axle must connect two wheels). The pattern could be interpreted in many different ways to solve particular problems that differ in their requirements for speed, durability, payload, fuel source, available materials, and other factors. Examples of the wheeled vehicle pattern are "automobile," "horse-drawn carriage," "ox cart," "moon buggy," and many others.

1.6.1 Hierarchy

A hierarchical organization of components based on a relationship of generalization/specialization is an important device in object-oriented programming. Although the power of such an organization can only be fully appreciated after more study, it is useful to at least hint at the role it will play. A generalization and its specializations are often said to be related by an "is-a" relationship. The relationship has this name because it is suggested by phrases such as "an aircraft is a vehicle" and "a lion is a carnivore." In these phrases the characteristics of a specialized entity, the aircraft and lion, are related to the characteristics of a more general category of entities, the vehicle and carnivore categories, respectively. The "is-a" terminology reflects that the specialization has all of the attributes and behavior of the generalization. Thus, an aircraft has all of the properties of vehicle plus an additional one that discriminates it as an aircraft apart from other types of vehicles. Similarly, a lion has all of the properties of a carnivore in addition to those that make it uniquely a lion.

A more comprehensive intuitive example of a generalization/specialization hierarchy is one that organizes and relates the characteristics of different types of vehicles. The diagram in Figure 1.19 illustrates a possible hierarchical structure for vehicles. The arrows in this diagram represent the "is-a" relation. For example, the arrow connecting the categories Aircraft and Vehicle is read as "Aircraft is a kind of Vehicle." The general concept of Vehicle is the root of the hierarchy. Properties shared by all vehicles might include the manufacturer's name, the type of fuel required, and the maximum speed. Two distinct groups of vehicles are those intended for use on land, Land Vehicles, and those designed to fly, Aircraft. Properties common to all land vehicles are the number of axles, and the vehicle identification number. Although these properties make sense for Land Vehicles, they are not relevant to Aircraft. Aircraft properties, however, might include a transponder signature and a tail number. Both Land Vehicles and Aircraft can be divided into Private and Commercial categories. Things in the Private category have a person-owner attribute whereas those in the Commercial category have a company-owner

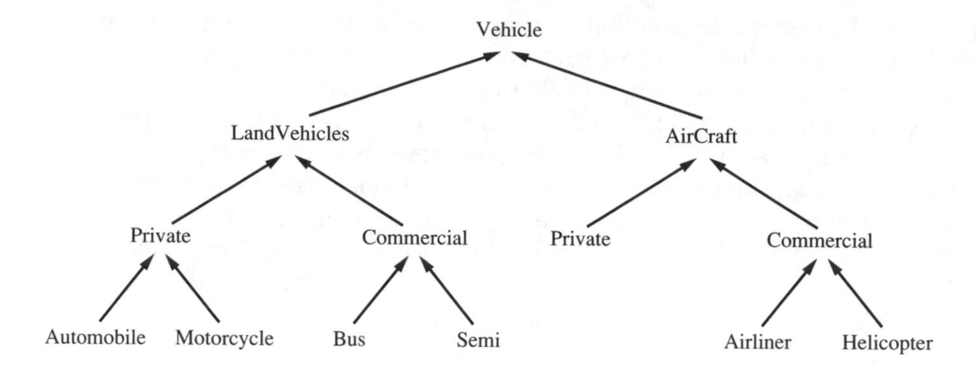

Figure 1.19 A Generalization/Specialization Hierarchy for Vehicles

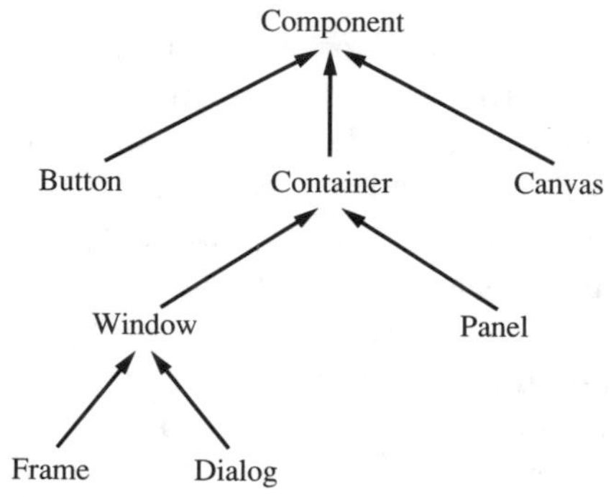

Figure 1.20 A Generalization/Specialization Hierarchy for Vehicles

attribute. Various specific types of vehicles are shown for the Land Vehicles categories and for the commercial subcategory of Aircraft.

Another example of a generalization/specialization hierarchy, this time from the domain of GUIs, is shown in Figure 1.20. The most general element, Component, has attributes of location (coordinates denoting where the component appears on the screen) and shape (height and width), and a behavior that allows the component to be repositioned and resized. Specialized kinds of Components include an area for drawing graphical shapes (Canvas), an interactive element for user control (Button), and a general collection of components (Container). Two specialized kinds of Containers are a Window, a Container that has a visible representation on the screen, and a Panel, a Container that maintains an arrangement of other Components. The Frame is a Window with a border and a Dialog is a Window specialized for the purposes of creating a text-oriented interaction with the user.

The notion of hierarchy in object-oriented programming can be defined as follows:

hierarchy: a generalization in which abstractions are organized into a directed a cyclicgraph whose arcs denote an "is-a" relation between a more generalized abstraction and the one or more derived specializations.

The most common case of hierarchy uses a tree structure to organize the abstractions, although more general organizations are possible.

A generalization/specialization hierarchy serves at least four major purposes. First, it provides a form of knowledge representation. A higher (more generalized) level in the hierarchy encodes an understanding of the general attributes and behavior possessed by all of its specialized descendents. Thus, it is possible to make statements such as: "All windows can be resized" and "All windows can be repositioned." Second, the names of the intermediate levels in the hierarchy provide a vocabulary that can be used among developers and between developers and domain experts (those knowledgeable about the application domain but not necessarily about computing). This vocabulary allows discussions to be less ambiguous because the terms in the vocabulary identify specific, clearly defined concepts. Third, the hierarchy can be extended by adding new specializations at any level. These additions are easier to make because they occur within an existing framework that defines some, perhaps many, of their attributes and behavior. For example, to add a new specialized kind of Panel, it is not necessary to redefine all of the attributes and behavior already defined in Container, Component, and Panel; these are assumed to be part of the more generalized nature of the specialized Panel being added. Fourth, new attributes and behavior can be added easily to the proper subset of specializations. For example, any new attribute or behavior that might be needed for all containers can beaded to the Container class. These additional attributes or behavior are then "automatically" part of all specialized kinds of Containers, but not of anything else.

1.6.2 Polymorphism

Polymorphism is a means of generalizing algorithms. The generality is achieved by allowing the algorithm to manipulate uniformly objects of different classes provided that the algorithm uses only common properties of the different classes. Any object known to possess the required common properties may be manipulated by the algorithm. Some object-oriented languages require that the compiler be able to verify at compile-time that an object possesses the required common properties. Other languages allow this verification to be deferred until run-time, risking a possible run-time error if, during execution, the object is discovered to be lacking one of the required common properties.

Polymorphism can be defined as follows:

polymorphism: the ability to manipulate objects of distinct classes using only knowledge of their common properties without regard for their exact class.

The meaning of polymorphism is reflected in the root phrases from which the term is derived. The phrase "poly" denotes "many" or "several," and "morph" refers to "shape," "form," or "appearance." Thus, polymorphism refers to things of many shapes or many forms. In the object-oriented programming sense, the "shape, form, or appearance" is taken to mean the interface or properties of an object. The "poly" aspect implies that the interfaces or properties are different or varied across the objects being considered. The challenge is how to manipulate these varied and different objects in a uniform manner.

Humans use polymorphism in many activities. One example is a store check-out clerk who determines the total amount of a customer's purchases. Each item being purchased has a bar code label that the clerk scans by passing it over a bar code reader. The bar code reader reads the identifying information on the bar code label, consults a database of merchandise, and reports the information to the cash register for totaling. The clerk follows a generalized algorithm that might be written as:

```
while ( more storeItems ) {
        pick up next storeItem;
        scan storeItem;
        put scanned storeItem in bag;
};
```

This algorithm does not refer to any of the many specific types of merchandise sold by the store. The algorithm only refers to a general "storeItem." The storeItem is only required to have a bar code label so that the item can be scanned. Any item of merchandise having such a label can be handled by the clerk. Conversely, any item not possessing a bar code label cannot be handled by the clerk. In this example, compile-time checking is equivalent to making sure that items have a bar code label when they are put on the shelf (i.e., when the "store" is "programmed"). Run-time checking is equivalent to having the clerk check for the presence of a bar code label and, if the item does not have such a label, the clerk calls a manager to report the problem. There are many every-day examples similar to the store clerk in which people act in a polymorphism way: shelving books in a library, driving different kinds of cars, and using different kinds of computers area few of these.

Polymorphism enables open-ended software. New classes possessing the required common properties can be incorporated into a polymorphic structure, the structure need not be changed in any way to accommodate the additional classes. The same is true for the store clerk algorithm. The store clerk does not need any additional training (reprogramming) when new kinds of merchandise are added to the store's inventory provided that the new merchandise possesses the required bar code label.

A mechanism called *dynamic binding* is needed to implement polymorphism whenever a customized response to a common invocation is needed. In this context, the term "binding" refers to the linking of an invocation made by the poly-

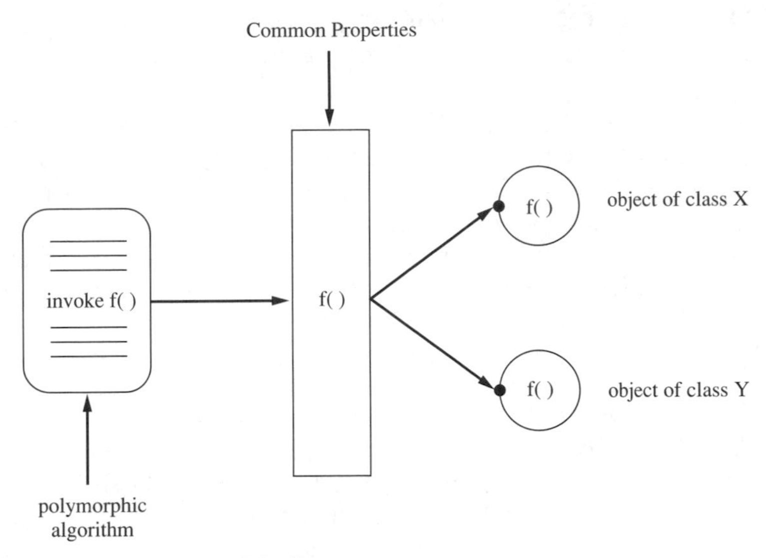

Figure 1.21 Dynamic Binding

morphic algorithm with the code of a method implemented by the receiving object. Because the polymorphic algorithm is unaware of the exact class of the receiver, the binding must be done dynamically because the same invocation may be bound to methods in different classes on different executions depending on what object is presented to the algorithm. Figure 1.21 depicts the act of dynamic binding. In this example the polymorphic algorithm invokes a method `f()` that is one of the common properties shared among a set of classes. The algorithm is unaware of the exact type of the object to which the invocation is directed. In the example, it is not known whether the object is of class X or class Y. The dynamic binding mechanism determines the type of the object and maps the invocation to the correct method in class X, if the object is of class X, or to the correct method in class Y, if the object is of class Y.

1.6.3 Patterns

A pattern is a generalized solution for a commonly occurring kind problem. A pattern does not give the detailed code for a particular solution but instead gives the general form of a solution for any problem of the particular kind. The user of the pattern must adapt the pattern to the particular case at hand and supply the missing details not given in the pattern. Experienced designers are believed to possess, perhaps even at an intuitive or subconscious level, a rich repertoire of patterns and the ability to recognize when a current problem can be solved by adapting a pattern used successfully as a solution for one or more previous problems. Lacking the collection of previous designs, novice designers are forced to solve each problem that is new to them as if it were a completely unsolved problem, often reinventing what previous generations of designers have already created.

Patterns are recognized at many level of scale and in many disciplines. In computer science, a large-scale pattern is often presented as an "architecture" or a "model." Examples of such large-scale patterns are the *client-server model*, *layered architecture*, and *micro-kernel architecture*. Small-scale patterns in computing are often called "plans" or "idioms" because they represent a common arrangement of programming language constructs. An example of a small-scale pattern is the "counted loop with early exit" plan. This plan might be used to scan an array of fixed length and terminate when the end of the array is reached or earlier if a given search criterion is satisfied. The plan specifies the initial conditions, the arrangement of the elements of the loop construct, and the termination conditions. The plan may be specified in a graphical or pseudo-code form so that it can be mapped by the user to different programming languages. Patterns are also common in other disciplines. The authors of the book DesignPatterns cite as part of their inspiration the role of patterns in the architecture of buildings and in literary forms.

A design pattern can be defined as follows:

design pattern: a named generalization describing the elements and relationships of a solution for a commonly occurring design problem.

A pattern contains four essential parts: a name, a problem, a solution, and the consequences. The four parts of a pattern are illustrated by a simple client-server pattern. The name of the pattern is intended to convey briefly and succinctly the subject matter of the pattern. For this example the name "client-server" is appropriate. The problem portion of the pattern identifies the conditions under which the pattern is applicable (i.e., for what problem is this pattern a solution). The client-server problem is one of providing a service to possibly multiple clients in a loosely-coupled manner. The solution specifies the elements that comprise the solution, their individual responsibilities, and the manner in which they collaborate to achieve the solution. The elements of the client-server pattern could be given in pictorial form as shown in Figure 1.22.

The client-server pattern identifies five elements in the pattern: Client, Server, request, reply, and Connection. The client is responsible for generating a request that is sent to the server, which, in turn, performs its service and delivers a response in the form a reply. The responsibility for conveying the requests and replies between the client and server is assigned to an intermediary knows as the "connection." The client and server each collaborate directly only with the connection (but only indirectly with each other). The collaboration between the elements is defined by the sequence of events beginning with the generation of a request by the client and its transmission to the server followed by the generation at the server of a reply and its transmission to the client.

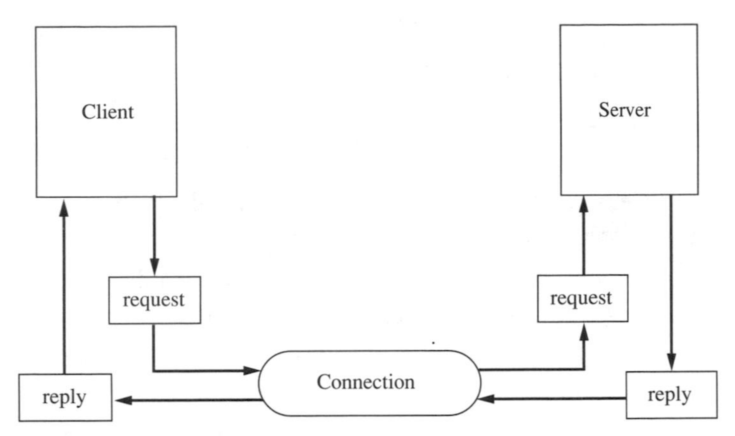

Figure 1.22 Client-Server Pattern

Notice that the pattern does not specify the nature of the service provided, it could be a name service, a time service, a location service, a file service, a security service, or any other. Also the pattern does not specify how the connection is to be implemented. The connection could be a memory buffer connecting two procedures within the same process, a memory buffer connecting two different processes on the same machine, or a network link between two processes on different machines. Although these details vary, the pattern remains the same.

A pattern also specifies the positive and negative consequences of using the pattern. Some of the positive consequences of the client-server pattern are that the client and server may be implemented on different machines allowing each to take advantage of local specialized hardware or software resources, the client and server may be totally or largely unaware of and insensitive to the actual location of each other, and the server may be made available to many clients at the same time. Two negative consequences of the client-server pattern are that the client may be left hanging if its request or reply is lost or if the server crashes, and the client cannot demand or control the service from the server—it can only request such service.

A pattern for an object-oriented design is expressed in terms of classes and objects. The elements of the pattern are represented by classes. The relationships among the elements are defined by association, aggregation, and/or hierarchy. The responsibilities and collaborations are understood in terms of the behavior of each class and the interactions among the classes as defined by their associations.

Exercises

1. Define a hierarchy for "Printed Material" that would include such specializations as books, magazines, textbooks, newspapers, and others.
2. Define a hierarchy for "Consumer Electronics" that would include such specializations as televisions, VCRs, radios, and others.
3. Define a hierarchy for "Athletic Games" that would include such specializations as soccer, basketball, football, tennis, track, and others.
4. Consider a librarian who is putting books back on the shelves after they have been returned. Each book has a catalog number printed on the spine of the book. Describe the actions of the librarian from the standpoint of polymorphism.
5. Consider a person working at a tollbooth who charges vehicles different amounts based on the number of axles: two-axle passenger vehicles are charged one amount, a track towing a trailer is charged a higher amount, and a one-wheeler is charged much more. Describe the actions of the tollbooth worker from the standpoint of polymorphism.
6. Define a design pattern for a "mail system." This pattern should be general enough to cover both a postal mail system, a package delivery service or courier service, and an electronic mail system. Identify the elements of the pattern, their responsibilities in the pattern, and their relationships to each other.
7. Define a "receptionist" design pattern. A receptionist holds arriving work for a boss, and passes the highest priority work to the boss whenever the boss is not occupied. This pattern should be general enough to cover both a real office environment and a computer-based scheduling system. Identify the elements of the pattern, their responsibilities in the pattern, and their relationships to each other.

1.7 Putting it All Together

To master object-oriented programming one must understand the connections among the design strategies, the software structures supporting the strategies, and the software engineering goals that the strategies and structures are meant to achieve. Some of the principal connections are shown in Figure 1.23. Understanding these connections enables the construction of useful and well-designed systems that solve important problems. This section identifies the key relationships among the many terms and concepts about object-oriented programming, Java, design, and software engineering that have been introduced in the first chapter. The relationships discussed here will be understood more deeply as the exploration of object-oriented programming unfolds. For ease of reference, the definitions introduced throughout the chapter are collected in summary form at the end of this section.

Although there is much to be learned about the design strategies, object-oriented software structures, and software engineering goals, two observations can be made:

> The structures of objects and classes are related to three of the four design strategies and one of the most important software engineering goals, reusability.

> Interfaces and inheritance relate to all of the software engineering goals, indicating the importance of understanding how to exploit these structures in creating quality software systems.

Other aspects of these relationships are discussed below.

1.7.1 Relationships to Design Strategies

Classes and objects are related to the strategies of abstraction and separation as well as the strategies for composition. The definitions of objects and classes makes evident the strong relationship between these basic concepts and the design strategies of abstraction and separation. An important task in system development is the identification of the core concepts in the application domain. The people performing this task are called system analysts, requirements engineers, or domain engineers. These people use the strategy of abstraction to identify the attributes and behavior essential to building useful application in the domain; complex entities are reduced to their essence. These abstractions, combining attributes and behavior, are translated directly into classes. The design strategy of separation is evident in the structure of class and objects that employ the notion of encapsulation to separate the public, external aspects of a class or object from it private, internal implementation. This separation confines the effects of changes to a class's implementation; improvements can be made in the implementation without creating “ripple effects” that require changes to other parts of the system that use the modified class.

Classes and objects are most often created so as to be used in conjunction with other classes and objects through composition. The notion of a “system” is one of differentiated parts interacting to achieve an overall behavior. Thus, to build an object-oriented system means to define classes and objects that are interrelated: they know about each other, they are designed to use each other's services, and they form organized structures. The two forms of composition, association and aggregation, have natural counterparts in object-oriented languages. Associations are created by classes whose objects can refer to each other and invoke each others methods. Aggregations are created when the implementation of one class encapsulates objects of other classes. Thus, classes and objects provide structures that support the design strategy of composition.

Abstract interfaces also support abstraction, separation, and composition. Like classes, interfaces are a means of expressing the behavior of some abstraction because both classes and interfaces allow a related collection of methods to be defined as a named entity. Abstract interfaces support separation even more strongly than classes because, unlike a class, there is no implementation associated with the definition of an abstract interface. With abstract interfaces, the definition of the abstraction's behavior is completely divorced from an implementation that is encapsulated in a class conforming to the requirements of the abstract interface. Abstract interfaces support the association form of composition because the methods defined in one abstract interface may refer to objects whose type is defined by another interface.

Inheritance and design patterns support generalization. Inheritance allows the definition of a hierarchical organization of classes so as to express the commonalities among them. Expressing these common attributes and behavior makes it easier to understand the entire collection of classes because the shared aspects of a generalization can be understood once for each specialization. The generalization/specialization hierarchy conforms to common ways of organizing information about complex, structured phenomena. Design patterns are a way of codifying the knowledge of experienced designers. A pattern presents a generalized solution to a frequently encountered design problem. The design pattern is a generalization in the sense that it is not a solution to a specific problem but a general guide that shows how to solve and specific instance of the design problem. Design patterns for object-oriented software are presented as a set of relationships among a collection of classes. Thus, a design pattern is a structure that must be adapted to the specifics of a particular problem.

1.7.2 Relationships to Software Engineering

Object-oriented programming is an evolutionary development in software engineering that addresses (at least) the three major software engineering goals shown in Figure 1.23: reusability, extensibility, and flexibility. The language features that address these issues are those of objects, classes, abstract interfaces, inheritance, and design patterns. The foundation for these language features were established by decades of software engineering experience. Also important were the widely recognized value of such software engineering techniques as information hiding, encapsulation, strict enforcement of interfaces, and layering.

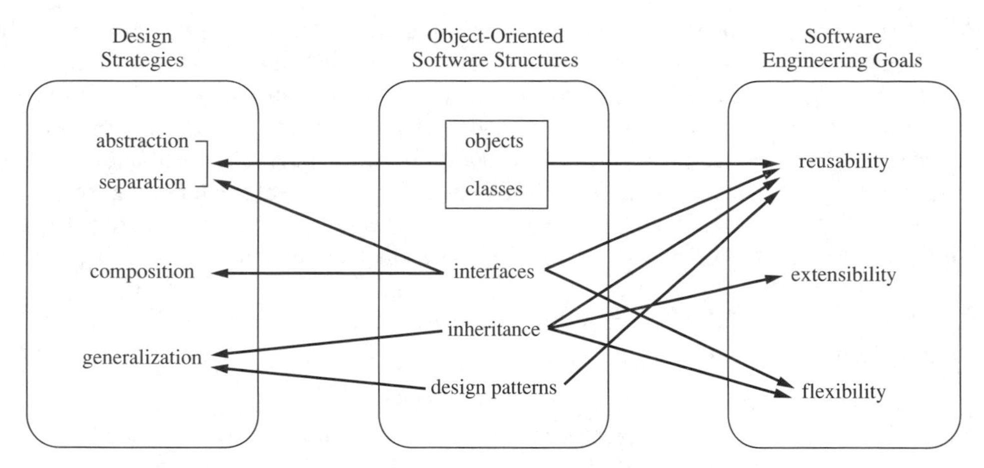

Figure 1.23 Connections Among Strategies, Structures, and Goals

Reusability is an important issue in software engineering for at least two major reasons. First, reusability is one means to cope with the pressures of producing ever larger and more functional systems in an ever-decreasing development cycle (time to market). Reusability allows developers to be more efficient because the same code can be developed once and used in many different applications. Second, reliability can be improved by reusing previously developed, and previously tested, components. The development of new code entails the additional costs in time and money of testing, validation, and verification of the new code. Much of these expenses can be avoided by using "off-the-shelf" components.

Software reuse is certainly not a goal unique to object-oriented programming. Although libraries of procedures proved this approach to be useful, in practice procedures were too primitive a unit to promote extensive reuse. Objects and classes are more sophisticated mechanisms for achieving software reuse because they bind together more completely all the aspects of an entire abstraction. Therefore, the abstraction can more easily be transported across applications. Interfaces promote software reuse because the software on either side of the interface may be reused independently of each other. That is, the classes implementing an interface can be used in any situation where the interface appears and, conversely, the code using an interface can be reused with a completely different set of classes implementing the interface. Any of the forms of generalization also contribute to reuse. A class in an inheritance hierarchy can be reused directly when it serves as a generalized base class from which a new class is derived by specialization. Design patterns allow design experience and success to be reused across designers.

Extensibility in software is important because software systems are long-lived and are subject to user's demands for new features and added capability. Object-oriented programming can help to satisfy this need through inheritance.

Recall that inheritance is a generalization/specialization hierarchy. Referring to the Component hierarchy discussed earlier, extensibility is possible in two ways. The first way in which a generalization/specialization hierarchy supports extensibility is that any new attributes or behavior that is added to a more generalized concept (e.g., Component) will automatically become part of the attributes and behavior of its specializations (e.g., Container, Window, Button). For example, as shown in Figure 1.24, if the Component abstraction is enhanced to include a color with which the Component is displayed on the screen, then the attribute "currentColor" and the behavior "setColor" might be added to Component. It would then be possible to manipulate the color of a Window as well as all of the other specializations of Component.

The second way in which a generalization/specialization hierarchy supports extensibility is that the hierarchy itself can be extended. New additions can be made under any existing node. For example, as shown in Figure 1.25, the Frame might be specialized to a HyperTextFrame by including additional attributes and additional behavior that distinguishes ordinary words or images in a Frame from those words or images that are hyperlinks and can be clicked on to cause the HyperTextFrame to display a new content.

Flexibility in software systems means, in part, that additions, variations, or modifications can be made without the need to modify numerous places in the system's code. Historically, many software systems were very brittle; the addition of a small change could only be accommodated by making modifications in many, and often apparently unrelated, parts of the existing system. This brittleness stood in marked contrast to the prevailing notion that, unlike hardware systems, software system were supposed to be extremely malleable and changes should be made easily. In addition, reducing the number of changes also reduces the introduction of bugs into the code.

Object-oriented programming contributes to flexibility in two ways. First, the separation of an interface from its implementation allows the user of the interface to remain unaffected by changes in the implementation. Thus, a modification can be made to the implementation (e.g., to improve its efficiency or reliability) without requiring any changes in the code that uses the interface. Second, polymorphism allows variations and additions to be made to the set of classes over which the polymorphism applies. For example, referring to the Component hierarchy, consider adding a new kind of button, a RadioButton. It would seem necessary to modify the Panel to allow a Panel to manipulate the newly created RadioButton. However, the Panel can use polymorphism so that the Panel's algorithms only rely on the more general attributes and behavior of an object (i.e., that it is a kind of Component) and does not need to be aware of the exact "type" (i.e., RadioButton) of the object. Using this approach, the Panel can be designed to operate on Components. Any newly created Component, even one-like the RadioButton—that is created after the Panel is already written, automatically can be manipulated by a Panel without changing the code of the Panel.

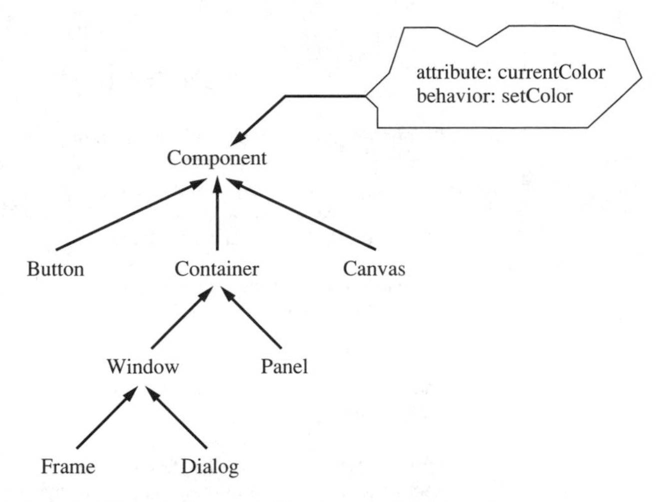

Figure 1.24 Adding New Attributes and Behavior

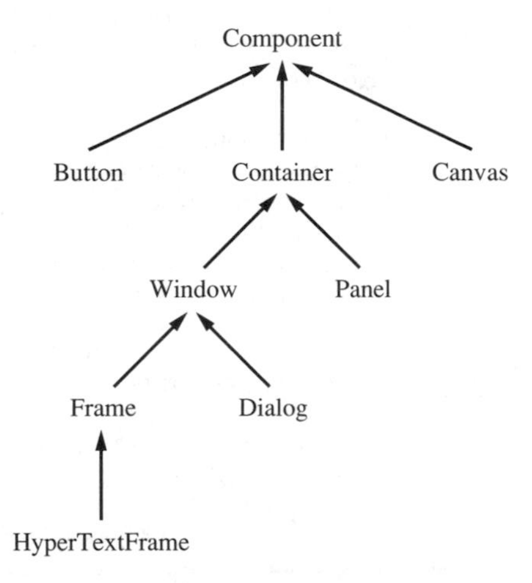

Figure 1.25 Adding New Specialized Classes

1.7.3 Summary of Definitions

The terms defined in this chapter are summarized below for ease of reference. The section number in which a term appeared is given in parenthesis after each term.

Term	Definition
Abstraction (1.2)	A named collection of attributes and behavior relevant to modeling a given entity for some particular purpose.
Software Interface (1.3)	The external, visible aspects of a software artifact by which the behavior of the artifact is elicited.
Software Implementation (1.3)	The programmed mechanism that realizes the behavior implied by an interface.
Separation (1.3)	In software systems, the independent specification of a software interface and one or more software implementations of that interface.
Class (1.4)	A named software representation for an abstraction that separates the implementation of the representation from the interface of the representation.
Encapsulation (1.4)	In object-oriented programming, the restriction of access to data within an object to only those methods defined by the object's class.
Object (1.4)	A distinct instance of a given class that encapsulates its implementation details and is structurally identical to all other instances of that class.
Abstract Interface (1.4)	A named software representation for an abstraction's behavior that is intended to be implemented by one or more classes.
Composition (1.5)	An organized collection of components interacting to achieve a coherent, common behavior
Association (1.5)	A composition of independently constructed and externally visible parts.
Aggregation (1.5)	A composition that encapsulates (hides) the parts of the composition.
Generalization (1.6)	The identification, and possible organization, of common properties of abstractions.

Term	Definition
Abstraction (1.2)	A named collection of attributes and behavior relevant to modeling a given entity for some particular purpose.
Hierarchy (1.6)	A generalization in which abstractions are organized into a directed a cyclic graph whose arcs denote an "is-a" relation between a more generalized abstraction and the one or more specializations derived from it.
Polymorphism (1.6)	The ability to manipulate objects of distinct classes using only knowledge of their common properties without regard for their exact class.
Design Pattern (1.6)	A named generalization describing the elements and relationships of a solution for a commonly occurring design problem.

CHAPTER 2

Using Objects of a Single Class

2.1 Introduction

In this section the basic aspects of classes and objects are presented. The outermost structure of a class definition is given along with several examples of classes that capture abstractions in a graphical user interface domain as well as an example from an ecological simulation domain. The basic mechanism for creating object is described and the role of variables in providing a way to refer to objects is examined. The close relationship between the concepts of a variable's type and an object's class is seen, lending credence to the idea that a class is a "user-defined type." Also described is the use of the `import` statement to guarantee that the compiler is able to see the definition of classes before use is made of these classes.

2.1.1 Giving a Name to a Class

In Java the keywords "class" and "public" are used to define a new class that is freely (publicly) available to other classes without restriction. Each class is given a distinctive name that conveys the meaning of the abstraction represented by the class. The following code defines the outer structure of a class named Frame that represents a "window" in a graphical user interface system.

```
public class Frame
{               // represent a graphical user interface window
   /* the body of the class definition
      goes in here between the curly braces */
}
```

Similarly, a class that defines an abstraction of a "prey" in a simulation of an ecological environment has the following general structure:

```
public class Prey
{               // represent a "prey" in an ecological simulation
   /* the body of the class definition
      goes in here between the curly braces */
}
```

The body of each classes' definition lies between the open and close braces. The body of the Frame class and the Prey class will be developed in the following sections.

Two-different forms of comments are illustrated in the Frame class definition above. An adjacent pair of slash marks "//" introduces a comment that ends at the end of the current line. A multi-line comment begins with the pair of characters "/*" and end with the matching pair of characters "*/."

An object-oriented program typically involves several, perhaps many, different classes. Other classes related to a windowing system might be:

```
public class Message {...}          // an unchanging line of text
public class TextBox {...}        z // editable lines of text
public class Button  {...}          // a selector that can be "pushed"
```

Other classes related to the ecological simulation might be:

```
public class Predator {...}            // a Predator that hunts Prey
public class Herd {...}             // a group of Prey
public class Pack {...}             // a group of Predators
```

These classes will be seen and used in this and subsequent chapters.

2.1.2 Creating Objects of a Class

Creating an object involves three steps: importing the definition of a class, declaring a variable (identifier) that will refer to an object of that class, and constructing the object. As in C, C++, and many other languages, Java requires that the definition of a class must precede the use of that class in the program text as seen by the compiler. The requirement is needed so that the Java compiler can more easily check that the definition of a class is consistent with its use in declarations and other statements. This is part of the character of Java as a statically typed object oriented language. The programmer must insure that the "declaration before use" rule is met by using the `import` statement to direct the compiler to search for and examine the definition of a given class. More details are in Section 4.9 on how the compiler knows where to search for the classes that are named in the `import` statement. The following code fragment illustrates how objects are created. The fragment's first two statements import the definitions of the Frame and Prey classes:

```
import Frame;       // find definition of Frame class
import Prey;        // find definition of Prey class
Frame display;      // declaration of a variable
Prey a Prey;        // declaration of a variable
...
display = new Frame(...);  // construct Frame object
a Prey = new Prey(...);    // construct Prey object
```

The third statement declares that the variable `display` will refer to an object of the Frame class. Similarly, the fourth statement declares that the variable `aPrey` will refer to an object of the Prey class. These declarations do **not** create the objects. All objects in Java are created by the `new` operator as shown in the last two statements. The ellipsis (i.e., the "...") is not part of Java syntax. This notation is used to denote the values that are typically required to initialize the object being declared. The values that should be given here will be seen when the complete definition of these classes is presented. The object created by the `new` operator is associated with an identifier (variable) by an assignment statement as shown in the last two statements. Defining a variable and creating an object can also be done in a single statement as follows:

```
Frame display = new Frame(...);
Prey aPrey = new Prey(...);
```

In these statements the object created by the new operator is assigned to a variable that is declared on the left-hand side of the assignment operator.

Many variables can be declared that refer to objects from the same class. For example, several variables that can refer to Frame objects and Prey objects can be created as follows:

```
Frame display, viewer;
Frame editor;
Prey rabbit, mouse;
Prey deer;
```

These two declarations create three variables that refer to Frame objects and three variables that refer to Prey objects. Notice that several identifiers (variables) can be created with one declaration, as is done with `display` and `viewer`. A comma must separate adjacent names in the same declaration. Also notice that, as in this example, the same class can be used in different declarations.

two-different variables may refer to the same object. For example, consider the following code that declares three variables:

```
Frame display, viewer;
Frame editor;
...
display = new Frame(...);
editor = new Frame(...);
viewer = display;
```

Two objects are created that are referred to by the variables `display` and `editor`. The last assignment statement means that the variable `viewer` will refer to the same object as that referred to by the variable `display`. In a complete program, some variables always refer to the same object whereas other variables refer to different objects at different times.

Although the variable and the object to which it refers are technically distinct, common terminology often emphasizes their close relationship. In discussing a program, programmers often say "the `display` object" instead of the technically correct "the object referred to by the `display` variable." Not only is the shorter phrase easier to say but it also emphasizes the fact that variables are created for the purpose of naming objects; manipulating an object is done by performing operations on a variable that refers to the object. It is occasionally necessary to use the more precise terminology when the distinction needs to be made between a variable and the object to which the variable refers.

The declaration of an identifier (variable) that refers to an object illustrates the strong connection between the concept of a "type" and the concept of a "class." Compare, for example the following three declarations:

```
int counter;
Frame display;
Prey aPrey;
```

The first declaration creates a variable whose type is "int" and that is named by the identifier "counter." The type "int" determines what operations can be applied to the variable. For example, "+," "-," "<" and "=" are some of the valid operations. The compiler will issue warnings or error messages if invalid operations are attempted. Similarly, the second declaration creates a variable whose type is "Frame" and that is named by the identifier "display," and the third declaration creates a variable whose type is "Prey" and that is named by the identifier "aPrey." As with all types, the compilerwill check that the operations applied to "display" and "aPrey" are appropriate for their types. Because Frame and Prey are programmer-defined types, the valid operations on objects of these types are exactly those given in the definition of the Frame class and the Prey class. The rules of type checking apply to assignment of objects just as they do to assignment of predefined types. For example, one object may be assigned to another object only (at least for now) if they are of exactly the same class. This rule is illustrated by the following code:

```
Frame display, viewer;
Prey aPrey, hunted;
...
display = viewer;     // correct types
aPrey = hunted;       // correct types
viewer = aPrey;       // incorrect types
hunted = display;     // incorrect types
```

It is permissible to assign `viewer` to `display` because these two variables refer to objects of the same class. However, `aPrey` cannot be assigned to `viewer` and `display` can not be assigned to `hunted`---in each case the two variables refer to objects of different classes, equivalently of different types.

2.1.3 UML Notation

The Unified Modeling Language (UML) provides graphical notations for representing classes and objects. Because only a very small part of the class and object concepts has been presented in this section, only a small part of the UML notation is described here. As more of the structure of classes and objects is revealed, more of the UML notation will be seen. The basic UML notation for a class is shown in Figure 2.1. UML allows a class to be represented at two-different levels of detail. A class is drawn as a rectangular box inside of which is written the name of the class. The left part of Figure 2.1 shows the Frame class using only this level of detail. The right part of Figure 2.1 shows the outline of the more detailed representation of the Frame class. The name of the class is written in the top-most compartment. The middle and bottom compartments are empty; the information that can be put in these compartments will be shown in following sections.

The UML representation for an object is similar to that for a class. An object of the Frame class is shown in Figure 2.2. The name of the object in this figure is "display." The name of the class is separated from the class of the object (in this case, the Frame class) by a colon. Both the name of the object and the name of the class are underlined to further distinguish the object notation from the class notation. The left part of Figure 2.2 shows only the basic information about an object. The right part of the figure shows that the object diagram may also have a second compartment. The information that can be placed in this additional compartment will be shown in the next section.

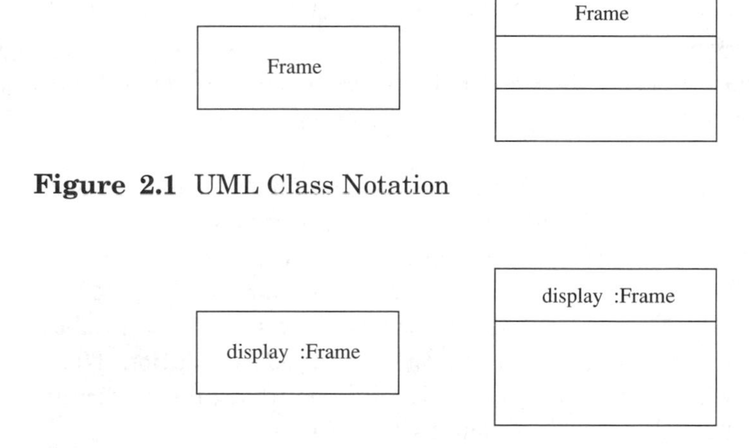

Figure 2.1 UML Class Notation

Figure 2.2 UML Object Notation

Exercises

1. Is it correct to have many classes with different names?
2. Is it correct have many objects of the same class?
3. Is it correct to define class int {...}; ?
4. Is it correct to declare "Frame Frame;"? That is, can an object and a class have the same name?
5. Is it correct to declare "Frame frame;" ?
6. Is it correct to declare "Frame aFrame;" ?
7. Write three declarations that create four Frame objects and two Message objects. Use the ellipsis notation to indicate where the initializing values would appear.
8. Write a different answer to the last question.
9. Write two declarations that create four Prey objects. Use the ellipsis notation to indicate where the initializing values would appear.
10. Write a different answer to the last question.
11. Name five other classes that might be part of a graphical user interface system. Present your answer in the form `public class ClassName {...}` where "`ClassName`" is the name of the class that you have chosen.
12. Name five other classes that might be part of an ecological simulation system. Present your answer in the form `public class ClassName {...}` where "`ClassName`" is the name of the class that you have chosen.
13. Give the declarations for the system described below in what you consider the best style.

    An application has two windows, one for receiving user commands and one for displaying status information. Each window has a message that identifies the window. The command window has two areas where editable text can be displayed, one area for a command and one for command options. The command window has two buttons, one used to execute the command and one to stop the command's execution. The status window has a second message that is used to display any error messages that result from a command's execution.
14. Compare your answer to the last question with someone who has a different style. Identify the ways in which they styles are different.

15. Draw UML diagrams for all of the classes mentioned in this section.

16. Draw UML diagrams for all of the objects mentioned in this section.

2.2 Structure of Classes and Objects

To use objects of an existing class it is necessary to understand something of their structure and operation, just as when learning to drive a car it is useful to understand something about the car's structure (where the driver sits, where the ignition key goes, etc.) and the car's operation (what the steering wheel does, what the accelerator pedal does, etc.).This section describes the structure of the publicly visible parts of a class and the operations that can be performed on objects of that class. These concepts are illustrated by examples from the two application domains introduced in the first section of this chapter: GUI systems and the simulation of a simple ecological model.

2.2.1 Public vs. Private Parts

For a programmer (re)using an existing class, the key element of the class' structure is the class's "public interface." The class's public interface defines the behavior of all objects created from this class definition. The public interface contains a set of methods (also called procedures, member functions, or operations) that can be used to manipulate the objects created from this class. The only way to manipulate an object is by using the methods defined in the public interface of the class from which the object was created.

A class (and any object created from it) also contains a private (hidden, internal, encapsulated) implementation. The user of an object has no concern with how the object is implemented, just as the driver of a car need not have any concern with how the engine is constructed. The internal details of an object's implementation can be ignored by the user of the object.

In Java the public and private portions of a class are denoted by the keywords public and private that are attached individually to method definitions and variable declarations. The use of the public and private keywords are shown in the outline of the Frame class in Figure 2.3. Notice that the class definition itself is denoted as public (`public class Frame`). This means that objects of this class can be created without restriction by any other classes in the program. It will be seen later that, for security, that it is possible to define non-public classes, classes that are restricted so that objects of these classes can only be created by a privileged set of other classes.

```
public class Frame
{
  private data1;    // private, encapsulated data
  private data2;    // private, encapsulated data

  public Frame (arguments)
  { implementation of constructor
  }

  public return-type method1 (arguments)
  {
    implementation of method2
  }

  public return-type method2 (arguments)
  {
    implementation of method2
  }
}
```

Figure 2.3 Use of Public and Private Keywords

In Java, the separation between the public interface and the private implementation is logical and not textual. Notice in the outline of the Frame class that the implementation of the methods is given directly in the definition of the class. Thus, the separation is not textual. A programmer examining the actual source text of the Frame class would be able to see both the private data of the class and the implementation of all of the class' methods. However, such knowledge does not allow the programmer to write code that accesses any of the private elements of the class. Any attempts to access the private elements will be detected as an error by the compiler. Thus, the separation is logical.

There is no required order for the public and private elements of the class definition. Typically, the private elements are grouped together as are the public elements. Some programmers prefer to put the public elements first because these are the most important (hence given first) elements as far as the user of the class is concerned. Other programmers prefer a different order. The order of the private and public elements has no effect on the meaning or use of the class; it is an issue of what the programmer considers the most readable.

The logical separation of the public interface from the private implementation is a major aspect of object-oriented programming. The public interface defines a contract between the object's implementor and the object's user. The contract specifies what service the implementor has agreed to provide. The contract limits the ways in which the user is allowed to manipulate the object. The separation of public interface from private implementation has several advantages:

- it promotes understanding and reuse by reducing the amount of information confronting the user of an object;
- it increases implementation flexibility by allowing the implementor to change the implementation (say to a more efficient one) so that in future programs the object looks and acts the same to the object's user who is unaware that a different implementation is involved;
- it eases the difficult task of debugging by providing a boundary that can be used to isolate the source of the error; and
- it improves the overall design of the system, allowing the system to be presented and understood as a collection of public interfaces.

These benefits will be understood more deeply as the ideas of object oriented programming are developed and as experience is gained in working with and building object-oriented systems.

2.2.2 Methods in the Public Interface

As shown in Figure 2.3, the public interface contains two-different kinds of methods:

1. constructors: methods that define how the object is initialized. There maybe (and commonly are) several constructors, allowing the object to be initialized in different ways. A constructor is invoked implicitly when an object is created. An object cannot be created without a constructor being invoked.
2. behavioral methods: these define how the object behaves or can be manipulated during its lifetime. These methods are often subdivided into:

    - accessors/interrogators/queries: methods that return information about the state of the object but do not change the state of the object, and
    - manipulators/mutators/actions: methods that (potentially) change the state of the object.

A class may also declare a `finalize` method that will be executed when the object is reclaimed by the automatic garbage collection system. The finalizer for an object is invoked when the system has determined that no variable in the program refers to that object. In such a case, the object is no longer visible or useful to the program and the memory resources used by that object can be reclaimed by the system. Through the finalizer, the system gives the object an opportunity to take any programmer-defined actions that are given before the object is deleted. However, the finalize methods are often not needed and are

Table 2.1 Comparison of Constuctors with Other Methods

Comparison	Constructor Method	Behavioral Method
Invoked	Implicitly	Explicitly
Return type	None	Always (at least `void`)
Name	Identical to class name	User chosen (may not be the class name)

usually not declared as part of the public interface to prevent their being called indiscriminantly. The finalizer method and garbage collection are discussed further in Section 2.9.

Constructors are different from behavioral methods in three ways. First, constructors are never invoked explicitly. Constructors are invoked implicitly when an object is created via the `new` operation. It is never correct to explicitly invoke a constructor. Second, constructors do not have are turned type. The nature of a constructor implies that what it produces is an initialized object of the class in which it is defined. Thus, it is syntactically incorrect to declare a constructor with a return type. All other methods, however, must have a return type; the type `void` is used if the method does not return a value. Third, the name of the constructor must be exactly the same as the name of the class in which it is declared. For example, the constructor for the Frame class is named `Frame`; the constructor for the Prey class is named `Prey`. The names are case sensitive so that a method named `frame` will not be recognized as a constructor for the Frame class. These differences are summarized in Table 2.1.

Table 2.1 Comparison of Constuctors with other Methods

2.2.3 An Abstraction for a GUI Window

The Frame class is the first of several *abstractions* from the domain of GUI systems. A GUI window has numerous capabilities as shown in Figure 2.4. A real-world GUI window has operation that can be performed on it to affect its placement and size; it is capable of displaying a wide range of information bearing elements (graphical, iconic, textual); and it affords a means of interacting with the user through control elements (buttons, menus, etc.). To avoid confronting all of these powerful capabilities in the first class being studied, a series of simpler abstractions will be shown. Figure 2.4 shows the first of these simpler abstractions.

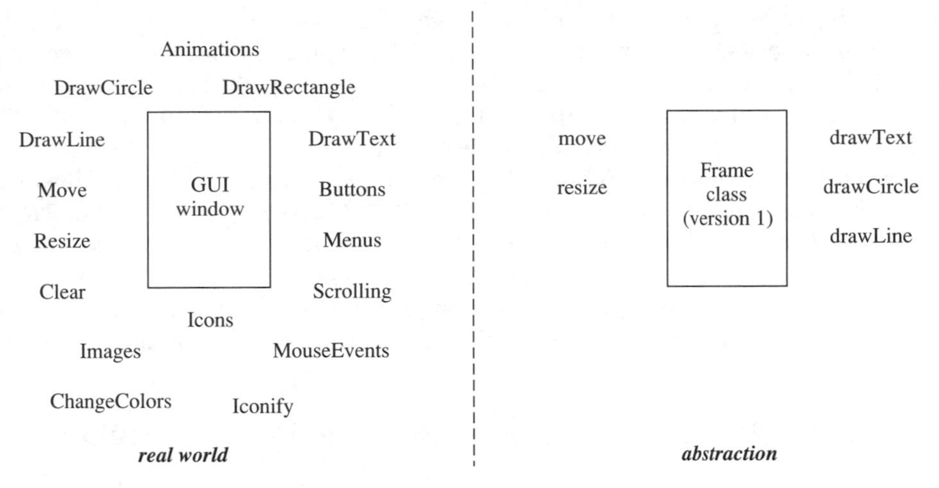

Figure 2.4 Abstraction of a GUI Window

```
public class Frame
{                       // Version 1

   // private implementation not shown

   public            Frame       (String name, int initXCoord, int initYCoord,
                                         int initWidth,  int initHeight)
   public void       resize      (int newHeight, int newWidth)
   public void       moveTo      (int newXCoord, int newYCoord)
   public boolean    isNamed     (String name)
   public void       clear       ()
   public void       drawText    (String text, int atX, int atY)
   public void       drawLine    (int fromX, int fromY, int toX, int toY)
   public void       drawCircle  (int centerX, int centerY, int radius)
}
```

Figure 2.5 Frame Class: version 1

Consistent with the ideas of mapping an abstraction to a class, the first version of the Frame class is defined as shown in Figure 2.5. Neither the private data of the class nor the implementation of the methods are shown in this definition. This is in keeping with the desire to hide all of the implementation details of an object—the user of the class cares only what operations are defined and not how these operations are implemented. The creator of the class must, of course, write the code for these methods and provide the other private data as well. We will see in Chapter 4 how this is done.

As shown in this example, the constructor method has the same name as the name of the class (Frame, in this case). This constructor requires five arguments giving the name to be associated with the Frame, the initial(x,y) coordinates of the

Frame's upper left corner (given by the pair [initXCoord, initYCoord]) and the Frame's initial dimensions (width and height). The `isNamed` method is an accessor method that allows the program to determine if the name of the Frame matches the method's input argument. All other methods are manipulator methods. The two methods `resize` and `moveTo` provide operations to relocate the Frame on the screen and to change its size. The `drawLine` and `drawCircle` methods allow simple graphical shapes to be drawn in the Frame. The method `drawText` allows text to be written into the Frame. The upper left-hand corner of the area where the text is written within the Frame is specified by the (atX, atY) coordinates. The `clear` method erases all text and graphics from the Frame. As noted, a real Frame class would have more methods, but these suffice for a number of interesting examples.

2.2.4 An Abstraction of a Prey in an Ecology Simulation

A second example captures the abstraction of a creature in a simple ecological system. The objects of this class will be used in developing a simulation of the ecological system. An ecological system is a complex interaction among creatures and between these creatures and the habitat that they occupy. As shown in the left part of Figure 2.6, the creatures have many properties, among which are those that determine the structure of the species, the required properties of its habitat, the interaction of the creatures and their habitat, the life-cycle of the creatures, the predators that hunt these creatures, the creatures' own prey, and the propagation characteristics of the species. The "Prey" abstraction shown in the right-hand part of Figure 2.6 ignores many of the detailed properties of real creature. This abstraction is named "Prey" because it does not hunt other creatures; in the simulation to be developed, "Prey" objects will be the targets of other creatures' hunting. The "Prey" abstraction models a single species that can move about in a rectangular part of a two-dimensional habitat. The habitat is divided into equal sized cells. The creature is always located in exactly one of these cells. The location of the Prey in the habitat is defined by the "coordinates" of the cell that the Prey occupies. A Prey creature moves randomly within the habitat, but must always remain within its rectangular area. A Prey creature can only roam a limited distance on each simulated "move"; these creatures live forever and do not propagate.

The definition in Java of a class capturing the Prey abstraction is shown in Figure 2.7. The constructor of the class defines the initial location of the prey in a rectangular area. The rectangular area in which the creature can move is defined by the remaining constructor arguments: the leastX and leastY values define the lower limits of the coordinates of the cell occupied by the creature whereas the rangeX and rangeY values define how far beyond this point the creature may move. The (x,y) coordinates of the creature's current location in the habitat can be found by the `getX` and `getY` methods. The `setRoam` method specifies how far the creature can move from its current location to its next location. That is, the x coordinate of the creature on its next move must lie between x and x+ roam and

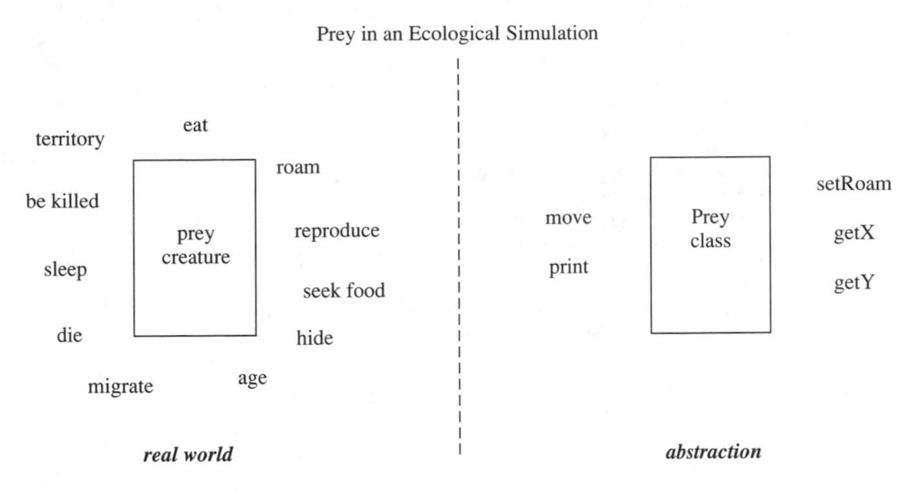

Figure 2.6 Abstraction of a Prey

```
public class Prey
{
   // private implementation
   public Prey(int whereX, int whereY, int leastX, int leastY,
               int rangeX, int rangeY)
   public void move()
   public int getX()
   public int getY()
   public void setRoam(int distance)
   public void print()
}
```

Figure 2.7 The Prey Class Definition

the y coordinate of the creature on its next move must lie between y and y+ roam. The `move` method causes the creature to move from its current location to its next location. The amount of movement is randomly determined. The print method outputs on a line the current location of the Prey object.

UML Notation: More About Classes and Objects

The Frame class in the UML notation is shown in Figure 2.8. Although the syntax is slightly different and the names of some of the parameters hasbeen shortened, the correspondence between the elements of the Frame class definition and its UML equivalent should be clear. As in the previous section, the top compartment of the UML diagram contains the name of the class. The middle compartment contains a description of attributes of the class and the bottom compartment contains the operations that collectively describe the behavior of

Frame
-xCoordinate : Integer -yCoordinate : Integer
+Frame(name :String, x: Integer, y :Integer, h: Integer, w: Integer) +resize(h : Integer, w: Integer) +moveTo(x: Integer, y :Integer) +isNamed(name :String) : boolean +clear() +drawText(text : String, x: Integer, y: Integer) +drawLine(x1 :Integer, y1 :Integer, x2 :Integer, y2 :Integer) +drawCircle(x :Integer, y :Integer, radius :Integer)

Figure 2.8 UML Notation for the Frame Class

Prey
-xCoordinate : Integer -yCoordinate : Integer
+Prey(x: Integer, y :Integer, minx: Integer, miny: Integer, rangeX :Integer, rangeY :Integer) +move() +getX() : Integer +getY() : Integer +setRoam(distance : Integer) +print()

Figure 2.9 UML Notation for the Prey Class

the class. The attributes and operations have several aspects in common. First, each is preceded by a plus ("+") or minus ("--") sign indicating whether the following element is public or private, respectively. In the Frame class all of the attributes are private and all of the operations are public. Second, a similar syntax is used to denote names and their types. Each attribute and each parameter has a name followed by a type with an intervening colon separating the name and the type. The general syntax of an operation is similar to that used to describe methods in Java with the operation's name followed by a comma-separated list of parameters. As shown by the `isNamed` operation, the type of value returned by an operation is given at the end of the operation following a colon that separates the returned type from the rest of the specification ofthe operation. The attributes given for the Frame class in the UML diagram are meant to be suggestive and not a definitive list. The x and y coordinate attributes are clearly attributes of the Frame class, although the user of the Frame class need not be aware of them explicitly. However, an actual Frame class has other attributes that are not discussed here because it involves too much of the underlying implementation.

The Prey class in the UML notation is shown in Figure 2.9. The syntax used in this diagram has already been explained. As with the Frame class, the correspondence between the Prey class definition in Java and the Preyclass representation in the UML diagram should be clear despite the differences in syntax. The attributes given for the Prey class are its x and y coordinates as these attributes can be queried by the `getX` and `getY` operations.

Exercises

1. Illustrate the difference between the public interface and the private implementation in the following ordinary objects:
   - Personal computer
   - Telephone
   - Radio

   For each ordinary object identify several operations in its public interface and name one or more things that are probably in its private implementation.
2. For one of the ordinary objects in the last question show how the public vs. private separation results in the advantages cited above (i.e, reuse, flexibility, debugging, design).
3. Write the public parts of a class definition for a "stack of integers" abstraction.
4. Write the public parts of a class definition for a "file of characters" abstraction.
5. Write the public parts of a class definition for a "calculator" that provides addition, subtraction, multiplication, and division of integer values. Be sure that you include a constructor that gives an initial value of the calculator. Also include methods to access the current value of the calculator and to reset the calculator's value to zero.
6. Extend the "calculator" class by adding methods to perform at least two other useful operations (e.g., squaring the current number).
7. Extend the "calculator" class by adding methods to save and restore the current value to a "memory."
8. Write a variation of the Frame class definition that includes a new method to move a Frame object by a relative amount (i.e., up/down a given number of units and left/right a given number of units).
9. Write a variation of the Frame class definition that includes a new method to change the size of a Frame by a fractional amount (e.g., makes it 50% bigger or 50% smaller).

10. Write a variation of the Frame class that includes new methods to draw rectangles and triangles in the Frame.
11. Write a variation of the Prey class that includes a new method to change the location of the Prey to a specific (x,y) coordinate.
12. Write a variation of the Prey class that includes two new methods to move the Prey a given distance in the x direction and a given distance in they direction.
13. Write a variation of the Prey class that includes two new methods, one of which determines whether the Prey is alive or dead and the other of which causes the Prey to die (i.e., to subsequently report that is dead when the first method is used).
14. Draw a UML diagram for the "stack of integers" class described in the exercises above.
15. Draw a UML diagram for the "file of characters" class described in the exercises above.
16. Draw a UML diagram for the "calculator" class described in the exercises above.

2.3 Manipulating Objects in a Java Application

This section uses the Prey class defined in Section 2.2 to illustrate how to create and manipulate objects in a Java application that can be compiled and executed from the command line. The next section describe show the GUI classes are compiled and executed. As will be seen, the steps for using the ecological simulation classes in a Java application are different from those to use the GUI classes. It is important in working with the code and the exercises to be clear on whether to use a Java application, as described in this section, or the execution environment described in the next section.

2.3.1 Applying Operations to a Prey Object

The code segment below shows the creation of an object of the Prey class. The constructed object, named `rabbit`, is initially located at the coordinates (200, 250) and is constrained so that the x-coordinate of the prey must be in the range from 100 to 300 (`leastX`=100, `rangeX`=200) and the y-coordinate must be in the range from 100 to 400 (`leastY`=100, `rangeY`=300).

```
import Prey;
...
Prey
rabbit(200,250,100,100,200,300);
...
rabbit.setRoam(10);
rabbit.move();

int x = rabbit.getX();
int y = rabbit.getY();

aPrey.print();
```

Once a Prey object is created, any of the methods defined in the Prey class can be applied to that object. In the example code segment, the `setRoam` method is applied to the `rabbit` object using the "dot" operator; the parameter of this operation is the constant integer value 10. Recall that the `setRoam` method defines how far the Prey object can "move" at one time. The `move` operation is applied to the `aPrey` object in a similar way, causing the object to randomly change its location in a way that is consistent with the constraints on its coordinates established by the object's constructor and the roaming distance imposed by the `setRoam` method. The current x-coordinate and the current y-coordinate of the Prey object can be found by applying to the object the `getX` and `getY` methods, respectively. The last line of code in the segment above shows how the current coordinates of the `rabbit` object can be output using the `print` method.

2.3.2 Constructing and Executing an Application

Because Java is an object-oriented language, a Java application takes the form of a class definition. The outline of a class for a Java application is shown in Figure 2.10. The keywords are shown in boldface. The import statement conveys to the

```
// must be in a file named Test.java
import Prey;

public class Test
{
  private Prey rabbit;

  public Test()
  { // create and manipulate rabbit object
  }

  public static void main( String[] args)
  {
    Test prog = new Test();
  }
}
```

Figure 2.10 General Structure of a Java Application

1. Create a user-defined class containing a `main` program; be sure that the signature of main method is correct.
2. Check that the .java file has the same name as the name of the user-defined class.
3. Compile the .java file to produce a corresponding .class file.
4. Run the program using the Java interpreter.

Figure 2.11 Checklist for Executing a Java Application

```
import Prey;

public class PreyDemo
{
   private Prey rabbit;

   public PreyDemo()
   { rabbit= new Prey(100,100, 200,300);
     rabbit.setRoam(20);
     rabbit.print();
     rabbit.move();
     rabbit.print();
   }

   public static void main(String[] args)
   { PreyDemo demo = new PreyDemo();
   }
}
```

Figure 2.12 An Example Program

Java compiler that the definition of the Prey class should be brought into the current compilation context. The compiler must have the definition of the Prey class so that it can perform type-checking to insure that Prey objects are used in a correct way. The import statement must come before the class definition in accordance with the "define before use" rule that is at the heart of the type-checking and safety guarantees of the Java language. Among these safety guarantees is that the object to which a method is applied does implement that method. The four steps to create, compile, and execute a Java command-line program are summarized in the checklist given in Figure 2.11. A complete example program is shown in Figure 2.12.

A Java application has two major features. First, a class must be defined that contains a `main` method as shown by the general form given in Figure 2.10. This step insures that the Java run-time environment will have a proper point at which the program's execution will begin. Programmers familiar with C or C++ will recognize Java's `main` method as the counterpart of the main function in these languages. The signature of the main method must be exactly as shown. The `public` attribute of the `main` method means that method is visible outside of the class so that it can be called by the Java run-time system. The `void` attribute means that the `main` method returns no result—it simply executes to completion. The `static` attribute is more subtle; it means that the Java run-time system will be able to call the `main` method without having created an object of the class containing the `main` method. It is not important at this point to understand the rationale for the static nature of the `main` method, but it is important that this attribute be used in declaring the `main` program. Notice also that the `main` method takes an argument—an array of strings. Second, the `main` method constructs an object of its own class. As shown above, the `main` method constructs a Test object. The constructor of the class creates and manipulates objects, a Prey object in this example.

The user must be sure that the name of the file containing the Java code for the class is in a file whose name is the same as the name of the user-defined class and has the ".java" suffix. For example, the program in the class named `Test` shown above must be in a file named `Test.java`. This naming convention must be followed for the program to execute properly. The naming is case sensitive, so "Test" with a capital "T" and "test" with a lower-case "t" are not the same.

The Java code must be compiled by a Java compiler. The compilation produces a file that has the same name as the Java code file but has the ".class" suffix. For example, the `Test.java` file would be compiled into a file named `Test.class`. The compiler may be the one distributed as part of the Java Development Kit (JDK) or a compiler embedded in anyof the various integrated development environments (such as Microsoft's Visual J++, Symantec's Cafe, or Borland's JBuilder). For simplicity, the publicly available JDK compiler is illustrated here. Additional information about using an integrated development environment is given in Chapter 6. The JDK compiler is invoked by the command

```
javac Test.java
```

where "javac" is the name of the JDK compiler. The result of compiling the file Test.java is a file named Test.class.

Finally, the compiled Java program is executed by the Java interpreter. The `Test.class` file produced by the Java compiler contains low-level instructions, called byte codes, for a "virtual machine." Because the instructions for the virtual machine are different from those of typical workstations, the compiled byte-code form of a Java program cannot be directly executed. Instead, an interpreter for the virtual machine is executed that simulates the execution of the byte-code instructions. There are versions of the Java intepreter for many contemporary workstations. The Java interpreter is executed with the name of the user-defined class as an argument. The command-line necessary to execute the compiled program in the Test.classfile is

```
java Test
```

where "java" is the name of the JDK interpreter that executes the compiled Java program contained in the file `Test.class`. Notice that it is not necessary to include the .class suffix when executing the interpreter.

2.3.3 An Example Program

A complete example program that creates and manipulates a Prey object is shown in Figure 2.12. This program conforms to the general outline given above. The main method creates an object of the PreyDemo class. The constructor performs a sequence of steps to create and then manipulate a Prey object. This program outputs the coordinates of the Prey object at its initial location and after its first move.

2.3.4 UML Object Notation

In addition to representing classes, UML provides a notation for representing individual objects created from those classes. An example of the UML object notation is shown in Figure 2.13 using as an object the `rabbit` object declared earlier in this section. An object diagram has two compartments. The upper compartment shows the name of the object (`rabbit`) and the name of the class (Prey). The object's name is given so that two-different objects of the same class can be differentiated. The class name is given so that it clear what type of object is being represented. Both the object name and the class name are underlined to further note that this is an object, and not a class, diagram. The lower compartment of the object diagram contains a list of attribute value pairs. In this example, only two of the attributes for a Prey object are shown. Both attributes are private, as indicated by the minus sign ("--") preceding the name of the attribute. The first attribute, `xCoordinate`, has the value 200, whereas the second attribute, `yCoordinate`, has the value 250. These two values are integer amount because the type of these attributes is declared as Integer in the UML diagram for the Prey class shown in the previous section.

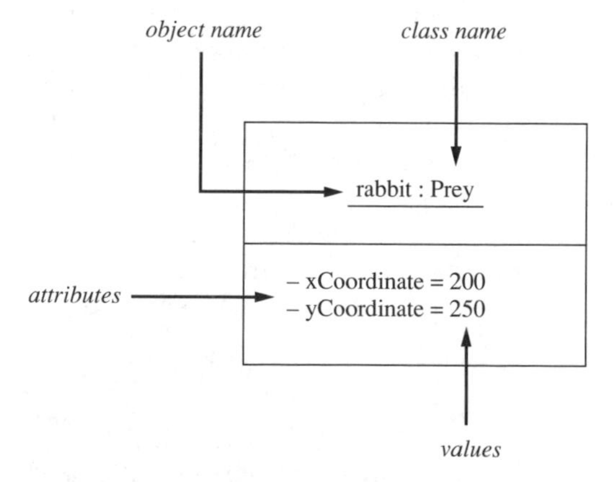

Figure 2.13 Representing an Object in UML

Exercises

1. Follow the steps described above to compile and execute the example Test application.
2. Edit the Test example application given above so that the static attribute is removed from the declaration of the `main` method. Attempt to compile and execute this revised example. At what step is there a problem? Be sure to note the error message that results so that you will be able to recognize this problem.
3. Copy the Test example application given above into a file named `Wrong.java`. Can you compile and execute the Wrong.java file? If not, note the errormessage(s) that results so that you will be able to recognize this problem.
4. What is one disadvantage to Java's "virtual machine" approach?
5. What is one advantage to Java's use of the "virtual machine" approach?
6. Write a Java application that creates a Prey object and prints out its location after each of its first 50 moves.
7. Write a Java application that creates a Prey object and finds out how far it is, in straight-line distance, from its initial starting point after 100 move operations.
8. Write a Java application that creates two Prey objects at the same location that can move in the same rectangular area. How far apart are the locations of these two objects after 100 `move` operations?
9. Extend the UML object diagram given in Figure 2.13 to show all of the attributes initialized by the Prey class constructor.
10. Draw a UML object diagram for a Prey object declared as follows:

```
Prey hare = new Prey(100,200, 300,300, 50,50);
```

2.4 Manipulating GUI Objects in a Simple Programming Environment

The previous section described how to construct and execute a Java application. This section describes how to create and manipulate Frame objects, and other

GUI objects introduced later, in a special programming environment that is provided with the software distributed with this text. One purpose of the special programming environment is to conceal a number of low-level details regarding the workings of the underlying Java libraries. A second purpose for the special programming environment is to provide a way for objects to be created and manipulated using a high-level iconic interface. It must be noted that this special programming environment is **not** part of the standard Java framework, it is only a device used in conjunction this book's software. However, the special programming environment is, in some respects, modeled after the form of a Java applet.

2.4.1 Applying Operations to a Frame Objects

A Frame object can be created and manipulated as shown in this code segment:

```
import Frame;
...
Frame display = new Frame ("Test Window", 10,20, 100, 200);
...
display.moveTo(50, 50);
display.resize(200,200);
display.drawText("Really Neat!", 50,50);
```

The import statement is used to access the definition of the Frame class. A Frame object named `display` is declared and constructed using the `new` operator. The Frame constructor method is called implicitly. The constructor arguments create a Frame whose upper left hand corner is at location (10,20) and whose height and width are 100 and 200, respectively. Once the `display` object has been constructed, it may be operated upon. In this example, the display object is first moved to location (50,50) using the `moveTo` method and then the size of the Frame is changed to a 200 by 200 square shape using the `resize` method. Finally, the `drawText` method is used to write the text “Really Neat!” in the Frame at the location (50,50) relative to the upper left-hand corner of the Frame. Notice that the “.” ("dot") operator is used to invoke a method of an object. Thus, “`display.moveTo(...)`” means to invoke the `moveTo` method on the object `display`. People programming in object-oriented languages often use phrasing like “ask the display object to move itself” to refer to operations being taken on objects. This phrasing reflects the point of view that an object is an entity that is capable of performing certain actions (e.g., a Frame object knows how to move itself to a new location).

Because there will be several extensions and revisions made to the Frame class, the definitions of the Frame classes are organized in separate directories in the software distribution accompanying this text. Which Frame class definition is accessed by the import statement depends on the setting of the CLASSPATH environment variable on your system and possibly the directory in which the file containing the import statement is located. These details are explained further in the notes supplied with the software distribution. Subsequent versions of the Frame class, and other classes that have versions, are organized and will be accessible in a similar way. In the following material, the import statement for a class always refers to the most recently defined version of a class.

2.4.2 Events and Reactive Systems

Programming with GUI objects—like objects of the Frame class and others that will be introduced later—involves a programming style that is qualitatively different from that typically seen in introductory programming courses. The difference in the programming style is due to the fact that GUI systems are ***event-driven*** or ***reactive*** systems. These terms reflect that the system is "driven" by the occurrence of external "events" (mouse clicks, clock alarms) to which the system must "react." The typical life-cycle of an event-driven or reactive system is:

- receive notification that an event has occurred,
- use information about the current state of the system to decide how to react to the event,
- react to the event by updating the display and changing the system's state information, and
- return and await the next notification.

The program does not "read" its inputs or control when such inputs occur, it simply reacts to their occurrence. Some simple examples using objects of the Frame class are given below.

The events in a GUI system come from two-different sources: the user and the hardware clock. In a typical workstation environment the user generates events by moving the mouse, pressing and releasing mouse buttons, or by pressing keys on the keyboard. With other peripheral devices the user might generate events by movements of a joystick, track-ball, or virtual reality devices (gloves, head-mounted displays, etc.). Only mouse events are dealt with in the first, simple programming environment. Timing events are generated by the hardware clock. These events are of interest because they are needed to create animated components in a user interface. A very simple example of this is blinking text that draws the user's attention to important information in the user interface. For the program to make the text blink, the program must have some idea of the passage of time. A sequence of timer events provides the program with this notion of time.

```
// This is the interface between the simple programming
// environment and the user-defined "program" class

public interface Program
{  public void onStart();
   public void onMouseEvent(String frameName, int x, int y, int eventType);
   public void onTimerEvent();
   public void onPaint();
}
```

Figure 2.14 The Program Interface

2.4.3 A Simple Programming Environment

A simple programming environment will be used to begin writing programs that create and manipulate GUI objects. Of course non-GUI objects, such as the Prey class, can also be used in this environment, although they will not have a visual representation in the user interface. This environment has several purposes. First, the environment assumes acknowledge of only the basic Java language features for creating and manipulating objects. Thus, programming can begin using only the language features that have been introduced so far. Second, the environment takes care of many details about windowing systems so that attention can be focused on learning and applying the concepts of object-oriented programming and the Java language without the need to understand, or even be aware of, the underlying details of windowing systems. Third, the programming environment supports in a simple and direct manner the reactive style of programming required by GUI applications. When the key parts of the Java language have been presented, the simple programming environment will be dropped and the details of the Java run-time environment that supports GUI objects will be seen (Figure 2.14).

As Java is an object-oriented language, a "program" takes the form of a class definition. To "execute" or "run" such a "program" in the simple programming environment means that an object of the class is instantiated and the methods defined for this object are invoked in some way. The single object created at the beginning of the program may create numerous other objects each of which may create other objects, and so on. Although the first programs will have only one or two objects, the point will be quickly reached where the complete program is populated by numerous interacting objects.

The simple programming environment defines an interface that a "program" class must implement. This interface defines how the environment will interact with the object of the user-defined class. As shown in Figure 2.14, this interface is named Program and consists of four methods.

The `onStart` method is called exactly once. This method can be used to initialize any objects and data as well as create the initial display that the user sees. The `onPaint` method is called whenever the system suspects that the user's display may have been "damaged" and should be redrawn. Common actions that trig-

onStart	Initialize global objects, global variables, and the user display
onPaint	Redraw the user display when needed
onMouseEvent	React to mouse clicks and/or mouse movement
onTimerEvent	React to a clock event

Figure 2.15 Summary of Functions in the Program Interface

```
import Frame;
import Program;

public class General implements Program
{

   // implementation of the four methods
   // defined in the Program interface
}
```

Figure 2.16 General Structure of a "Program" Class

ger this method being called are when a window is moved, resized, or exposed to view after being partially, or completely, obscured by an overlapping window. Whenever, within the display area of a Frame object, the user clicks a mouse button or moves the mouse, the `onMouseEvent` method is called. This function has input parameters giving the name of the Frame object in which the event occurred, the x and y coordinates of the mouse's current location, and information about the type of the event that has occurred. The `onTimerEvent` function is called whenever a clock alarm occurs. The role of each of the four functions in the simple programming environment is briefly summarized in Figure 2.15.

A program is written for the simple programming environment by defining a class that implements the Program interface. To properly implement the Program interface, the user-defined class must contain at least the four methods that are defined in the Program interface. If the program does not intend to use a method in the Program interface (e.g., the program is not designed to use mouse events), the body of an unused method in the user-defined class can contain no code; the method exists but takes no action. It is important that all of the four methods be implemented in the user-defined class, even if the body of the method contains no code.

A class that creates Frame objects and represents a program to be executed by the simple programming environment is shown in Figure 2.16. The first import statement conveys to the Java compiler that the definition of the Frame

```
1. Create a user-defined class that implements the Program interface.
2. Check that the .java file has the same name as the name of the
   user-defined class.
3. Compile the .java file to produce a corresponding .class.
4. Run the simple programming environment.
```

Figure 2.17 Checklist for Executing a Program in the Simple Programming Environment

class should be brought into the current compilation context. The implements keyword is used to declare that the class intends to provide an implementation for all of the methods defined in the Program interface. This commitment is checked by the compiler, that is, it checks to see that the class claiming to implement an interface actually does implement each of the methods defined in the interface. Some example programs are shown below.

To prepare a program for execution, the user must take four steps. First, a class must be defined that implements the Program interface. This step insures that the simple programming environment will be able to properly interact with the objects instantiated from this class. Second, the user must be sure that the name of the file containing the Java code for the class is in a file whose name is the same as the name of the user-defined class and has the ".java" suffix. For example, if the user completes the definition of the class named General shown in Figure 2.16, then this code must be in a file named General.java. Third, the Java code must be compiled by the Java compiler. This produces a file that has the same name as the Java code file but has the ".class" suffix. Fourth, the simple programming environment is executed with the name of the user-defined class as an argument. The simple programming environment is itself written in Java. The name of this environment is "jake," a shorthand for JULIUS (Java Utility for Learning about Interactive User interface Systems). The command-line necessary to execute the simple programming environment is:

```
java jake
```

where "java" is the name of the Java interpreter that executes the Java program "jake." These four steps are summarized in the checklist in Figure 2.17.

When executed, the simple programming environment displays two windows: a "Start" window that provides controls for initiating the program, terminating the program, and controlling a simple timer; and a "Simulator" window that allows classes and objects to be manipulated through icons. These two windows and the relationships between them are explained below.

2.4.4 The Start Window

The "Start" window is shown in Figure 2.18. The exact appearance of the window might be slightly different on different platforms because Java uses the native windowing system to generate the low-level user interface components. Thus, a button or slider bar may appear slightly differently on a Windows 95 platform

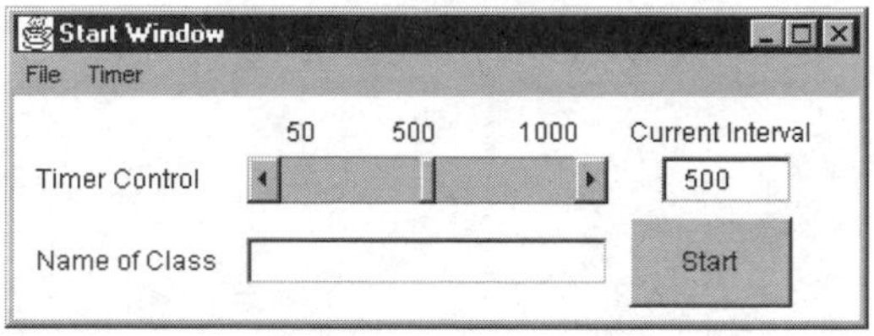

Figure 2.18 The Start Window

than on a Sun/Solaris platform. Although the appearance may vary, the operation of the controls in the "Start" window are the same on all platforms.

The controls in the "Start" window operate in the following way. The name of a class that implements the Program interface should be entered in the text area located in the bottom center of the "Start" window. When the "Start" button is pressed the Environment attempts to instantiate an object of the class whose name was entered in the text area. If this object cannot be created, an error dialogue appears that, when dismissed, returns the user interface to its original condition. In the event of an error, make sure that all of the items in the checklist were done correctly and that the name of the class was typed correctly keeping in mind that class names are case sensitive. If the object is created, the "Start" button is removed from the user interface and the `onStart` method of this object is invoked. At any time, the entire program can be terminated by selecting the "Quit" item in the "File" menu. The "Timer" menu contains two items for turning on and off a timer (a source of timer events). The occurrence of a timer event will cause the `onTimerEvent` method to be called. The interval of this timer (the duration between alarms) is controlled by the slider bar labeled "Timer Control." The slider and the timer are calibrated in milliseconds. The initial slider setting is at 500 milliseconds (one-half a second). The range of timer settings is between 50 milliseconds (one-twentieth of a second) and 1000 milliseconds (one second). The timer interval may be changed either while the timer is running or when the timer is turned off.

2.4.5 The Simulator Window

The "Simulator" window provides a specialized visual programming environment that simulates the operations performed on classes and objects in an object-oriented program. The "Simulator" window is shown in Figure 2.19. The window is divided into two parts by a solid vertical line. The left part of the window is labeled "Class Space" and the right part of the window is labeled the "Object Space." The labels on these spaces suggest the types of entities that are represented by the icons appearing in them. Initially, the class space contains a single icon and the object space is empty. The icon appearing in the class space is a visual representation of the Frame class; the visual appearance of the icon and

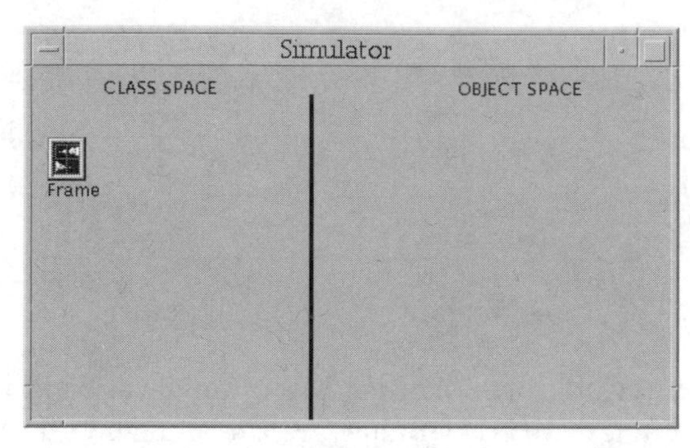

Figure 2.19 The Simulator Window

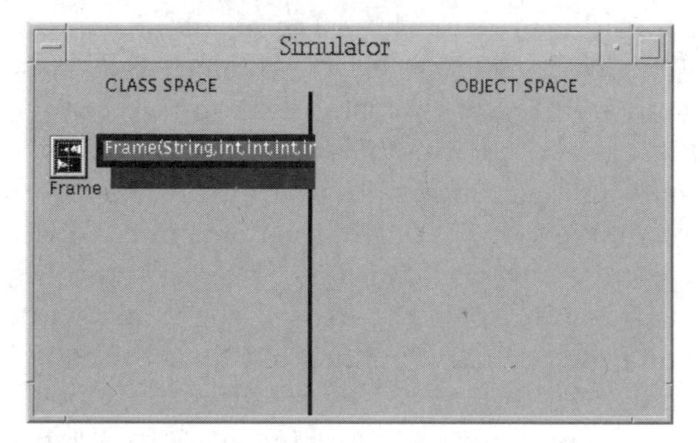

Figure 2.20 The Constructor Menu

its label convey this relationship. The icon can be manipulated in ways that are suggestive of how a class definition is used in a program. As explain below, the Frame class icon can be manipulated to create one or more Frame objects. For each Frame object that is created an icon will appear in the object space and a new window will appear on the user's display. The icon for an object provides a way to execute the methods of the Frame object. The effect of executing the method can be seen in the position, dimensions, or contents of the window corresponding to the icon. The class space for the code related to this chapter will only contain the single Frame icon. In the next chapter more icons will appear as additional classes are added to the simple programming environment.

A Frame object can be created using the Simulator window as follows. Performing a control-click on the Frame icon in the class space causes a menu to appear immediately adjacent to the icon. The control-click can also be used to dismiss the menu. This menu, as shown in Figure 2.20, contains one entry for each constructor defined for the class. The constructor menu is for the first version of the Frame class that contains only a single constructor. The constructor menu for later versions of the Frame class will contain multiple entries. Notice that the constructor menu shows the signature of the constructor, it gives the types of the arguments as they must appear when the constructor is used.

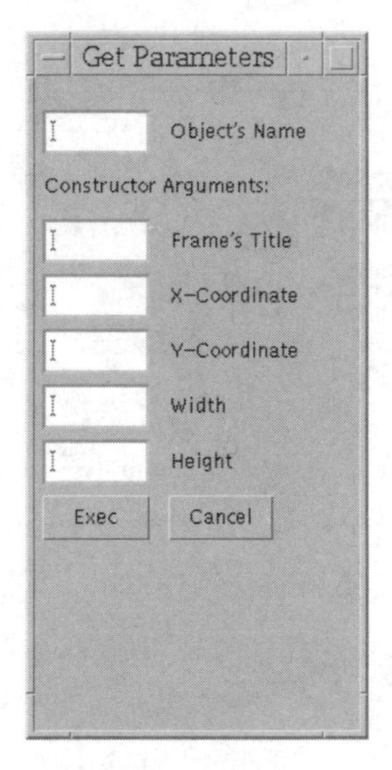

Figure 2.21 Constructor Dialogue Box

For example, the first argument in the constructor shown below must be a String and the remaining arguments must be simple integer values.

Clicking on an entry in the constructor menu indicates that an object should be created using that constructor. To construct an object, values must be given for each of the constructors arguments. For this purpose, the constructor selected from the constructor menu presents a dialogue box whose entries correspond to the required constructor arguments. The dialogue box for the constructor shown in Figure 2.20 is pictured in Figure 2.21. The dialogue box consists of three logical area from top to bottom. The topmost part of the dialogue box is a text area labeled "Object's Name." The name entered in this field is used as a label for the icon that will appear in the object space portion of the Simulator window. The middle part of the dialogue box contains a series of fields, one for each of the constructor's arguments. The user should enter appropriate values into all of these fields. The bottom part of the dialogue box contains two control buttons. The "Exec" button causes the constructor to be run whereas the "Cancel" button dismisses the dialogue box and terminates the constructor operation as if it was never attempted. Pressing the "Exec" button causes an icon to appear in the object space part of the Simulator window and an actual window to appear on the users display. The title, location, and shape of the window correspond to the values entered by the user in the constructor dialogue box.

Figure 2.22 shows the effect of executing the selected constructor in the Simulator window. Not shown is the actual window that appears on the user's display. The icon for the constructed object appears in the object space part of the Simulator window. The icon used for the object is the same as that used for the

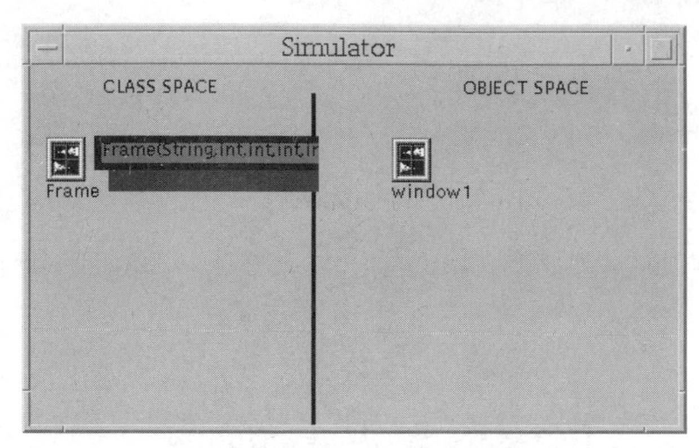

Figure 2.22 An Object Icon in the Object Space

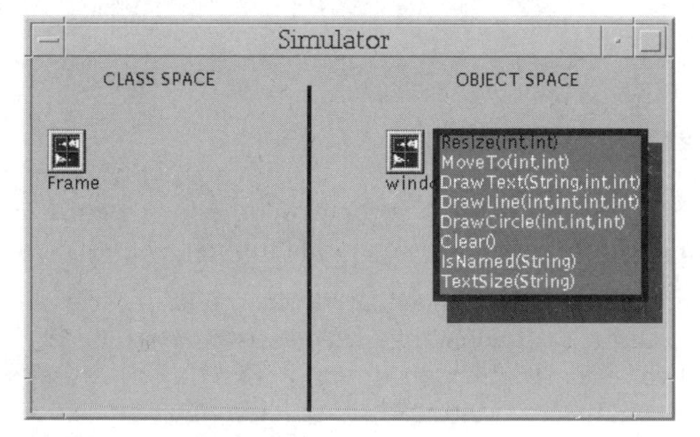

Figure 2.23 The Menu of Methods for an Object

class to reflect that the object was constructed from the class. Thus, the relationship between a class and the objects of that class is visually apparent. This visual similarity will be useful later when there are multiple objects of several classes. The object icon is labeled "window1" assuming that this is the text string entered by the user in the "Object's Name" field of the constructor dialogue box. Also notice that the constructor menu remains visible in the class space. By selecting the constructor menu entry again (by clicking on the menu entry), additional Frame objects can be created. The constructor menu can be dismissed by a control-click operation on the Frame icon in the class space.

The actual window on the user's display created by the above steps can be manipulated using the Frame icon that appears in the object space part of the Simulator window. The list of methods that can be applied to the object are shown to the user in a menu that appears by control-clicking on the icon in the object space. The menu of methods for the Frame object is shown in Figure 2.23. The menu appears adjacent to the icon and can be dismissed by control-clicking on the icon again. A method can be selected by clicking on it and, as with constructors, a dialogue box will appear into which the value of the required arguments can be given. This dialogue box also contains "Exec" and a "Cancel" buttons that execute the method or cancel the operation, respectively.

Two other mouse actions can be applied to an icon in the object space. The shift-control-click combination on an icon in the object space causes the icon and the corresponding object (and for a Frame object its corresponding window) to be deleted. For an icon representing a Frame object a shift-click combination exposes a small window adjacent to the icon that shows the x and y coordinates of the cursor within that window and the up/down state of the mouse button.

The Simulator window can be used in two-different ways. First, as a standalone visual programming environment the simulator window can be used to explore visually the concepts of object construction and method execution. Second, when a program is executed in the simple programming environment, using the Start window as described above, the objects created by that program will be represented by icons in the object space of the Simulator. The feedback provided by the appearance of these icons can sometimes be used as testing or debugging aid when working with the initial classes defined in these chapters. The object created by the program (whose icons appear in the object space of the Simulator window) can also be manipulated directly through the Simulator window.

2.4.6 Sample Programs

Two simple programs are presented that illustrate the simple programming environment. The first program is a simple "Hello World" program that illustrate show to display a string of text in a Frame. The second program adds to the first program the use of timer events to create a "Hello World" text that blinks. An example program that uses the `onMouseEvent` method is shown in the next section. The exercises at the end of this section contain a number of interesting small programs that can be written using the Frame class and the simple programming environment.

The "Hello World" program is shown in Figure 2.24. This program uses the first version of the Frame class definition to declare a Frame object named `window` that is located at position (200,200) on the display and is 400 pixels wide and 400 pixels tall. This window will have a title of "Hello World Program" when it appears on the display. Both the `onStart` and the `onPaint` methods clear the window object and write the string "Hello World!" near the upper left-hand corner of the window. The HelloWorld class satisfies its commitment to implement the Program interface by providing the definitions of all of the method defined in the Program interface. Because they are not used, there is no code for the `onMouseEvent` and `onTimer` event methods.

The execution of the HelloWorld1 program is shown in the snapshot in Figure 2.25. There are three windows shown in the figure. In the lower left-hand

```
import Frame;
import Program;

class HelloWorld1 implements Program
{
 private Frame window;

   public void onStart()
   { window = new Frame("Hello World Program", 200, 200, 400, 400);
     window.clear();
     window.drawText("Hello World!", 20, 20);
   }

   public void onMouseEvent(char *frameName, int x, int y, int eventInfo)
   {
   }

   public void onTimerEvent(){}

   public void onPaint()
   { window.clear();
     window.drawText("Hello World!", 20, 20);
   }
}
```

Figure 2.24 The First Hello World Program

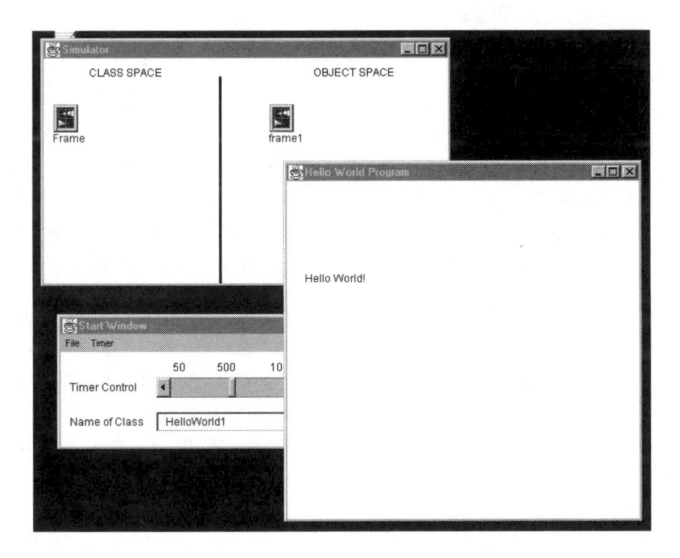

Figure 2.25 The Window Created by the First Hello World Program

part of the figure is the Start Window. As can be seen, the name `HellowWorld1` has been entered in the text area to identify the program to execute. The Simulator window is shown at the top of the figure. Notice that there are two icons in

```
import Frame;
import Program;

class HelloWorld2 implements Program
{
 private Frame window;
 private boolean visible;

  public void onStart()
  { window = new Frame("Hello World Program", 200, 200, 400, 400);
    window.clear();
    window.drawText("Hello World!", 20, 20);
    visible = true;
  }

  public void onMouseEvent(String frameName, int x, int y,
                            int eventInfo)
  {
  }

  public void onTimerEvent()
  { window.clear();
    if (visible) visible = false;
    else
    { visible = true;
      window.drawText("Hello World!", 20, 20);
    }
  }

  public void onPaint()
  { window.clcar();
    if(visible) window.drawText("Hello World!", 20, 20);
  }
}
```

Figure 2.26 Hello World Program with Timer Events

the Simulator window: a Frame icon in the area labeled "Class Space" that represents the Frame class and a Frame icon in the area labeled "Object Space" that represents the window created by the HelloWorld1 program. The Simulator does not know what name the HelloWorld1 program uses to refer to this window, so the Simulator labels the Frame objectic on with the generated name `frame1`. The window that is generated by the HelloWorld1 program is shown on the right. Notice that the title bar at the top of this window displays the string "Hello World Program" given by the HelloWorld1 program. Also notice that the string "Hello World!" is drawn in this window as a result of the `drawText` method in the HelloWorld1 program. The three windows in this figure were captured on a Windows 95 system. Remember that the exact appearance of these window may be different on other machines because the underlying Java libraries use a local, or native, GUI components to preserve that platform's "look and feel" characteristics.

The second example program, shown in Figure 2.26, illustrates how timer events are handled. In this program the "Hello World!" string is turned into blinking text by alternately clearing and writing the string on successive timer events. The rate of blinking is controlled by the timer interval. Remember that the timer events will not occur until the timer is turned on using the "Timer" menu in the Start window. Also remember that the slider bar in the Start window controls the timer interval (the time between timer events). The program uses additional state information, the variable `visible`, to record whether the string is or is not visible at the current time. In addition to the `onTimerEvent`, the `onPaint` method uses this state information to decide whether or not to write the string of text in the window when the window is refreshed.

2.4.7 UML Object Notation

The UML notation for objects was described at the end of the Section 2.3 and is briefly repeated here for completeness. Figure 2.27 shows and example of using the UML notation to represent an object of the Frame class. The Frame object depicted in this figure is the one used in the Hello World example programs above. As shown in the top compartment of the UML diagram, the name of the object is `window` and it is an object of the Frame class. Note that the object's name and the name of the class are both underlined in the object diagram. The diagram shows five private attributes and the values given to these attributes by the Frame class constructor used in the example programs. For example, the `name` attribute has the value "Hello World Program" and the `xCoordinate` attribute has the value 200.

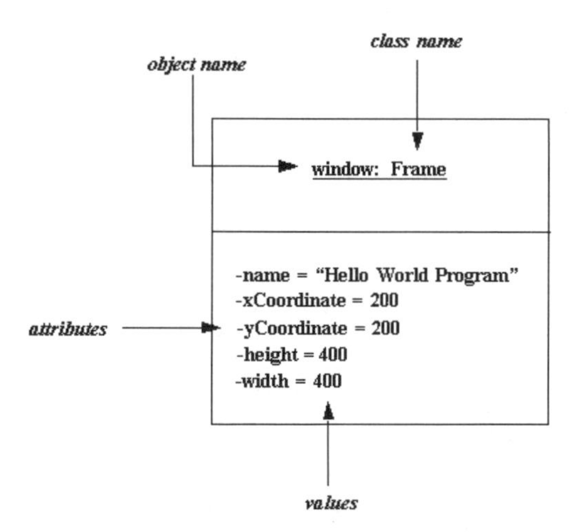

Figure 2.27 Representing a Frame Object in UML Notation

Exercises

1. Write a declaration that creates a Frame object at location (20, 30) with a width of 150 and a height of 175.
2. Write a declaration that creates a Frame object at location (20, 30) with a width of 150 and a height of 175.
3. Write a declaration that creates a Frame object at location (20, 30) with a width of 150 and a height of 175.
4. Write a segment of code to move the Frame you created in the step above to location (50,50) and change its size to a width of 100 and a height of 200.
5. Write a program that displays your full name approximately centered in a Frame that is itself approximately centered on the screen. Note that you may have to do some experimentation with the sizes and locations.
6. Remove the code from the onPaint method in the Hello World program. Experiment with this program to determine how this changes its behavior.
7. Write a program that draws a circle of radius 20 in each corner of a Frame of size 400 by 400.
8. Analog Clock: write a program that draws a picture of an analog clock in a Frame. A circle can be used for the clock face and a single line can be used to draw one hand on the clock. Place the hand pointing straight up.
9. Two-Handed Analog Clock: write a program that draws a picture of an analog clock in a Frame. A circle can be used for the clock face and two line scan be used to a shorter (hours) hand and a longer (seconds) hand. Place the hands so that the time on the clock reads 3 o'clock.
10. Analog Clock with Numbers: modify the Analog Clock program so that the numbers 1 through 12 appear around the outside of the clock face.
11. Animated Analog Clock: modify one of the Analog Clock programs so that the hand(s) move. On each timer event move the hand(s) to the next position.
12. Corner Tour: Write a program that places a circle in the upper left corner of a Frame. The program then moves this circle to the upper right, lower right, and lower left corners before returning the circle to its original position. Repeat this cycle ten times. At each position, display

in the window a line of text appropriate for the current position of the window such as "Upper Left," Upper Right," "Lower Right," "Lower Left."

13. Border Walk: write a program that moves a circle in small steps around the outside border of the screen starting from an initial location in th eupper left hand corner of the screen. Can you make the motion appear smooth?

14. Plot in a Frame object the first 100 locations of a Prey object. Represent the position of the Prey by a small circle whose center coordinates are the x and y coordinates of the Prey object.

15. Plot in a Frame object the first 100 locations of a Prey object. Represent the movement of a Prey by drawing a straight line between successive locations of the Prey object.

16. Draw a UML object diagram for the display object used in the example code at the beginning of this section.

17. Draw a UML object diagram for a Frame object whose name is "drawing" that is located at the position (20, 30) with a width of 150 and a height of 175.

18. Draw a UML object diagram for a Frame object that is created by the following statement:

```
Frame viewer = new Frame("View Window", 100, 300, 500, 600);
```

2.5 Named Constants

2.5.1 Role of Named Constants

It is often useful to define a named, constant value that represents a significant or special value in the application. The name conveys the meaning of the constant value. The constant value cannot be changed: its value is fixed, immutable. In some cases constants are used to define mathematical values such as pi (3.14159...). In other cases constants are used to define program limits, such as the length of array, or special values that have application-specific meaning, such as a code that means whether a file can be read, written, or both read and written. The best way to organize special values is to define them in a class that is related to the nature of the constants. It will be shown below, for example, how special codes for mouse button events are defined in the Frame class whereas special values for the roaming ability of Prey objects is defined in the Prey class.

There are several advantages to defining named, constant values. Three of these advantages of this practice are:

1. It promotes platform independent: if the values relate to system resources, the natural values to use on different platforms (operating systems, libraries, etc.) may be different. In this case, the user's code is able to operate correctly on different platforms because the code only refers to the constant values by their name (not the actual values of these constant variables). The implementation of the class on each platform defines the value for the named constant appropriate for that platform. For example, if different platforms use different values to denote that the mouse button was pressed when a mouse event occurs, then a named constant can be defined to represent the value. Any program that uses the named constant for the value, as opposed to the actual value, can then run on any platform because the program is not tied to the value, which changes with platforms, but to the name of the constant, which does not change with platforms.
2. It increases the implementor's flexibility: the user's code is only dependent on the name of the constant value, not on the specific value of the constant. The implementor can change these values without "breaking" the user's code. Thus, adding new values or reorganizing the values is easy for the implementor. For example, if an implementor changed the value denoting that the mouse button was pressed, only the named constant definition would need to be changed. The Java code that uses the named constant remains unchanged. However, any Java code that used the actual value would no longer be correct, such code would have to be found (a potentially difficult job) and changed.
3. It improves the readability of the code: placing the actual values in the detailed code does not convey much information about the programmer's intention. However, the name of a constant value is chosen to convey suggestive, intuitive meaning. By using these names, the programmer's code is easier to read and understand. For example, the name MOUSE_DRAG is more readable and suggestive of the program's meaning than the value 3.

Although the names of the constant values are given in documentation, the values need not be. Even if the programmer using the named constants knows the actual value of the constant, good programming practice requires that only the name of the constant be used in the code.

Named constants may be either private to a class or declared to be public so that they can be accessed outside of the class in which they are defined. The mathematical constants, such as pi, are most naturally defined in a mathematics-related class that makes them public so that these constants can be accessed wherever they are needed. Codes that have application-specific meaning are also naturally defined as public constants. The read/write code for a file would naturally be defined in a file-related class and made public so that classes that use files can access these codes. However, a value that represents the length of an array used internally within a class is better declared as a private named constant because its meaning is restricted to that class.

2.5.2 Declaring Named Constants

The Frame class needs to define a set of codes that define the type of the mouse event that has occurred in a window represented by a Frame object. The type of the event is communicated to the user's code through the last parameter (`eventType`) of the `onMouseEvent` method. There are four types of mouse events that correspond to depressing the mouse button (`MOUSE_DOWN`), releasing a depressed mouse button (`MOUSE_UP`), moving the mouse (`MOUSE_MOVE`), and dragging the mouse (`MOUSE_DRAG`). Dragging is a movement of the mouse while holding the mouse button down. Each of these events is given a unique integer value. By testing the value passed as the `eventType` parameter of the `onMouseEvent` method, the user's code is able to determine what type of mouse event occurred and can react accordingly. For example, some program may react to drag events but not to move events.

The syntax for defining named constants in Java is illustrated by an extension to the Frame class that defines a set of codes for the types of mouse events. The extensions to the Frame class are shown in Figure 2.28.

The syntax for declaring a named constant as shown in the Frame class involves:

1. The name of the constant. In the example above the names of the constants are MOUSE_DOWN, MOUSE_UP, MOUSE_DRAG, and MOUSE_MOVE. It is only a stylistic convention that the names of constants are given in capital letters with underscore characters separating words for readability. This convention is useful in easily distinguishing named constants from variables. Technically, the name of a constant must obey the same rules as that for a variable name.

```
public class Frame
{
   public static final int MOUSE_DOWN = 1;
   public static final int MOUSE_UP   = 2;
   public static final int MOUSE_DRAG = 3;
   public static final int MOUSE_MOVE = 4;
   //...
   // other parts of Frame class unchanged
   //...
}
```

Figure 2.28 Named Constants in the Frame Class

2. The value of the constant. In the Frame class the constants are assigned the values 1 through 4. Each constant must be assigned a value in the declaration. Failing to assign a value to the constant is a syntax error. As expected of a constant, the value of the named constant cannot be changed during the execution of the program.

3. Four modifiers that define a constant in Java. These are:

   a. **int** (or more generally, the type of the constant)—this modifier determines the type of the constant. The type may be any built-in type (int, float, etc.), any Java-defined type (e.g., String), or any user-defined type (e.g., Frame).

   b. **final**—this modifier specifies that the given value is the final value, the value cannot be modified. It is this modifier that gives the "constant" aspect to the named constant.

   c. **public** (or private) — this modifier determines the accessibility of the object. Using public means that the named constant can be accessed outside of the class in which it is declared. Using private means that the named constant can only be accessed within the class where it is declared. In the example of the Frame class the named constants are declared as public so that they can be used outside of the Frame class.

   d. **static** — this modifier specifies that the named constant is associated with the class in which it is declared and not with the objects of the class. This is a subtle distinction. In the case of the Frame class this modifier means that the four integer constants need not be repeated in each object of the Frame class, allowing each Frame object to be represented in a smaller amount of memory. Other aspects of the static declaration will be considered later.

   These parts of the constant declaration are also shown in Figure 2.29.

2.5.3 Accessing Named Constants

A variation of the Hello World program that responds to mouse events method is used to illustrate how to access the named constants declared in the Frame class. This version of the Hello World program is shown in Figure 2.30. In this program, the string "Hello World!" is written wherever in the window the user clicks the mouse button or drags the mouse. Recall that the `onMouseEvent` method is called whenever the mouse is moved, dragged, or a mouse button is clicked or released. In this program, the `onMouseEvent` method checks to see if the `eventType` parameter indicates that the mouse button has been clicked (i.e., depressed) or if the mouse is being dragged. If either of these kinds of mouse

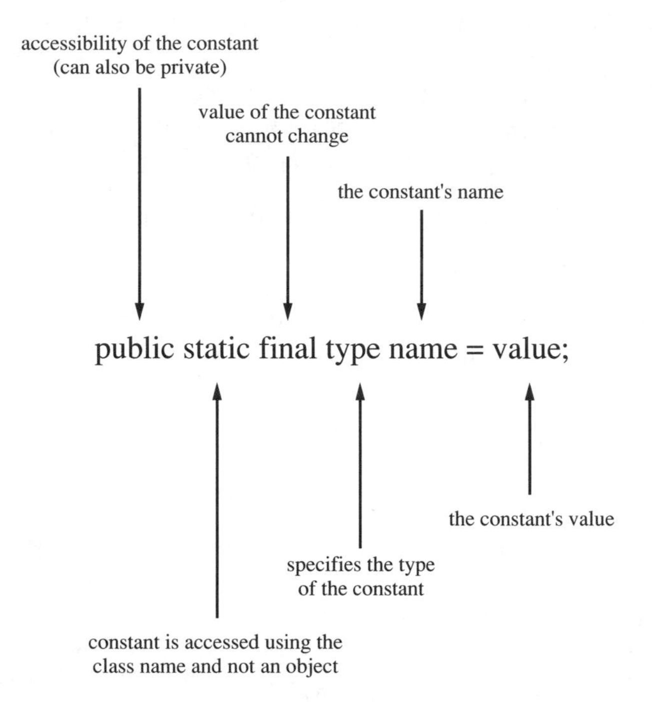

Figure 2.29 Declaring a Named Constant

events has occurred, the window is cleared and the string "Hello World!" is written at the coordinates of the mouse event. The named constants in the Frame class are used to determine what kind of mouse is being reported to the `onMouseEvent` method. The kind of mouse event is given by the `eventType` parameter.

The "." (dot) operator applied to the class name is used to access a named constant. In the modified Hello World program, the value of the `eventType` parameter is compared with the named constants defined in the Frame class by the code:

```
if( eventType == Frame.MOUSE_DOWN ||
    eventType == Frame.MOUSE_DRAG) ...
```

Notice especially that the class name, Frame, is used rather than the name of a variable referring to an object of the Frame class. The class name is used because the named constants were declared with the static modifier, making the constants associated with the class and not with a specific object of the class.

Also important in this program is the private data to record the current "state" of the program. This state information is represented by the variables `lastX` and `lastY` that record the position of the last place where the "Hello World!" string was written. It is necessary to keep track of this state information so that the `onPaint` method will know where in the window the string should

```
import Program;
import Frame;

public class HelloWorld3 implements Program
{
   private int lastX, lastY;
   private Frame window;

   public void onStart()
   { window = new Frame("Hello World Program", 200, 200, 400, 400);
     window.clear();
     window.drawText("Hello World!", 20, 20);
     lastX = 20;
     lastY = 20;
   }

   public void onMouseEvent(String frameName, int x, int y, int eventType)
   { if (eventType == Frame.MOUSE_DOWN ||
         eventType == Frame.MOUSE_DRAG    )
     { window.clear();
       window.drawText("Hello World!",x,y);
       lastX = x;
       lastY = y;
     }
   }
   public void onTimerEvent(){}

   public void onPaint()
   { window.clear();
     window.drawText("Hello World!", lastX, lastY);
   }
}
```

Figure 2.30 Hello World Program with Mouse Events

be placed when the window needs to be redrawn. Notice that `lastX` and `lastY` are initialized in the `onStart` method and updated in the `onMouseEvent` method.

2.5.4 Named Constants in the Prey Class

In the Prey class named constants can be used to establish meaningful programming terminology for distinguished kinds of creatures. In a given application domain, the species of prey being modeled differ in their roaming characteristics; on a single move the prey of one species may move much farther than the prey of another species. These differences can be captured in a series of named constants that associate a meaningful name with a given integer value intended to be used as the argument to the `setRoam` method. The additions to the Prey class that

```
public class Prey
{
   // ...
   // use these named constants as an argument
   // for the setRoam method   public static final int IMMOBILE =  0;
   public static final int SLOW     = 25;
   public static final int NORMAL   = 30;
   public static final int FAST     = 50;
   public static final int RANGING  = 75;
   //...
}
```

Figure 2.31 Declaring a Named Constant

introduce a set of named constants is shown in Figure 2.31. Only the additions to the class are shown.

A code segment using the named constants in the Prey class is shown below. In this code, a Prey object is created and its roaming distance is set using the Prey.FAST named constant.

```
Prey fastPrey;
//...
fastPrey = new Prey(50, 75, 0,0,300,300);
fastPrey.setRoam(Prey.FAST);
```

This code segment is not, of course, a complete application; only the code related to the Prey class and its object are shown.

2.5.5 UML Notation for Named Constants

The UML notation provides a means of representing named constants. The use of the UML notation to show the named constants for the Prey class is illustrated in Figure 2.32. The named constants are placed in the attributes compartment of the class diagram. Recall that the plus sign ("+") in front of each named constant signifies that it is publicly accessible. The name and type of each named constant is the same as for ordinary attributes. Each named constant is given a value where an equal sign ("=") separates the type name from the value. At the end of each attribute is the keyword "invariant" in parenthesis. The invariant keyword denotes in UML the constant aspect of the named constant. Finally, notice that each of the named constants are underlined. The underlining is the UML equivalent of the Java `static` keyword, meaning that the named constant is a class-level property. Such class level properties hold for all instances of the class.

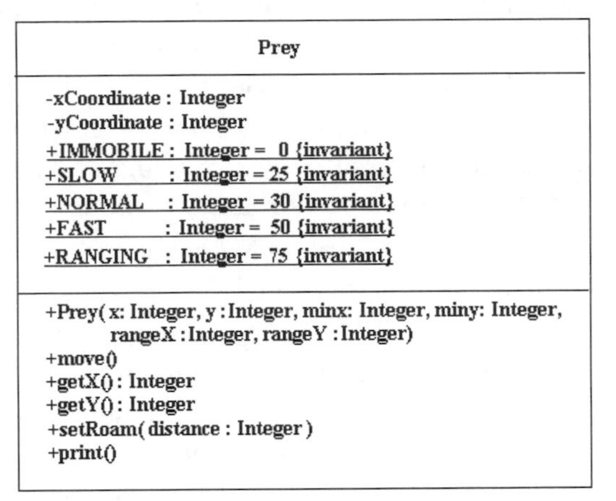

Figure 2.32 Invariant Values in UML Notation

Exercises

1. Write the declaration of the mathematical constant for pi in the form of a Java named constant.
2. Write the declarations of two named constants, YES and NO, that have the values `true` and `false`, respectively.
3. Rewrite the Hello World program so that the coordinates at which the string "Hello World" is written are defined as publicly accessible named constants. Compile and test your revised class.
4. Rewrite the Hello World program so that the String that is written is defined as publicly accessible named constants. Compile and test your revised class.
5. Rewrite the Hello World program so that the height and width of the Frame are defined as private named constants. Compile and test your revised class.
6. Write and test an application that attempts to change the value of one of the named constants. When is this error detected? at compile time? At run-time?

7. Consider a Calculator class that can perform simple mathematical operations on floating point values. Write the declarations of two named constants that would be appropriate for this class.
8. Write a Java application that creates two Prey objects. Use the named constants in the Prey class to create a fast-moving and a slow-moving creature. Compare the distances they roam over 50 moves.
9. Draw a UML diagram for the complete Frame class including the named constants introduced in this section.
10. Draw a UML diagram for a Switch class. A switch can be either "on" or "off" and the class has methods to set the switch to one of these states and to get the current status of the switch. Represent the "on" and "off" values as named constants in the diagram.
11. Draw a partial UML diagram for a Money class that has named constants representing the value of a penny, nickle, dime, quarter, half-dollar, and dollar. You do not need to show the operations of the class.

2.6 Overloaded Methods

In some situations, frequently with constructors, overloaded method maybe defined in a class to provide alternative ways of performing the same operation. Overloaded methods are simply a set of methods that have the same name but with different argument lists. The argument lists may differ in the number of arguments, in the type of at least one of the arguments, or both.

The use of overloaded methods is a common and encouraged practice because:

1. It allows the methods to be applied using different types of information. In this case the overloaded methods differ in the types, and possibly number, of their parameters. This form of method overloading is useful when it is anticipated that in different programming contexts the required information will be available in different forms. Providing the overloaded methods for the operation eliminates the necessity of converting the various forms of information into the single form required by a single method.
2. It allows the methods to give varying degrees of control over how the operation will be performed. In this case the overloaded methods differ in how many arguments appear in the parameter list. Consider a complex operation that has many parameters. In many programming contexts, most of these parameters are given standard, default values,

whereas only a few of the parameters are typically supplied by the user. To cater to this case, one version of the overloaded method has only those parameters that are typically changed. The implementor uses the standard, default values in the implementation of this method. To provide for those less common situations where the user requires more control over the operation, another overloaded method is provided that contains more of the operation's parameters. Finally, another overloaded method may have all of the parameters, giving the user complete control over the parameters of the operation. Also note that it is correct to have an overloading that takes no parameters, allowing the implementor of the method to select all of the values.

A critical aspect of overloaded methods is that they represent the same conceptual operation. Although it is technically possible, it is clearly poor design to have two unrelated methods with the same name.

2.6.1 Overloaded Methods in the GUI Classes

The use of overloaded methods, including overloaded constructors, is shown in a second version of the Frame class. The extended version of the Frame class is shown in Figure 2.33. The first constructor requires five arguments—the first argument for the name, the next two arguments for the placement of the window on the screen, and the last two arguments for the size of the window. The second constructor specifies only the name and the placement arguments. When this constructor is used, the two arguments determine where the window is placed on the screen, but the object's constructor determines, by an algorithm or by a simple default, the size of the window. In the third constructor, the user provides the name for the window but the constructor itself determines, by an algorithm or by simple defaults, both the placement and size of the window. Finally the last constructor, with no arguments, allows the object's constructor to select the object's name, placement, and shape.

Examples of using the overloaded constructors are:

```
Frame exact  = new Frame("First Window",  50, 50, 100, 200);
               // exact is constructed using the first  constructor
Frame here   = new Frame("Second Window", 50, 50);
               // here is constructed using the second constructor
Frame simple = new Frame("Third Window");
               // simple is constructed using the third  constructor
Frame any    = new Frame();
               // any is constructed using the fourth  constructor
```

This collection of overload constructors gives the user of the Frame class more flexibility in the amount of control the user of the class wants over the construction of the object.

```
public class Frame
{                    // Version 2
   // private implementation not shown
   public Frame(String name, int initXCoord, int initYCoord,
                             int initWidth,  int initHeight);

   public Frame(String name, int initXCoord, int initYCoord);
   public Frame(String name);
   public Frame();
   public void resize(int newHeight, int newWidth  );
   public void resize(float factor );

   public void clear();
   public void clear(int x, int y, int w, int h);

   public int  getTextHeight();
   public int  getTextWidth(String s);

    // other methods the same as in version 1
}
```

Figure 2.33 Frame Class: Version 2

The `resize` method shows how overloading is used for non-constructor methods. The version with two integer parameters resizes the window to the specified width and height. The second version of `resize` changes both of the window's dimensions by a given factor. Factors larger than 1.0 cause the window to expand in both width and height. Factors less than 1.0 cause the window to shrink in both width and height.

The `resize` method is used in the following ways:

```
exact.resize(100, 100);        // change to a 100 X 100 square
exact.resize(1.5);             // enlarge by 50%
exact.resize(0.5);             // shrink to 50%  current size
```

The `clear` method is also overloaded. The version of this method with no arguments clears the entire frame. The version of the `clear` method with four arguments allows a rectangular area within the frame to be cleared without erasing anything outside of this rectangle.

To make the overloaded clear method usable for erasing text, two convenience methods, named `getTextHeight` and `getTextWidth`, are added to the Frame class that determines the height and width of the rectangular area occupied by a text string. A simple example using the convenience functions to find the rectangular dimensions of the text "Hello World" is as follows:

```
int width, height;      // variables to hold the result
height = exact.getTextHeight();
width  = exact.getTextWidth("Hello World")
```

Notice that the height of the string is independent of the actual string (the fixed font is always the same height) but the width of the string depends on the actual string itself.

A more complete use of the overloaded `clear` method is shown below. This segment of code erases from a Frame object one text string (the "Hello World" string) leaving a second text string visible (the string "This is Great!").

```
Frame window = new Frame("Clear Test", 100,100, 200,200);

window.drawText("Hello World", 20, 20);
window.drawText("This is Great!", 50,50);

int height = exact.getTextHeight();
int width  = exact.getTextWidth("Hello World");

window.clear(20, 20, width, height);// erase "Hello World"
```

The overloaded `clear` method can, of course, be used to erase any rectangular region of a Frame, not just one containing text. It is the programmer's responsibility, however, to insure that the rectangular area contains only what is intended to be erased.

2.6.2 Overloaded Methods in the Prey Class

The Prey class constructor can be overloaded to allow more flexible ways of creating Prey objects. Figure 2.34 shows the revised Prey class's original constructor and three additional constructors. The constructor with seven integer values allows the constructor to specify the roaming value in addition to the six arguments present in the original constructor that specify the location and rectangu-

```
public class Prey
{
  //...

  public Prey(int whereX, int whereY, int leastX, int leastY,
              int rangeX, int rangeY, int roam)
  public Prey(int whereX, int whereY, int leastX, int leastY,
              int rangeX, int rangeY)
  public Prey (int whereX, int whereY)
  public Prey()

  public void move()
  public void move(int steps)

  //...
}
```

Figure 2.34 Revised Prey Class with Overloaded Methods

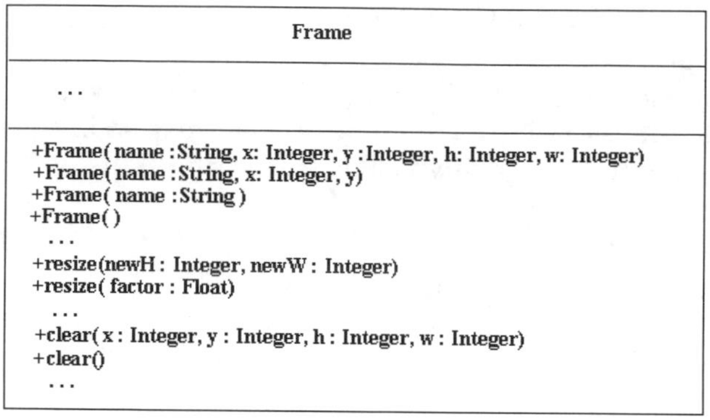

```
Frame
--------------------------------------------------------------------------
...
--------------------------------------------------------------------------
+Frame( name :String, x: Integer, y :Integer, h: Integer, w: Integer)
+Frame( name :String, x: Integer, y)
+Frame( name :String )
+Frame( )
...
+resize(newH : Integer, newW : Integer)
+resize( factor : Float)
...
+clear( x : Integer, y : Integer, h : Integer, w : Integer)
+clear()
...
```

Figure 2.35 Overloaded Methods in UML

lar area in which the prey can move. The constructor with two arguments allows the initial location to be specified; the rectangular area in with the prey can move is given default values. The constructor with no arguments chooses the initial location randomly within the default rectangular area. The values are used as defaults are conveyed by comments or documentation.

The revised Prey class also contains an overloading of the `move` method. The move method with an integer argument is designed for those cases where it is necessary to move the Prey object a number of times in sequence. The number of times the prey is moved is given by the argument's value. Thus, to move a prey object five steps, the program can either call the `move()` method in a loop or call `move(5)` once.

2.6.3 Overloaded Methods in UML

Overloaded methods are represented in UML in the same was as non-overloaded methods. No additional syntax is needed in UML. To illustrate this, a portion of the UML diagram for the Frame class is shown in Figure 2.35. An ellipses ("...") is used in this diagram to indicate missing pieces and is not part of the UML notation. Notice that each of the overloaded methods, both constructors and other methods, is written in the usual UML syntax. UML and Java have the same requirement for overload methods: no two methods in the same class may have the same signature, that is, the same name and list of argument types. The overloaded constructors have different signatures as do the overloaded `resize` and `clear` methods.

Exercises

1. Construct a window using the constructor with no arguments and see what name it chose for the name of the window. Create two such windows and compare their names.
2. **Simple Button:** Write a program that displays within a frame your first name towards the top and, near the middle, a circle around the text "PushHere." When the user clicks anywhere inside the circle, erase just your first name and replace it by your last name. Clicking again within the circle should cause your last name to be erased and your first name to be displayed. Subsequent clicks within the circle should alternate in this way showing either your first or last name.
3. **Shrinking Window 1:** Write a program that places a window of size 500 by 500 near the center of the screen. Leaving its position fixed, resize the window 19 times, each time making it smaller by an additional 25 units. Use the version of Resize that takes two integer arguments.
4. **Shrinking Window 2:** Write a program that places a window of size 500 by 500 near the center of the screen. Leaving its position fixed, resize the window 19 times, each time making it smaller by 10 percent of its current size. Use the version of Resize that takes a single float argument.
5. **Heart Beat 1:** Write a program that first shrinks and then expands a window back to its original size using the approach in the Shrinking Window 1 problem.
6. **Heart Beat 2:** Write a program that first shrinks and then expands a window back to its original size using the approach in the Shrinking Window 2 problem.
7. Examine the documentation for the Prey class. How will a Prey object be initialized by the constructor that takes no arguments?
8. Define another constructor for the Prey class. Specify the type(s) and intended meaning(s) of each of its parameters.
9. Define an overloading of the setRoam method. Specify the type(s) and intended meaning(s) of each of its parameters.
10. Write a Java application that uses the overloaded move method to determine how far a Prey object moves in 50 steps.

11. Draw a UML diagram for the revised Prey class that contains overloaded methods.

12. Draw a UML diagram for a Date class. The Date class provides one constructor to initialize a Date object using three integers representing the month, day, and year (5, 3, 1987) or as a single string ("May 3, 1987"). The Dateclass also has a `next` method that moves the date forward one day and a `next(int)` method that moves the date forward by number of days specified by the parameter.

2.7 Overloaded Methods in Java Classes

Overloaded methods are frequently used in the Java library classes. Two examples of how the Java libraries use overloaded methods will be presented here: one of the basic input and output (I/O) classes and the String class. Aside from illustrating the utility of overloaded methods these two classes are often useful in many programming situations.

2.7.1 Overloaded Methods in Interactive I/O

Method overloading is a key element in programming I/O in Java. Method overloading is useful for I/O because the same operation (input or output) is being performed, but it is being performed on different types. This is exactly the situation that method overloading is meant to address. In the Java I/O classes, a method to perform an input or output action is frequently overloaded for each of Java's predefined types. Thus, the programmer only needs to remember a single name for the operation, not a different name for each type. At compile time the actual type of the data being input or output determines which of the overloaded methods will be used.

In Java, I/O is based on a stream model. In a stream model the input data is viewed as a continuous stream of data that flows from a source into the sequence of variables presented to the input stream. The type of the variable determines how the input stream is interpreted to provide values for the variables. On output, the values of variables flow into a (logically) continuous steam to the destination. The source (for input) and the destination (for output) may be the user's display/keyboard or a file.

Interactive stream I/O is provided by two classes:

```
class InputStream {...}          // stream input
class PrintStream {...}          // stream output
```

and the standard Java environment includes three predefined variables:

```
InputStream System.in;           // keyboard input
PrintStream System.out;          // output to user's display
PrintStream System.err;          // error message
```

Because these classes use elements of the Java language that have not been covered yet, only a cursory study of these classes is made here. A more detailed study of the Java I/O classes given in Chapter 8. For now, a minimal understanding of how to use these classes is sufficient.

The most extensive use of overloaded methods is in the PrintStream class. The PrintStream class defines two methods, `print` and `println`, that are overloaded for each of the basic Java types (int, float, double) and for the String class. The `print` method takes a single argument the character representation of which is appended to the stream of output characters. The `println` method is similar except that it adds an extra character to the output stream to cause the next character in the stream to begin on a new line. Examples of using these overloaded methods are:

```
System.out.print(10);                  // output an integer
System.out.print(1.234);               // output a float
System.out.print('x');                 // output a character
System.out.print("Hello World." );     // output a string
System.out.println();                  // end current line
```

In the last statement of this example, the `println` method was invoked with no arguments. Used this way, the method appends to the output stream only the character that will cause the beginning of a new line. The `println` method is also overloaded so that it can also be invoked with a single argument. The last two lines in the above example can be rewritten as the single line:

```
System.out.println("Hello World." ); // output a string and end line
```

Alternatively, each value could be printed on its own lines as follows:

```
System.out.println(10);                // output an integer
System.out.println(1.234);             // output a float
System.out.println('x');               // output a character
System.out.println("Hello World." );   // output a string
```

For readability, blanks are often inserted into the output stream as in this extension of the above example:

```
System.out.print(10);                  // output an integer
System.out.print("  ");                // add two blanks
System.out.print(1.234);               // output a float
System.out.print("  ");                // add two blanks
System.out.print('x');                 // output a character
System.out.print("  ");                   // add two blanks
System.out.print("Hello World." );     // output a string
System.out.println();                  // end current line
```

that inserts two blanks between each pair of values being output.

Notice that there is no relationship between the number of lines of code that produce output and the number of lines of text that appear in the output.

For example, the following three code fragments each output the same two lines of text:

```
(1)  System.out.println(10);
     System.out.println(20);

(2)  System.out.print(10);
     System.out.println();
     System.out.println(20);

(3)  System.out.print(10);
     System.out.println();
     System.out.print(20);
     System.out.println();
```

The values of variables can be output using the PrintStream objects as shown in the following example:

```
int x, y;                  // two integers
char c;                    // a character
String s= "Hello";         // a string
float z = 1.415;           // a floating point value

x = 100; y = 200; c ='!';

System.out.print(x);
System.out.print("  ");
System.out.println(y);
System.out.print(s);
System.out.println(c);
System.out.println(z);
```

Produces the output stream:

```
100  200
Hello!
1.415
```

The output will appear as three lines because the `println` method is used three times.

2.7.2 Stream Output to a Window

A variation of the Frame class, named TextFrame, is introduced to allow stream output to a window. This class presents an interface similar to that of the PrintStream class in that it uses overloaded `print` and `println` methods to provide a means of displaying the values of different built-in types (int, long, float, double, char, and String). A partial definition of the TextFrame class is shown in Figure 2.36. The constructors for a TextFrame are similar to those for a Frame

```
public class TextFrame
{

   // encapsulated data and implementation not shown
   public TextFrame(String name, int x, int y, int w, int h)
   public TextFrame(String name, int x, int y)
   public TextFrame(String name)
   public TextFrame()

   public void     moveTo( int x, int y)           // change position
   public void     resize( int width, int height)  // change shape
   public void     resize( float factor)           //
   public int     isNamed(Sting n)                 // is this your name?

   public void print(int i)                  // output integer
   public void print(float f)                // output float
   ...
   public void println(int i)                // output integer and new line
   public void println(float f)              // output float and new line

}
```

Figure 2.36 TextFrame Class Definition

```
Frame window1 = new Frame("Window1", 100,100, 200, 200);
Frame window2 = new Frame("Window2", 400,400, 200, 200);
TextFrame out = new TextFrame("Display", 400,20, 300,200);

OnStart()
{ window1.drawText("Click in this window", 20,20);
  window2.drawText("Click in this window", 20,20);
  out.println("Name of window clicked in will appear below");
}

OnPaint()
{ window1.drawText("Click in this window", 20,20);
  window2.drawText("Click in this window", 20,20);
}

OnMouseEvent(String frameName, int x, int y, int eventType)
{ out.println(frameName);
}

OnTimerEvent() {}
```

Figure 2.37 Using the TextFrame Class

object as are the `moveTo` and `resize` methods except that the height and width of a TextFrame a measured in units of characters. Thus, specifying a width of 80 and a height of 20 means that the TextFrame will be large enough to hold 20 lines each of up to 80 characters in length. Keep in mind that the TextFrame class is not part of the standard Java library; like the Frame class, it is only part of the materials used here for learning about Java.

The TextFrame class can be used as shown in the code in Figure 2.37. This code creates two Frame objects and a TextFrame object. The code output to the TextFrame the name of the Frame object in which each mouse event occurs. Notice that the Shape parameter for the TextFrame is measured in rows and columns, not pixels. However, both the Frame and TextFrame Locations are measured in terms of pixels.

The TextFrame class is useful in displaying textual information to a user and is also convenient for displaying status information during development, testing, and debugging.

2.7.3 Overloaded Methods in the String Class

The handling of string-oriented data is a commonplace programming requirement. In some case the data is best represented as a character string (e.g., a person's name, a password, a message) whereas in other cases the data is presented or encoded as a character string and will be converted to another type (e.g., when data is read from the keyboard it is initially presented as individual characters or as characters strings). The Java libraries contain a utility class to facilitate the handling of string-oriented data.

The String class captures the abstraction of a fixed character string. String objects can be created, compared for equality with other String objects, and examined using a variety of substring operations. Only a few of these operations are presented here. A String object is created and given a value by assignment as illustrated by the following code segment:

```
String title = "Object-Oriented Software Design";
String buttonLabel;
...
buttonLabel = "Press Here";
```

Alternatively, a String object is given a value using the String constructor that is overloaded to accept either another String object or an array of characters. These two possibilities are shown in the following code segment:

```
String duplicate = new String(title);  // create a copy of the title String
char[] school = {'T' , 'E' , 'C' , 'H'};
String university = new String(school);// create String from array of char
```

Regardless of how it is created, the individual characters in a String cannot be changed except by giving the String object a completely new value.

Java's String class uses overloaded methods to perform conversions between the basic types and a String. The name of the method is `valueOf` and it takes a single argument. The value of the argument is converted to a String representation that becomes the value of the String itself. For example:

```
String intString  = new String();
String boolString = new String();
int count = 123;
boolean onoff = true;
...
intString  = String.valueOf(count);
boolString = String.valueOf(onoff);
```

Notice that intString and boolString initially refer to objects that are created with a no-argument constructor. This constructor creates a null string object—a String object with no characters. Overloadings for the `valueOf` method are also defined for the other built-in types.

For convenience, Java uses overloading to define a shortcut means of concatenating character strings. This shortcut uses the "+" operator to denote string concatenation. However, the Java compiler accepts overloaded uses of this operator among String and other built-in types because the compiler knows how—using the String class—to convert the built-in types to String values. The use of this shortcut are shown in the following segment:

```
String labeledValue;
String label = "The value of X is: ";
int X = 123;
labeledValue = label + X;
```

This produces as the value of `labeledValue` the equivalent of the character string "The value of X is: 123." Here the integer value of X has been automatically converted to a String that is concatenated with `label`. This shortcut often appears in output statements to generate a String that represents a line of output. For example:

```
int quantity= 123;
float unitPrice= 2.14;
...
System.out.println("Order " + quantity + " units " at a price of "
                 + unitPrice + " each.")
```

The code for the necessary conversions are automatically supplied by the compiler.

Exercises

1. **Mouse Tracker:** write a program that displays in a Frame the current mouse coordinates. The coordinates should be written in the form (x,y) — including the parentheses and comma — at the current mouse location. Use String objects to format the string to be written in the Frame.

2. **Simplest Timer:** write a program to output to a TextFrame the current value of an integer variable that is incremented and output on each timer event. The TextFrame should initially display a zero.
3. **Mouse Reporter:** write a program to output to a TextFrame a line each time the left mouse button is clicked in a Frame object. The line of output should be of the form (x,y)—including the parentheses and comma—where x and y are the coordinates of the mouse event.
4. **Mouse Reporter 2:** write a program that extends the Mouse Reporter program by having two Frame objects and the line of output in the TextFrame is of the form name: (x,y) where name is the name of the Frame in which the mouse click occurred and x and y are the coordinates of the mouse event.
5. **Mouse Reporter 3:** write a program that extends the Mouse Reporter program by having a line of output written to a TextFrame describing each mouse event that occurs in a Frame object. The description should give the coordinates of the mouse event an a string describing the event (e.g, move, drag, up down).
6. **Event Timing:** write a program that at each timer event output the number of mouse events that have occurred in a Frame object since the last timer event and, as a floating point value, the running average of mouse events that have occurred per timer event since the start of the program.

2.8 Arrays of Objects

An array of objects can be declared just as an array of any built-in type. Each element of the array is an object of the same class. Being able to declare arrays of objects in this way again underscores the fact that a class is similar to a type. Some of the syntax and conventions for arrays are adopted from the C language. This section describes the way Java treats arrays and gives examples using arrays of one dimension and arrays of two-dimensions. Both the GUI classes and the ecological simulation classes are used in the examples.

2.8.1 Declaring Arrays of Objects

Creating an array in Java consists of three distinct steps:

1. **Declaration—**state the name of the array and the type of the elements that the array will contain. All elements in the array are constrained to be of the type used in this declaration.

2. **Construction—**create an object that represents the array as a whole. This object will be referred to as the array object. Each element in the array is assigned a default value. For built-in types a predefined default value is defined by the Java language (e.g., 0 for int arrays). If the array is an array of objects, each array element is set to `null`, a special Java keyword that refers to a non-existent object.
3. **Initialization—**assign values or objects to positions in the array.

The last step can be skipped for arrays of built-in types provided that the default value is a suitable initialization for each array element.

The code below shows the declaration of array whose elements are objects of user defined classes and an array of the built-in int type. The declaration of an array is the same regardless of whether the type of the array elements is built-in or user-defined.

```
Frame frames[];
Prey hunted[];
int   width[];
...
frames = new Frame[3];
hunted = new Prey[100];
width  = new int[10];
```

The pair of square brackets are used in the declaration of the array name to indicate that an array of objects is being declared and not a single object. The number of elements in the array is not part of the declaration; the declaration simply introduces the array name and specifies the type of the array's elements. In the code above, the number of elements in the `frames`, `hunted`, and `width` arrays are not given in the first two statements. The number of elements in the array is specified in the construction step when the array object is created. This step is shown in the last two lines of code above. As with any object, the `new` operator is used to create the array object. The Java syntax allows the brackets in the declaration to be placed after the array name, as above, or after the type, as follows:

```
Frame[] frames;
int[]   width;
```

These two-different forms are entirely equivalent.

An important fact about arrays of objects in Java is that declaring and constructing the array object (the declaration and construction steps above) does not automatically create the objects that are the values of the array, even for arrays of built-in types. When an array of objects is declared and constructed, all elements in the array are initialized to the special value `null`. A run-time error will result if any method is applied to a `null` value. Thus, the elements in an array cannot be manipulated until after the initialization step, that is until objects have been constructed and assigned to the elements of the array. Separating the initialization from the other steps in creating an array of objects is useful in those cases where the constructor information for the array elements will not be known until sometime during the computation. In this case, the array can be declared and constructed wherever it is convenient while the initialization is deferred until the constructor information is discovered. For example, the user may be asked to supply the name of a file that contains the desired locations and shapes for constructing an array of Frame objects. This information can be read from the file and each array element can be constructed accordingly.

The initialization of an array of objects (i.e., creating the objects that are the elements of the array) can be done using assignment statements. For example, the array of Frames declared above can be initialized as follows:

```
// initialization step
for(int i=0; i<3; i++)
{ frames[i] = new Frame("Frame"+i, 300*i, 100, 200, 150);
}
```

In this code three Frame objects are created and assigned to the successive positions in the `frames` array. This initialization code completes the creation of the `frames` array. Notice that, as in C, the subscripts of an array being at zero. The logical structures of the *frames* array is shown in Figure 2.38. Similarly, the array of Prey objects is initialized as shown in this code segment:

```
// initialization step
for(int next=0; next<100; next++)
{ hunted[next] = new Prey();
}
```

In this segment, the overloaded constructor with no arguments is used to construct each Prey object.

The declaration and construction of an array can be done in a single statement as shown in this code fragment:

```
Frame frames[] = new Frame[3];
Prey hunted[]  = new Prey[100];
int width[]    = new int[3];
```

The effect of these statements is exactly the same as when the declaration and construction steps are performed separately. It is often only a question of convenience or style whether to combine or separate these steps.

By means of an initializer list it is possible to create an array in a single statement. The initializer list is illustrated in the following code:

```
int width[] = {100, 200, 50, 60, 70, 300, 0, 110, 5, 1000};
Frame frames[] = { new Frame("Frame0",   0,100, 200, 150),
                   new Frame("Frame1", 300,100, 200, 150),
                   new Frame("Frame2", 600,100, 200, 150)
                 };
```

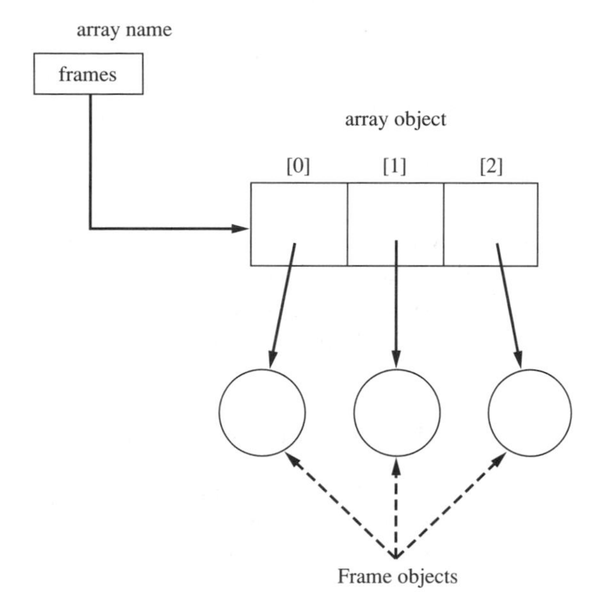

Figure 2.38 Structure of an Array of Frame Objects

The declaration of the array name is as before except that this declaration is followed by an assignment operator and an initializer list. The initializer list defines a series of value or objects of the same type as the array elements. The length of the initializer list (i.e., the number of value or objects in the list) determines the number of elements in the array. In this example, the `width` array has ten elements because there are ten integers in the corresponding initializer list. The `frames` array has three elements. The array elements are initialized in the order of appearanceof the value or objects in the initializer list. Thus, `width[0]` is initialized to 100, `width[1]` is initialized to 200, and `frames[1]` is initialized to an object that has the name "Frame1" that is located at (300,100) and has a width of 200 and a height of 150. The number of elements in the array is completely determined by the length of the initializer list, it is not possible to specify the length in any other way. For large arrays, such as the `hunted` array of 100 Prey elements, using an initializer list is often impractical. It is often more convenient to initialize large arrays using loops.

If there are overloaded constructors, as there are for the Frame class, an object in an array can be constructed using any of the constructors. For example, if it was only desired to specify the name and initial location, but not the shape, for each object in the array then the following declaration would suffice:

```
Frame frames[] = { new Frame("Frame0",  0, 100),
                   new Frame("Frame1", 25, 100),
                    new Frame("Frame2", 50, 100)
                 };
```

In this case the overload constructor will determine the shape of each object. It is also possible to use different constructors for each objects as shown here:

```
Frame frames[] = { new Frame("Frame0", 100, 100, 100, 100),
                   new Frame("Frame1",  25, 100),
                   new Frame()
                 };
```

In this version, the first object in the array is constructed by explicitly providing each constructor argument. The constructor for the object named "Frame1" specifies only the location. The constructor for the object at subscript position 2 specifies no constructor arguments, allowing all defaults to apply, including the name.

2.8.2 Manipulating Objects in an Array

An object in an array can be manipulated by a combination of the subscripting operator "[ ]," used to select which object of the array is to be manipulated, and the "." (dot) operator, used to apply the operation to the selected object. This code is as follows:

```
frames[1].moveTo(100, 50);
int i = 53;
hunted[i].move();
int xLoc = hunted[0].getX();
```

The first statement moves the object with subscript 1 in the frames array to a new position. Remember that the subscripts begin with 0. The third statement operates on the object whose position in the array is given by the value of a variable. In this statement, the selected Prey object is asked to compute a new simulated location. The last statement illustrates that an operation on an object in an array may also return a result. In this statement, the x coordinate of the first Prey object in the array is assigned to the variable xLoc. Notice again that array subscripting begins with 0.

One of the advantages of working with arrays of objects is that it is easy to program the same operation over all of the objects. For example, a single loop can move all of the Prey objects as follows:

```
for (int i = 0; i<100; i++)
    hunted[i].move();
```

More complex operations involving the elements in the array are also possible. For example the following loop positions the windows along a diagonal fromupper left toward lower right and makes them all of the size:

```
for (int i = 0; i<3; i++;)
{
   frames[i].moveTo(10*i+1, 10*i+1);
   frames[i].resize(50, 50);
}
```

Subscripting is checked automatically by the Java run-time system to detectinvalid subscripts. This is part of the safety guarantees that are a criticalpart of the design of the Java language. If an invalid subscript is used, an exception will be generated.

2.8.3 Handling Arrays

The number of elements in an array is commonly defined by a *named constant.* This is a useful practice because many parts of the code may be dependent on the size of the array, for example, the code that constructs the objects for the array, code that manipulates all the elements of thearray, and code that checks if a subscript bound is valid. This code segmentshows the use of named constants in a class that represents a group offrames:

```
public class FrameList
{ private static final int FRAMES_LENGTH = 3;
  private frames[];

  public FrameList()
  { frames = new Frame[FRAMES_LENGTH];
  }

  public void moveTo(int whichFrame, int newX, int newY)
  { if (0 <= whichFrame && whichFrame < FRAMES_LENGTH)
  frames[whichFrame].moveTo(newX, newY);
  }
  ...
}
```

In this code a private named constant, `FRAMES_LENGTH`, is usedto define the length of the array frames that is also declared as partof the private data of the FrameList class. The named constant is also used in the `moveTo` method to insure that the parameter `whichFrame` is a valid subscript for the `frames` array.

Because an array name is declared separately from the array object to which the name refers, it is possible for the array name to refer to different arrays at different times. This possibility is illustrated by an array of ints in the code below:

```
int width[] = new int[3];
...
width = new int[10];
...
```

In this case the array name `width` is first associated with an array with three elements. Later, a new array object is created and associated with the same array. After this assignment, the array name refers to an array of ten elements each of which has the default value 0; the original values of the width array are not preserved. In other words, the array is replaced by a new array, it is not extended (if the new array is larger)or truncated (if the new array is shorter).

Because an array name is declared separately from the array object to which the name refers, it is also possible for two array names to refer to the same array. This possibility is illustrated by the two array names in this code:

```
int width[] = {0,1,2,3,4,5};
int other[];
...
other = width;   // both names refer to the same array
other[2] = 6;    // changes both other[2] and width[2]
```

In this case, the two array names `width` and `other` refer to the same array. The fact that they refer to the same array is shown by the last assignment statement. This statement changes the value of the element subscripted by 2 to the new value 6 (its previous value was 2). If at this point both the array named `other` and the array named `width` were examined, they would both have the values {0,1, 6, 3, 4, 5}.

Because an array name can refer to arrays with different number of elements during a program, Java allows the programmer to query an array to determine its current length. An example of this is shown in the following code:

```
int width[] = new int[3];
...
int current = width.length;    // number of elements is now 3
...
width = new int[10];
int newlength = width.length; // number of lements is now 10
...
```

The syntax `arrayname.length` in Java returns the number of elements in the array referred to by the name `arrayname`. This syntax is often used in code that iterates through an array as follows:

```
for(int i=0; i<width.length; i++)
{
  // manipulate width[i]
}
```

The use of `width.length` in the for loop test guarantees that the loop will be correct for the array width regardless of the number of elements in the array at the time the for loop is executed.

Although arrays in Java are of a fixed size, the effect of a varying length array can be simulated because the array name can be bound to different array objects at different times. The FrameList class used above is modified to show this possibility.

```
public class FrameList
{ private static final int INITIAL_LENGTH = 3;
  private static final int INCREMENT = 2;
  private frames[];
  int next = 0;

  public FrameList()
  { frames = new Frame[INITIAL_LENGTH];
  }

  public void addFrame(String name, int atX, int atY)
  { if (next == frame.length)                        // if at capacity...
      { Frame newFrames[] =
             new Frame[frame.length + INCREMENT]; // make bigger array
      for (int i=0; i<frame.length; i++)       // copy old frames
         newFrame[i] = frame[i];
      frames = newFrames;                          // use bigger array
      }
      frames[next] = new Frame(name, atX, atY);
      next = next + 1;
      }
  ...
}
```

In this example, the FrameList class has an initial number of Frames that it can maintain. Each time it is asked, via the `addFrame` method,to construct and maintain a new Frame, it checks to see if the current array is of sufficient size to hold another reference to a Frame object. If all elements of the `frames` array have already been assigned to a Frame object, then the `frames` array is effectively enlarged by creating a new array with `INCREMENT` additional elements, initializing the new array using the existing `frames` array, and associating the array name `frames` with the new, larger array object.

2.8.4 Two-Dimensional Arrays

Variables can be declared that refer to arrays having two or more dimensions, allowing multi-dimensional data organizations to be programmed in a straightforward way. The syntax for declaring two-dimension arrays of different types are shown below. The three declarations define two-dimensional arrays of integers, Frame objects and Prey objects, respectively. Notice that the length of the two-dimensions are not specified.

```
int[][] board;
Frame[][] displays;
Prey [][] herd;
```

As with one-dimensional arrays, declaring a two-dimensional array only creates a variable that can refer to such an array, it does not create the array structure or any objects of the array's type. For example, the declaration of the herd variable above neither creates an array nor constructs any Prey objects.

Constructing the two-dimensional array can be done in several ways. The shortest way to construct the array is to declare the size of each dimension as follows:

```
board = new int[100][50];
displays = new Frame[3][3];
```

The first of these statements constructs an array capable of holding 5,000 integer values arranged in 100 rows, each of which has 50 columns. The second statement constructs an array with three rows and three columns, each element of which is a Frame object. Neither statement creates any values for the array elements. An alternative way to construct an array that emphasizes that each row of a two-dimensional array is itself a one dimensional array is as follows:

```
herd = new Prey[3][];
herd[0] = new Prey[5];
herd[1] = new Prey[5];
herd[2] = new Prey[5];
```

The first line creates an array of three rows; the subsequent statements create each row. The row can be constructed in any order and it is not necessary that they all be created at once. It is even possible that a given row might never be constructed or that the different rows may have different number of columns. two-dimensional arrays with varying number of columns per row are sometimes needed when the structure of the data is irregular. An irregular array is created by the following code segment:

```
Herd[ ][ ] irregular = new Prey[3][ ];
irregular[0] = new Prey[10];
irregular[1] = new Prey[3];
irregular[2] = new Prey[7];
```

An irregular array can be processed because the number of elements of each array can be accessed through the array's length attribute. The following code segment initializes the irregular array defined above:

```
for(int i=0; i<irregular.length; i++)
  for(int j=0; j<irregular[i].length)
     irregular[i][j] = new Prey();
```

The outer loop is controlled by the expression `irregular.length`, which in this example has the value 3 because "irregular" is an array of length 3, each of whose elements are themselves arrays. The inner loop is controlled by the expression `irregular[i].length` that determines the number of elements in the *I*-th element of the irregular array; for i=0t he expression evaluates to 10, whereas for i=2 the expression evaluates to 7.

Exercises

1. **Frame Wave:** write a program that has an array of ten windows. The windows are the same shape and are aligned horizontally with the vertical edges of adjacent windows touching. From left to right, each window has one of the numbers from 1 to 10 written in it. Each "wave" beings with the leftmost window moving up vertically and then back to its original position. This same action is repeated for each window from left to right. Repeat this for a few waves. In this version declare the array so that the constructor with no arguments is used.
2. Modify the "Frame Wave" program so that each object in the array is constructed by giving values for each constructor argument.
3. Modify either version of the "Frame Wave" program so that a new wave begins when the previous wave has reached the middle of the line of windows.
4. **Moving Ball:** write a program that has an array of five windows all of the same size and arranged in a horizontal (or vertical) line. The first (leftmost or topmost) window has a circle drawn in it. The circle should move from the current window to the adjacent window. When it reaches the last (rightmost or bottommost) window, it reappears in the first window. Repeat this process indefinitely.
5. **Tic-Tac-Toe:** write a program with ten windows. Nine windows (the game windows) are in a two-dimensional array that has three rows and three columns. The windows in the two-dimensional array are displayed on the screen in a three-by-three grid pattern as in tic-tac-toe. The tenth window (the restart window) is placed off to one side. Initially all the game windows are empty. When a left mouse click occurs in an empty game window either an "O" or an "X" will appear beginning with an "O" and alternating thereafter. Make the "O" with a circle and the "X" out of two lines. Clicking in a game window that is not empty has no effect. Clicking in the tenth window causes all of the game windows to become empty.
6. **Leap Frog:** write a program that has an array of five windows. The windows are of the same size and all have the same y coordinate. The first window is placed near the left edge of the screen. The second window is placed somewhat to the right of the first window and overlapping the first window; the third window is similarly placed to the right of and overlapping the second window; and so on. On successive itera-

tions the left-most window is moved so it is somewhat to the right and overlapping the right-most window. The window just moved is now the new right-most window. Continue this movement for some number of iterations.

7. Write a Java application that maintains 20 Prey objects in an array. Output the initial locations of each of the prey and their final locations after each prey has moved 100 steps.
8. Write a Java application that outputs the location of the "center" of a herd of 100 prey after each of 100 steps. The center of the herd is a location based on *minx*, *miny*, *maxx*, *maxy* where *minx* is the smallest x coordinate of any prey, *maxx* is the largest y coordinate of any prey and similarly for *miny* and *maxy*. The center is: (minx + (maxx - minx)/2, miny + (maxy - miny)/2).
9. Write a Java application that uses a two-dimensional array to represent the area within which a given Prey can move. Each element of the two-dimensional array is a boolean value that is true if the prey has even been at the location corresponding to that element and false otherwise. Simulate the movement of the Prey for 1000 steps. Output the number of locations visited by the prey (those whose array elements are true) and the number of locations not visited by the prey (those whose array elements are false).
10. Extend the last exercise by simulating 20 prey instead of just one.
11. What kind of array structure would be needed to store the x and y coordinates of 50 prey in each of 100 time steps? How many dimensions does this array have? What is the range of index values for each dimension?

2.9 Managing Objects

Managing objects refers to the steps required to create and delete objects during the execution of an object-oriented program. The creation of objects is never an issue; programmers have a clear sense of when a new object should be created or when an existing object should be manipulated. However, less obvious is the correct deletion of objects. Of course, objects should only be deleted when the object is no longer needed by any part of the program. But how can a programmer know, particularly for a system constructed out of reusable components, when an object is no longer needed?

Java provides a powerful run-time mechanism for managing objects: garbage collection. Garbage collection means that the system is able to determine when an object is no longer needed by a Java program. Such unneeded objects, termed "garbage," are automatically collected. This collection of garbage objects is important because objects consume memory space. Without the recycling effect created by the garbage collector long-running Java programs would eventually exhaust the system's memory. Garbage collection, however, reclaims the memory used by unneeded objects and uses this reclaimed memory to create new, needed objects.

Java's garbage collection mechanisms is automatic; the programmer need take no explicit actions to insure that garbage objects are reclaimed. The automatic nature of Java's garbage collection is a major improvement over object oriented languages, such as C++, that require explicit programmer management of object reclamation. It is well known that errors in object management are the most difficult types of bugs to detect and correct in languages that require explicit programmer management of objects. The convenience and power of automatic object management comes at a price: there is additional space and execution time required by the run-time system to maintain, update, and process information about objects so that the garbage collection can be performed.

An object can become garbage in one of two ways. First, the end of the scope of a variable that refers to an object may be reached. The scope of a variable is that portion of the program where the variable is visible (i.e., where it can be manipulated). When the end of the scope is reached, the variable ceases to exist and the object to which the variable referred is referenced by one fewer variables. Second, a variable referring to an object may be explicitly set to the special `null` value by the programmer. In this case, the object is no longer referenced by the variable. When an object is no longer referenced by any variable in the program the object can be reclaimed by the garbage collector. Because there is no way for the program to refer to the object the absence of the object can have no effect on the program's execution. Thus, it is safe for the garbage collector to consider the object as garbage and reclaim the memory space allocated to the object.

If a garbage object has a finalizer, a method declared as `void finalize()`, it is called immediately before Java's run-time garbage collector deallocates and reclaims the object. The finalizer allows the object to take any actions that are necessary to safely terminate the object's lifetime. Because of its role in an object's life, the finalizer method is sometime described as the object's "last wishes." Common actions that occur in a finalizer are to take any final actions on the objects encapsulated resources (e.g., closing open files, closing windows), writing any log entries that record the history of the computation, or issuing error messages if the object is being deallocated under inappropriate circumstances.

The example program shown in Figure 2.39 illustrates the two ways that an object can become garbage. This program declares three variables that can refer to Frame objects. The variables `permanentFrame` and `nullFrame` are declared as private data of the class. These two variables will exist as long as the object of which they are a part exists. The third variable, `scopeFrame`, is

```
import Program;
import Frame;

public class GCDemo1 implements Program
{
  private Frame permanentFrame;
  private Frame nullFrame;

  public void onStart()
  { Frame scopeFrame;
    scopeFrame     = new Frame("Out of Scope",     100, 100, 200, 200);
    permanentFrame = new Frame("Permanent Frame", 310, 100, 200, 200);
    nullFrame      = new Frame("Null Frame",      520, 100, 200, 200);
  }

  public void onMouseEvent(String name, int x, int y, int eventType)
  { if(eventType == Frame.MOUSE_DOWN )
    {  nullFrame = null;
    }
  }

  public void onPaint()
  {
  }

  public void onTimerEvent()
  {
  }
}
```

Figure 2.39 How Objects Become Garbage

declared in the `onStart` method; this variable will only exist during the single execution of the `onStart` method. When `onStart` is invoked, three Frame objects are constructed and assigned to the three variables. The variable `scopeFrame` ceases to exist when the `onStart` method returns, causing the Frame object to which it refers become a garbage object. When any `MOUSE_DOWN`event occurs, the `nullFrame` variable is set to `null`, causing the object to which it refers to become garbage.

The unpredictable timing of Java's garbage collector, however, causes the program above to behave in an unexpected way. Despite the fact the two of the Frame objects become garbage, all three windows continue to be visible on the screen. It would seem more natural for each window to disappear when the Frame object for that window becomes garbage. This behavior is explained by the fact that the garbage collector runs according to rules that are known only to the garbage collector itself. Furthermore, these rules may vary among virtual machine implementations that use different garbage collection strategies. For example, some garbage collectors may only run when the Java run-time system suspects that too much of the available memory is consumed by garbage objects,

```
public class GCDemo2 implements Program
{
   ...
   public void onMouseEvent(String name, int x, int y, int eventType)
   { if(eventType == Frame.MOUSE_DOWN )
     { nullFrame = null;
       System.gc();          // trigger garbage collector
     }
   }
   ...
}
```

Figure 2.40 Triggering the Garbage Collector

```
public class Frame
{
   ...
   public void dispose();
   ...
}
```

Figure 2.41 Triggering the Garbage Collector

whereas other garbage collectors maybe more aggressive, running at fixed periods of time regardless of the memory usage. The run-time system is designed to avoid running the garbage collector too often so that the execution of the garbage collector does not take the processor resources from the application. From the programmer's perspective, the times at which the garbage collector run are unpredictable.

The program in Figure 2.40 shows that the unexpected behavior is due to the timing of the garbage collector. The Java run-time system provides a way for the programmer to trigger the running of the garbage collector. The program's onMouseEvent method is modified as shown below. The statement `System.gc()`is a request for the Java run-time system to run the garbage collector. When this program is executed, the two windows that correspond to the two garbage objects disappear immediately after the first `MOUSE_DOWN` event because the garbage collector detects these garbage objects and calls their finalize method which deallocate the windows.

Although most classes do not require the immediate freeing of their resource, classes that require prompt actions to free resources, such as the Frame class, should include for this purpose specific methods that can be invoked explicitly. Explicitly triggering the garbage collector is not a good design practice and was used above only to illustrate the characteristics of the garbage collector. The Frame class is revised as shown in Figure 2.41 to include a new method, `dispose`, that can be used to dispose of the window on the screen and release the system resources associated with this window. A Frame object continues to exist after its `dispose` method has been called, but, of course, the methods of the object no longer have any effect. If the Frame object itself becomes garbage, it will be garbage collected the next time the garbage collector runs.

It is emphasized again that in most cases the Java programmer does not need to be concerned about the releasing of resources. Most of the time the natural scope of variables, the manner in which variables reference objects, and the automatic running of the garbage collector by the run-time system are the best means of managing objects. Some types of objects, such as Frame objects, do require more detailed management by the programmer. The programmer should, of course, assume this additional management task only when it is strictly necessary.

Exercises

1. Add a fourth Frame variable as part of the private data of the example program that also refers to the `nullFrame`. Explicitly trigger the garbage collector and observe what happens. Explain this behavior.
2. Rewrite the example program so that the dispose operation is used at the end of the onStart method and in the onMouseEvent method to release the sources associated with the `scopeFrame` and `nullFrame` objects, respectively. Run this revised program and observe its behavior.
3. Rewrite the example program so that an array of three Frame objects is used instead of three separate variables. The array can be declared as:

```
Frame frames[3];
```

   In the onMouseEvent method set `frames=null` and explicitly trigger the garbage collector. Explain the behavior that you observe.
4. In addition to class scope (such as that of the variables `permanentFrame` and `nullFrame`) and method scope (such as that of the variable `scopeFrame`), name three other programming constructs that create an associate scope.

CHAPTER 3

Using Objects of Different Classes

3.1 Introduction

One major aspect of the design of an object-oriented system is defining objects to represent the often-complex information that is communicated between interacting objects. In some cases, interacting objects use simple, built-in types to exchange information. However, when the information being exchanged is more complex, objects are often used to structure the data involved in the interaction.

A second major aspect of the design of an object-oriented system is organizing the relationships among objects so as to reflect the temporal and structural properties of the interaction. The temporal properties of an interaction refer to the period of time during which the objects conduct their interaction. In some cases, object interacts over a brief period of time whereas in other cases the interaction extends over a long period of time. Objects with longer-lived interactions usually require some programmed structure to support their communication over time. The structural properties of the interactions among objects refers to whether it is better to create connections that are static and cannot be changed by other parts of the system or to create connections that allow dynamic changes in the connections among the objects. Static connections lead to systems that are more secure and more easily reused but are less flexible whereas the reverse is true for the dynamic case.

3.1.1 Complex Information

Using an object to exchange complex, structured information is a natural use of the organizing power of classes. The information can be encapsulated as the private data of an object and made accessible through access or methods. One advantage of using an object for this purpose is that it is more compact to exchange a single object than the multiple data elements that comprise the object. A second advantage of using an object is that the name of the object's class and the name of the object can be used to convey the meaning, role, and purpose of the data. Section 3.2 uses the GUI and ecological simulation classes to explore how objects can be used to communicate information.

The communication of information from a sender object to a receiver object can be done by:

Parameter passing: a method of the receiving object's class takes an object as one (or more) of its parameters. In this case the caller plays the role of the sender whereas the object containing the method being invoked plays the role of the receiver.

Return value: the value returned by a method may be an object. In this case the object whose method is returning the object plays the role of the sender and the object accepting the returned result plays the role of the receiver.

Both of these means of exchanging information will be seen as ways of communicating complex information and establishing interactions among objects.

Java has a simple rule for how data is exchanged among objects: all objects and arrays are passed by reference and all built-in types are passed by copy (also known as passing by value). Passing objects by reference communicates the *identity* of the object or array being passed instead of a copy of the object or array. Passing an object by reference avoids the cost of copying the object and allows the sender and receiver to share the same object. In the simple form, passing objects by reference also allows the sender to observe any changes that the receiver might make intake shared object. Often times, observing these changes is how the communication between the sender and the receiver is achieved. Passing a built-in type "by copy" has this name because a copy of the value is passed to the receiver. Because it is only a copy of the value held by the sender, any change made to the data by the receiver does not change the value as seen by the sender.

It is the Java programmer's responsibility to create a means of passing an object by copy. It is sometimes necessary to pass an object by copy to guarantee to the sender that the exchanged information is unchanged by actions of the receiver. There is a standard technique for creating copies of an object that can be used by developers of classes wishing to support passing objects of the class by copy. Aside from defining a means of copying an object, the programmer is responsible for using this device to actually copy the object and pass the duplicated object—there is no automatic mechanism in Java for duplicating objects or passing duplicated objects as parameters or return values.

3.1.2 Relationships Among Interacting Objects

An object-oriented system is an organized group of interacting objects forming *associations* and/or *aggregations*. Each object in the system performs a specialized role and communicates with other objects as needed to perform its role as an individual and as a collaborating member of a larger assembly. The interacting objects maybe of different classes or of the same class. When the interacting objects are of different classes, the definition of one class must refer to objects of another class. When the objects are in the same class, the definition of the class must refer to itself in some way.

In an association, each object must be able to invoke the methods of one or more of the other objects in the association. An object that uses other objects in this way is said to" "know about," "be connected to," or "communicate with" those other objects. It is exactly the knowledge, connections, and communication paths among objects that gives the sense of unity, purpose, integrity and meaning to the association. Two objects in an association form either a client-server connection or a peer connection. A client-server connection is a unidirectional relationship where one object, the client, knows about the other object, the server. The client invokes methods of the server; the server may return information to the client via a return value but the server does not invoke methods of the client. A peer connection is a bi-directional relationship where each object knows the other and each is able to invoke methods of the other. Section 3.3 and 3.4 show how to build sequences of interactions and simple associations; more complex associations are presented in Section 3.6.

The use of Java's interface construct can improve the reusability and flexibility of objects that are intended to be a part of an association. A Java interface specifies a set of methods that the using object (e.g., the client object) requires of a used object (e.g., the server object). The using object does not need to know the class of the used object; it only needs to know that the used object provides the methods specified in the interface. Because the using object does not know the class of the used object, objects of different classes can be substituted for the used object, provided only that each of these classes provides all of the methods specified in the interface. The Java compiler will verify that a class claiming to implement a given interface fulfills the obligation to implement all of the interface's methods. Section 3.5 describes Java interfaces and gives several examples showing how interfaces allow more flexible associations to be designed and implemented.

3.2 Using Objects for Communicating Data

An object being used for communication can be passed as an input parameter to a method of a receiving object or the object can be the returned result of a method. Both of these cases will be illustrated by refining the interface of the

Frame class into a more object-oriented form. The ecological simulation classes will be enhanced in a similar way to illustrate how objects are used for communicating data. The examples and discussion in this section will show that there are numerous advantages to using objects as a form of communicating data, including better readability, easier maintainability, and better program structure.

3.2.1 Using Objects for Communication in the GUI Classes

The examples that follow make use of two new classes. In the original definition of the Frame class the location and shape of the frame were described by four integer values. However, the abstractions of "location" and "shape" can be captured in classes as shown in Figure 3.1. Remember that this is largely what "real" object-oriented programming is about—building classes that capture the concepts of some application domain. A good class need not be one that has an "important looking" interface. The Location and Shape classes are modest ones that cleanly capture a simple, but useful, concept. The methods `getX`, `getY` in the Location class and `getHeight` and `getWidth` in the Shape class are often called "accessor" methods because they allow you to access, albeit indirectly, some information about the state of the object.

The Frame class can now be redefined to use the definitions of the Shape and Location classes as shown in Figure 3.2. An advantage of defining the Shape and Location classes is seen in the first two overload constructors. Because Shape and Location are distinguished classes it is possible to define constructors that take them in either order. This cannot be done when the shape and location information is represented by four integer values. Another advantage is seen in

```
public class Location                          // Version 1
{
       // encapsulated implementation not shown

   public      Location(int x, int y)          // specific location
   public      Location()                      // default location
   public int getX()                           // return x-axis coordinate
   public int getY()                           // return y-axis coordinate
}

public class Shape                             // Version 1
{
       // encapsulated implementation goes here

   public      Shape(int width, int height) // specific shape
   public      Shape()                      // default shape
   public int getHeight()                   // return height
   public int getWidth()                    // return width
}
```

Figure 3.1 The Location and Shape Classes

```
public class Frame                              // Version 3
{
       // encapsulated implementation not shown

 public   Frame(String name, Location p, Shape s) // exact description
 public   Frame(String name, Shape s, Location p) // exact description
 public   Frame(String name, Location p)          // default shape
 public   Frame(String name, Shape s)             // default location
 public   Frame(String name )                     // name only
 public   Frame();                                // all defaults
 public void moveTo(Location newLocation)         // move the window
 public void resize(Shape    newShape)            // change shape
 public void resize(float factor)                 // grow/shrink by factor
       ...                                        // other methods below
}
```

Figure 3.2 Frame Class: Version 3

the overloaded constructors "`Frame(String, Shape)`" and "`Frame(String, Location)`." The effect of both of these constructors did not (and could not) exist in the earlier version (Version 2) of the Frame class. When the location and shape information is represented as four integers, what does a constructor with only two integers mean? For example, consider the following two object declarations:

```
Frame square = new Frame("Square",100,100);
Frame center = new Frame("Center",500,500);
```

where the intent of declaring the object square is to create a window whose height and width are both equal to 100 pixels and the intent of declaring the object `center` is to create a window in the center of the user's display. However, the implementor of the class must decide what a constructor with two integer values means: does it mean the height and width (as for the `square` object)? Or does it mean the x and y coordinates (as for the `center` object)? Clearly the implementor of the class must make a choice because it cannot mean both! However, both overloadings are possible by introducing different classes that distinguish the two integers that are the shape from the two integers that are the location.

The code segment below shows how to declare Location, Shape, and Frame objects. In the example code, a set of *named constants* are used to define invariant Location and Shape objects. These invariant objects are then used in constructing a set of Frame objects.

```
public final static Location nearTop     = new Location(20, 20);
public final static Location nearCenter  = new Location(500, 500);
public final static Shape    smallSquare = new Shape(50, 50);
public final static Shape    largeSquare = new Shape(500, 500);
...
private Frame smallTop      = new Frame("Square Near Top", nearTop, smallSquare);
private Frame largeCenter   = new Frame("Big at Middle", nearCenter, largeSquare);
private Frame someWhere     = new Frame("Big Somewhere", largeSquare);
private Frame someSize      = new Frame("At Middle", nearCenter);
private Frame anyKind       = new Frame("Name Only - Rest Defaults");
```

```
public class Frame                     // Version 3 (continued)
{
   ... // other methods as above

   public void drawText(String text, Location loc)
   public void drawLine(Location end1, Location end2)
   public void drawCircle(Location center, int radius)
   public void clear()
   public void clear(Location corner, Shape rectangle)

   ...
}
```

Figure 3.3 Frame Class: Version 3 (continued)

The declarations of the Location and Shape objects above show that named-objects can convey useful information to the reader about the intention of the programmer. The name "largeSquare" is more suggestive about the intention to have a window that is large and square than are the two integers 500 and 500 used in a parameter list with two other integers and one or more other values.

The Location and Shape classes have uses beyond those for which they were immediately conceived. Because the Location class captures a reasonably abstract notion—a point in a two-dimensional coordinate system—it maybe useful anywhere such a coordinate system appears. For example, just as the Location class helps to record "where on the screen should a window be placed," it can also be used by other interface items to record "where within a window should an item be placed." The text and graphical items that can be displayed within a Frame also use the concepts of location and shape. For example, the `drawText` method specifies that a given text string should be displayed at a given location. Also the `drawLine` method specifies the endpoints (two locations) of a line segment. These and similar methods of the Frame class can also benefit from the Location and Shape classes as shown in the continuation of the redefinition of the Frame class given in Figure 3.3. Notice that the `clear` method uses both the Location and the Shape classes because this method needs to specify both the placement and dimensions of a rectangular area within the Frame. This illustrates the point made above: the Location and Shape classes are useful wherever a two-dimensional coordinate system is used to specify placement or where rectangular dimensions are required, whether this is information about a Frame on a screen or, equally well, an item displayed within that Frame.

The several advantages of defining the Location and Shape classes can be summarized as follows:

- increased ease of use made possible by more combinations of overloading constructors and other methods
- improved readability through the suggestive naming of objects
- better maintainability through the use of invariant objects
- increased productivity by reusing classes in other contexts

These advantages show the utility and power of defining classes for even relatively simple concepts, such as those for a Location and a Shape.

Returning Objects: Frame Example (Continued)

Objects can also be returned as the result of a method's execution. Returning an object, rather than a single primitive type, allows the method to communicate a complex entity as its result. Two examples are given to illustrate how objects are returned by the methods of a class. One example uses the Frame class and one example uses two new classes.

The `getHeight` and`getWidth` methods in the Frame class should be redefined to return an object. The `getHeight` and `getWidth` methods compute the dimensions of the rectangular area occupied by a given text string. This computation depends on the font used by the Frame, the length of the string, and the characters in the string (some characters, like "w" and "m" are wider than other characters, such as "i" and "t"). The earlier Frame class declared these method as:

```
public class Frame        // Version 1
{
    ...
    public int getHeight()
    public int getWidth(String msg)
    ...
}
```

where the dimensions were returned as two distinct integers values. However, this definition has two problems:

1. It does not clearly capture the responsibility of the Frame class's methods to return the dimensions of a rectangular area. It is not obvious from the definition that `getHeight` and `getWidth` are related methods. It might even be mistakenly believed that `getHeight` returns the height of the window and not the text.
2. The results returned by the two methods do not match closely the parameters of other related methods (e.g., the `clear` method) in the Frame class.

The following example code that displays and then erases a text string illustrates how the `getHeight` and `getWidth` methods do not match the parameters of the `clear` method:

```
Frame    display = new Frame(...);
int width, height;
String msg = "Hello World!";
Location msgLocation= new Location(50,50);
...
display.drawText(msg, msgLocation);
...
int height = display.getHeight();
```

```
public class Frame
{                   // Version 3 (continued)
    ...
public Shape getTextSize(String msg)
    ...
}
```

Figure 3.4 Returning an Object by the getTextSize Method

```
int width   = display.getWidth(msg);
Shape msgShape= new Shape(width, height);
display.clear(msgLocation, msgShape);
```

Notice that the code writer must explicitly create the `msgShape` object. This must be done so that the two integer values returned by the `getHeight` and `getWidth` methods can be put into the form (a Shape object) that is required by the `clear` method.

The `getHeight` and `getWidth` methods can be replaced by a single method that returns a Shape object. The definition of this single method is shown in Figure 3.4. Notice that this definition more clearly expresses the responsibility of the method: to compute and return an object (of the Shape class) that describes the dimensions of a rectangular area on the screen.

With this definition of the `getTextSize` method, the earlier example of displaying and then erasing a text string can be written more succinctly as follows:

```
Frame display = new Frame(...);
String msg = "Hello World!";
Location msgLocation = new Location(50,50);
...
display.drawText(msg, msgLocation);
...
Shape msgShape = display.textSize(msg);
display.clear(msgLocation, msgShape);
```

Notice that the returned result of the `getTextSize` method now matches the parameters required by the `clear` method. Also notice that the declaration of the `msgShape` object can be given at thepoint in the code where the `msgShape` object is first used. Alternatively, the declaration could be given earlier as in:

```
Shape msgShape;
...
msgShape = display.getTextSize(msg);
...
```

Some prefer to place the declaration at the point of first use, particularly if this is the only use of the object, because it helps to improve the readability of the code. Others prefer to place all declarations together at the beginning, particularly if the object is used several times in different places in the code, because this makes it easier to find the declaration of any object by simply looking in this one place. Alternatively, the explicit declaration of the `msg-`

Shape variable can be entirely avoided by using the returned result directly in the clear method invocation where the returned results is needed, as shown in this example:

```
display.clear(msgLocation, display.getTextSize(msg) );
```

This usage assumes that the returned Shape object is needed only in the clear method. However, if the Shape object is needed somewhere else then a variable must be declared to refer to the returned Shape object. Objects that are created and used without being given a name are discussed further in the subsection below on anonymous objects.

Revised Frame Class

All of the methods in the Frame class that can take advantage of passing information by copy have been redefined. The individual changes are collected together in Figure 3.5. It should be clear that by using the Location and Shape classes the readability and utility of the Frame class has been significantly improved.

Anonymous Objects

In some cases an object is needed only temporarily. Explicitly introducing a variable to name this temporary object can be avoided by creating an anonymous object. An anonymous object is an object in every sense except that it has no name. Consider the following example:

equals: a Location object is to decidc if it has the same screen coordinates as another Location object,

```
public class Frame                                   // Version 3
{
  // private implementation not shown
  public       Frame(String name, Location p, Shape s) // exact description
  public       Frame(String name, Shape s, Location p) // exact description
  public       Frame(String name, Location p)          // default shape
  public       Frame(String name, Shape s)             // default location
  public       Frame(String name )                     //  name only
  public       Frame()                                 // all defaults;
  public int   isNamed(String aName)                 // is this your name?
  public void  moveTo(Location newLocation)          // move the window
  public void  resize(Shape    newShape)             // change shape
  public void  resize(float factor)                  // grow/shrink by factor
  public void  drawText(String text, Location loc)   // display text string
  public Shape getTextSize(String msg)               // get shape of string
  public void  drawLine(Location p1, Location p2)    // draw line segment
  public void  drawCircle(Location center,
                          int radius)                // draw circle
  public void  clear()                               // erase entire Frame contents
  public void  clear(Location corner,
                     Shape rectangle)          // erase rectangular area
}
```

Figure 3.5 Complete Frame Class (Version 3)

`equals`: a Shape object is to decide if it has the same height and width as another Shape object

In each case the operation needs as its parameter an object in the same class as the one containing the operation. A similar situation occurs when a method of a class returns an instance of that class as a result. Some examples of methods that return objects in their own class are the following:

`resize`: a Shape object returns a new Shape object, each of whose dimensions are some percentage less or more than the size of the original Shape object

`xMove`, `yMove`: a Location object returns a new Location object that is horizontally or vertically offset from the original Location object

In these cases the methods in the Shape and Location classes return another object in their own class.

The Location and Shape are extended to include the methods named above that take as a parameter an object of the class executing the method and returning from a method an object of the class containing the method. The extensions to these classes are shown in Figure 3.6.

Anonymous Objects

In some cases an object is needed only temporarily. Explicitly introducing a variable to name this temporary object can be avoided by creating an anonymous object. An anonymous object is an object in every sense except that it has no name. Consider the following example:

```
public class Location
{
    public      Location(int x, int y)       // specific location
    public      Location()                   // default location
    public int getX()                        // return x-axis coordinate
    public int getY()                        // return y-axis coordinate
    public boolean equals (Location other)
    public Location xMove(int amount);          // move right/left
    public Location yMove(int amount);          // move up/down
}
public class Shape
{
    public      Shape(int w, int h)             // specific shape
    public      Shape()                         // default shape
    public int getHeight()                      // return height
    public int getWidth()                       // return width
    public boolean equals (Shape other)
    public Shape resize(float factor)
}
```

Figure 3.6 Revised Location and Shape Classes

The `equals` methods in the revised Location and Shape classes can be used in the following way:

```
Location loc1 = new Location(...);
Shape shape1 = new Shape(...);

Location loc1 = new Location(...);
Shape shape1 = new Shape(...);

// are the two location the same?

if (loc1.equals(loc2))
   { // the two locations are the same
   }

// are the two shapes the same?

if (shape1.equals(shape2))
   { // the two shapes are the same
   }
```

In this code segment the two Location objects, `loc1` and `loc2`, are tested for equality using the Location class's `equals` method while a similar test for equality is made between two Shape objects, `shape1` and `shape2`, using the Shape class's `equals` method. Because the `equals` method determine equality, the two tests above could also be performed by exchanging the roles of the objects as follows:

```
if (loc2.equals(loc1))
   { // the two locations are the same
   }

// are the two shapes the same?

if (shape2.equals(shape1))
   { // the two shapes are the same
   }
```

Using these revisions to the Shape and Location class we can operate on a window as follows:

```
Location nearTop = new Location(...);
Shape largeSquare = new Shape(...);
Frame window(nearTop, largeSquare)
Shape    newShape         = largeSquare.resize(0.9)
Location newLocation      = nearTop.xMove(50);
window.moveTo( newLocation );window.resize( newShape );
```

In this example a window is made smaller by 10% and moved to a location that is 50 units to the right of its starting location. The variables introduced in the preceding code segment are not strictly necessary. The same effect can be achieved as follows:

```
Location nearTop = new Location(...);
Shape largeSquare = new Shape(...);
Frame window(nearTop, largeSquare);
window.moveTo( nearTop.xMove(50) );
window.resize( largeSquare.resize(0.9)  );
```

In this code segment, the Location object returned by the `xMove` method is used directly as the input value to the `moveTo` method. Similarly, the Shape object returned by the Shape's `resize` method is used directly as the input value to the Frame's `resize` method.

3.2.2 Using Objects for Communication in the Ecological Simulation

The definition of the Prey class can be revised to structure the arguments and return values as objects of classes rather than as primitive types. The Location class introduced above is also suitable for describing the concepts of the position of a Prey object in its environment. The "range" attributes of the prey abstraction can be captured in a new class whose name and methods reflect the qualities of a "range." The Range class is defined in Figure 3.7. The Location and Shape classes play a natural role in the definition of the Range class because a "range" represents a rectangular area within which a Prey can move. This rectangular area can be represented by the location of its "least" point (i.e., its smallest x and smallest y coordinates) and the "shape" of the area.

The Prey class is redefined using the Location and Range classes as shown in Figure 3.8. The first two constructors use Location and Range classes to define the types of its input parameters for the location and range of the Prey object. The Location class is used to define the type of the object returned by the `getLocation` method. This single method replaces the two previous methods name `getX` and `getY` that returned the x and y coordinates, respectively. The `getLocation` method combines these two methods and returns a single object that carries both the x and y coordinates. If the individual x or y coordinates need to be known, they can be extracted from the Location object using the Location class's `getX` and `getY` methods. A new query method, `getRange`, is also introduced that returns a Range object describing the "range" of the prey modeled by the object to which the method is applied.

```
public class Range
{
  public  Range(Location least, Shape dimensions)     // specific Range
  public  Range()                                     // default Range
  public Shape shape()                         // return dimensions
  public Location  location()                  // return"least"point
}
```

Figure 3.7 The Range Class

```
import Location;
import Range;

public class Prey                    //version 2
{

   public Prey(Location where, Range range)
   public Prey(Location where, Range range, int roam)
   public Prey(Location where)
   public Prey()

   public void move()
   public void move(int steps)

   public Location getLocation()
   public Range getRange()

   public void setRoam(int distance)
   public void print()

}
```

Figure 3.8 Redefined Prey Class (Part 1)

Modifying a Communicated Object

The receiving object may modify an object communicated as an argument to another object's method. To illustrate the need for modifying a communicated object, the ecology simulation is extended to include the definition of a class representing "predators" in the environment. Predators are similar to prey in that they move about in a defined part of the environment but differ from prey in that a predator must capture prey in order to survive. The mortality of the predators and prey is reflected in that a predator has a given "lifetime" within which it must capture a prey or else the predator is assumed to die, whereas being captured kills a prey. A predator captures a prey when the locations of the predator and the prey are within a given distance of each other. The distance within which a prey can be captured is an attribute of the individual predator, making it possible to model different species of predators.

The Prey class is extended to provide methods to query whether the prey is alive and a method that allows the prey to be marked as dead. These two methods are shown in the extension of the Prey class presented in Figure 3.9. The `isAlive` method returns a true value if the prey is alive and false otherwise. A prey will always be alive unless the kill method has previously been invoked to change the object's state from alive to not alive. All other aspects of the Prey class are as shown previously.

```
public class Prey
{
  //... as above
  public boolean isAlive()
  public void kill()
}
```

Figure 3.9 The Prey Class (Part 2)

```
import Location;
import Range;
import Prey;

public class Predator
{

  public static final int IMMOBILE =  0;
  public static final int SLOW     = 25;
  public static final int NORMAL   = 30;
  public static final int FAST     = 50;
  public static final int RANGING  = 75;

  public Predator(Location where, Range range,
                  int lifetime, int killZone)
  public Predator(Location where, Range range,
                  int roam, int lifetime, int killZone)
  public Predator(Location where, int lifetime, int killZone)
  public Predator(int lifetime, int killZone)

  public boolean hunt(Prey aPrey)

  public void move()
  public void move(int steps)
  public boolean isAlive()
  public Location getLocation()
  public Range getRange()
  public void setRoam(int distance)
  public void print()
}
```

Figure 3.10 The Prey Class (Part 2)

The Predator class is defined in Figure 3.10. The Predator and Prey classes are very similar because their abstractions are also very similar. The constructors for the Predator class are similar to those for the Prey class except that they include two extra arguments to model the lifetime and the hunting characteristics of the prey. The `lifetime` of the prey determines how many moves the predator can survive without having captured a prey. If the `lifetime` interval is exceeded without capturing a prey, the predator is assumed to die. The current lifetime for a Predator is decrement by one on each invocation of the Predator's `move` method. A predator captures a prey by discovering that it is within a specified distance, the `killZone`, of the prey.

The hunt method in the Predator class has as its parameter a Prey object that the receiving Predator object may modify. As part of its execution, the hunt method computes the distance between the Prey parameter object and the Predator object executing the method. If this distance is less than the Predator object's killZone, the Predator object will call the kill method of the Prey object, causing the internal state of the Prey object to be changed from alive to not alive. Thereafter, the Prey object will respond false when its isAlive method is invoked. The hunt method will reply true if the Prey object was caught by the predator. A by-product of the hunt method is to reset the Predator's current lifetime back to its original value if the predator captured the prey.

A program illustrating the use of the Predator class and the revised Prey class is shown in Figure 3.11. This program creates one Predator object and one Prey object that move about in the same area (i.e., their Locations and Ranges are the same). The Prey object is constructed with a roaming distance (how far it can move on one move) of 15 compared to the Predator that can roam a distance of 50 on each move. The Predator constructor sets the lifetime of the Predator to 100 moves. Finally, the Predator can capture the Prey if the distance between then is does not exceed 25. The program simulates the movement of the Predator and Prey objects for up to 100 steps or until the Predator captures the Prey.

```
import Predator;
import Prey;
import Location;
import Range;

public class EcoSim
{
    private Predator predator;
    private Prey     prey;

    public EcoSim()
    { predator = new Predator(new Location(50,50), 100, 25);
      predator.setRoam(50);

      prey = new Prey();
      prey.setRoam(15);

      for(int i=0; i<100; i++)
      {
        if (predator.hunt(prey))
         { System.out.println("prey caught at step " + i);
           predator.print();
           prey.print();
           return;
         }
        predator.move();
        prey.move();
      }
    }

    public static void main(String[] args)
    { EcoSim simulation = new EcoSim();
    }
}
```

Figure 3.11 Using the Predator and Prey Classes

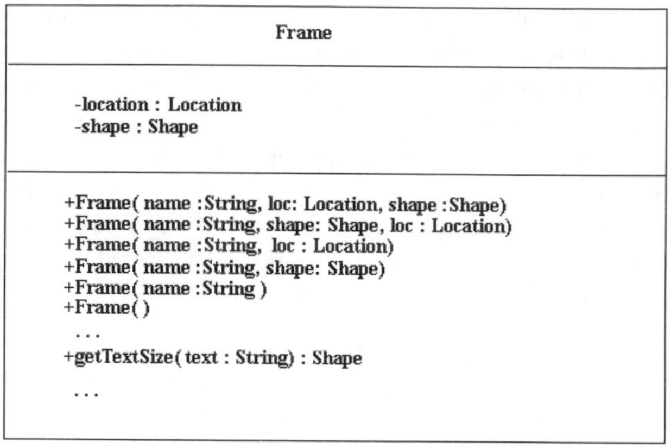

```
Frame
--------------------------------------------------------------
-location : Location
-shape : Shape
--------------------------------------------------------------
+Frame( name :String, loc: Location, shape :Shape)
+Frame( name :String, shape: Shape, loc : Location)
+Frame( name :String, loc : Location)
+Frame( name :String, shape: Shape)
+Frame( name :String )
+Frame( )
 ...
+getTextSize( text : String) : Shape
 ...
```

Figure 3.12 Showing Objects as Parameters and Return Values in UML

The most significant line of code in the EcoSim program in Figure 3.12 is the statement

```
if (predator.hunt(prey))
```

that has two effects. First, the expression `predator.hunt(prey)` yields a boolean value that indicates whether the prey was captured by the predator. Second, if the prey was captured the `prey` object will be modified as a result of the `predator` object invoking the `kill` method on the `prey` object. This expression is significant because it illustrates how a receiving object can modify another object passed to the receiver as a parameter.

Showing Communication Using Objects in UML

The UML notation easily and directly represents passing objects as parameters or returning an object from a method. Just as in the Java syntax, the class of the object is used to describe the object's type in a parameter list or as a returned value in exactly the same way that built-in types have been used in the previous UML diagrams. To illustrate how this appears in UML, Figure 3.12 shows a part of the redefined Frame class. The private data of the Frame class uses the Location and Shape classes as the types of its attributes. Similarly, the arguments for the constructors are defined as being objects of the Location or Shape classes. Finally, the `getTextSize` method is defined so that its returned type, denoted by the "`: Shape`" syntax, is an object of the Shape class.

Exercises

1. Give at least two other good names that could be used for the Shape class.
2. Give at least two other good names that could be used for the Location class.
3. Give the declarations of at least four Location objects that are on the top and left-hand side of the display.
4. Give the declarations of at least four Shape objects that are thin rectangles that are short or long in length.
5. Give the declarations of at least four Frame objects that use different combinations of the Location and Shape objects defined in the last two questions.
6. Draw a picture of a screen showing how the Frame object declared in the last question would appear on the screen. Label each Frame in the picture with the name of the object that it represents.
7. Write a program that creates a 200 by 200 size window near the middle of the screen with your complete name displayed near the middle of that window.
8. Write a program that creates a 200 by 200 size window near the middle of the screen with your first name centered at the top of the window and your last name centered at the bottom of the window.
9. **Expanding/Contracting Line:** Write a program to display a horizontal line of length 200 near the middle of the screen that contracts and expands as follows. Initially, each timer event causes the line to become shorter on both of its ends; the line should appear to be contracting towards its midpoint. The contracting continues until the length of the line is zero. Each timer event should then cause the line to become longer on both ends; the line should appear to be expanding outward from its midpoint. Continue this contracting and expanding indefinitely. Experiment with the amount by which the line contracts and expands—pick an amount that "looks right" to you.
10. Describe a method of the Prey class that would take a Prey object as a parameter.
11. Describe a method of the Prey class that would return a Prey object as a result.

12. Revise the EcoSim program so that there are 5 Prey objects and 1 Predator object. Use an array to hold the Prey objects.

13. Revise the EcoSim program so that there are 5 Predator objects and 1 Prey object. Use an array to hold the Predator objects.

14. Revise the EcoSim program so that there are 5 Predator objects and 5 Prey objects. Use an array to hold the Predator objects and an array to hold the Prey objects.

15. The Appointment class given below is used to define meetings and other reserved blocks of time as part of a calendar management system. This class uses only primitive types. Improve this class by redefining it to use objects of at least two new classes that you define. Use these new classes to create more useful overloadings for the class's constructors and to simplify parameter lists and return values. Show the definitions of the two new classes that you define as well as the redefined Appointment class.

```
public class Appointment
{
 public Appointment(int hour, int min, String month, int day, int duration);
 public void moveTo (String newMonth, int newDay);
 public void moveTo (int newHour, int newMin);
 public void cancel();
 public int whatHour();
 public int whatMin();
 public String whatMonth();
 public int whatDay();
 public int howLong();
}
```

16. The Cargo class given below is used to define packages that are tracked by a worldwide parcel delivery system. This class uses only primitive types. Improve this class by redefining it to use objects of at least two new classes that you define. Use these new classes to create more useful overloadings for the class's constructors and to simplify parameter lists and return values. Show the definitions of the two new classes that you define as well as the redefined Cargo class.

```
public class Cargo
{
  public Cargo(int width, int height, int depth, String country, String city,
            int deliveryDays, int weight);
  public void rerouteTo(String newCountry, String newCity);
  public void deliverIn(int newDays);
  public boolean deliveredYet();
  public boolean fitInBox(int width, int height, int depth);
  public String whatCity();
  public String whatCountry();
  public String whatMonth();
  public int whatDay();
```

```
    public int howLong();
}
```

17. The Airliner class given below is used to define the aircraft monitored by an air traffic control system. This class uses only primitive types. Improve this class by redefining it to use objects of at least two new classes that you define. Use these new classes to create more useful overloadings for the class's constructors, and to simplify parameter lists and return values. Show the definitions of the two new classes that you define as well as the redefined Airliner class.

```
public class Airliner
{
    public Airliner(int latitude, int longitude,
                    int altitude, String company, int flightNumber, int heading);
    public void changeHeading(int newHeading);
    public void changeLocation(int newLongitude,
                    int newLatitude, int newAltitude);
    public String whatCompany();
    public int whatflightNumber();
    public int whatLatitude();
    public int whatLongitude();
    public int whatAltitude();
    public int whatHeading();
}
```

18. Think of a familiar application domain or type of system such as those in the exercises above for calendar management, parcel delivery, and air traffic control. Define a class for a concept or abstraction in this application domain such that the constructors and other methods of this class have as their argument objects of other classes in this application domain. Show the definitions of all of the classes involved.

19. Complete the UML diagram shown in Figure 3.12 by including all of the methods in the redefined Frame class.

20. Draw a UML diagram for the redefined Prey class.

21. Draw a UML diagram for the Appointment class described in the exercise above.

22. Draw a UML diagram for the Cargo class described in the exercise above.

23. Draw a UML diagram for the Airliner class described in the exercise above.

3.3 Sequences of Interactions

The simplest form of interaction is one in which a controlling object performs a sequence of operations over a set of objects. The defining characteristic of a sequence of interactions is that the objects in the set do not directly interact with each other. Rather, the controlling object interacts with each of the objects in the set, passing to each object the data needed for that object to perform its operations and receiving from that object any results that are generated. The controlling object manages any information that must be transmitted between objects in the set. Although the logical flow of data may be from one object in the set to another object in the set, the actual flow of data is indirectly through the controlling objects. A real-world scenario that operates in a sequenced manner is the activity of an operator in a telemarketing company. The operator interacts with the customer to obtain the details of the merchandise that the customer wants to purchase. The operator then interacts with the company's warehouse to deliver the items to the shipping area. Finally, the operator interacts with a parcel delivery service to arrange for the delivery of the materials. In this section, the continuing GUI set of classes and the classes in the ecological simulation are extended to illustrate how a sequence of operations can be used to construct simple systems.

3.3.1 UML Sequence Diagrams

A UML sequence diagram shows a time-ordered series of method invocations among a set of objects. The important elements of the diagram are the objects involved and the sequencing of the invocations among them. The compact, direct way in which the sequence of invocations is presented in the diagram starkly contrasts with the obscure manner in which the same relationships exist in the source code. In the source code, the sequence of interactions is dispersed, with each class's code containing one part of the sequence. The invocations are also interspersed with the other code in each class. The sequence diagram, however, extracts the essential information and presents it in a single, integrated, and succinct form.

The basic UML notation for representing a sequence of interactions among objects is shown in Figure 3.13. Other aspects of the sequence diagram notation are given in later examples in this section. The vertical axis in a sequence diagram represents time; time flows from the top of the diagram to the bottom. The horizontal axis shows the object participating in the interactions. In Figure 3.13 there are three objects whose classes are `Controller`, `Object1`, and `Object2`. Notice that each object is drawn as a box containing the class of the object. The name of the object's class is underlined and preceded by a colon. The underlining and the use of the colon in the class name are consistent with the naming of objects in the object diagrams seen in Chapter 2. The execution state of each

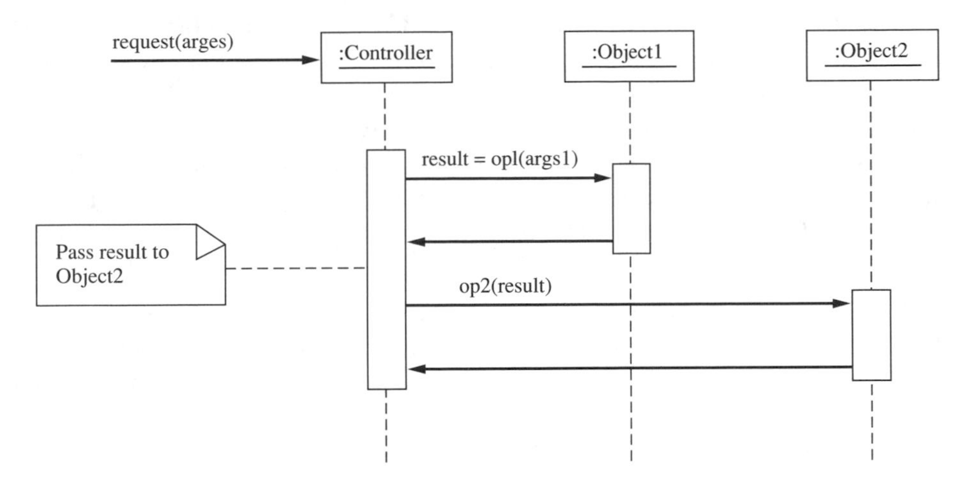

Figure 3.13 UML Notation for a Sequence of Interactions

object is drawn vertically below the object with a dotted line, denoting that the object is inactive, and a thin, vertical rectangular box, denoting that the object is active. The horizontal, arrowed lines that point to the right represent invocations and the arrowed lines that point to the left represent returns from these invocations. The invocations may be labeled to indicate which of the target object's methods is invoked. The returns are not labeled. The arrowheads on the invocations and returns are drawn differently to further convey the differences in their natures. The return arrows may be omitted from the diagram if no loss of readability results.

The sequence diagram illustrates how the `Controller` object responds to the invocation of its `request` method where `args` is provided as the method's arguments. As part of its computation, the `Controller` object invokes the `op1` method of `Object1` passing `args1` as the arguments. This invocation is represented by the labeled horizontal arrowed line that goes from the thin vertical rectangle denoting the active execution state of the `Controller` object to the `Object1` object. In response to the invocation, `Object1` becomes active; the dotted line denoting its execution state changes to a thin vertical rectangle. When `Object's` method completes, it returns to the `Controller` object; the return arrow that is directed from Object1 to the Controller object denotes the return. After returning, `Object1` again become inactive; its execution state reverts to a dotted line. The `op1` method generates an output value that the Controller identifies by the name `result`. After completing the invocation involving `Object`, the `Controller` objects invokes the `op2` method of `Object2` passing `result` as the arguments. The diagram shows that `Object2` becomes active, performs its computation, and returns control to the `Controller` object. This completes the sequence of operations depicted in the diagram.

The graphic in the left part of Figure 3.13 that resembles a page with a turned down upper right-hand corner is UML notation for a note. A UML note is similar to a comment in programming languages. The text written inside of the border of the note is intended to be informative for the reader to clarify or explain something that might not be clear from the diagram itself. The note graphic is connected by a dotted line to a part of the diagram to which the note is relevant. In Figure 3.13 the note is attached to the activity of the Controller object.

Sequence diagrams do not show actual execution times, rather they show that a computation has begun but is not yet completed. In other words, the vertical axis is not a linear measure of time. In the diagram in Figure 3.13, for example, the heights of the vertical boxes denoting execution activity are not significant. These boxes only have meaning to show the relative occurrence of an object's execution in the sequence. Thus, it is not correct to say that the execution times of `Object1` and `Object2` are approximately the same because the vertical boxes denoting their executions have approximately the same height. Also, the vertical boxes denoting activity are not perfectly matched with the idea of the object actively executing. After invoking the `op1` method of `Object1`, the `Controller` object is still depicted as active even though execution control will pass to `Object1`. The `Controller` object is still active after this invocation because the computation of its `request` method has begun but has not yet completed.

3.3.2 A Sequence of Interactions with GUI Objects

The sequence of operations necessary to display an image (e.g., a ".gif" image) are used to illustrate a simple system based on sequenced interaction. The steps to display the image are:

- ask the user for the name of the file containing the image,
- create the image using the contents of the named file, and
- draw the image in a Frame.

The structure of a simple system to perform this sequence of steps is shown in Figure 3.14 as a UML sequence diagram. It is possible, of course, to add other steps (such as verifying that the named file exists and does, in fact, contain an image) or to combine some of these steps (program the Frame object to receive the file name so that it can both create and draw the image). Although the exact steps may change, the central idea is that the system is built around a sequence of actions taken by independent objects.

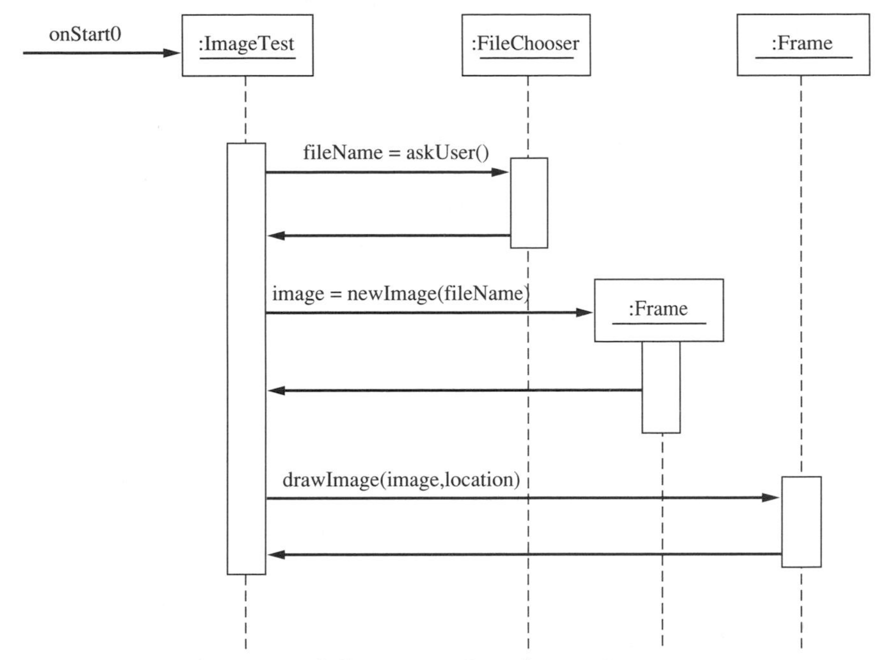

Figure 3.14 A Sequenced System to Display an Image

The UML diagram in Figure 3.14 contains four objects. The `ImageTest` object is assumed to be a program written for the simple programming environment. When its `onStart` method is invoked, the `ImageTest` object performs the three basic steps outlined above. First, the `askUser` method of a `FileChooser` object is used to solicit the name of a file from the user. The file with this name presumably contains a graphical image. The file name obtained from the user is denoted by "`fileName`" in the UML diagram. Second, an `Image` object is created using the name of the file as a constructor argument. The newly created `Image` object is referred to as `image` in the UML diagram. Third, the dynamically created `Image` object is drawn in the user interface by invoking the `drawImage` method of the `Frame` class passing the `Image` object as a parameter.

One new aspect of UML sequence diagrams shown in Figure 3.14 is how to represent object creation as part of the sequence of operations. In this diagram, after the file name is obtained from the user, the Image object is dynamically created. This is shown in the UML diagram because the invocation labeled "`new Image(fileName)`" is directed to the box containing the name of the Image class. The activity that is directly attached below this box represents the activity of the Image object's constructor.

Two new classes are introduced that can be used to perform the sequence of operations to display an image: FileChooser and Image. The FileChooser class

```
public class FileChooser
{
  public FileChooser()          // create a FileChooser object
  public void askUser()         // initiate dialog with user
  public String getFileName()   // return filename selected by user
  public String getDirectory()  // return path where filename exists
}
```

Figure 3.15 The FileChooser Class

```
public class Image
{
  public Image(String imageFileName) // create an image object
                                     // from the specified file
  public int getHeight()             // report the height of the image
  public int getWidth()              // report the width of the image
}
```

Figure 3.16 The Image Class

initiates a dialog with the user through which the user is able to select a file containing the desired image. Given a file name, an Image object is responsible for loading and constructing an image based on the contents of a file. Adding a method that draws an Image also extends the Frame class. The FileChooser, Image, and Frame classes can be operated upon in a variety of ways to produced simple but interesting systems based on the notion of a sequence of operations. One example is shown and the exercises at the end of the section contain a number of ideas for other simple systems.

The FileChooser class, shown in Figure 3.15, allows the user to navigate through the local file system, moving up and down in the directory hierarchy, until the desired file is located and selected by the user. When the dialog is completed, the getFileName and getDirectory methods can be used to obtain strings that describe the file selected by the user. For example, if the user selected the file named "clown.gif" in the directory "C:\Java\Gifs," then the getFileName method would return "clown.gif" and the getDirectory method would return "C:\Java\Gifs." The FileChooser class does not restrict what file the user selects. It does not know, for example, that the intention in this context is to select only a ".gif" file. Any such validation must be done by the code using the FileChooser. The example system shown in Figure 3.16 illustrates how such checking can be done.

The Image class has a simple interface. The definition of the Image class is given in Figure 3.16. The constructor takes a single string argument that is the name of a file that must contain a ".gif" image. The filename given as the constructor argument must be sufficient for the Image class to locate the file. This

```
public class Frame
{
   // other methods as in version 3...
   public void drawImage(Image image, Location where) // draw Image in Frame
   // ...
}
```

Figure 3.17 Frame Class (extended to version 3)

```
import Program;
import Frame;
import Location;
import Shape;
import Image;
import FileChooser;

public class ImageTest implements Program
{
   private Frame window;
   private Image image;

   public void onStart()
   { window = new Frame("Hello World Program",new Location(100,100),
                                            new Shape(300,300));
     FileChooser chooser = new FileChooser();
     chooser.askUser();
     String fileName = chooser.getFileName();
     if ( fileName.endsWith(".gif") )
       { String dirName = chooser.getDirectory();
         image = new Image(dirName + fileName);
         window.drawImage(image, new Location(40,40));
       }
   }

   public void onPaint()
   { if (window != null) window.drawImage(image, new Location(40,40));
   }

   public void onMouseEvent(String frameName, int x, int y, int eventInfo)
   {
   }

   public void onTimerEvent()
   {
   }
}
```

Figure 3.18 A Sequence of Operations to Draw an Image in a Frame

means that if the complete path is not given (e.g., a name like "clown.gif" is given), then the desired file is assumed to exist in the current directory at the time of execution. To insure that the file can be located the complete path may need to be given (e.g., "C:\Java\Gifs\clown.gif"). The height and width of the image (in pixels) can be obtained by the `getHeight` and `getWidth` methods, respectively. The height and the width must be known in order to erase an Image from a Frame or to arrange a display so that the image does not overlap other information being presented.

The Frame class is modified so that it includes a method to display an Image. The extension to the Frame class is a single method, `drawImage`, which takes an Image object and a Location object as parameters. The Frame will display the ".gif" image represented by the Image object in the Frame where the upper-left-hand corner of the image is at the specified Location. This extension to the Frame class is shown in Figure 3.17.

A system that displays an Image in a Frame is shown in Figure 3.18 to illustrate a sequence of operations. In this simple system the ImageTest object plays the role of the controlling object. A FileChooser object is used to obtain a file name from the user. This name is tested using the String `endsWith` method to insure that the file is at least named correctly (this is, of course, not a guarantee that the contents of the file are actually a gif image, only that the file is named to indicate that it does). If the file has the expected suffix, an Image object is constructed using the concatenated directory name and file name as the constructor argument. Finally, the Image object is drawn in the screen. If the user selects a file that does not have the expected suffix the window will remain blank.

3.3.3 A Sequence of Interactions Using the Predators and Prey Classes

The ecological simulation can also be used to illustrate how a sequence of interaction is applied to Prey and Predator objects. In this example, a simple simulation is constructed in which a single predator hunts for members of a group of prey. To build this simulation the Herd class is introduced to represent the group of Prey objects. The Herd class is defined in Figure 3.19. A Herd object can be constructed by specifying the initial number of Prey in the herd; the constructor populates the herd with Prey having randomly generated locations and with default values for other characteristics. Alternatively, an empty Herd can be constructed to which individual members are added explicitly. The `add` method allows a Prey to be added to the Herd. This method can be used regardless of how the Herd was constructed (i.e., with an initial size or empty). There is no fixed bound on the size of the Herd. The individual members of the herd can be accessed via the `member` method that returns the individual Prey at a given index position in the herd. The `move` method causes each of the members of the herd to move to a new location. The number of members in the Herd is returned by the `size` method. Because a predator can kill individual Prey, the number of members of the herd alive is returned by the `alive` method.

```
import Prey;

public class Herd
{
   public Herd(int size)        // create a herd of size Prey
   public Herd()                // create a herd with no members
   public void add(Prey aPrey) // add another Prey to the herd
   public Prey member(int i)    // return the ith Prey of the herd
   public void move()           // move all the Prey in the herd
   public int size()            // what is the size of the herd
   public int alive()           // how many Prey in the herd are alive
}
```

Figure 3.19 The Herd Class

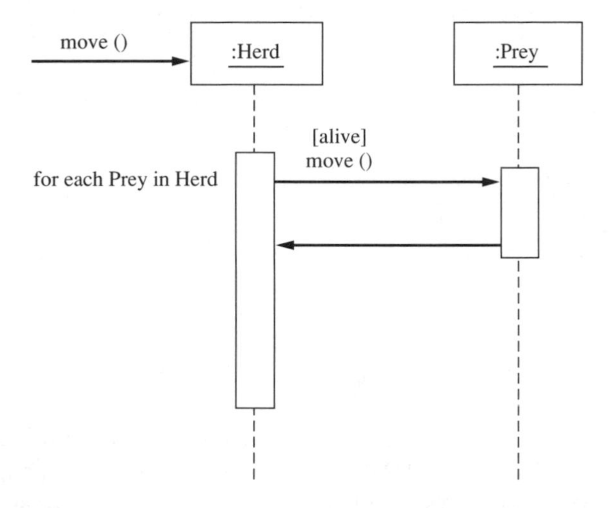

Figure 3.20 Representing Iterations and Conditions in UML Diagrams

The Herd class is used to illustrate annotations that can appear on UML diagrams to denote iteration and conditional action. The UML diagram in Figure 3.20 shows the interaction between the Herd class and the Prey class when the Herd classes `move` method is invoked. The annotation that reads "for each Prey in Herd," termed a script in UML, is used in this case to convey the fact that the invocation of the Prey class's `move` method is performed repeatedly. The script indicates that the `move` method is invoked on each Prey object that is a part of the Herd. The arrowed line denoting the invocation of the Prey class's `move` method also bears an additional annotation that reads "`[alive]`." The annotation denotes a condition; the `move` method only has effect if the Prey object is "alive." Recall that the Prey class has an attribute indicating if the simulated prey is alive or dead and that this attribute can be tested by the `isAlive` method in the Prey class.

```
import Prey;
import Herd;
import Predator;

public class PreySequence
{

   public PreySequence()
   {
     Herd herd = new Herd(10);
     Predator predator = new Predator(20, 30);

     for(int step=0; predator.isAlive() && step<100; step++)
     { predator.move();
       herd.move();

       for(int next=0; next < herd.size(); next++)
         { predator.hunt(herd.member(next));
         }
     }

     int alive = herd.alive();

     predator.print();
     System.out.println("Surviving prey: " + alive);
   }

   public static void main(String[] args)
   { PreySequence seq = new PreySequence();
   }
}
```

Figure 3.21 Sequences of Interactions in a Small Simulation

A small Java application that uses a sequence of interactions to implement the simulation is shown in Figure 3.21. In this application, a Herd of 10 Prey is constructed along with a single Predator object. The simulation repeats a basic step 100 times (or until the predator itself dies). On each basic step, the predator and the herd are moved to their new locations and the predator hunts. The hunting of the predator involves calling the hunt method of the predator successively with each member of the herd. The simulation concludes by outputting the status of the predator and the number of surviving herd members. This small simulation application illustrates a sequence of interactions in several ways. First, the controlling object invokes the `move` methods on the Predator object and the Herd object in a sequenced fashion. Second, in the basic simulation step each element of the Herd is extracted from the herd by the `member` method and passed to the Predator object's `hunt` method. This sequence of interactions in this basic step is repeated for each member of the Herd. Finally, the `alive` and `print` methods of the Herd and Predator classes, respectively, are used to determine the output from the simulation.

Exercises

1. **Dual Images:** write a program that displays two different images in a Frame.
2. **Blinking Image:** write a program that creates a blinking image effect by alternately drawing and clearing an image in a Frame on successive timer events.
3. **Alternating Images:** write a program that displays two images alternately on successive timer events.
4. **Draggeable Image:** write a program that allows the user to drag an Image around in a Frame.
5. **Bordered Image:** write a program that displays an Image and draws a box (four line segments) around the Image.
6. **Image Info:** write a program that displays in a Frame several Images that you have gathered from the web. When the user clicks on an Image a short description of the gif image should be drawn in the Frame.
7. **Image Gallery:** write a program that allows a user to browse an "image gallery." Find a collection of related gif images on the web (famous paintings, historic locations, famous people) and place these in a common directory. The user is presented with a Frame containing an initial Image. Each time the user clicks in the Frame the Frame is cleared the user is allowed to select, via a FileChooser, a file whose Image is displayed in the Frame.
8. Revise the PreySequence application so that the Herd is initially empty and 10 Prey objects are added to the Herd.
9. Revise the PreySequence application so that the Herd is initially empty and 5 Prey objects are added to the Herd for the first 50 steps of the simulation. Five additional Prey are then added to the Herd for the last 50 steps of the simulation.
10. Revise the PreySequence application so that there are two Predator objects.
11. Revise the Prey Sequence application so that there is an array of Predator objects.
12. Define the interface of a class named Pack that contains a group of Predator objects. The relationship between the Pack and Predator classes is similar to that between the Herd and Prey classes.

13. Draw a UML sequence diagram for the telemarketer example given in the introductory paragraph of this section.

14. The UML sequence diagram shown in Figure 3.20 for the `ImageTest` object does not represent accurately how the `FileChooser` and `Frame` objects are created. Draw a more accurate UML sequence diagram, correctly depicting the creation of these objects.

15. The UML sequence diagram shown in Figure 3.20 for the `ImageTest` object does not represent the complete sequence of method invocations involving the `FileChooser` object as given in the code in Figure 3.21. Identify the missing steps and draw a more complete UML sequence diagram.

16. Draw a UML diagram that shows the interaction between the PreySequence object and Herd object in Figure 3.19. In this diagram, ignore the Predator object. Use scripts and conditions as appropriate.

17. Draw a UML diagram that shows the interactions among the PreySequence, the Herd, and the Predator objects in Figure 3.19. Use scripts and conditions as appropriate.

3.4 Simple Associations

Association can be used to build systems of interacting, collaborative objects. A robust collection of classes allows the system to be constructed with little additional programming, the objects are simply instantiated and hooked together to build the system. This method of building systems by composition is often referred to as the "plug and play" technique because the builder simply "plugs" the objects together and "plays" with (experiments, validates, evaluates) the system.

Several new classes will be introduced to illustrate building systems by association. In the case of the GUI classes, a "message" class is defined that represents a text string, a "counter" is introduced that represents a simple incrementing or decrementing counter, and a simple "timer" class is give. Though these three classes are simple, they can be configured to form a number of interesting systems. The classes are also very specialized because only a part of the Java language is used to define them. Techniques that will be learned later can be used to extend the generality of these classes. In the case of the ecological simulation, a Pack class, representing a group of predators, is added to complement the Herd class that represents a group of prey. In addition, a simple simulation class is introduced that performs a simulation using associated Pack and Herd objects.

3.4.1 Forming an Association in the GUI Classes

A simple association will be created using a newly defined class, the Message class, and the existing Frame class. The Message class is an abstraction of a displayable text string. A Message object knows what text should be written to a Frame and where within the Frame the text should appear. In addition, a Message object will be responsible for erasing its text from the Frame and for updating the Frame when the Message is changed. The definition of the Message class is given in Figure 3.22.

An association can be represented in UML notation as a relationship between classes. Figure 3.23 shows a UML diagram for the association between the Message class and the Frame class. Each class is represented simply by a box that contains the name of the class. Additional details about the attributes and methods of a class may be given in the diagram; alternatively, the details of each class may be placed in a separate diagram, allowing the association diagram to focus on the relationships between the classes. The line connecting two classes represents the association. The line maybe annotated in various ways to provide additional information about the nature of the association. The association in Figure 3.23 between the Message and Frame classes has four annotations. First, the label "appears in" gives a name to the association. This name serves to describe the purpose or function of the association. The names given to associations are usually verbs. Because class names are usually nouns, this allows a simple sentence to be read from the diagram. For example, the naming used in Figure 3.23 yields the sentence: "A Message appears in a Frame." Second, the

```
public class Message
{
  public         Message (String textString, Location whereAt)
  public         Message (Location whereAt)
  public void    displayIn (Frame whichFrame)
  public void    moveTo (Location newLocation)
  public void    setText(String newText)
  public String  getText()
  public void    clear()
  public void    draw ()
}
```

Figure 3.22 The Message Class

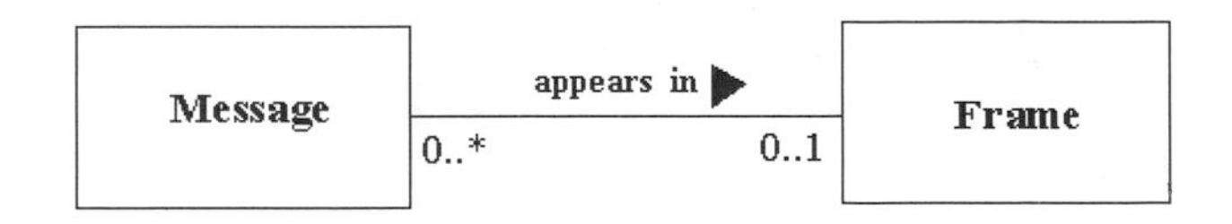

Figure 3.23 A Simple Association in UML

```
public class Message
{
   //encapsulated implementation

   private String   msgText;             // display this text string
   private Frame    msgFrame;            // in this Frame
   private Location msgLocation;         // at this Frame Location

   ...

   public void displayIn (Frame whichFrame)
   { msgFrame = whichFrame;
   }
}
```

Figure 3.24 Private Elements of The Message Class

association between a Message and a Frame is a one-way relationship. That is, the Message object knows the Frame object with which it is associated, but the Frame object does not know what Message object may be associated with it. Examples will be show later of associations that are bidirectional. The direction of an association is shown by the solid triangle whose tip point in the direction of the association. Third, the annotation “0..1” is one of several ways to indicate multiplicity. This annotation means that each Message object may be associated with zero or one Frame objects. This means that (1) a Message object may not be associated with any Frame object and, (2) it is not possible to associate a single Message with two or more Frame objects at the same time. This annotation does not preclude the possibility that a single Message object may be associated with two or more different Frame objects at different times. Fourth, the annotation “0..*” is another multiplicity indicator. This annotation means that zero or more Message objects may appear in the same Frame object. The number of such Message objects is unbounded.

To make the idea of association concrete, a portion of the Message class' implementation is examined. The private data of the Message class contains variables that refer to the text string that the Message object displays and to the Frame object in which the string will be displayed. The Message also contains a Location object indicating where the text string appears within the Frame. The private data of the Message class is shown in Figure 3.24 along with the implementation of the `displayIn` method. The `displayIn` method creates the association between a Message object and a Frame object. This method takes as a parameter the Frame object with which the Message object will be associated. The `displayIn` method simply assigns to the `msgFrame` variable in its private data the associated Frame object. Thus, `msgFrame` in a Message object will refer to the Frame object that was passed as the parameter of the `displayIn` method.

The following code segment creates an association between a Message object and a Frame object:

```
// declaring the variables
    Frame window;
    Message greeting;
```

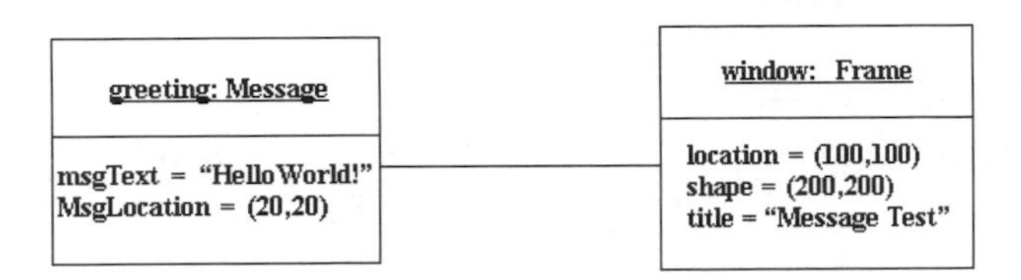

Figure 3.25 A Simple Association Between Objects

```
// constructing the objects
    window = new Frame("Message Test", new Location(100,100), Shape(200,200));
    greeting = new Message("Hello World!", new Location(20,20));
// creating the association
    greeting.displayIn(window);
```

This code will create an association between the greeting object and the window object that can be pictured as shown in Figure 3.25. This association is created because the `greeting` object retains as part of its private data a reference to the `window` object. This reference will remain valid until it is changed by the `greeting` object (i.e., the `displayIn` method is called to have the Message point to a different Frame object) or the `greeting` object itself is destroyed.

The association between the object created by the above code segment are shown in the UML object diagram in Figure 3.25. This diagram shows the attributes of the `window` object and the `greeting` object. The types of these objects are also given in their respective boxes in the diagram where a colon (":") is used to separate the object name from the class name. As before, the names are underlined because the boxes represent objects, not classes. A single line is drawn between the greeting object and the window object denoting the association between these objects. The annotation information for the association is not given in the object diagram because this information was given in the class diagram.

An association can be used by the methods of a class to perform its operation. For example, the association between the Message object and the Frame object is used by the `clear` method in the Message class. The code for this method is shown in Figure 3.26. This code uses the private data member's `msgFrame` and `msgText` to obtain from the Frame object the shape of the text displayed by the Message object. The `clear` method of the Frame class is then used to erase the rectangular area containing the Message object's text. Note that `msgText`, `msgFrame`, and `msgLocation` are private data members that are part of the Message object. These data members are visible to the methods of the Message object; these data members exist as long as the object itself exists (though the value of these data members may change). The Shape object `msgShape`, however, is a local object of the `clear` method; this object exists only during the execution of the `clear` method itself.

```
public class Message
{
   public void clear()
   {
      Shape msgShape = msgFrame.getTextSize(msgText);
      msgFrame.clear(msgLocation, msgShape);
   }
   ...
}
```

Figure 3.26 Implementation of the `clear` Method

```
public class BlinkingText implements Program
{
   private Frame window;
   private Message greeting;
   private boolean visible;

   public BlinkingText()
   {
     window = new Frame("Message Test", new Location(100,100),
                                        new Shape(200,200));
     greeting = new Message greeting("Hello World!", new Location(20,20));
     visible = false;
   }

   void onStart() {
      greeting.displayIn(window);
      greeting.draw();
      visible = true;
   }

   void onTimerEvent() {
        if (visible) { greeting.clear(); visible = false; }
        else { greeting.draw(); visible = true; }
   }

   void onPaint() {
      if (visible) greeting.draw();
   }

   // ...
}
```

Figure 3.27 The Blinking Text Revised

Also notice that both the Message class and the Frame class have a `clear` method. There is no confusion about which method is intended in a given invocation because the class of the object to which the method is applied determines which method is executed. For example, the invocation

```
greeting.clear();
```

Invokes the clear method in the Message class because greeting is an object of the Message class. Similarly, the invocation

```
window.clear();
```

invokes the clear method in the Frame class because window is an object of the Frame class.

A more complete example of using an association between a Message object and a Frame object is the Blinking Text example shown in Figure 3.27. This version of the Blinking Text problem is considerably simpler than the one that would result without the Message class. The Message class contains the machinery necessary for a Message object to manage itself more completely. Thus, to erase the text from the screen it is only necessary to tell the Message object to clear itself—it is not necessary to manipulate the Frame object directly.

3.4.2 Simple Counters and Timers

Simple systems of three or four objects will be built that count discrete events, either individual user-interface actions or ticks of a timer. The existing Message and Frame classes will be used. In addition, two new classes, Counter and Timer, will be defined. These classes are defined so that they can be composed together in an association to form a small system. More complex examples are considered later.

The Counter class models a simple integer counter that can count upwards or downwards depending on how it is constructed. The Counter displays its current value in a Message. If the Message object is itself displayed in a Frame object, the value of the Counter object will appear on the display. The `reset` method allows the Counter object to be returned to its original state. The class definition is shown in Figure 3.28.

In the first constructor, the Counter counts upwards by one if `start` is less than `stop` and it counts downward by one otherwise. The second constructor defines a counter that counts upward by one without bound. The current value of the Counter is displayed in the Message object specified in the `connectTo` method. The current value of the Counter is incremented or decremented by the `next` method. Whenever the value of the Counter is changed by the `next` method, the Message object, if any, to which the Counter object is connect is

```
public class Counter
{
  public Counter (int start, int end);  // count up/down from start to end
  public Counter();                     // count upwards from zero
  public void next();                   // increment/decrement by 1
  public void reset();                  // reset to original state
  public void connectTo(Message msg);   // show current value here
}
```

Figure 3.28 The Counter Class

```
public class ClickCounting implements Program
{
   private Frame window;
   private Message countDisplay;
   private Counter clickCount;

   public ClickCounting()
   { window = new Frame("Click Counting", Location(100,100), Shape (200,200));
     countDisplay = new Message(Location(10,10));
     cclickCount = new Counter();
   }

   public void onStart()
   { window.clear();
     countDisplay.displayIn(window);
     clickCount.connectTo(countDisplay);
   }

   public void onPaint()
   { countDisplay.draw();
   }

   void onTimerEvent() {}

   void onMouseEvent() {String frameName, int x, int y, int eventType)
   {  if (eventType == Frame.MOUSE_DOWN)
          clickCount.next();
   }
}
```

Figure 3.29 Click Counting Program

updated accordingly using the Message object's `setText` method. The `reset` method causes the Counter object to be restored to its initial state.

A simple system that counts mouse click events is shown in Figure 3.29. This system uses a Counter to count the number of mouse click events, a Message object to display the Counter object's current value and a Frame object to make this display visible to the user. There are two significant things to observe in this example:

1. the `onStart` method "plugs" the parts of the system together. The Message object is associated with the Frame object and the Counter object is associated with the Message object;
2. the `onMouseEvent` method has little processing to do: it simply informs the Counter object to performs its `next` method whenever a mouse click is detected.

When the `next` method in the Counter object is called, a series of actions is triggered among the parts of the system so that the Counter object's internal count is incremented, its corresponding Message representation is changed, and

```
public class Clock
{
 public Clock (int interval);               // milliseconds between "ticks"
 public void connectTo(Counter count);  // change count on each "tick"
 public void on();                          // (re)start Clock
 public void off();                         // halt Clock
}
```

Figure 3.30 The Clock Class

```
public class SimpleTimer implements Program
{
   private Frame   window;
   private Message label;
   private Message display;
   private Counter seconds;
   private Clock   timer;

   public SimpleTimer()
   {
      // create objects
      window = new Frame("Timer", Location(100, 100), Shape(200, 200));
      label = new Message("Seconds:", Location(10,10));
      display = new Message("", Location(100,10));
      seconds = new Counter();
      timer = new Clock(1000);
   }

   public void onStart()
   {
      // create associations
      timer.connectTo(seconds);
      second.connectTo(display);
      display.displayIn(window);
      timer.on();
   }

   public void onPaint()
   {
      display.draw();
   }

   public void onTimerEvent() {}

   public void onMouseEvent(String frameName, int x, int y,
                            int buttonState) {}
}
```

Figure 3.31 A Simple Timer System

the Message object changes what is being displayed in the Frame object visible to the user.

The Clock class is an abstraction of the system's interval timer. The Clock class increments a Counter at fixed intervals of time. The resolution of the Clock (i.e., the timer's interval) is set on construction. The Clock can be started and stopped. The definition of the Clock class is show in Figure 3.30. The constructor specifies the interval of time, in milliseconds, between successive clock "ticks."

On each "tick" of the clock, the Clock calls the `next` method in the Counter to which the Clock is connected. The connection between the Clock and a Counter is established by the `connectTo` method. The `start` and `stop` methods can be used to control the Clock.

An example of how a Clock and a Counter can be used to build a simple timer systems is shown in Figure 3.31. This examples creates a one second Clock connected to a Counter that counts upwards from 0. The value of the Counter is presented in a Message labeled "Seconds" that is visible in the window Frame.

3.4.3 Using Association in the Ecological Simulation

The principle of association can be used to create a simple simulation system involving some additional classes that are introduced in this subsection. The basic form of the association is shown in Figure 3.32. The Ecology class embodies the basic logic of a simulation step in which the predators and prey move to their locations and then the predators hunt among the prey. In effect, the sequence of interactions shown in the *PreySequence* example in the previous section is internalized by the Ecology class. Rather than having the Ecology class manage individual Predator and Prey objects, the *Herd* class introduced in the last section is used to organize the Prey objects and provide a simpler interface for the management of the prey. A similar class, named Pack, is added hereto organize the Predator objects. Two associations are created: one between the Ecology and the Herd, and one between the Ecology and the Pack. These two associations create the linkages necessary for the Ecology to function. The UML diagram in Figure 3.32 shows that an Ecology has exactly one associated Pack and exactly one associated Herd. Also, both the Pack and the Herd may be in at most one Ecology at a time. The Pack consists of zero or more Predators; this allows the Pack to be empty or to contain an unbounded number of Predator objects. Similarly, the Herd may be empty or contain an unbounded number of Prey objects. The diagram makes no statement about whether a given Predator may be in zero, one, or more Packs at the same time. The diagram is similarly silent on whether a given Prey maybe in zero, one, or more Herds at the same time. These details are omitted if they are not considered relevant to understanding the relationships involved in the diagram.

The Pack class is shown in Figure 3.33. The two constructors allow either an empty Pack or a Pack with an initial number of Predators whose characteristics are all given default or random values. Regardless of how the Pack was constructed, new Predators can be added at any time using the `add` method. There is no limit on how many Predators can be in a Pack. The current number of Predators in the Pack is returned by the `size` method. The individual Predators of the Pack can be retrieved by using the `member` method. The `move` method causes all of the Predators in the Pack to move to new locations. Finally, the `alive` method returns the number of Predators that are currently alive.

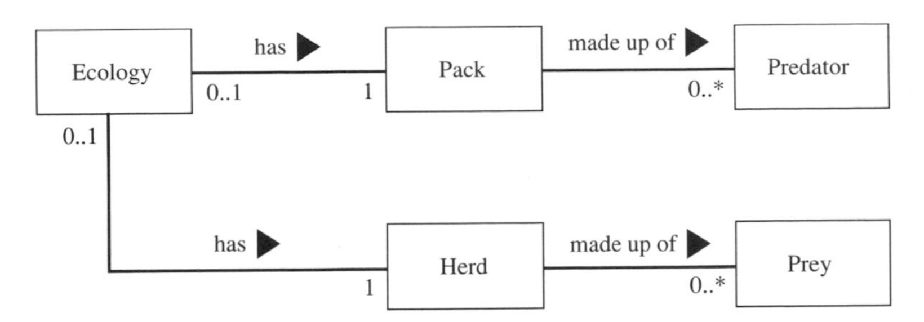

Figure 3.32 Representing Associations between Simulation Classes in UML

```
import Predator;
public class Pack
{
    public Pack()
    public Pack(int size)
    public void add(Predator newPredator)
    public Predator member(int i)
    public void move()
    public int size()
    public int alive()
}
```

Figure 3.33 The Pack Class

The Ecology class shown in Figure 3.34 is defined so that associations are created between an Ecology object and a Pack object and also between an Ecology object and a Herd object. These two associations allow the Ecology methods to manipulate the Pack and Prey objects that are constructed independently. These two associations are created when the Ecology object is constructed as indicated by the two constructor arguments of the Ecology constructor. To emphasize the role and mechanics of an association, the code for the constructor and a part of the code of the `next` method are also shown. The Ecology class defines two private variables, `pack` and `herd`, that are initialized by the constructor to refer to the Pack and Herd objects that are passed as the parameters of the constructor. An Ecology object "remembers" the associated Pack and Herd objects by means of its internal, private data (in this case the `pack` and `herd` variables). The `next` method is able to manipulate the associated Pack and Herd objects through the internal references to these objects recorded in the `pack` and `herd` variables. The overloaded `next` method has a parameter to indicate how many simulation steps should be taken at one time.

A Java application that uses the Ecology class in association with a Pack object and a Herd object to construct a simple simulation system is shown in Figure 3.35. This application constructs a Herd with 15 members(named `hunted`)

```
public class Ecology
{
   private Pack pack;
   private Herd herd;

   public Ecology(Pack aPack, Herd aHerd)
   { pack = aPack;
     herd = aHerd;
   }

   public void next()
   { pack.move();
     herd.move();
     ...
   }

   public void next(int steps)
}
```

Figure 3.34 Defining the Ecology Class Using Associations

```
import Ecology;
import Pack;
import Herd;

public class EcoSim2
{

   public EcoSim2()
   { Herd hunted  = new Herd(15);
     Pack hunters = new Pack(5);

     Ecology ecoSystem = new Ecology(hunters, hunted);

     ecoSystem.next(100);

     int numHunters = hunters.alive();
     int numHunted  = hunted.alive();

     System.out.println("Surviving Predators: " + numHunters);
     System.out.println("Surviving Prey:      " + numHunted);
   }

   public static void main(String[] args)
   { EcoSim2 simulation = new EcoSim2();
   }
}
```

Figure 3.35 Building a Simulation with Associations

and a Pack with 5 members (named `hunters`). An Ecology object (named `ecoSystem`) is then constructed that has associations with the `hunted` and `hunters` objects. Notice that the three objects, `ecoSystem`, `hunted`, and `hunters`, are constructed independently and all of them are visible in the application. This independent construction and visibility are the standard features of an association. The overloaded `next` method is used to run the simulation for 100 steps, after which the number of surviving predators and surviving prey are printed.

Exercises

1. **Hit Counter:** using association, write a program that counts the number of mouse button clicks that occur within a circle that is drawn in the Frame. The number should appear approximately in the middle of the circle.
2. **Hit and Miss Counter:** using association, write a program that counts the number of mouse button clicks that occur within a circle that is drawn in the Frame and the number of mouse button clicks that occur outside of the circle. The number that records the mouse button clicks within the circle should appear approximately in the middle of the circle. The number that records the mouse button clicks outside the circle can appear anywhere outside of the circle.
3. **Controlled Clock:** using association, implement a system that implements a simple, controllable timer. Use a mouse button click to control whether the displayed number is incremented. The first mouse button click "starts" the timing (the number increments once each second). The second mouse button click "stops" the timing. Thereafter, alternate mouse button clicks start and stop the timing.
4. **Two Valued Clock:** using association, implement a system that displays the value of two Clocks, one operating on a one second interval and one on a 0.1-second interval. Each Clock is connected to a different counter. Both counters display their values on the screen with appropriate labels.
5. **Chess Clocks:** using association, implement a system of two clocks such that only one of the clocks is running at any time. Each clock is displayed in its own Frame. The two Frames are named "Black's Time" and "White's Time." Initially, the clock in the "White's Time" Frame is incrementing. Clicking in the Frame of the running clock stops that clock and starts the clock in the other Frame. Clicking in the Frame of a stopped clock has no effect.
6. Revise the EcoSim2 application so that the Prey are added to the Herd *after* the association between the Ecology object and the Herd object is established.
7. Revise the EcoSim2 application so that both the Predators and the Prey are added to the Herd *after* the association between the Ecology object and the Herd object is established.

8. Revise the EcoSim2 application so that 10 new Predators and 10 new Prey are added to the Pack and Herd after the first 100 steps of the simulation. Continue the simulation for another 100 steps after the addition of the new Predators and Prey.

9. Revise the EcoSim2 application so that the simulation stops only when the number of Predators or the number of Prey reach zero. At the end of the simulation output information about the length of the simulation and the state of the number of remaining Predators or Prey.

10. Revise the EcoSim2 application so that there are two Herds, one Pack, and two Ecology objects. Each Ecology object is associated with one of the Herds whereas both Ecology objects are associated with the same Pack.

11. **Prey Births:** write a Java application that extends the EcoSim2 application. The extended application should add one new Prey object to the herd after every 5 time steps.

12. **Predator Births:** write a Java application that extends the EcoSim2 application. The extended application should add one new Predator object to the herd after every 5 time steps.

13. **Predator/Prey Births:** write a Java application that extends the EcoSim2 application. The extended application should add one new Predator and one new Prey object to the herd after every 5 time steps.

14. **Visual Simulation:** write a program that displays in a Frame the current state of an ecological simulation by drawing an "X" in the Frame to denote the position of a predator and an "O" to denote the position of a prey. Clicking in the window should cause the simulation to move to its next state.

15. **Visual Simulation 2:** extend the Visual Simulation exercise so that the current simulation step is displayed in the Frame. Use association with a Counter object and a Message object to keep track of the current simulation step.

16. Draw a UML diagram that represents the fact that a car must have exactly four wheels. Assume there is a class Car and a class Wheel.

17. Draw a UML diagram that shows a Car object and its four Wheel objects. Assume the Wheel class has an attribute `side`, with values either `right` or `left`, and an attribute `end`, with values either `front` or `back`.

18. Draw a UML diagram showing the association between the Counter and Message classes. Use as many of the annotations as possible to describe the nature of the association.
19. Draw a UML diagram showing the association between the Clock and Counter classes. Use as many of the annotations as possible to describe the nature of the association.
20. Draw a UML sequence diagram with the Message and Frame classes that shows the Message class responds to an invocation of its `clear` method.
21. Draw a UML sequence diagram with the Counter, Message, and Frame classes that shows how the Counter class responds to an invocation of its `next` method.
22. Draw a UML diagram for the SimpleTimer system in Figure 3.31.

3.5 Interfaces

A Java interface definition is a realization of the concept of a software interface. A Java interface defines a named collection of methods and, consistent with the idea of an interface, does not provide any implementation of these methods. The absence of an implementation is the primary difference between a class (that must provide an implementation) and an interface (that can not provide an implementation).

The examples in this section, involving both the GUI classes and the ecological simulation classes, will illustrate that interfaces can be used to provide flexibility to a system's design. The flexibility manifests itself in two different ways. First, during design, associations can be made more flexible because an association can be formed between an object of one class and any object conforming to a specified interface. Several classes may conform to the specified interface and any of their objects can be used in the association. This is more flexible than forming associations only between two specific classes. Second, during the extension to an existing system, new classes can be designed and implemented that conform to the specified interface. Objects of these classes can also participate in the association even though they were not part of the original design or implementation of the system.

3.5.1 The Role of an Interface in the GUI Example

The associations formed using the *Clock* and *Counter* class are inflexible in the sense that a Clock object may only be associated with a Counter object and a Counter object may only be associated with a Message object. The inflexibility

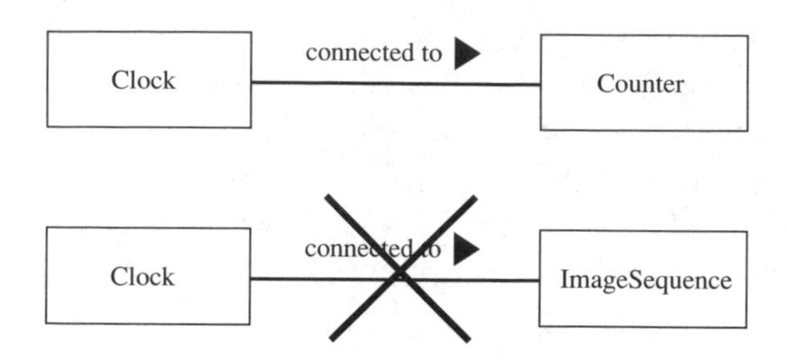

clock.connectTo(imageSequence); // not allowed

Figure 3.36 Inflexibility in the Clock Class

arises in these classes because they defined and implemented so that they can only interact with objects of specifically named classes. For example, the `connectTo` method in the Clock class takes as its argument an object of the Counter class and the `connectTo` method in the Counter class takes as its argument an object of the Message class. This inflexibility is a problem when the capabilities of these classes are needed in associations that involve objects of other classes. For example, a class named *ImageSequence* is introduced below that can be used to create simple animations. To create the sense of animation, each image in the sequence must be shown for a short period of time and then replaced by the next image. The time-driven aspect of the animation could be easily handled if a Clock object could be associated with an ImageSequence object. However, the definition of the Clock class does not permit this possibility. The inflexibility in the Clock class is illustrated in Figure 3.36.

An interface increases the flexibility of classes that are used in associations by expressing the minimal requirements needed to form the association. The definition of the Clock class expressed "too much" about the objects with which it could be associated. In effect the Clock class definition insisted that the associated object have all of the methods defined in the Counter class (`next`, `reset`, `connectTo`). However, the Clock class does not use all of these methods. The only method that the Clock uses of the Counter class is the `next` method. An interface, the *Sequenced* interface, will be used to expresses this more limited requirement. The Clock class can then be defined so that it can connect to any object that supports the Sequenced interface, regardless of which class the object is an instance. This greater flexibility in creating associations is shown in Figure 3.37. The UML notation used in this figure represents the interface by a small labeled circle. The label is the name of the interface. A solid line connects the circle to a class that conforms to the interface. Thus, solid lines are drawn between the circle denoting the Sequenced interface and the Counter and ImageSequence classes. A dashed arrow is drawn toward the circle from a class, the Clock class in this case, that forms an association with an object through the interface. As

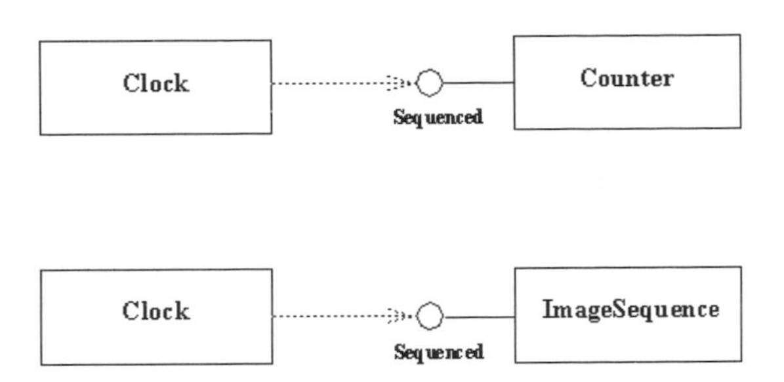

Figure 3.37 Representing Associations Involving Interfaces in UML

shown, it is the interface that establishes the requirements for the association between objects and not the class of the objects.

3.5.2 Defining an Interface

An interface definition in Java uses the keywords "abstract" and "interface" as shown in the definition of the Sequenced interface given in Figure 3.38. The Sequenced interface defines two methods, `next` and `reset`, both of which take no arguments and return no results. The keyword "abstract" in an interface definition emphasizes that there is no implementation provided by the interface. In this context, the "abstract" keyword is used only for emphasis and can be omitted without changing the meaning of the interface definition. In other contexts, the "abstract" keyword has a richer meaning. Although it is only a matter of emphasis, some prefer to retain the "abstract" keyword to reinforce the meaning of the interface concept as a matter of style.

Methods in an interface definition may have arguments and return results, as do methods in a class declaration. In this sense there is no difference between a method signature (name, return type, argument list) that appears in a class definition and one that appears in an interface definition. The Text interface (see Figure 3.39) contains methods that take arguments and/or returns values. In the Text interface the arguments and return types are both String. In general, however, the argument list may have as many arguments of the same or different

```
public abstract interface Sequenced
{
  public void next();
  public void reset();
}
```

Figure 3.38 The Sequenced Interface Definition

```
public abstract interface Text
{
   public void setText(String newText);
   public String getText();
}
```

Figure 3.39 The Text Interface Definition

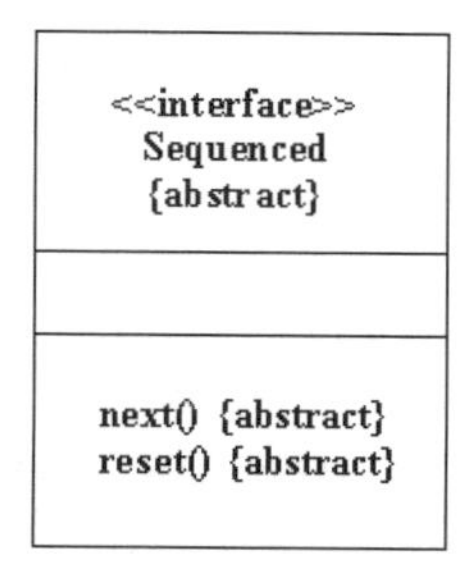

Figure 3.40 Defining an Interface in UML

types and both the argument types and the returned types may be predefined by Java or defined by the user.

An interface must be declared in a .java file and, even though it contains no executable code, it must be compiled. For example, the Sequenced interface should be placed in a file named `Sequenced.java` and, when compiled, a file named `Sequenced.class` will be created.

UML provides a notation for representing the definition of an interface. The Sequenced interface in UML notation is shown in Figure 3.40. The overall shape of the interface graphic resembles that of the graphic notation used for a class. This similarly in appearance is deliberate; the syntax for defining a Java interface is very similar to that for defining a class. Just as the Java syntax provides additional keywords to discriminate between an interface and a class definition, the UML notation similarly provides some additional annotations. The stereotype "<<interface>>" and the attribute "{abstract}" are used in the name compartment to highlight the difference between a class definition and an interface definition. Notice also that the "{abstract}" notation is used for each method defined in the interface.

3.5.3 Implementing an Interface

A Java class definition must explicitly indicate that the class provides the methods defined in a given interface by using the keyword "implements" in the class definition. The Counter class is redefined to indicate that the Counter class implements the Sequenced interface as shown in Figure 3.41. The only new feature introduced in this redefinition is the "`implementsSequenced`" part of the

```
public class Counter implements Sequenced
{
  // all methods as defined in the earlier
  // Counter class
}
```

Figure 3.41 Counter Class Implementing the Sequenced

```
public class ImageSequence implements Sequenced
{

  public ImageSequence()
  public void  showIn(Frame frame)     // show images here
  public void  add(Image image,        // add this image next
  Location location)                   // ... display it here
  public void  reset()                 // go back to first image
  public void  next()                  // show next image
  public void  redraw()                // redraw current image
  public Image current()

}
```

Figure 3.42 ImageSequence Class

class definition. The Counter class implements the `next` and `reset` methods as required by the Sequenced interface. Notice that nothing need be changed in the definition (or the implementation) of the *Counter* class except the addition of the implements clause in the class declaration. This means that classes that were originally not created for a given interface can be easily retrofitted to declare that they implement that interface. The compiler will check, of course, that the Counter class defines and implements all of the methods specified in the Sequenced interface. A compile-time error message will be generated if a method defined in the interface is not defined and implemented in the class. The signature of a method defined in an interface must match exactly (in name, number and type of arguments and return type) with a corresponding method in a class declared to implement that interface. A class may, and usually does, have more methods than those defined in the interface. The only requirement is that the class have at least those methods defined in the interface.

Typically, several classes will implement the same interface. The ImageSequence class defined in Figure 3.42 also implements the Sequenced interface. This class represents a sequence of Image objects that it displays in a Frame one after the other. The `next` method clears the current Image from the Frame and draws the next Image in the sequence into the Frame. The sequence of Images is determined solely by the order in which they are inserted to the ImageSequence by the `add` method. When each Image is added, it must also specify a Location at which the Image should be drawn in the Frame object. Thus, different Images may be drawn in different parts of the Frame. Only one of the Images of the ImageSequence is ever visible at any one time. The `redraw` method redraws the current image. This method is useful in methods such as the `onPaint` method

```
public class TextSequence implements Sequenced
{
  public TextSequence()
  public void showIn(Frame frame)
  public void add(String text, Location location)
  public void reset()
  public void next()
  public void redraw()
  public String current()
}
```

Figure 3.43 The TextSequence Class

where it is necessary to redisplay the current image. The `current` method returns the Image object that is currently being displayed in the ImageSequence.

Another class implementing the Sequenced interface is the TextSequence class whose definition is shown in Figure 3.43. This class is conceptually similar to the ImageSequence except that the sequence is an ordered collection of Strings instead of Images. The TextSequence class fulfills the requirements of the Sequenced interface because the class defines and implements a `next` method and a `reset` method. The `showIn` method creates an association with a Frame object in which the sequence of Strings will be drawn. The `add` method is used to append another String to the current TextSequence. A location at which the String should be displayed is also given to the `add` method. The `reset` and `next` methods allow the TextSequence to be repositioned at the beginning of the sequence, and display the next String in the sequence (after clearing the current String), respectively. The `redraw` method redraws the current text string. The `redraw` method is useful in cases where the string is displayed in a Frame that needs to be refreshed by, for example, `onPaint`. The current method can be used to determine which String is the one currently being displayed.

3.6 Declaring Parameters of an Interface Type

An interface name may be used as the type of a method's parameter in the same way that a class name may be used as the type of a parameter. Declaring the type of a method's parameter by using an interface name is sensible for two reasons. First, the class containing the method is conveying that the only operations that the parameter object must support are those defined by the interface; the actual object may have additional operation, but these are not relevant. Second, the type of a parameter determines what operations may legitimately be performed upon that parameter by the receiving object. When an interface name defines the type of a parameter, it is clear that the only operations that may be applied to the parameter are those defined in the interface. The *Clock* class is redefined as shown in Figure 3.44 to use the Sequenced interface as the type of the parameter in the definition of the `connectTo` method.

```
public class Clock
{
   public void connectTo(Sequenced target);
   // other method the same as in
   // the original Clock class
}
```

Figure 3.44 An Interface Used as a Parameter Type

An object of a class that implements an interface can be passed to a method that accepts an argument of the interface type. For example, a Counterobject can be passed to the Clock class's `connectTo` method because the Counter class implements the Sequenced interface and the `connectTo` method of the Clock class accepts a parameter of the Sequenced interface type. For the same reasons, an ImageSequence object can be passed to the `connectTo` method of the Clock class.

Using an interface name to describe the type of an object radically increases the flexibility of the software. As shown by the Clock example above, the class is able to interact with any object that conforms to the requirements of the Sequenced interface. A class's implementor need no longer be constrained to interact only with a specific type of object known in advance. By using interface names to describe the type of objects, even objects of a class that did not exist at the time the interface was defined can be manipulated. Strategic use of interfaces allows software to be constructed that can be more easily extended—by defining new classes that conform to the required interfaces.

3.6.1 Building Associations with Interfaces

The flexibility in building associations is illustrated by using the revised Clock class (that can be connected to objects implementing the Sequenced interface), the ImageSequence class, and the revised Counter class that implement the Sequenced interface. Figure 3.37 showed pictorially how the Sequenced interface could be used to establish an association between a Clock and a Counter object and a Clock and an ImageSequence object. The outline the code to establish such associations is shown in Figure 3.45.

As shown in Figure 3.45, the two Clock objects (`timer` and `sequencer`) form associations with a Counter object (`elapsedTime`) and with an ImageSequence object (`images`). The crucial point is that the Clock objects are unaware of the exact class of the object with which they are forming an association; the Clock objects only care that the associated objects implement the Sequenced interface. Notice that the two uses of the Clock's `connectTo` method are indistinguishable in the sense that the form of the invocation does not depend on the exact class of the object passed as an argument.

```
...
import Counter;
import ImageSequence;
import Clock;
...

public class ImageSequenceTest implements Program
{
  ...
  private Counter elapsedTime;
  private ImageSequence images;
  private Clock   timer;
  private Clock   sequencer;

  public ImageSequenceTest()
  {...
    elapsedTime  = new Counter();
    images = new ImageSequence();
    timer  = new Clock(1000);         // a one second timer
    sequencer = new Clock(60);        // a 60 millisecond timer
  }

  public void onStart()
  { ...
    timer.connectTo(elapsedTime);   // form an association with
                                    // a Counter object
    sequencer.connectTo(images);    // form an association with
                                    // an ImageSequence object
    timer.on();
    sequencer.on();
  }
  ...
}
```

Figure 3.45 Program Segments Using the Sequenced Interface

3.6.2 Interfaces in the Ecological Simulation Example

The inflexibility of the ecological simulation classes developed in the previous sections become evident by considering the effect of adding to the simulation a different kind of prey. The current Prey class captures the notion of a creature that moves in an unpredictable fashion; in fact, the class is implemented to change the location in a random way. However, another type of creature might have a known pattern of movement; the creature stays in the same area and moves in a relatively predictable pattern.

An inappropriate course of action is to modify the exiting Prey class so that its behavior has either a random or predictable pattern of movement depending on how the object is constructed. This is inappropriate philosophically because it weakens the abstraction represented by the Prey class by including in the class two dissimilar and mutually exclusive behaviors. From a pragmatic viewpoint modifying the existing Prey class is also objectionable because it complicates the code and data needed for the class. The data must contain the variables to generate a random movement as well as the data needed to generate a fixed pattern of movement. Similarly, the code will contain logic for both cases. The basic flaw in this approach is that any given Prey object would only use a part of the total data and code that the object contains. Furthermore, even if we were willing to follow this approach for two different kinds of prey, the defects in the approach are even more clearly evident as a larger number of prey kinds are incorporated into the simulation.

However, introducing a new class for the migratory prey has problems of its own if objects of these classes can only be referred to by their specific class names. To illustrate the problems, consider the effect on those classes that use the Prey and MigratoryPrey classes. One such using class is the Predator class whose `hunt` method is defined as:

```
public class Predator
{
   ...
   public boolean hunt (Prey aPrey)
   ...
}
```

The `hunt` method can only be invoked with a Prey object as the parameter. A MigratoryPrey object cannot be used because the method explicitly uses the Prey class name to identify the type of the parameter object. A solution to this problem is to overload the `hunt` method as follows:

```
public class Predator
{
   ...
   public boolean hunt (Prey aPrey)
   public boolean hunt (MigratoryPrey migPrey)
   ...
}
```

This solution is far from ideal for two reasons. First, the `hunt` method must be overloaded again for each new type of prey introduced into the simulation system. This requires repeated recoding of the Predator class (and all other similar classes that manipulate objects representing different kinds of prey). Second, the code for the overloaded `hunt` methods is virtually identical, differing only in the class name used to describe the kind of prey. Any changes that need to be made in the `hunt` method (for correction of errors, performance improvement, or extension) would need to be laboriously included in each of the overloaded methods. What is more desirable is a solution in which there is a single `hunt` method that can handle any kind of prey object.

Defining the Hunted Interface

Greater flexibility in handling different kinds of prey can be achieved by defining an interface that captures the methods common to all classes representing an abstraction of some kind of prey. The Hunted interface defined in Figure 3.46

```
import Location;
public interface Hunted
{ public void kill();
  public boolean isAlive();
  public Location getLocation();
  public void move();
}
```

Figure 3.46 The Hunter Interface

serves this purpose. This interface specifies that any class desiring to have its objects accessible through the use of this interface must implement the four methods given in the body of the interface's definition. These methods characterize a hunted entity as a creature 1) that can be killed, 2) has an alive/dead status that can be determined, 3) has a current location, and 4) can move to a new location.

Notice that the interface does not specify any constructors because it is not possible to create objects using an interface. For example, the statement

```
Hunted animal = new Hunted();        // WRONG!
```

is incorrect—it is not possible to use the new operator with an interface as shown in this statement. Objects cannot be created using the interface because there is no implementation associated with the interface; the implementation is provided by classes that conform to the requirements of the interface.

3.6.3 Implementing the Hunted Interface

The original Prey class can be rewritten and a new MigratoryPrey class can be defined in terms of the Hunted interface as shown in Figure 3.47. Notice that the declarations of the Prey class and the MigratoryPrey classes include the clause `implements Hunted`. This part of the class declaration is a promise that these classes will implement the methods defined in the Hunted interface. The compiler will check that this promise is fulfilled. The compiler will verify that each method defined in the interface has an exact corresponding method in the class; the corresponding method must have the same name, the same number and types of parameters, and the same returned type. For the Prey and MigratoryPrey classes, it can easily be seen that they implement the required four methods (`kill`, `isAlive`,`getLocation`, and `move`).

3.6.4 Declaring Parameters Using the Hunted Interface

The Predator class is modified to take advantage of the flexibility provided by the Hunted interface. The `hunt` method in the Predator class creates a relationship between the Predator class and the Prey and MigratoryPrey classes. It is desired that the Predator be able to “hunt” a prey of either kind without knowing which

```
import Hunted;
public class Prey implements Hunted
{
  public Prey(Location where, Range range)
  public Prey(Location where, Range range, int roam)
  public Prey(Location where)  public Prey()  public void move()
  public void move(int steps)
  public boolean isAlive()
  public void kill()
  public Location getLocation()
  public Range getRange()
  public void setRoam(int distance)
  public void print()
}

import Hunted;
public class MigratoryPrey implements Hunted
{
  public MigratoryPrey(Location[] path)
  public void move()
  public void move(int steps)
  public boolean isAlive()
  public void kill()
  public Location getLocation()
  public void print()
}
```

Figure 3.47 Defining the Prey and MigratoryPrey Classes

kind of prey it might be hunting in a given instance. For a Predator object to hunt a prey, it is only necessary that the Predator be able to determine the location of the prey (is the prey within the predator's `killZone`) by the prey's `getLocation` method, to discover if the prey is alive by the prey's `isAlive` method, and to effect the prey by invoking the prey's `kill` method. Because these three methods are defined in the Hunted interface, an object of any class that implements the Hunted interface can be passed as the parameter of the Predator class's `hunt` method. This change in the definition of the Predator class is shown in Figure 3.48. Notice that the parameter of the `hunt` method is declared as Hunted. This declaration means that the object passed as the actual parameter at run-time can be from any class that implements the Hunted interface. In this example, it means that the `hunt` method may receive a Prey object on some invocations and a MigratoryPrey object on other invocations. However, the Predator class is able to treat these two cases uniformly because it only relies on the common properties of the Prey and MigratoryPrey classes as expressed in the Hunted interface. A portion of the implementation of the Predator class is shown to illustrate how the Predator class uses the methods defined in the Hunted interface.

The relationship involving the Hunted interface, the revised Predator class, and the two prey classes is shown in Figure 3.49 using the UML notation. The

```
import Hunted;
public class Predator
{
  //...
  private int x;
  private int y;
  private boolean alive = true;
  private int lifetime;
  private int lifeLeft;
  private int killZone;
  //...
  private boolean captures(Hunted aPrey)
  { double xdist = (double)(aPrey.getLocation().xCoord() - x);
    double ydist = (double)(aPrey.getLocation().yCoord() - y);
    return (int)(Math.sqrt(xdist*xdist + ydist*ydist)) < killZone;
  }
  public boolean hunt(Hunted aPrey)
  { if (!alive) return false;
    if(captures(aPrey) && aPrey.isAlive())
        { aPrey.kill();
          lifeLeft = lifetime;
          return true;
        }
    else return false;
  }
  //...
}
```

Figure 3.48 Revising the Predator Class to Use the Hunted Interface

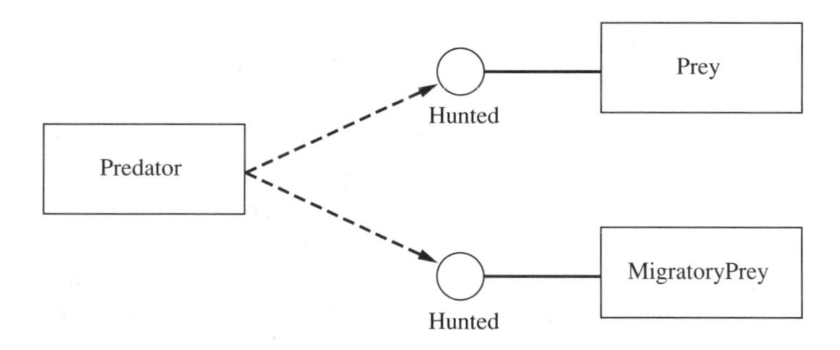

Figure 3.49 The Role of the Hunted Interface Shown in UML

diagram shows that the Hunter interface is implemented by both the Prey and MigratoryPrey classes. This is denoted by the solid lines connecting the symbols for the Hunted interface (the circles labeled Hunted) to the symbols for the two classes. The Predator class uses objects of the Hunted interface as indicated by the dashed arrows from the symbol of that class to the symbols for the Hunter interface.

The Herd class is also redefined to exploit the flexibility of the Hunted interface. The Herd class initially represented a group of Prey. By using the Hunted interface to identify the prey objects, the Herd class will be capable of

```
import Hunted;
public class Herd
{
    //...

  public void add(Hunted newPrey)
  public Hunted member(int i)
    //...
}
```

Figure 3.50 Using the Hunted Interface in the Herd Class

representing a more diverse group of objects, a group that is a mixture of Prey and MigratoryPrey objects. As shown in boldface in Figure 3.50, the important changes in the Herd class are in the `add` and `member` methods. The `add` methods includes a new member in the herd. Because the type of the `add` method's parameter is defined by the Hunted interface, the actual object passed at run-time can be of any class that implements the Hunted interface. Because the parameter is defined by the Hunted interface, the implementation of the add method can only apply to its parameter object those methods defined in the Hunted interface. The `member` method is redefined so that it returns an object whose only known type is that defined by the Hunted interface. The Hunted interface is a sufficient description of the objects that the Herd class manages because the Herd class only needs to be able to `move` the prey and ask if the prey `isAlive`; both of these methods are included in the Hunted interface.

3.6.5 Type Casting

An application can use the flexibility of the Hunted class to create simulations where a predatory is hunting among a mixed group of prey, some of which are represented by Prey objects and some of which are represented by MigratoryPrey objects. An example of this is the EcoSim3 application shown in Figure 3.51. The most significant part of this application is the two lines shown in boldface. In the first line, a Prey object is passed as the parameter to the `hunt` method whereas in the second line a MigratoryPrey object is passed as the parameter. The Predator object receives and manipulates these two objects even though the parameters are from two different classes. This is a clear illustration of the flexibility and power for the interface construct. If any number of classes are added that model new kinds of prey, the Predator class would remain unchanged and completely usable as long as the new prey classes implement the Hunted interface.

The flexibility illustrated in the EcoSim3 application is made possible by type casting. The EcoSim3 application uses explicit type casting in the two invocations of the `hunt` method. The type casting is shown in boldface in these two lines:

```
predator.hunt((Hunted)prey)
...
predator.hunt((Hunted)migPrey)
```

```
import Predator;
import Prey;
import MigratoryPrey;
import Location;
import Range;

public class EcoSim3
{
  private Predator predator;
  private Prey     prey;

  public EcoSim3()
  { predator = new Predator(new Location(50,50), 100, 25);
    predator.setRoam(50);
    prey = new Prey();
    prey.setRoam(15);

    Location[] path = new Location[6];
    path[0] = new Location(120,120);
    path[1] = new Location(150,150);
    path[2] = new Location(150,180);
    path[3] = new Location(180,180);
    path[4] = new Location(160,180);
    path[5] = new Location(140,180);

    MigratoryPrey migPrey = new MigratoryPrey(path);

    for(int i=0; i<100; i++)
    {
      if (predator.hunt((Hunted)prey))
        { System.out.println("prey caught at step " + i);
          predator.print();
          prey.print();
          return;
        }
      if (predator.hunt((Hunted)migPrey))
        { System.out.println("migratory prey caught at step " + i);
          predator.print();
          migPrey.print();
          return;
        }
      predator.move();
      prey.move();
      migPrey.move();
    }
  }
  public static void main(String[] args)
  { EcoSim3 simulation = new EcoSim3();
  }
}
```

Figure 3.51 An Application that Uses the Hunted Interface

The syntax `(Hunted)` preceding an object specifies the programmer's claim that the object may be treated as an instance of a class conforming to the `Hunted` interface. If this claim is correct, then it is safe to apply to the object any of the methods defined in the Hunted interface. The compiler will, of course, verify the

```
//imports

public class EcoSim4
{
  private Ecology ecoSystem;

  public EcoSim4()
  { Herd hunted  = new Herd();
    Pack hunters = new Pack(5);

    for(int i=0; i<10; i++)
      hunted.add(new Prey());

    Location[] path = new Location[6];
    path[0] = new Location(120,120);
    path[1] = new Location(150,150);
    path[2] = new Location(150,180);
    path[3] = new Location(180,180);
    path[4] = new Location(160,180);
    path[5] = new Location(140,180);

    MigratoryPrey migPrey = new MigratoryPrey(path);
    hunted.add(migPrey);

    ecoSystem = new Ecology(hunters, hunted);
  }

  public void simulate()
  {
    // do simulation using ecoSystem
  }

  public static void main(String[] args)
  { EcoSim4 simulation = new EcoSim4();
    simulation.simulate();
  }
}
```

Figure 3.52 Using the Revised Herd Class

programmer's claim by checking that the object's class fully implements the Hunted interface.

Type casting does not change the actual object. For example, in the EcoSim3 application, the prey and migPrey objects are not changed when they are passed to the `hunt` method that knows them by the Hunted type; these objects remain objects of the Prey and MigratoryPrey classes, respectively. This situation is similar to the following real-world analogy. In asking a friend to return to the library an object-oriented design book that I checked out, I might say "Can you return this library book for me?" For my friend to perform this task it is not necessary that the exact type of the book is agreed upon; my friend only needs to know that it is a library book. I know the more exact type of the book whereas my friend has a more generic view of the type of the book, but when I hand the book to my friend, the book itself does not change.

Although good style strongly argues in favor of always using explicit typecasting, Java allows implicit type casting as well. The EcoSim4 application shows an example of implicit type casting using the modified Herd class. A portion of this application is shown in Figure 3.52. The two statements shown in boldface are the key aspects of this application. The `add` method is used in the first statement to include a Prey object in the group. The `add` method is used in the second statement to include a MigratoryPrey object in the group. Notice that neither statement uses the explicit typecasting syntax. The compiler will note that the type of the parameter objects (i.e., Prey and MigratoryPrey) do not match exactly the type of the parameter declared for the `add` method in the Herd class (i.e., Hunted). The compiler will then perform the checks for type casting as if the programmer had written the code for explicit type casting. Thus, in situations such as those illustrated by this example, the type casting checks are always performed, regardless of whether or not the programmer used the explicit type casting syntax.

3.6.6 Implementing Multiple Interfaces

A class may implement several interfaces. When objects of the class are used in several different contexts, each context may use only a subset of the methods provided by the class. If other classes also implement one or more of these subsets, it is useful to capture this common subsets of methods in an interface definition. The interface is particularly well motivated if it is believed that other classes might be introduced in the future that also will implement these interfaces. As noted above, the introduction of such interfaces makes the collection of classes more flexible.

In the ecological simulation, an example of a class that is used in two different contexts is a one representing a "weak predator." A weak predator models a creature that is able to hunt for prey but is also susceptible to being hunted by other predators. The three kinds of creatures—prey, predators, and weak predators—allow the simulation to more accurately represent a "food chain" in which those creatures at the top of the chain are pure predators, those at the bottom of the chain are pure prey, and those in the middle are a prey to some and a predator to others.

Because the WeakPredator class introduces a variation of the existing Predator class it is useful to define an interface that identifies their common set of methods that distinguish them as abstractions of hunting creatures. The Hunter interface that captures the common behavior of the two predator classes is shown in Figure 3.53. This interface indicates that any class intended to represent a "hunter" must implement the three specified methods. A "hunter" is able to move about in search of prey, it can hunt a prey, and its state of being alive can be determined. The Hunter interface plays the same role with respect to the classes representing different kinds of predators as the Hunted interface plays for the classes representing different kinds of prey. Notice in particular the dec-

```
import Hunted;

public interface Hunter
{
  public boolean isAlive();
  public boolean hunt(Hunted prey);
  public void move();
}
```

Figure 3.53 The Hunter Interface

laration of the `hunt` method in the Hunter interface. The parameter of the `hunt` method is an object conforming to the Hunted interface. The use of the Hunted and Hunter interfaces allows system to be built that can have any type of hunter hunt for any type of prey. This is, again, an illustration of the flexibility provided by the interface structure.

The same method may appear in more than one interface. This occurs with the `isAlive` and `move` methods that appear in both the Hunted and the Hunter interfaces. When a method appears in more than one interface it simply reflects the fact that the behavior represented by that method is viewed as a part of the concepts represented by each interface. The ability to move, for example, is a natural part of a prey's behavior as captured in the Hunted interface as well as a natural part of a predator's behavior as captured in the Hunter interface.

The revision of the Predator class and the important parts of the definition of the WeakPredator class is shown in Figure 3.54. The Predator class is revised to show that it implements the Hunter interface because the Predator class contains the `move`, `isAlive`, and `hunt` methods required by that interface. The WeakPredator class implements both the Hunter and the Hunted interfaces as appropriate for its dual role as a predator with respect to the Prey and MigratoryPrey classes and as a prey with respect to the Predator class. Notice that the WeakPredator class satisfies the requirements of each interface. Also notice that the `isAlive` method and the `move` method are used to satisfy the requirements of both the Hunted and the Hunter interfaces, the `kill` and `getLocation` methods are used to satisfy only the requirements of the Hunted interface, and the `hunt` method is used to satisfy only the requirements of the Hunter interface.

The UML notation to represent a class that implements multiple interfaces is shown in Figure 3.55. In this diagram the Weak Predator class is related to both the Hunter interface and the Hunted interface. As before, each of the two interfaces is drawn as a circled labeled by the name of the interface. The solid line connecting each interface to the WeakPredator class denotes that the class implements the interface. If a class implements more than two interfaces, each additional interface would be depicted by another labeled circle connected to the class by a solid line.

```
import Hunter;
import Hunted;

public class Predator implements Hunter
{
    //...
  public boolean hunt(Hunted aPrey)     // Hunter interface
  public boolean isAlive()              // Hunter interface
  public void move()                    // Hunter interface}


import Hunted;
import Hunter;

public class WeakPredator implements Hunter, Hunted
{
  public WeakPredator(Location where, Range range, int lifetime, int killZone)
  // other constructors as in Predator class
  public boolean hunt(Hunted aPrey)     // Hunter interface
  public Location getLocation()         // Hunted interface
  public void kill()                    // Hunted interface
  public boolean isAlive()              // Hunted and Hunter interfaces
  public void move()                    // Hunted and Hunter interfaces

  //other methods
}
```

Figure 3.54 Implementing Two Interfaces in the WeakPredator Class

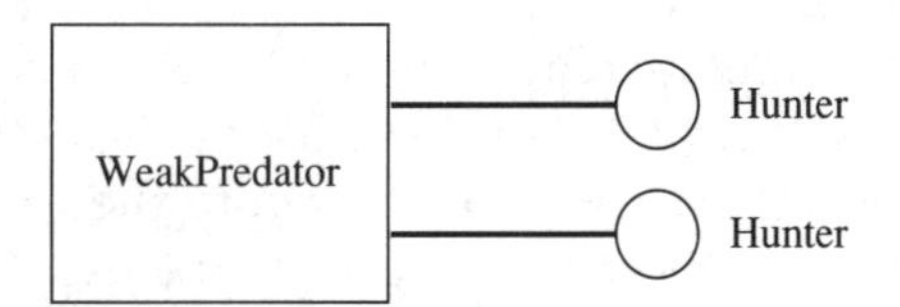

Figure 3.55 Implementing Multiple Interfaces in UML

The Pack class can be redefined to take advantage of the Hunter interface. This redefinition is similar to that done for the Herd class, in this case allowing any object to be added to a pack provided that the object's class implements the Hunter interface. The revised Pack class is shown in Figure 3.56. Due to the redefinition of the Pack class's `add` method either a Predator or a WeakPredator could be added to a pack as shown in this code fragment:

```
Predator regularPredator  = new Predator(...);
WeakPredator weakPredator = new WeakPredator(...);
Pack predators = new Pack();
...
predators.add((Hunter)regularPredator);          // add a Predator
objectpredators.add((Hunter)weakPredator);       // add a WeakPredator object
```

```
import Hunter;
public class Pack
{
  public Pack()
  public void add(Hunter newHunter)
  public Hunter member(int i)
  public void move()
  public int size()
  public int alive()
}
```

Figure 3.56 Revising the Pack Class to Use the Hunter Interface

In this code fragment, a Pack object has two objects added to it: one object is an instance of the Predator class and one object is an instance of theWeakPredator class. Note that explicit type casting is used to change the view of these objects to object conforming to the Hunter interface.

Exercises

1. **Image Viewer:** using the Sequenced interface, implement a system that allows a user to view a sequence of Images. The next image in the sequence is presented when the user clicks the mouse anywhere within the window containing the image.
2. **Image Viewer2:** using the using the Sequenced interface, implement a system that allows a user to view a sequence of Images. The next image in the sequence is presented when the user clicks the mouse anywhere within the displayed image. Mouse clicks outside of the image are ignored.
3. **Image Scanner:** using the Sequenced interface, implement a system that allows a user to view a sequence of Images. Each image remains visible for five seconds.
4. **Simple Animation:** using the Sequenced interface, implement a system that presents a sequence of images in sufficiently rapid sequence to create the effect of an animation.
5. **Freeze-Frame:** using the Sequenced interface, implement a system that allows the user to control a sequence of images that is present in sufficiently rapid sequence to create the effect of an animation. The user can "freeze" the animation by pressing (without releasing) the mouse button in the Frame where the animation is presented. The

animation remains unchanged as long as the mouse button is depressed. The animation resumes when the mouse button is released.

6. **Simple Timer:** using the Sequenced interface, construct a system that displays a number that is incremented once each second.
7. **Start/Stop Timer:** using the Sequenced interface, construct a system that allows the user to start and stop a simple timer. A simple timer displays a number that is incremented once each second. Initially the simple timer is running. The user stops the timer by clicking in the frame where the simple timer's number is displayed. When the timer is stopped, another mouse click restarts the timer.
8. **Pausing Timer:** using the Sequenced interface, construct a system that allows the user to pause a simple timer. A simple timer displays a number that is incremented once each second. Initially the simple timer is running. A MOUSE_DOWN event causes the timer to stop and a MOUSE_UP event causes the timer to restart. This means that the timer is stopped for as long as the user hold down the mouse button.
9. **Dual Clocks:** using the Sequenced interface, construct a system that displays two incrementing numbers in the same frame. One number is incremented at each one second interval and the other number is increment at a 0.1 second interval. Both number should be appropriately labeled.
10. **Text Display:** using the Sequenced interface, construct a system that shows a sequence of text arranged in some pattern in a window. For example, the sequence "Buy Now!," "Prices Never Lower!!," and "No Offer Refused!!!" might appear in sequence across the diagonal of a frame or from top-to-bottom.
11. **Multimedia System:** using the Sequenced interface, construct a system that presents an animation (a rapid sequence of related images) in a frame. During the animation, a sequence of text is displayed around the outside of the animation area (e.g., at the top, then the right, then the bottom, then the left).
12. Modify the EcoSim3 application so that the simulation has two migratory prey.
13. Modify the EcoSim3 application so that the simulation has an array of 5 migratory prey.
14. Modify the EcoSim3 application so that the simulation has a single array of 10 prey objects, 5 of which are objects of the Prey class and 5 of which are objects of the MigratoryPrey class. The array can be declared and initialized as

```
Hunted[] prey = new Hunted[10];
```

that uses the interface name as the type of the array.

15. Modify the `simulate` method of the EcoSim4 program so that after the number of surviving predators and prey are printed the locations of all surviving prey are printed. Accomplish this by using the `member` and `size` methods of the Herd class. You should notice in your answer that the prey are manipulated only by using the Hunter interface and not the specific class names Prey or MigratoryPrey.

16. Using the Hunter interface, show how the definition of the Pack class should be modified so that it can contain both Predator and Weak-Predator objects.

17. The Herd class uses only the move and `isAlive` methods of the Prey and MigratoryPreyclasses. Write the definition of an interface that captures this usage. Show how the definitions of the Prey, MigratoryPrey, and Herd classes should be changed.

18. The Pack class uses only the move and `isAlive` methods of the Predator class. Write the definition of an interface that captures this usage. Show how the definitions of the Predator and Herd classes should be changed.

19. Review the previous two exercises. Define a single class that can replace both the Pack and the Herd classes.

20. The three creature classes—Prey, MigratoryPrey, and Predator—all have a `print` method that outputs a description of the creature. Write an interface that captures this common behavior. Change the definition of these three classes to use your new interface. Write an application that demonstrates the flexibility offered by your interface. The application must show how an object's information can be displayed without the code depending on exactly which of the three classes the object belongs to.

21. Draw a UML diagram for the TextInterface interface similar to Figure 3.61.

22. Draw a UML diagram for the Hunted interface similar to Figure 3.61.

23. Draw a UML diagram that shows the relationship between the Text-Sequence class and the Sequenced interface.

24. Draw a UML diagram that shows the relationships among the classes and interfaces used in the ImageSequenceTest program shown in Figure 3.66.

25. Draw a UML diagram that shows the relationships among the Herd class, the Prey class, the MigratoryPrey class, and the Hunted interface.
26. Draw a UML diagram that shows the relationships among the Pack class, the Predator class, the WeakPredator class, the Hunter interface, and the Hunted interface.
27. Draw a UML diagram that shows the relationships among the classes and interfaces used in the EcoSim3 program shown in Figure 3.72.
28. Draw a UML diagram that shows the relationships among the classes and interfaces used in the SimpleTimer system described in one of the exercises above.
29. Draw a UML diagram that shows the relationships among the classes and interfaces used in the DualClocks system described in one of the exercises above.
30. Draw a UML diagram that shows the relationships among the classes and interfaces used in the Multimedia system described in one of the exercises above.

3.7 More Complex Associations

Realistic object-oriented systems involve associations among numerous objects from a variety of classes. Commercial software systems might use many tens of classes and hundreds or thousands of objects. The examples involved here do not approach that scale. However, several additional classes will be introduced that use the same techniques and illustrate how such complex and realistic systems are structured. The GUI classes are restructured to make them more realistic. This restructuring introduces more associations among the existing and new classes. The ecological simulation classes are also extended to show how more complex associations among its classes lead to the construction of more complicated, but more useful, systems. The exercises at the end of the section describe a number of small systems that can be constructed by creating more complex associations among objects.

3.7.1 Associations in Complex User Interfaces

A more realistic version of the Frame class will be devised that employs association. Association is necessary because the interface of the Frame class would become unbearably complex if all of the rich functionality of a window were captured directly and exclusively in this one interface. For example, only two shapes are currently drawable (a line and a circle). But there are many more shapes that are commonly available including ovals, rectangles, splines, and polygons. Also there are a variety of properties that can be defined for each shape such as its color, line thickness, line pattern, and fill pattern. Clearly, attempting to control all of these details through the Frame interface alone would create an extremely long and complex interface. In addition, the Frame class also needs to be extended to include a wide range of interactive elements through which the user can manipulate the user interface. These interactive elements include buttons, editable text, sliders, check boxes, scrollable lists, radio buttons, and others. Even adding one or two methods to the Frame class for each of these interactive elements is clearly a step toward a large and unruly interface that lacks cohesion.

The responsibilities for the graphical and interactive elements of a window will be partitioned among three associated classes:

Frame: a rectangular area on the display screen that may be moved and resized.

Canvas: an area within a Frame for drawing text and graphics and responding to mouse movements.

Panel: an area within a Frame that contains interactive elements.

The Frame class is simplified so that it retains only those responsibilities not assigned to the Canvas and Panel classes. The Canvas class assumes the responsibilities for all drawing functions. Mouse events with a Canvas area are now associated with the Canvas and not the Frame. The Panel class assumes all responsibilities for managing interactive elements.

3.7.2 Reorganizing the Frame and Canvas Classes

The definition for the revised Frame class is shown in Figure 3.57. The Panel and Canvas classes will be presented next. Notice that all of the methods related to drawing (e.g., `drawText`, `drawling`) have been removed from the Frame class. The methods that remain in the Frame class are those that are specifically, and only, having to do with the definition and management of the Frame itself. In this way, the Frame class presents an abstraction of a bordered area on the user's display that can, under program control, be changed in position and shape. The "contents" of the Frame are defined by what other objects (e.g., objects of the Canvas

```
public class Frame
{                                   // Version 4

  public Frame(String name, Location p, Shape s)  // exact description
  public Frame(String name, Shape s, Location p)  // exact description
  public Frame(String name, Location p)           // default shape
  public Frame(String name, Shape s)              // default location
  public Frame(String name )                      // name only
  public Frame()                                  // all defaults;
  public boolean isNamed(String aName)            // is this your name?
  public void   moveTo(Location newLocation)      // move the window
  public void   resize(Shape    newShape)         // change shape
  public void   resize(float factor)              // grow/shrink by factor

  public void   add(Canvas canvas)                // add canvas to Frame
  public void   add(Panel panel)                  // add panel to Frame
}
```

Figure 3.57 The Frame Class (Version 4)

```
public class Canvas
{
  public Canvas(String name, Location p, Shape s)
  public Canvas(String name, Shape s, Location p)
  public Canvas(String name, Location p)
  public Canvas(String name)
  public Canvas()

  public boolean isNamed(String name)
  public void drawText(String s, Location loc)
  public Shape getTextSize(String s)
  public void drawLine(Location p1, Location p2)
  public void drawRectangle(Location corner, Shape size)
  public void drawCircle(Location center, int radius)
  public void drawImage(Image image, Location where)
  public void clear()
  public void clear(Location corner, Shape rect)

  public void setBackground(Color color)
  public void setColor(Color color)
  public void drawFilledRectangle(Location corner, Shape size)
  public void drawFilledCircle(Location center, int radius)
}
```

Figure 3.58 The Canvas Class

and Panel classes) are added to the Frame. It is the programmer's responsibility to ensure that multiple Canvas and Panel objects placed within the same Frame are arranged within the Frame so that their areas do not overlap.

The Canvas class assumes many of the responsibilities previously allocated to the Frame class. The definition of the Canvas class is given in Figure 3.58. Notice that the Canvas class contains the methods for drawing text and graphical shapes as well as the methods for erasing the Canvas, either in whole or in part. The name given to a Canvas object is used to identify that object as the source of mouse events. Mouse events that occur in a Canvas object will be intercepted by the Canvas object and the `onMouseEvent` method will be invoked using the name

```
public class Color
{
  public Color(int red, int green, int blue)
  public Color()  public void addRed(int more)
  public void addGreen(int more)
  public void addBlue(int more)
  public int getRed()
  public int getBlue()
  public int getGreen()
  public void setRed(int red)
  public void setBlue(int blue)
  public void setGreen(int green)
}
```

Figure 3.59 The Color Class

of the Canvas object as the first parameter. Previously, the name of the Frame object was passed as the name parameter. In the revised design presented here, mouse events are associated with the Canvas in which they occur and not the Frame containing that Canvas. Notice that the Canvas class has also been extended to allow text or shapes to be drawn in color. Each canvas has a background color that can be set by the `setBackground` method. Each canvas also has a current drawing color that can be set by the `setColor` method. The current drawing color is used to display any text or graphical shape that are drawn in the canvas. In addition, the circle and rectangle shapes can be drawn in one of two ways: unfilled or filled. The `drawRectangle` and `drawCircle` methods draw their shapes so that the outline of the shape is drawn using the current drawing color; the interior of the shape has the same color as the background color. The drawFilledRectangle and drawFilledCircle methods draw their shapes so that the outline and the interior of the shape are completely in the current drawing color. Colors can be created using the Color class (described next).

The Color class represents a color by a combination of three primary colors (red, blue, green). The Color class is shown in Figure 3.59. Each of the three primary colors has an intensity value associated with it. Each of the three get methods (`getRed`, `getBlue`, `getGreen`) returns the intensity value for the color corresponding to the name of the method. The range of intensity values determines how many different color scan be produced. If we assume that the intensities are in the range 0-255, then a light red color can be created by using a moderate intensity for the red color and a zero intensity for the green and blue colors. For example, this code segment creates an object representing this color:

```
Color lightRed = new Color(100, 0, 0);
Color paleRed  = new Color( 75, 0, 0);
```

A more intense red shade can be created in one of three ways, as shown in the following statements:

```
(1) Color deepRed = new Color(200, 0, 0);     // create new Color
(2) lightRed.setRed(200);     // make red intensity be 200
(3) paleRed.addRed(125);      // increase red intensity by 125
```

The first statement simply creates a new Color object with a higher intensity for the red color. The second and third statements create the more intensity color by modifying an existing Color object. The `setRed` method changes the object's red intensity to the value specified by the parameter. Thus, the `lightRed` object will be changed to have a red color of 200. The `addRed` method increases the object's red intensity by the parameter's amount. Thus, the `paleRed` object will be changed by adding 125 to its red intensity. The set and add methods for the other colors operate in the same way.

Adding Interactive Elements

We will now introduce three additional classes defining interactive control elements. By using objects of these new classes, an interactive user interface can be created. Although the number of interactive controls is very limited (there are only two), it should be clear that additional interactive controls could easily be added. The intention here is to illustrate the use of association in building more complicated systems and not to make possible the construction of complex user interface. These three classes are:

Panel: mentioned earlier, it is an area within a Frame that contains interactive elements, like Button and TextBox objects.

Button: captures the abstraction of a simple, pushable, named button that the user can "push" by clicking within the boundary of the button's displayed image. The button is displayed as a rectangle containing the button's name.

TextBox: provides a mechanism for the user to edit a passage of text that may be read subsequently by the program.

Together, these three classes provide basic controls for the user to enter data and trigger actions to be taken by the program.

The definition of the Panel class is given in Figure 3.60. The overloaded constructors provide a way for the Location and Shape of the Panel to be specified. When a Panel object is added to a Frame, the Panel's Location determines where within the Frame the Panel will be placed; the Panel's Shape determines how much of the Frame's space is occupied by the Panel. The Panel itself is not visible in the Frame. The interactive elements that are placed in a Panel are visible. Where the interactive elements appear in a Frame depend on where the element is placed in its Panel and where the Panel is placed in the Frame. The overloaded `add` method allows any number of Buttons and TextBoxes to appear in a Panel. It is the programmer's responsibility to ensure that interactive elements placed in the same Panel are arranged so that the visible representation of these elements do not overlap in the Panel.

```
public class Panel
{
   public Panel(Location loc, Shape sh)
   public Panel(Shape sh, Location loc)
   public Panel(Location loc)
   public Panel()

   public void add(Button  button)       // add a button to the Panel
   public void add(TextBox  tbox)        // add a textbox to the Panel
}
```

Figure 3.60 The Panel Class

```
public class Button
{
   public Button(String name, Location loc, Shape sh)
   public void addListener(ButtonListener listener)
}

public abstract interface ButtonListener
{
   public void onPush(String buttonName);
}
```

Figure 3.61 The Button Class and ButtonListener Interface

The Button class captures the abstraction of a pushable user interface control. The definition of the Button class is given in Figure 3.61. The Button class constructor requires that the "name" of the Button object be defined along with the Location of where the Button will appear in a Panel and the Shape of the Button. The Button's name appears on the user's display as the label on the Button's graphical representation. Thus, a Button object named "Start" will appear as a bordered rectangular box on the screen surrounding the word "Start." The Shape of the Button should be large enough to allow the full "name" to be visible. Only a portion of the Button's name will be displayed if the Shape is a smaller area than that required to display the entire "name."

The Button class has a related interface, the ButtonListener interface, that is also shown in Figure 3.61. The ButtonListener interfaces defines how a Button object interacts with another object that will perform actions when the Button is "pushed." The object performing the actions is referred to as a "listener" because it "listens" for the Button to the pushed. When the user "pushes" a displayed Button object (i.e., the user clicks within the bordered rectangular box corresponding to the Button) the `onPush(String)` method is called in the listener object. The Button's "name" is passed as an argument to the `napes` method so that a single listener object can be attached to several Button objects. The "name" parameter allows such a listener to determine which Button was pushed among the several Button objects.

An example of a class that implements the ButtonListener interface is the SequenceControl class shown in Figure 3.62. This class can be used to allow a But-

```
import ButtonListener;
import Sequenced;

public class SequenceControl implements ButtonListener
{

  public static final String NEXT_NAME = "Next";

  public SequenceControl()
  public void connectTo(Sequenced s)
  public void setName(String newName)
  public void onPush(String buttonName)
}
```

Figure 3.62 SequenceControl Class

```
public class TextBox
{
  public         TextBox( Location p, Shape s)
  public         TextBox()  public String getText()
  public void    setText(String val)
}
```

Figure 3.63 The TextBox Class

ton object to trigger the `next` method in any object that implements the Sequenced interface (e.g., the Counter class and the ImageSequence class). The `connectTo` method in the SequenceControl class establishes an association between the SequenceControl object and an object that implements the Sequenced interface. The SequenceControl object will be added as a listener to one or more Buttons. When one of the buttons is pushed by the user the `onPush` method of the SequenceControl will be called and the name of the Button is given as a parameter. If the Button's name matches the name set by the `setName` method (or the name "Next" by default), the SequenceControl will invoke the `next` method in the object with which it has been associated through the `connectTo` method. An example using the SequenceControl is given in Figure 3.62.

The TextBox class, defined in Figure 3.63, allows the user to edit and/or enter data. Each TextBox appears to the user as a bordered rectangular area in which a typing cursor will appear when the mouse cursor is moved within the TextBox area. When this cursor is visible, the user may edit (erase, add to) any text that is visible in the TextBox. The TextBox will scroll long lines of text so that only a portion of the text may be visible at any one time. The current value of the TextBox may be set or queried by the program using the TextBox's methods `setText` and `getText`. The Location of a TextBox defines where within its containing Panel the TextBox object will be placed. The Shape of the TextBox must be wide enough to hold the string that the program will display or the user is expected to enter.

A Simple Example

A small system, ButtonCounter, is developed to illustrate how many of the new classes are used. This simple example presents a single button to the user that, when pushed, increments an integer value that is displayed to the user. The user interface structure and the object structure of this system are shown in Figure 3.64. From a user interface perspective, the window on the user's display is composed of two parts: a Canvas area and a Panel area. The Panel area contains the Button labelled "Next." The Canvas area shows the current value of the number. This user interface is constructed by an association among several objects. The Canvas and Panel objects are added to the Frame object to create the overall structure of the interface. The Button object is added to the Panel. A Counter object maintains the numeric value which it display to the user through a Message object that is associated with the Canvas object. The SequenceControl object invokes the Counter object's `next` method whenever the Button is pushed.

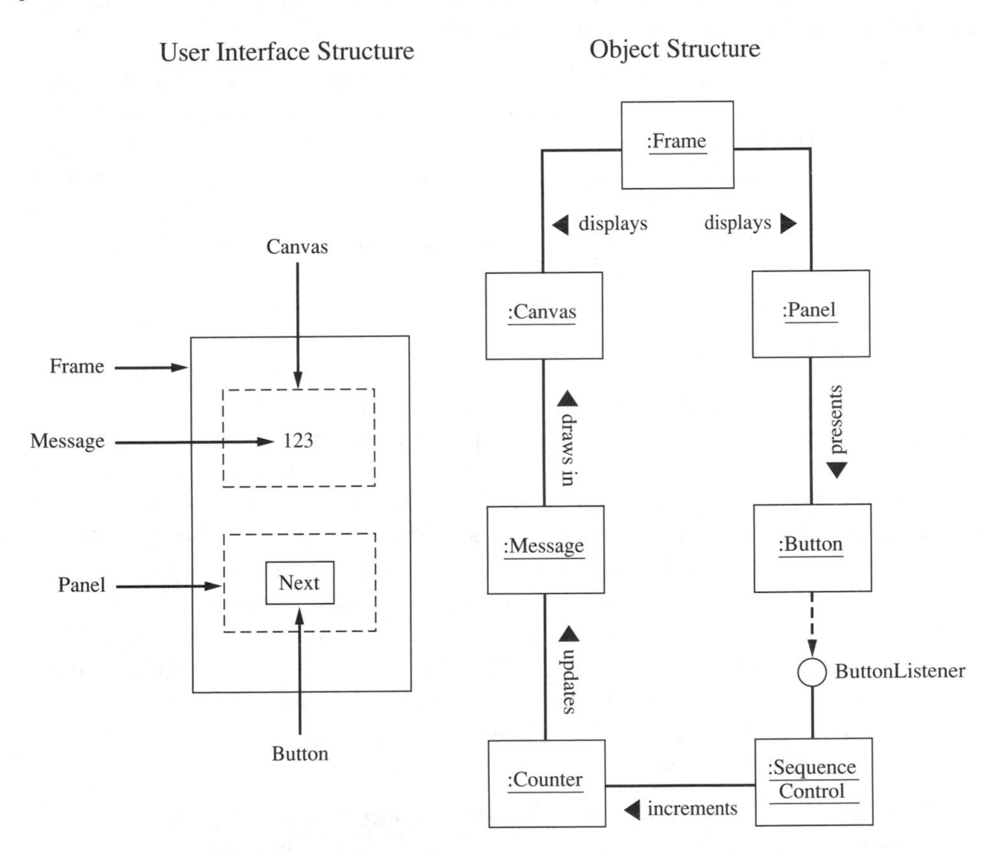

Figure 3.64 User Interface and Object Structure of the ButtonCounter System

The ButtonCounter system operates in the following way. When the user presses the "Next" button in the user interface the listener registered with the corresponding Button object is informed via the listeners `onPush` method. In the code for the ButtonCounter system shown in Figure 3.65, this means that the `onPush` method of the SequenceControl object named control will be invoked. Because the name of the button that was pressed matches the default name expected by the SequenceControl object, the SequenceControl object will call the `next` method of the Counter object named `count`. The Counter object will increment its internal value and invoke the `setText` method of the Message object named `currentValue` a String representation of the current integer value of the Counter object is passed as a parameter to the `setText` method. The Message object will use the `drawText` method of the Canvas object to update the text shown in the Canvas. The Panel object is necessary because it holds the Button object. The Frame object is used to support both the Panel object and the Canvas object because the Canvas and the Panel's controls are only visible to the user if they are associated with a visible Frame object.

Notice that a true "system" has been created. Together the constructor method and the on Start method instantiate a set of objects and create associations among these objects. Once the associations are established the system operates autonomously. This can be seen in that the system operates even though no further code in the SequenceControl Test program is executed (except for the single line of code needed in `onPaint` to redraw the contents of the Canvas area).

A More Complex Example

A slightly more complicated example of an association is that of an interactive adding calculator. The user interface of this system has a TextBox in which the user can enter an integer number. When the "Add" button is pressed the number in the TextBox is added to a total and the updated total is displayed. The user interface and the object structure of this system are shown in Figure 3.66. As in the previous example, the association among the Frame, Panel, and Canvas objects are used to create the basic structure of the user interface. The two interactive elements, the Button object and the TextBox object, are associated with the Panel object, whereas a Message object, used for displaying the calculators current value, is associated with the Canvas object. Objects of two new classes, the Calculator class and the Calculator Control class, are also used. These classes are explained below.

The Calculator class captures the abstraction of a simple, hand-held calculator. The code for this class is shown in Figure 3.67. The interface of the Calculator class provides methods for adding to, subtracting from, and setting its current value. The current value of the calculator is displayed in a Message object. The association with the Message object is created by the `connectTo`

```
import Frame;
import Panel;
import Canvas;
import Message;
import Button;
import Program;
import Location;
import Shape;
import SequenceControl;
import Counter;

public class ButtonCounter implements Program
{
  private Frame           window;
  private Canvas          canvas;
  private Panel           panel;
  private Button          nextButton;
  private SequenceControl control;
  private Message         currentValue;
  private Counter         count;

  public ButtonCounter()
  {window       = new Frame("Calculator Test", new Location(200, 200),
                                        new Shape(400, 400));
   canvas       = new Canvas("Calculator Value", new Location(100,50),
                                        new Shape(200,100));
   panel        = new Panel(new Location(100,175), new Shape(200, 100));
   nextButton   = new Button("Next", new Location(10,20), new Shape(30,20))
   currentValue = new Message(new Location(100,50));
   count        = new Counter();
   control      = new SequenceControl();

  }

  public void onStart()
  {
    window.add(canvas);
    window.add(panel);
    panel.add(nextButton);
    currentValue.displayIn(canvas);
    count.connectTo(currentValue);
    control.connectTo(count);
    nextButton.addListener(control);
  }

  public void onPaint()
  { currentValue.draw();
  }

  // ...
}
```

Figure 3.65 Code for the ButtonCounter System

method that takes a Message object as a parameter. The overloaded `connectTo` method allows an association to be created between the Calculator object and a

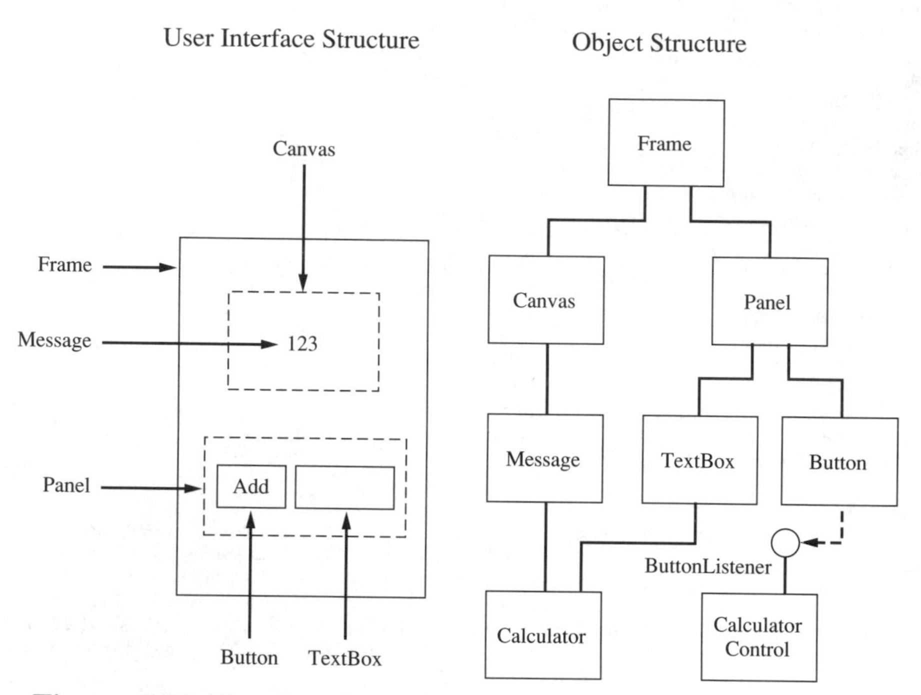

Figure 3.66 User Interface and Object Structure of the Adding Calculator

TextBox object. The numeric value entered in the TextBox by the user is used by the Calculator in its add, subtract, and set operations. For example, the add operation adds the numeric value in the TextBox to the Calculator object's current value. The subtract and set operations are similar. Whenever the current value of the Calculator changes, the Message object is updated accordingly.

The CalculatorControl class, also shown in Figure 3.67, allows the user to control the operation of the Calculator. Through the `connectTo` method an association can be created between a CalculatorControl object and a Calculator object. The CalculatorControl class implements the ButtonListener interface so that a Button object may add a CalculatorControl object as the Button's listener. The CalculatorControl is designed to listen for up to three buttons whose default names, defined by named constants, are "Add," "Subtract," and "Set." Each of these names can be changed by the three methods `setAddName`,`setSubtractName`, and `setSetName`. When a listened for button is pressed, the CalculatorControl object will invoke the corresponding method in the Calculator object with which it is associated.

The code for the adding calculator system is shown in Figure 3.68. Almost all of the code is contained in the constructor that creates the objects needed to form the system and the `onStart` method that creates the required associations.

```
import TextBox;
import Message;

public class Calculator
{

  public Calculator()
  public void connectTo(TextBox textbox)
  public void connectTo(Message msg)
  public void add()
  public void subtract()
  public void set()
}

public class CalculatorControl implements ButtonListener
{

  public static final String ADD_NAME        = "Add";
  public static final String SUBTRACT_NAME   = "Subtract";
  public static final String SET_NAME        = "Set";
  public CalculatorControl()
  public void connectTo(Calculator c)
  public void onPush(String buttonName)
  public void setAddName(String newName)
  public void setSubtractName(String newName)
  public void setSetName(String newName)
}
```

Figure 3.67 Calculator and CalculatorControl Classes

For example, the `add` method in the Panel class is used to create associations with the Button and TextBox objects. The Message object's `displayIn` method creates an association between the Message object and the Canvas object. The `connectTo` methods in the Calculator and CalculatorControl classes are used to create the association between themselves and the Message and TextBox objects (for the Calculator object) and the Calculator object (for the CalculatorControl object). Finally, the `addListener` method creates the association between the Button object and the CalculatorControl object. The only other code is the single statement in the `onPaint` method that is needed to redraw the contents of the Canvas when required.

One additional class that implements the ButtonListener interface, ClockControl, is used in the exercises. The ClockControl class is given in Figure 3.69. An association can be created between a ClockControl object and a Clock object using the `connectTo` method in the ClockControl class. A ClockControl object listens for two buttons whose names by default are "Start" and "Stop." When the `onPush` method is called by a button labelled "Start" the ClockControl object invokes the `on` method in the Clock object with which it is associated. When the `onPush` method is called by a button labelled "Stop" the ClockContol object invokes the `off` method in the Clock object. The names of the buttons to which

```
import Frame;
import Message;
// ... other imports

public class AddingCalculator implements Program
{
  private Frame              window;
  private Canvas             canvas;
  private Panel              panel;
  private Button             addButton;
  private TextBox            number;
  private Calculator         calculator;
  private CalculatorControl control;
  private Message            currentValue;

  public AddingCalculator()
  {window       = new Frame("Calculator Test", new Location(200, 200),
                                               new Shape(400, 400));
   canvas       = new Canvas("Calculator Value", new Location(100,50),
                                                 new Shape(200,100));
   panel        = new Panel(new Location(100,175), new Shape(200, 100));
   addButton    = new Button("Add", new Location(10,20), new Shape(30,20));
   number       = new TextBox(new Location(100, 20), new Shape(70,20));
   currentValue = new Message(new Location(100,50));
   calculator   = new Calculator();
   control      = new CalculatorControl();

  }

  public void onStart()
  {
    window.add(canvas);
    window.add(panel);
    panel.add(addButton);
    panel.add(number);
    currentValue.displayIn(canvas);
    calculator.connectTo(currentValue);
    calculator.connectTo(number);
    control.connectTo(calculator);
    addButton.addListener(control);
  }

  public void onPaint()
  { currentValue.draw();
  }

  //...
}
```

Figure 3.68 The AddingCalculator System

ClockControl object will react can be changed by the two methods `setStartName`, to change the name of the "Start" button, and `setStopName`, to change the name of the "Stop" button.

```
import ButtonListener;
import Clock;

public class ClockControl implements ButtonListener
{

  public static final String START_NAME = "Start";
  public static final String STOP_NAME  = "Stop";

  public ClockControl()
  public void connectTo(Clock c)
  public void onPush(String buttonName)
  public void setStartName(String newName)
  public void setStopName(String newName)
}
```

Figure 3.69 The ClockControl Class

3.7.3 More Complex Associations in the Ecological Simulation

The classes used in the ecological simulation are revised and extended to illustrate how a series of associations can be used to create more elaborate simulation systems. Interfaces will be used to improve the flexibility of the associations created among the existing and new classes. The revisions and extensions will add to the ecological simulation means that models birth and death processes among both the predator and the prey populations. Classes representing a single, simple birth process and a single, simple death process are used to illustrate the associations, although it should be clear that additional classes for more complex birth and death processes can easily be added. Interfaces are designed so that the classes representing the birth and death processes can be applied to groups of predator and/or groups of prey.

The first step in creating associations is to determine what information the birth and death processes need from the various types of creatures on which they operate. Although there are many ways of approaching this issue, a reasonable approach that is in line with the existing predator and prey classes is captured in the Creature interface shown in Figure 3.70. The Creature interface has two query methods, `isAlive` and `getLocation`, that provide information about a creature. The `isAlive` method is included in the interface because a death process would need to know whether a creature is alive or had already been killed. The `getLocation` method provides useful information to both the birth and death processes because these processes may depend on where the creature is in the environment or on its proximity to other creatures. The Creature interface has two other methods, `kill` and `spawn`, that allow the death and birth processes, respectively, to simulate the death of the creature and to generate a new creature that is an identical copy of the existing creature. The cloning approach used in the spawn method is only one simple and reasonable way, among many, to introduce new creatures into the simulated environment.

```
import Location;

public interface Creature
{
  public void kill();
  public boolean isAlive();
  public Location getLocation();
  public void spawn();
}
```

Figure 3.70 The Creature Interface

```
public class Prey implements Hunted, Creature
{
  //...
  public void join(Herd herd)
  public boolean isAlive()
  public void kill()
  public void spawn()
  public Location getLocation()
  //...
}

public class Predator implements Hunter, Creature
{

  public void join(Pack pack)

  public void spawn()
  public boolean isAlive()
  public void kill()
  public Location getLocation()

}
```

Figure 3.71 Adding New Associations to the Predator and Prey

The second step is to extend the existing predator and prey classes to conform to the Creature interface; this will require adding new associations in addition to new methods. These changes are illustrated for the Predator and Prey classes, as shown in Figure 3.71. Similar changes are made for other classes implementing variations of predators and prey. The Creature interface is added to the list of interfaces implemented by the Prey and Predator classes. To satisfy the Creature interface, a `spawn` method is added to both classes and a `kill` method is added to the Predator class. One aspect of the `spawn` method is problematic: if an existing Predator object is a member of a Pack, how does the newly cloned Predator also become a member of that Pack? The same issues arises between a Prey and the Herd of which it is a member. Currently, the Pack and Herd classes maintain a one-way association with the predators and prey that are in their groups. To allow a spawning creature to add its cloned progeny to its own group, the spawning creature will need to know which group it is a member

```
import Creature;

public interface CreatureGroup
{
  public int size();
  public Creature member(int i);
}
```

Figure 3.72 The CreatureGroup Interface

of. In technical terms, each individual creature object will need to have an association with the object, Pack or Herd, representing the creature's group. To create this association, the Predator and Prey classes include a `join` method that allows the required association to be created. The following code fragment illustrates how the `join` method is used to create the bidirectional association:

```
Herd herd = new Herd();
Prey prey = new Prey();
...
herd.add(prey);      // create association Herd —> Prey
prey.join(herd);     // create association Prey —> Herd
```

In this fragment, the Herd's `add` method is used to create the association by which the Herd knows about the Prey that is its member and the Prey's join method is used to create the association by which the Prey knows about the Herd that it is a member of. Associations between a Pack and Predator objects are created in a similar way.

The third step is to design the birth and death processes so that they can be used with any groups of creatures. This design goal is preferred to the more costly alternative of constructing a separate set of birth and death processes for each distinct group of creatures. Concretely in the ecological simulation example, the birth and death processes must be able to be associated with either a Herd object or a Pack object. To gain the needed flexibility, the CreatureGroup interface is defined as shown in Figure 3.72. This interface requires only two methods of any group: a `size` method that reports the number of creatures in the group, and a `member` method that returns a Creature object whose index in the group is given as a parameter. Using the size and member methods, the birth and death processes are able to iterate through groups of creatures, using the Creature interface to extract information about the state of the creature and causing the creature to be killed or spawn a clone of itself.

The Birth and Death classes are defined in terms of the CreateGroup interface. These classes are shown in Figure 3.73. The constructor for each class creates an association between the Birth or Death object and an object conforming to the CreatureGroup interface. The Birth class's `generate` method examines the current creatures in the group with which it is associated and spawns new creatures in that group. The Birth class follows a simple rule: every other alive creature in the CreatureGroup is asked to spawn itself. In a similar way, the Death class constructor is used to create an association with a CreatureGroup so

```
import CreatureGroup;

public class Birth
{
  public Birth(CreatureGroup source)
  public void generate()
}

import CreatureGroup;

public class Death
{
  public Death(CreatureGroup source)
  public void reduce()
}
```

Figure 3.73 The Birth and Death Processes

that the Death class's `reduce` method can examine the creatures in the associated CreatureGroup and require some members of the group to be killed. Like the Birth class, the Death class employs a simple rule: every fifth alive creature in the CreatureGroup is killed. Of course, other and more sophisticated birth and death processes can be simulated. However, it is important to note that new classes implementing more elaborate birth and death processes can be introduced easily using the structure of classes and interfaces built up to this point.

The last step in creating the associations is to resolve a conflict between the CreatureGroup interface and the Pack and Herd classes. The conflict is centered on the type of the object returned by the member method in the Pack and Herd classes. The conflicting declarations are:

```
Herd class:      public Hunted member(int i);
Pack class:      public Hunter member(int i);
CreatureGroup: public Creature member(int i);
```

As can be seen from these declarations, the `member` method of the Herd and Pack classes are specifically designed to returned objects that are typed by the nature of the creature each contains: the Herd returns objects conforming to the Hunted interface and the Pack returns objects conforming to the Hunter interface. Neither of these member method matches the returned type of the CreatureGroup interface. Because the Birth and Death classes are defined in terms of the CreatureGroup interface, the conflict between the CreatureGroup and the Pack and Herd classes must be resolved to make it possible for Birth and Death objects to interact with a Pack or Herd object.

An "adaptor" class is used to allow a Herd or Pack object to be accessed via a CreatureGroup interface. An alternative to the adaptor class is to change the Herd and Pack classes so that their `member` methods return a Creature object. Instead of changing the Herd and Pack classes, the adaptor technique is presented because it is generally useful, avoids possible changes to other classes (such as the Ecology class) that depend on the current definition of the Herd and

```
import CreatureGroup;
import Creature;
import Herd;

public class HerdAdaptor implements CreatureGroup
{
  private Herd herd;

  public HerdAdaptor(Herd aHerd)
  { herd = aHerd;
  }

  public int size()
  { return herd.size();
  }

  public Creature member(int i)
  { return (Creature) (herd.member(i));
  }
}
```

Figure 3.74 An Adaptor Class

Pack classes, and demonstrate show the conflict can be resolved without changing the Herd or Pack classes. One of the two adaptor classes, HerdAdaptor, is shown below. The PackAdaptor class is similar.

The full implementation of the HerdAdaptor is shown in Figure 3.74 to illustrate its simplicity and to give a concrete sense of its role informing an association. First, note that the HerdAdaptor implements the CreatureGroup interface. Thus, Birth and Death objects can form an association with a HerdAdaptor. The argument for the constructor of the HerdAdaptor is a Herd object with which the HerdAdaptor forms an association. As seen in the constructor code, forming the association is simple: the HerdAdaptor merely keeps a reference to the Herd given by the constructor argument. Second, the `size` and `member` methods of the HerdAdaptor simply uses the corresponding methods in the Herd with which it is associated. This is sometimes referred to as "forwarding" the invocation. Notice that the `member` method of the HerdAdaptor type casts the object returned by the member method Herd (an object conforming to the Hunted interface) to an object conforming to the Creature interface. This type cast is needed to meet the requirements of the CreatureGroup interface.

The key parts of a small example, named EcoSim6, that uses associations to build a simulation from the newly defined classes and interfaces is described using UML in Figure 3.75. The outline of the code for this example appears in Figure 3.76. There are four important associations created in this system. First, the Herd and Pack objects maintain an association with each prey and predator added to them, respectively. This association is needed so that the Herd or Pack can access each of its members. Second, each prey and predator object maintains an association with the single Herd or Pack of which it is a member. This association allows the prey or predator to spawn a duplicate of itself in the same group.

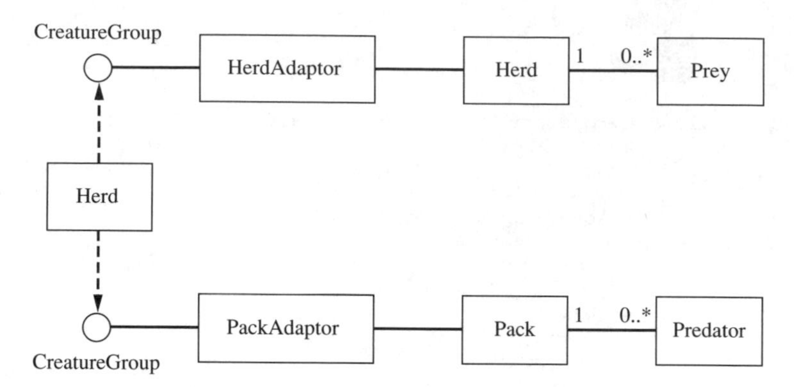

Figure 3.75 UML Diagram of EcoSim6

```
public class EcoSim6
{
  public EcoSim6()
  { Herd herd = new Herd();
    // initialize herd creating associations between
    // the herd and Prey objects

    Pack pack = new Pack();
    // initialize herd creating associations between
    // the pack and Predator objects

    HerdAdaptor herdAdaptor = new HerdAdaptor(herd);
    PackAdaptor packAdaptor = new PackAdaptor(pack);

    Birth preyBirths     = new Birth((CreatureGroup)herdAdaptor);
    Birth predatorBirths = new Birth((CreatureGroup)packAdaptor);


    preyBirths.generate();
    predatorBirths.generate();

    //...
  }

  public static void main(String[] args)
  { EcoSim6 simulation = new EcoSim6();
  }

}
```

Figure 3.76 Code for EcoSim6

Third, the HerdAdaptor is associated with the Herd object and the PackAdaptor is associated with the Pack object. As described above, these adaptors conform to the CreatureGroup interface. Fourth, the Birth object maintains an association with an adaptor for either a Pack or Herd object. In this example, two Birth objects are created, one connected to a PreyAdaptor and one connected to a PredatorAdaptor. Notice that type casting is used with the constructor argument for the Birth objects; type casting changes the type of the objects from PreyAdaptor and PredatorAdaptor to the type defined by the CreatureGroup interface.

Exercises

1. **Canvas Click Count:** using the Frame, Canvas, Message, and Counter classes, implement a system that displays the count of the number of mouse button clicks that occur in the Canvas area.
2. **Two Canvas Click Count:** using the Frame, Canvas, Message, and Counter classes, implement a system that has two Canvas areas. Each Canvas area should displays the count of the number of mouse button clicks that occur within it. Use additional Message objects to label the counts that appear in each Canvas.
3. **Three Button Calculator:** extend the AddingCalculator system so that it can also subtract and be set. Use the default button names "Add," "Subtract," and "Set."
4. **Three Button Calculator 2:** extend the Adding Calculator system so that it can also subtract and be set. Label the buttons with the names "Increment," "Decrement," and "Reset."
5. **Image Viewer:** implement a system that allows a user to view a sequence of Images. The next image in the sequence is presented when the user presses a button labelled "Next Image."
6. **Image Scanner:** implement a system that allows a user to view a sequence of Images. Each image remains visible for three seconds or until the user presses a button labelled "Next Image."
7. **Image Scanner 2:** implement a system that allows a user to view the sequence of Images. Each image remains visible for three seconds. A button labelled "Pause" allows the user to keep the current image visible until a button labelled "Resume" is pressed.
8. **Image Scanner 3:** implement a system that allows a user to view the sequence of Images. Each image remains visible for three seconds or until the user presses a button labelled "Next." A button labelled "Pause" allows the user to keep the current image visible until a button labelled "Resume" is pressed or until the "Next" button is pressed.
9. **One-Button Timer:** Implement a system that provides a simple one-second timer controlled by a single button. Pushing the Button for the first time "starts" the timing (the displayed number increments once each second). Pushing the Button a second time "stops" the timing.

Thereafter, pushing the Button alternately starts and stops the timing.

10. **Two-Button Timer:** Implement a system that provides a simple one-second timer controlled by two buttons. Pushing the button labelled "Start" causes the timer to start (the displayed number increments once each second). Pushing the button labelled "Stop" causes the incrementing to stop. Pushing the Start (Stop) button when the timer is already started (stopped) has no effect.
11. **Dual Timers:** Implement a system that has a pair of Two Button Timers (see above). Each timer can be started and stopped independently.
12. Suppose there are 10 Predator objects and 10 Prey objects created in theEcoSim6 system. How many total associations of all types are there in the system?
13. Use the adaptors and other interfaces to build and test a simulation that has both a birth process and a death process attached to a group of prey.
14. Use the adaptors and other interfaces to build and test a simulation that has both a birth process and a death process attached to a group of predators.
15. **Birth/Death Simulator:** use the adaptors and other interfaces to build and test a simulation having both a birth process and a death process attached to a group of predators and separate birth and death processes attached to a group of prey.
16. Use the adaptors and other interfaces to build and test a simulation that has two death processes attached to the same group of predators.
17. Use the adaptors and other interfaces to build and test a simulation that has two birth processes attached to the same group of prey.
18. Draw a UML diagram of the three button calculator described in an exercise above.
19. Draw a UML diagram of the Image Scanner 2 system described in an exercise above.
20. Draw a UML diagram of the Image Scanner 3 system described in an exercise above.
21. Draw UML diagram of the Birth/Death Simulator described in an exercise above.

CHAPTER 4

Implementing a New Class

4.1 Introduction

Understanding how to implement a new class or modify an existing class is a basic skill in object-oriented programming. Although it is always preferable to reuse intact an existing class that is suited to the needs of the system being built, it is often the case that a suitable class does not exist or that the existing class does not fully provide the attributes and behavior that are required. In these cases is it necessary to design and implement a new class or alter the design and implementation of an existing one.

4.1.1 Properties of a Good Class

A good class design and implementation must have a number of desirable properties. Because a *class* captures an abstraction, the class must have all of the *properties* of a good abstraction. But, as an executable representation, a class must also have three major properties beyond those of an abstraction:

1. **Correct:** an object of the class must maintain its state properly and respond to invocations of its methods with the expected results. The most stringent level of correctness is a formal proof, though such proofs are usually reserved for safety-critical components due to the high cost of proving correctness of software. More common are less-stringent levels achieved through testing. No amount of testing establishes the formal correctness of a class. However, useful and measurable degrees of reliability and dependability can be achieved through rigorous testing.

2. **Safe:** when used in obvious ways, an object of a class should not produce unexpected or harmful consequences. In particular, an object should behave safely when passed as a parameter or copied. Furthermore, an object should detect and report conditions that interfere with its normal operation so that the object does not cause a failure of the system.
3. **Efficient:** the object should make efficient use of processor and memory resources. The most important means for ensuring efficiency reside in the overall system design and the choice of critical data structures and algorithms.

Given the desired properties of abstractions and those of a class, it is clear that good object-oriented design and implementation are creative and challenging activities.

Implementing a new class is a challenging activity because it involves the interaction of several very different types of knowledge and abilities, among which are:

Aggregation: the conceptual foundation of a class. A good class cannot be designed without a good understanding of how to recognize aggregations, identify the parts of the aggregation, and define the relationships among these parts.

Language features: the programming foundation of a class. To implement a class it is necessary to have a thorough understanding of the syntax and meaning of the parts of the language that bear on the structure and operation of an object. For example, it is necessary to understand how to properly construct, organize, and manage objects with complex internal structures.

Design: the design of a system—the assignment of responsibilities and the organization of collaborations—largely determines the performance and software engineering properties (e.g., maintainability) of the system. A good design results from the combination of insight, understanding, inspiration, experience, and hard work. A critical aspect of design is how to recognize abstractions that should be represented as classes.

Debugging: a collection of newly designed and implemented classes inevitably contain errors that are revealed through testing or usage. There are systematic strategies for discovering the cause of these errors. Knowledge of these strategies and proficiency in their application are important.

Documentation: knowledge of how to use a class must be conveyed to other developers to promote the effective reuse of the class. The knowledge is conveyed through well-written and informative documentation that disconnected to the documentation of other related classes.

Packaging: almost any system involves not a single new class but many new classes. It is usually necessary to organize the classes into logically cohesive packages so that classes within a package can interact in ways that are denied to classes outside of the package. The packaging also is critical for distributing the classes conveniently to potential reusers.

Because all of these areas of knowledge and skills are interwoven, they cannot be perfectly separated for individual study. Any approach to learning these topics must focus on some and defer others, not because the deferred topics are less important but only because some place must be chosen as the starting point. This chapter is covers the concept of aggregation and the language features of Java that are needed to implement a new class. The topics of design, documentation, debugging, and packaging are covered in Chapters 5.

4.2 Implementing a Class

4.2.1 General Concepts

Implementing a class consist of defining:

1. Data—the encapsulated (hidden, private) variables that record the current state of the object, and
2. Code—the methods (operations, actions) that perform computation using the object's data and the method's own input parameters.

The data is often referred to as the *state* variables or the *instance* variables of the class. The term "state" reflects the point of view that an object changes from one internal condition to another as directed by the execution of its methods. For example, when the `moveTo` method is applied to a Frame object, the object is changed from a state in which it is at one location to a state in which it is at a different location. In the same way, the `next` method of a Prey object changes the state of the object so as to reflect that object's new simulated position. The term "instance" denotes the fact that each object is an instance of the class; each instance of a given class is distinct from all other instances and possesses its own private data. For example, the instance variables of a Predator object denote that particular predator's aliveness, lifetime, and location.

The encapsulated data in a class is accessible to the methods of that class. Such access is allowed, of course, because the methods and the data are parts of the same implementation: to be coded, the programmer of the code must know

```
public class Location
{

  private int currentX;
  private int currentY;

  public Location(int x, int y)
  { currentX = x;
    currentY = y;
  }

  public Location()
  { currentX = 0;
    currentY = 0;
  }

  public int getX()
  { return currentX;
  }

  public int getY()
  { return currentY;
  }
}
```

Figure 4.1 Implementation of the Location Classes

the details of the data. The encapsulated data is, however, completely inaccessible to all methods that are outside of the class.

4.2.2 A Simple Example

The Location class, used in both the GUI classes and the simulation classes, illustrates the syntax and placement of the data and the code for a class. The complete implementation for the Location class is shown in Figure 4.1. Notice that the implementation, the private data and the code for each method, is textually visible in the class definition. In some object-oriented languages, the interface and the implementation are separated textually. In C++, for instance, the definition of the class's methods and the implementation of the class's methods are placed in separate files. Java, however, follows the practice of other object-oriented languages, including Smalltalk, that combines the definition and implementation in one file. The advantages of combining the two is that it makes the compiler's job somewhat easier and it avoids additional syntax, as is required in C++, to indicate which method implementation corresponds to which method definition.

The general syntax of the implementation of a method is:

```
Access ReturnType MethodName ( ArgumentList ) { Statements }
```

where

Access is a keyword that determines whether the method is visible outside of the class. The keyword `public` is the only keyword seen in this example.

ReturnType is the type of the value returned by the method; the returned value may be a primitive type (e.g., int) or a class of.

MethodName is the name that is the same as the class's name for a constructor or a name suggesting the effect of the method (e.g., getX) for non-constructor methods.

ArgumentList is a comma-separated list of the arguments for this method (e.g., x and y for the first constructor); the list is empty if there are no arguments as shown in the second constructor.

Statements is the code that defines what the method does when it is invoked.

The Location class does not show an example of a method returning an object; an example of this is shown later in Figure 4.3 (see page XX).

The general syntax for declaring the encapsulated data of a class is

```
Access DataType VariableName = InitialValue;
```

where

Access is a keyword that determines whether the method is visible outside of the class. The keyword `private` is the only keyword seen in this example.

DataType is the type of data being declared, either a predefined type (e.g., int) or the name of another class.

VariableName is the name of the variable chosen to suggest its purpose in the class.

InitialValue is an optional initial value for the variable may be given after the equal sign (=); this value may be changed by a constructor.

The Location class example does not assign initial values to its private data. An example of this is shown later in the Prey class in Figure 4.3.

There is no technical significance to the ordering of the data and methods in a class definition. Although it is common practice to group together the private data and to group together the constructors and put them before any other methods, the compiler assigns no significance to such grouping or arrangement. The arrangement is significant as a matter of style and the extent to which a given arrangement assists or impedes the readability of the implementation.

Each public class must be in a file whose name matches that of the class. For example, the Location class must be placed in a file named Location.java. The Java compiler will issue an error message if this naming scheme is not followed.

4.2.3 Invocations Among Methods in the Same Class

The implementation of a method may invoke another method that is in the public interface of the same class. This is a useful technique to avoid repetitive code in a class's implementation. The Message class's implementation, shown in Figure 4.2, illustrates this situation. Except for its `setText` and `moveTo` methods the implementation of the Message class is straightforward. The Message class defines three private variables that are: 1) the Message's text string (`msgText`), 2) the position of where this text should be drawn in a Canvas (`msgLocation`), and 3) the Canvas in which the text is drawn (`msgCanvas`). The overloaded constructors allow the text string and the text position to be defined, whereas the `displayIn` method defines the Canvas. The current text string of a Message object is returned by the `getText` method. The `clear` and `draw` methods cause the text string to be erased and displayed, respectively, provided that the Message has an associated Canvas object that provides the low-level methods to manipulate text in the user interface. A reference to the Canvas object is held in the private variable `msgCanvas` that is initialized to the special value `null` in both constructors. The condition (`msgCanvas == null`) in the `clear` and `draw` methods tests if the reference is still `null` and, if so, simply returns. Thus, it is safe to invoke a Message object's `clear` and `draw` methods even if the Message is not associated with a Canvas object.

The `moveTo` and `setText` methods each invoke the `clear` and `draw` methods of the Message class. When the `moveTo` method is invoked, it must use the current position to erase the Message's text from the user interface, change its position to that indicated by the `moveTo` method's parameter, and display the text at the new position. To avoid repeating the code that erases and displays the Message's text, the `moveTo` method simply invokes the `clear` and `draw` methods that are already defined for these purposes. Similarly, the `setText` method also calls the `clear` and `draw` methods. Notice that the method invocations do not use the dot (.) operator—the presumption is that the implied object to perform the invocation is the object making the invocation. In other words, if a Message object named `msg` is executing its `moveTo` method, the invocation `clear()` is treated as `msg.clear()` by the compiler.

The Prey class also illustrates how one method of a class can invoke other public methods in its own class. A portion of the Prey class is shown in Figure 4.3. This class contains an overloaded `move` method; with no arguments, the `move` method simulates a single movement of the prey whereas the `move` method with a single integer argument simulates that many successive movements of the prey. The implementation of the `move(int)` method repeatedly calls the `move()` method to achieve each individual simulated movement.

```
import Location;
import Canvas;
import Shape;

public class Message
{
  private String   msgText;
  private Location msgLocation;
  private Canvas   msgCanvas;

  public Message(String textString, Location whereAt)
  { msgText     = textString;
    msgLocation = whereAt;
    msgCanvas   = null;
  }

  public Message(Location whereAt)
  { msgText     = "";
    msgLocation = whereAt;
    msgCanvas   = null;
  }

  public void displayIn(Canvas whichCanvas)
  { msgCanvas = whichCanvas;
  }

  public String getText()
  { return msgText;
  }

  public void clear()
  { if(msgCanvas == null) return;
    Shape msgShape = msgCanvas.getTextSize(msgText);
    msgCanvas.clear(msgLocation, msgShape);
  }

  public void draw()
  { if(msgCanvas == null) return;
    msgCanvas.drawText(msgText, msgLocation);
  }

  public void moveTo(Location newLocation)
  { clear();          // invokes own clear() method
    msgLocation = newLocation;
    draw();           // invokes own draw() method
  }

  public void setText(String newText)
  { clear();         // invokes own clear() method
    msgText = newText;
    draw();          // invokes own draw() method
  }
}
```

Figure 4.2 Implementation of the Message Classes

```
public class Prey implements Hunted, Creature
{
  //...
  private Location current;
  private int roamDistance;
  private boolean alive = true;
  private PreyMove moves;

  public static final int IMMOBILE =  0;
  public static final int SLOW     = 25;
  public static final int NORMAL   = 30;
  public static final int FAST     = 50;
  public static final int RANGING  = 75;

  //...

  public void move()
  { if(!alive)return;
    current = moves.next(current, roamDistance);
  }

  public void move(int steps)
  { for(int i=0; i,steps; i++)
     move();                       // invoke Prey move() method
  }

  //...

  public Location getLocation()
  { return current;
  }

}
```

Figure 4.3 Partial Implementation of the Prey Class

4.2.4 Defining and Invoking Private Methods

A private method is one that is not visible outside of the class, although it is visible to other methods in its class and may be invoked from other methods in its class. Private methods may be used when there is replicated code in public methods, but no public method that performs the action of this replicated code. The method containing the replicated code is declared private so that it is not visible outside of the class but can still be invoked by other methods in the class. Private methods may also be used to make code more readable. A complicated expression may be placed in a private method. The private method is given a suggestive name, one that conveys the intent of the expression it replaces. Whenever a public method needs to evaluate this expression, the private method is invoked.

The SimpleCounter class defined in Figure 4.4 shows an example of a private method named `update`. In the SimpleCounter class, the methods `next`, `reset`, and `connectTo` each need to cause the associated Message object, if there is one, to alter the string that it displays so that it reflects the current value of the SimpleCounter. Updating the Message object involves three steps: 1)

```
import Message;

public class SimpleCounter
{
  private int     value;
  private Message message;

  private void update()
  { if(message != null)
    { String newText = String.valueOf(value);
      message.setText(newText);
    }
  }

  //...

  public void next()
  { value = value + 1;
    update();              // invoke private method
  }

  public void reset()
  { value = initial;
    update();              // invoke private method
  }

  public void connectTo(Message msg)
  { message = msg;
    update();              // invoke private method
  }
}
```

Figure 4.4 A Private Method in the SimpleCounter Class

checking that there is an associated Message object, 2) and if one exists, converting the Counter's numeric value to a string, and 3) invoking the `setText` method of the Message. Rather than duplicating this code in each of the three methods, each one calls a utility method, named `update`, that performs the three steps to update the Message object. The `update` method must be accessible to the methods of the Counter class, but it is not intended that users of a Counter object would be able to invoke it. Therefore, the `update` method is declared with the keyword `private`. As with private data, private methods can be accessed by the methods of the class in which they are declared, but are inaccessible to any code outside of the class's methods.

The difference between public and private methods is illustrated in this segment of code:

```
SimpleCounter test = new SimpleCounter(10);
...
test.next();     //OK, next is public, next invokes update
...
test.update();   // ERROR, update is private
```

```
public class Predator implements Hunter, Creature
{
  //...
  private int x;
  private int y;
  private boolean alive = true;
  private int lifetime;
  private int lifeLeft;
  private int killZone;

  //...

  private boolean captures(Hunted aPrey)
  { double xdist = (double)(aPrey.getLocation().xCoord() - x);
    double ydist = (double)(aPrey.getLocation().yCoord() - y);

    return (int)(Math.sqrt(xdist*xdist + ydist*ydist)) < killZone;
  }

  public boolean hunt(Hunted aPrey)
  { if (!alive) return false;
    if(aPrey.isAlive() && captures(aPrey))
       { aPrey.kill();
         lifeLeft = lifetime;
         return true;
       }
    else return false;
 }

  //...
}
```

Figure 4.5 Private Methods in the Predator Class

The invocation of the `next` method on the object `test`is valid because `next` is declared as a public method. However, because `update` is declared as a private method, it cannot be invoked except from within the methods of the SimpleCounter class. Except for its restricted visibility, a private method is like any other method—it can access the private data of the class, and invoke other public or private methods of the class.

Another example of a private method is shown in the Predator class in Figure 4.5. In this class, the `hunt` method must determine the distance of the predator from the prey object passed as a parameter. If the prey is both alive and within the predators reach, the predator extends its own lifetime by capturing the prey. To simplify the programming of the `hunt` method's compound test, that is checking both the state of the prey and the distance to the prey, the test for proximity to the prey is placed in the private `captures` method. This method is private because it is not intended to be part of the public interface of the Predator class; it is only a convenience method used internally as part of the hidden implementation of the class. Private methods of this form—ones that separate out a part of another method's computation—are often encountered because they help improve the readability of the code. The code's readability is enhanced both through the name chosen for the private method and the simplification it makes in the invoking method's own control flow.

4.2.5 Using Interface Variables

A variable, though not an object, may be declared using an interface name as its type. For example, the following code segment shows variables being declared using the Sequenced interface:

```
import Sequenced;
...
Sequenced pageNumber;
Sequenced numberofInvocations, linesPrinted;
```

The import statement is needed because the definition of an interface must be seen by the Java compiler before any use is made of that interface. Notice that the syntax of a variable declaration is the same as seen previously. The only difference is that interface names are used to specify the type of the variables declared.

A variable whose type is an interface name can only refer to objects that are instances of classes that implement the interface. For example, the variable `pageNumber` declared above can only refer to objects that are instances of a class that implements the Sequenced interface. Because the revised Counter class implements the Sequenced interface, the following assignments are correct:

```
import Counter;
...
pageNumber = new Counter(0,100);
linesPrinted = new Counter();
```

It is also possible to combine the variable declaration and the object assignment in one step. For example:

```
Sequenced cardCount = new Counter();
```

For assignment of objects to variables whose type is an interface name, the compiler will check that the object is an instance of a class that implements the interface. For the `cardCount` variable the compiler will check that the class of the object assigned to `cardCount` (in this case Counter) implements the Sequenced interface. The assignment above to `cardCount` is correct because the Counter class (version2) does implement the Sequenced interface. The relationship between a variable whose type is an interface name and an object can also be established more indirectly, as shown in this code segment:

```
Sequenced intervals;
...
Counter intervalCount = new Counter();
intervals = intervalCount;
```

This example illustrates that the same object may be known both by its actual class (intervalCount of type Counter) and by an interface name (intervals of the Sequenced interface).

Any method defined in an interface may be applied to the object referred to by a variable whose type is defined by the interface. Because the Sequenced interface defines the next and reset methods, the following examples are correct:

```
pageNumber.next();
linesPrinted.reset();
cardCount.next();
```

These examples are clearly correct because the compiler has verified that each method is in the Sequenced interface and the compiler has already verified that the actual object performing the operation has such methods because the compiler has verified that the class implements the Sequenced interface.

Only methods defined in an interface may be applied to the object referred to by a variable whose type is defined by the interface, as shown in the following segment:

```
Message msg = new Message(...);
Sequenced current = new Counter();
...
current.connectTo(msg);      // compile-time error - connectTo not
                             // in Sequenced interface
```

The important point made by this example is that it does not matter whether the object actually has a given method—the current object does, in fact, have a connectTo method. However, the connectTo method cannot be applied to the object referred to by current because the connectTo method is not defined in the Sequenced interface.

An instance variable of a class may be of an interface type. When such a variable is used to create an association, the variable may refer to objects of different classes, even to objects of different classes at different times during execution. The SequenceControl class, shown in Figure 4.6, contains an instance variable whose type is defined by the Sequenced interface. Recall that the SequenceControl class is designed to be registered as a listener for a Button object and, accordingly, implements the ButtonListener interface that requires the implementing class to have an onPush(String) method that will be called when the Button is pushed. The SequenceControl is also designed so that its onPush method will invoke the next method of an associated object that implements the Sequenced interface. Recall that objects of the Sequenced interface must define a next method.

The connectTo method creates an association between a SequenceControl object and an object of a class that implements the Sequenced interface. The parameter of this method is declared as "Sequenced," meaning that the actual object passed as the parameter must be an object of a class that implements the Sequenced interface. To construct an association, the SequenceControl must

```
import ButtonListener;
import Sequenced;

public class SequenceControl implements ButtonListener
{
  private Sequenced sequence;
  private String nextName;

  public static final String NEXT_NAME = "Next";

  public SequenceControl()
  { sequence = null;
    nextName = NEXT_NAME;
  }

  public void connectTo(Sequenced s)
  { sequence = s;
  }

  public void setName(String newName)
  { nextName = newName;
  }

  public void onPush(String buttonName)
  { if (sequence != null && buttonName.equals(nextName))
        sequence.next();
  }
}
```

Figure 4.6 Using Interface Types to Declare Instance Variables

maintain a reference to the object that is passed as the parameter of its `connectTo` method, but by design, the SequenceControl does not know the actual class of this object. Therefore, the SequenceControl cannot declare an instance variable whose type is the class of the parameter object. Instead, the SequenceControl declares an instance variable whose type is the interface Sequenced; this is the variable `sequence` in the SequenceControl class.

The `onPush` method of the SequenceControl class uses the `sequence` instance variable to invoke the `next` method of the object with which it is associated, provided that such an object exists (i.e., the condition `sequence != null`) and that the pushed Button matches the name expected by the SequenceControl object (i.e., the condition `buttonName.equals(nextName)`).

Notice that the variable of an interface type is critical to implementing a flexible and type-safe SequenceControl class. The flexibility comes from the fact that the SequenceControl can be associated through its `connectTo` method with any object of a class that implements the Sequenced interface. The safety comes from the fact that the compiler will check that the actual parameter object passed to the `connectTo` method is of a class that implements the Sequenced interface. The invocation `sequence.next()` is type-safe because the associated object is, therefore, guaranteed to have a `next` method.

```
public class Predator implements Hunter, Creature
{
  //...

  public boolean hunt(Hunted aPrey)
  { if (!alive) return false;
    if(aPrey.isAlive() && captures(aPrey))
       { aPrey.kill();
         lifeLeft = lifetime;
         return true;
       }
    else return false;
  }

  //...
}

public interface Hunted
{
  public boolean isAlive();
  public Location getLocation();
  public void kill();
  public void move();
  public void print();
}
```

Figure 4.7 Interface Variables in the Predator Class

The Predator class also illustrates how interface names are used as the types of parameters. The `hunt` method of the Predator class is shown in Figure 4.7. The type of the `hunt` method's single parameter, `aPrey`, is defined by the Hunted interface, which is also shown in the figure for reference. The `hunt` method applies to the `aPrey` object the two methods `isAlive` and `kill`. Using these two methods is correct because both of them are defined in the Hunted interface.

The compiler can verify that the `aPrey` object provides the two methods used by the `hunt` method because it can verify at the point of the invocation whether or not the class of the actual object implements the Hunted interface. For example, in this code segment

```
Predator predator = new Predator(...);
Prey aPrey = new Prey(...);
...
predator.hunt((Hunted)aPrey);
```

the compiler can verify if the explicit type cast on the invocation of the `hunt` method is correct. In this case the compiler will refer to the definition of the actual class of the `aPrey` object (i.e., Prey) and note that this class implements the Hunted interface.

4.2.6 Encapsulation Revisited

To gain a deeper understanding of the concept of encapsulation, consider a method that allows two Location objects to be compared. This method determines if the two Location objects represent the same point in the coordinate sys-

```
public class Location
{
  private int xCoord;
  private int yCoord;

  //...

  public boolean equals (Location other)
  { return (xCoord == other.xCoord) && (yCoord == other.yCoord);
  }
}
```

Figure 4.8 The Equal Method in the Location Class

tem; that is, whether the encapsulated integer data values of the two objects are equal. Two locations can be compared by using the `getX` and `getY` methods to extract the x and y coordinates of both locations and comparing the corresponding coordinates. To avoid having to repeat these steps whenever a comparison is required, the Location class provides a utility method for this purpose. One way of implementing the method is shown in Figure 4.8.

Because encapsulation is a class property, and not an object property, the implementation of the `equal` method does not violate the encapsulation property. On the surface, encapsulation appears to be violated because the internal data of the "other" object is accessed directly and not via a public accessor method. Specifically, the expressions "`other.xCoord`" and "`other.yCoord`" directly accesses the supposedly encapsulated data of the "other" object. However, encapsulation must be understood from a class perspective: the private data defined within a class can only be accessed by methods of that class. Because the `equal` method is a member of the Location class it may access any of the private data members of that class in any Location object to which it has access. This does not violate the notion of encapsulation because the benefit of encapsulation derives from the limitation on which methods, not which objects, can access the private data of a class. To underscore this idea, suppose that the name or type of the internal value in the Location class were changed. The only code that would have to be altered to accommodate this change is in the Location class itself.

Exercises

1. Rewrite the Location class so that the x and y coordinates are initialized to zero by assignment in their declarations. How does this change the constructors?
2. Show how to define and implement a `distance` method in the Location class that determines the straight-line distance between two Location objects.

3. Show how to define and implement a `withinRange` method that returns a boolean value indicating if a given Location object is within a given distance. Implement this method by calling the distance method developed in the exercise above.
4. Show how to define and implement an `equal` method in the Location class that determines if the x and y coordinates of two Location objects are the same. Implement this method using the accessor methods `getX` and `getY` of the Location class.
5. Show how to define and implement a `lessThan` method in the Counter class that determines if the value of one Counter object is strictly less than the value of another Counter object.
6. Without looking at the software distribution, show how to implement the Shape class.
7. Define and implement an extension to the Location class that adds a method `moveBy(int dx, int dy)` that changes the coordinates of the Location object to which it is applied by the amount given by the two parameters. For example, if a Location object has the coordinates (100,100), applying the operation `moveBy(20, -10)` changes the coordinates of the object to be (120, 90).
8. Design, implement, and test a class to represent simple fractions. For example, the class might be used as follows:

```
Fraction half(1,2);
Fraction quarter(1,4);
Fraction sum = half.plus(quarter);
```

   Add other interesting and useful methods to the class.

4.3 The Role of Aggregation

4.3.1 The Concept of Aggregation

The term *aggregation* describes a structure in which one component, the whole, contains the other components, the parts. In object-oriented programming terms, the contained components are "sub objects" that are encapsulated within an enclosing object. The enclosing (outer, whole) object uses the functionality provided by the sub objects to implement its own behavior. Although the Location class contains only built-in types (two ints), it is more common to find classes that use other classes in addition to built-in types to define their private data. Numerous examples of such classes will be seen in this section.

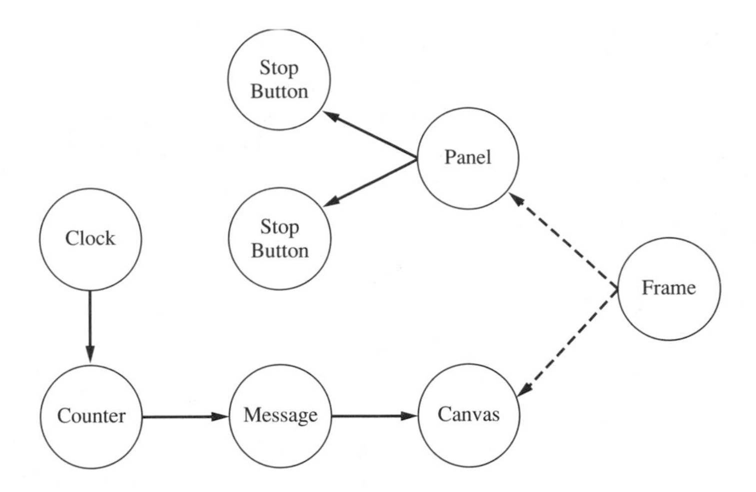

Figure 4.9 Using Association to Build a Stop Watch

Aggregation is related to, but distinct from, *association*. The difference between aggregation and composition is illustrated in the following figures that show the objects making up a *timer system*. As shown in Figure 4.9, creating the timer system by association involves creating the Clock, Counter, Message, Panel, Canvas, and Button objects individually, and using their methods to build up the desired structure of connections among them. In this figure, the solid-line arrows show objects connected by references. The Counter object, for example, maintains a preference to the Message object to which it communicates its current value. The dotted-line arrows in the figure represent the relationship between a Frame object and the user interface components that are displayed in that Frame.

Figure 4.10 shows how the same system would appear when aggregation is used. With aggregation, the basic machinery of the timer system is encapsulated inside another object whose class, StopWatch, will be developed throughout this section. The public interface of the StopWatch class provides methods that allow the timer system to be manipulated as a whole.

A given class, for example the Clock class, may be used in several different aggregations. For example, a different timer system might not need user-control buttons. Such a system, a SimpleTimer, could be built using aggregation, as shown in Figure 4.11. In this aggregation, the timer lacks any control elements. The SimpleTimer aggregation is less functional because it does not provide built-in buttons for allowing the user to control the timer. However, the SimpleTimer might be more reusable because it makes no assumptions about how the control should be provided. The greater reusability of the SimpleTimer is evident in an application where the program, and not the user, is intended to be in control of the timer.

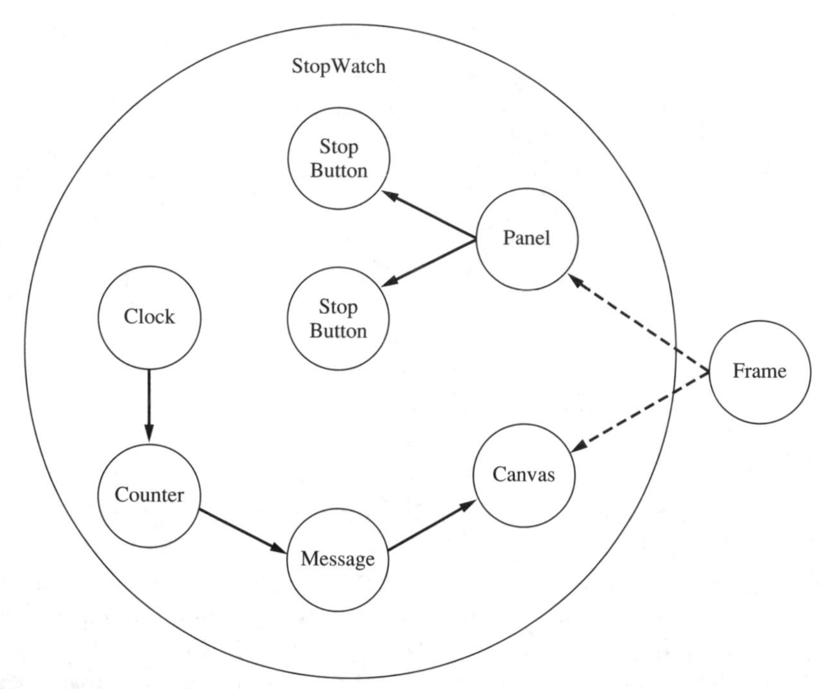

Figure 4.10 Using Aggregation to Build a Stop Watch

Another timer system using aggregation is shown in Figure 4.12. This timer system, the InteralTimer, lacks both control elements and any means of displaying its value in the user interface. The InternalTimer might be used in situations where only a measurement of time is required. For example, if the program maintains the amount of time that the user has been using the application, perhaps for billing purposes, only the very simple services provided by the modest InternalTimer aggregation are required.

Examples of aggregations can also be found in the classes developed for the ecological simulation. A very complex aggregation is pictured in Figure 4.13. This aggregation contains a complete simulation system: the predators and prey are fixed within the aggregation, the birth and death processes are selected and connected to the groups of prey and predators, and the basic simulation step is driven by the Ecology class. An aggregation of this form is useful to encapsulate many of the design decisions about the simulation, allowing a user to specify some high-level parameters (e.g., the number of predators or prey, the size of the simulated environment) and receive some high-level results (e.g., the number of surviving predators and prey after an elapsed simulated time). This aggregation encapsulates so many aspects of the simulation that it gives little latitude to the user in configuring the internal components used by the simulation.

Aggregation can be used to build a more flexible but less complete simulation system, as shown in Figure 4.14. In this aggregation, the individual preda-

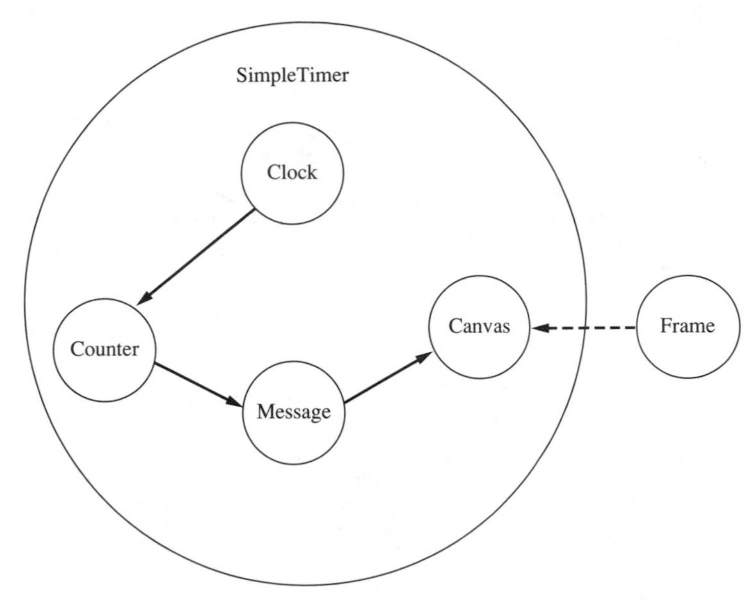

Figure 4.11 SimpleTimer Aggregation

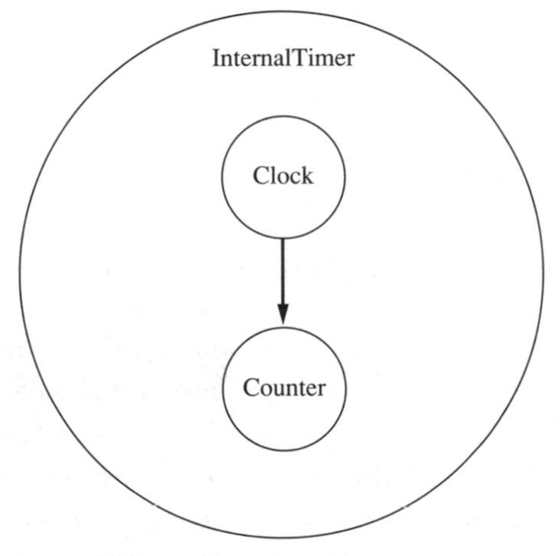

Figure 4.12 InternalTimer Aggregation

tors and prey objects are not fixed. However, the aggregation does provide both the organizational structure to hold predators and prey (a Pack object and a Herd object, respectively) and the objects for the birth and death process to act on these structures. In this system, the user of the aggregation is given both the choice and the responsibility to define and add individual predator and prey objects; once added the aggregation is capable of performing the simulation.

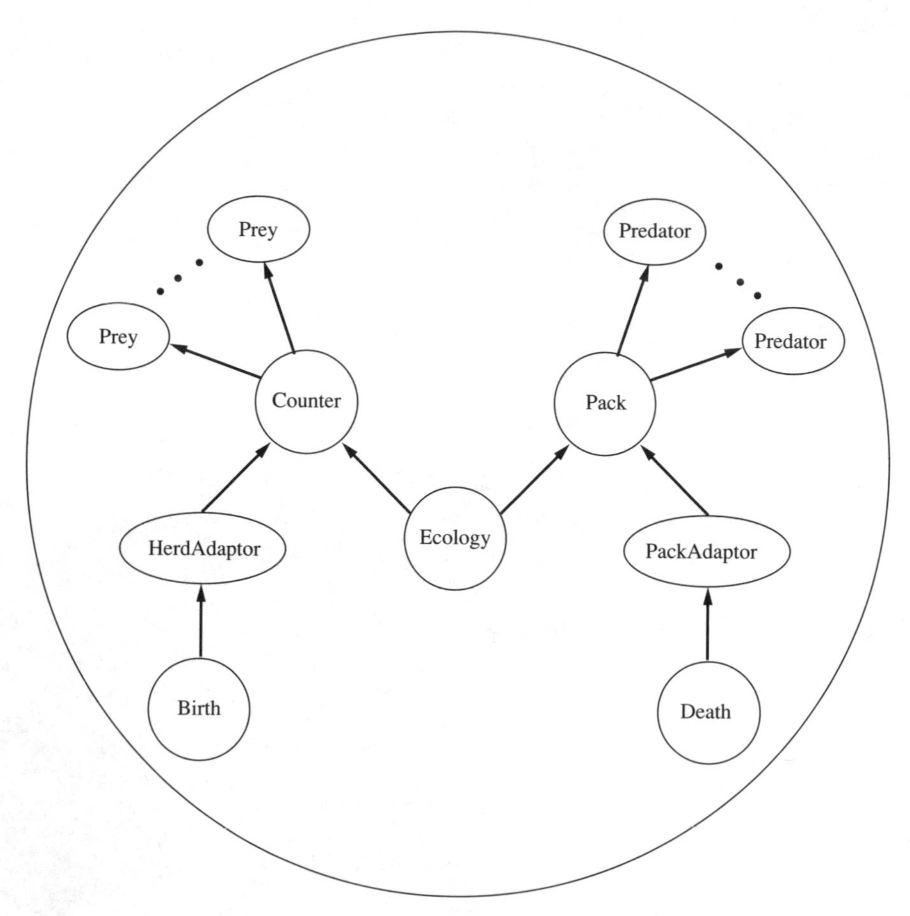

Figure 4.13 A Complete Simulation Aggregation

Thus, the user of this aggregation has more control over the nature of the simulation but must bear more of the work in configuring the components of the simulation. This aggregation illustrates a trade-off between flexibility (greater ability to control) and responsibility (required work not encapsulated in the aggregation) frequently encountered in the design of aggregation structures. Knowing what to reveal and what to encapsulate is often a difficult design choice.

A final aggregation, one that provides a minimal simulation structure is shown in Figure 4.15. In this case, the aggregation encapsulates only the most basic machinery for conducting the simulation; these encapsulated objects would be part of any simulation. The Pack and Herd objects provide a means of holding the predator and prey objects that would be added to the simulation. The Ecology object provides the basic simulation step. The advantage of this aggregation is

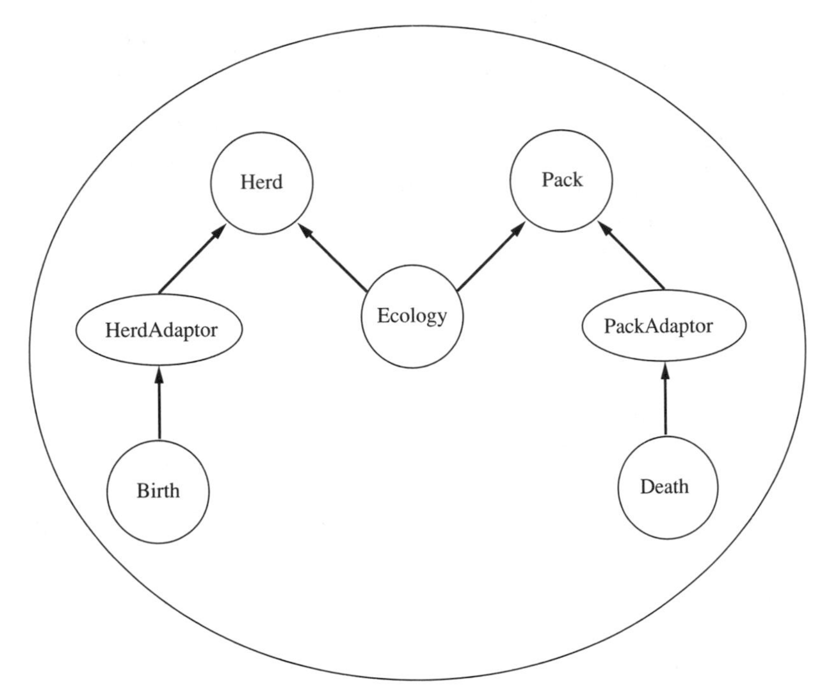

Figure 4.14 Flexibility vs. Responsibility in an Aggregation

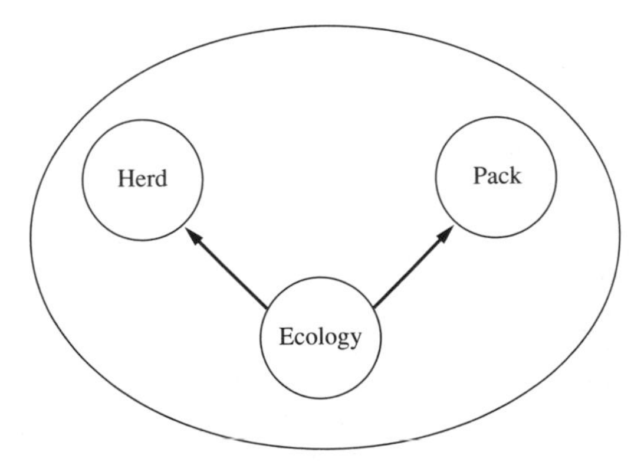

Figure 4.15 An Aggregation with Minimal Structure

that it imposes minimal restrictions on the user of the aggregation but correspondingly invests most of the responsibility for building the simulation on the user. The user of the simulation must define and add all of the predator and prey objects along with any birth and death processes.

A final aggregation, one that provides a minimal simulation structures is shown in Figure 4.15. In this case, the aggregation encapsulates only the most basic machinery for conducting the simulation; these encapsulated objects would be part of any simulation. The Pack and Herd objects provide a means of holding the predator and prey objects that would be added to the simulation. The Ecology object provides the basic simulation step. The advantage of this aggregation is that it imposes minimal restrictions on the user of the aggregation but correspondingly invests most of the responsibility for building the simulation on the user. The user of the simulation must define and add all of the predator and prey objects along with any birth and death processes.

4.3.2 Advantages of Aggregation

Aggregation confers several advantages, most of which flow from the use of encapsulation. These advantages are:

1. **Simplicity:** the aggregating class or object allows the entire assembly of encapsulated sub objects to be referred to as a single unit. This makes it easier to construct and manage multiple, independent instances of the system of sub objects. Imagine, for example, the difference in building a system that has three independent timer systems. Using composition, the code would directly manipulate fifteen different objects (three Clock objects, three Counter objects, three Textbox objects, and six Button objects) in addition to one Frame object. Using aggregation, the code would directly manipulate only three objects (three StopWatch objects) in addition to one Frame object.
2. **Safety:** through encapsulation the sub objects of the timer system are protected from accidental misuse by elements outside the timer system itself.
3. **Specialization:** the public interface of the StopWatch class can provide operations that:
   - **a.** apply to several (or all) of the sub objects as a group. For example, a single method in the StopWatch class can be defined to display the three user interface sub objects (the TextBox and the two Buttons).
   - **b.** are named more meaningfully to distinguish them from the generic name of the sub object's operation. For example, the number of timer intervals that have occurred when the timer has been activated is held in the Counter object. The Counter's internal number can be retrieved by applying the `value` method to the Counter object. However, it may be more meaningful to define an `elapsedTime` method that returns this value (by itself invoking

the Counter's `value` method), as this name more directly conveys the intent of the method.

3. **Structure:** the existence of the encapsulating boundary captures the designer's intent that the components of the timer system are intended to function as a unit. Their organization and relationships are expressed directly in the StopWatch class, which can be studied and understood as a separate entity apart from any specific application.
4. **Substitution:** an alternative implementation of the object defined by aggregation can be substituted without affecting other parts of the system as long as the public interface of the aggregating object remain unchanged.

It is clear from these advantages that developing skill in defining and implementing aggregations is an important goal in becoming a proficient developer of object-oriented systems.

4.3.3 Types of Aggregation

There are two types of aggregation: static aggregation and dynamic aggregation. In static aggregation, the lifetimes of the sub objects are identical to the lifetimes of the containing object. The sub objects are explicitly declared in the class of the containing object, they are constructed when the containing object is constructed, and they are become garbage when the containing object becomes garbage. In dynamic aggregation, at least some of the objects known only to the containing object are created dynamically, via the new operator, at run-time.

An intuitive example that illustrates the difference between static and dynamic aggregations is the contrast between an automobile, which has a fixed number of tires, and a tire store, where tires arrive from the factory and are sold to customers. For the automobile, the number of tires is known in advance. However, for the tire store, the type of its contents (i.e., automobile tires) is known, but the number of tires at any one time is variable and cannot be determined in advance.

Static aggregations are usually simpler, safer, and more efficient for a system to manage and thus should be used whenever possible. However, dynamic aggregations are needed for those equally important cases where the type, but not the number, of sub objects is known at design time. Both forms of aggregation are useful, and a good designer must be able to distinguish between them and use whichever type is appropriate for the problem at hand.

```
import Point;

public class Rectangle
{
  private Points corner[];
  private Point center;
  private Canvas canvas;

  public Rectangle (Location corner, Shape shape)
  public Rectangle (Shape shape, Location corner)
  public Rectangle (Location location)
  public Rectangle (Shape shape)
  public Rectangle ()
  public void drawIn(Canvas canvas)
  public void rotate(int degrees)
  public void moveUp(int pixels)
  public void moveDown(int pixels)
  public void moveRight(int pixels)
  public void moveLeft(int pixels)
  public void moveTo(Location newPlace)
  public void draw()
  public void clear()
}
```

Figure 4.16 Partial Definition of the Rectangle Class

4.4 Simple Static Aggregation

The concept of a static aggregation is illustrated by a class capturing the abstraction of a rectangle that can be rotated about its center point. The Rectangle class will be responsible for rotating the rectangle and drawing itself in a specified canvas. The initial position of a Rectangle object within a Canvas will be defined by a Location object that gives the coordinates of the upper-left-hand corner of the Rectangle. The height and width of the rectangle are defined by a Shape object that is passed as an argument to the Rectangle's constructor. A partial definition of the Rectangle class, and an associated Point class, is shown in Figure 4.16. In addition to the `rotate` method that rotates the rectangle a given number of degrees about its center point, the Rectangle class is also provided with public methods to identify the Canvas on which the rotating rectangle is drawn (`drawIn`), to draw itself on a canvas (`draw`), and to erase itself from a canvas (`clear`).

The Rectangle class maintains its state information to facilitate its drawing operations. First, the `rotate` method involves mathematical operations whose accuracy must be maintained over time to avoid accumulated round-off errors that would distort the shape of the rectangle. Because the Location class only provides integer values, a similar class, the Point class, is introduced that holds double values. The interface of the Point class is shown in Figure 4.17. Second, drawing a rectangle on a Canvas is accomplished by four separate `drawLine`

```
public class Point
{ double x;
  double y;
  public Point(double xcoord, double ycoord)
  public Point(int xcoord, int ycoord)
  public double xCoord()
  public double yCoord()
  public Location asLocation()
}
```

Figure 4.17 The Point Class

operations, each of which requires two Location objects that specify the end-points of the line. To expedite the drawing of the rectangle, each of the four Point objects specifies the coordinates of one of the corners of the rectangle and the Point class provides a method to return a Location object that is the nearest integer-valued coordinates to the real-valued coordinates maintained by the Point object.

The Rectangle class is an example of a static aggregation because of the following properties of the four Point sub objects aggregated in each Rectangle object. First, the sub objects are not visible outside of the class in which they exist because: the sub objects are created as private data within the Rectangle class, there is no method of the class that returns any of these objects and the Point objects are not passed as parameters to other methods. Second, the lifetime of the aggregated sub objects is bounded by that of the aggregating object: the Point sub objects are constructed when the Rectangle object of which they are a part is constructed and they are reclaimed as garbage objects when that Rectangle object is reclaimed.

4.4.1 Aggregation in the Ecological Simulation

Another example of using aggregation to simplify the structure of a complex object is found in the implementation of the Prey class. One of the major responsibilities of the Prey class is computing successive locations for the simulated prey. It makes sense to invest this responsibility in an aggregated sub object because:

- the computation of a new random location within a bounded distance from the current location involves some detailed coding (generating the random numbers, keeping the new location within bounds, etc.) that is useful to separate from the coding of the rest of the Prey class because it improves the readability of the code of the Prey class;
- a number of low-level design decisions are involved with choosing the next location; isolating these decisions from the other decisions made in the Prey class is a better design because it allows the decisions on how the

```
import PreyMove;

public class Prey implements Hunted, Creature
{
  private Herd herd;
  private int roamDistance;
  private Location current;
  private Range territory;
  private boolean alive = true;
  private PreyMove moves;

  public Prey(Location where, Range range, int roam)
  { current = where;
    territory = range;
    roamDistance = roam;
    moves = new PreyMove(territory);
  }

   public void move()
  { if(!alive)return;
    current = moves.next(current, roamDistance);
  }

  //...
}
```

Figure 4.18 An Aggregrated Sub Object in the Prey Class

next location is determined to be changed without impact on the rest of the Prey class; and

- the actions associated with computing the next location are easily separable from the other actions in the Prey class; using an aggregated sub object is an organized way to achieve this separation.

For these reasons, the Prey class contains an aggregated sub object whose existence is completely unknown outside of the Prey class itself.

A portion of the code for the Prey class is shown in Figure 4.18. The private data of the Prey class includes a sub object of the class PreyMove. The PreyMove class assumes the responsibility for computing the next location for the simulated prey. The highlighted lines of code in Figure 4.18 show what the Prey class code does to determine the prey's next location. This amounts to constructing the PreyMove sub object in the Prey class's constructor and calling the `next` method of the PreyMove to compute the next location. Clearly, the simplicity of the Prey class's code confirms the advantage of using the sub object. The implementation of the PreyMove class is discussed in the next subsection.

4.4.2 Shared Sub Objects

It is sometimes, though not often, necessary to create a sub object that is *shared*

```
import java.util.Random;

public class PreyMove
{
  private Location min;
  private Shape    bounds;
  private static long seed = 987654;
  private Random control;

  public      PreyMove(Range range)
  { min     = range.location();
    bounds  = range.shape();
    control = new Random(seed);
    seed    = control.nextInt();
  }

  private int minX()
  { return min.xCoord();
  }

  private int maxX()
  { return min.xCoord() + bounds.width();
  }

  // minY and maxY similar...

  public Location next(Location at, int max)
  {
    int x = at.xCoord() + control.nextInt() % max;
    int y = at.yCoord() + control.nextInt() % max;
    if(x < minX()) x = minX();
    if(x  maxX())  x = maxX();
    if(y < minY()) y = minY();
    if(y  maxY())  y = maxY();
    return new Location(x,y);
  }
}
```

Figure 4.19 A Shared Sub Object in the PreyMove Class

among the objects of a given class. This sharing is in contrast to the usual access to sub objects in which each object has its own distinct, private copy of each sub object. In the Prey class, for example, each Prey object has its own private instance of a PreyMove object, Location object, and so on. In most cases, non-shared sub objects are exactly what is required by the nature of the data. In the Prey class, the Location sub object is not shared because each Prey object has its own current location independent of any other Prey object's current location. A shared subobject is also referred to as a "class variable" because it acts like an attribute of the class rather than a private attribute of each object of that class. The defining characteristic of a class variable is that it is accessible to all objects of the class and any change made to the class variable is seen by all objects of the class.

The PreyMove class, given in Figure 4.19, shows how to declare shared sub objects (class variables) in Java. The highlighted line of code shows the declaration and initialization of a shared sub object (class variable) named `seed` that is a `long` data type. This line includes the additional keyword `static` as part of the declaration. The `static` keyword identifies `seed` as a class variable (shared sub object). Although the PreyMove class only requires a class variable that is of a built-in type (`long`), the same technique can be applied in declaring a class variable of any user-defined class. The `private` keyword in the declaration of the `seed` means that the `seed` can only be accessed by the methods of the PreyMove class.

The PreyMove class must use a shared sub object because of the way in which random numbers are generated. Java provides a class for generating random numbers. This class is imported by the full name java.util.Random. The constructor for the Random class requires a single `long` value that is used to initialize the random number generator. Once initialized, the `nextInt` method may be used to generate the next integer number in the sequence. The numbers generated by the `nextInt` method are "psuedo random" in the sense that they are computed by mathematical steps that guarantee certain properties of randomness. The specific sequence of numbers depends on the initial seed; two random number generators starting with the same seed will produce the same sequence of numbers. The dependence of the number sequence on the seed value is useful for debugging and repeatability of simulation experiments. However, the question arises as to how the seed value can be chosen when multiple random number generators are instantiated. In the PreyMove class, notice that the Random object, named `control`, is initialized by the long value `seed`. If seed were not a class variable, it would have the same value in each PreyMove object, implying that the `control` objects in each PreyMove object would be initialized with the same `seed` and hence generate the same sequence of random numbers. This would not be desirable because the prey in the simulation would appear to move in a coordinated pattern, not in a random manner. Each `control` object must, therefore, be initialized with different `seed`. One way to accomplish this initialization is shown in the PreyMove class using a class variable. As shown in the highlight code in Figure 4.19, the `control` object is initialized with the current `seed` value and the `seed` value is then changed to whatever random number is first generated by that `control` object. Because the `seed` value is a class variable, the next PreyMove object to use the `seed` will find a different value than the previous PreyMove object found. Finally, notice that generating random numbers in a given range is straightforward. As shown in the last highlighted code in Figure 4.19, the integer value returned by `nextInt` can simply be taken modulo the desired range to obtain a number that falls within that range.

Exercises

1. Demonstrate your understanding of static aggregation by defining, implementing, and testing a Circle class that has Point sub object

defining the center of the circle and an integer value defining the radius of the Circle. Your Circle object should be able to draw, erase, and move itself on a Canvas.

2. Demonstrate your understanding of static aggregation by defining, implementing, and testing a Triangle class that has three Point sub objects defining the vertices of the triangle. Your Triangle object should be able to draw, erase, and move itself on a Canvas.

3. Demonstrate your understanding of static aggregation by defining, implementing, and testing a PossumPrey class. The PossumPrey class encapsulates a Prey object and behaves exactly like a Prey object except that the PossumPrey "lies" about whether it is dead or alive in order to avoid being captured by a Predator. The live PossumPrey lies by alternately telling its true state (alive) and a false state (dead) when the `isAlive` method is invoked. A dead PossumPrey always reports that it is dead. Can you implement the PossumPrey class so that one of its objects can be used just like aPrey object in the simulation?

4. Demonstrate your understanding of static aggregation by defining, implementing, and testing a ColonyPrey class. A ColonyPrey encapsulates a Prey object and behaves exactly like a Prey object except that all of the ColonyPrey die when their total number falls below a given threshold. The current total number of ColonyPrey must be maintained as a shared attribute of the ColonyPrey class.

4.5 More Complex Static Aggregation

In this section, two classes are implemented to illustrate more complex aggregations. In these classes the aggregated sub-objects are more functional than those seen in the previous section. Also, the problems of properly constructing these aggregation are more challenging. One class presented in this section is a StopWatch class. The StopWatch class provides a one-second timer that is visible on the user's display that the user can control through simple buttons. The second class presented in this section is a Simulation class. The Simulation class aggregates all of the machinery to conduct a complete execution of the ecological simulation. The user of the class has high-level control over the general parameters of the simulation. Before considering the details of these more elaborate aggregations. We will first describe a general design issue, involving the degree to which the internal sub-objects of the aggregation are implicitly revealed through the aggregation's public interface. This issue is termed "*indirect control.*"

4.5.1 Indirect Control

When developing an aggregation, indirect control refers to the extent to which the object's user is aware of the type or number of aggregated objects and to what extents the detailed organization or operation of these aggregated objects can be affected. Indirect control can be provided either through the constructors or the behavioral methods of the aggregating class. In the StopWatch example, the following indirect control questions arise:

- Where in a window are the control buttons and the time value displayed?
- What is the relative placement of the buttons and the time value in a window? Buttons beside? Buttons below? Buttons above?
- What is the time interval? Is it fixed? User selectable? Set by the program?
- How many digits can appear in the time value?
- What are the names of the buttons as they appear in a window?
- Does the StopWatch object always start at time zero or can it be given an initial value?

The Simulator class also has aspects related to indirect control, among which are the answers to these questions:

- How many predators and prey are present?
- What is the size of the ecological system?
- What are the characteristics of the predators (lifetime, range of movement, etc.)?
- What are the characteristics of the prey (range of movement, speed, etc.)?
- Are birth and death processes involved? If so, how are they related to the predators and prey?
- How long is the simulated time?

As can be seen, these questions touch on the encapsulated sub-objects in the StopWatch class and in the Simulator class.

Ideally, no indirect control over the encapsulated objects should be allowed, but this may not always be reasonable or possible. Beware, though, that providing excessive indirect control over the encapsulated objects begins to weaken the advantages of aggregation. In the extreme case, the aggregating class relinquishes complete control of its sub-objects, becoming little more than a weak wrapper to hold the sub-objects together as a group. The design of a good class must strike a balance between providing sufficient indirect control of the encapsulated objects so that they are usable in different applications yet not so much that the benefits of aggregation are lost.

The designer of an aggregating class has several options for dealing with the issue of sub-object control. First, several similar classes can be designed, each providing a different degree of control. At the expense of creating and naming several classes, this approach allows a spectrum of choices for programmers who may have varying needs for control over the sub-objects. Second, the interface of the aggregating class may use overloaded constructors so that control reverts to the aggregating class itself in those constructor where the initialization for sub-objects is not specified. Although this approach also promises a spectrum of choices, the constructors become more complicated and more difficult to design. Due to the choices offered by the constructors, a user of the aggregating class may find it necessary to assume more control than is desired. Third, one or more auxiliary classes can be defined for specifying the control information. An instance of this auxiliary class is provided as an argument to the aggregating class. The auxiliary class may have a default constructor so that users may assume no indirect control. In the case of the StopWatch class, the arrangement of the user interface components can be collected into a StopWatchLayout class, which would contain all of the placement and labeling information for a StopWatch. The default StopWatchLayout constructor would provide standard (default) values for this information. The constructor for the StopWatch class would have a StopWatchLayout argument whose default value is a StopWatchLayout object constructed by the default constructor of the StopWatchLayout class.

Indirect Control in Constructors

The constructor for a sub-object may be related to the constructor of the aggregating class in one of three ways:

1. Independent: the sub-object constructor is fixed and independent of the arguments of the aggregating class.
2. Direct: the sub-object constructor depends directly on one or more arguments of the aggregating class's constructor.
3. Indirect: the sub-object constructor depends on one or more values computed from the aggregating class's constructor arguments.

These relationships are shown pictorially in Figure 4.20. In the independent case, the sub-object has a fixed constructor that does not depend in anyway on the construction of the aggregating class. Examples of this will be seen in the StopWatch and Simulator classes. In the StopWatch design, the sub-object that maintains the time value is always initialized to zero regardless of any other properties of the StopWatch object being constructed. In the Simulator design the Birth and Death processes are constructed in a fixed manner, independent of the class's constructor arguments.

The direct case is one in which an aggregated sub-object or variable is initialized directly from a constructor argument. This case is illustrated by the Clock sub-object in the StopWatch class. Here, the Clock object's constructor argument, the timer interval, is taken exactly from the StopWatch constructor

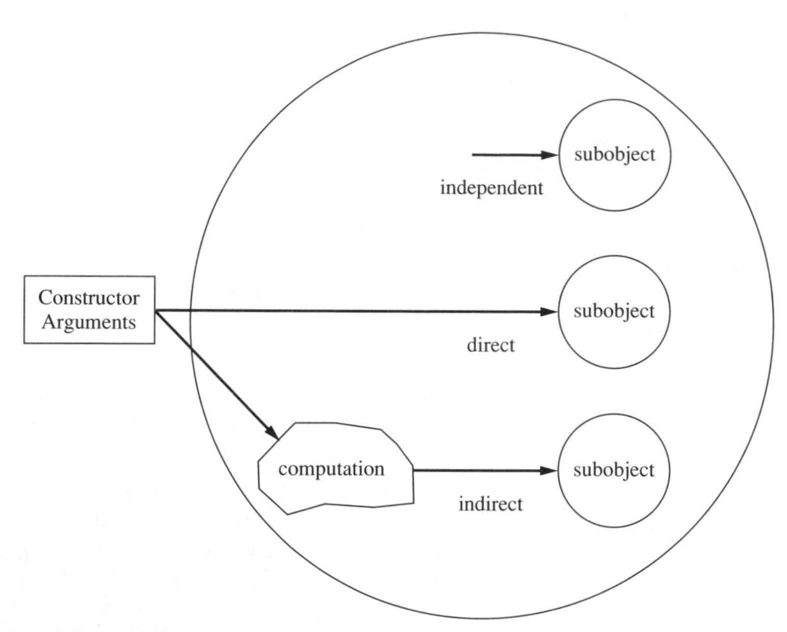

Figure 4.20 Sub-Object Construction

argument; no change is made in this value. In the Simulator class, the number of steps in the simulation is taken directly from a constructor argument.

In the indirect case, a constructor argument partially determines the initialization of the sub-object. This case is illustrated by the construction of the Canvas and Panel sub-objects of the StopWatch. The StopWatch constructor has a single Location argument and these two user interface objects are positioned relative to it. The locations of the Canvas and the Panel sub-objects are determined by offsets from the specified Location argument. In the Simulation class, the initialization of the aggregated Herd and Pack objects are partially dependent on the constructor arguments that specify the number of creatures in group, but not on any other characteristics of these creatures.

4.5.2 Implementing the StopWatch Class

The definition of the StopWatch class is given in Figure 4.21. The public interface provides methods to start and stop the StopWatch from the program, to identify a Frame in which the StopWatch should display its user interface components (Message and Buttons), and a method to redraw itself. Notice that this design makes a number of decisions about the control issues raised earlier. For example, the StopWatch class allows the user to select the time interval and to start and stop the timing. However, the user cannot affect the detailed layout of the StopWatch's components in the user interface nor determine the number of digits in the displayed time value. This is not to suggest that these are the right decisions; they are only reasonable and illustrative ones.

```
public class StopWatch
{
  private Button              startButton;
  private Button              stopButton;
  private Clock               clock;
  private ClockControl        control;
  private Counter             count;
  private Message             message;
  private Canvas              canvas;
  private Panel                panel;
  public StopWatch(Loction at, in interval)
  public void showIn(Frame frame)
  public void start()
  public void stop()
  public void redraw()
}
```

Figure 4.21 Definition of the StopWatch Class

```
public class StopWatch
{
  public void showIn(Frame frame)
  { frame.add(canvas);
    frame.add(panel);
  }

  public void redraw()
  { message.draw();
  }

  public void start()
  { clock.on();
  }

  public void stop()
  { clock.off();
  }

}
```

Figure 4.22 StopWatch Class Implementation

The methods of the StopWatch class can be implemented as shown in Figure 4.22. This code illustrate how the methods of the StopWatch class achieve their effect by manipulating the internal sub-objects. For example, the `showIn` method adds its Canvas and Panel sub-objects to the Frame that is passed as a parameter. The StopWatch `start` and `stop` methods simply calls the `on` and `off` method of the Clock sub-object. Similarly, the `redraw` method simply invokes the `draw` method of the Message sub-object.

The StopWatch constructor has a single Location argument relative to which the user interface components of the StopWatch are positioned. This allows the user of the class a simple, though minimal, way to control the appear-

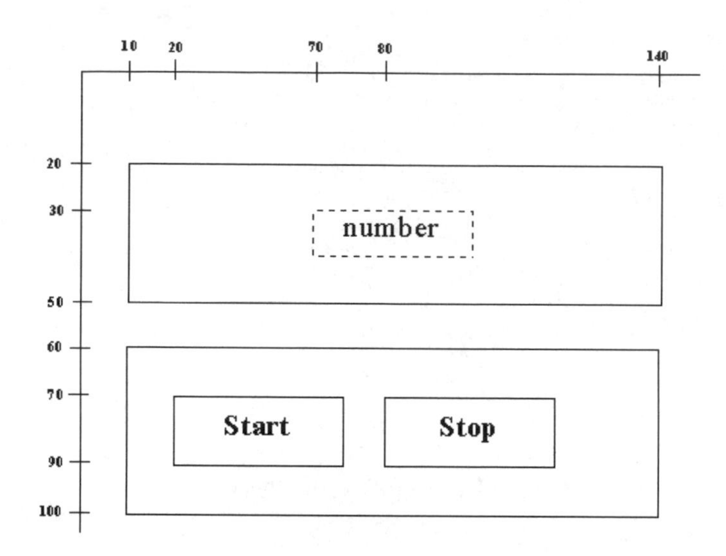

Figure 4.23 Layout of the StopWatch User Interface Sub-Objects

Message:	Location(60,10) in Canvas (shape determined by number of digits)
StartButton:	Location(10,10) in Panel Shape(50,20)
StopButton:	Location(70,10) in Panel Shape(50,20)
Canvas:	Location(at.getX() + 10, at.getY() + 20) in Frame Shape(130, 30)
Panel:	Location(at.getX() + 10, at.getY() + 60) in Frame Shape(130, 40)

Figure 4.24 Location and Shape of User Interface Sub-Objects

ance of the StopWatch object in the user interface. The user is able to control only one aspect of the object's appearance: where the object will appear. The user is not able to control the relative placement of the user interface components nor the total amount of screen space used. It is assumed for the StopWatch class that the user interface subobjects are positioned as shown in Figure 4.23. Of course, many other arrangements of the components or the spacing of the components are possible.

Using the layout picture in Figure 4.23 and the Location given as a constructor argument, the locations of the user interface sub-objects can be determined. The computation of the sub-object locations involves invoking methods

```
public StopWatch(Location at, int interval)
{ count = new Counter();
  message = new Message("0", new Location(70,10));
  startButton = new Button("Start", new Location(10,10),
                              new Shape(50,20));
  stopButton = new Button("Stop", new Location(80,10),
                              new Shape(50,20));
  clock = new Clock(interval);
  control = new ClockControl();
  canvas = new Canvas("Timer Display",
                new Location(at.getX() + 10,
                            at.getY() + 20),
                new Shape(130,30));
  panel = new Panel(new Location(at.getX() + 10, at.getY() + 60),
                new Shape(130,40));
  control.setStartName("Start");
  control.setStopName("Stop");

  count.connectTo(message);
  clock.connectTo(count);
  control.connectTo(clock);
  message.displayIn(canvas);
  panel.add(startButton);
  panel.add(stopButton);
  startButton.addListener(control);
  stopButton.addListener(control);
}
```

Figure 4.25 StopWatch Class Constructor

(`getX` and `getY`) of the StopWatch constructor argument (`where`), performing simple addition, and constructing new (anonymous) Location objects. The computation of the location for each of the user interface components is summarized in Figure 4.24.

By using the layout decisions made above the constructor for the StopWatch class can now be written. The constructor's code is shown in Figure 4.25. In this constructor, the Counter, Message, Button, and ClockControl objects are initialized in an independent way without any dependence on the StopWatch constructor arguments. The Clock object is constructed in a direct way—its constructor argument is directly that of the StopWatch constructor. The other objects, the Canvas objects and the Panel object, are constructed in an indirect way depending on a computation that involves the StopWatch constructor arguments.

4.5.3 Implementing the Simulator Class

The definition of the Simulation class is given in Figure 4.26. Contained in this aggregation are several sub-objects. The Ecology, Herd, Pack, Birth, and Death objects form the principal elements of the simulation. Recall that the Ecology class is associated with a Pack and a Herd upon which it performs the basic simulation step. The Ecology, Herd, and Pack classes are completely invisible outside of the Simulation class; nothing about their existence is conveyed by the

```
public class Simulation
{
  private Ecology ecology;
  private Herd    herd;
  private Pack    pack;
  private Birth   birth;
  private Death   death;
  private int     steps;
  private int     betweenBirths;
  private int     betweenDeaths;
  public Simulation(int numberOfSteps,
                    int numberOfPrey,
                    int numberOfPredators,
                    int stepsBetweenBirths,
                    int stepsBetweenDeaths)

  public void perform()
  public int survivingPrey()
  public int survivingPredators()
}
```

Figure 4.26 Definition of the Simulation Class

value or types of the arguments in the methods of the class. The Birth and Death objects are indirectly mentioned by the constructor arguments that give the number of simulated steps between application of the birth and death processes. The constructor of the class also allows for the specification of the number of steps in the simulation, the initial number of predators, and the initial number of prey. The other methods provide ways to perform the simulation, and to query the number of surviving predators and prey. This class provides an extremely simplified interface to the class's user. Notice that this design makes a number of decisions about the control issues raised earlier. For example, the user has no control over whether the birth and death processes apply to the predators or the prey, this is strictly determined by the programming of the Simulation class. Also, although the number of predators and prey can be given, the class's user has no control over the characteristics of the predators and prey (e.g., their mobility and range).

The non-constructor methods of the Simulation class can be implemented as shown in Figure 4.27. This code illustrates how the methods of the Simulation class achieve their effect by manipulating the internal sub-objects. For example, to determine the number of surviving prey the `survivingPrey` method inquires of the Herd sub-object how many of its members are alive. Similarly, the `survivingPredators` method invokes the `alive` asks the Pack sub object. The `perform` method synchronizes the steps of the simulation. In each step of its loop, one step of the simulation is performed by invoking the `next` method of the Ecology class. Recall that the `next` method moves each predator and prey to their new locations and allows each predator to hunt for nearby prey. The `perform` method also keeps track of when to apply the birth and death processes given the values specified in the constructor. It is not possible to tell from these

```
public class Simulation
{

  private Ecology ecology;
  private Herd    herd;
  private Pack    pack;
  private Birth   birth;
  private Death   death;
  private int     steps;
  private int     betweenBirths;
  private int     betweenDeaths;

  //...

  public void perform()
  { int timeToNextBirth = betweenBirths;
    int timeToNextDeath = betweenDeaths;
    for(int i=0; i<steps; I++)
    { ecology.next();

      if (--timeToNextBirth == 0)
        { birth.generate();
          timeToNextBirth = betweenBirths;
        }

      if (--timeToNextDeath == 0)
        { death.reduce();
          timeToNextDeath = betweenDeaths;
        }
    }
  }

  public int survivingPrey()
  { return herd.alive();
  }

  public int survivingPredators()
  { return pack.alive();
  }
}
```

Figure 4.27 Simulation Class Implementation

methods group of creatures the birth and death processes apply to nor to tell how many predators and prey were initially present. These issues are dealt with in the Simulation class constructor.

The Simulation class's constructor initializes the elements of the simulation as shown in Figure 4.28. The basic infrastructure of the simulation consists of the Ecology, Pack, Herd, Birth, and Death objects that are created and associated, as shown in the first part of the constructor's code. The Ecology, Birth, and Death objects are created independently of any of the constructor arguments. The three assignment statements in middle part of the constructor's code directly initialize variables in the Simulation from the constructor arguments. The two iterations at the end of the constructor completes the initialization of the Pack and Herd objects; these objects are initialized indirectly from the con-

```
public class Simulation
{

  private Ecology ecology;
  private Herd    herd;
  private Pack    pack;
  private Birth   birth;
  private Death   death;

  private int     steps;
  private int     betweenBirths;
  private int     betweenDeaths;

  public Simulation(int numberOfSteps,
                    int numberOfPrey,
                    int numberOfPredators,
                    int stepsBetweenBirths,
                    int stepsBetweenDeaths)
  { herd = new Herd();
    pack = new Pack();
    ecology = new Ecology(pack, herd);
    birth = new Birth (new HerdAdaptor(herd));
    death = new Death (new PackAdaptor(pack));

    steps = numberOfSteps;
    betweenBirths = stepsBetweenBirths;
    betweenDeaths = stepsBetweenDeaths;

    for(int i=0; i<numberOfPrey; i++)
    { herd.add((Hunted)new Prey());
    }
    for(int i=0; i<numberOfPredators; i++)
    { pack.add((Hunter)new Predator());
    }
  }

  //...
}
```

Figure 4.28 Simulation Class Constructor

structor arguments because the constructor arguments specify how many creatures are contained in each.

Exercises

1. Add a label (a Message sub object) to the StopWatch class so that the label appears above the existing Message displaying the numeric value of the StopWatch. Add appropriate constructor arguments to the StopWatch constructor to give a character string for the label.

2. Implement and test the *InternalTimer* class described above.
3. Modify the StopWatch class so that the names of the two Buttons can be given by the StopWatch constructor.
4. Modify the StopWatch class so that the constructor can specify whether the Buttons appear above or below the incrementing value. You will need to redesign and re-implement portions of the constructor to achieve a good solution.
5. Modify the StopWatch class so that the StopWatch contains a TextBox and a Button "Reset" that sets the Clock value to whatever value has been entered by the user in the TextBox prior to pressing the "Reset" Button.
6. Implement and test the *StopWatchLayout* class defined above.
7. Implement and test a modified version of the StopWatch class that allows the layout to be customized by the user without changing the code. This customization should be achieved by reading the layout information from a file when a StopWatch object is constructed.
8. Modify the Simulator class so that the Predator and Prey objects are explicitly added by the user. This will require changes in the existing constructor and the addition of two new methods.
9. Modify the Simulator class so that the user can specify whether or not the birth and death processes should be used.
10. Modify the Simulator class so that the Pack and Herd sub objects are both affected by birth and death processes.
11. Modify the Simulator class so that the user can provide the Birth and Death objects, if any, that apply to the predators and those that apply to the prey.
12. Modify the Simulator class so that an auxiliary class, SimulationParameters, has `get` and `set` methods for each of the parameters of the Simulation. The Simulation constructor takes a single argument, an object of the SimulationParameters class.
13. Modify the Simulator class so that the characteristics of the predator and prey objects are given as constructor arguments.
14. Modify the Simulator class to include query methods that return the number of predators and prey that are not alive.
15. Implement and test a modified version of the Simulation class that allows the simulation to be customized by the user without changing the code. This customization should be achieved by reading the simulation parameters from a file when a Simulation object is constructed.

4.6 Dynamic Aggregation

The distinguishing feature of a dynamic aggregation is that at least some of the objects encapsulated within such an aggregation are dynamically created (via the new operator) at run-time. Dynamic aggregations are needed when the *type* of the encapsulated sub-objects is known when the class is defined but the *number* of such objects is not. At run-time the dynamic aggregation must allocate and manage new sub-objects. The sub-objects in a dynamic aggregation are automatically reclaimed by the garbage collector when the aggregating object is reclaimed.

Two techniques for implementing dynamic aggregations are shown in this section. The first technique uses a linked-list structure to maintain the dynamically allocated sub-objects. As each new sub-object is created it is added to the end of the linked list. A simple linked-list traversal allows access to each of the sub-objects. The second technique uses a utility class in the Java libraries. This utility class, named Vector, provides a storage structure that will expand to contain elements as they are added to it. The Vector internally allocates storage to hold each additional element. Both techniques are presented because they are both valuable. The linked list technique is independent of the language; it can be used equally well in other object-oriented languages. The Vector class is a commonly-used structure in Java applications because of its simplicity. The linked list technique is used to implement a dynamic aggregation for a common user interface component. The Vector technique is used in the implementation of the Herd and Pack classes.

4.6.1 Implementing Dynamic Aggregations Using Linked Lists

An abstraction that must be represented as a dynamic aggregation is a closed polygon-like shape that has an arbitrary number of sides. A class that captures this abstraction, the PolyShape class, is shown in Figure 4.29. This class will allow the vertices of the shape to be defined dynamically at run-time. The class must maintain a list of vertices whose length is not known in advance. When required to draw itself on a canvas, the class is responsible for drawing lines between each successive pair of points, treating the last vertex and the first vertex as adjacent. Thus, if there are n vertices, n lines will be drawn: the first line is drawn from vertex 0 to vertex 1, the second line from vertex 1 to vertex2, and so on, with the last line being drawn from the vertex n-1 to vertex0.

A PolyShape object is constructed with the Location, the `x` and `y` coordinates, of its first vertex. These coordinates are used to initialize the current location of the PolyShape, represented by the state variables `currentX` and `currentY`. The `up`, `down`, `left`, and `right` methods change the current location by the amount of the method's parameter. The name of the method suggests which coordinate of the current location is affected and in what manner. For

```
public class PolyShape
{
  private LocationNode head;
  private LocationNode tail;
  private int currentX;
  private int currentY;
  private int length;
  private Canvas canvas;

  public PolyShape(int x, int y)
  public void up    (int n)
  public void down (int n)
  public void left (int n)
  public void right(int n)
  public void mark()
  public void drawIn(Canvas c)
  public void draw()
}
```

Figure 4.29 PolyShape Class Interface

example, if the current location is (100, 100) then the method `up(10)` changes the y coordinate so that the current location becomes (100, 90), a location "up" in the sense that it is closer to the top of the canvas area. Similarly, the call `right(20)` would change the current location (100, 100) to become (120, 100), a location 20 pixels toward the right edge of the canvas. The implementation of these methods is shown in Figure 4.30. The `mark` method adds the current location to the linked list of Locations maintained by the PolyShape object. The `draw` method draws the PolyShape in the canvas specified by the `drawIn` method. The implementation of these two methods is discussed further below.

A significant issue for the designer of the PolyShape class is how to maintain the ordered list of vertex Locations. Because the number of vertices is unknown (at least unknown at design-time and compile-time), dynamic aggregation based on a linked-list data structure is used. The Location class provides a convenient means to maintain an (x,y) coordinate pair but it does not provide a capability for Location objects to be members of a list. Although the Location class could be changed to add the necessary data and methods to provide a linked-list capability, this approach is not followed. Three reasons argue against modifying the Location class in this way:

1. There is nothing inherent in the abstraction of a Location to suggest that it is a member of a list of Locations. Thus, modifying the Location class would weaken the abstraction on which the class is based.

2. The additional methods and data are costs incurred by all Location objects regardless of whether they are needed. Thus, modifying the Location class lessens the efficiency of Location objects in many situations. In the worst case, applications that do not use a list of Locations receive no benefit from the list mechanisms added to the Location class.

```
public class PolyShape
{
 private int currentX;
 private int currentY;
 // additional instance variables introduced below

 public PolyShape(int x, int y)
  { head = new LocationNode( new Location(x,y));
    tail = head;
    currentX = x;
    currentY = y;
  }

  public void up    (int n)
  { currentY = currentY - n;
  }

  public void down (int n)
  { currentY = currentY + n;
  }

  public void left (int n)
  { currentX = currentX - n;
  }

  public void right(int n)
  { currentX = currentX + n;
  }
```

Figure 4.30 Basic Methods of the PolyShape Class

3. This approach may not always be possible. In some situations, the objects to put on a list are instances of classes that cannot be changed. This occurs when the class is a library class provided by a vendor and the source code is not available to be changed.

Instead of modifying the Location class to add linked-list features, another approach that allows lists of Location objects will be used, one that does not modify the Location class.

The linked-list technique used in the PolyShape class depends on an auxiliary class, the LocationNode class that provides the ability to form a linked list of Location objects. The relationship between a PolyShape object, the LocationNode objects, and the Location objects is shown in Figure 4.31. As illustrated, each LocationNode object contains a reference (`contents`) that identifies the Location object with which the LocationNode is paired. The LocationNode also contains a reference (`next`) that identifies the next LocationNode (if any) in the list of LocationNodes. The two references in each LocationNode provide the abilities to form a list, by using the `next` reference, and to represent a Location object, by using a reference to the associated Location object. As illustrated in the figure and shown in the PolyShape class definition, a PolyShape object maintains two references, `head` and `tail`, that indicate the first and last elements in the linked list of LocationNodes.

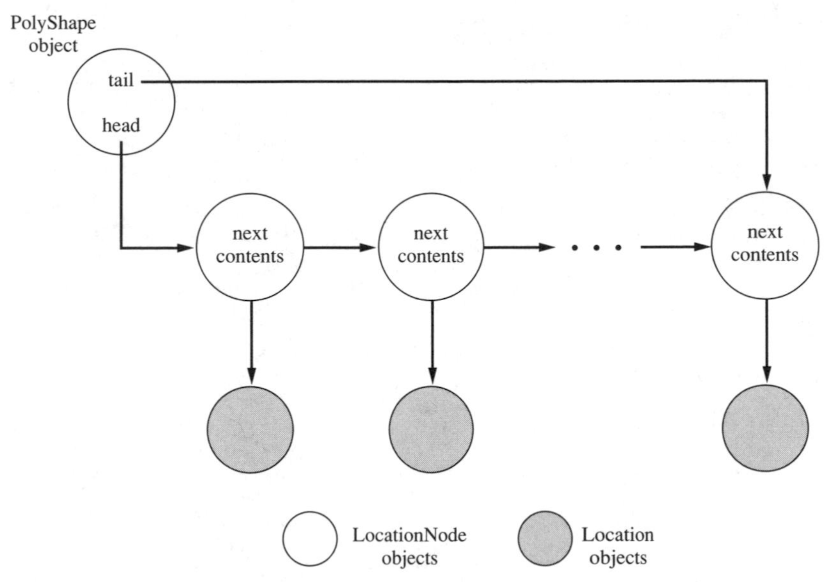

Figure 4.31 Relationships Among PolyShape, LocationNode, and Location Objects

```
public class LocationNode
{
  private LocationNode next;
  private Location location;

  public LocationNode(Location loc)
  { location = loc;
    next = null;
  }

  public void followedBy(LocationNode after)
  { next = after;
  }

  public LocationNode next()
  { return next;
  }

  public Location contents()
  { return location;
  }
}
```

Figure 4.32 LocationNode Class

The code for the LocationNode class is given below in Figure 4.32. Notice that no changes are needed in the Location class in order to implement the LocationNode class. Thus, the three problems noted earlier are avoided by the design of the LocationNode class.

```
public class PolyShape
{
  private LocationNode head;
  private LocationNode tail;
  private int length;
  private Canvas canvas;
  // other instance variable defined above

  public PolyShape(int x, int y)
  { head = new LocationNode( new Location(x,y));
    tail = head;
    length = 1;
    // other constructor action defined above
  }

  public void mark()
  {
    Location newPoint     = new Location(currentX, currentY);
    LocationNode newNode = new LocationNode(newPoint);
    tail.followedBy(newNode);
    tail = newNode;
    length = length + 1;
  }

  public void drawIn(Canvas c)
  { canvas = c;
  }

  public void draw()
  { if (length == 1) return;
    LocationNode node, next;
    node = head;
    for(int i=0; i<length-1; i++)
    { next = node.next();
     canvas.drawLine(node.contents(),
                    next.contents());
      node = next;
    }
  }
   // other methods defined above
}
```

Figure 4.33 Using the LocationNode Class to Implement PolyShape

The `mark` and `draw` methods of the PolyShape class operate on the linked list of LocationNodes as shown in the code below. The `mark` method creates a new Location object using the current location of the PolyShape and creates a new LocationNode object whose contents points to the Location object just created, then adds the just-created LocationNode to the tail of the linked list of LocationNodes. The `draw` method uses the `drawLine` method of the Canvas class to draw a sequence of lines. Each line is drawn between a pair of consecutive Location objects extracted from the linked list of LocationNodes. The code for the `mark` and `draw` methods is shown in Figure 4.33.

4.6.2 Implementing Dynamic Aggregations Using Vectors

A second technique for implementing a dynamic aggregation uses the Vector class. Because the Vector class is specific to programs written in Java, this technique is less general purpose than the linked-list technique presented above, but in Java programs the use of the Vector class is a common way to implement a dynamic collection of objects. A partial description of the Vector class is shown in Figure 4.34. The Vector class maintains a collection of elements of the class Object. In Java, an object of any class can be treated as if it were also an instance of the Object class. More specifically, any object can be type cast to the Object class. The reason behind this ability will not be explained here because it involves the inheritance mechanism that is explained in Chapter 6. Suffice it to know at this point that the type cast is possible. Because any object can be treated as an instance of the Object class, the Vector class is highly reusable. The Vector class maintains an ordered collection of objects. Objects can be added to a Vector in one of two ways: 1) the `addElement` method appends the specified object to the end of the current collection, and 2) the `insertElementAt` method inserts the object into the collection at the specified index position. The lowest numbered index position is zero (0). Similarly, objects can be removed from the Vector in one of two ways: 1) the `removeElement` method removes a specified object from the collection, and 2) the `removeElementAt` method removes the object at a given position in the ordered collection. An object can be retrieved from the Vector using the `elementAt` method to obtain the object as a given position in the ordered collection. The final method shown is the `size` method that returns the number of elements currently in the Vector. The complete Vector class contains other methods for examining or manipulating the objects in the Vector. The methods described here are the most commonly used ones and ones that are sufficient for many uses.

The Herd class uses a Vector object to implement a dynamic aggregation. The Herd class is shown in Figure 4.35. Notice that the import statement specifies java.util. Vector as the name of the class to be imported. This longer name is due to the fact that the Vector class is defined in the "java.util" package. The concept of packages for organizing a group of classes is explain in Section 4.9. The single instance variable in the Herd class is a Vector object named `prey`. The

```
public class Vector
{
  public  Vector()
  public void addElement(Object obj)
  public void insertElementAt(Object obj, int index)
  public Object elementAt(int index)
  public void removeElement(Object obj)
  public void removeElementAt(int index)
  public int size()
}
```

Figure 4.34 The Vector Class

```
import Hunted;
import java.util.Vector;

public class Herd
{
  private Vector prey;

  public Herd()
  { prey = new Vector();
  }

  public void add(Hunted newPrey)
  { prey.addElement((Object)newPrey);
  }

  public Hunted member(int i)
  { if(0<=i && i<prey.size())
          return (Hunted)prey.elementAt(i);
    else return null;
  }

  public void move()
  { for(int i=0; i<prey.size(); i++)
      ((Hunted)prey.elementAt(i)).move();
  }

  public int size()
  { return prey.size();
  }

  public int alive()
  { int alive = 0;
    for(int i=0; i<prey.size(); i++)
     if( ((Hunted)prey.elementAt(i)).isAlive() ) alive = alive + 1;
    return alive;
  }
}
```

Figure 4.35 The Herd Class

Herd class constructor shows how the `prey` object is initialized. The `add` and `move` methods are examined in detail to illustrate the mechanics of using a Vector object. The `add` method in the Herd class adds another prey to its collection. Recall that the Hunted interface was defined so that various kinds of specific prey classes could be defined and manipulated in a uniform way. Thus, the `add` method does not take an object of the Prey class but any object of a class that implements the Hunted interface; the Prey class is one such class. The `add` method's parameter is explicitly type cast to the Object class (recall that any object can be type cast to an Object) when it is used as the parameter of the `addElement` method applied to the `prey` Vector object. Because the ordering of the creatures in the Herd is not relevant, the newly added Hunted object is simply appended to the end of the collection using the `addElement` method. The goal of the Herd's `move` method is to invoke the `move` method of each of the creatures in the Herd; that is, moving the herd is accomplished by moving each member of the herd. The iteration in the `move` method uses the Vector class's `size` method to determine the current number of elements in the prey Vector. For each index position the following statement is executed:

```
((Hunted)prey.elementAt(i)).move();
```

This statement is executed as follows. First, the elementAt method is applied to the prey Vector using the current value of the iteration variable, i, as the parameter; this obtains the next object from the Vector. Second, as indicated by the parenthesis, the object returned by the elementAt method is type cast using the Hunted interface. This type cast is legitimate because only objects conforming to the Hunted interface are added to the prey Vector by the add method. Finally, the move method is applied to the Hunted object. The member and alive methods use similar programming steps to manipulate the contents of the prey Vector. The size method simply returns whatever value is reported by the size method of the prey Vector.

Exercises

1. Use the linked-list technique developed in this section to define and implement a linked list of Message objects without changing the Message class. A partial specification of the MessageList class interface is given below. The draw method should invoke the draw method in each Message object on its list. Similarly for the clear method.

```
public class MessageList
{...
   public MessageList()
   public void add(Message msg)
   public void draw()
   public void clear()
}
```

2. Implement the MessageList class described above using the Vector technique.
3. Rewrite the Herd class by adding a clear method that removes from the Herd all Prey that are not alive.
4. Rewrite the Herd class using the linked-list technique.
5. Rewrite the PolyShape class using the Vector technique.
6. Use the linked-list technique to implement a dynamic aggregation for a BarChart class. The interface of the BarChart class should be similar to the following:

```
public class BarChart
{ public BarChart()
  public void add(int height)                  // height of next bar
  public void setWidth(int width)              // of all bars
  public void draw(Canvas c, Location p) // draw bar chart
}
```

7. Implement the BarChart class using the Vector technique.
8. Use the linked-list technique to implement a dynamic aggregation for a PieChart class. The interface of the PieChart class should be similar to the following:

```
public class PieChart
{ public PieChart()
  public void add(int percent)       // size of next pie segment
  public void setRadius(int radius) // of pie chart
  public void draw(Canvas c, Location p) // draw pie chart
}
```

9. Implement the PieChart class using the Vector technique.
10. Use the linked-list technique to implement a dynamic aggregation for a LineGraph class. The interface of the LineGraph class should be similar to the following:

```
public class LineGraph
{ public LineGraph()
  public void addPoint(float x, float y) // next point on line graph
  public void draw(Canvas c, Location p) // connect the points to draw
                                         // a line graph
}

// The line graph drawing should include a vertical and a horizontal axis.
```

11. Implement the LineGraph class using the Vector technique.

4.7 The "this" Variable

An object may refer to itself within any of its methods by using a special predefined variable named "`this`" whose type is defined to be a reference to an object of the class in which the variable appears. For example, if the `this` variable is used in a method of class X, then its assumed type is "reference to an object of class X." The `this` variable may appear in several classes and in each case it is defined to refer to an object of the class in which it appears. The `this` variable need not, and indeed cannot, be explicitly declared. Its nature is predefined in the Java language and is understood by the compiler. There are several contexts in which the `this` variable is useful: chaining constructors, variable and method reference, an object passing itself as a return result, and an object passing itself as a parameter. Each of these uses is explored in this section.

```
public class Rectangle
{
  public Rectangle (Location at, Shape size) // constructor 1
  public Rectangle (Shape size, Location at) // constructor 2
  public Rectangle (Location at)             // constructor 3
  public Rectangle (Shape size)              // constructor 4
  public Rectangle ()                        // constructor 5
  //... other methods
}
```

Figure 4.36 Overloading Constructors in the Rectangle Class

4.7.1 Chaining Constructors

In some cases, overloaded constructors perform closely related initializations, often the same code with slightly different values. By allowing a constructor to invoke another constructor the duplication of code among similar constructors is avoided. The Rectangle class will be extended with additional constructors to illustrate this situation. The extended Rectangle class is shown in Figure 4.36.

The term "chaining constructors" is used to describe the circumstance where one constructor invokes another constructor. Because constructor are not explicitly invoked, Java provides a special syntax that uses the "`this`" variable to allow one constructor to invoke another constructor. This special syntax can only be used within a constructor and only to invoke another constructor of its own class. The syntax for chaining constructors, as shown in the implementation of the Rectangle class's constructors, uses the `this` variable in an invocation-style syntax to suggest that "`this`" object is being constructed with the arguments provided. The "chaining" effect may involve more than one step. For example, consider what happens when constructor number 4 (see the comments in Figure 4.37 for the number of each constructor) is used to construct a Rectangle object. Constructor number 4 has a Shape object as its only parameter. Constructor number 4 creates an anonymous Location object (`new Location(1,1)`) which, together with the Shape object is used to invoke constructor number 2 using the "`this(...)`" notation. Constructor number 2 simply reorders its parameters and invokes constructor number 1.

4.7.2 Removing Ambiguity

The `this` variable can be used to disambiguate an identifier name that is used both as an instance variable and as a parameter. This situation arises because the programmer chooses to use the same descriptive name for both the instance variable of a class and the parameter that is used to initialize that instance variable. When an instance variable and a parameter have the same name the use of the name in a method is ambiguous because it is not clear which of the two objects is the one being referred to.

```
public class Rectangle
{
  private Point corner[];
  private Point center;
  private Canvas canvas;

  public Rectangle(Location at, Shape size)      // constructor 1
  { corner = new Point[4];
    corner[0] = new Point(at.xCoord() , at.yCoord());
    corner[1] = new Point(at.xCoord() + size.width(), at.yCoord());
    //...
    center    = new Point(at.xCoord() + (size.width()/2),
                          at.yCoord() + (size.height()/2));
    canvas = null;
  }

  public Rectangle(Shape size, Location at)      // constructor 2
  { this(at,size);
  }

  public Rectangle(Location at)                  // constructor 3
  { this(at, new Shape(100,100));
  }

  public Rectangle(Shape size)                   // constructor 4
  { this(size, new Location(1,1));
  }

  public Rectangle()                             // constructor 5
  { this(new Location(1,1), new Shape(100,100));
  }

  //...other methods
}
```

Figure 4.37 Chaining Constructors in the Rectangle Class

An example of this situation is shown in Figure 4.38 where the same name is used for the instance variable that denotes the Canvas where a Rectangle should be drawn and the parameter of the `drawIn` method that is used to initialize the instance variable. The assignment statement `canvas=canvas` is clearly ambiguous. Although the programmer clearly intends that the identifier `canvas` on the right-hand side of the assignment refer to the parameter and the identifier `canvas` on the left-hand side of the assignment refer to the instance variable, there are situations where the opposite interpretation is desired. Therefore, the compiler treats this as an error.

The ambiguity can be removed by using the `this` variable to identify which names refer to instance variables, as shown in Figure 4.39. In this case, the expression `this.canvas` names the instance variable whereas the simple identifier `canvas` is taken to mean the parameter object. This interpretation is sensible because an expression that begins "`this.`" refers to a private or public element of the current object such as an instance variable but does not refer to

```
public class Rectangle
{
  private Canvas canvas; // canvas where Rectangle should be drawn

  // ...

  public void drawIn(Canvas canvas)
  { canvas = canvas;       // WRONG - ambiguous
  }

  // ...
}
```

Figure 4.38 Ambiguous Identifier Names

```
public class Rectangle
{
  private Canvas canvas; // canvas where Rectangle should be drawn

  // ...

  public void drawIn(Canvas canvas)
  { this.canvas = canvas;      // OK - not ambiguous
  }

  //...

}
```

Figure 4.39 Using "`this`" to Remove Ambiguity

parameters that are not public or private elements of the object. As a matter of style, some programmers use the "`this.`" notation even when it is not strictly required to emphasize that the variable or method being named is an element of the current object.

4.7.3 Returning "`this`" as a Result

In some cases, an object may want to return itself as the result of one of its own methods. The PolyShape class will be used to illustrate why an object may be designed to return itself as the result of one of its own methods. The code in Figure 4.40 shows a typical use of the PolyShape class to draw a polygonal shape. Notice that sequences of statements are needed to perform each operation one at a time.Instead of using sequences of statements, it might be desirable to provide an interface so that related operations can be strung together. This clearly makes the use of the class's methods more natural and readable. The PolyShape class can be redesigned to allow the code above to be written as shown in Figure 4.41. Although expressions such as `quad.left(20).mark()`may seem strange at first, they are no more unusual than arithmetic expressions like "a + b - c." In each case, the sub-expression yields a result (an object) that is the subject of the next operation to be performed.

```
PolyShape quad = new PolyShape(20,20);

...

quad.right(100);
quad.down(50);
quad.mark()
quad.left(20)
quad.mark();
quad.down(30);
quad.left(50);
quad.mark();
quad.draw();
```

Figure 4.40 Using the PolyShape Class

```
import PolyShape2;

PolyShape2 quad = new PolyShape2(20,20);

...

quad.right(100).down(50).mark();
quad.left(20).mark();
quad.down(30).left(50).mark();
quad.draw();
```

Figure 4.41 Revising the Polyshape Class to Allow a Sequence of Method Calls

The existing definition of the PolyShape class will not allow its methods to be applied in sequence in one expression. The methods `up`, `down`, `right`, and `left` all return `void` as a result. Thus, an expression like

```
quad.left(20).mark();
```

cannot be done because the result of `quad.left(20)` would be `void` and the subsequent invocation would be the illegal and meaningless expression `void.mark()`. What is needed is a way for each of the operations `up`, `down`, `left`, and `right` to return as a result the same object on which they themselves operated. This involves changes in both the definition and implementation of the PolyShape class. These changes are shown in the code in Figure 4.42.

The methods being changed return a result of type PolyShape. The role of the `this` variable is seen in the code for the revised `up` method. After changing the state variables of the object, the code must be able to indicate that the return value is the same PolyShape object as that which the current method is operating upon. The `this` pointer can be used for this purpose. The `left`, `right`, `down`, and `mark` methods are similar in their use of the `this` variable.

The expression:

```
quad.left(20).mark();
```

where `quad` is assumed to be a PolyShape object, is now interpreted as follows. The expression is evaluated left-to-right. The sub-expression `quad.left(20)`

```
public class PolyShape
{ private ... // same as before

  public PolyShape up(int n)
  { currentY = currentY - n;
    return this;
  }

  public PolyShape down(int n)
  { currentY = currentY + n;
    return this;
  }

  public PolyShape left(int n){...}
  public PolyShape rightint n) {...}
  public PolyShape mark(){...}
}
```

Figure 4.42 Using the "*this*" Pointer in the Polyshape Class

returns a modified PolyShape object on which the second sub-expression performs `mark()` operation. Another way of viewing the effect of this sequence of operations is as follows:

```
PolyShape temp = quad.left(20);
temp.mark();
```

where the sequence has been divided into two statements and a temporary variable used to refer to the PolyShape object. Both the single sequence and the two statements have the same effect on the PolyShape object.

4.7.4 Passing the "`this`" Variable as a Parameter: Callbacks

An object may use its **`this`** variable to pass itself as a parameter to another object's method. The receiving object often uses the parameter to establish an association with the invoking object (i.e., the object passing its **`this`** variable) so that it can invoke one of the methods of the invoking object at a later point in time. Such an arrangement is called a "callback" because the receiving object "calls back" to the invoking object to inform it of some event or action that has occurred in the receiving object.

A pop-up window is used to illustrate how an object passes itself as a parameter to create a callback arrangement. The pop-up window consists of two parts whose relationship is shown in the diagram in Figure 4.43. The first part is the visible window that contains a button for the user to press when the window should be dismissed. The second part is the PopupWindow object that creates the visible window, listens for the dismiss button to be pressed, and—when the button is pressed—disposes of the window. Because it listens for the button to be pressed, the PopupWindow class implements the ButtonListener interface. As shown in the diagram, the PopupWindow object must register itself as a listener with the Button object that is in the visible window.

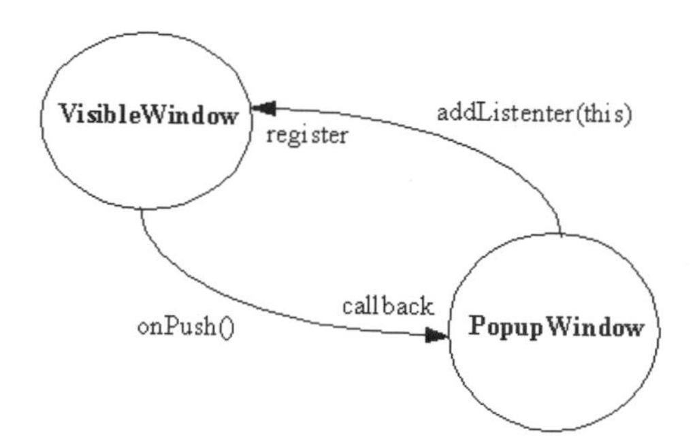

Figure 4.43 A Callback Relationship

```
public class PopupWindow implements ButtonListener
{
  private Frame window;
  private String text;
  private Canvas canvas;

  public PopupWindow(String txt)
  { text = txt;
  }

  public void show(Location at)
  { window         = new Frame("Information",  at,...);
    canvas         = new Canvas(...);
    Panel panel    = new Panel(...);
    Button dismiss = new Button("Dismiss", ...);

    dismiss.addListener(this); // adds itself as a listener
    panel.add(dismiss);
    window.add(panel);
    window.add(canvas);
    canvas.drawText(text, new Location(20,50));
  }

  public void onPush(String buttonName)
  { window.dispose();
  }

  public void redraw()
  { canvas.drawText(text, new Location(20,50));
  }
}
```

Figure 4.44 The Popup Window Class

The key parts of the PopupWindow class are shown in Figure 4.44. The constructor takes a string argument that is drawn in the visible window. The `show` method's argument is a Location specifying where the visible window will be placed on the user's display. The show method creates and organizes the window, including the objects that are needed to draw a string (a Canvas object) and present a Button (a Panel object). The line of code in bold uses the `this` variable to add the PopupWindow object as a listener of the Button object that appears in the visible window. The PopupWindow object implements the ButtonListener interface, and its `onPush` method disposes of the visible window.

Exercises

1. Revise the Prey class using chaining of constructors to eliminate duplicate code in the constructors.
2. Revise the Predator class using chaining of constructors to eliminate duplicate code in the constructors.
3. Revise the Prey class so that its move method can be used as follows:

```
Prey prey = new Prey(...);
prey.move().move();
```

4. Revise the Predator class so that its move and hunt methods can be use as follows:

```
Predator predator = new Predator(...);
predator.move().move().hunt(prey).move();
```

5. Implement a Number class that provides operations for simple integer operations that can be used as follows:

```
Number num(10);          // initially 10
num.plus(5).minus(3).minus(20).times(4).divide(-4);
```

6. Revise the relationship between the Herd and Prey classes by changing the implementation the `join` method in the Prey class and the `add` method in the Herd class as follows. The `join` method should add the current Prey object to the Herd that it is joining. The `add` method should be sure that the same Prey object is not already a member of the Herd.
7. Revise the relationship between the Pack and Predator classes by changing the implementation the `join` method in the Predator class and the `add` method in the Pack class as follows. The `join` method should add the current Predator object to the Pack which it is joining. The `add` method should be sure that the same Predator object is not already a member of the Pack.

4.8 Copying Mutable Objects

4.8.1 Mutable Objects

Mutable objects have methods allowing the object's state to be changed after the object has been constructed. Methods that change the object's state are called mutator methods. A Color object is a mutable object because its set and change methods (e.g., `setRed`, `addRed`) change the color represented by the object, as shown in the following code segment:

```
Color original = new Color(100,0,0); // sightly red
// ...
original.addRed(100);                 // now much more red
```

The `original` Color object is constructed with red intensity of 100. The red intensity is increased by the `addRed` method.

An immutable object does not have mutator methods; once an immutable-object is constructed, its state cannot be altered. Variables that refer to immutable objects change their values by changing what object the variable refers to. For example, objects of the Location class are immutable because the Location class has no mutator methods. Aside from its constructor, the Location class has only inspector or accessor methods that leave the state of the object unchanged. For example, consider the following code segment:

```
Location where = new Location(10,10);
Location different = new Location(20,20);
// ...
where = new Location(30,30); // changes value of where, or
where = different;           // changes value of where
```

Because it is not possible to change the state of an existing Location object, the value of the variable `where` can only be changed by changing the object to which it refers by creating a new object for this pupose or by using another existing Location object. If the previous object to which `where` referred is no longer referenced it will be reclaimed by the garbage collector.

Sharing mutable objects among different components must be done carefully because of the possibility that the mutable object might be changed by one of the components without proper agreement or coordination with the other components. An example is given below that illustrates the problems that can arise from shared mutable objects.

The Problem

A ColoredRectangle captures the abstraction of a rectangle whose interior is drawn with a specified color. The definition of the ColoredRectangle class is shown in Figure 4.45. The constructor specifies the Location of the upper left-hand corner of the rectangular area, its dimensions, and an initial color. The

```
public class ColoredRectangle
{
  private Location corner;        // upper left-hand corner
  private Shape    size;          // width and height
  private Color    currentColor;  // color inside rectangle
  private Canvas   canvas;        // where to draw

  public ColoredRectangle(Location where, Shape shape, Color initialColor)
  { corner = where;
    size   = shape;
    currentColor = initialColor;
    canvas = null;
  }

  public void drawIn(Canvas c)
  { canvas = c;
  }

  public void draw()
  { if (canvas == null) return;
    canvas.setColor(currentColor);
    canvas.drawFilledRectangle(corner, size);
  }

  public void changeRed(int amount)
  { currentColor.addRed(amount);
  }

  // ... other change color methods

  public void moveTo(Location newCorner)
  { corner = newCorner;
  }
}
```

Figure 4.45 The ColoredRectangle Class

`drawIn` method associates the rectangle with the Canvas in which the rectangle will draw itself. A set of methods allow the rectangle's color to be altered (see the `changeRed` method shown below) whereas the `moveTo` method allows the position of the rectangle to be changed.

A small program that uses the ColoredRectangle class is shown in Figure 4.46. This program creates two ColoredRectangles that are drawn side-by-side in the same Canvas. Successive mouse clicks in the Canvas area should cause one of the ColoredRectangles to change its color from red (its initial color) to blue. This behavior is reasonably expected because the `addRed` method is applied only to one of the rectangles. However, the MutableObjectTest program does not behave as expected. When the user clicks in the Canvas area, *both* rectangles change their color. Although this unexpected behavior is not desired, its cause, and remedy are not readily apparent.

The MutableObjectTest program fails to behave as expected because the ColoredRectangle objects inadvertently share a mutable object. The object refer-

```
public class MutableObjectTest implements Program
{
  private Frame window;
  private Canvas canvas;
  private ColoredRectangle rectangle1, rectangle2;

  public MutableObjectTest()
  {window = new Frame(...);
   canvas = new Canvas(...);
  }

  public void onStart()
  { window.add(canvas);
    canvas.clear();
    Color initialColor = new Color(255,0,0);
    Shape rectShape = new Shape(100,100);
    rectangle1 = new ColoredRectangle( new Location(20,20),
                                       rectShape, initialColor);
    rectangle2 = new ColoredRectangle( new Location(200,20),
                                       rectShape, initialColor);
    rectangle1.drawIn(canvas);
    rectangle2.drawIn(canvas);
    rectangle1.draw();
    rectangle2.draw();
  }

  public void onPaint()
  { canvas.clear();
    rectangle1.draw();
    rectangle2.draw();
  }

  public void onMouseEvent(String canvasName, int x, int y, int eventType)
  { if(eventType == Canvas.MOUSE_DOWN)
    { rectangle1.addRed(-10);
      rectangle1.addBlue(+10);
      onPaint();
    }
  }
}
```

Figure 4.46 Using the ColoredRectangle Class

enced by the variable `initialColor` is passed as a parameter to the two ColoredRectangle objects, each of which keeps a reference to that object. When one of the ColoredRectangle objects changes its color by using the mutator methods of the Color object, the color of the other ColoredRectangle object is also changed because they each have a reference to the *same* Color object. In other words, each ColoredRectangle object is treating its Color object as an aggregated sub object, whereas the Color object is actually associated with both ColoredRectangle objects.

The sharing of a mutable object can be resolved by copying the object. The copy can be made by the invoking component—in which case a different copy is passed as a parameter, or the copy can be made by the component receiving the parameter. It does not matter which of these two strategies is adopted; what is important is that all of the objects make the same assumptions about which strategy is in force. As the example program demonstrates, erroneous behavior can result when some components treat an object as an aggregated subobject and other components treat the same object as part of an association.

Copying Objects

An object can be copied in one of two ways: through a special constructor called a copy constructor or through a special method that returns copy of the object to which it is applied. Both of these techniques will be illustrated and then the circumstances under which one may be preferred are described.

A class's copy constructor defines how instances of the class are copied. A copy constructor uses an existing object's attributes (data, state, instance variables) to initialize the new object being created. A copy constructor has a distinguishing signature, and like all other constructors cannot be called explicitly, but only implicitly as a result of a new object being created. A copy constructor for the Color class can be defined as shown in Figure 4.47. The copy constructor has a single argument: a reference to an object of the same class (i.e., the Color class in this case) that is not changed as a result of the copying. In the case of the Color class, the copy constructor simply assigns to the instance variables of the new object the values of the corresponding instance variables of the exist in gobject. Because *encapsulation is a class property*, it does not violate the principle of encapsulation for the copy constructor to access the instance variables of the object being copied.

The copy constructor is used as shown in the following code segment:

```
Color red = new Color(255,0,0);
//...
Color redCopy = new Color(red);
```

where a new Color object (`redCopy`) is created based on an existing Color object (`red`).

An alternative technique for copying an object uses a non-constructor method that takes no arguments and returns a copy of the object executing the

```
public class Color
{
   private int red;
   private int green;
   private int blue;
   public Color(Color other)     // copy constructor
   { red   = other.red;
     blue  = other.blue;
     green = other.green;
   }
   //... other methods
 }
```

Figure 4.47 Copy Constructor for the Color Class

```
public class Color
{
   private int red;
   private int green;
   private int blue;
   public Color makeClone()     // clones the current object
   {
        return new Color(red, green blue);
   }
   //... other methods
}
```

Figure 4.48 Using a Clone Method to Copy an Object

```
public abstract interface Cloneable
{
  public Cloneable clone();
}

public class Checkpoint
{
  private Cloneable saved;

  public Checkpoint()
  { clone = null;
  }

  public void save(Cloneable object)
  { saved = object.clone();
  }

  public Cloneable restore()
  { return saved;
  }
}
```

Figure 4.49 Cloning and Object through an Interface

method. Figure 4.48 shows a method that returns a clone of a Colorobject using the `makeClone` method. The `makeClone` method uses an existing constructor and the instance variables of the existing object to create the cloned object.

The cloning technique is used as shown in the following code segment:

```
Color red = new Color(255,0,0);
//...
Color redClone = red.clone();
```

where the existing Color object creates a duplicate of itself that it returns as a result of the `makeClone` method.

Although the choice between using a copy constructor and a cloning method is often a matter of style, one circumstance where the cloning technique is required occurs when an object is known by an interface that it implements rather than by its class. The Checkpoint class defined in Figure 4.49 illustrates this situation. The Checkpoint class is designed to save and restore a copy of an object that is defined by the Clonable interface. The Checkpoint class is very general purpose; it will work for objects of any class that implements the Clonable interface. The Checkpoint class itself has no knowledge of the actual class of the object that it saves and restores, it simply knows that the object has a clone method by which the Checkpoint class can make a copy of the object. Because the Checkpoint class does not know the actual class of the objects that it copies, it cannot create the copies by means of a constructor because the constructor's name is tied to knowledge of a specific class. In this case, only a clone method will work.

Exercises

1. Add a copy constructor to the Shape class. Test your code with a simple main program.

2. Add a copy constructor to the Location class. Test your code with a simple main program.

3. Add a copy constructor to the PolyShape class defined in Section 4.6. Test your code with a simple main program.

4. Add a clone method to the Shape class. Test your code with a simple main program.

5. Add a clone method to the Location class. Test your code with a simple main program.

6. Add a clone method to the PolyShape class defined in Section 4.6. Test your code with a simple main program.

7. Examine the Predator and Prey classes. Which form of copying is implemented in these two classes?

8. Examine the StopWatch class implementation given in Section 4.5. Describe how you would make a copy of a StopWatch object.

9. There are two terms that describe different ways of copying an object: a deep copy makes a duplicate of the object and all of the object's aggregated objects; a shallow copy makes a duplicate of the object but not of the object's aggregated objects. Consider the Herd class. Under what circumstances would it be preferable to perform a deep copy and under what circumstances would it be preferable to perform a shallow copy.

CHAPTER 5

Producing an Object-Oriented System

5.1 Introduction

Developing a complete object-oriented system involves more than simply writing the code for individual classes. Four major considerations beyond the implementation of a class are:

1. **Design:** developing strategies, skills, and intuitions for discovering good abstractions that lead to good classes.
2. **Debugging:** systematic strategies for identifying the source of errors in the code that are revealed by executing the system in a test environment.
3. **Packaging:** organizing groups of related classes together so that they can be distributed and reused as a unit more easily and conveniently.
4. **Documentation:** providing several levels of natural language description to aid a reusing developer in understanding whether and how to make use of the classes that have been designed, implemented, debugged, and packaged.

These four issues are, of course, interrelated. A well-conceived design is usually one that can be debugged more easily, packaged more effectively, and documented more clearly. Correspondingly, a weak design is usually one that is troublesome to debug, is not as readily packaged in cohesive units, and is harder to explain through documentation. In debugging a system, its design or packaging structure may help to provide boundaries that limit the scope of the debugging activity. Good documentation may also give information that is useful to the debugging process.

This chapter presents strategies for design and debugging, introduces the Java language structure for packaging together related classes into a single manageable unit, and describes the documentation facility that is part of the standard Java development kit. Readers should recognize, however, that the material presented here is the bare beginning. The design and debugging strategies must be applied, not merely studied, to develop the skill in these tasks. Also, developers must be proficient users of tools that automate the mechanical aspects of producing and debugging a system, especially as the size and complexity of the system increases. Familiarity with tools that automate the (re)compilation of changed classes and other classes affected by these changes is critical to being an efficient and effective developer. Similarly, debugging tools yield information about the system during execution without the need for any preprogramming. These tools make it easier for the developer to examine the state of the executing system and control the system's execution during the debugging task. The developer does not need to insert and later remove code specifically added to obtain this information and control. There are numerous tool sets and integrated development environments for Java that embody these tools. The systems are numerous enough and diverse enough that they are not discussed here; only the common strategies and language features are treated.

5.2 Designing a Class

The ability to design a class is fundamental to developing good object-oriented systems because the class is the basic programming unit. A good designer is one who can generate ideas for possible classes from a problem description and shape these ideas into a concrete class. Knowledge of good class design is represented in the form of heuristic rules for *discovering* a class design and guidelines for *evaluating* a class design. The heuristics rules suggest things to look for in a specification that might indicate a possible class. These rules have arisen from the accumulated experience of designers. However, designers must remember that heuristic rules do not guarantee a successful design, they may not apply in all cases, and they indicate only a starting point for further work. The guidelines are qualitative measures for evaluating a design. These can be viewed as a checklist of features that a good design should possess. The designer must make an assessment of whether or not the class possesses each feature. Because the measures are qualitative, good judgement on the part of the designer is important in applying these measures.

The heuristic rules and qualitative measures are used together in an iterative manner. It is not uncommon that a rule can suggest the beginning of a good class design—the rule triggers some thought in the mind of the designer that, though it usually lacks the detail of a complete class design, yields the qualitative measures that can be applied to assess the emerging design as it is developed. The measures can also help in making decisions about which design of

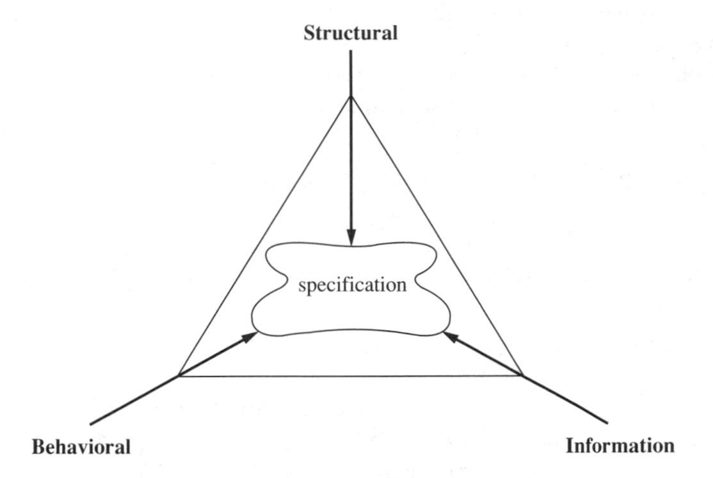

Figure 5.1 Three Perspectives on Class Design

several alternatives is most appropriate. The measures may suggest continuing with the design, backtracking and considering other alternatives, or even eliminating the idea from further consideration.

5.2.1 Discovering Class Design

Ideas for classes can be generated by considering the system specification from different perspectives. As shown in Figure 5.1, three different perspectives are:

1. *behavioral perspective*, emphasizing the actions of a system;
2. *structural perspective*, emphasizing relationships among components; and
3. *information perspective*, emphasizing the role of information and its manipulation.

Each perspective inspires ideas for possible classes by suggesting general categories of entities to look for in the specification, posing certain kinds of questions that might be asked about the system, and focusing on a particular dimension of the overall system to concentrate the designer's thinking. The *combination* of these three perspectives is a large category of commonly encountered classes.

***Behavioral Perspective*:** The behavioral perspective centers on the actions that a system takes. The analysis of actions is a natural starting point because systems are often described in terms of what the system does. In a similar sense, software is developed to accomplish some end and is purchased because of what

What object initiates the action?
What objects collaborate in performing the action?
What objects are altered by the performance of the action?
What objects are interrogated during the action?

Figure 5.2 Behavioral Perspective Questions

it can do. Terms such as "accomplish" and "do" illustrate the fundamental role of a system's activity.

The purpose of identifying an action is to reveal the object that performs the action. In the object-oriented view of software an action is performed by the method(s) of some object(s). Simple actions might be performed by a single object. More complex actions might require the collaboration of several objects. In each case, the actions emanate from one or more objects. Natural questions to ask about each action are given in Figure 5.2; the answers to these questions begin to reveal the components and organization of the underlying object structure.

The study of a system's actions often leads to objects that fall into well-known general categories. General categories of objects that are often associated with actions are: *actor, reactor, agent,* and *transformer.*

An "actor" has a specific purpose, mission, agenda, goal, outcome, or plan. An actor knows what result a part of the system is meant to achieve and it is equipped with the programming to drive the system toward this result. An actor object may embody knowledge about, and enforce the sequencing of, activities that must occur; it may contain strategies for evaluating and selecting among different ways to achieve the result; and it may have ways of coping with exceptional conditions by recovery, back tracing, or graceful termination.

A "reactor" responds to events that are characterized by the fact that they are asynchronous and cannot be scheduled in advance, such as in an interactive drawing program, where the user may be allowed to select a shape on the screen by clicking a mouse button at any time. Events may originate from a variety of sources, three categories of which are:

1. **Internal events:** events generated by other objects within the system itself. For example, a timer object may generate an event that signals the end of a prescribed time interval. The reactor object must determine what should occur at this time and initiate the corresponding action. A specific situation is an animation sequence in which the reactor must arrange for the next step in the animation to occur.
2. **External events:** events originating in another system. A toolkit, for instance, may have several interacting programs that share data. When one of the programs updates the data, the other programs must

react accordingly. A specific case of this is a spreadsheet program that creates the data for a table appearing in a document-formatting program. When the spreadsheet recomputes new values for the table, the formatting system must update its document in response.

3. **Interface events:** events initiated by the user through mouse movements (dragging, clicking), keyboard actions (pressing or releasing keys), or interactive user-interface components (buttons, sliders). The system may contain different reactor objects for these different types of user events.

Regardless of the event's source, the reactor object must determine the appropriate reaction and initiate the response. Some reactor objects maintain a state or history of past events, and their reaction to the current event is conditioned by this history. For example, a mouse-event reactor that needs to distinguish between a single click and a double click needs to keep track of information about the recent past. Other reactor objects are stateless and always have the same reaction. For example, a "centertext" button always reacts in exactly the same way, whatever the data.

In the third category of objects associated with actions is an "agent" which is an intermediary that assists other objects in some way. The purpose of the agent is twofold: first, to relieve the other objects of the responsibility for performing the service that the agent provides; second, to conceal or hide the details of how the agent performs its service. Agent objects promote reuse because they can be used in any system where their service is needed. Agent objects improve the reliability and flexibility of a system through information hiding because no other part of the system is aware of how the agent's service is implemented. An agent may play one of several roles:

1. **Messenger:** this type of agents provides a data-delivery service through which one part of the system can relay information to other parts of the system. Like postal systems and package delivery companies, the messenger relieves the sender of the responsibility of locating the recipient, arranging for the transportation, tracking the progress of the item, and arranging the delivery. Distributed mail systems, for example, depend on message agents.
2. **Server:** this type of agent is essential to the client-server model; commonly servers are used as producers or consumers of data. The server relieves its clients of the burden of knowing where and how the data is stored. Servers may obtain the data from local tables, disk files, network connections to remote databases, or generate the data via simulation. In all cases, the client is protected from the details of how the server performs its task.

3. **Finder:** this type of agent locates particular data or other objects. For example, the messenger agent may employ the services of a finder agent to locate a recipient, or the server agent may use one to locate a particular record in a database. The finder contains knowledge of how and where to search for the desired entity and how to recognize the sought for entity when it is discovered.
4. **Communicator:** this type of agent engages in dialogue with the user. A variety of user-interface devices may be used by the communicator to provide its service; for example, a communicator interacting with the user to obtain the name of a file where data is to be found or placed might conduct a simple fill-in-the-box dialog, allowing the user to select a file from a list of file names that the communicator found in a particular directory, or allowing the user to navigate through the file system seeking the desired file.

Many other kinds of agents exist. These four are meant only to suggest the kinds of objects included in this category.

In the fourth and final category of objects associated with actions is a "transformer." A transformer object alters in some way the data that passes through it. A transformer often has very little knowledge of either the producer or the consumer of the data and little understanding of the meaning of the data that it is manipulating. These limitations reflect the narrow scope of the transformer object. Two examples of transformers are:

1. **Formatter:** this type of transformer changes the appearance of the data. Commonly encountered formatters are displayers, marshallers, and encoders. A displayer object renders its data in a human readable form. Low-level displayers are similar to the stream I/O objects that change the binary (internal) representation of a value into the string representation shown to the user. A high-level displayer is a paragraph object that knows how to align the text contained in a paragraph and arrange for line breaks, hyphenation, and spacing. A marshaller object is responsible for creating a linearized representation of its data. Marshaller objects are used in file operations to pack data into blocks for more efficient use of disk operations and are used in remote operation systems to pack the arguments of an operation into a single buffer. An encoder object is used to change the appearance of the data, though not into a human-readable form. Encoders are used to convert data into a standard representation format so that it can be exchanged with other programs and encrypt the data for secure communication over untrusted networks.

What objects are involved in the relationship?
What objects are necessary to sustain (implement, realize, maintain) the relationship?
What objects not in the relationship are aware of and exploit the relationship?
What objects not in the relationship are used by the related objects?

Figure 5.3 Structural Perspective Questions

2. **Filters:** this type of transformer screens the data for certain characteristics. The filter removes from the data any item that does not meet its criteria. For example, a filter may remove all lines in a text file that do not contain a search keyword. Other filters might look for patterns in the data, or for other more complex search criteria. Web search engines and library catalog searchers are large-scale examples of filters.

Transformer objects are often used in a sequenced or pipelined arrangement; a filter transformer may select data from a database, pass the selected items to a displayer transformer to put it into human-readable form, and pass this data through an encrypter transformer for secure transmission.

Structural Perspective

Classes can be discovered by focusing on the relationships described or implied by a specification. A relationship defines a pattern, organization, or structure among a set of entities. Because the entities are likely candidates for classes, discovering and analyzing the relationships is a way of discovering classes. This is a productive approach because the statement of a system's functionality often involves the use of relationships to explain the intended nature of some part of the systems; words or phrases like "consists of," "uses," "enforces," "maintains," and "group" of all indicate relationships. A relationship can be analyzed by asking questions that identify the classes and objects it implies. Figure 5.3 lists some of the questions that are part of analyzing a relationship. The answers to these question lead the designer from the relationship to classes of objects that are in some way involved with it. The study of a system's structure often leads to objects that fall into well-known general categories. General categories of objects that are often associated with particular structures are: *acquaintance, containment,* and *collection.*

The first category of objects that can be discovered from the structural perspective is "acquaintance." In an acquaintance structure, some objects know about one or more of the other objects. This is the simplest form of structural relationship that allows one object to interact with another. Concretely, one object would have a reference to the object that it knows about. There are two kinds of acquaintance relationships: symmetric and asymmetric.

1. **Symmetric:** an acquaintance in which the objects are mutually acquainted; they know about one another. For example, in a drawing

tool, a Rectangle object and a Canvas object may know about each other. The Canvas is acquainted with the Rectangle, and other similar objects that appear on the Canvas, so that the Canvas knows how to redraw itself. The Rectangle is acquainted with the Canvas because the Rectangle object contains the detailed information on how the Rectangle should be drawn (location, shape, color, etc.) using the methods provided by the Canvas (e.g., drawLine).

2. **Asymmetric:** an acquaintance is which the known object is unaware of the knowing object. For example, in a system where a Clock object is started by the user pressing a "Start" Button, the Button object must know about the Clock object but the Clock object need not know about the Button object

There are certain properties that apply to both forms of acquaintance. The acquaintance may be persistent or transitory. A persistent acquaintance is one that lasts for a substantial period of time, perhaps even throughout the entire execution of the system. A transitory acquaintance lasts for only a short time, maybe just the duration of one method invocation. The acquaintance may also be direct or indirect. In a direct acquaintance, one object may immediately refer to the other. In an indirect acquaintance, some intermediary object must be accessed in order to refer to the known object.

Containment objects also may be discovered from the structural perspective. In a containment structure the objects form a part-whole structure. Terms in the specification like "contains," "consists of," and "has" are indicative of a containment relationship. Two uses of the containment relationship are:

1. **Collaborator:** a structure in which the whole is created by the interaction of it parts. Two different areas of a system where collaborative relationships might be sought are in the description of the application-specific entities and in the user interface. An application-specific entity description might state: "A StopWatch consists of a clock display, a Start button, and a Stop button. The clock display has two hands and the numerals 1 through 12 arranged in a 12-hour clock manner." A containment relationship occurs twice in this description. First, the StopWatch is described as having three components contained within it: a clock display and two buttons. Second, the clock display is described as having two components: the hands and the numerals. In a containment relation, the containing entity is represented as a class whose aggregated objects are of classes defined by the contained entities. In the StopWatch example, the StopWatch class would aggregate objects of the ClockDisplay and Button classes. Similarly, the class ClockDisplay would aggregate objects of the ClockHands and ClockNumerals classes. Containment relationships can

also be found in the description of the user-interface structure; as in "The drawing tool interface has a drawing area and three menus through which the user can control the operations of the tool." The word "has" denotes the containment relationship between a DrawingTool class and the aggregated objects it contains, namely, an object of the DrawingArea class and three objects of the Menu class.

2. **Controller:** a controller object exerts substantial, and possibly total, control over their objects. An example of a controller is the Boss in the Boss-Worker model: in this model, units of work, called tasks, are presented to the Boss by client objects. The Boss delegates a task to a Worker that performs the tasks and delivers the result to the Boss. The result then is forwarded to the client. In a controller structure, the Workers are completely concealed by the Boss, and are invisible to the client. The Workers usually have no contact with each other and even may have no contact with other objects except for the Boss object. In some cases, the Workers perform identical actions and the Boss delegates the task to the next available Worker. This situation frequently arises in parallel-processing computations where each Worker may be on a separate processor, or in programs with multiple independent threads where each Worker has its own thread of control. In other cases, each Worker performs a distinct computation. For example, the Boss may play the role of a DataSource while each Worker represents a different, specific source (a LocalFile Worker, a RemoteFile Worker, a DataBase Worker, etc.).

The structural perspective may also reveal "collection" objects. In a collection structure, the individual objects maintain their external visibility. Collection is similar to containment in that both are groupings, but collection differs from containment in that collection does not totally conceal the grouped objects, whereas containment completely aggregates and hides them. The variations among collections are determined by the nature and the degree of control that is imposed on the group. Three kinds of collections are peer, iteration, and coordinator. The first two of these exert limited control on their objects, but coordinators have greater influence over their members. The three kinds of collections are:

1. **Peer:** a collection in which objects are of equal status (hence the name) and are undifferentiated by the collection that imposes no control over them. The collection exists simply to give a name to the logical structure of the objects that it contains and, perhaps, to provide resources for these objects to use. Such a form of collection is described in the statement: "The user interface has three buttons to start, stop,

and reset the system." The three buttons form a logical grouping; the word "has" suggests a possible containment relation. However, the object may not be completely aggregated by the grouping and so a peer collection might be more appropriate. Thus, a class ControlButtons might be created to represent the group. In practical terms, the ControlButtons might provide resources that are needed by the button objects in the GUI system. The three button objects are peer objects within the ControlButtons group.

2. **Iterator:** a collection providing some indexing (ordering, sorting) function over its objects. The grouped objects are not necessarily of the same class but they have a shared interface that allows the group to realize the indexing function. The indexing may beas simple as the order in which the objects were added to the collection (as, for example, items in a pull-down menu) or more complicated (as, for example, items in a database indexed by a key field).

3. **Coordinator:** a collection designed to maintain some property or invariant condition among its objects. For example, a RadioButton collection may enforce the property that only one among all of the Button objects in the RadioButton may be in the "pushed" state at any one time. Thus, pushing one of the buttons has the side effect of unpushing any other previously pushed button. The coordinator exerts some control over the objects in the collection, but the coordinated objects maintain their visibility, and can be known and operated upon by objects outside of the collection. The collection is intended not to conceal the coordinated objects but to assist these objects in implementing a group-wide property.

***Information Perspective*:** Classes can be discovered by examining the information content of a system and the way such information is manipulated. This point of view is useful because information processing is a significant aspect of most software systems, as reflected by terms such as "information systems" and "information age" in relation to computerized systems. In some cases, information-processing capabilities are the most important services a system can offer to its users. The specifications of these systems are especially concerned with describing the information and its manipulation.

Information can be viewed as data or state. In simple terms, data is the information processed by the system and state is the information used by the system to perform that processing. As an example of the difference between data and state, the specification of a document preparation system might refer to the notion of a paragraph. The user of the system defines the words that make up the paragraph, i.e., the paragraph's data. When processing this paragraph, the system may have state information such as a variable that determines if the end

Factor	Data	State
Primary Focus	Application/User	Program/System
Role	Processed by system	Guides processing
Lifetime	Exists beyond program execution	Same as program's execution
Source/Visibility	User	System

Figure 5.4 Distinctions Between Data and State

What objects are needed to represent the data or state?
What objects read the data or interrogate the state?
What objects write the data or update the state?

Figure 5.5 Information Perspective Questions

of paragraph has been reached. This variable determines whether the paragraph processing will continue or terminate. Although the distinction between data and state information cannot always be perfectly drawn, the differences are often clear enough that it is useful to make the distinction.

The four factors that distinguish data from state information are given in Figure 5.4. Data is user-centered information and is defined in terms of concepts in the application domain. In contrast, state information is primarily an artifact of the system itself: the state information may change if the system design changes, but the data usually remains unaffected by changes in the system (except, of course, if the system is changed to require different data or data in a different format). The lifetime of data exceeds the lifetime of the system's execution, whereas state information does not.For example, in the document-preparation system, the paragraph data exists before, during, and after the execution of the system. However, the state information indicating the end of paragraph has been reached only has meaning and existence while the program is executing. Finally, data is of direct concern to the user, who is using the system precisely because the system processes the data in some manner. However, the user is not interested in the state information that the system maintains for its own use.

When data or state information is referred to in a specification, some of the questions that can be asked about the information in order to identify classes and objects related to the information are shown in Figure 5.5. The study of a system's information often leads to objects that fall into well-known general categories. Some of the object categories often relevant to data are discussed next.

General categories of objects that are frequently relevant to data and state information are:

1. **Source or sinks:** a repository of data outside of the system. A source is any entity outside of the program (system) that generates data, and a sink is any entity outside of the program (system) that receives data. An entity can be both a source and a sink; an updatable database is an example. Sources and sinks include local files and databases, remote files and databases, and servers. Objects that directly represent the sources and sinks should always be considered in the design. Reader objects and writer objects are obvious kinds of objects to consider for each source and sink, respectively.
2. **Query:** the description of the data sought from a source. In the simplest case—reading sequentially from the source—the description is empty; the mere fact that the query is attempted implies what is sought by the program. For a randomly accessed source, the query may simply contain an index of the required record or block of data. In more complicated cases—highly structured databases, for example—the query may contain a wealth of information indicating how to select, combine, reduce, and reorder information in the database. The role of the query object is to provide a simply programmed interface by which this complex information can be managed most effectively.
3. **Result:** the data returned by a source or directed to a sink. In the simpler cases, the result may be nothing more than a block of data. More complex cases arise when dealing with more complicated data organizations. For example, a digital library system might return as the result of a query a set of titles that satisfy the query and rank them by some relevance criteria. Here, the object that represents the result has a more intricate structure and a more sophisticated interface. Correspondingly, the program may generate a complex result that has to be transmitted to the sink ina sequence of more primitive, lower level operations. The purpose of the result object is to provide an interface that relieves the other parts of the system of the burden of being aware of the lower level details of how the complex data is communicated to sources or sinks.
4. **Buffer:** multiple logical data items contained in one physical unit. The data is transferred from the source or to the sink in terms of the physical units of data. Buffers are often used to improve the performance of lower level I/O operations. For example, more efficient use is made of network bandwidth and disk controllers if data is written in fewer, larger blocks. A buffer for a sink gathers the data written to it by the program and actually transmits this accumulated data as one physical unit when the buffer is sufficiently full. A buffer for a source reads the data in larger physical units and delivers this data as

requested by the program. When the buffer is empty, another physical unit is obtained from the source.

5. **Cache:** an object anticipating the need for data not yet requested by the program. A cache for a source might read ahead, trying to guess what data the program will request next. If the cache's guess is a good one, the program will discover that its requested data is readily available. This effect, improving the latency of lower level I/O operations, is the principle motivation for a cache. The extent to which a cache is successful depends on how accurately it can guess the future needs of the program. In some situations, effective caching strategies are possible; for instance, a cache for a sink might retain previously written data in expectation that this data might be requested again in the near future. Another example is in a digital library system where it may be a good guess that additional data about the titles given in response to a user's query are likely to be requested in the near future.
6. **Synchronizers:** enforcers of timing or sequencing constraints. Constraints are usually necessary to ensure the correct operation of a source or sink. For example, a source may only work correctly if read operations are performed sequentially (i.e., each read operation is issued only after the previous read operation has completed). More complex constraints might exist for an updatable database that imposes the restriction that write operations cannot take place while a read operation is in progress. In this case, a synchronizer object is needed to regulate the reading and writing activity.

In addition to these classes of objects, iterators and transformers, discussed earlier in this section, are also frequently relevant to the information perspective. *Iterators* and *transformers* can be discovered from the structural or behavioral perspectives, respectively.

General categories of objects that are frequently relevant to state are:

1. **Recorder:** a representation of the current state of the system. All information needed to evaluate the current condition of the system is contained in recorder objects. The state information stored includes the processing options that currently apply (e.g., the current drawing color), the current mode of the system (e.g., "add" or "delete" mode), the prevailing boundary conditions ("there can be no more than 100 sides on a polygon"), and program flags (e.g., "shape currently selected"). Because the state information is of such varied character, there may be several classes each of which represent a related part of the current state of the system.

2. **Scheduler:** able to prioritize a system's currently available courses of action. In sequential programs, any one of a variety of actions may possibly produce the desired answer. For example, in a maze search program, there are several alternative paths to test at each intersection. The role of the scheduler is to determine in what order these possibilities are evaluated. In concurrent programs—programs with multiple independent threads of control—the scheduler is responsible for selecting which thread to execute next from among all threads that are capable of executing. The scheduler may take a variety of application-specific details into account in making its selection.
3. **Maintainer:** determine the actions to take in the current state of the system and determine the next system state. In simple systems, every action of which the system is capable can be performed at any time. In such simple systems the maintainer is trivial and perhaps not even needed. However, in more complex systems, the system's response is dependent on previous actions ("a paste can only occur after a cut or copy operation"), the current mode of the system ("in add mode a new shape is placed where the user clicks whereas in delete mode the shape where the user clicks is removed"), or the current recorded state ("if a shape is selected, then highlight the shape"). In these more complex systems, the maintainers must be more highly structured; the correct design and implementation of the maintainers can be the most challenging issue faced by the developer.

Combining the Three Perspectives

Figure 5.6 summarizes the combined categories of classes that are discussed above. Though these categories are not exhaustive and are meant only to illustrate the varied kinds of objects that can be discovered by analyzing a specification, they provide a useful foundation for beginning the analysis of a specification.

The three perspectives are meant to be used together and in combination. For example, an initial analysis of a specification may discover a datasource (information perspective), and study of the data source reveals the need for a filter (behavioral perspective) to process the data from the source. Further analysis may discover that the filter has an asymmetric acquaintance (structural perspective) with a communicator (behavioral perspective). The communicator conveys its output to a buffer (information perspective) that is connected to a sink (information perspective). As illustrated by this example, discovering an object in one perspective may lead to the discovery of objects using a different perspective.

Behavioral	Structural	Information
Actor	Acquaintance	Data
Reactor	• symmetric	• sources/sink
• system events	• asymmetric	• query
• external events	•	• result
• user events		• buffer
		• cache
Agent	Containment	• synchronizer
• messenger	• collaborator	
• server	• controller	
• finder	•	
• communicator		
Transformer	Collection	State
• formatter	• peer	• recorder
• filter	• iterator	• scheduler
•	• coordinator	• maintainer

Figure 5.6 Combining All Three Perspectives

Abstraction: does the class capture a useful abstraction?
Responsibilities: does the class bear a reasonable set of responsibilities?
Interface: is the interface of the class clean and simple?
Usage: is the class design consistent with how it is actually used?
Implementation: is there a reasonable implementation for the class?

Figure 5.7 Class Design Evaluation

5.2.2 Evaluating a Class Design

A proposed class design must be evaluated to determine whether the proposed design should be accepted, revised, or rejected. In the early stages of design many ideas for classes may be discovered. In fact, it is a good practice to generate as many ideas as can be thought of in a brainstorming and uncritical mode. The goal of this early phase is to discover possible classes. At a later stage a possible class must be analyzed to determine if it is substantial enough to be represented as a class, if it duplicates or overlaps with another class, or whether it should be refined into two or more other classes. Five aspects of a proposed class design should be evaluated as shown in Figure 5.7. All of these aspects should be considered for each class. It may also be useful to apply them in the order listed because this ordering proceeds from the highest to the lowest level of detail.

The abstraction captured by the class is the first aspect of a class design to evaluate. Recall that capturing an abstraction is the most fundamental role of a class, so this is most critical. The abstraction may come from the application domain (e.g., Automobile or Employee), from the user interface (e.g., StartButton or FileChooser), or from the computation (e.g., ListManager or MenuBar). Specific tests to determine the adequacy of the abstraction are:

1. **Identity:** simple and suggestive names for the class and for all of its operations can be found if a class captures an abstraction. Difficulty in finding a good name for a class or its operations is usually a sign of a weak abstraction, as are names that contain vague modifiers. For example, terms such as "simple" or "complex" in a name should be questioned, particularly if they are not derived from application domain terms. If an application has some labels that contain only letters and digits and other labels that can contain any character, referring to these as "SimpleLabel" and "ComplexLabel" is not helpful. Unless there are more meaningful application terms for these labels, better names might be AlphaNumeric Label and Label. In these names, the vague meaning of "simple" has been replaced by a more specific indication of the class's intent and the vague meaning of "complex" has been dealt with by simply eliminating the modifier. The same rule applies to the methods of a class.
2. **Clarity:** the meaning of a class can be given in a brief, dictionary-style definition. The definition should be short (the equivalent of one or two short, declarative sentences), use precise terms, and fully convey the intent of the class. A definition of this form is difficult to write because it requires careful thought and precise use of language. However, the effort to construct this definition leads to a confirmation that the class is well defined, creates a compact reference for potential reusers of the class, and establishes a basis for the class's documentation.
3. **Uniformity:** the operations defined for the class should have a uniform level of abstraction. This means that the names and arguments of the class's methods must be at a similar level of conceptualization. For example, consider the following partial class definition:

```
public class ShapeManager
{...
    ...
    public void addShape(Shape s)
    public void removeShape(Shape s)
    public void replaceShape(Shape by, Shape with)
    public void findRectangle(Rectangle r)
    ...
}
```

In the ShapeManager class, all of the methods refer to objects of the class are the second aspect of a class design to evaluate. Shape except for the single method `findRectangle`, whose name and argument refers to a lower level concept. The uniformity of this class can be improved by eliminating the `findRectangle` method or replacing it with a `findShape` method that is consistent with the level of conceptualization of the other methods of the class.

The responsibilities assigned to the class. A class's responsibilities are what it is expected to remember over time, the effects it is expected to have on other parts of the system, and the services that it is expected to provide for other objects in the system. Specific qualities determine the adequacy of a class's responsibilities test the extent the responsibilities are:

1. **Clear:** it should be easy to determine whether or not the class is charged with a specific responsibility. Any doubts about a class's responsibilities signal danger because it raises the possibility that the specifier, the implementor, and the user of the class may all have different interpretations of the class's responsibilities. This lack of common understanding can only lead to unwelcome situations.
2. **Limited:** the responsibilities placed upon a class should not exceed those required by the abstraction on which it is based. Adding extraneous responsibilities obscures the purpose of the class, confounds (re)users, and increases the difficulty of implementing the class.
3. **Coherent:** the responsibilities of a class should make sense as a whole. Coherence is lost when two distinct abstractions are represented by the same class. When this occurs, the responsibilities of the class will represent the union of the responsibilities associated with each of the two abstractions. Because the abstractions are distinct, though perhaps similar, the overall responsibilities of the class loses coherence.
4. **Complete:** the responsibilities given to a class must completely capture those of the corresponding abstraction. Not only does a missing responsibility weaken the class of which it should be a part, but it also disturbs the coherence of the other class(es) in which the responsibility is placed.

The interface of the class is the third aspect of a class to be evaluated. A well-designed class interface is clearly important; it is the concrete programming device by which objects of the class are manipulated. Programmers are more likely to (re)use, and to (re)use correctly, a class that has a well-designed interface. Specific aspects of a class's methods to assess are:

1. **Naming:** the names of the methods should contain active verbs and should clearly express the method's intended effect on the object. Methods that return a `boolean` value should be named to indicate their truth value. For example, the method name `lightIsOn` is better than the name `lightStatus`. Methods that have different effects should be given names that are distinctly different. A class can be confusing and even hazardous if the names of methods with different effects are too similar. For example, consider the following class interface:

```
public class ItemList
{
  public void delete(Item item); // take Item's node out of list and delete Item
  public void remove(Item item); // take Item's node out of list but do not delete Item
  public void erase (Item item); // keep Item's node in list, but with no information
};
```

   Each of these methods has a different effect on the List and on the Item parameter, but their names are easily confused. Many programming mistakes could easily arise if `delete` is used when `remove` or `erase` is intended. The remedy for this situation might be deeper than a simple change of names in the interface; the entire class design might need to be reconsidered.

2. **Symmetry:** if a class has a pair of inverse operations, the names and effects of the corresponding methods should be clear. A typical example of symmetric operations is the pair of accessor methods for a class property X that might be named `getX` and `setX` to reflect their mutual relation to the property X. The interface should be reexamined if it has only one of a pair of inverse operations (e.g., a get method but not a set method). Is there a sound design decision to provide only one of the pair? If not, include the missing operation.
3. **Flexibility:** the methods of the class, particularly the constructor, should be overloaded to provide a variety of different uses. There are three ways in which overloading increases the flexibility of the interface. First, it allows the method to be invoked using the form of data that is most readily available at the invoking site. For example, consider the class interface

```
class ItemList
{
  public void addItem(Item item, int index)
  public Item findItem(int index)
    ...
}
```

that identifies Item objects by their position ("index") in a list. If it is known that character string data is often available at the invoking site (the index has been read as a character string), then it is reasonable to consider adding overloaded `addItem` and `findItem` method that allow the index to be given as a character string. Via this overloading, the class assumes the responsibility of converting the character string to an integer index.

Second, overloading allows only the necessary arguments to be supplied. The interface can be tailored to allow the invocation to assume more or less control over the details of the operation: the more parameters in an overloading, the more control is given to the invocation. For example, the class below contain several overloadings of a `draw` method:

```
class DrawingArea
{
   public void draw(Shape s);
   public void draw(Shape s, Color outline);
   public void draw(Shape s, Color outline, Color fill);
  ...
};
```

The programmer using a DrawingArea object can ignore the Color parameters if they are not relevant or if the Colors selected by the DrawingArea object itself are acceptable. However, the programmer is able, when needed, to use the overloadings that allow one or both of the Colors to be specified.

Third, overloading can be used to relieve the programmer of remembering the order of arguments. For example, the AddItem method in the ItemList class above requires both an Item and an index. An overloading could be provided so that the Item and the index could be specified in either order. Overloading should only be used, of course, when the overloaded methods all have exactly the same effect on the object.

The fourth aspect of a class to be evaluated is its usage. An otherwise well-designed class may lack useful methods because it is often difficult for the class designer to foresee all of the important contexts in which the class may be used. By examining how the objects of the class are used in different contexts, it is possible to discover these missing operations. For example, consider the following definition and use of the Location class:

```
class Location
{ private:
      int xCoord, yCoord; // coordinates
  public:
      Location(int x, int y);
      int getX(); // return xCoord value
      int getY(); // return yCoord value
};
...
//usage
Location point(100,100);
...
point = Location(point.getX()+5, point.getY()+10); // shift point
```

The code to shift the point relative to its current coordinates is possible using the existing interface of the Location class. If the Location class is commonly used in this way, the class designer should consider adding a new method. The revised definition and use are:

```
class Location
{ private:
      int xCoord, yCoord;               // coordinates
  public:
      Location(int x, int y);
      int getX();                     // return xCoord value
      int getY();                     // return yCoord value
      void shiftBy(int dx, int dy);    // shift point relative to
                                               current coordinates
};
...
//usage
Location point(100,100);
...
point.shiftBy(5,10); // shift point
```

This change in the class design improves both the simplicity and readability of the code using the Location class.

The implementation of the class is the fifth and final aspect to be evaluated. The implementation is the most detailed, the most easily changed, and the least important of all of the aspects of a class. A class that represents a sound abstraction and has a well-designed interface can always be given a better implementation if the class's existing implementation is weak. The implementation can, however, point to two ways in which a class can be improved. First, an unwieldy and complex implementation may indicate that the class is not well conceived or is simply not implementable. In this case, the design of the class and its underlying abstraction reconsidered. Second, an overly complex implementation may also indicate that the class has been given too much responsibility. If this is the case, then either the class can be partitioned into two or more classes, or new classes can be developed that are used internally by the original class. The first strategy is visible to the users of the class whereas the second strategy is invisible. In either instance, new classes are developed that may help to reveal previously missing abstractions in the application domainor may simply be useful classes in the computational structure.

Exercises

Read the following description of a data visualization system and then answer the questions below.

Specification of a Data Visualization System

Many applications in science and engineering disciplines generate large volumes of data that must be understood by the scientist or engineer. Because of the volume of data (megabytes of numerical data) it is difficult or impossible to easily understand the meaning of the data or to recognize a critical aspect of the data.

Develop a data visualization systems that provides a scientist or engineer with a two dimensional graphical representation of a large set of data. Through computer graphics techniques and effective use of colors, the system allows the user to navigate within the displayed representation, to request specific details of a particular part of the data, to see the representation change over time, or to filter the data on which the representation is based.

The basic functions of the visualization systems are:

Selection: the user must be able to select the file containing the data that is input to the visualization system. The user initiates the selection through a button in the user interface.

Representation: the data is limited to display on a two-dimensional x-y coordinate system. The axis of this system must be drawn and some labeling of the axis must be given. The user, through the file format or through the user interface, must have some means of determining what symbol will be used to represent the data (e.g., a small filled point, an alphabetical letter, a cross-hair).

Filtering: the user must be able to set the limits of the x-y coordinates that are presented in the display. For example, a user might specify that the data to be displayed must have an x coordinate between -100.0 and +100.0 while the y value must be in the range from 50.2 to 125.5. Data values outside of this range are ignored. The axis in the representation must be scaled so that the selected range extends across the entire area allocated to the representation. In other words, by selecting successively smaller ranges, the user will have the effect of "zooming" in on a part of the data.

Timed display: the user must have a way of requesting that the data be displayed in a time sequence with additional data appearing at each time step. It is possible that a different file format may be required to support this option.

The user interface for the data visualization system contains a display area (a Canvas object) on which the data is displayed on a x-y axis. The user interface also contains a number of TextBoxes in which the user enters the limits of each axis for filtering the data. A number of buttons are present to control different options or initiate different functions (e.g.,open a new file, begin timed display).

1. Using the behavioral perspective, identify several classes for the Data-Visualization System.
2. Evaluate the class that are found in terms of the abstraction, responsibilities, and interface.
3. Using the behavioral perspective, identify several classes for the Data-Visualization System.
4. Evaluate the class that are found in terms of the abstraction, responsibilities, and interface.
5. Using the behavioral perspective, identify several classes for the Data-Visualization System.
6. Evaluate the class that are found in terms of the abstraction, responsibilities, and interface.

5.3 Designing Complex Logic

Complex logic is often need to control programs with numerous actions and states, especially when current state determines whether, which, or how actions are performed. User-interface systems, communication protocols, interactive systems, and embedded systems typically exhibit complex logic. As an example of a state-dependent action, consider a user-interface system with cut and paste commands. The paste command should only be possible after a cut operation has been performed; the state of the system reflects whether this has happened. The logic of such systems is complicated to program due to the state dependence of actions and the usually large number of states.

Complex logic is difficult to design. In realistically sized systems, the combinatorial explosion of (state, action) pairs creates such a large space that attempts at easy solutions are usually defeated. In addition, the design difficulty is compounded if the system specification is stated in an informal manner (e.g., in natural language). It is difficult to analyze informal specification for crucial properties such as freedom from internal contradiction (consistency), freedom from external contradiction (correctness) absence of ambiguity (clarity), and coverage of all relevant cases (completeness).

Complex logic may also seem difficult to capture in an object-oriented style. It may not be clear how the if-then-else, or case statement form, of the logic can be transformed into an object structure. Also, it may not be apparent how the other objects in the application relate to the states and actions of the system. If the actions are made methods of some objects, how does the object know the state of the system so that the object can decide on the proper way to deal with the action? On the other hand, turning the states into objects may not seem natural or in keeping with the object-oriented philosophy.

> The graphical editor presents the user with an initially clear drawing area and waits for the user to draw, move, and resize any of a set of predefined shapes. To draw a shape, the user clicks outside of any currently drawn shape and is presented with a pop-up menu of possible shapes to choose from. The user selects one of these shapes and then clicks again in the drawing area to indicate where the selected shape should be placed. The user may select an existing shape to manipulate by depressing the mouse button inside or on the border of the shape. A selected shape is displayed with a border that is thicker than normal to reflect the fact that it is selected. To move a selected shape, the user depresses the mouse button inside the shape and then drags the shape to its new position. To resize a shape, the user depresses the mouse button on the border of the shape and then drags the mouse. Dragging away from the border increases the shape's size and dragging in toward the shape reduces it.

Figure 5.8 Specification for the Graphical Editor

The processing of mouse events in a simple graphical editor will be used in this section as an example of how to design and implement complex logic in an object-oriented form. The key ideas developed by this example are how to present the processing logic in a graphical, semiformal representation, and transliterate this graphical representation into code. The real design work is accomplished in the first of these steps, for the transliteration step is straightforward. Two different transliterations are given; one is much more object-oriented than the other. This section's example is small so that it can be presented completely. However, it should be clear that the same technique used here can be used for larger, more complex problems as well.

Given in Figure 5.8 is a natural-language statement describing how mouse events should be handled in a simple graphical editor system. Only two mouse events are used: depressing the left mouse button and dragging (moving the mouse while the left mouse button remains in the depressed state). The specification details how the user creates and manipulates shapes. Clearly, this specification could be complicated further by introducing more actions (e.g., grouping shapes together, ungrouping shapes, rotating shapes, saving to a file), and employing alternative user-interface mechanisms (e.g. using a pulldown menu in addition to the popup menu to select the shape to be drawn). The technique for handling the simpler case described below can also be applied to these more complicated cases.

5.3.1 UML State Diagrams

A UML state diagram will be used to represent the specification of the graphical editor's logic in a visual, semiformal manner. The state diagram is visual because UML uses rounded rectangles, arrowed lines, and textual annotations to express the editor's logic. The state diagram is semi-formal because it lies between the informality of a natural-language expression, where no direct analysis can be done, and the full formality of a mathematical expression that can be subject to rigorous analysis.Thestate diagram has a prescribed form (a syntax) and there are heuristic rules that can detect certain weaknesses in the specification.

A state diagram depicts states of the system, drawn as rounded rectangles, and transitions between states, drawn as arrowed lines. In other contexts, a state diagram is also called a state-transition diagram. Each state hasa name suggestive of the system condition to which it corresponds. States of the graphical editor system that will be developed include these:

- **Awaiting:** no shape is currently selected.
- **Moving:** the user is dragging a shape to a new position.
- **Resizing:** the user is changing the size of a shape.
- **Drawing:** a new shape is being selected for drawing.

A state is drawn as a rounded rectangle with the name of the state written inside. In some cases the mere name of the state is sufficient to describe the role of that state in the system's logic. In other cases, the state may be drawn with three compartments that contain the name, state variables used to represent the information relevant to that state, and activities that consists of actions or events manipulating the state variables. Three standard events that appear in the activities section are referred to as "*entry*," "*exit*," and "*do*." An "entry" activity happens whenever thc state is entered and an "*exit*," activity happens when the state is exited. A "do" activity can happen once or repeatedly while in the state. The general form of a state in UML is shown in Figure 5.9. A state diagram must indicate a single initial state; the initial state for the graphical editor system is the state in which it is awaiting a user action. The initial state has a transition directed to it from a small filled circle. Termination is represented by a transition from a state that is directed to a special symbol drawn as a filled circle surrounded by a larger circle.

Transitions are indicated by arrowed lines that connect two states. The transition is drawn as a directed arrow from a starting state (or the initial symbol) to a target state (or the termination symbol). The transition is labelled by an annotation that conveys the event or circumstance that causes the change from the starting state to the target state to occur. The transition may also contain an annotation of a condition that must hold for the transition to occur and a set of actions that are taken as a result of the transition. A given transition may only be taken if the condition specified for that transition holds. The condition may use actual program variable names or operations that can clearly be computed from the information available in the starting state. The set of actions for a given transition is executed when the transition is taken. The general form of transitions in UML is shown in Figure 5.10.

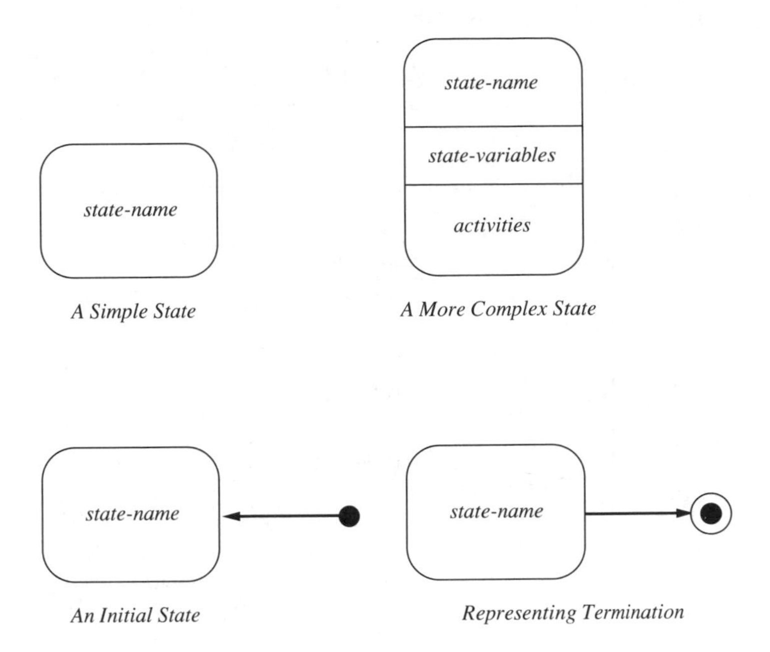

Figure 5.9 Representing States in UML

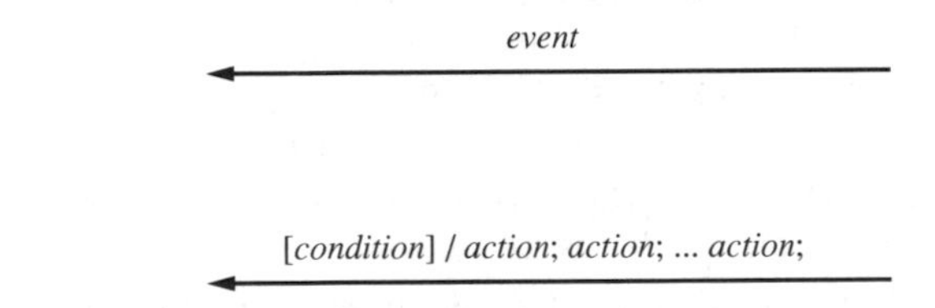

Figure 5.10 Representing Transitions in UML

The operation of a state diagram is captured in the following steps:

1. if the system is in a given state,
2. and if the condition is true of a transition directed away from that state,
3. then perform the actions associated with the transition,
4. and enter the state to which the transition is directed.

If none of the conditions for a state hold, then the system remains in the current state and no action is taken. In a properly formed diagram at most one of the conditions can be true at any one time. These steps are applied in a state

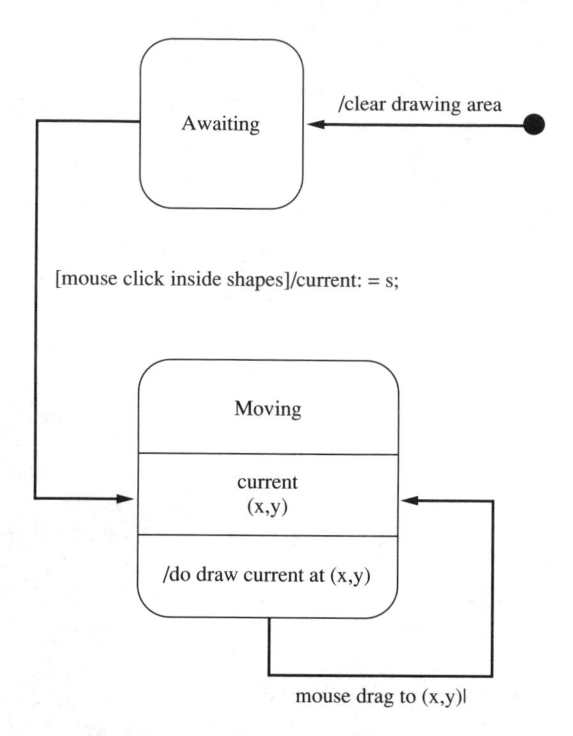

Figure 5.11 State Diagram with Awaiting and Moving States

until a transition is taken to another state, where the steps are applied again until another transition is taken, and so on. This process continues until a transition to a termination symbol is taken. In a properly constructed state transition diagram, every execution of the real system corresponds to a sequence of transitions in the diagram and every sequence of transitions in the diagram corresponds to a legal execution of the real system.

Using State Diagrams to Represent and Analyze Complex Logic

A part of the logic for the graphical editor system is captured by the state diagram shown in Figure 5.11. This diagram focuses on two states: Awaiting, the initial state, and Moving. The initial transition into the Awaiting state specifies that the drawing area is cleared when the system begins. Note that this transition has an action, but no condition. Two other transitions and their associated annotations are also shown. The first transition, from Awaiting to Moving, is taken when a mouse click occurs within a shape. This shape is referred to in the condition part of the annotation by the name "s," which is also used in the action part of the condition where "s" is assigned to the program variable current. When the condition is true (i.e., a mouse click occurs inside of some shape), the action is taken and the Moving state is entered. The second transition shows a case where the starting and ending state of the transitions are the same. The Moving states represents the fact that moving a shape causes the system to remain in a state where that shape can be moved again. Notice that the Moving state has two state variables, current and the coordinate pair (x,y). The action labelled "mouse drag to (x,y)" denotes that the coordinate pair maintained by the Moving state will be changed as a result of the user dragging the mouse to a new location. Notice also that the Moving state contains an activity. This activity begins with "/do" to signify an activity that is taken while in the Moving state. Thus, the Moving state maintains an idea of the currently selected shape and the coordinates at which to draw this shape. By dragging the mouse, the user is able to reposition the shape.

The state diagram easily reveals that the written specification is incomplete. An inspection of the state diagram shows that the only transition from the Moving state leads back to the Moving state. This means that once the Moving state is entered, the system stays in that state forever. Clearly this is an oversight. Although it would be difficult to recognize this oversight in the written specification, the graphic form directly exposes this weakness. Lacking this insight, the question of how to terminate the moving of a shape might not otherwise arise until the coding phase at which point it is more expensive and more difficult to resolve the oversight. The written specification is amended and the resulting state transition diagram, including the Resizing state, is shown in Figure 5.12. The written specification is amended to include the statement: "The dragging operation is terminated when the user releases the left mouse button." This same issue arises for the Resizing state and a similar statement is added to the specification: "The resizing operation is terminated when the user releases the left mouse button."

However, examination of the transition actions for the corrected specifications for the Moving and Resizing states reveals that the wording and structure the user may select an existing shape to "manipulate" and that a selected shape highlights its border. Ambiguity arises because the word *"may"* is open to several interpretations. In its stronger sense "may" could be interpreted as a mandatory act, but in its weaker sense "may" could be interpreted as describing a permissible, but not a required act. A second source of ambiguity lies in the structure of the specification. That statement of how to "select" a shape for manipulation immediately precedes the description of the moving operation. Is the specification of selection to apply only to the moving operation? Or to the resizing operation that follows later as well? Furthermore, the term "select" is used in two places in the specification, once in reference to how to choose an item from the popup menu ("The user selects one of the shapes") and again in the context of identifying a shape for manipulation. Are these the same or different operations? Does the highlight apply to both cases in some way, or only to the latter case?

When ambiguities in the written specification are corrected, the state diagram will be as shown in Figure 5.13. The diagram indicates that the stronger sense of "may" is used and that highlighting applies to both moving and resizing operations. The written specification will use different terms to describe choosing

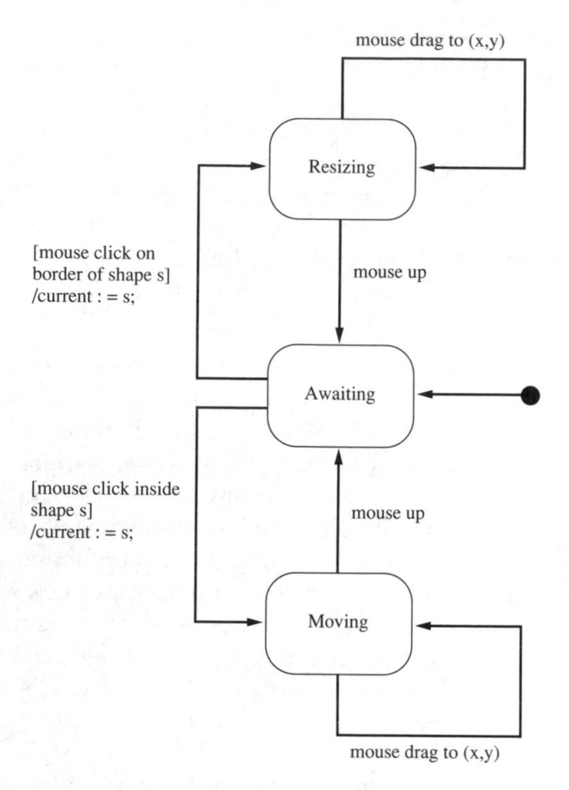

Figure 5.12 State Diagram for Corrected Moving and Resizing States

from a menu item and selecting a shape. Notice that the transitions into the Moving and Resizing states include as their actions the highlighting of the selected shape and that transitions out of these two states include the actions to unhighlight the selected shape.

The final step in the development of the state transitions diagram deals with that part of the specification for drawing a new shape. Drawing a new shape is defined in two steps: 1) choosing a new shape from a menu, and 2) placing the new shape within the drawing area. These two steps are modeled by two states named Choosing and Placing. In defining the conditions and the actions related to these two states the written specification is found to be incomplete in these two ways:

1. the specification does not say how the user selects an item from the menu, and
2. the specification does not say whether the menu remains visible after the selection, if the menu is automatically dismissed, or if the user must take some action to dismiss the menu.

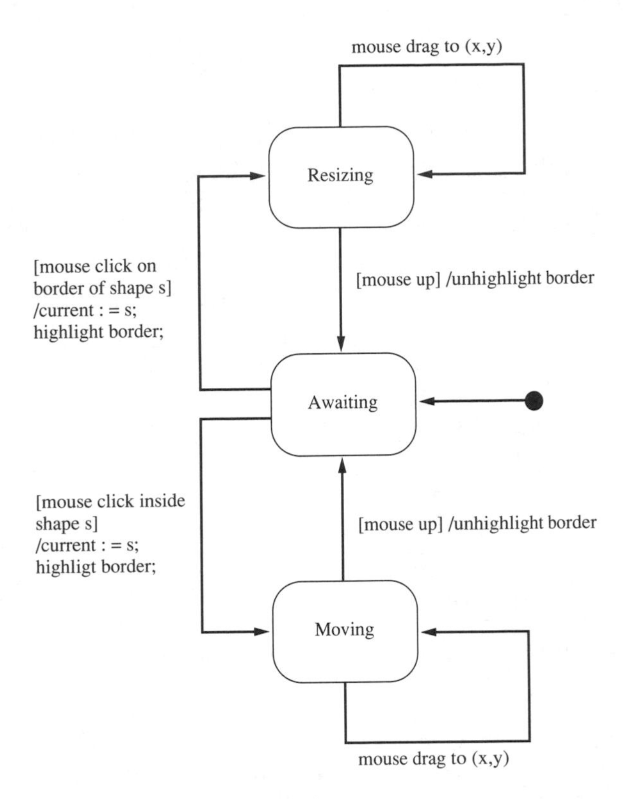

Figure 5.13 Correcting the Transitions for Highlighting Actions

The written specification will be revised yet again to indicate that the user selects a menu item by a mouse click and that the menu should be automatically dismissed after the selections. With these changes in the specification, the Choosing and Placing states are added to the state transition diagram as depicted below in Figure 5.14. The annotations for the previous transitions are not repeated again in this figure.

The written specification, incorporating all changes thus far, is repeated below in Figure 5.15 with the changes in bold. Clearly, the original specification was incomplete and ambiguous in several important areas. The development of the state transition diagram served as a useful device to discover these problems and to represent the specification in a more precise way. In addition, the state transition diagram, as a graphical representation, more clearly shows the structure of the system's behavior: the major conditions in which the system exists are modeled as states and the actions that drive the system among its states are modeled as transitions.

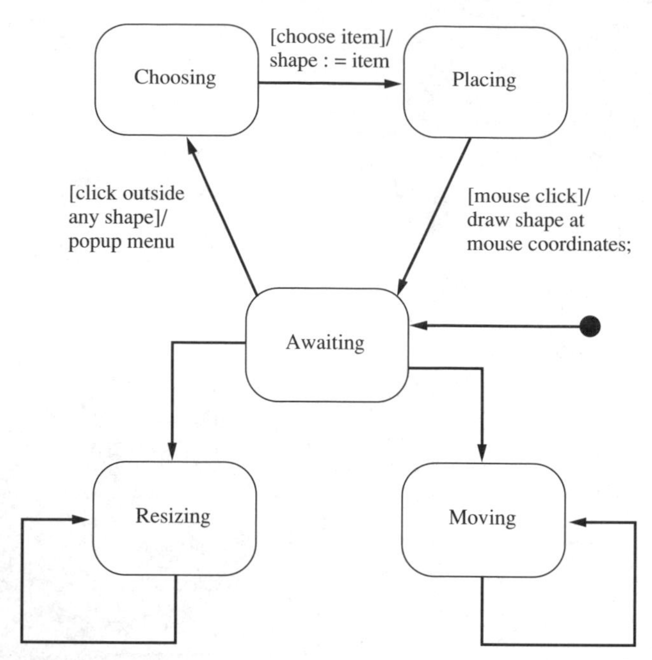

Figure 5.14 Adding the Choosing and Placing States

The graphical editor presents the user with an initially clear drawing area and waits for the user to draw, move, and resize any of a set of predefined shapes. To draw a shape, the user clicks outside of any currently drawn shape and is presented with a pop-up menu of possible shapes to choose from.The user **chooses** one of these shapes **by clicking on one of the menu items. After the choice is made, the pop-up menu disappears.** The user then clicks in the drawing area to indicate where the selected shape should be placed. The user **must** select an existing shape to **move or resize** by depressing the mouse button inside or on the border of the shape. A selected shape is displayed itself with a border that is thicker than normal to reflect the fact that it is selected. To move a selected shape, the user depresses the mouse button inside the shape and then drags the shape to its new position. **The moving operation is terminated when the user releases the mouse button.** To resize a shape, the user depresses the mouse button on the border of the shape and then drags the mouse. Dragging away from the border increases the shape's size and dragging in toward the shape reduces it. **The resizing operation is terminated when the user releases the mouse button.**

Figure 5.15 Revised Specifications for the Graphical Editor

Implementing the Design

A state-transition diagram can be transformed into an object-oriented structure by representing each state by a class. The implementation of the class represent-

```
public class SystemData
{ // system-dependent data that represents
  // (1) the current condition of the system as required
  //     to test the conditions on transitions, and
  // (2) system components that are operated upon in
  //     the actions of the transitions.
}
```

Figure 5.16 General Class for Representing System Data

```
public abstract interface State
{
  public State next (SystemData condition);
}
```

Figure 5.17 Base Class for Classes Representing States

ing a given state is derived from the annotations of all transitions that exit from that state in the state-transition diagram. The implementation includes code for:

- testing the conditions of each transition leaving the state,
- performing the actions of the transition whose condition holds, and
- returning an object that represents the state of the system after the actions have been taken.

A state is represented by a class because each state has a distinct set of transitions with distinct conditions to evaluate and distinct actions to take. Note that the use of classes to represent states is counter-intuitive. Usually, it is expected that there will be multiple objects of a given class in use at one time. However, in this case, only one object of a class will exist at any one time.

Each class must have access to those parts of the system that it needs to test its conditions and perform its actions. For example, in the graphical editor system, the conditions and actions make reference to the system components current, shape, and mouse coordinates. Testing the condition "outside of any shape" implies that the class has access to a list of all of the current shapes and a means of determining whether the mouse coordinates lie outside of a shape. Finally, the action "draw shape at mouse coordinates" implies that the class has access to the drawing area. Of course, the specific components that are accessed by the states are system dependent. Thus, the structure of this system data can only be defined in the most general terms. The SystemData class shown below (Figure 5.16) introduces a name to refer to this collection of system-dependent information.

All classes that represent states have the same interface, which is captured in an abstract interface. Figure 5.17 below shows this shared interface that has a single method, `next`, taking as its parameter the collection of system data needed by any state to properly interrogate the system's condition and modify the system as required by the state's actions. The value returned by the `next` method is a State object representing the new state of the system.

```
public class Moving implements State
{
   public Awaiting()
   {}

   public State Next (SystemData condition)
   {
      if (condition.MouseEvent == DragEvent)
      { ...update SystemData for drag event
        return this; // stay in Moving state
      }
      if (condition.MouseEvent == LeftUp)
      { ...update systemDate for button release
        return new Awaiting(); // change to Awaiting state
      }
   }
}
```

Figure 5.18 The Class for the MovingState

An example of a class for a specific state is coded below in Figure 5.18. Here, the Moving state is defined as a derived subclass of the abstract base class State. This derived class implements the `next` method as required by the base class. The Moving class also provides a constructor which has no code because the Moving state maintains no state-dependent information. Classes for other states may have state-dependent information and may also provide methods other than the `next` method. The implementation of the Moving class's `next` method is the critical part of this class. This method tests the SystemData to determine whether a relevant event has occurred. As shown in the state diagrams, the two relevant events in the Moving state are a drag event that leaves the system in the Moving state and a mouse-button-up event that returns the system to the Awaiting state. The `next` method achieves this change of states by returning a state object for the correct state of the system. If the system remains in the Moving state, the `next` method simply returns the current object (itself an object representing the Moving state). If the system should return to the Awaiting state then a new object representing that state is constructed and returned.

Exercises

Read the description below of the control logic for the Circle-PlacementSystem and answer the questions that follow.

Circle-Placement System

The Circle Placement Systems allows a user to create, position, move, and delete fixed-sized circular shapes in a drawing area. The user interface operates in the following way:

- The user can create a new circle by left-clicking outside of the boundary of any existing circle; a new circle is created whose center is at the position where the user left clicked.
- The user can change the position of an existing circle by positioning the cursor within the boundary of the circle and dragging (i.e., moving the mouse/cursor with the left mouse button depressed). The dragging ends when the user releases the left mouse button.
- The user can delete an existing circle by positioning the cursor within the boundary of a circle and doing a shift-left click (holding down the shift key while clicking the left mouse button).
- The user can change the position of an existing circle by positioning the cursor within the boundary of the circle and doing an alt-left click (holding down the alt key while clicking the left mouse button).The circle is moved one radius to the left.
- The user can change the position of an existing circle by positioning the cursor within the boundary of the circle and doing an alt-right click (holding down the alt key while clicking the right mouse button). The circle is moved one radius to the right.

1. Draw a state-transition diagram for the Circle Placement System.
2. Construct the class hierarchy for the states in the Circle Placement System.
3. Construct the data should be part of the SystemData class for this system.
4. Implement and test the Circle Placement System using the class hierarchy that represents the system states and the SystemData class developed in this section.
5. The specification of the graphical editing system does not describe a method for termination. Write one or two sentences describing a termination for the system and modify the state diagram accordingly.
6. Figure 5.12 shows the highlighting steps as actions on the transitions. Draw a revised state diagram that uses the entry and exit events for this purpose instead.

5.4 Debugging

5.4.1 Errors, Faults, and Failures

Debugging is difficult because it is primarily concerned with correcting mistakes in the thinking of the developer and only secondarily concerned with correcting the statements in the program. Setting aside problems that are due to simple mechanical transcription mistakes (e.g., the developer mistakenly typed "+" instead of "-"), a problem revealed by running the system began in the mind of the developer. The developer may have formed an inaccurate mental model of the systems's goals and constraints, conceived of an algorithm that is incomplete or incorrect, misunderstood a programming language feature (e.g., inheritance), or misused a library component. The term error is often defined to mean these invalid models, incorrect concepts, and misunderstandings that are in the mind of the developer. During system development the developer's errors become manifest in the system's code. Such code is said to contain one or more faults.When the code containing a fault is executed, the system enters an unintended state and eventually the system experiences a failure. A failure is an observed departure of the system from its intended behavior. The failure is the outward manifestation of the problem created by the fault(s). Harmless failures are those that affect the appearance of the system. For example, the output may not be formatted correctly or a button may have the wrong label. A more severe kind of failure produces incorrect results but allows the continued execution of the system. The most severe failures cause the system to terminate immediately and abnormally with possible loss of data or corruption of other resources.

The steps in debugging a system are shown in Figure 5.19. First, the failure of the system is observed during a test. The term "test" in this sense is very broad, including an informal execution of the system by the developer during development, a formal test conducted under controlled conditions by an independent team of testers, and production use by the end-user. Second, the fault(s) in the code are located. During this step other tests of the system are usually conducted to recreate the failure so as to isolate and identify the code that is involved in causing the failure. Third, the errors on the part of the developer are discovered. This step involves questioning the models and concepts employed by the developer in creating the faulty code. Fourth, once the misunderstandings are identified, a correct model or concept can be formed. The developer may reexamine the system specification, other documentation, or consult with other team members to form a correct model or concept. Fifth, the fault(s) in the code are repaired by adding to, removing from, and/or modifying the system's code. The repairs made in this step may be very localized if the error was a mistake about details or the repairs may require widespread changes if the error was a fundamental mistake. Sixth, the repaired system is retested to insure that the system does not fail as previously observed. This step also helps to insure that the repaired code did not itself introduce any new faults into the system.

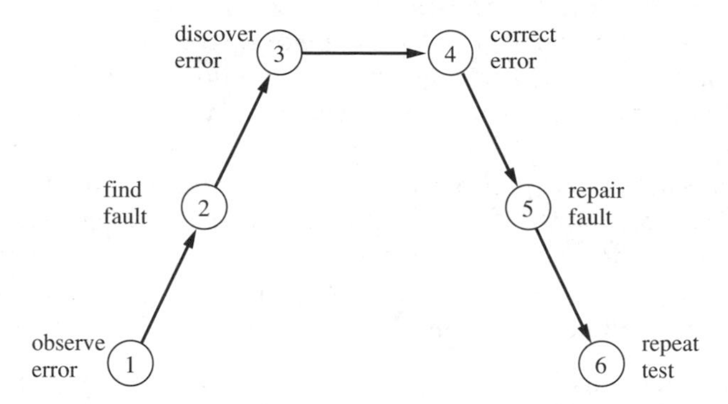

Figure 5.19 Steps in Debugging a System

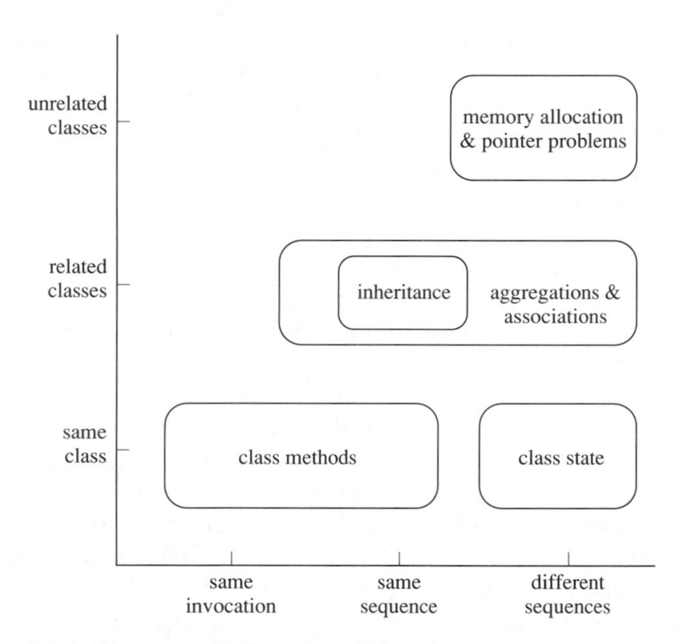

Figure 5.20 Common Debugging Situations

The code containing a fault and the code that is executing at the time of the failure may not be the same and may have different spatial and temporal relationships. Various spatial and temporal relationship between these two segments of code are shown in Figure 5.20. The term "spatial" as used here refers to the relationship between the classes containing the two segments of code. The spatial relationships shown in the figure are based on whether the two segments are in the same class, in different but related classes, or in unrelated classes. Classes are related through inheritance or because objects of these classes form associations or aggregations. The term "temporal" as used here refers to the points in time when the two segments of code are executed. Significant temporal relationships that are shown in the figure are whether the two segments are both executed within a single method invocation, that is not within the same method invocation but within the same sequence of method invocations, or in different method invocation sequences. A method invocation sequence is an ordered list of method names such that at a given point in time during the execution each method in the sequence, except the last, has invoked the next method in the sequence and the invocation has not yet returned; the last method in the sequence is the method being executed at the given point in time.

Commonly occurring debugging problems can be identified by their spatial and temporal characteristics. Figure 5.20 shows five commonly occurring situations. These five examples are meant to illustrate different situations and are not meant to be an exhaustive list of all possible debugging problems. First, the most limited and most easily fixed cases are those where the two segments of code are in the same class and in either the same invocation or the same invocation sequence. Often, the problem is a small mistake in the detailed coding of the class's methods. Second, a slightly more difficult case is one where the two segments are in the same class but each segment is executed in a different execution sequence. Because different execution sequences are involved, a typical problem is the way in which the two segments are using the state information of the object that they are both a part of. This state information is the most immediate thing that ties together the two segments of code. Third, the two segments of code may lie in different classes that are related through inheritance and are executed in the same invocation sequence. These problems are often due to misunderstandings or misuse of inherited methods, unintentionally overriding a base class method so that other base class methods no longer work correctly, or conflicts over the use of protected data that is accessed by both the base class and the derived class. Fourth, the two segments of code may lie in different classes that are related because the objects of these classes are parts of an aggregation or parts of an association. These problems are harder to diagnose because they involve multiple classes and, possibly, different method-invocation sequences. These problems are frequently due to misunderstanding the behavior or responsibilities of a class, this is to say the developer made incorrect assumptions about how the class acts. Fifth, the most difficult problems to locate and correct are those that "cannot happen." This category of problems are those that occur between unrelated classes and at unrelated points in time. Furthermore, these problems often are not deterministic, that is, the failure happens under different conditions or the same conditions do not always produce the failure. In sequential programs problems of this kind are most often due to attributed to improper use of pointers or related memory allocation effects (e.g., using an object after it has been deleted). Many of these problems do not occur in Java because Java does not allow pointers and uses garbage collection. However, similar problems can occur in programs that use multiple, independent threads of execution that are not correctly synchronized. Threads and synchronization are described in Chapter 9.

5.4.2 The Role of Debugging Tools

Debugging tools are useful for efficiently completing the first two steps in debugging: observing failure and locating faults. These two steps essentially deal with reporting the occurrence of interesting or unusual events, providing snapshots of the system as it executes, and allowing the developer to interrogate and control the system's execution. Effective debugging tools provide support for all of these activities. The subsequent steps in debugging—identifying the errors, correcting the errors, and repairing the faults—cannot be automated.

The developer can employ one of two strategies in observing failures. The first strategy is simply to run the system and wait for the system to fail. This strategy is often the first one employed because the developer may have no reason to anticipate if or when a failure will occur. The second strategy is to set "watch" conditions, conditions that are tested to determine if the system is in a valid state. When an invalid state is detected, the system is halted with an informative message. The second strategy is often used when the developer is attempting to recreate a previously observed failure or if the developer is wary of a particular part of the system being tested, perhaps because this part is new, complex, or not well understood. The watch conditions may stop the system short of the actual failure but at a point close to the true fault. The watch conditions may be dynamically inserted in the system using a debugging tool or they may be preprogrammed by the developer. Inserting watch conditions dynamically depends on the details of the debugging tool.

To accomplish the second step in debugging, locating the faults in the code, it is necessary to accumulate three different kinds of information about the system's execution at the point of failure:

1. the state of objects in the system;
2. the current execution sequence; and
3. previous execution sequences

The state of each object in the system reflects what information that object-currently contains and what other objects it knows about. Collectively, the entire system state is represented by the union of the states of all of the objects in the system. The current execution sequence shows the sequence of events that immediately preceded the failure. Knowing this sequence gives an indication of the processing actions that were being attempted at the point of failure. In simple cases, knowing the state of key objects and the current execution sequence is sufficient to locate the fault. In more complicated cases, where the execution of the code with the fault and the execution of the code that causes the failure are more distant in time from each other, an execution history that extends farther back in time is needed.

5.4.3 The Debugging Environment

Understanding key components of the system's execution environment—the "heap" and the "run-time stack"—is helpful in becoming a proficient user of debugging tools and more adept at locating faults in the code. The space for dynamically created objects is allocated from a memory area referred to as the system's heap. The heap memory allocated for an object contains the object's data (and possibly some other information generated by the compiler for run-time purposes). The object's `this` pointer points to the beginning of the object's memory area in the heap. For three object identified as A, B, and C, Figure 5.21 below shows the memory allocated for the objects and their respective `this` pointers.

The run-time stack provides the memory space for all automatically allocated objects including local variables (named objects declared within a method and anonymous objects) and parameters. The high-level view shown in Figure 5.22 illustrates the contents of the run-time stack for an invocation sequence in which a method in object A invokes a method in object B that in turn invokes a method in object C. A "stack frame" (also known as an "activation record") is pushed onto the stack each time than an invocation is made. When the current invocation returns, its stack frame is popped from the run-time stack and control is returned to the method invocation corresponding to the new top of the run-time stack. Conceptually, each stack frame has two parts containing the parameters passed to the invoked method and the local variables.

The organization of the execution environment helps to explain some of the difficulty of debugging and the limitations of debugging tools.

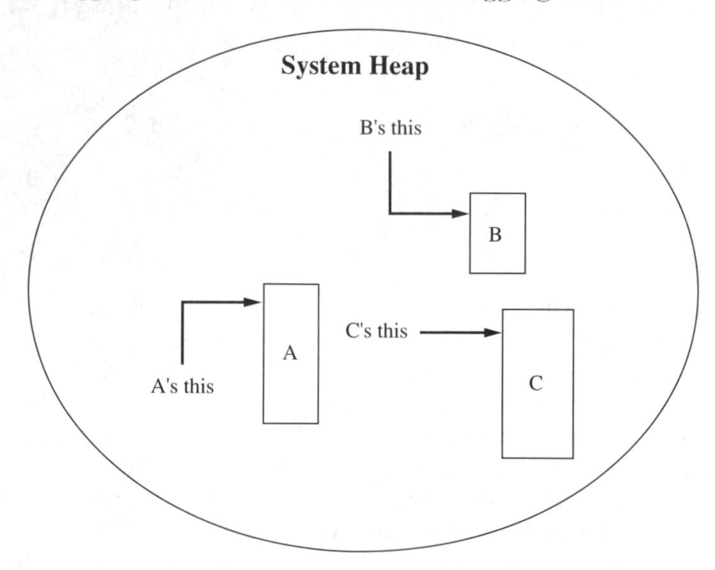

Figure 5.21 The System Heap

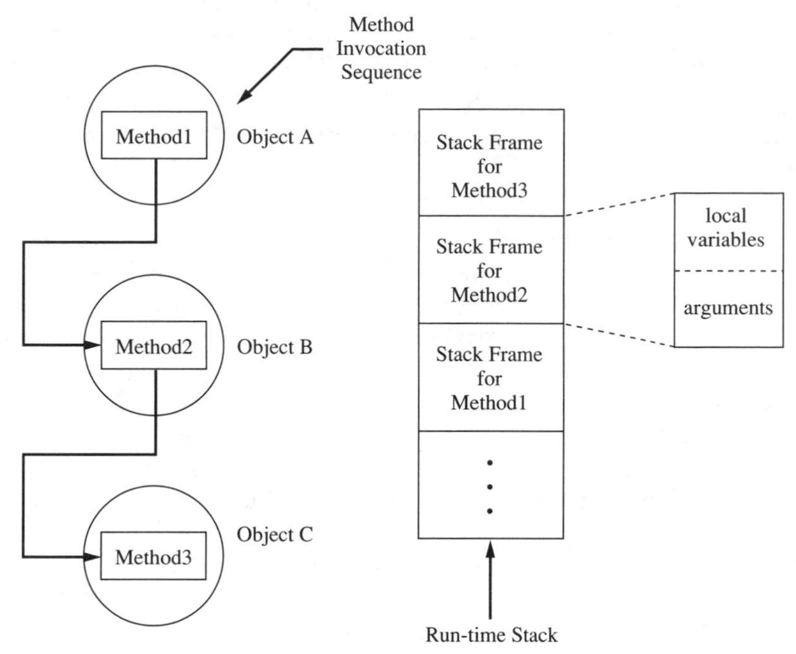

Figure 5.22 The Run-Time Stack

- To examine the state of a dynamically created object a reference to the object is needed. Because the dynamically created object resides in the memory allocated by the heap, there is no way to access such objects except via a reference.
- It is easy to access information about the current execution sequence. Information about the current execution sequence is contained on the run-time stack and easily available to the debugging tools. Typically, debugging tools provide commands for moving among the various stack frames in the run-time stack. By using these commands to view stack frames that are deeper in the stack, the developer is able to trace backward in time in the current execution sequence to determine exactly how the computation was performed.
- It is not easy to obtain information about previous execution sequences. The run-time environment has certain irreversible actions that make it impossible to recover information about some aspects of the past history of the computation. First, when a method returns, its stack frame and all the information that it contained, is lost and cannot be recovered. Second, when a dynamically created object is deleted, the memory occupied by that object is returned to the heap and cannot be recovered. This implies that if

the execution of the code containing the fault(s) is sufficiently removed in time from the execution of the code that results in the failure, the debugger tools may not be able to provide sufficient information to identify the code that contains the faults; by the time the failure occurs the stack frames and objects used in the code containing the faults may have been lost.

The evident strength of automated debugging tools is in examining the execution sequence and existing objects at the time of the failure. In some cases, this information is sufficient to identify the fault. In other cases more extensive means must be used to gather information about past events in the history of the computation.

"Breakpoints" and "logs" are two strategies for gaining information about execution sequences that occur before the failure. Although both strategies provide information about prior execution sequences, they do so in very different ways. Breakpoints are a means of controlling the forward execution of the program starting at a point in time before the failure occurs. Logs are a means of examining a recorded past history to unravel the sequence of events that led to the failure. Breakpoints do not require preprogramming whereas logs are preprogrammed.

Breakpoints are used in the following manner. The developer dynamically inserts breakpoints into the system prior to the system's execution using the commands provided by a debugging tool. A breakpoint can be inserted immediately before any executable line of code. During execution the program will halt whenever a breakpoint is reached and allow the developer to examine the state of objects, examine the current execution sequence, set new breakpoints or remove existing breakpoints, and control the forward execution of the system. The developer controls the forward execution of the system using commands provided by the debugging tool. These commands allow:

- executing a single line of code and then halting,
- executing a fixed number of lines of code and then halting, and
- executing until the next breakpoint or until the point of failure.

When the line of code being executed is an invocation the user has additional options to:

- trace the invocation on a line-by-line basis,
- execute the invocation as a single instruction, and
- after tracing an invocation, run until the invocation returns.

These commands allow the user to control the forward execution of the system and to examine the state of the system at any point in time. The difficulty of using the breakpoint approach is that the user must have a means of setting the breakpoint so that the execution will be halted by the breakpoint before and near the point of failure. In some cases it is difficult or impossible to set a convenient breakpoint. For example, the developer may know that the failure occurs in a given method. However, if that method is executed thousands of times before the failure occurs, setting a breakpoint at the beginning of the method's code is of little use.

A log is a preprogrammed means of gaining information about the past history of the execution. In this approach the developer builds into the code output statements that write selected information to a log file. The information recorded in the log file gives information about the sequence of events that occurred during the system's execution. The preprogrammed output statements typically write to the log file entries indicating when a method has begun and/or completed execution, when the values of parameters or other objects at the time an invocation occurs and/or completes, and relevant information at other points in the execution. The advantage of the log approach is that the complete history is available (at least as much as the developer is willing to preprogram) in a stable form. The developer may use this log to reconstruct the sequence of events that led to the failure or compare the logs of different tests to determine at what point the execution resulting in a failure diverges from a normal execution.The difficulty of the log approach is that it requires the expense of preprogramming; the developer must have a reasonable idea in advance of what information to capture in the log file, and the log file for an execution may be so huge that the critical information needed by the developer is lost in the mass of extraneous log entries.

5.4.4 Debugging Strategies

Developers must employ debugging tools with a strategy in mind. A debugging strategy uses the debugging tools in a deliberate, calculated way that enhances the probability of most rapidly identifying the fault(s) in the system. As with all tools, possessing a powerful debugging tool is not a guarantee of efficiency or effectiveness in debugging. The developer must know and put into practice strategies that help to guide the debugging tool's use.

It may be useful to think of debugging strategies in terms of a game metaphor. The player's (developer's) objective is to navigate a robot (the system state) through a terrain that contains hidden opponents (faults). The opponents can convincingly lie to the robot (make it think that the way ahead is clear when in fact it is on the edge of a cliff). A large unexplored terrain will usually contain many opponents and many hiding places. Two opponents may sometimes collaborate to conceal each other's presence or to create together a harmful effect on the robot that neither one is capable of producing by itself (one opponent distracts the robot while the other pushes it into a hole). The opponents are devious and may set a time-delay bomb on the robot and then run away causing the robot

Proactive	Reactive
Incremental development scope restriction	fault isolation deductive reasoning trap setting model testing

Figure 5.23 Debugging Strategies

to crash when the opponent is not near the robot. The player is allowed to search the terrain (using the debugger) and execute the system under different conditions so as to reveal the presence of an opponent. Although this metaphor is inaccurate in some respects, it does suggest some obvious strategies that the player might use: create a terrain that is easier to examine for possible opponents; don't give the opponents many places to hide; isolate a part of the terrain and search it for opponents; follow the trail backward from the site of a crashed robot looking for clues about the opponents and their hiding places; set traps to catch opponents. These strategies have counterparts in debugging of real systems.

Debugging strategies are either proactive or reactive. Proactive strategies are practices that the developer can use in designing and building the system to limit the introduction of faults. Reactive strategies are practices that the developer can use in locating faults that, despite the best use of proactive strategies, have been introduced into the system. The debugging strategies considered here are shown in Figure 5.23.

The first proactive debugging strategy is "incremental development." Software development projects of any size are always implemented in progressive and incremental manner. It is never the case that all of the code is written before any of it is tested, evaluated, and possibly modified to remove errors or to change parts of the overall design. The many, small progressive tasks that define the incremental strategy for a given system are usually planned in advance. Each step in the incremental development is carefully selected so that it is both testable and minimal. The ability to test each step is necessary to ensure that it is implemented correctly and that it operates correctly with the code that was added in previous steps. There is little point in adding a small bit of code if is so incomplete that there is noway to test it to determine these properties. At the same time, a step represents the smallest incremental addition that can be made that is still testable. If the steps are too large (i.e., introduce too much new functionality and code), it becomes difficult to test it as completely as would be desired. Some experience is usually required to gain a proficiency with identifying a good set of incremental steps. However, once learned, the ability to develop systems in testable, minimal steps will yield numerous advantages.

Although it may seem strange, this development practice is one of the most effective strategies for creating a debugged system because it follows two of the strategies suggested by the game metaphor: "create a terrain that is easier to examine for possible opponents," and "don't give the opponents many places to hide." The first step in incremental development creates the smallest system possible (the least amount of code) to achieve its goal. This gives faults in the program the fewest places to hide and makes it easier to examine simply because there are fewer places to look. Each addition to the system adds a small increment of code. Thus, each debugging step is simpler than one in which a large body of undebugged code is added in a single step. Because less code is introduced, it is easier to discover where mistakes in the code have been made—there are simply fewer places to look. Lessening the interactions between new and old code is important because problems with the code from previous steps may only be revealed by the introduction of code in later steps.

The second proactive debugging strategy is to build systems that use "scope restriction" through encapsulation, information hiding, aggregation, and other design techniques that limit the visibility and accessibility of system components. This design approach creates systems that are more easily debugged because it follows the game strategy of "create a terrain that is easier to examine for possible opponents." Encapsulation and other scope-restricting techniques are the equivalent of building protective walls in the terrain that trap opponents either inside or outside of the wall. Thus trapped, the opponents are easier to find and have more limited ability to cause damage.

The first reactive debugging strategy is "fault isolation." In this strategy the system is made smaller by removing (commenting out) or disabling (turning off) suspected parts of the system. The smaller system is then tested again using the same test conditions that produced the failure. If the failure still occurs, then the removed or disabled part of the system did not contain the fault and the strategy is repeated by removing or disabling an additional part of the system. At each step the fault becomes isolated in a smaller part of the system. At some point the failure will not occur. When the failure does not occur the removed or disabled code contains the fault. The most likely site for the fault is in the last code that was removed or disabled. More extensive and detailed debugging of this can now be done with the debugger. This strategy follows the game metaphor notions of "don't give the opponents many places to hide" and "isolate a part of the terrain and search it for opponents." Notice that the debugging tools did not come into play until after the strategy had yielded a smaller area to examine.

The second reactive debugging strategy is "deductive reasoning." Debugging is like the work of a detective: starting at the point of failure (scene of the crime) the system state contains information (clues) from which deductions can be made about how the failure occurred. Possible causes (suspects) for the observed system state can be tested (interrogated), which either reveals the fault (culprit) or produces new information (additional clues) for further deduction and tests. Unlike real detectives, the developer has the advantage of using the debugging tools to replay the system's execution (the crime) and examine in detail a possible cause (suspect). Notice that the use of the debugging tool is important, though secondary—the use of the tool is guided by the strategy that determines what to look for and where to look for it. As with legendary detectives, sharp deductive reasoning is better than a powerful debugging tool.

The third reactive debugging strategy is "trap setting." Difficult cases to debug are those where the developer knows in what way the system state has been damaged but cannot gather much evidence about how or when the damage occurred. For example, the system may fail because a state variable has an incorrect value but this value can be changed as a result of many actions in the system. This situation is often one where the execution of the code that causes the failure is in a different execution sequence from the one that executed the code containing the fault. A starting point for debugging can be found by setting a trap to identify when and where the system state is damaged. A trap can be set using a debugging tool to set a *watch condition*. Both of these techniques allow the developer to be notified when the damage to the system state occurs. With this starting point the other strategies can be used to locate the fault.

The fourth reactive debugging strategy is "model testing." In some cases the system being debugged is too complex to apply the other strategies. If the developer has an idea of what components are involved in the failure, a scaled-down model of the system can be built and tested. The model must be able to exhibit the same failure as the real system. If such a model can be constructed, locating the fault in the simpler model can also reveal the fault in the more complex, real system. Although this may sound difficult, it is often easy to construct the model for testing. For example, in a graphical editor system if there is a problem with the resizing of polygons, then a special test program can be built that creates a single, hard-coded polygon. This model system can be tested.

Some other hints and suggestions about debugging are:

- Find the fault that caused the failure. The system may contain several faults. Simply finding some fault does not mean that this fault caused the observed failure. Although the discovered fault should be corrected, the debugging should continue in search of the fault that caused the observed failure. Retesting the system after correcting the fault will easily reveal if the right fault has been found. It is also a good idea to be able to explain how the fault caused the failure. Without such an explanation either the wrong fault has been found or the developer may not know how to correct the fault.
- A fault may remain undiscovered for some time. If the testing is not thorough it is possible for a fault to remain dormant for many steps in the incremental development of the system. When the failure does occur, the "obvious" places to look—in the most recently added code—are not the right places. This does not mean that incremental development and fault isolation should be abandoned; it does mean that the developer needs to be aware of the possibility of a long-dormant fault.
- Do not replace one fault with another. The reason the fault was introduced into the system was due to an error in the mind of the developer. The

developer must be sure that this misconception has been corrected before attempting to correct the fault in the code or else a likely outcome is that the original fault is replaced by a new fault.

- Avoid hopeful corrections. Developers may sometimes change code "hoping" that the change will fix the failure even if there is little or no evidence that the original code contains a fault. This practice has little chance of succeeding. The developer must be disciplined enough to reject an ill-conceived and unjustified change. The surest way to avoid hopeful corrections is to insist on explanation for how the fault produced the failure. In absence of such an explanation, there is no reason to believe that the change will have the desired effect. At best the change will mask the real fault, in which case an even more difficult debugging task is left for later—discovering and removing the masking code and then finding the underlying fault.
- Avoid frustration. Debugging can easily lead to unproductive frustration especially when the writer of the code is also the person doing the debugging.Frustration results from the combined knowledge that the developer cannot find the problems and that the problem is of the developer's own making. Adopting a game-playing attitude may help. Envision the faults as opponents in the game metaphor.
- Get help. Because faults are due to errors on the part of the developers, the developer may not be able to see past the misconception that lies at the heart of the problem. It may be useful to get another mind involved that does not share the misconception. Another team member may be useful in this role. Sometimes it is enough simply to try to explain the failure to someone else. The mere act of articulating one's thinking can force the misconception out in the open.

Even with these strategies and hints, the developer must realize that there is no shortcut in the difficult work of debugging—patient determination, consistent application of effective strategies, and knowledgeable use of debugging tools are the only real paths to success.

Exercises

1. For the debugging tool that you are using, find out how to set watch conditions or watch points.

2. For the debugging tool that you are using, find out how to examine the current execution history and navigate among its stack frames (activation records).
3. For the debugging tool that you are using, find out how to examine an object's data given a variable that is a reference to that object.
4. For the debugging tool that you are using, find out how set breakpoints in the program's execution and control the flow of execution once the breakpoint is reached.
5. Name all of the features of the Java language that contribute to scope restriction.

5.5 Organizing Related Classes in Packages

A Java package is a named collection of classes that are related to each other because they act together to provide a common service, are typically used together, or are implemented to share protected information. Examples of packages in the Java development environment are shown in Figure 5.24. We have already seen the Vector class (described in Section 4.6) and some of the I/O classes (in Section 2.7). The swing package is described in detail in Chapter 7 and the I/O package is presented in Chapter 8. This section describes the mechanism the Java developers used to organize these collection of classes into related groups using the Java package feature.

5.5.1 Uses of Packages

Packages are used to accomplish one or more of three important goals: organization, security, and naming. A developer uses packages to systematically arrange a large collection of classes just as folders are used in a desktop environment to arrange a large collection of documents and files. Also like folders, packages can

swing	basic GUI classes (Chapter 7)
io	input/output (Chapter 8)
net	classes for networking and distributed communications (Chapter 9)
util	utility classes and basic data structures (e.g., Vector)

Figure 5.24 Example Java Packages

be arranged in a hierarchical, nested structure. The physical organization of a package's contents allow packages to be conveniently stored and archived as a single file (i.e., as a zip or tar file) for dissemination to others. The package organization also allows the developer to create a rational structure within which it is easier to locate a desired class for reuse.

Security is the second reason for creating a package because the classes in a package may create data and methods that are only accessible by other members of the package. This feature allows the implementor of a package's class to expose sensitive information or operations that are needed by other trusted classes—those in the same package—without exposing these methods or operations to general use by untrusted classes outside of the package.

The third major use for packages is to create a structured name space in which classes with the same name can coexist without conflict. This need arises because it is not unusual for common terms such as HelpMenu, FileDialogue, and StartButton to be used by different implementors or vendors as names of classes that have nothing in common other than their names. The package provides an additional layer of naming that allows classes with the same name to be used together in the same application because a class named StartButton in the package Controls can be distinguished from the class named StartButton in the package InterfaceComponents. Packages help to avoid name conflicts in the same way that a file system allows files in different directories or folders to have the same name. Similar problems and solutions apply to the names of packages: two packages with the same name must themselves be placed in distinctly named packages. One proposal for a global (literally!) package naming scheme uses a reverse form of an organization's World Wide Web URL. In this scheme, a company named `Marvel.com` would have a highest level package named `com` that contained a single package named `Marvel`. All the package names within the `Marvel` package could then be safely chosen by Marvel's developers without fear of conflict with other vendors. In a large organization, individual projects or departments could be assigned package names within the Marvel package and given the authority to create package names within their assigned package. This is similar to the way that an administrator of a shared file system assigns a top-level directory to each user who is then free to create their own subdirectory names that are guaranteed not to be confused with subdirectories of other users even if the names of these sub-directories are identical.

5.5.2 Creating a Package

A class declares its membership in a package by means of a statement that uses the keyword `package` as shown in Figure 5.25 for the PolyShape class that adds itself to a package named Shape. The package is not explicitly created—its existence is implied by the fact that a class adds itself to the package. Other classes, such as the Rectangle class, could also add themselves to the Shape package by using the same package statement.The package statement must be the first

```
package shape;
//... import statements
public class PolyShape
{
   //...
}
```

Figure 5.25 The Package Statement

```
package graphics.shapes;        package graphics.window;
// ... import statements        // ... import statements
public class PolyShape          public class Color
{                               {
  //...                           // ...
}                               }
```

Figure 5.26 Hierarchical Package Naming

statement in a file. A class may only be in one package and any class that does not explicitly declare its membership in a package is added to a default, unnamed package.

A hierarchical package organization can be created by using multipart, structured package names of the form X.Y.Z, which means that the class is adding itself to a package Z that is included in a package Y that is included in a package X. The various Java packages, for example, are included ina top-level package named java so that the classes in the I/O package declare themselves to be members in the package `java.io` and the classes in the networking package declare themselves to be members of the package `java.net`. To show how a hierarchical package organization is created, suppose that the PolyShape and related classes are to be grouped into a package named `shapes` whereas the Canvas, Color, and their related classes are placed in a package named `window`. Furthermore, the two packages `shapes` and `window` could be grouped themselves in a package named `graphics`. As shown in Figure 5.26, the declaration of the PolyShape and Color classes simply use the hierarchical names graphics.shapes and graphics.window to name the package in which they should be included.

5.5.3 Importing A Class

A class is imported simply by naming the class and its package—including any hierarchical package names—in an import statement. For example, the following code imports the Polyshape and Color classes using the hierarchical package organization given in Figure 5.26:

```
import graphics.window.Color;
import graphics.shapes.PolyShape;
// ...
```

```
Color red = new Color(255,0,0);
PolyShape polygon = new PolyShape(...);
```

Notice that once the class has been imported only the simple name of the class need be used, not the hierarchical name.

A convenient notation allows all of the classes in a package to be imported. The following statement imports all of the classes in the `graphics.shape` package:

```
import graphics.shape.*;
```

where the asterisk (*) is used to denote all of the classes in the package.This use of the asterisk is similar to the way a wildcard in a filename pattern-matching expression, such as `example.*`, is used to identify all files in a directory that have a base name of `example` and any file extension (e.g., `example.zip` and `example.gif`). In an import statement the asterisk may only appear as the last part of a hierarchical name; thus `graphics.*.shape`, `graphics.*.*` and similar expressions are not allowed.

If a class's package—but not the class itself—has been imported, the class must be named in the code by using a hierarchical naming notation similar to that used in the import statement itself. For example, in the following code segment:

```
import graphics.shape;
// ...
shape.PolyShape polygon = new shape.PolyShape(...);
```

the hierarchical name `shape.PolyShape` is needed in the code to complete the naming of the intended class.

Using a hierarchical name in the code is needed to deal with the possible ambiguity arising in cases where the same class name is used in two different packages. Suppose that both the `shape` and the `window` package search contained a class named Edge; Edge in the `window` package is used to describe the width and color of the edge of a window whereas Edge in the `shape` package is used to describe the two points that are connected by an line. The hierarchical names must be used to disambiguate references to these two classes as shown in the following code segment:

```
import graphics.shape;
import graphics.window;
//...
shape.Edge line = new shape.Edge(...);         // Edge in Shape package
window.Edge border = new window.Edge(...);     // Edge in Window package
```

5.5.4 Storing and Finding Packages

The compiled .class files for classes that are members of a given package must be stored in a directory whose name matches that of the package. For example, because the PolyShape and Rectangle classes are members of the package shapes, the PolyShape.class and Rectangle.class files must be placed in a directory named shapes. This same rule applies to hierarchical package structure. Because the PolyShape and Rectangle classes are members of the package graphics.shapes, the shapes directory must be a subdirectory of a directory named graphics.

The CLASSPATH environment variable specifies a set of places to look in the file system for directories that correspond to packages. The Java compiler and other Java-related utilities use the CLASSPATH environment variable to locate directories that contain the compiled .class files for classes that are members of packages. Continuing our working example, suppose that the complete path name of PolyShape.class file in the file system is:

```
c:\Courses\Java\graphics\shapes\PolyShape.class     (Windows95/98/NT system)
/home/user/Courses/Java/graphics/shapes/PolyShape.class  (Unix system)
```

Although the directory names graphics and shapes are specified by the package statement in the PolyShape definition, the location of these directories in the complete file system is not specified. The CLASSPATH variable for the continuing example might be:

```
CLASSPATH=C:\JavaStuff\Code;.;C:\Courses\Java      (Windows95/98/NT system)
CLASSPATH=/home/user/JavaStuff/Code:.:/home/user/Courses/Java (Unix system)
```

where the value of the CLASSPATH variable is an ordered list of directory names to be searched. Adjacent directory names are separated by a semicolon (;) in Windows95 system or by a colon (:) in Unix systems. In the example above, each CLASSPATH specifies three directory names. The dot (.) symbol denotes the "current working directory"—that is, the directory at run-time of where the program is executing. These CLASSPATH variables specify that the Java compiler should search, in order, the directories:

```
Windows95/98/NT system                  Unix system

C:\JavaStuff\Code                       /home/user/JavaStuff/Code
.(current working directory)            . (current working directory)
C:\Courses\Java                         /home/user/Courses/Java
```

The directory names in the CLASSPATH variable and the package names an import statement are used to locate the .class file. Thus, the import statement:

```
import graphics.shapes.PolyShape;
```

would cause the compiler to look for a .class file whose name matched one of the following:

```
Windows95/98/NT system:
    C:\JavaStuff\Code\graphics\shapes\PolyShape.class
```

```
1. create the logical organization of the packages
   by defining and compiling the class definitions
   that contain the package statements.

2. create the physical organization of the packages
   by making a directory structure that corresponds
   to the logical organization of the packages.

3. initialize the physical organization by copying
   each .class file to its corresponding place
   in the physical organization.

4. enable the importing of the package members by
   adding to the CLASSPATH variable the name(s) of
   the root directory or directories of the physical
   organization.
```

Figure 5.27 Steps in Using Packages

```
    .\graphics\shapes\PolyShape.class
    C:\Courses\Java\graphics\shapes\PolyShape.class

Unix system:
    /home/user/JavaStuff/Code/graphics/shapes/PolyShape.class
    ./graphics/shapes/PolyShape.class
    /home/user/Courses/Java/graphics/shapes/PolyShape.class
```

The search is terminated when the first file matching the required filename is found. If no such file can be found, the Java compiler issues an error message.

The steps to organize and use a set of packages are summarized in Figure 5.27.

5.5.5 Restricting Access to Package Members

Using the package structure, classes, method, and instance data may be declared so that they are accessible only by other members of the package; these classes, methods, and instance data are not accessible by code that is in any class outside of the package. This addition level of accessibility provides a way for package members to share among themselves abilities that are not allowed for non-package members. A developer may make use of this level of accessibility for two reasons. First, classes can be hidden in the package that are used only as part of the implementation of other classes in the package and not intended to be used by classes outside of the package. An example of this will be given below. Second, for performance reasons, methods of classes may allow access to the internal subobjects of a class so that they may be accessed by other classes in the package; the developer may not want non-package classes to be able to access these subobjects as it would weaken the encapsulation of the class more than is desired.

```
//file LocationNode.java

package shapes;

class LocationNode  // not public
{//...
}

//file PolyShape.java

package shapes;

public class PolyShape
{ private LocationNode head;
  private LocationNode tail;
  //...
}
```

Figure 5.28 Accessibility Within a Package

To illustrate one reason for using packages to restrict access, consider the PolyShape class. The PolyShape class uses the LocationNode class to implement a dynamic aggregation. The LocationNode class is purely part of the implementation mechanism for the PolyShape class: the PolyShape class does not return objects of the LocationNode class nor does it have input parameters of this class. No class other than the PolyShape class needs to know about the existence of the LocationNode class. A revised outline of these two classes is given in Figure 5.28 using the package named `shapes` introduced above. Notice that both the LocationNode class and the PolyShape class declare themselves as members of the `shapes` package. Also notice that the LocationNode class is not declared as public. The absence of an accessibility modifier (e.g., `public`) in front of the `class` keyword denotes package-level access. In other words, by removing the public keyword from the class declaration, the accessibility of the class becomes limited to other package members. Because the PolyShape class is also a member of the `shapes` package, it is able to access the LocationNode class definition. This definition is used to define part of the PolyShape's aggregated data as shown in the bottom part of Figure 5.28. Other classes in the `shapes` package would also be able to use the LocationNode class as part of their implementation. However, no classes outside of the `shapes` package would be able to use the LocationNode class.

Package accessibility can also be given to individual methods and instance variables of a class. The Prey class is modified to show how an individual method's accessibility can be restricted. Suppose that the developer wanted to restrict the `spawn` method of the Prey class so that Prey objects could only be spawned by other code that was developed as part of the same package as the Prey class. Figure 5.29 shows a part of the Prey class with two changes that accomplish this restriction. First, the Prey class declares itself to be a member of the `ecosim` package. Second, the `spawn` method is declared with no public modifier. Because no accessibility modifier has been given for the `spawn` method, this method's accessibility is taken to be package-level access. This means that the

```
package ecosim;

public class Prey ...
{
  //...
  void spawn()      // package accessibility
  {...
  }
}

package ecosim;

public class Birth
{
  public void generate()
  { //...
     creature.spawn();  //invoke restricted method
    //...
}
```

Figure 5.29 Restricting Method Accessibility

spawn method can only be invoked by code of a class that is also declared as part of the ecosim package. For example, if the Birth class is also declared as part of the ecosim package, the generate method of the Birth class could invoke the spawn method as shown in the bottom part of Figure 5.29.

Exercises

1. By examining the CLASSPATH variable for your system find where the java.util package is stored on your system.
2. Revise the classes that are part of the ecological simulation so that they are in a single package. Move this package to a different place in your file system and reset the CLASSPATH variable for your system accordingly. Revise one of the ecological simulation test programs to import your package. Execute the revised program to verify that the classes in your package were found.
3. Write some test code to determine if a single class can be in two packages at the same time.
4. Hypothesize about the effect of creating a class whose constructors are declared with package-level accessibility. Write test programs to explore your hypothesis. Can you think of a situation where this would be useful?

5.6 Documenting a Class

5.6.1 External Documentation

A class must be well documented to be (re)usable. Although the critical role of documentation is clear when we are the ones attempting to use someone else's code, a common failing among developers, especially among novice programmers, is to focus on the design and implementation with little regard for documentation. The bias against documentation comes from several sources. First, documentation is demeaned with respect to design and implementation, which are considered the technical and interesting aspects of development, whereas documentation is merely a recording or reporting activity lacking in creative challenge. Second, writing and communication are often not coherently integrated into the educational programs through which most developers have been trained. Writing and programming are compartmentalized, without a clear connection suggesting the important role that written and oral communication play in the total software development process. Third, although the execution properties of a system can be easily demonstrated and graded, sometimes even by automated graders, documentation can only be evaluated for content by more time-consuming methods. Thus, documentation often plays much less of a role in the evaluation of work produced by learning programmers. Despite these factors, documentation is essential. A simple thought experiment to demonstrate the important role of documentation is to consider any reasonably complicated set of classes; for example, Java's GUI classes in the Swing Toolkit (see Chapter 7). Imagine trying to use these classes in the absence of any documentation.

There are several forms of documentation. Taking the view that documentation encompasses all of the non-executable parts of a system, the UML diagrams are a form of documentation; they convey in an annotated, semi-structured, graphical language the essence of the overall design. Aside from such design documentation, other forms of documentation include internal documentation, external documentation, and user manuals. Internal documentation refers to comments that are placed within the code to explain the detailed role of a statement of a group of statements. For example, variable declarations are often commented to describe what is represented by the value of the variable. Similarly, decisions and iterations are often preceded by comments indicating their overall intended effect. External documentation refers to descriptions at the class and method level. The class description conveys the abstraction captured by the class. The description of each method indicates the behavior that it elicits, the conditions under which it can be invoked correctly, and what information must be given as parameters of the method's invocation. The internal and external documentation are closely tied to the organization of the code. A user manual provides a narrative description of how to use the system from the user's perspective. This level of documentation refers only incidentally to code or design issues and is organized around user's tasks and concepts and not those of the design or implementation.

External documentation, documentation at the class and method level, is the focus of this section. Beginning programmers are exposed to the use of comments for internal documentation and the writing of user manuals is an extensive topic in its own right. External documentation is the middle ground that is needed for the communication between class developers and class (re) users. In this sense, external documentation is communication between developers. Thus, the vocabulary and level of discourse may remain at the technical level. Finally, external documentation is considered here because there are automated tools to assist with the mechanical aspects of producing the documentation in a useful form.

5.6.2 The "javadoc" Utility

The Java Development Kit (JDK) provides a tool to assist with external documentation, javadoc. Javadoc is a document generator that produces an indexed collection of web pages based on structured comments that are embedded in Java code. The javadoc tool overcomes two common problems that make documentation difficult. First, because the structured comments are embedded in the Java code itself, javadoc facilitates consistency between the code and its documentation that is often lacking in other approaches. Java programmers using javadoc can change the code and its documentation in the same file at one time. Rerunning javadoc automatically generates the updated documentation. In other approaches, the external documentation is maintained in a separate structure from the code allowing for inconsistencies to develop more easily between them. Second, javadoc automatically constructs an indexed collection of HTML documents. The index allows for easy access to the documentation for each class and the hyperlinked structure allows easy cross-referencing between related classes. For example, if a method's parameter is an object of another class, a hyperlink will be generated automatically from the parameter to the external documentation for its class. The documentor can also easily add other hyperlinks to related classes and methods. The javadoc approach, embedding external documentation comments in the code, does have one drawback. With the embedded comments it is more difficult to see the code itself. Arguably, this makes it slightly more difficult to work with the code during development than if the comments were not present.

The javadoc utility produces a three-part browsable documentation file (i.e., an `.html` file) for each class. For a class defined in the file `ClassName.java`, javadoc produces a documentation file named `ClassName.html`. The documentation file is in a standard format that organizes the information given in the class's embedded structured comments. The documentation file consists of three logical parts: the class description, the constructor/method index, and the con-

Class Location

```
java.lang.Object
  |
  +--Location
```

---

public class **Location**
extends java.lang.Object

This class captures the abstraction of a location in a two dimensional rectangular coordinate system. The location is defined by an (x,y) coordinate pair. Both coordinates are integer values. The x and y coordinates can be specified when the Location object is constructed. Accessor methods return the x and y coordinates individually.

Figure 5.30 The Class Description Part of a Documentation File

Constructor Summary
`Location()` Construct a location object using the default coordinates (0,0).
`Location(int x, int y)` Construct a Location object given its x and y coordinates.

Method Summary	
int	`getX()` Returns the x coordinate of the current (x,y) location.
int	`getY()` Returns the x coordinate of the current (x,y) location.

Figure 5.31 The Constructor/Method Index for a Documentation File

structor/method descriptions. The Location class is used to illustrate these three sections.

The first part of the documentation file for a class contains the overall description of the class. This part of the documentation file for the Location class is shown in Figure 5.30. Above the horizontal rule (line) is the name of the class and an inheritance diagram whose meaning will be made clear in Chapter 7. By default, all classes are related to the predefined Java class named Object. Below the horizontal rule is the name and description of the class. The text for the description is taken from that given in the structured comments embedded in the Location.java file.

The second part of the documentation file is the constructor/method index. This part of the documentation file for the Location class is shown in Figure 5.31. The constructor index gives the signature and one sentence description of each constructor defined in the class. The name field in the signature is a hyper-link to

Constructor Detail

Location

```
public Location(int x,
                int y)
```

Construct a Location object given its x and y coordinates.
Parameters:
x - the x coordinate of the (x,y) location
y - the y coordinate of the (x,y) location

Method Detail

getX

```
public int getX()
```

Returns the x coordinate of the current (x,y) location. The x coordinate is not changed.
Returns:
the x coordinate of the location

Figure 5.32 Constructor/Method Descriptions in a Documentation File

the more complete description of the constructor in the third part of the documentation file. The method index is similar.

The third part of the documentation file is a detailed description of each constructor and method in the class. Portions of this part of the documentation file for the Location class is shown in Figure 5.32. The top part of Figure 5.32 shows the documentation for one the two constructors of the Location class. The signature of the constructor is given followed by a description of the constructor. The text for this description is taken from the embedded comments in the Location.java file. Following the description is a "Parameters:" section that lists the parameters used in the constructor. Documentation text for each parameter is given as supplied in the Location.javafile. The bottom part of Figure 5.32 shows the documentation for the `getX` method of the Location class. The layout of the documentation for a method is similar to that of a constructor with the addition of a "Returns:" section. This section documents the meaning of the value returned by the method. In this example, the method does not have a parameter list, but if one were present it would have a section for documenting each parameter as was shown with the constructor in the upper part of the figure.

The javadoc utility makes extensive use of hyperlinks to provide documentation that is easily navigable. Some use of hyperlinks was seen in the constructor/method index in Figure 5.31. Thus, clicking on the name of a constructor or method in the index causes the browser to advance to that part of the file containing the detailed description of the constructor or method. One other use of hyperlinks was not shown in this example. If the parameter of a method is an object of a class, the signature given in the detailed constructor or method description will contain a hyperlink to that class. Thus, when examining the documentation for a method it is easy to follow the hyperlink to the documentation for the objects that must be used to invoke the method. Similarly, a hyperlink is created when returned values are objects of a class.

The javadoc utility also produces three hyperlinked indices. One index, contained in a file named tree.html, lists all of the classes by name and shows the inheritance relationships among them. Inheritance is covered in Chapter 6 and the significance of this index will become fully clear then. For now, this index provides a simple listing of each class by name in alphabetical order. A second index, contained in a file named AllNames.html, is an alphabetical list of all "names" encountered by javadoc, including the names of methods, classes, fields, and packages. This index is useful for locating the documentation of any named entity. The third index, contained in a file named packages.html, is an alphabetical list of all packages that are defined in the classes processed by javadoc. The role of packages is explained later in this chapter.

5.6.3 Structured Comments and Tags in javadoc

The documentation text intended to be processed by javadoc are placed in special comments sometimes referred to as doc-comments. A doc-comment begins with the characters "`/**`"and end with the characters "`*/`." To the compiler, a doc-comment appears as regular comment because it begins with "`/*`" and ends with "`*/`," the form of a regular comment. Thus, doc-comments do not require any special treatment by the Java compiler. Doc-comments should be placed immediately before the class declaration (`public class ...`) and immediately before each method. The doc-comments before the class declaration should be used to describe the overall purpose of the class whereas those before each method should describe the method's role and operation. The placement of the doc-comments is important because it implies to javadoc how the doc-comments are related to the elements of the class definition. For example, the doc-comments that come immediately before the class declaration are used by javadoc to produce a class index that gives a summary for each class. If the doc-comments for a class are moved elsewhere in the Java code, javadoc has no way of recognizing it as a doc-comment for the class. Finally, the first sentence in each doc-comment for a class or method should be a one sentence summary of the class or method because javadoc will use this sentence by itself in certain of its generated index files. The rule for doc-comments are summarized in Figure 5.33.

In addition to ordinary text, doc-comments may include two different kinds of tags that give special meaning or formatting to the tagged information. One kind of tags are defined by javadoc. These tags identify the meaning of the infor-

- Text intended for javadoc must be placed in doc-comments that begin with `"/**"` and end with `"*/"`
- Doc-comments for a class must be placed immediately before the class declaration
- Doc-comments for a method must be placed immediately before the method declaration
- The first sentence for a doc-comment should be a one-sentence summary of the class or method being documented

Figure 5.33 Conventions for javadoc Doc-Comments

@see ***classname***
: generates a "See Also:" entry referring to the class "classname" (e.g., `@see Frame`)

@see ***full-classname***
: generates a "See Also:" entry referring to the class whose name is "full-classname" (e.g., `@see java.awt.Frame`)

@see ***full-classname#method***
: generates a "See Also:" entry referring to the specified method of the specified class (e.g., `@see java.awt.Frame#setTitle`)

@version ***text***
: generates a "Version:" entry with the "text" used as the version identification (e.g., `@version Version 1.1.5`). This tag may only appear in a doc-comment for a class, not a method.

@author ***text***
: generates an "Author:" entry with the "text" used as the identify of the author (e.g., `@author John Q. Programmer`)

@param ***name text***
: generates an entry in the "Parameters:" list for the current method where "name" is the parameter's name as used in the Java code and "text" is a description of the parameter's role and meaning.

@return ***text***
: generates a "Return:" entry for the current method where text is used as a description of the return value's meaning.

Figure 5.34 javadoc Tags

mation that follows the tag. The other kind of tags are a subset of HTML markup tags. These tags give more control over the appearance of the text in the web pages generated by javadoc. The format of the javadoc tags is "`@tag`" where tag is one of several keywords. For example, the `@param` tag is used to define documenting text for a method's parameter and the `@return` tag is used to define documenting text for a method's return value. The more commonly used javadoc tags are given in Figure 5.34.

```
/**
   This class captures the abstraction of a location
   in a two dimensional rectangular coordinate system.
   The location is defined by an (x,y) coordinate pair.
   Both coordinates are integer values. The x and y coordinates
   can be specified when the Location object is constructed.
   Accessor methods return the x and y coordinates individually.
*/

public class Location                              // Version 1
{
  /**
   Construct a Location object given its  x and y coordinates.

   @param <Bx</B the x coordinate of the (x,y) location
   @param <By</B the y coordinate of the (x,y) location
   */

  public      Location(int x, int y)      // specific location
  { //...
  }

  /**
   Construct a location object using the default coordinates (0,0).
   */
  public      Location()                  // default location
  { //...
  }

  /**
   Returns the x coordinate of the current (x,y) location.
   The x coordinate is not changed.

  @return the x coordinate of the location
   */

  public int getX()                      // return x-axis coordinate
  { return xcoord;
  }

  /**
   Returns the x coordinate of the current (x,y) location.
   The x coordinate is not changed.

  @return the y coordinate of the location
   */

  public int getY()                      // return y-axis coordinate
  { return ycoord;
  }
}
```

Figure 5.35 The Doc-Comments in the Location Class

The doc-comments may also contain a subset of HTML markup tags that can be used to affect the appearance of the documentation. These tags are usually in pairs that bracket the text to which they apply with a tag of the form <tag-name preceding the text and a tag of the form </tag-name at the end of the text. The angle brackets are a required part of the syntax. For example, text can be emphasized by

making it **boldface** using the pair of tags `<B` and `</B` or by putting it in *italics* using the pair of tags `<I` and `</I`. To include extra vertical space a break tag, `<BR`, can be used. Not all HTML markup tags can be used in doc-comments because they interfere with the HTML tags generated by javadoc itself.

5.6.4 An Example

The doc-comments used to generate the documentation for the Location class are shown in Figure 5.35, previous page. The first doc-comment gives an overall description of the class. This doc-comment must come immediately before the class declaration because it is intended to be taken by javadoc as the class-level documentation. The doc-comments for the first constructor contains the text describing the constructor and a pair of `@param` tags, one for each parameter of the constructor. Notice also that the name of the parameter will appear in boldface in the generated HTML because of the `<B` and `</B` tags. The doc-comment for each constructor and each method must also precede the constructor or method which they document. The doc-comment for the `getX` method shows the use of an `@return` tag to document the value returned by a method.

Exercises

1. Browse the web and find other available tools similar to javadoc. Compare their features and decide which one you would prefer to use. Download this tool and make it available in your local environment.
2. Examine the javadoc generated documentation for one of the Java libraries (e.g., the swingx library for building GUIs). What features of javadoc can you see being used?
3. Use javadoc to develop external documentation for one of the classes that you implemented earlier. Run javadoc and view the generated HTML files.
4. Modify the Location.java file so that the doc-comment for the class is moved from being immediately before the `public class Location` declaration to immediately after this line. What effect does this have on the generated documentation.
5. Modify the Location.java file so that an "Author:" section is generated by javadoc naming you as the author.
6. Modify the Location.java file so that a "Version:" section is generated with the version being 1.2.3.

CHAPTER 6

Inheritance

6.1 Introduction

Generalization captures the shared aspects of abstractions. It is not unusual to find such generalizations in everyday experience. For example, the statement "all computer workstations have a monitor" expresses a generalization about computer workstations: it identifies a common attribute among the various abstractions for a computer workstation. Similarly, the statement "all telephones can make connections through the telephone switching system" expresses a similarity in behavior: all abstractions of telephones will possess a behavior that allows them to make connections. In a programming context, when a group of abstractions in an application domain share similar features, the classes representing these abstractions may also be similar. This is natural because a class is intended to reflect the attributes and behavior of an abstraction. Thus, similarities in the abstractions will result in similarities among the classes representing them.

A Java interface is one way of expressing generalization. The definition of an interface contains the set of methods that are common to a set of classes. Several examples of interfaces were seen in earlier chapters. In Section 3.5, the Sequenced interface described the methods (i.e., `next` and `reset`) that were common to abstractions that maintained information in a sequential order. The generalization expressed by the Sequenced interface applied to the ImageSequence class, that maintained images in a sequential order, and the Counter class, that maintained numeric values in a sequential order. The Hunted and Hunter interfaces were also seen in Section 3.5. These two interfaces described generalizations of the "prey" and "predator" abstractions, respectively, in the ecological simulation application. Java interfaces are limited, however, in that the only generalization that can be expressed are the signatures of methods.

Inheritance is a mechanism for expressing a generalization more completely than is possible with interfaces. The generalization expressed by inheritance includes not only signatures of methods, but may also include the implementation of these methods and the data structures manipulated by them. Inheritance extends the class concept to distinguish between a base class that defines the shared interface and implementation, and a derived class that inherits the shared elements from the base class. Equivalent terminology used in other object-oriented languages are superclass and subclass, referring to base and derived classes, respectively. The derived class is endowed automatically with all of the methods and implementation of its base class. Derived classes may add new methods and implementation, creating a more specific or specialized abstraction than that represented by the base class. Several derived classes may have the same base class and a derived class may itself serve as the base class for its own collection of derived classes. Thus, the inheritance relationships define a tree or hierarchical structure among the classes.

Conceptually, inheritance is often described as an "is-a" relation between a generalized abstraction and one or more specializations. For example, a "vehicle" abstraction captures the notion of a mechanical device that is used to transport people and/or things from one place to another using some medium. Specializations of the vehicle abstraction might include "car," "bus," and "truck," objects that are all land-based wheeled vehicles, as well as "airplane," "helicopter," and "blimp," objects that are all airborne vehicles. The statement "car is a vehicle," illustrates why the inheritance is referred to as an "is-a" relationship. As noted in the paragraph above, the inheritance, or "is-a", relationship can create a hierarchical tree structure among abstractions. For example, the "car" abstraction may be further specialized to describe "taxi cabs," "rental cars," and "personal cars," each of which "is-a" car but with different notions of the ownership and driver. The airplane abstraction can also be specialized to capture more specific abstractions such as "jet airplane," and "propeller airplane," or it can be specialized in a different way to capture other specialization such as "commercial airplane" and "private airplane."

Inheritance is arguably the most critical aspect of object-oriented programming because it has implications in three important dimensions:

1. **Programming**: expressing the similarities among a related set of classes in a single base class makes unnecessary the repetition of code in each of the derived classes. Not only does this create an immediate savings for the classes at hand, but it also establishes a foundation on which future derived classes can be built more efficiently.
2. **Design**: in the largest sense, software design is a form of knowledge engineering, because it attempts to represent in software a model of the real world. A good designer does more than organize software structures; he or she tries to reflect in the software the existence and

organization of abstractions in the problem domain. Thus, if there are similarities among the abstractions, there should be a corresponding way to represent these similarities in the software. The more direct and explicit the software can be in representing these similarities, the better a model it will be of the application domain.

3. **Software engineering**: software has a long lifetime and undergoes many changes and extensions during its existence. Therefore, important qualities of software are the degrees to which it is flexible, that it can be modified to add new features, and extensible, that is to say that it can accommodate the creation of new elements not originally anticipated.

Learning how to exploit the power of inheritance is the hallmark of a successful object-oriented programming. The most successful users of inheritance are those who are able to combine its ability to organize concepts coherently via the "is-a" relation and achieve significant practical advantage through the sharing of implementations.

6.2 Using Inheritance to Share Implementation

Using inheritance to share implementation is illustrated by two examples in this section. The first example is related to the graphical user application used in previous chapters. In the first example, the complete implementations of two numeric classes, Number and Cycler, are shown, assuming that each was developed as an independent class. Then, a base class that captures those aspects of the implementation common to the two classes is defined. Finally, the original classes are then reimplemented using inheritance. Objects of the two new derived classes will have the same interface and behavior as objects of the original classes. The second example used in this chapter is derived from the ecological simulation application. In this example, the predator and prey abstractions are generalized and their corresponding classes are redesigned and reimplemented using inheritance.

6.2.1 Generalizing Two Numeric Classes

The definition of the Number class is given in Figure 6.1. This class captures the abstraction of an integer value that can be incremented by one without limit. Objects of this class can be used to count the occurrence of some event. The constructor specifies the starting value for a Number object, zero by default. The `next` operation increments the value of the Number object by one. The current value of a Number object is returned by the `value` accessor method. The Number class also provides a facility to display its current value to the user in a Text-

```
public class Number
{
   private  int value;
   private  TextBox textBox;

   public Number(int initValue)      // start at initValue
   public Number()                   // start at 0
   public void showIn(TextBox tbox)  // place to display/read value
   public void show()                // display current value
   public void next()                // increment
   public void reset()               // get new value from user
   public int  value()               // reply current value
}
```

Figure 6.1 The Number Class

```
public class Cycler
{
   private int value;
   private int base;
   private TextBox textBox;

   public Cycler(int b)                  // modulo base b
   public Cycler()                       // base 10
   public void showIn (TextBox& tbox) // place to display value
   public void show()                    // display current value
   public void next()                    // increment
   public void reset()                   // get new value from user
   public int  value()                   // reply current value
}
```

Figure 6.2 The Cycler Class

Box as a character string. The `showIn` method creates an association with a TextBox where the Number's value should be displayed. The `show` method triggers the actual displaying of the current value in the TextBox. Finally, the `reset` method allows the user to provide a new value for the Number. This method assigns a new value to the Number by converting to an integer the character string read from the TextBox.

The Cycler class is similar to the Number class, except that the integer value maintained by the Cycler is constrained to a range determined by the base of the Cycler. The base value is specified when the Cycler object is constructed. The value of a Cycler object must always be in the range from 0 to base-1. Cycler objects are useful for counting events that are numbered cyclically, such as seconds in a minute (0-59) or hours in a day (0-23). Like a Number, the Cycler also contains methods for creating an association with a TextBox that will display its current value in the TextBox and for obtaining a new value from the user. The definition of the Cycler class is shown in Figure 6.2.

The similarities in the Number and Cycler classes are evident in their definitions and include both the data that each maintains and the code for some of their methods. Specifically, the similarities are:

```
Data/Attributes:
        value      : an internal integer value
        textBox    : a reference to a TextBox

Code/Behavior:
        showIn     : provide a TextBox where value is displayed
        show       : display the current value in the TextBox
        reset      : use the TextBox to get new value from user
        value      : returns the current internal value
```

Notice that the `next` method is *not* similar: its implementation distinguishes the classes from each other. Notice also that the constructors are not the same; because the constructor take its name from the class, it is not possible for them to be shared among classes with different names.

Identifying the similarities among classes is a process of generalization resulting in a new class. The new class is referred to as the base class (also sometimes called the superclass or the parent class). The classes over which the generalization is made are referred to as the derived classes (or subclasses or child classes). The base class is named so that it reflects its role as a generalization. In the example, the generalization is formed over classes that have a numeric property (Numbers and Cyclers have numeric values) and a property of being displayable to the user. Thus, one name for the generalized (base) class is DisplayableNumber; other names such as InteractiveNumber, GUIValue, and VisualNumeric are possible.

The classes over which the generalization is formed are viewed as specializations. Each of these classes contains distinctive properties (data and/or methods) that are beyond the similar properties captured in the base class. These distinctive properties also differentiate a class from other classes that are specializations of the same generalization. Thus, both Number and Cycler are specializations of DisplayableNumber; each is a particular kind of DisplayableNumber. The specializing property in this example is the `next` method. The `next` method is not part of the generalization because it has a different meaning in the two classes. A generalization-specialization hierarchy is used to organize the generalized class and its specializations. The generalization-specialization hierarchy for the example is shown in Figure 6.3 using UML notation.

The properties of inheritance can be seen in the inheritance structure shown in Figure 6.3. Each derived class inherits from the base class the base class's code and data; these need not be repeated in the definition of the derived class. For example, because the Number class inherits from the DisplayableNumber class, the Number class implicitly has all of the data and methods of the DisplayableNumber class. The only elements defined in the Number class are the specializing features that make it distinctive. In this case, only a `next`

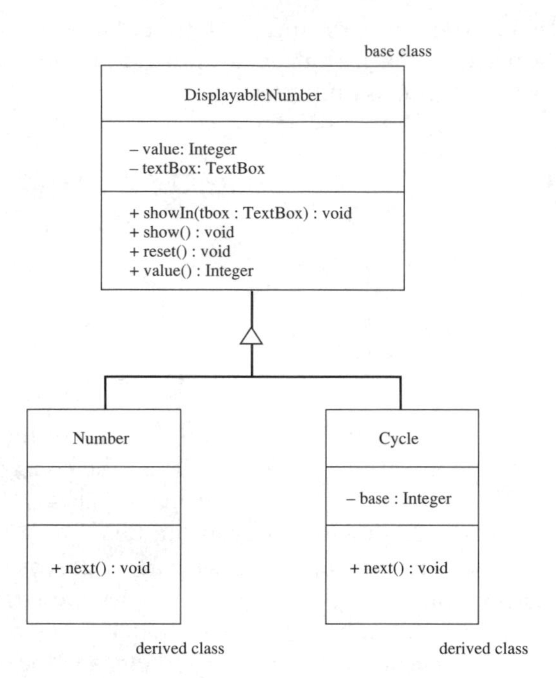

Figure 6.3 Generalization-Specialization Hierarchy in UML

method is added by the Number class. This method is distinctive in the sense that the generalization does not contain a `next` method and the `next` methods of the other specializations of DisplayableNumber are different from the Number class's `next` method. Similarly, the Cycler class inherits all of the data and methods of the DisplayableNumber class and adds to that inherited data a new data element, the base of the Cycler, and an additional method, `next`.

The programming advantage of inheritance is that the definition and implementation fixed in the base class does not have to be repeated in the derived classes. Clearly, this reduces the amount of coding that has to be done to add a new derived class. Perhaps more importantly, because the base class may have existed for a long period of time its implementation is, therefore, more likely to have been tested and debugged. In this way inheritance aids in the more efficient development of more reliable software systems.

Object Structure

The structure of an object instantiated from a derived class may be thought of as a series of layers, each layer corresponding to one level in the inheritance hierarchy. For example, the structure of a Cycler object is shown in Figure 6.4. Cycler objects have two layers, one corresponding to its base class, DisplayableNumber, and one layer corresponding to its derived class, Cycler. Each layer adds the data and methods defined by the corresponding class definition. Thus, the object pos-

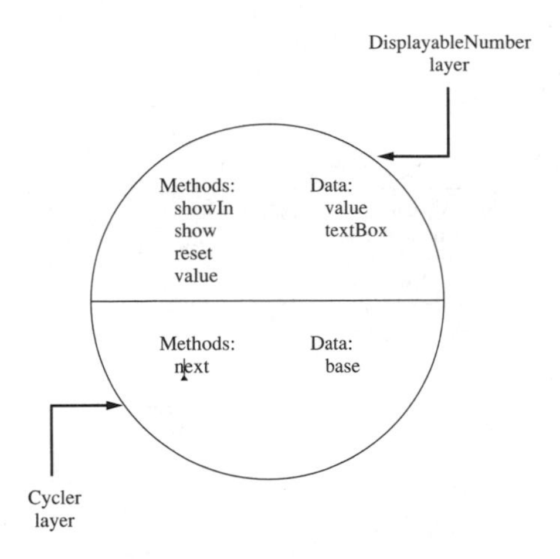

Figure 6.4 Logical Structure of a Cycler Object

sesses the union of all of the methods and data of all of the classes from which it directly or indirectly inherits.

The layered object structure helps to explain why a derived class object is able to respond to methods that are defined and implemented in the base class. An example of this is shown in the following code:

```
Cycler octal = new cycler(8);
...
TextBox tbox = new TextBox(...);
...

octal.showIn(tbox);          // apply base class method
octal.next();                // apply derived class method
octal.show();                // apply base class method
```

As seen in this code, a Cycler object is able to perform those methods defined in the derived class (i.e., `next`) as well as those defined in the base class (i.e., `showIn` and `show`).

Multiple Levels of Inheritance

A derived class can itself be a base class whose implementation may be shared by classes derived from it. In this manner, inheritance extends over several, and perhaps many, levels. The example using DisplayableNumber and Cycler had only two levels, but more extensive use of inheritance to share implementations is possible and even common.

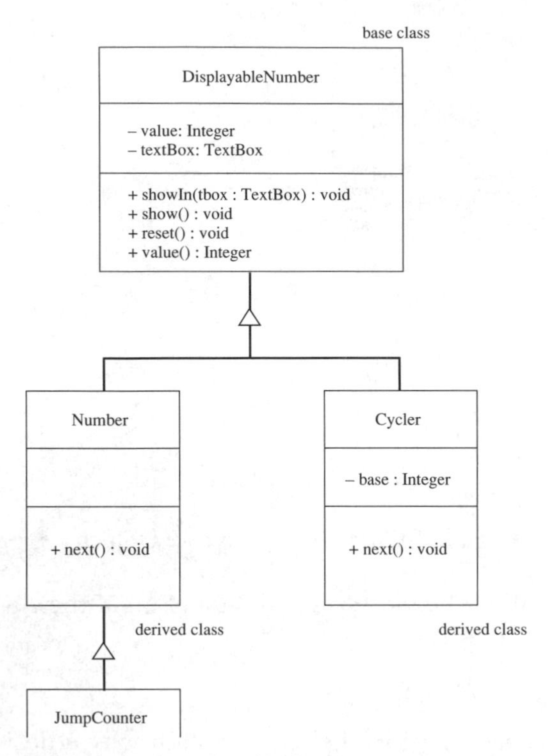

Figure 6.5 Mutiple Levels of Inheritance

To illustrate multiple levels of inheritance, consider a JumpCounter that can be incremented by one or by an arbitrary amount. Such an object might be used to show the current length of a file where the length of the file may be changed by appending a single character (increment by one) or by appending an entire string (increment by the length of the string). Alternatively, the JumpCounter may represent the current page number in a document. In some cases the user turns the pages one at a time. In this case the JumpCounter should be able to increment its value by one each time its `next` method is called. In other cases, the user may jump ahead many pages, by following a link or reference. In this case the JumpCounter should be able to change by an arbitrary integer amount.

The inheritance needed to define a JumpCounter is shown in the diagram in Figure 6.5. Because the Number class has all of the functionality necessary to implement a JumpCounter except the ability to increase the internal value by a given amount, the JumpCounter class is derived from the Number class. Recall that the Number class is itself derived from the DisplayableNumber class.

Notice that the JumpCounter class overloads a method that is defined in a class from which it inherits. The `next` method is defined in the Number class and the JumpCounter class defines an overloading of this method, `next(int)`. In general, many overloadings are possible, either defined within a single class

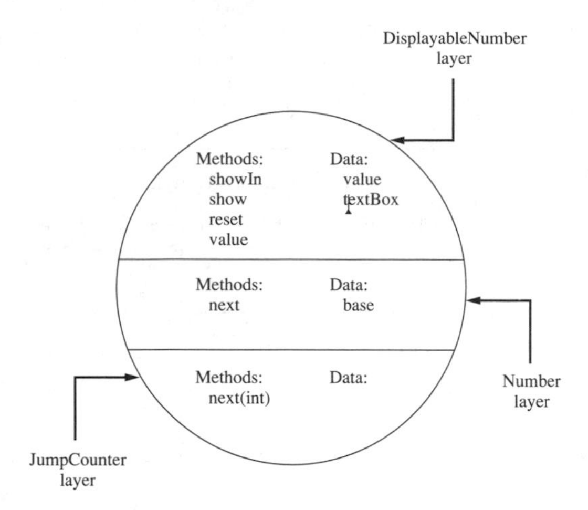

Figure 6.6 Object Structure of a JumpCounter Object

or accumulated across several levels of inheritance. An overloading that is introduced in a derived class should maintain the conceptual integrity of the method's name. In the case of the JumpCounter, the two variants of the `next` method have conceptual similarity; the two methods provide alternative ways of increasing the value of the Number. By contrast, the conceptual similarity would be violated by introducing an overloading of the Next method that had the meaning "this is the amount by which the next increment should increase the value." Such an overloading weakens the meaning of `next` by confusing whether it applies to the current operation or to a future operation.

The essential point is that a JumpCounter object responds to all methods of its immediate class (JumpCounter) as well as to all of the methods of its ancestor classes (Number and DisplayableNumber). This is illustrated by the following code:

```
JumpCounter  fileLength = new JumpCounter();
TextBox      lengthDisplay = new TextBox(Location(100,100), Shape(50,20));
...
fileLength.showIn(lengthDisplay);    // uses method in DisplayableNumber
fileLength.show();                   // uses method in DisplayableNumber
...
fileLength.next();                   // add 1 using method in Number
...
fileLength.next(50);                 // add 50 using method in JumpCounter
...
fileLength.reset();                  // uses method in DisplayableNumber
```

The layered structure of an object helps to explain the behavior of the JumpCounter object in this code. A JumpCounter object has three layers, one for the derived class, JumpCounter, a second for the base class of JumpCounter, Number, and the third for the base class of Number, namely DisplayableNumber. The structure of a JumpCounter object is shown in Figure 6.6.

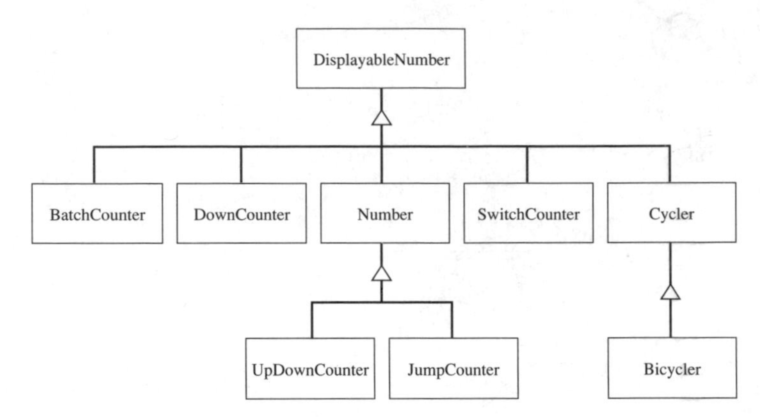

Figure 6.7 An Inheritance Hierarchy of Displayable Numbers

In general an inheritance diagram may form a deep and/or broad tree structure. Each node in the tree denotes a class that inherits from its parent (base class) and also serves as a base class for its descendents. The exercises below, when completed, will build an inheritance diagram that looks like the one shown in Figure 6.7. Designing a new derived class by inheritance commonly makes the introduction of a new variation or extension of an existing class easier than would be reimplementing the class entirely from scratch. It will become clearer as more is learned that designing the "right" inheritance structure is both important and difficult. Much of the effort in object-oriented programming is invested in the search for good inheritance structures.

6.2.2 Generalizing the Predator and Prey Abstractions

The abstractions for predators and prey in the ecological simulation have a number of shared, or generalizable, properties that can be effectively captured in an inheritance hierarchy. Among the generalizable properties are:

```
Data/Attributes:
        location  : where the creature is located
        range     : size of the creatures habitat
        roam      : distance the creature can move at one time
        alive     : whether the creature is alive
        age       : the simulated age of the creature

Code/Behavior:
        getlocation    : examine the creature's location
        get range      : examine the size of the creature's habitat
        getroam        : examine the distance the creature can move
        get/set alive  : examine/change the creature's state
        get age        : examine the creature's age
```

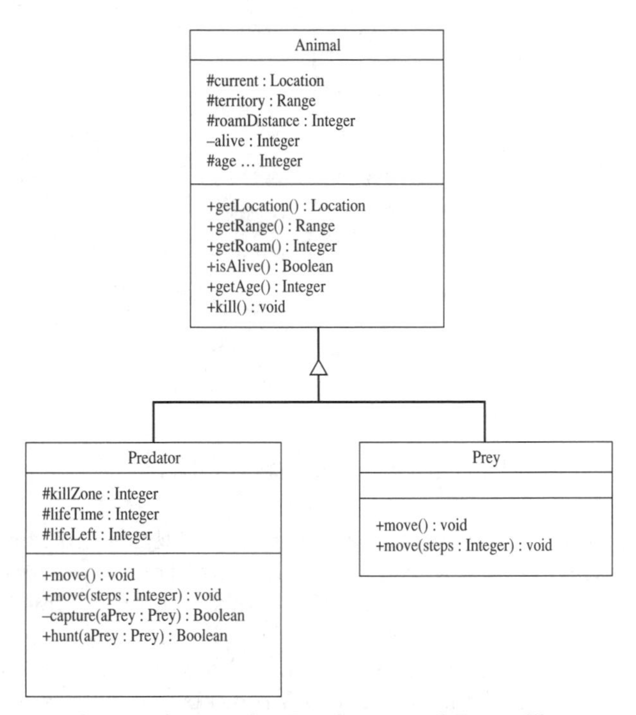

Figure 6.8 Generalizing the Predator and Prey Classes

The common characteristics of the predator and prey abstractions can be explicitly represented in the simple inheritance hierarchy shown in Figure 6.8. This UML diagram shows that the base class, named Animal, contains all of the general properties of the predator and prey abstractions. These shared properties are inherited by the specialized Predator and Prey classes that are derived from the Animal base class. The inheritance relationship is shown in the UML diagram by the large arrowhead that points in the direction of the base class. As shown in the diagram, the Predator and Prey classes have overloaded `move` methods in addition to the methods inherited from the Animal base class. The `move` methods are not promoted to the base class because the have different implementations in the Predator and Prey classes. It will be seen later how to express in inheritance that the signature of the method is shared, but not the implementation. For now, only those properties that are identical among the derived classes will be elevated to the base class.

Inheritance introduces an additional level of security that can be afforded to data and/or methods of a class. The hash mark or pound sign ("#") shown in Figure 6.8 is used to denote data or methods that are "protected." The protected attribute specifies an intermediate level of security between public and private. Protected data or methods are not visible in the public interface of the object; in this sense protected is like private. However, protected data and/or methods are visible to, and may be accessed by, methods in derived classes. For example, in

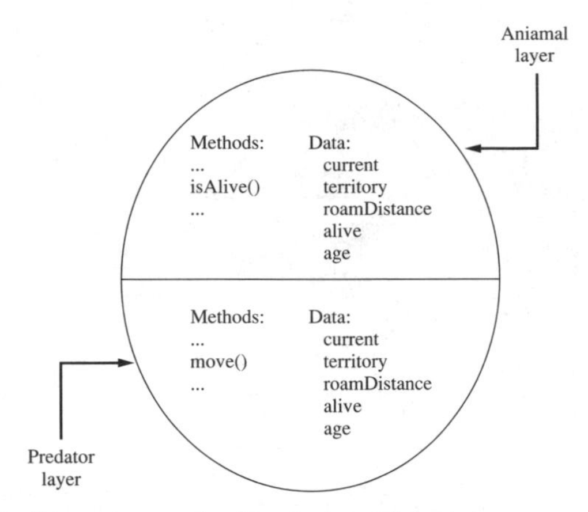

Figure 6.9 Structure of a Predator Object

the inheritance diagram in Figure 6.8, the `age` data is annotated as being protected. This means that the `age` variable is not in the public interface of the Animal class nor in the public interface of any derived class. However, the methods of derived classes, such as the `move` method in the Predator class or the Prey class, may access the `age` data. Notice that the age of an Animal can be discovered by using the `getAge` method of the Animal class that, as a public method, is in the public interface of the Animal class. Notice also that the `alive` data of the Animal class is annotated as private. Because the `isAlive` and `kill` methods provide the only manipulation of the alive data that is possible, there is no need to expose this data to derived classes. In general, it is desirable to restrict the access of data and methods as tightly as possible.

The effect of inheritance can be seen in the following code fragment illustrating that a Predator object possesses all of the attributes and behavior defined in the Predator class as well as all of the attributes and behavior defined in the Animal class.

```
Predator pred = new Predator(...);
pred.move();                          //derived class method
boolean alive = pred.isAlive();       //base class method
```

In this code fragment, the Predator object responds to both the `move` method that is defined in the derived class (Predator) and the `isAlive` method that is defined in the base class (Animal). To further emphasize the effect of inheritance the structure of a Predator object is shown in Figure 6.9. This figure illustrates that a Predator object has two logical layers, one layer defined by the base class and one layer defined by the derived class. Thus, the complete Predator object possesses the cumulative attributes and behavior defined in the Animal and Predator classes. The same is true of Prey objects. Each Prey object possesses all of the attributes and behavior defined in the Prey class in addition to those defined in the Animal class.

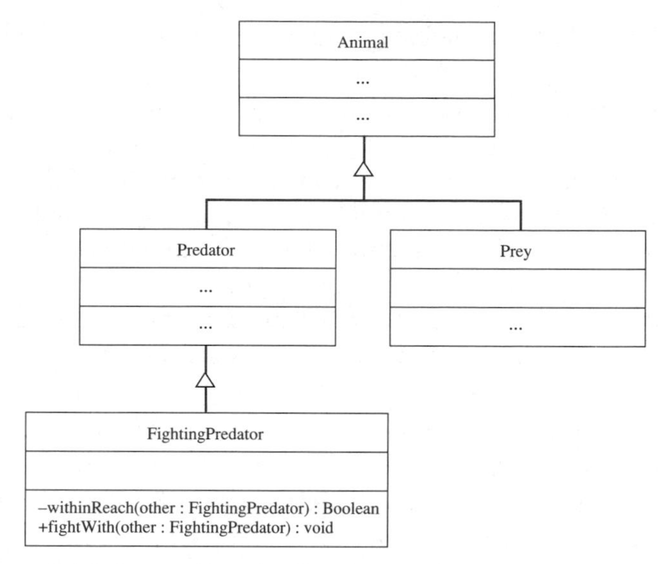

Figure 6.10 Extending the Predator Class

Extending the Predator Class Through Inheritance

Any class, even a derived class, can play the role of a base class that can be extended through inheritance. To illustrate this possibility consider a class, FightingPredator, that is like a Predator in every respect expect that it has one additional, specialized aspect. Two FightingPredators will fight if they are sufficiently close, with the older of them dying as a result. The FightingPredator class can be easily defined using inheritance because most of its properties are already defined in the Animal and Predator classes. The FightingPredator class can be defined by extending the Predator class as shown in Figure 6.10. The `fightWith` method introduced in the FightingPredator class determines which, if either, of the two predators will die. Notice that the FightingPredator class also defines a private method, `withinReach`, that is used by the `fightWith` method to determine if the two predators are sufficiently close.

Exercises

1. The class DownCounter maintains an integer counter whose nonnegative value, given initially by a constructor argument, is decremented by one on each call to its Next operation until the value reaches zero. Upon reaching zero, subsequent calls on Next will have no effect; the value remains at zero. The value of a DownCounter object can be displayed in a TextBox. Using an inheritance diagram, show how the

DownCounter class is defined by inheritance from DisplayableNumber.

2. The class UpDownCounter maintains an integer counter whose non-negative value, given initially by a constructor argument, is incremented by one on each call to its Next operation. The UpDownCounter class also has a Previous method that decrements the counter's value by one. The counter's value cannot be decremented lower than its initial value. The value of a UpDownCounter object can be displayed in a TextBox. Using an inheritance diagram, show how the UpDownCounter class is defined by inheritance from Number.
3. The class BiCycler is to be defined that maintains an integer counter that is incremented modulo the base given by the constructor. The BiCycler class also has a Previous method that decrements the counter's value by one. When the internal value is zero, the Previous operation sets the internal value to the largest possible value (i.e., base-1). Using an inheritance diagram, show how the BiCycler class is defined by inheritance from Cycler.
4. The class SwitchCounter maintains an integer counter that is incremented or decremented by the Next method depending on the current direction of the SwitchCounter. Initially the SwitchCounter is directed up. When up, the value is incremented by one when Next is called. When in the "down" direction the value is decremented by 1 when Next is called. The Switch method changes the direction to the opposite of its current setting. Using an inheritance diagram, show how the SwitchCounter class is defined by inheritance from DisplayableNumber.
5. The class BatchCounter maintains an integer counter that is incremented by one only when the Next operation has been called n times. The value of n is given as a constructor argument. This class counts batches of Next operations. It may be used, for example, to increment a one-minute counter only after its Next method has been called sixty times by a one-second Clock. Using an inheritance diagram, show how the BatchCounter class is defined by inheritance from DisplayableNumber.
6. Draw a layered diagram showing the structure of an FightingPredator object.
7. Draw an inheritance diagram that would show how to create an FightingPrey class.
8. Draw an inheritance diagram "vehicles" that would include derived classes for such things as airplanes, trains, trolleys, automobiles, etc.

6.3 Inheriting Methods and Data

In Java, the relationship between a base and derived classes is represented syntactically as follows:

```
public class DisplayableNumber {...}                 // base class
public class Number extends DisplayableNumber {...} // derived class
public class Cycler extends DisplayableNumber {...} // derived class

public class Animal { ... }                          // base class
public class Predator extends Animal {... }          // derived class
public class Prey extends Animal { ... }             // derived class
```

The additional syntax "extends *classname*" is used in the definition of each derived class to name the base class from which the derived class inherits. The keyword "extends" means that all of the public, private, and protected methods and data defined in the base class (DisplayableNumber or Animal) become part of the corresponding part of the derived classes (Number, Cycler, Predator, Prey). These inherited methods represent the code sharing that is achieved by inheritance. Protected methods and data are described later in this section.

6.3.1 Inheritance Using the DisplayableNumber Class

The public interface of the classes DisplayableNumber, Number, and Cycler are shown in Figure 6.11. The same basic class structure is used to define both a base and a derived class. Both base and derived classes have constructors and behavioral methods: the only difference between a base and a derived class is their roles in the inheritance relationship that relates them to each other.

Notice that the base class DisplayableNumber forms a complete class, that is it defines an unchanging integer that can be displayed in a TextBox. In some limited cases this may be all that is needed. For example, a portion of an interactive testing system may need to display a final score to the user as follows:

```
TextBox scoreBox = new TextBox(Location(100,100), Shape(75, 50));
int score;

// interact with user; determine final score

DisplayableNumber finalScore(score);
finalScore.showIn(scoreBox);
finalScore.show();
```

The classes derived from DisplayableNumber introduce the ability to change the number dynamically. Each new derived class embodies a different way to change the value.

The critical point is that through inheritance Number and Cycler objects not only have those methods defined in the Number and Cycler classes but also

```
public class DisplayableNumber

{
   public DisplayableNumber(int initValue)
   public void showIn(TextBox tbox)
   public void show()
   public void reset()
   public int  value()
}
public class Number extends DisplayableNumber
{
   public Number(int initValue)
   public Number()
   public void next()
}

class Cycler : public DisplayableNumber
{
   public Cycler(int base, int initValue)
   public Cycler(int base)
   public Cycler()
   public void next()
}
```

Figure 6.11 Syntax of Inheritance

those methods inherited from the public interface of the base class Displayable-Number. For example:

```
Number count  = new Number(10);      // initially 10
Cycler binary = new Cycler(2);       // base 2

TextBox display = new TextBox(Location(10,10), Shape(50,50));
TextBox onoff   = new TextBox(Location(20,20), Shape(50,50));

count.showIn(display);
binary.showIn(onoff);

count.next();             // increment by 1
binary.next();            // increment by 1 modulo 2

count.show();             // display updated value
binary.show();            // display updated value

int c = count.value();  // get value of Number object
int b = binary.value(); // get value of Cycler object
```

As this example illustrates, the Number and Cycler objects can respond both to the methods defined in their immediate classes (`next`) and to the inherited methods (`showIn`, `show`, `reset`, and `value`) that are defined in the base class DisplayableNumber.

Protected Data

Data can be placed in the base class and made accessible to both the base and derived classes. As shown in Figure 6.12, the `value` and `textBox` variables declared in the DisplayableNumber base class. The variable `textBox` is used only in the methods `showIn`, `show`, and `reset`, all of which are in the base class (DisplayableNumber). Thus, the `textBox` variable can be declared as private data of the base class. The variable `value`, however, is needed in both the base class, where it is used by the `show` and `reset` methods, and in the derived class, where it is used in the `next` method. Data to be accessible in both the base and derived classes are declared using the `protected` keyword in the base class. The `next` method of the Number class is also shown in Figure 6.12 to illustrate that the protected data defined in the base class is directly accessible in the methods of the derived classes. Similarly, the Cycler class would have direct access to the protected data in DisplayableNumber.

The protected level of access is needed because neither private nor public access are adequate for the data shared between the base and derived classes. If the shared data is declared as private to the base class it is inaccessible to the derived classes. This is, of course, contrary to what is needed. If the shared data is declared as public in the base class, then although it is accessible to the derived classes, it is also accessible in the public interface of the base and derived class, which means that the data loses its encapsulation; this is also contrary to what is required. The protected data (and operations) are accessible to the base class and derived class but inaccessible everywhere else. In other words, pro-

```
public class DisplayableNumber

{
   private TextBox textBox;   // place to display value
                              // accessible only in this class

   protected  int  value;     // internal counter
                              // accessible in this class and in
                              // all derived classes

   public DisplayableNumber(int init)
   public void showIn(TextBox tbox)
   public void show()
   public void reset()
   public int  value()
}

public class Number
{
  //...
  public void next()
  { value = value + 1;        // can access protected data
  }
}
```

Figure 6.12 Example of Protected Data

```
public class DisplayableNumber

{

   private TextBox textBox;          // place to display value
   private int     value;            // internal counter

            // the following accessor methods
                        // are visible in derived classes

   protected void setValue(int v);   // sets "value"
   protected int  getValue();         // gets "value"

   public // ... as before
}

public class Number
{
  // ..

  public void next()
  { setValue( getValue() + 1);
  }
}
```

Figure 6.13 Using Protected Accessor Methods

tected data (and operations) are not part of the public interface of either the base class or the derived classes.

Even though the protected data is not part of the public interface, many designers argue that the data should remain private to the base class and protected accessor methods should be defined in the base class that allows access to the shared data. This way, the data remains the private concern of the class in which it is declared and can still be accessed by the derived classes. Using this approach the DisplayableNumber class would be written as show in Figure 6.13. Because the accessor methods are in the protected section, they are not part of the public interface of the base or any derived class. The accessor methods are, however, visible to the derived classes. Thus, the Number's `next` method would be written as shown above using the `getValue` and `setValue` methods. Although the `getValue` and `setValue` methods are accessible in the derived classes these methods are not part of the public interface of either the base or derived classes. The `next` method's implementation also illustrates why some developers argue against the accessor method approach: two method invocations are necessary to simply increment the value of the Number by one. This overhead may be disproportionate to the additional encapsulation gained by the accessor-method approach.

Constructors

The constructors for derived classes, such as those for the Number and Cycler classes, must be related to the constructors of their base classes, such as DisplayableNumber. The constructor for the Number class has an integer argument that should be used to initialize the Number's internal value. However, the DisplayableNumber class also has a constructor for that purpose. In this case, the Number's constructor argument should simply be passed on to the DisplayableNumber's constructor. The Java syntax for this is shown in Figure 6.14. The additional syntax "`super(initValue)`" means that the base class constructor is invoked using the Number class's constructor argument (`initValue`). The keyword `super` reflects the terminology used in some object-oriented programming languages, notably Smalltalk, that refers to the class being extended as the superclass and the extending class as the subclass. In this case, no other initialization is done in the derived class (the body of the Number's constructor has no code other than the invocation of the super class's constructor). The superclass cannot be named explicitly; it is referred to only by the keyword `super`. This is deliberate in Java so that the name of the base class, or superclass, can be changed without requiring any change in the derived class, or subclass.

The Cycler class illustrates a different relationship between the constructors of the derived and base classes. The constructors of the Cycler class are shown in Figure 6.15. The first constructor has two integer arguments: the first integer, `initBase`, is used to initialize the `base` of the Cycler and the second integer, `initValue`, is used to initialize the `value` of the Cycler. The initial base value is used by the Cycler constructor itself whereas the initial value is passed to the superclass constructor. In the other two constructors, the constant zero (0) is passed as a default value to the superclass constructor and the base value is initialized either by the constructor argument `initBase` or by the default value 10.

When the `super(...)` syntax is used, it must appear as the first statement in the derived class constructor because the constructors of the base and derived classes are executed in a prescribed order: the base class is constructed first, then the class immediately derived from the base class, etc. The order in

```
public class Number extends DisplayableNumber

{
   // ...

   public Number(int initValue)
   { super(initValue);            // passing data to the
                                  // base class constructor
   }

   // ...

}
```

Figure 6.14 Number Class Constructor

```
public class Cycler extends DisplayableNumber
{
   private int base;

   public Cycler(int initBase, int initValue)
   { super(initValue);   //must be first
     base = initBase;
   }

   public Cycler(int initBase)
   { super(0);            // must be first
     base = initBase;
   }

   public Cycler()
   { super(0);           // must be first
     base = 10;
   }
}
```

Figure 6.15 Cycler Class Constructors

```
public class DisplayableNumber
{ privateint value;
  public DisplayableNumber(int initValue)
  { System.out.println(""DisplayableNumber Constructor " + initValue);
  }
}

public class Cycler extends DisplayableNumber
{ private int base;
  public Cycler(int initBase, int initValue)
  { System.out.println("Cycler Constructor " + initBase);
  }
}

//...

    Cycler cycler= new Cycler(8, 2);}
```

Figure 6.16 Order of Constructor Execution

which the constructors are executed is illustrated by the code shown in Figure 6.16. This code uses trivialized classes but has the same inheritance relationships and the same constructors as the real classes for which they are named. The output from the main program clearly shows that the base class constructor is the first one to be executed, followed by the constructor of its derived class. The output from this program is

```
DisplayableNumber Constructor 2
Cycler Constructor 8
```

which clearly shows that the DisplayableNumber base class constructor is executed before the constructor of the derived Cycler class. It also confirms that the

```
public class Cycler extends DisplayableNumber
{
   private int base;

   public Cycler(int initBase, int initValue)
   { super(initValue);   //must be first
     base = initBase;
   }

   public Cycler(int initBase)
   { super(0);              // must be first
     base = initBase;
   }

   public Cycler()      // first version
   { this(10);          // uses Cycler(int)
   }

   public Cycler()      // second version
   { this(10,0);        // uses Cycler(int,int)
   }
}
```

Figure 6.17 Using `this(...)` and `super(...)` Together

second argument of the Cycler's constructor (2) has been passed from the Cycler constructor to the DisplayableNumber constructor.

In summary, the constructor arguments are distributed from the bottom up (i.e., proceeding from the most derived class to the base class) and then the constructors are executed top down (i.e., proceeding from the base class to the most derived class). The execution of the constructors guarantees a derived class that the base class layers have been properly initialized before the derived class constructor is executed. This is useful in those cases where derived classes use the data or methods of the base class to perform their own initialization.

A derived class's constructors can use the `super(...)` and `this(...)` syntaxes in different combinations. Recall that using the `this(...)` syntax is referred to as chaining constructors. The Cycler class's default constructor—the one with no arguments—is rewritten two different ways to illustrate how both of these syntaxes can be used together. Bear in mind that both versions of the default constructor are shown in this figure for illustration; only one of them, however, could be used in defining the actual class. The revised constructors for the Cycler are shown in Figure 6.17. The first version for the default constructor uses the `this(...)` notation with the constant value 10 to invoke the Cycler constructor with a single integer argument. This constructor, in turn, uses the `super(...)` notation with the constant value 0 to construct the base class and uses the argument value (`initBase`) to initialize the `base` variable. Similarly, the second version for the default constructor uses the `this(...)` notation with two constant values, 10 and 0, to invoke the Cycler constructor with two integer arguments. This constructor, in turn, uses the `super(...)` notation with one of its arguments (`initValue`) to construct the base class and uses the other argument value (`initBase`) to initialize the base variable.

The Complete Derived Classes

Having declared the protected data in the base class, the code for two derived classes, Number and Cycler, are shown in Figure 6.18. The programming efficiency of inheritance is clearly reflected in the relatively small amount of code needed to implement each derived class. Keep in mind that each derived class definition must be placed in its own .java file. Thus, the Number class would be defined in a file named Number.java and the Cycler class would be defined in a

```
//file Number.java
import DisplayableNumber;

public class Number extends DisplayableNumber
{
  public Number(int initValue)
  { super(initValue);
  }

  public Number()
  { super(0);
  }

  public void next()
  { value = value + 1;
  }
}

// file Cycler.java
import DisplayableNumber;

public class Cycler extends DisplayableNumber
{
  private int base;

  public Cycler(int initBase, int initValue)
  { super(initValue);
    base = initBase;
  }

  public Cycler(int initBase)
  { super(0);
    base = initBase;
  }

  public Cycler()
  { super(0);
    base = 10;
  }

  public void next()
  { value = (value + 1) % base;
  }
}
```

Figure 6.18 The Complete Number and Cycler Classes

file named Cycler.java. Each derived class file begins by importing the base class as shown in Figure 6.18.

6.3.2 Inheritance Using the Animal Class

The inheritance mechanism is used to create the Predator and Prey classes by deriving them from the Animal base class. Figure 6.19 shows the structure of the code for these three classes. Inheritance is denoted in the definition of the Predator and Prey classes by the clause "`extends Animal`." The "`extends`" keyword conveys the sense that the derived class being defined is an extension of the named base class. This figure shows only the methods defined in each of the classes. As explain above and in the previous section, the utility of inheritance is

```
public class Animal

{ ...
  public Animal (Location start, Range range, int roam)
  public Animal (Range range, int roam)
  public boolean isAlive()
  public void kill()
  public Location getLocation()
  public Range getRange()
  public int getRoam()
  public int getAge()
}

public class Predator extends Animal
{ ...
  public Predator(Location where, Range range, int lifetime, int
killZone)
  public Predator(Location where, Range range,
                  int roam, int lifetime, int killZone)
  public Predator(Location where, int lifetime, int killZone)
  public Predator(int lifetime, int killZone)
  public Predator()
  public void move()
  public void move(int steps)
  public boolean hunt(Prey aPrey)
}

public class Prey extends Animal
{ ...
  public Prey(Location where, Range range)
  public Prey(Location where, Range range, int roam)

  public Prey(Location where)
  public Prey()
  public void move()
  public void move(int steps)
}
```

Figure 6.19 Deriving the Predator and Prey Classes Using Inheritance

```
public class Animal

{
  protected int roamDistance;
  protected Location current;
  private   Range territory;
  private   boolean alive = true;
  protected int age = 0;

  public Animal (Location start, Range range, int roam)
  { current = start;
    territory = range;
    roamDistance = roam;
  }

  ...
}

public class Predator extends Animal
{
  private Mover mover;      // generates random locations
  protected int lifeTime;
  protected int lifeLeft;
  protected int killZone;
  public static final int IMMOBILE =  0;
  public static final int SLOW     = 25;
  public static final int NORMAL   = 30;
  public static final int FAST     = 50;
  public static final int RANGING  = 75;

  ...

  public void move()
  { if(!isAlive()) return;
    if(lifeLeft==0)
      { kill();
        return;
      }
    current = mover.next(getLocation(), getRoam());
    lifeLeft = lifeLeft - 1;
  }
}
```

Figure 6.20 Protected Data and Public Constants

that objects of the derived classes possessed in addition to those methods defined in their immediate class, all of the methods defined in the named base class. Thus, the Predator class's public interface contains all those methods defined as public in the Predator class and also all the public methods defined in the Animal class.

The use of protected data to allow access by the derived classes to data defined in the base class is illustrated by examining portions of the Animal and Predator classes as shown in Figure 6.20. The Animal base class declares as `protected` a number of data items, such as the variable `current` that denotes the present location of the predator. These protected variables are accessible both within the Animal class itself and also in all derived classes such as the Predator class. The Animal class defines the boolean variable `alive` as private, however, because the Animal class provides set/get methods for this value via the `isAlive` and `kill` methods. Thus, any access required by a derived class is available through these set/get methods. The Predator class also defines a number of protected variable in anticipation of other classes that might be derived from the Predator class and that might need access to the data introduced by the Predator class. The Predator class also defines a private variable, `mover`, that is used to compute the next simulated position of the Predator.

The `move` method defined in the Predator class (see Figure 6.20) shows how the public methods and the protected data in the Animal base class are accessed along with the data defined in the derived class itself. The first `if` statement accesses the public `isAlive` method in the base class. Notice that only the name of the `isAlive` method is used in this statement; no explicit reference is made to the object that is to execute this method. When no explicit object is named it is assumed that the current object is the one to execute the method. In the case of a Predator object, this turns out to be the `isAlive` method defined in the Predator class's base class. The condition in the second `if` statement tests the variable `lifeLeft` defined in the Predator class itself. Similar to the invocation of the `isAlive` method, the move method also invokes the `kill` method of the base class. The next to the last line of code in the `move` method shows that the Predator class's method have access to the protected data of the base class. Notice that this statement assigns a value to the variable `current` that is declared as a protected variable in the Animal class from which Predator is derived. Through inheritance and protected access, it is possible for the `move` method to change the value of the `current` variable.

Constructing a Predator object involves initializing the variables defined in the Predator class and also the variables defined in the Animal class that it extends in a sequence that is well-defined in the Java language. For a Predator object the construction process is carried out in three steps:

1. the Predator class constructor invokes the Animal class constructor passing appropriate arguments,
2. the Animal class constructor executes; it initializes the variables defined in the Animal class, and
3. the Predator class constructor continues; it initializes the variables defined in the Predator class and possibly initializes or changes the values of protected variables to which it has access in the Animal class.

In general, the constructor process first distributes initialization values from the most derived class to the top-level base class followed by the execution

```
public class Animal

{
  protected int roamDistance;
  protected Location current;
  private   Range territory;
  protected boolean alive = true;
  protected  int age = 0;
  public Animal (Range range, int roam)
  { territory = range;
    roamDistance = roam;
  }

  ...
}


public class Predator extends Animal
{
  private Mover mover;
  protected int lifeTime;
  protected int lifeLeft;
  protected int killZone;

  ...
  public static final int NORMAL   = 30;
  ...

  public Predator(int lifetime, int killZone)
  { super(new Range(), Predator.NORMAL);
    this.lifeTime = lifetime;
    this.lifeLeft = lifeTime;
    mover = new Mover(getRange());
    current = mover.next();
  }

  ...
}
```

Figure 6.21 Constructing a Predator Object

of the constructors, beginning with the top-level base class and ending with the execution of the most derived class.

This sequence of events is illustrated by the constructors shown in Figure 6.21. Assume that a Predator object is being constructed as a result of this line of code:

```
Predator pred = new Predator(100, 20);
```

that invokes the Predator class constructor with two integer arguments. This constructor is the one shown in Figure 6.21. The first line of code in the Predator class constructor ("`super(..)`") invokes the constructor of the base class. The term `super` is used to identify the base class. The arguments passed to the base class constructor are a newly created Range object and an integer value that is a defined constant in the Predator class. This completes the first of the three steps given above. The second of the three steps is to execute the base class constructor, in this case the one shown for the Animal class in Figure 6.21. The Animal class constructor simply initializes the `territory` and `roamDistance` variables using the constructor arguments. Notice that the `alive` and `age` variables are also initialized by the values given in their declarations (e.g., age is initialized to 0). However, the `current` variable is not initialized by the Animal class constructor. The third step in the construction of the Predator object is for the Predator class constructor to complete its execution. The three statement following the "`super(...)`" statement initialize the variables introduced in the Predator class (i.e., `mover`, `lifeTime`, and `lifeLeft`). The last statement in the Predator class constructor uses the Mover object's `next` method to generate a random location in the predator's range; this location is used to initialize the `current` variable that is inherited from the base class. It is possible for the Predator constructor to perform this initialization because `current` is declared with protected access in the base class.

Exercises

1. Implement and test the DownCounter class. Your test program should show a DownCounter object's value in a TextBox and have a button labelled Next, which when pressed causes the object's `next` operation to be executed.

2. Implement and test the UpDownCounter class. Your test program should show a UpDownCounter object's value in a TextBox and have buttons labelled Next and Previous, which when pressed cause the object's `next` and `previous` operations, respectively, to be executed.

3. Implement and test the BiCyler class. Your test program should show a BiCyler object's value in a TextBox and have buttons labelled Next and Previous, which when pressed cause the object's `next` and `previous` operations, respectively, to be executed.

4. Implement and test the SwitchCounter class. Your test program should show a SwitchCounter object's value in a TextBox and have buttons labelled Next and Switch, which when pressed cause the object's `next` and `switch` operations, respectively, to be executed.

5. Implement and test the BatchCounter class. Your test program should show a BatchCounter object's value in a TextBox and have a button labelled Next, which when pressed causes the object's `next` operation to be executed.

6. Explain in detail what the expression "`new Mover(getRange())`" does in the Predator class constructor shown in the Figure 6.21.
7. Create a new class derived from Animal that models a sedentary animal. A sedentary animal is one that is created is a given place and stays there until it reaches the end of its lifetime.
8. Write a small simulation program using a single Predator object and a single Prey object. After each 10 simulated steps, output the state and current locations of the simulated predator and prey. Annotate your code to indicate which methods invoked on the Predator and Prey objects are defined in the base class and which are defined in the derived class.
9. Rewrite the Animal class so that the `age` variable is private to the Animal class without changing the public interface of the Animal class. Remember that methods can also be declared as protected.
10. Revise the Animal class hierarchy to model the fact that all Animals have a fixed lifetime. When an Animal's age reaches its lifetime the alive variable should be set to false as if the Animal had been killed.
11. Implement a class FightingPredator that is derived from the Predator class. A FightingPredator has an additional method "`fight(FightingPredator other)`". The older of the two FightingPredators is killed.

6.4 Replacing Inherited Methods

A derived class is capable of redefining an inherited by overriding it, method, replacing the inherited method with one that is specifically designed for the derived class. Because they are suited to its behavior, the derived class may want to inherit many of the base class's methods. This section considers how to selectively replace an inappropriate base class method with an appropriate one for the derived class. The invocation of a method that has been replaced will result in the replacing method being invoked rather than the replaced method. The replacement is transparent to the code performing the invocation because the replacing method has the same signature (name and ordered list of argument types) as the method it replaces.

The substitution achieved by replacement is often referred to as the receiving object "doing the right thing," The receiving object is aware of its internal structure, and in response to an invocation selects an appropriate method for execution. The invoker of the method is unaware of how the receiving object determines which of its methods to execute. Of course, the receiving object is restricted to executing a method that matches the signature (name and ordered list of argument types) of the invocation.

6.4.1 Replacing a Method in the Number Class

The RestartCounter class is an example of a class in which method replacement is needed. A RestartCounter object is just like a Number object, except that the Reset method always sets the internal value back to an initial value that is given when the RestartCounter is constructed. The RestartCounter does not use the TextBox to obtain the value to which it is reset.

Below is the inheritance diagram for the RestartCounter class (see Figure 6.22). This diagram implies that a RestartCounter object has the following methods:

- `showIn`, `show`, `value` (from DisplayableNumber),
- `next` (from Number), and
- `reset` (from RestartCounter).

The Reset method defined in DisplayableNumber has been overridden by the `reset` method defined in RestartCounter.

Notice the difference between overloading and overriding. Overloaded methods have the same name but different argument lists (signatures). Overridden methods have the same name and the same arguments (signatures). In the JumpCounter class the `next` method is overloaded because the two methods `next(int)` in the JumpCounter class and `next()` in the Number class have different signatures. Thus, a JumpCounter object has both of the `next` methods.

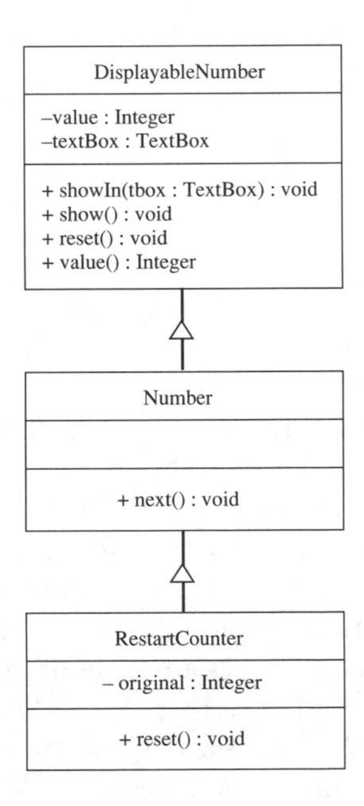

Figure 6.22 Inheritance Diagram for RestartCounter Class

```
import Number;

public class RestartCounter extends Number
{
    private int original;
    public RestartCounter (int initValue)
    { super(initValue);
      original = initValue;
    }

    public RestartCounter ()
    { super(0);
      original = 0;
    }

    public void reset()
    { value = original;
    }
}
```

Figure 6.23 Overriding an Inherited Method in the RestartCounter

However, a RestartCounter object has only one `reset` method—the one defined in the RestartCounter class. The definition of the RestartCounter class and its code are given in Figure 6.23.

To emphasize again the role of inheritance, the following code illustrates that a RestartCounter object includes all of the (non-overridden) methods of its ancestors (Number and DisplayableNumber):

```
TextBox display = new TextBox ( new Location(100,100), new Shape(50,50));
RestartCounter restart(7);
restart.next();               // from Number
restart.showIn(display);      // from DisplayableNumber
restart.show();               // from DisplayableNumber
restart.reset();              // from RestartCounter (overrides
                              //    DisplayableNumber's Reset()
```

Method Lookup

When an invocation is received by an object with a layered structure (i.e., an object whose structure is defined through inheritance) a method lookup occurs to determine which method in the layered object to execute in response to the invocation. This method lookup is performed by the receiving object transparently to the invoker. The method lookup described below should be viewed only as a conceptual aid and should not be taken as the actual process used by the Java run-time system. However, the method lookup described is conceptually correct and gives an intuitive way to understand the notion of overriding.

Method lookup is a bottom-up search; it always begins in the level corresponding to the class specified in the method invocation. For a JumpCounter object, the method lookup begins in the JumpCounter layer; for a Number object, the method lookup begins in the Number layer. If a method matching the invocation is found, it is selected

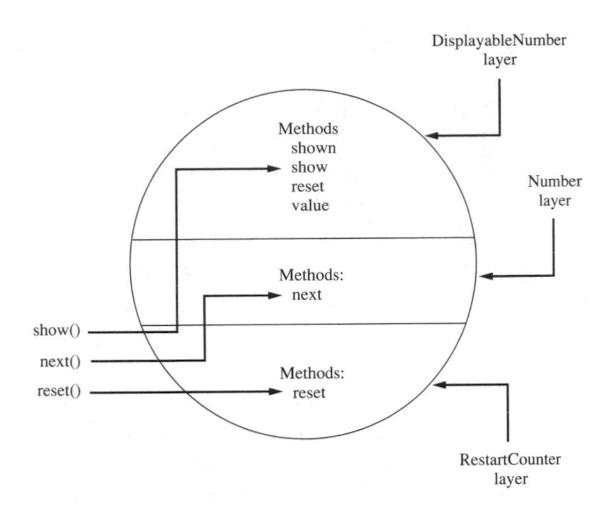

Figure 6.24 Method Lookup in a RestartCounter Object

for execution and the method lookup is complete. If a matching method is not found, the method lookup continues the search by moving to the layer immediately above the current layer. The layered structure for a RestartCounter object illustrates overriding and method lookup. As shown in Figure 6.24, a RestartCounter object has three layers: RestartCounter, Number, and DisplayableNumber. The figure shows the invocation of the methods `next`, `restart`, and `show`.

The invocation of `reset` is simple because a matching method is immediately discovered in first layer (RestartCounter). Thus, the invocation of `reset` on a RestartCounter object is bound to the reset method defined in the RestartCounter class. This illustrates the effect of overriding because the method lookup will always finds the `reset` in the RestartCounter layer as opposed to the `reset` method in the DisplayableNumber level. The invocation of `next` is bound to the method `next` defined in the Number class because the method lookup:

- begins at the RestartCounter layer but did not find a matching method, and
- continues at the next higher layer (i.e., the Number layer), where the lookup finds the matching method `next`.

Finally, the method lookup for the invocation of the `show` method is:

- unsuccessful at the RestartCounter layer,
- unsuccessful at the Number layer, and
- successful at the DisplayableNumber layer.

Thus, the invocation of `show` on a RestartCounter object is bound to `show` method defined in the DisplayableNumber class.

6.4.2 Replacing a Method in the Predator Class

The notion of replacing an inherited method by one more appropriate for the derived class is also illustrated by considering a specialized type of predator, one that kills a prey within its reach only with some probability of success. A class for this less lethal predator, a WeakPredator class, can be implemented by inheriting from the existing Predator class. The WeakPredator class inherits all of the attributes and behavior of the Predator class, including one that is not desired. The `hunt` method in the Predator class is not an appropriate method for the WeakPredator class because it is exactly the difference in hunting behavior that distinguishes a Predator from a WeakPredator. The WeakPredator class must then define its own hunt method as shown by the UML diagram in Figure 6.25.

The code for the WeakPredator class is shown in Figure 6.26. The critical part of the WeakPredator class's code is the `hunt` method. The signature of this method is exactly the same as the `hunt` method defined in the Predator class that is extended by the WeakPredator class. Because the signatures are the same, the definition of the `hunt` method in the WeakPredator class will be used by an WeakPredator object on which the hunt method is invoked. For example, in this code fragment

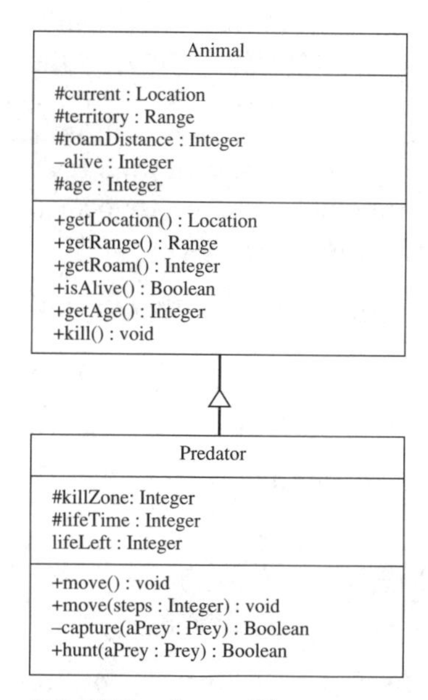

Figure 6.25 The WeakPredator Class

```
public class WeakPredator extends Predator

{

  private boolean killsPrey = true;

  public WeakPredator(Location where, Range range, int lifetime, int killZone)
  { super(where, range, lifetime, killZone);
  }

  //... other constructors similar

  private boolean captures(Prey aPrey)
  { double xdist = (double)(aPrey.getLocation().getX() -
                            this.getLocation().getX());
    double ydist = (double)(aPrey.getLocation().getY() -
                            this.getLocation().getY());

    return (int)(Math.sqrt(xdist*xdist + ydist*ydist)) < killZone;
  }

  public boolean hunt(Prey aPrey)
  { if (!alive) return false;
    if(captures(aPrey) && aPrey.isAlive())
       { if (killsPrey)
            { aPrey.kill();
              lifeLeft = lifeTime;
              killsPrey = false;
              return true;
            }
         else
            { killsPrey = true;
              return false;
            }
       }
    else return false;
  }
}
```

Figure 6.26 The WeakPredator Class

```
Prey prey = new Prey(...);
WeakPredator weak = new WeakPredator();
weak.hunt(prey);
```

the actual method invoked in the last line of code is the hunt method defined in the WeakPredator class because the object is of the WeakPredator class.

The implementation of the `hunt` method in this example uses a very simple mechanism for deciding if the WeakPredator is able to kill a prey that is within its reach. A simple boolean variable, `killsPrey`, is used so that only every other prey within reach is killed by the WeakPredator. Notice how this variable is manipulated in the hunt method defined in Figure 6.26. Notice also that the WeakPredator class must redefine the `captures` method that was declared as a private method of the Predator class. Because this method was declared private in the Predator class it is inaccessible even to a derived class such as the Weak-Predator class.

Exercises

1. Write a set of trivialized classes that have the same interfaces as the DisplayableNumber, Number, and RestartCounter classes. The methods in these trivialized classes should simply output messages indicating which method was executed. Using these trivialized classes, write a test program that creates a RestartCounter object and invokes the `next`, `reset`, and `show` methods on it. Use the output of the program to confirm the method bindings given in this section.
2. Write a set of trivialized classes that have the same interfaces as the DisplayableNumber, Number, and JumpCounter classes. The methods in these trivialized classes should simply output messages indicating which method was executed. Using these trivialized classes, write a test program that creates a JumpCounter object and invokes the `next` and `next(10)` methods on it. Explain the output of the program.
3. Implement and test a class CheckpointCounter that is derived from the Number class. A CheckpointCounter object is like a Number except that the value to which the Number is set by the `reset` operation is determined by a `checkPoint` method. The `checkPoint` method saves the value of the CheckpointCounter when it is called. It is to this saved value that the CheckpointCounter is reset. Note that the CheckpointCounter will need to introduce additional data and will also need to override the `restart` method in the DisplayableNumber class.
4. Implement and test a class SetpointCounter. A SetpointCounter is like a Number except that it contains an additional method, `setPoint`, that defines the value to which the object should be set by the next `reset` operation applied to it. The current setpoint value performs this function until changed by a subsequent invocation of the `setPoint` method. Use the initial value of the object as its initial setpoint.
5. Modify the Predator class so that the `captures` method is accessible to derived classes but is not part of the public interface of the Predator class. Test your change by removing the `captures` method from the WeakPredator class. Compile and test the revised classes.
6. Define a new class, WeakFightingPredator, that extends the FightingPredator class defined in the exercises in Section 6.3. A younger WeakFightingPredator kills another WeakFightingPredator that is within reach only with a certain probability. Compile and test your new class.

7. Define a new class, PossumPrey, that extends the Prey class. Every other time it is asked whether it is alive or dead, a live PossumPrey will falsely reply that it is dead. Compile and test your new class. Notice that the method being replaced is one inherited from the Prey class's base class, not the Prey class itself.
8. Define a new class, StationaryPredator, that extends the Predator class. A StationaryPredator always remains at the same point at which it was created. Compile and test your new class.

6.5 Extending Inherited Methods

Extending an inherited method is a variation of replacing a method. The distinguishing features of extending an inherited method is that the extending method in the derived class overrides the inherited method (i.e., the extending method has the same signature as the inherited method), and invokes the inherited method to perform part of its work. Because the overriding method itself uses the method that it overrides, it appears to extend the inherited method by adding new actions to the method's execution.

6.5.1 Extending a Method of the Cycler Class

An example of extending an inherited method occurs in the Cycler class. As the class was defined earlier, it inherits a Reset method from the DisplayableNumber class. However, this inherited method allows any number to be entered by the user, possibly one outside the range of the Cycler. If this occurred, the program could access this erroneous value, via the Value method. To prevent this problem from occurring, a safer (more restricted) Reset method is needed in the Cycler class. To override and extend the inherited Reset method, the Cycler class would be redefined as shown in Figure 6.27.

In this method, the overridden base class method is itself invoked. To distinguish between the two `reset` methods, the syntax "`super.reset`" is used in the Cycler's `reset` method to indicate the `reset` method in the base class (DisplayableNumber). Without this additional syntax to specify the base class name, it would be assumed that the Cycler's `reset` method was making a recursive call on itself, when that is clearly not what is desired here.

Figure 6.28, using the Cycler class as an example, depicts the sequence of events that occurs when an extended method is executed. In step 1, an invocation of the `reset` method occurs. Because the derived class method overrides the inherited method, this invocation will result in the execution of the derived class method (`reset` in the Cycler class). In step 2, the derived class method invokes the inherited method (`reset` in the DisplayableNumber class). When the base

```
public class Cycler extends DisplayableNumber

{
   private int base;

   public Cycler (int initBase, int initValue)
   public Cycler (int initBase)
   public Cycler ()
   public  void next()

   public  void reset()     // overrides and extends the Reset
                            // method inherited from DisplayableNumber
   {                        // no preprocesing
     super.reset();         // invoke overridden method
     value = value % base;  // postprocesing
   }
}
```

Figure 6.27 Extending an Inherited Method in the Cycler Class

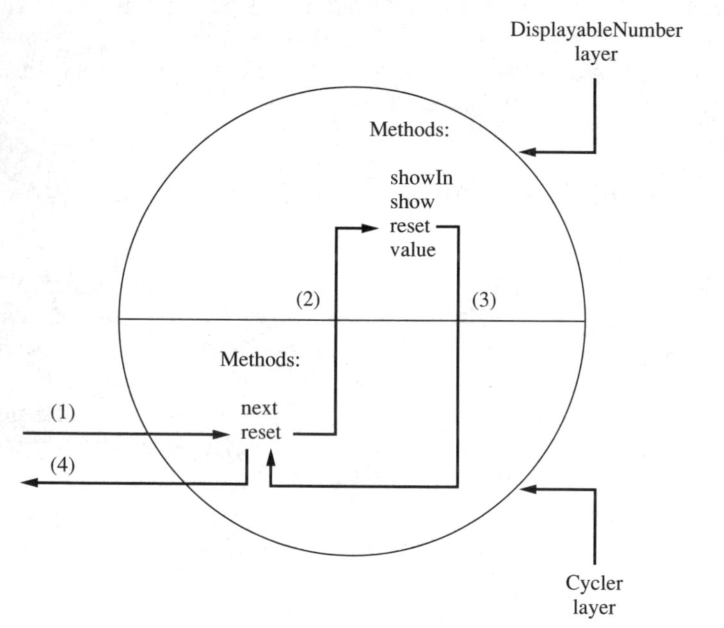

Figure 6.28 Extending an Inherited Method

class method returns, in step 3, it returns to the Cycler class's `reset` method. Finally, in step 4, the derived class method returns, completing the invocation. Because the control begins and ends in the derived class method, the derived class method can perform any necessary preprocessing actions before invoking the base class method (after step 1 and before step 2) and can perform any necessary postprocessing actions before returning (between steps 3 and 4).

6.5.2 Extending a Method in the Predator Class

Consider how the abstraction of an "aging predator" might be implemented as an extension of the predator abstraction. An aging predator is like a normal predator except that it becomes a less capable hunter as its age increases. The decline in an aging predators hunting abilities could be reflected by reducing its roaming distance, by reducing the zone within which it can capture a prey, or both. Whichever lessening of capability is chosen, the AgingPredator class must be able to alter the corresponding attributes defined in the Predator class in a way that is related to its age. The age of the predator is determined by the number of times it has been asked to move; each movement is one simulated period of time. How the AgingPredators movements are simulated is not at issue and need not be changed. However, the AgingPredator class must extend the inherited `move` method so that actions can be taken each time the age of the AgingPredator changes due to the invocation of the move method.

The essential aspects of the AgingPredator class are presented in Figure 6.29. In this class the decline in the predators hunting ability is achieved by reducing the distance that the predator can move at one time. The amount by which the roaming distance is reduced on each simulated time step is controlled by the variable `roamingLoss` that can be set via the `setLoss` method. Each time the AgingPredator is asked to move, its `move` method first invokes the inherited `move` method using the `super` notation, as shown by the line of code in bold in Figure 6.29. After moving to is new location, the aging predator is now one simulated time step older. Therefore, the aging predators roaming distance is reduced by the current amount of loss. The reduction is tempered so that at any age the aging predator has a roaming distance of at least 5. Notice that an

```
import Predator;

public class AgingPredator extends Predator
{

  private int roamingLoss = 0;

  //..constructors not shown

  public void setLoss(int loss)
  { roamingLoss = loss;
  }

  public void move()
  { super.move();          //invoke inherited move method
    roamDistance = roamDistance - roamingLoss;
    if (roamDistance < 5) roamDistance = 5;
  }
}
```

Figure 6.29 Extending the `hunt` Method in the AgingPredator Class

aging predator whose `roamingLoss` is 0 behaves the same was as a Predator with no loss of hunting capability over time.

Exercises

1. Implement and test a class AutoCounter. An AutoCounter object is like a Number object except that the Next method in the AutoCounter object does both the incrementing of the value and the update of the TextBox display. Use the technique described in this section to override and extend the Number class's Next method in the AutoCounter class.
2. Reimplement and test the BatchCounter class. In this case, BatchCounter inherits from the Number class. However, the BatchCounter class now overrides and extends the Number class's Next method.
3. Implement and test a MonotonicCounter class derived from the Number class. A MonotonicCounter is like a Number except that the value to which it reverts by a Reset operation can never be smaller than its value prior to the Reset operation. In other words, the value given by the user is ignored if it is less than the current value of the MonotonicCounter.
4. Reimplement and test the BatchCounter class. In this case, the BatchCounter class has, as a private data member, a Cycler object. The Cycler object is used to keep track of the number of Next operations that have been done in the current batch of Next operations.
5. Implement a variation of the AgingPredator class that reduces the size of the zone within which the aging predator can capture a prey. Devise and execute a test program for your class.
6. Implement a MeasuredPredator class that keeps track of how far the predator has traveled during its lifetime. Devise and execute a test program for your class.
7. Implement a CountingPredator class that keeps track of how many prey the predator has captured during its lifetime. Devise and execute a test program for your class.
8. Implement a SatisfiedPredator class that does not capture a prey unless it is hungry. A SatisfiedPredator is initially hungry but, after capturing a prey, it not hungry for the next 5 simulated time steps (5 move operations). Devise and execute a test program for your class.

6.6 Hiding Inherited Methods

6.6.1 The Problem

It is occasionally, though rarely, necessary to prevent a base class method from appearing in the public interface of a derived class. Such hiding must happen, however, if the inherited method is inappropriate to objects of the derived class and when the action taken by the inherited method is in conflict with the specialization introduced by the derived class. A small example is explored below that illustrates this situation, and describe three ways of hiding inherited methods.

Hiding inherited methods is a controversial technique. Some argue that it is a violation of the "is-a" principle that underlies inheritance. The standard for judging the appropriateness of inheritance is whether the derived class "is a" kind of the base class. Strictly interpreted, a hidden method is an exception to the "is-a" rule: the derived class is a kind of the base class, but it cannot perform this action defined in the base class. This argument is clearly correct if the hiding is too extensive because with sufficient hiding two very dissimilar abstractions can be related through inheritance. For example, if the class Dog defines the properties "bark," "fetch," and "eat food," then a class Cat can be derived from Dog by hiding "bark" and "fetch" and adding "purr" and "sleep." In this case, the inheritance does not reflect a meaningful relationship in the underlying abstractions. Others argue, however, that hiding is acceptable if used judiciously in limited circumstances. In their view, some specializations are, in fact, defined by a limitation on a more generalized notion. For example, a Window class could define many operations (show, hide, move, resize, change color, and iconify, among others) all of which, except for the resize operation, are needed to define a FixedSizedWindow abstraction. In this case, hiding the single operation seems acceptable.

The example of inheriting an inappropriate method involves the Rectangle class shown in Figure 6.30. The Rectangle defines a number of methods that are useful in defining a Square class. However, if class Square is derived from the Rectangle class, it will inherit the **`setShape`** method, which is not an appropriate method for the Square class because it would allow a Square object (by definition, with equal height and width) to be set to an arbitrary Shape. There is no guarantee that the argument passed to the setShape method would object the restrictions of the derived Square class.

```
public class Rectangle
{ //...

   public  Rectangle(Shape shape)
   public  void setLocation(Location loc)
   public  void setShape(Shape shape)
   public  void draw()
   public  void clear()
   public  void rotate()
}

public class Square extends Rectangle
{
  // inherits SetShape method
}
```

Figure 6.30 Inheriting an Inappropriate Method

6.6.2 Solutions

There are three means of dealing with an inappropriate inherited method: the developer can define a harmless overriding method, use aggregation, or revise the class hierarchy. Each of these approaches has its own advantages and drawbacks that will be seen by applying them to the examples given above.

Solution One: Overriding the Method

A simple way to deal with an inappropriate method is to retain the method in the public interface but remove its unwanted effect by overriding it and replacing it with a derived class method that either does nothing or takes a benign action. The relevant parts of the code for the Square class using this approach is shown in Figure 6.31. This overriding `setShape` method guarantees that if the `set-Shape` method is applied to a Square object, the dimensions of the Square are unaffected. In effect, the invocation is silently ignored.

Alternatively, the `setShape` method could be redefined in the Square class to take one of the dimensions of the Shape object passed as the argument for the new height and width of the Square. The code for this alternative is

```
public class Square extends Rectangle
{

    public Square(int side)            //constructor sets the Shape
    public void SetShape(Shape shape) //override inherited method
    { // no code - do nothing
    }
}
```

Figure 6.31 Overriding the Inappropriate Method in the Square Class

```
public vid setShape(Shape shape)
{ super.SetShape(new Shape(shape.Width(),shape.Width()));
}
```

where only the width of the Shape parameter is used.

The drawback of the do-nothing and benign overriding methods is that they potentially convey misleading information about the class to programmers using the class. It is not unreasonable that a programmer would expect a method to have some effect, especially when the method involved (such as `setShape`) is known to have effects on objects of all other classes.

Solution Two: Use Aggregation

Instead of using inheritance, aggregation can be used to relate the Square and Rectangle classes. In this approach, as shown in Figure 6.32, the Square class encapsulates a Rectangle object. Many of the methods of the Square class, such as **`setLocation`**, simply invoke to corresponding method of the encapsulated Rectangle object. This style of invocation is sometimes called "forwarding the invocation" because the Square class's method do not take any action except to reroute the invocation to its counterpart in the Rectangle class. The constructor for the Square has a single parameter that defines the size of the four sides of the

```
public class Rectangle
{ //...

   public  Rectangle(Shape shape)
   public  void setLocation(Location loc)
   public  void setShape(Shape shape)
   public  void draw()
   public  void clear()
   public  void rotate()
}

public class Square
{
  private Rectangle rectangle;

  public Square (int side)
  { rectangle = new Rectangle(new Shape(side,side));
  }

  public setSide(int newSide)
  { rectangle.setShape(new Shape(newSide, newSide);
  }

  public setLocation(Location loc)
  { rectangle.setLocation(loc);
  }

  //...other methods similar
}
```

Figure 6.32 Using Aggregation to Hide an Unwanted Method

```
pubic class Quadrilateral
{ //...

   public  Quadrilateral(Shape shape)
   public  void setLocation(Location loc)
   public  void setShape(Shape shape)
   public  void draw()
   public  void clear()
   public  void rotate()
}

public class Rectangle extends Quadrilateral
{

   public  Rectangle(Shape shape)
   public void setShape(Shape shape)
}

public class Square extends Quadrilateral
{

   public  Square(int side)
   public  void setSide(int side)
}
```

Figure 6.33 Altering the Inheritance Hierarchy

square. This single value is used to construct a Shape object that is then used to construct the encapsulated Rectangle object. Similarly, the **setSide** method has a single parameter representing the new length of the four sides of the square. The **setSide** method constructs a new Shape object, one whose height and width equal the new length specified by the method's parameter, and uses the **setShape** method of the Rectangle class to change the shape of the encapsulated **rectangle** object.

There are three essential aspects of this approach. First, the Square class simply forwards to the `rectangle` object all operations that are the same between the Square and the Rectangle classes; in this sense the aggregation is being used to simulate the effect of inheritance. Second, the Square class insures that non-identical operations are properly limited or conditioned by a method of the Square class before a similar operation is invoked on the encapsulated object. Third, methods of the encapsulated object that have no counterparts in the public interface of the encapsulating object are effectively hidden.

Solution Three: Revise the Inheritance Hierarchy

In some cases changes in the class hierarchy can eliminate cases where an inappropriate method is inherited. In both of the examples, Square and ProgramControlledCounter, the inappropriate method was one that allowed the object to be changed in a manner that conflicted with the meaning of the derived class. The nature of this change can be used to divide the class hierarchy into two parts: those classes for which the change is appropriate and those classes for which the change is not appropriate. To reflect this division it may be necessary to introduce a new base class that contains the methods needed by both of the sets of classes.

The problem with the Square and Rectangle classes can be resolved by factoring the common methods into a new base class, Quadrilateral, and establishing two derived classes, Rectangle and Square. The revised class definitions are outlined in Figure 6.33. Each of the derived classes introduces methods that allow their dimensions to be altered as appropriate for their class. In this revised class hierarchy, no inappropriate methods are inherited. The Rectangle class inherits all of the methods of the Quadrilateral class and adds a method that allows both dimensions of a Rectangle object to be changed. Similarly, the Square class inherits all of the methods of the Quadrilateral class and adds a method that allows only a change in dimensions that will affect both dimensions simultaneously.

Exercises

1. Consider how a StationaryPrey could be introduced into the Animal class hierarchy. The `move` method defined in the Prey class is clearly inappropriate for the SolitaryPrey class. Solve this problem using each of the three strategies presented in this section. Compare and contrast the resulting class designs.
2. Consider how a StationaryPredator could be introduced into the Animal class hierarchy. The `move` method defined in the Predator class is clearly inappropriate for the SolitaryPredator class. Solve this problem using each of the three strategies presented in this section. Compare and contrast the resulting class designs.
3. Suppose that there are a Triangle class, representing objects with three vertices, and a Polygon class, representing objects with an arbitrary number of vertices. The Polygon class has a method to add a new vertex and a method to report the current number of vertices. Identify what inappropriate behavior would be inherited by defining the Triangle class as an extension of the Polygon class. Solve this problem using each of the three strategies presented in this section. Compare and contrast the resulting class designs.

6.7 Type Casting

6.7.1 Concept

Type casting is the act of viewing an object of a derived class as an object of its base class. For example, a Number object may be viewed as an object of the class

Number or as an object of the class DisplayableNumber. Alternatively, a Predator object can be viewed as an object of the Predator class or as an object of the Animal class. Viewing an object of a derived class as an object of the base class is sensible because, through inheritance, the derived class object has all of the attributes and behavior (data and code) of the base class. Because any operation that can be applied to a base class object can also be applied to a derived class object, it is safe to use an object of the derived class where an object of the base class is expected. Type casting does not change the object; it only changes what parts of the object are visible through that type case. For example, a single derived class object might be viewed in two different ways as shown in Figure 6.34. When viewed as a base class object, the single object reveals only the base class portion of its structure, but when viewed as a derived class object, all of the object's structure is revealed.

Type casting is the foundation for a powerful form of *polymorphism*. In the sense that it is used here, polymorphism refers to the ability to manipulate in a uniform manner objects that are of different classes. A base class defines the uniform set of methods that can be applied to any objects of the base class and, more importantly, an objects of any of its derived classes. The term type casting describes this technique because the exact "type" (i.e., class) of an object is "cast" away in favor of a more generic type (the base class of the object). Through polymorphism it is possible to create flexible and extensible software structures. A software structure that is defined only in terms of the properties of a base class can, without change, accommodate any object of a derived class by type casting the derived class object to its base class type. In this sense, the software structure is very flexible as it can be applied to a wide class of specific objects.

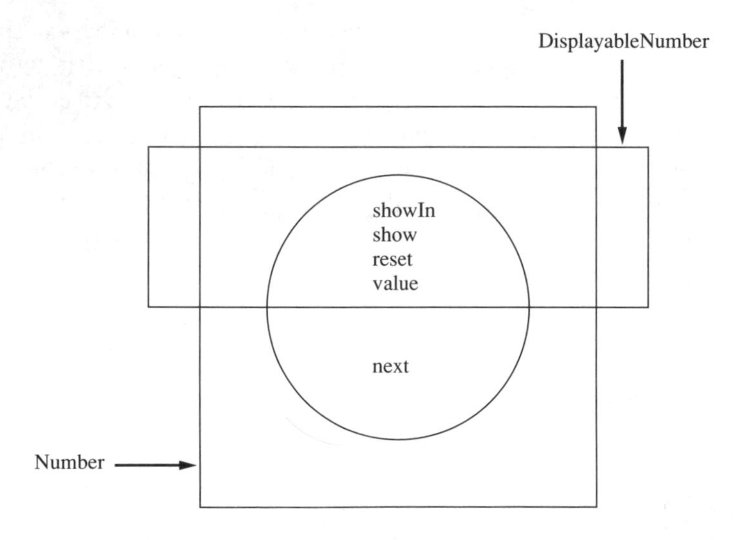

Figure 6.34 Type Casting

Syntax: The syntax for expressing a type cast in Java is shown in the following code fragment that assumes that the DerivedClass extends the BaseClass:

```
BaseClass baseObject;                                  // variable of  base class
DerivedClass derivedObject = new DerivedClass(...);   // object of the derived class
baseObject = (BaseClass) derivedObject;                // type cast
derivedObject.derivedMethod(...);                      // access as derived class object
baseObject.baseMethod(...);                            // access as base class object
```

In this code fragment, a single derived class object is accessed through two references: the first, `derivedObject`, is of type DerivedClass and the second, `baseObject`, is of type BaseClass. A single object is created and a reference to this object is assigned to the variable `derivedObject`. When accessed through the `derivedObject` variable, the object is treated as an object of the DerivedClass because that is the type of the variable. Thus, the `derivedMethod` operation defined in the DerivedClass class can be applied to the object using the variable `derivedObject`. In other words, the variable `derivedObject` gives a DerivedClass view of the object, a view that contains the `derivedMethod` operation. When the same object is accessed via the variable `baseObject`, it is treated as an object of the BaseClass because that is the variable's type. Thus, the `baseMethod` operation can be applied to the object identified by the variable `baseObject` because this operation is defined in the BaseClass class.

Methods can only be invoked when they are in the view defined by the type (or class) of the variable used to access the object. An example of an errors is shown in this code fragment:

```
BaseClass baseObject;
DerivedClass derivedObject = new DerivedClass(...);
baseObject = (BaseClass) derivedObject;             // type cast
derivedObject.derivedMethod(...);                   // OK
baseObject.derivedMethod(...);                      // ERROR
```

The second invocation of `derivedMethod` is in error because it attempts to use an operation that is not defined for the BaseClass portion of the object. The object certainly has a `derivedMethod` operation, but the view that is taken of that object (as a BaseClass object) does not reveal that aspect.

Implicit Vs. Explicit Type Casting

Type casting may be explicit or implicit. When explicit, the program contains code that directs the exact type casting that is done, as shown in the code fragments above. This is explicit type casting because the program code clearly states the casting from a derived type to a base type. Implicit type casting occurs when objects are assigned or passed as parameters without an explicit type cast. For example, the assignment shown in this code fragment:

```
BaseClass baseObject;
DerivedClass derivedObject = new DerivedClass(...);
baseObject = derivedObject;                          // implicit type cast
```

is an implicit type cast because an object of the DerivedClass class is assigned to a variable that holds a reference to an object of the BaseClass class, but no explicit type cast appears in the code.

Implicit and explicit type casting commonly occurs in parameter passing. When used in this way, the formal parameter type is declared using the base type, whereas the type of the actual argument value is declared using a derived class. For example, a method of a class `UserClass` might be declared as

```
public void add(BaseClass  bc);
```

This method might be called with either explicit or implicit type casting. The `add` method is called with an explicit type cast in the following example:

```
UserClass user = new UserClass(...);
DerivedClass dc = new DerivedClass(...);
user.add((BaseClass)dc);
```

In this case, the formal parameter type is BaseClass, whereas the actual argument is of type DerivedClass. On the call to the `add` method, the actual argument is explicitly type cast to agree with the type of the formal parameter. The parameter can also be passed using implicit type casting as shown in the following code segment:

```
UserClass user = new UserClass(...);
DerivedClass dc = new DerivedClass(...);
user.add(dc);
```

In this case, the DerivedClass object is passed without explicit type casting as an argument to a method defined to accept a BaseClass as its parameter. The example illustrates implicit type casting in that the program does not directly specify the type cast, but merely implies that one should be performed.

Although implicit type casting is legal when assigning a derived class object to a variable that is a reference to the base class type, it is strongly recommended that implicit type casting be avoided so that the programmer's intent is clearly expressed in the code. The explicit type cast conveys visibly that the programmer was aware of the casting and deliberately chose to enact the cast. In the absence of an explicit type cast, other programmers (testers, maintainers, various members of the development team) cannot be certain about the programmer's intent. Is the absence of a type cast merely an oversight? Or is it a mistake?

Safety: The safety of implicit or explicit type casting is determined by whether the casting widens or narrows the type of the object. A type cast is said to widen the type of an object when a derived class object is type cast to a base class object. The term widen is used because the object type resulting from the cast applies to a wider collection of classes than the original type (class). For example, the type BaseClass is a wider type than the type DerivedClass. A type cast is said to narrow the type of an object when a base class is type cast to a derived class object. The term "narrow" or "narrowing" is used in this case to reflect that the type cast describes the object as being in a more limited class of objects. For example, type casting a BaseClass object to a DerivedClass object makes the type of the object more determined.

A type cast that widens the type of an object is always safe, but a type cast that narrows the type of an object cannot be guaranteed to be safe. Widening an object's type is always safe because the object has all of the method of the wider type through inheritance. For example, the type cast that widens a DerivedClass object to a BaseClass type is safe because a DerivedClass object has all of the methods of the BaseClass class. However, if a BaseClass object is type cast to one of its derived classes, there can be no guarantee provided by the compiler that the operations on the resulting object are safe. Consider the following example that has two dissimilar derived classes extending the same base class:

```
BaseClass BCref;
DerivedClass1 derivedObject = new DerivedClass1(...);
DerivedClass2 DC2ref;

BCref = (BaseClass)derivedObject; // safe; it widens
DC2ref = (DerivedClass2)BCref;    // run-time error
DerivedClass1 DC1ref;
DC1ref = (DerivedClass1)BCref;    // checked at run-time, no error
```

The first type cast is safe; it widens the type of the number object from a DerivedClass object to a BaseClass object. The second type cast is unsafe and, in this example, is erroneous, because the narrowing type cast from BaseClass to DerivedClass2, although legal to the compiler, results in the variable DC2ref referring to a DerivedClass1 object and not a DerivedClass2 object. Because the compiler cannot determine whether the narrowing operation is valid, the compiler generates code that will check a narrowing type cast operations at run-time. In the example above, a run-time error would result from the narrowing of the object referred to by `BCref` to a DerivedClass2 object. This is an error because the object is not an object of the DerivedClass2 class. The second narrowing operation, type casting the object referred to by `BCref` to a DerivedClass1 object, is also checked but is considered valid because the actual object is of the DerivedClass1 class.

Java provides a mechanism to check whether a type cast will result in a run-time error so that programmers may deal with erroneous situations more proactively in their code. The `instanceof` syntax may be used as a relational operator to test whether a given reference is an instance of a given class. The `instanceof` operator is used in the following code fragment:

```
if (ref instanceof DerivedClass1)
  { DerivedClass1 DC1ref = (DerivedClass1)ref;
    // apply derived class methods to DC1ref
  }

else
  { // handle ref in some other way
  }
```

In this fragment the object referred to by the variable ref is tested to see if it is an instance of the class DerivedClass1 (or any of its subclasses). If the test is true, then the type cast of ref to DC1ref will be valid. After this type cast, the derived class methods may be applied to the object referred to by DC1ref. If the test is false, then some other way of handling the object referred to by ref is programmed by the developer.

6.7.2 An Example Using DisplayableNumber

In this example, type casting is used to create a polymorphic NumberPanel class. The NumberPanel manages a collection of three objects of the DisplayableNumber class or any of its subclasses. The NumberPanel class hides the existence of the TextBoxes used to display the objects and thus simplifies the management of several DisplayableNumber objects. Also, the NumberPanel defines a **show** operation that will be applied to each of the objects it manages. Because the NumberPanel is a specialization of a Panel, NumberPanel is defined by inheritance from the Panel class. The definition of the NumberPanel is shown in Figure 6.35. The NumberPanel defined below exemplifies the flexibility achieved by polymorphism. The NumberPanel is a manager for objects that are derived from DisplayableNumber; it treats the objects that it manages as DisplayableNumbers only, unaware of their exact derived class type. Thus, it is possible for a NumberPanel to manage any collection of Number, Cyclers, or Bicyclers objects, and so on. The NumberPanel also illustrates why polymorphic structures are extensible: because they can be applied to any class derived from the base class, the derived class need not even be known at the time the polymorphic structure is designed and implemented. Thus, the NumberPanel can manage objects whose classes did not exist at the time the NumberPanel was built. *Extensibility* means

```
import Panel;

public class NumberPanel extends Panel
{
  private DisplayableNumber number[];       // contents of NumberPanel
  private int howMany;                      // how many in the NumberPanel
  public NumberPanel(Location loc)
  public void add(DisplayableNumber num)    // add another to NumberPanel
  public void show()                        // show each DisplayableNumber
}
```

Figure 6.35 Interface of the NumberPanel Class

```
import Panel;

public class NumberPanel extends Panel
{
  private DisplayableNumber number[];
  private int howMany;

  public NumberPanel(Location loc)
  { super(loc, new Shape(200, 40));
    number = new DisplayableNumber[3];
    howMany = 0;
  }

  public void add(DisplayableNumber num)
  { if (howMany < 3)
    { TextBox tbox = new TextBox(new Location(10 + 50*howMany, 20),
                                 new Shape(40, 20));
      num.showIn(tbox);
      this.add(tbox);
      num.show();
      number[howMany] = num;
      howMany = howMany + 1;
    }
  }

  public void show()                // show each DisplayableNumber
  { for(int i=0; i < howMany; i++)
    { number[i].show();
    }
  }
}
```

Figure 6.36 Implementation of the NumberPanel Class

that a software system can be extended by adding new derived classes whose objects can be manipulated by other, existing parts of the system.

The NumberPanel interface defines an `add` method to add another DisplayableNumber to the NumberPanel and to display its value in a given Frame when required by the `show` method. Notice that the DisplayableNumber added to a NumberPanel does not provide a TextBox in which its value is displayed; a TextBox is automatically supplied by the NumberPanel. The implementation of the NumberPanel is shown in Figure 6.36. A number of low-level design decisions have been made in the NumberPanel implementation. For example, the location and size of the TextBox created for each DisplayableNumber is defined by simple constants. These low-level decisions are made for simplicity because they are not the main issue in this example. More sophisticated layout strategies could, of course, be used instead of these simple ones. The interesting aspect of the NumberPanel is that it can accommodate any specialized kind of DisplayableNumber. This means that it is not necessary to build several classes such as CounterPanel, CyclerPanel, or SwitchCounterPanel. The NumberPanel works for any single subclass of DisplayableNumber, or for any combinations of subclasses: a

```
public class NumberPanelTest implements Program
{
  private Frame frame;
  private NumberPanel numbers;
  private Number number1;
  private Number number2;
  private Cycler cycler;

  public NumberPanelTest()
  { frame = new Frame("Number Panel Test", new Location(200,200),
                      new Shape(300,300));
    numbers = new NumberPanel(new Location(20,50));
    number1 = new Number(100);
    number2 = new Number (200);
    cycler  = new Cycler(8,5);
  }

  public void onStart()
  { numbers.add(number1);
    numbers.add(number2);
    numbers.add(cycler);
    frame.add(numbers);
  }

  public void onTimerEvent()
  { number1.next();
    number2.next();
    cycler.next();
    numbers.show();
  }

  //...
}
```

Figure 6.37 Implementation of the NumberPanel Class

NumberPanel may contain two Number objects and one Cycler object, or one Number object, one Cycler object, and one SwitchCounter object, for example. The NumberPanel can provide this level of generality because it is built to depend only on the methods defined in the DisplayableNumber class.

The code shown in Figure 6.37 illustrates the NumberPanel's flexibility. In this code, the NumberPanel is managing two different kinds of DisplayableNumbers (two Number objects, and a Cycler object). The type cast used in calling the NumberPanel's `add` method, however, allows the NumberPanel object to treat them all as objects of their common base class (DisplayableNumber). This is possible because the NumberPanel uses only the methods defined in the base class.

6.7.3 Type Casting in the Java Libraries

In Java, every class is a subclass of a standard class named Object that is defined in the java.lang package. This implicit inheritance is implemented by the compiler because it will treat the class definition

```
public class Vector
{
   public Vector()
   public void addElement(Object obj)
   public Object elementAt(int index)
   public void removeElementAt(int idex)
   public void removeElement(Object obj)
   public int size()

     // ...
}
```

Figure 6.38 Partial Interface of the Vector Class

```
import Panel;
import java.util.Vector;

public class NumberPanel2 extends Panel
{
  private Vector number;

  public NumberPanel2(Location loc)
  { super(loc, new Shape(200, 40));
    number = new Vector();
  }

  public void add(DisplayableNumber num)
  { TextBox tbox = new TextBox(new Location(10 + 50*(number.size()), 20),
                                 new Shape(40, 20));
      num.showIn(tbox);
      this.add(tbox);
      num.show();
      number.addElement(num);
  }

  public void show()                    // show each DisplayableNumber
  { for(int i=0; i < number.size(); i++)
    { DisplayableNumber num = (DisplayableNumber)number.elementAt(i);
      num.show();
    }
  }

}
```

Figure 6.39 Using a Vector: Type Casting to/from the Object Class

```
public class Example { ...}
```

as if the definition were actually written as

```
public class Example extends java.lang.Object {...}
```

A class such as Object from which all other classes are derived is sometimes referred to as a root class because it is at the root position in a tree structure that represents the inheritance hierarchy.

The standard Java utilities exploit the existence of the root Object class to provide a variety of general-purpose data structures whose flexibility stems from safe type casting between the Object class and programmer-defined classes. Table 6.1 summarizes a number of these utility classes. In this section the Vector class will be used to show how type casting can be used to achieve the flexibility of these generic data structures.

A partial description of the Vector interface is given in Figure 6.38. The single constructor shown here takes no arguments. The `addElement` method adds a new Object at the end of the current ordered collection of objects. The `elementAt` method returns the object at a given position in the Vector's ordered collection. An object can be removed from the Vector by its identity, using the `removeElement` method, or by its position in the Vector, using the `removeElementAt` method. When an element is removed, the index of all object after the removed element are reduced by one. The `size` method returns the current number of objects in the Vector.

To illustrate type casting involving the Object root class, the NumberPanel is extended to allow it to manage an arbitrary number of DisplayableNumbers. The revised class definition is shown in Figure 6.39 where the changes to use the Vector are shown in bold. In comparison with the previous version of NumberPanel, this version uses a Vector rather than an array to keep track of the DisplayableNumbers. Notice that in the `add` method implicit type casting is used when a DisplayableNumber object is passed as an argument to the Vector's `addElement` method. Type casting is also used in the `show` method. To manipulate each DisplayableNumber, an iteration retrieves each object from the Vector using the Vector's `elementAt` method. The `elementAt` method returns an entity of type Object that is type cast to a DisplayableNumber. Recall that this narrowing operation will be checked at run-time. After the type cast, the retrieved object can be treated as a DisplayableNumber; as illustrated the `show` method is applied to each retrieved object.

Table 6.1 Utility Classes in java.util Package

Class Name	Purpose
Vector	Ordered, unbounded list of elements that can be accessed by position or by object identity
Hashtable	An unordered collection of key-value pairs designed to allow rapid location of a value associated with a given key
Properties	A specialization of Hashtable allowing the key-value pairs to be read from an input source
Stack	A last-in, first-out collection of objects

```
public class SimStat

{ private int totalAge = 0;
  private int alive    = 0;
  private int dead     = 0;
  private int number   = 0;

  //...

  public void add(Animal animal)
  { totalAge = totalAge + animal.getAge();
    number = number + 1;
    if (animal.isAlive())
      alive = alvie + 1;
    else dead = dead + 1;
  }

  public double averageAge()
  { return (double)totalAge / (double)number;
  }

  //...
}
```

Figure 6.40 Type Casting in the SimStat Class

6.7.4 Type Casting Using the Animal Class

Suppose that the ecological simulation is required to produce a set of statistics at various points during the execution of the simulation. The statistics might include the average age of the overall population, the number of live and dead members of the population. Because the information required (age and liveliness) are attributes maintained in the Animal class, it is possible through type casting to implement a class that uniformly handles all of the many different types of creatures that exist in the simulation. The outline of a class named SimStat is shown in Figure 6.40 . The SimStat class maintains various counts that are initialized to zero and incremented appropriately for each Animal object that is presented using the `add` method. The various reporting methods, such as `averageAge`, compute and return one of the individual statistics based on the current value of the counts.

The flexibility gained through type casting is that any Animal object and any object of a class derived from Animal, such as the several Predator classes and the several Prey classes, can be given to the SimStat's `add` method. This is illustrated in the following code fragment:

```
SimStat statistics = new SimStat();

Predator predator = new Predator(...);
Prey prey = new Prey(...);
AgingPredator agedPredator = new AgingPredator(...);
```

```
//conduct simulation using the various predators and prey

statistics.add((Animal)predator);
statistics.add((Animal)prey);
statistics.add((Animal)agedPredator);

double averageAge = statistics.averageAge();
```

In this fragment there are objects of three classes derived from the Animal class (Predator, Prey, and AgingPredator). However, as shown in the three invocations of the add method, each of these can be safely type cast to the Animal base class. The type cast is safe because it is a widening form of type cast, type casting from a derived class to a base class.

Exercises

1. Implement and test a NumberPanel class as described in this section.
2. Implement and test a program that uses a NumberPanel to manage two Number objects and a Cycler object.
3. Implement and test a program that uses a NumberPanel to manage an UpDownCounter object, a BiCycler object, and a SwitchCounter object.
4. Implement and test a class BiDisplay that allows a single DisplayableNumber object to be displayed in two different Frames simultaneously. The BiDisplay's Show() method connects the DisplayableNumber to a TextBox in one Frame and the uses Show to display the value there. The BiDisplay then repeats these actions for a TextBox in the other Frame.
5. Implement and test a class Summation that displays in a TextBox the total of all of the values of the DisplayableNumber objects that have been Added to the Summation object. The class should be able to handle up to five DisplayableNumber objects.
6. Extend the NumberPanel class to include a Reset method that resets each of its constituent DisplayableNumbers objects.
7. Implement and test a class SplitDisplay that manages a single DisplayableNumber or one of its derived classes. The SplitDisplay creates two TextBoxes for the DisplayableNumber, both displayed in the same Frame. The Frame is passed as an argument of the SplitDisplay's ShowIn method. One of the two TextBoxes is always used to show the current value of the DisplayableNumber. The other TextBox is used only for the user to enter a new value during a Reset operation.

8. Implement the SimStat class described in this section. Write and execute a test program to demonstrate that your class is properly defined and implemented. Be sure that your test program uses a variety of Predators and a variety of Prey.

9. Extend the SimStat class to be able to report the statistics separately for Predators and Prey. Use the `instanceof` operator in Java to distinguish whether an Animal object is a Predator (or one of its subclasses) or a Prey (or one of its subclasses). Write and execute a test program to demonstrate that your class is properly defined and implemented.

10. In the code fragment showing how the SimStat class can be used, are all of the type casts needed to invoke the add method?

11. Consider a variation of the SimStat class that has overloaded add methods defined as:

```
public void add (Predator predator);
public void add (Prey prey);
```

What advantage, if any, is there in this approach?

6.8 Dynamic Binding, Abstract Methods, and Polymorphism

6.8.1 Concepts

Static and Dynamic Binding

The term "*binding*," or *method lookup*, refers to the act of selecting which method will be executed in response to a particular invocation. In some languages, such as C, the binding is done completely at compile-time, even if overloaded methods are involved. Binding done at compile-time is also called "static binding" because once the binding is set, it does not change during the execution of the program. However, when type casting and inheritance are involved, the binding cannot be done completely at compile-time because the actual body of code to execute when a method is invoked may depend on the actual class of the object, something that may not be known at compile-time. Dynamic binding refers to binding that is performed at run-time. The interesting case of dynamic binding occurs when type casting, inheritance, and method overriding are combined.

```
public class Base
{
   public void operation()
}

public class Derived1 extends Base
{

   // does not override operation method
}

public class Derived2 extends Base
{

  public void operation()
}
```

Figure 6.41 An Inheritance Hierarchy to Illustrate Dynamic Binding

The role of dynamic binding is illustrated by two examples using the simple class hierarchy given in Figure 6.41. In this class hierarchy two classes are derived from the same base class. The Base class and the Derived2 class contain a definition of a method named `operation`. The Derived1 class does not override the definition of `operation`. The question of interest in the case of the overridden `operation` method is which of the methods is executed under different conditions involving type casting. The question is illustrated in the following code segment:

```
Derived1 first  = new Derived1(...);
Derived2 second = new Derived2(...);
Base generic;
generic = (Base)first;
generic.operation();
generic = (Base)second;
generic.operation();
```

In the first invocation of `operation` the actual object is of the class Derived1. Because the Derived1 class does not override the `operation` method the invocation will cause the execution of the Base class's `operation` method. In the second invocation of `operation` the actual object is of the class Derived2, which does override the `operation` method defined in Base. In this later case, which of the two `operation` methods is invoked? In Java, dynamic binding always executes an overridden method based on the actual type of the object. Thus, in the code segment above, the second invocation of the `operation` method is bound to the Derived2 class's `operation` method. Because the actual type of the object may not be known until run-time, the binding is referred to as dynamic to distinguish it from bindings that can be determined purely at compile-time. Dynamic binding is sometimes referred to as the object "doing the right thing" because the object is aware of its exact class and binds invocations to its methods based on the knowledge of its own class even when, and especially when, the invoking code is unaware of the exact class of the target object.

Abstract Methods

To allow a derived class method to be executed using dynamic binding, the method must be defined in the base class. In negative terms, the derived class method cannot be invoked when the base class does not contain a definition of the method that the derived class can override. For example, type casting a Number object to a DisplayableNumber yields an interface that does not include the **next** method. Similarly, type casting a Predator or Prey object to an Animal yields an interface that does not include the **move** method. Thus, it is not possible to create an extended NumberPanel that would allow it to invoke the **next** method on each of the DisplayableNumbers that it maintains. Similarly, it would not be possible to build a Simulator class that handles Animal objects with the intention of having the Simulator be able to invoke the **move** method to advance the simulation. In both of these cases, it is clear that the objects have the desired method (the classes derived from DisplayableNumber have a **next** method and the classes derived from Animal have a **move** method). The difficulty is that the methods are not visible in the base class to which the objects are type cast.

To enable dynamic binding, the method that can be overridden in the derived class must be defined in the base class in one of three ways:

1. A method with a default implementation
2. A method that has no code
3. An abstract method

For the DisplayableNumber class the first two of these alternatives is shown in Figure 6.42. Each alternative defines a `next` method that will be inherited and can be overridden by the derived classes. The first alternative simply increments the value by one as a default implementation. With this alternative it would not be necessary to define the Number derived class that uses the same implementation of the next method. By default, any derived class that did not override the inherited `next` method would use the base class implementation. The second alternative defines a method that does nothing. For this alternative the Number derived class must be defined as before. Any derived class that did not override the inherited `next` method would use the inherited `next` method that has no effect. The first two alternatives for the Animal class are also shown in Figure 6.42. The default implementation simply increments the age of the ani-

```
public class DisplayableNumber  // alternative 1
{
  public void next()
  { value = value + 1;
  }
}

public class DisplayableNumber  // alternative 2
{
  public void next()
  {
  }
}

public class Animal             // alternative 1
{
  public void move()
  { age = age + 1;
  }
}

public class Animal             // alternative 2
{
  public void move()
  {
  }
}
```

Figure 6.42 Two Alternatives of Base Class Methods

mal without changing its location. The second alternative is one which has no code. The third alternative for both example is discussed in detail below.

In some cases, a default implementation cannot reasonably be given in a base class. It is, perhaps, questionable whether it is a good design decision to provide an empty `next` method in the DisplayableNumber class, because providing a class with a `next` method suggests that something will happen to advance the state of the object when the method is invoked. The fact that nothing happens may reasonably be viewed as counterintuitive or misleading. In other cases, it is clear that no reasonable default implementation can be given for a method. Consider, for example, the design of a base class that generalizes the concept of a geometric shape. Although it is desirable to be able to require that each particular shape (Rectangle, Circle, etc.) be able to draw themselves via a `draw` method or report their screen area by an `area` method, there is clearly no default implementation of either of these methods that passes any reasonable standard.

An "*abstract method*" is one that is declared in the base class using the keyword `abstract` as shown in Figure 6.43. No implementation of an abstract method can be given; this is the sense in which it is abstract. An abstract method serves as a placeholder for an overriding method that must be supplied by the derived class. Intuitively, an abstract method makes a promise on behalf of its derived classes that these derived classes will implement the abstract method. The two examples in Figure 6.43 show how an abstract `next` method is declared

```
public class DisplayableNumber    // alternative 3
{
  public abstract void next();

}

public class Animal
{
   public abstract void move();
}
```

Figure 6.43 Defining an Abstract Method

in the DisplayableNumber class and an abstract `move` method in the Animal class.

A class containing one or more abstract methods is referred to as an "*abstract class.*" If a derived class does not implement all of the abstract methods that it inherits from an abstract class, then the derived class is also considered an abstract class. In contrast, the term "*concrete class*" is used to refer to a class that does not defined abstract methods and has given implementations for all inherited abstract methods. The term abstract in this context is used to mean that the nature of the class is only partially specified. A concrete class, on the other hand, denotes a fixed, specific type of object. Because an abstract class is not fully specified—its abstract methods are defined but not implemented—it is not possible to create objects of abstract classes. For example, the following code would not be allowed:

```
DisplayableNumber adn = new DisplayableNumber(...);     // not allowed
Animal creature = new Animal(...);                      // not allowed
```

This restriction enforces the guarantee that an abstract method will be implemented by a derived class. Thus, objects with unimplemented abstract methods cannot be created. This restriction is reasonable because an abstract base class is incomplete, it does not provide the implementation of its abstract methods.

Although it is not possible to create an object of an abstract class, it is possible, and often done, to have a reference to abstract base classes that refers to an object of a derived, concrete class. Such references are needed in order to be able to refer to a derived class object without knowing its exact type. Because the abstract method is visible in the base class it is possible to invoke an abstract method on a derived class object that has been type cast to the base class. Two examples of this are shown. First, the following code segment illustrates that the `next` method can be invoked using an object reference of type DisplayableNumber.

```
Cycler octal = new Cycler(8);        // object of concrete derived class
DisplayableNumber numRef;            // reference, not an object
numRef = (DisplayableNumber)octal;   // type cast to abstract base class
numRef.next();                       // execute method defined in derived class
```

A similar example code segment uses the Animal and Predator classes:

```
Predator predator = new Predator(...); // object of concrete derived class
Animal animalRef;                      // reference, not an object
animalRef = (Animal)predator;          // type cast to abstract base class
animalRef.move();                      // execute method defined in derived
                                         class
```

The crucial point illustrated by these code segments is that an object of a concrete derived class object (i.e., Cycler or Predator) can be manipulated through a reference to the object's abstract base class.

Manipulating an object of a concrete class through a reference to its abstract base class is both powerful and safe. It is powerful because it allows very flexible systems to be invented; the system can manipulate a wide variety of concrete objects knowing only their general (abstract class) properties. It is also safe to manipulate objects in this way because the abstract methods are guaranteed to be implemented in the concrete object; that is what makes them concrete. For example, the invocation of the `next` method or the `move` method in the code segment above is safe because these methods are guaranteed to be implemented in whatever concrete object is refered to by the variable whose type is the abstract base class.

Polymorphism

Dynamic binding enhances the polymorphism afforded by type casting. The term *polymorphism* is used to describe how objects of different classes can be manipulated uniformly. Through polymorphic techniques it is possible to write code that manipulates objects of many different classes in a uniform and consistent manner without regard for their exact type. The flexibility and generality of polymorphic structures is one of the significant advantages of object-oriented programming. Learning how to recognize opportunities to exploit this possibility takes practice.

The strategy for developing a polymorphic structure begins with identifying the common methods across a group of similar but not identical types of objects. A class hierarchy is then defined in which the common methods are placed in a base class, whereas the remaining methods are organized into classes derived from this base class. The interface of the base class defines an interface through which an object of any of the particular subclasses may be manipulated. It is important to remember that although methods of the shared interface must be **declared** in the base class, they may be left abstract with the subclasses assuming the responsibility for providing the **definition** (code) for the abstract methods. The general class structure for polymorphism is shown in Figure 6.44. The base class contains one or more methods (vm1, vm2, vm3) that represent the shared interface through which the objects of the derived classes may be manipulated. These methods may be given default implementations in the base class, or they may be defined as abstract methods. If the base class methods are abstract ones, then the methods must be defined in a derived classes from which objects are to be instantiated. If the base class methods are implemented in the

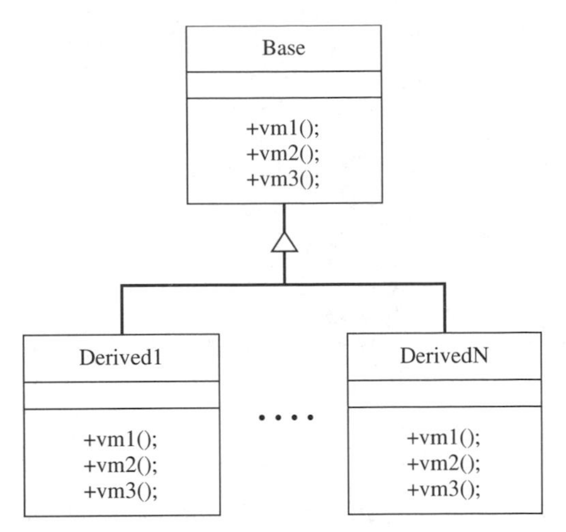

Figure 6.44 Defining an Abstract Method

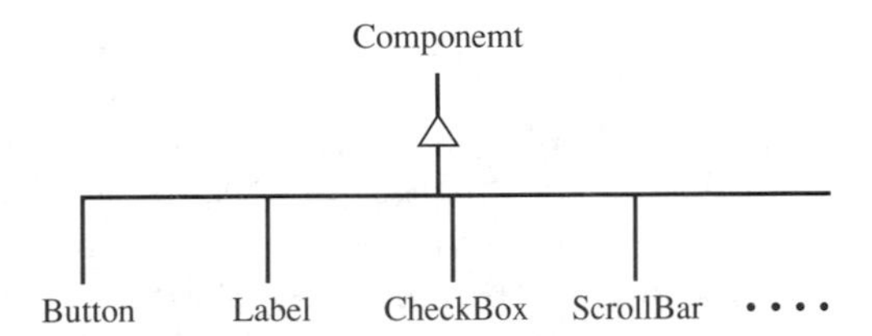

Figure 6.45 The Component Class Hierachy

base class, then the methods may be overridden in the derived classes. Objects can be instantiated from the derived class even if the base class methods are not overridden provided that all abstract methods have been implemented.

One powerful example of polymorphism can be found in the AWT class hierarchy. This class hierarchy is part of the Java run-time environment and the classes are written in Java. A portion of the AWT class hierarchy is shown below in Figure 6.45. The Component class is the base class for numerous derived classes, only some of which are shown in the following figure. This base class represents the shared interface of a range of different entities that can appear in a user interface built with Java and the AWT. The Component class includes a method `inside(int, int)` that determines if the point defined by the two integer input parameters lies inside the given component. This method is useful, for example, in determining if the user has just clicked on a button—it can check if the current coordinates of the mouse are inside a button when a click event occurs. Exactly how a component checks for inside will depend on its nature and

```
public class ComponentManager
{
  private Component member[10];
  private int       number = 0;
        ...
  public void enroll(Component cmp)
  { member[number++] = cmp;
  }

  public Component inside(int x, int y)
  { for(int next = 0;  next<number; next++)
        if (member[next].inside(x,y) )
                        return member[next];
     return NULL;
   }
   ...

}
```

Figure 6.46 Use of Polymorphism: Component Example

geometry. Nonetheless, it is meaningful to inquire of any component whether the coordinates are inside of that component.

Using the polymorphism enabled by the Component class, the essential pieces of a simple ComponentManager are shown below in Figure 6.46. The critical element of this ComponentManager is its ability to manipulate any of the subclasses of Component. When the "*inside*" method of the ComponentManager is invoked, it in turn queries the Component objects that it knows about in search of one that contains the coordinates (x,y). If such a Component is found, then a pointer to that Component is returned. Otherwise, a null value is returned, indicating that the point does not lie inside of the Components managed by the ComponentManager.

6.8.2 Examples

The first example uses dynamic binding to extend the NumberPanel class developed earlier by adding a reset method as shown in Figure 6.47. Due to dynamic binding the **reset** method that is executed is determined dynamically by each object of a class that extends DisplayableNumber. Thus, Number objects will execute the **reset** method defined in DisplayableNumber because the Number class does not override the **reset** method that it inherits from the DisplayableNumber class. However, Cycler objects will execute the **reset** method that is defined in the Cycler class. Dynamic binding allows the NumberPanel class to invoke the "right" method for each specific class of object even when the NumberPanel is itself unaware of the exact class of an object.

```
public class NumberPanel
{
  private Vector number;                     // holds DisplayableNumbers
                                             // as Objects

  public void add(DisplayableNumber num) // add to Vector

  //...

  public void reset()
  { DisplayableNumber num;

    for(int i=0; i<number.size(); i++)
    { num = (DisplayableNumber)nummber.elementAt(i);
      num.reset();
    }
  }
}
```

Figure 6.47 Extending the NumberPanel Class

```
public class Simulation
{
   private Vector animals;                  // holds Animals objects as
                                            // as java.lang.Objects

  public void add(Animal animal) // add to Vector
  { animals.addElement(animal);  // implicit type cast to
                                 // java.lang.Object
  }

  //...

  public void moveAll()
  { Animal animal;

    for(int i=0; i<animals.size(); i++)
    { animal = (Animal)animals.elementAt(i);
      animal.move();
    }
  }

}
```

Figure 6.48 Dynamic Binding and Abstract Methods

The second example uses abstract methods along with dynamic binding. Suppose that the Animal class has been revised as shown in Figure 6.43; the revised Animal class contains an abstract `move` method. Recall that both the Predator and the Prey classes implement the `move` method. The Simulation class shown in Figure 6.48 provides a general mechanism to move each member of a set of simulated animals. The animals are added to the set by the `add` method whose parameter is an Animal type. Through type casting the actual argument passed to the add method may be an object of any class that extends the Animal class. The Animal objects are stored in a Java Vector. The critical aspect of the

Simulation class is the `moveAll` method. This method extracts each object from the Vector and uses type casting to refer to the object as an Animal type. The `move` method is then invoked using the Animal reference. The actual `move` method that is executed depends on the actual type of the object. Thus, if the variable `animal` refers to an object of the Predator class, the Predator class's `move` method will be invoked as appropriate for that object. However, if the variable `animal` refers to an object of the Prey class, the Prey class's `move` method will be invoked as appropriate for it.

Exercises

1. Define and implement a TextDisplay base class that captures the common properties of the TextBox and Message classes. The intent of this base class is to exploit polymorphism so that other classes can manipulate an object of type TextDisplay without being aware of, or dependent upon, knowledge of the exact class of the object.
2. Using the TextDisplay class, define and implement a class FlexCounter by revising the Number class. A FlexCounter can be connected to either a TextBox or a Message object. Be sure to exploit the polymorphic properties of the TestDisplay class.
3. Using the TextDisplay class, define and implement a class FlexDisplayableNumber by revising the DisplayableNumber class. A FlexDisplayableNumber is defined so that its method showIn can accept either a TextBox object or a Message object as a parameter.
4. Illustrate the flexibility properties gained through inheritance by finding the number of associations that can be built using the Clock class (as revised in this section), the TextDisplay, and the FlexDisplayable-Number.
5. Define and implement a revised Button class named VirtualButton to serve as a base class for a wide range of specific types of buttons. Include in the VirtualButton class a method "void onPush()" that defines an action that the button object should perform when its corresponding button the screen is pushed. The default behavior for this method is to do nothing. A do-nothing button would be used as follows:

```
VirtualButton vButton = new VirtualButton("Test", Location(20,20), Shape(60,20));
Frame window = new Frame("ButtonTest", Location(100,100), Shape(200,200));
Panel panel = new Panel(window, Location(20,20), Shape(100,50));
//...
```

```
panel.add(vButton);

//...

void onPush(char* buttonName)
{ if (vButton.isEqual(buttonName) vButton.onPush();
}
```

6. Define and implement a revised Button class named AbstractButton that functions like a VirtualButton except that the `onPush` method is declared to be an abstract method.
7. Define and implement a class StartButton that is derived from VirtualButton. A StartButton object can be connected to a Clock object in an association. The `onPush` method of the StartButton should call the Clock's `start` method.
8. Define and implement a class StopButton that is derived from VirtualButton. A StopButton object can be connected to a Clock object in an association. The `onPush` method of the StopButton should call the Clock's `stop` method.
9. Complete the implementation of the Simulation class started in Figure 6.48. Write a test program to demonstrate that your implementation works. Be sure that your test program uses objects of several different classes derived from Animal that have different `move` methods.
10. Using inheritance and dynamic binding, show how to implement the Pack and Herd classes. Recall that the Pack (Herd) class is a collection of Predator (Prey) objects. The Pack and Herd classes report how many Predators or Prey, respectively, they contain and the number of those that are currently alive. Each class also provides a set of iteration methods to allow each contained Predator or Prey object to be returned.
11. Using inheritance, dynamic binding, and abstract methods show how to implement the Birth and Death classes. The Birth class causes selected members of a Pack or Herd to spawn an identical copy of themselves. The Death class causes selected living members of a Pack or Herd to die.

6.9 Refactoring of Base Classes

Developing a derived class may lead to a redesign or a refactoring of the base class that is done so that the derived class can be accommodated without sacrificing the integrity of the base class itself. In general, the interface between the base class and its derived classes is as important, and requires as much effort to develop and maintain, as the interface between an object and the object's clients. The example given in this section illustrates a situation in which base class redesign is needed to accommodate a new derived class.

Refactoring a base class is often required to preserve the base class's information-hiding properties of the base class. Information hiding is a software engineering principle stating that knowledge of design decisions (the information) should have the narrowest possible dissemination (the hiding). This principle helps to insure the independence of different parts of the system. Furthermore, information hiding promotes easier maintenance and adaptation of software, because a change in a design decision does not have a widespread impact if information about that design decision has been circumscribed. However, if many, or seemingly unrelated, parts of the system are conditioned on knowledge of that design decision, then a change in the design decision may render invalid these other parts of the system.

As an example, the DisplayableNumber class must be refactored to accommodate an OctalNumber class because the `show` method is inappropriate for the new class. An OctalNumber object is just like a Number object, except that the OctalNumber object's value is displayed using octal number (base 8) notation and not as a decimal value. For example, an OctalNumber object with the decimal value 23 would be displayed in its octal representation as 27. Although most of the methods in the Number and DisplayableNumber classes are exactly those needed to implement an OctalNumber, the `show` method is inappropriate because it displays values in a decimal notation.

Simply overriding the `show` method in the OctalNumber class leads to a loss of information hiding. A first approach to modifying the `show` method is to provide an overriding `show` method: the inherited `show` method must be replaced (overridden) by a `show` method that displays the value in octal notation. However, overriding the `show` method leads to a dilemma regarding the sharing of data between the base and derived classes. The `show` method uses the TextBox variable to display the DisplayableNumber's current value. To override the `show` method in a derived class, the TextBox variable must be declared as a protected member of the base class. This change, although workable, significantly enlarges the scope (i.e., weakens the protection) of the TextBox variable, as the base class no longer completely encapsulates the existence of the TextBox variable. Therefore, both the base class and its derived classes are dependent on the following design decisions:

- the DisplayableNumber's value is displayed in a TextBox,
- the TextBox is accessed via a reference,
- the name of the reference is textBox, and
- the TextBox has a `setText` method.

```
public class DisplayableNumber
{
   private TextBox textBox;
   protected int value;

   //...

   protected String format()              // produce string to display
   { return Integer.toString(value, 10);
   }

   public void show()
   {
      if (textBox) textBox-SetText(format());
   }

}
```

Figure 6.49 Refractoring the DisplayableNumber Class

If any of these design decisions change, then both the base class and all of its derived subclasses are vulnerable to change. Notice how serious a problem this is: a derived class (OctalNumber) may need to be changed because of a change in a class (TextBox).

The cause of the problem is that the `show` method performs two related but separable actions that are formatting the character string to be displayed, and displaying the string in the TextBox. The design dilemma is easily resolved by recognizing that the OctalNumber class only needs to override the first action, and only the second action requires knowledge of the TextBox class and the TextBox variable. A new virtual method, "`String format()`", is added to the base class to perform the first action. The revised `show` method will use the `format` method to perform the second action. Separating the two actions of the `show` method leads to the revised definition and implementation of the DisplayableNumber class shown in Figure 6.49. Notice that the `format` method can be overridden in a derived class; such an overriding method will be used in preference for the default one (decimal formatting) given in the DisplayableNumber class.

However, refactoring of the DisplayableNumber class shown in Figure 6.49 is incomplete because the `reset` method has not been accounted for. When `reset` is called, it is expected to produce a new value for the DisplayableNumber by parsing the string obtained from the TextBox. However, this parsing is done assuming that the string represents a decimal value. Once again, this is inappropriate for the OctalNumber class because the string "77" parsed as a decimal value is clearly different from this same string parsed as an octal value. In the `reset` method there are found again two separable actions: obtaining from the user the string that represents the new value, and parsing this string to determine the new value. Following the principle of information hiding, the first of these actions will remain the private concern of the base class. The second action will be established as a protected method of the base class. The additional changes needed in the DisplayableNumber are shown in Figure 6.50.

```
public class DisplayableNumber
{
   private TextBox textBox;
   protected int value;
   public void reset()
   {
      if (textBox) value = parse(textBox-getText());
   }

   protected int parse(String input)     // convert user input to value
   {  return Integer.valueOf(input,10);
   }
     // ...
}
```

Figure 6.50 Additional Refactoring of the Base Class

```
public class OctalNumber extends Number
{

   public OctalNumber(int value)
   { super(value);
   }

   protected int parse(String input)     // convert user input to value
   {  return Integer.valueOf(input,8);
   }

   protected String format()               // produce string to display
   { return Integer.toString(value, 8);
   }

}
```

Figure 6.51 Defining the Octal Number Class

Using this revisions made to the DisplayableNumber class as shown in Figures 6.49 and 6.50, implementing the OctalNumber class is straightforward. The code for the OctalNumber class is shown in Figure 6.51. Because OctalNumber inherits from Number, the only methods that the OctalNumber must implement are the `format` method and the `parse` method. The `format` method and the parse method are declared as protected methods of the OctalNumber class so that they does not become a part of the public interface of this class.

Exercises

1. Implement and test the refactored DisplayableNumber and OctalNumber classes described in this section.

2. Implement and test a class HexNumber that is like a Number except that it displays itself in hexadecimal notation. Develop this class as a subclass of Number using the refactored DisplayableNumber class.
3. Implement and test a PageNumber class that is like a Number except that it displays itself with the string "Page " preceding the decimal value of the number. Develop this class as a subclass of Number using the refactored DisplayableNumber class.
4. Implement and test a DollarNumber class that is like a Number except that it displays itself with the character $ preceding the decimal value of the counter. Develop this class as a subclass of Number using the refactored DisplayableNumber class.
5. Use the techniques presented in this section to revise the Animal class hierarchy by adding a `print` method that outputs a description of the objects simulated state. As an example, the output from a Predator object would contain the following items in the order given: (1) the string "predator" (that should be printed by a Predator class method), (2) its current location, age and alive/dead status (that should be printed by an Animal class method), and (3) its remaining lifetime (that should be printed by a Predator class method). The only method added to the public interface of the class should be the `print` method itself.

6.10 Designing a Class Hierarchy

6.10.1 Basic Principles

The design of a class hierarchy embodies a scheme for classifying a set of related classes according to a generalization-specialization principle. As shown in Figure 6.52, there are three directions in the tree-structured hierarchy. Classes toward the top of the hierarchy (toward the root of the tree) are more generalized classes. The similarities among classes at one level are elevated to the classes at the next higher (more generalized) level. In the opposite direction, the classes descending from a given class are specializations of that class. Each specialization adds behavior and/or data that simultaneously makes the specialized class more specific, more capable, and less general. The specializing class is a refinement of the more general base class from which it is derived. The third direction in the hierarchy is across the classes that have the same immediate parent class. Each of these peer classes specializes the parent class in a different way, creating variety among the derived classes.

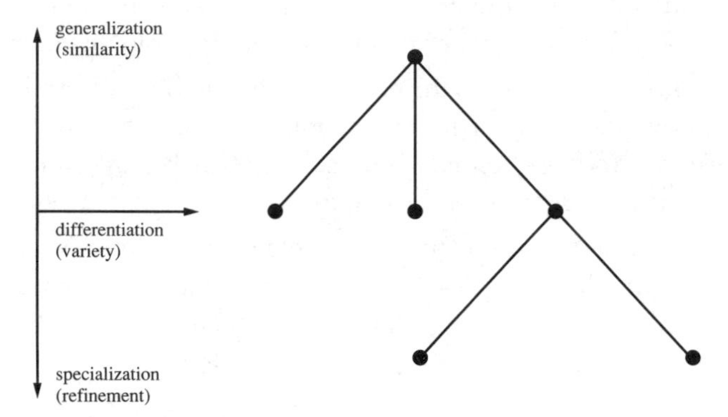

Figure 6.52 Inheritance Dimensions

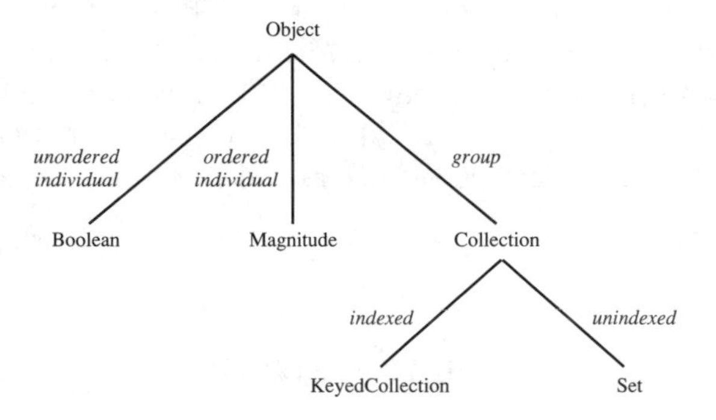

Figure 6.53 A Rationalized Class Hierarchy

The role of the class hierarchy designer is not only to design the class hierarchy but also to create a rationalization of the class hierarchy. Rationalization in this sense means the creation of a logical, well reasoned (i.e., a rational) explanation for the organization of the hierarchy. The rationalization is concretely presented in the form of a logical condition that describes the refinement introduced by each specializing class. The logical conditions serve two purposes. First, the logical conditions identify the way in which the generalized (base) class is refined by the specialized (derived) class. Thus, the generalization-specialization direction in the class hierarchy is rationalized. Second, the difference between two peer classes can be understood by comparing their logical conditions. Through this comparison the variety (differentiation) direction in the class hierarchy is rationalized.

As an example of a rationalized class hierarchy, a small portion of Smalltalk's much more elaborate class hierarchy is shown in Figure 6.53. In this portion of the class hierarchy, the universe of all Objects is divided into three classes: Boolean represents an object with unordered values, Magnitude represents individual objects that can be ordered with respect to each other, and Collection represents groups of objects as opposed to individual values. Individual ordered objects (i.e., the derived classes of Magnitude) are distinguished by the nature of the scale that determines how the objects are compared. The Char class has no scale; it is a simple predefined ordering of it elements. Individual objects of the Char class can be compared with each other but there is no sense of distance in the ordering. For example, the character *A* comes before the character *B*, but there is no sense that *A* is closer to or farther away from *B* than *B* is from *C*. The Number class is defined by a one-dimensional scale (such as for integers or floating-point numbers) where distance is an integral part of the nature of the values of this class. The Point class is defined by a two-dimensional scale, such as a Cartesian space or a computer screen. In contrast to ordered values are groups of objects represented by the Collection class. Two different collections are shown: Set and KeyedCollection. The rationalization for these two subclasses is that the objects of a KeyedCollection are indexed by the key value associated with each object, whereas the objects in a Set are unindexed. This rationalization of the class hierarchy makes it easier to understand the organization of the concepts in the hierarchy and guides where extension should be made if new classes are added to the hierarchy.

There is a general strategy for finding a class hierarchy and its rationalization. The strategy has three steps:

1. Analyze all classes that have the same immediate parent (or, at the beginning, all classes).
2. Divide the classes into groups based on discriminating properties; all classes in a group should share the discriminating property associated with that group, which no class outside of the group has.
3. Establish a base class for each group; the discriminating properties are the rationalization of the base classes.

These three steps are repeated iteratively until all the classes have been categorized, at which point there is a rationalization for the class hierarchy. It may be that not all of the classes can be placed into groups in the second step. These other classes can be considered again in a later iteration. The *Flight Control Panel* example below applies this general strategy in the design of a class hierarchy.

The rationalization of a class hierarchy is an important element in object-oriented software design for numerous reasons. It is a test of the adequacy of the class hierarchy. An inability to define the logical conditions among classes is a sign that the class hierarchy is not well founded. Additional work or a different approach is needed to complete the rationalization. It is a way of explaining and justifying the class hierarchy. The names of the classes and the logical conditions among them create a vocabulary and a set of relationships through which the designer can articulate the design of the class hierarchy. This vocabulary also lends insight into how the designer conceives of the concepts in the application domain. Rationalization creates a concrete artifact for debate and discussion. A class hierarchy embodies a way of thinking about the concepts in the application domain; members of the development team can use it as a device to test whether their conceptualizations of the application domain entities are similar. Such a comparison is impossible without a concrete, shared, external representation such as the one provided by the class hierarchy. Similarly, it provides a means of understanding the class hierarchy. A (re)user of the class hierarchy can use the logical conditions to learn about its structure and organization. The more logical and systematic the rationalization, the easier it will be for the (re)user to develop an understanding of the class hierarchy. The rationalization is a handy guide for locating a desired class in the hierarchy. A (re)user needing a particular class can start at the root of the hierarchy and ask which of the logical conditions of its subclasses best describes the desired class. By iterating through this process, either a suitable class will be found or it will be clear that the class hierarchy does not contain a suitable class. As the class hierarchy is extended, rationalization gives an indication of where further variety is possible. If the logical conditions attached to the classes derived from a given class are exhaustive, then additional variety is not possible because the existing derived classes have accounted for all possibilities. However, if this is not the case, then new subclass can be introduced and the nature of these subclasses might be hinted at by what is left over by the existing conditions.

Designing and rationalizing the class hierarchy is an evolutionary process. Hence, the class hierarchy designer must approach the task of identifying and classifying the common properties among classes with the realization that there may be more than one good class hierarchy, so alternatives should be explored. Exploring the design may involve backtracking to an earlier point and moving forward again in a new direction. Alternative designs can be compared on the basis of the clarity of their rationalization and the possibility of further extension. Additionally, the designer must proceed knowing that use and iteration are necessary to refine the class hierarchy; it is unlikely that the complete hierarchy will be seen at the start except for a hierarchy that is very small or one which is virtually identical to an existing hierarchy. For example, the class hierarchy at the heart of the Smalltalk system evolved over the period of many years of use and refinement. Creating a good class hierarchy is both a challenging and a rewarding task.

6.10.2 An Example of Designing a Class Hierarchy

The principles of designing a class hierarchy are illustrated through the Flight Control Panel example described below. This panel is part of a larger flight simu-

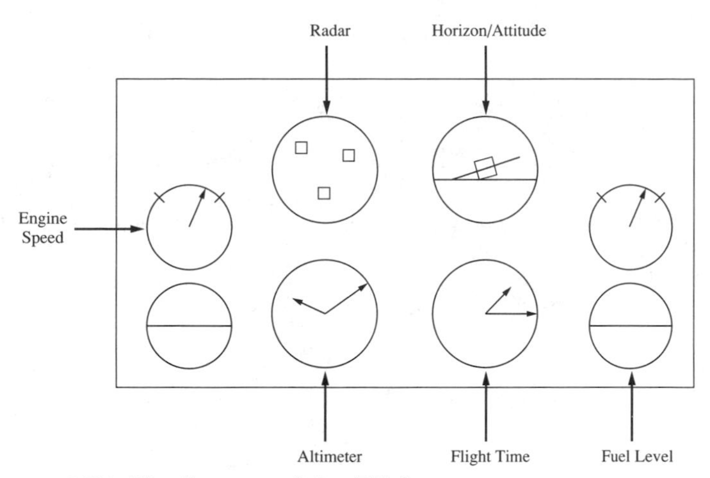

Figure 6.54 The Layout of the Flight

lator. Designing a good class hierarchy is important in this project because the Flight Control Panel may be modified during development, expanded in later version of the flight simulator, and components of the panel might be reused on other projects that have some of the same instrumentation.

The flight control panel consists of different types of dials, gauges, and displays that provide the pilot with status information during the simulated flight. The panel is organized as shown in Figure 6.54. The simulated aircraft has two engines and two fuel tanks. The left and right sides of the panel have a pair of instruments that show the engine speed and the fuel-tank level. The bottom center of the panel contains an altimeter and a clock. The two hands of the altimeter display the current altitude of the aircraft; one hand is calibrated in 1000-foot units and the other is calibrated in 100-foot units. The clock gives the elapsed time since takeoff in hours and minutes. The top center of the panel features a radar and a horizon/attitude display. The radar shows various icons and text representing other aircraft in the vicinity, whereas the horizon/attitude display's small centered icon represents the aircraft. This icon rotates about its center point to indicate the alignment of the aircraft's vertical axis to the ground. A horizontal line in this display indicates the alignment of the aircraft's horizontal axis with the ground. When the line is in the middle of the display, the aircraft is in level flight. The degree to which the line is toward the top or bottom of the display indicates how much the aircraft is descending or ascending.

An initial set of class is easy to find in this problem. Each of the different types of instruments is a candidate for the definition of a class. These classes might be named:

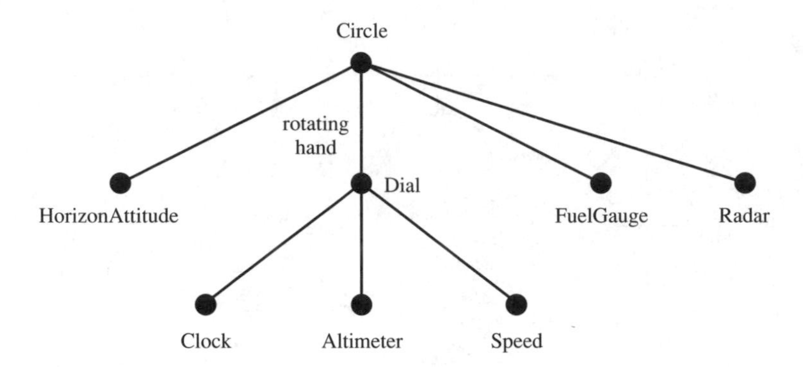

Figure 6.55 Flight Control Panel Hierarchy: First Iteration

- Altimeter
- Clock
- Radar
- FuelGauge
- HorizonAttitude
- Speed.
-

The more difficult issue is how to organize these classes into a class hierarchy.

Several iterations of the a class hierarchy design for the Flight Control Panel are shown. Each iteration deepens the organization of the classes. The rationalization of the class hierarchy is developed at the same time as the hierarchy itself.

First Iteration: The first step in organizing the Flight Control Panel's classes is to identify any properties common to all of them. One evident property is that all of the elements are circular in shape. This property can be captured in a base class. All of the classes derived from this base class will inherit the property of being circular. There is no other evident property shared by all of the instruments. Therefore, groups of classes that share a new common property are sought. Some of the instruments convey information by a rotating hand; the classes representing these instruments are FuelGauge, Altimeter, and Clock. These three classes can be organized into a sub hierarchy whose base class is named Dial. The rationalization for the Dial class is "rotating hand." The class hierarchy at this point in shown in Figure 6.55.

Second Iteration: Following the general strategy, the immediate descendents of the Circle class, Radar, Dial, Speed, and HorizonAttitude are analyzed. Notice that this set of classes is a mixture of original classes (Radar, Speed, Hori-

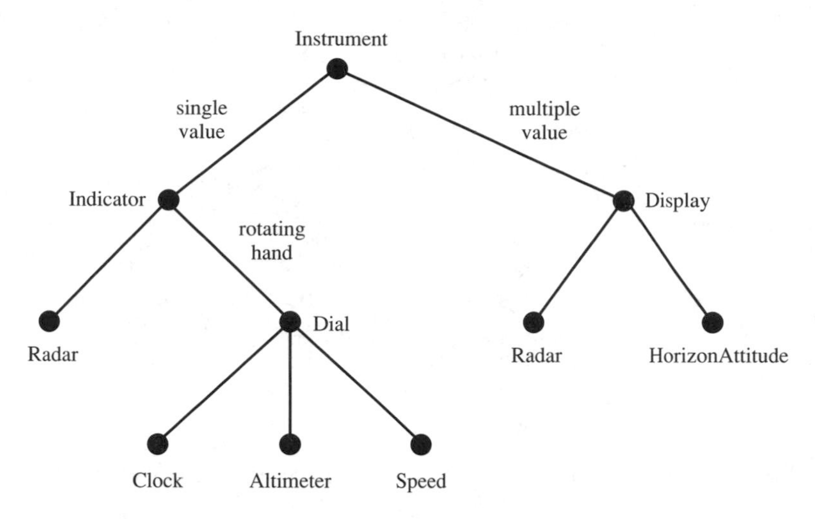

Figure 6.56 Flight Control Panel Hierarchy: Second Iteration

zonAttitude) and a base class (Dial) created in the first iteration. A discriminating property among these four classes is that the Dial and Speed classes display a single value or condition whereas the Radar and HorizonAttitude classes display multiple values or conditions. Using these groups as a guide, two new base classes may be invented: Indicator, a base class for single-value instruments, and Display, a base class for multiple-value instruments. The rationalizations for the Indicator and Display classes leads to a reconsideration of the name of the Circle class: the rationalization for the Indicator class would be read as "an Indicator is a single-value Circle," but the term Circle is inappropriate in this context. A more precise statement is "an Indicator is a single-value Instrument that is shaped like a Circle." The name Instrument is more suggestive in this context and, thus, the name of the Circle class is changed to Instrument. Figure 6.56 shows the class hierarchy after the second iteration.

Third Iteration: In this iteration, the classes derived from Indicator and those derived from Display are considered. Of the two classes derived from Indicator, Dial and FuelGauge, the rationalization "rotating hand" has already been developed for the Dial class. This leads naturally to finding the corresponding rationalization for the FuelGauge class. Instead of a rotating hand, the FuelGauge indicates its value with a horizontal line that moves up and down to show the level of the fuel in the tank. FuelGauge may therefore be described as "is a sliding-position Indicator." In addition, neither of the two classes derived from Display, Radar and HorizonAttitude, has a rationalization. One essential difference between these two classes is that the Radar has a varying, unbounded number of items that it can display, whereas the HorizonAttitude class works with a fixed, bounded number of items. The rationalizations "varying number" and "fixed number" can be used for these classes. To check that this makes sense, the

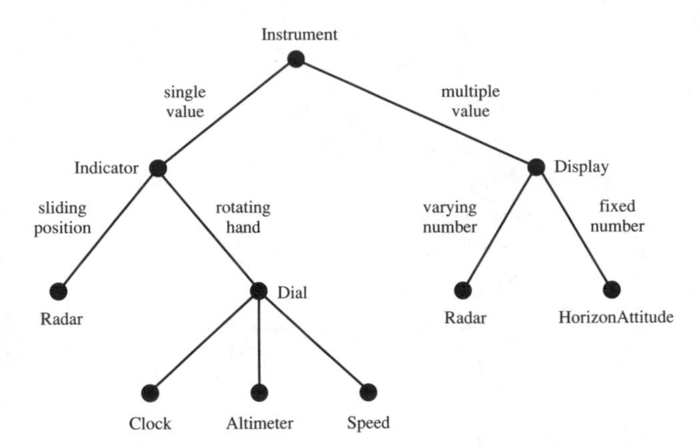

Figure 6.57 Flight Control Panel Hierarchy: Third Iteration

rationalization would indicate that "a Radar is an Instrument for a varying number of multiple values" and that "a HorizonAttitude is an Instrument for a fixed number of multiple values." Because these interpretations are consistent with the understanding of these classes, the rationalization is acceptable. The class hierarchy after the third iteration is shown in Figure 6.57.

Fourth Iteration: The fourth and final iteration reconsiders the classes derived from the Dial base class: Speed, Altimeter, and Clock. In searching for discriminating characteristics, it can be found that the Altimeter and the Clock have two rotating hands but the Speed indicator has only one. As there may be more specific kinds of indicators introduced in future versions of the system, it could be useful to make this distinction explicit. Therefore, a new base class, TwoHandDial, may be introduced as a class derived from Dial that becomes the class from which both Altimeter and Clock are derived. Clearly the rationalization for the TwoHandDial class would be "two hands," whereas the rationalization for the Speed class would be "one hand." To check that the accumulated rationalizations are sensible, the Clock class would be described as "an Instrument that displays a single value using two rotating hands" where the single value is understood to be the elapsed flight time. It is also sensible to describe the Speed class as "an Indicator that displays a single value using a single rotating hand." To complete the rationalization, the subclasses of TwoHandDial, Clock and Altimeter, should be considered. One essential difference between these two classes is that the Altimeter is bidirectional: its hands can move both clockwise and counterclockwise. The Clock, however, is unidirectional, as its hands can only move forward in the clockwise direction. If these properties are used for the rationalization of these two classes, the class hierarchy design is complete. The final class hierarchy is shown in Figure 6.58.

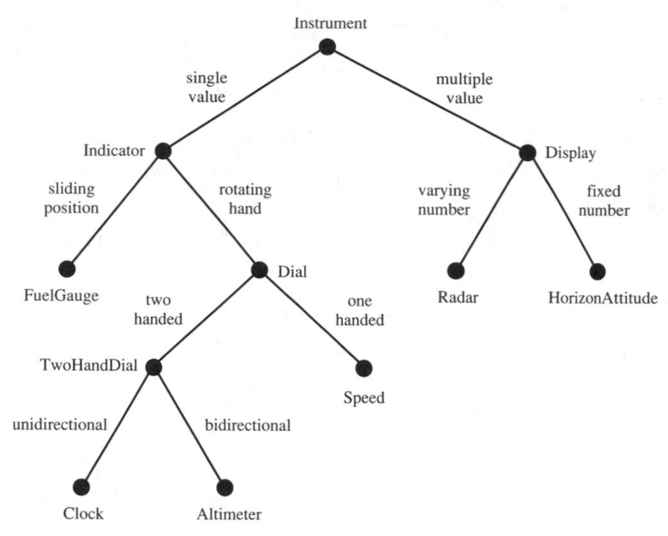

Figure 6.58 Flight Control Panel Hierarchy: Fourth Iteration

Exercises

1. Revise the fourth-iteration class hierarchy developed for the Flight Control Panel assuming that the FuelGauge was changed so that it had a single hand indicating positions between a position marked "empty" and a position marked "full."

2. Revise the fourth-iteration class hierarchy developed for the Flight Control Panel assuming that the HorizonAttitude instrument was split into two instruments, the Horizon instrument and the Attitude instrument.

3. Revise the fourth-iteration class hierarchy developed for the Flight Control Panel assuming that a new instrument is added to indicate the position of the landing gear by displaying one of three text strings: "retracted," "extended," or "locked."

4. Revise the fourth-iteration class hierarchy developed for the Flight Control Panel assuming that a new kind of instrument is added to the panel, a status light for the engine temperature. The light is either green, indicating a temperature for normal operations, or red, indicating a temperature that is too high.

5. Revise your answer to question number 4 by adding two other kinds of status lights. One kind of status light blinks when it changes to the red state, and the other kind beeps when it changes to the red state.
6. The FuelGauge and the HorizonAttitude display are similar in that both have a movable horizontal line. Give specific advantages and disadvantages of revising the fourth-iteration class hierarchy developed for the Flight Control Panel so that the HorizonAttitude class inherits from the FuelGauge class.
7. The class hierarchy developed in this section for the Flight Control Panel was organized on the basis of the appearance of the instruments. Develop an alternative class hierarchy on the basis of some other characteristic of the instruments.

6.11 Design Patterns

6.11.1 Definition and Structure of a Design Pattern

Once represented, a design may itself be reused by designers other than the original one. Individual designers have always been able to reuse their own designs or those that they had learned about informally from others. However, a broadly understood design representation makes it possible for a designer to communicate well-understood, well-tested designs to other practitioners faced with similar design problems and to students learning about object-oriented design concepts.

A reusable design must include more information than just the design diagrams. Among other things, the problem that the design is meant to address must be defined. This information is important because it allows potential reusers, faced with a particular problems, to identify available designs that are candidates for reuse. Another kind of information that is needed in a reusable design concerns the trade-offs implied by the design. Typically, designers must achieve a balance between such competing goals as efficiency, flexibility, fault tolerance, and simplicity. A single problem may give rise to several useful designs, each offering a different balance among the design factors.

A "**design pattern**" is a proposed format for presenting a reusable design. The structure of a design pattern is defined in the book *Design Patterns* by Gamma, Helm, Johnson, and Vlissides (p. 360) as:

> A design pattern systematically names, motivates, and explains a general design that addresses a recurring design problem in object-oriented systems. It describes the problem, the solution, when to apply the solution, and its consequences. It also gives

implementation hints and examples. The solution is a general arrangement of objects and classes that solve the problem. The solution is customized and implemented to solve the problem in a particular context.

The first sentence of the definition expresses the intent of a design pattern: to present in a consistent and coherent manner the solution to a recurring design problem. The next two sentences of the definition outline the content of a design pattern. The last two sentences explain the usage of a design pattern. The usage makes clear that a design pattern is not a program or code; it is a design that must be tailored to fit the specific requirements of a particular problem and then implemented. The book *Design Patterns* contains a collection of design patterns, one of which is studied in detail here.

A design pattern includes the following twelve elements:

1. **Name:** each pattern has a unique, short descriptive name. The collection of pattern names creates a specialized vocabulary that designers can use to describe and discuss design ideas.

2. **Intent:** the intent is a succinct (one to three-sentence) description of the problem addressed by the design pattern. The intent is useful in browsing design patterns and aids in recalling the purpose of a pattern when the name alone is not a sufficient reminder.

3. **Motivation:** the motivation explains a typical, specific problem representative of the broad class of problems that the pattern deals with. It should be clear from the motivation that the problem is widespread and not trivial. The motivation usually includes class diagrams and/or object diagrams along with a textual description.

4. **Applicability:** this element is a list of conditions that must be satisfied in order for a pattern to be usable. The conditions express goals that the designer is trying to fulfill (e.g., the ability for clients to be able to ignore the difference between compositions of objects and individual objects), complicating aspects of the problem (e.g., an application uses a large number of objects), and constraints (e.g., storage costs are slight because of the sheer quantity of objects).

5. **Structure:** a description of the pattern using class diagrams and object diagrams. The class and object names are generalizations of those that appear in the specific example given in the motivation. For example, the Builder pattern motivation uses an example that has a base class named TextCon-

verter with derived classes ASCIIConverter, TeXConverter, and TextWidgetConverter. The class diagrams in the structure section names the base class Builder and has a single representative derived class named ConcreteBuilder.

6. **Participants:** each class in the structure section is briefly described. The description is a list of each class's responsibilities and purpose in the design.

7. **Collaborations:** the important relationships and interactions among the participants are described. Object-interaction diagrams may be used to illustrate complex interaction sequences.

8. **Consequences:** this section explains both the positive and negative implications of using the design pattern. Positive implications might be increased flexibility, lower memory usage, easier extensibility, support for particular functionality, or simplified usage. Negative implications might be inefficient behavior in particular cases, complex class structure for certain problems, loss of guarantees of system behavior, or overly general design with attendant loss of performance or storage costs. It is important that authors of design patterns present, and readers of design patterns understand, positive as well as negative consequences. All designs achieve a compromise among many competing forces and no design can avoid have some negative consequences.

9. **Implementation:** a representative implementation is shown for the classes given in the structure section. Because the structure section is generalized, so also is the implementation provided in this section. This section is meant as a high-level guide on how to represent the pattern in a given programming language.

10. **Sample code:** the essential code for a typical problem (often the one presented in the motivation) is given. This code illustrates in detail how the pattern would be applied to the particular problem.

11. **Known uses:** this is a list of systems, libraries, tools, or frameworks that have dealt with the design problem addressed by this design pattern. The example systems may have used a variation of the design pattern as a solution.

12. **Related patterns:** other design patterns that are thought to be useful in combination with this pattern are listed. This list

provides additional guidance to designers by offering pointers to other patterns that could potentially help.

6.11.2 An Example of a Design Pattern

The "Composite" pattern, given in *Design Patterns*, will be used as an example of a design pattern. The *name* of the pattern is "Composite," suggesting the pattern deals with composing objects. The *intent* of the pattern is stated as follows:

> Compose objects into tree structures to represent part-whole hierarchies. Composite lets clients treat individual objects and composites of objects uniformly.

The intent expresses both the subject matter of the pattern (trees of objects related by a part-whole relation) as well as the goal of the pattern (uniformity of treatment). The *motivation* presented for this pattern describes a typical graphical drawing tool that allows users to draw a variety of predefined basic shapes (rectangles, lines, circles, rounded rectangles, polygons, etc.) and also allows shapes to be composed together. A composite shape is treated as a newly defined basic shape in that it can be composed with other basic or composite shapes. A set of operations (draw, move, resize, etc.) can be applied to any shape (basic or composite). Both a class diagram and an object diagram are used to illustrate a design solution. The class diagram is shown in Figure 6.59.

The *applicability* section defines two conditions: (1) part-whole hierarchies are being represented, and (2) uniformity of treatment for parts and a whole is sought. The conditions mirror the basic ideas presented in the statement of the pattern's intent. The *structure* section contains the generalized class diagram shown in Figure 6.60. In the generalized class diagram, the specific kinds of parts are represented by a single class "Leaf," whereas the class named "Composite" represents a whole. The abstract base class, "Component," defines an interface that must be implemented by Leaf classes and the Composite class. The abstract base class reflects the uniform treatment of Leaf and Composite objects. Note also that the generic "Operation" method is an abstraction of some application-specific operation.

The *participants* section lists the responsibilities of each of the four classes that appear in the structure (Component, Leaf, Composite, Client). For example, the responsibilities of the Composite class are to define the behavior of "a composition of objects, to store the composed (sub)objects, and to implement the operations defined in the abstract base class."

The *collaborations* section defines how the Composite pattern's participants work together to meet their individual responsibilities and achieve the effect intended for the pattern. For instance, in this example, in the Composite pattern, the client interacts with the Leaf or Composite objects only through the abstract

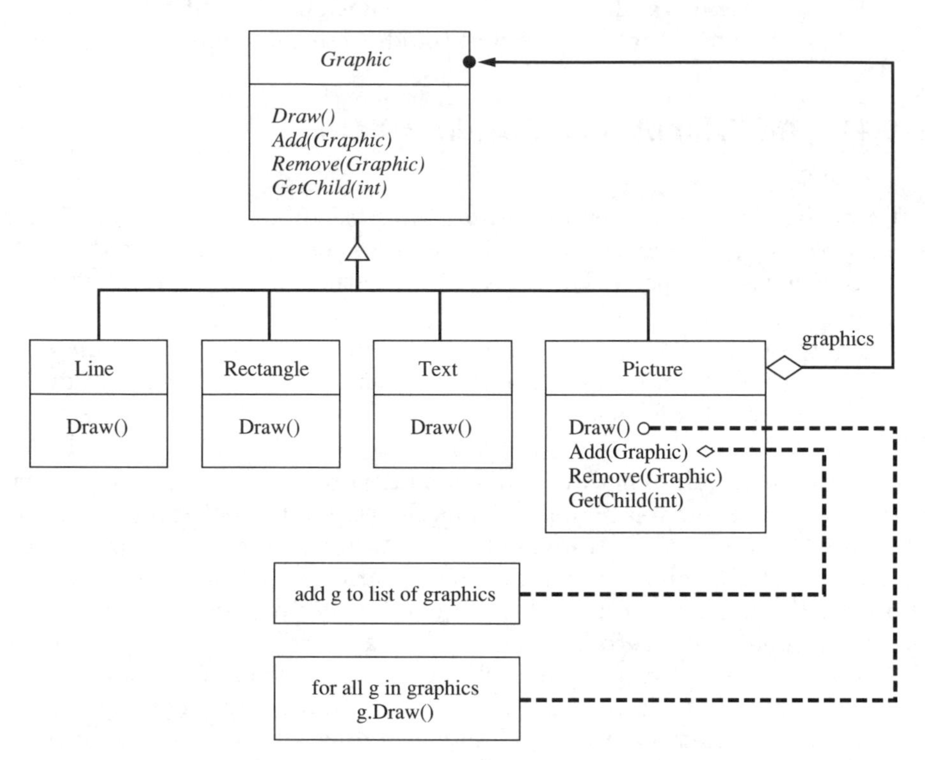

Figure 6.59 Composite Pattern example

interface defined in the Component class. This collaboration captures a key feature of the pattern: the client is able to manipulate Components without regard for whether they are Leaf class objects or Composite class objects.

Two of the *consequences* of using the Composite pattern are that it makes it easy to add new kinds of basic components (i.e., Leaf classes)—they are simply added as another class derived from Component—and it can make the design overly general in those cases where only certain combinations of objects have semantic meaning (for example, a document may be viewed as a Composite of paragraphs, tables, sections, and so on. However, a correct document must have exactly one title and a table may not have sections within it. It is difficult to enforce these kinds of restrictions with the Composite pattern as the pattern places no limitations on the way in which a Composite can be formed. Notice again that both the strengths and the limitations of the pattern are identified.

The *implementation* section presents issues relevant to the detailed coding of the classes in the pattern. For example, the trade-off between safety and transparency is considered in this section of the Composite pattern. This trade-off involves where to place the methods for manipulating the children of a Composite. If these methods are placed only in the Composite class, it is safer

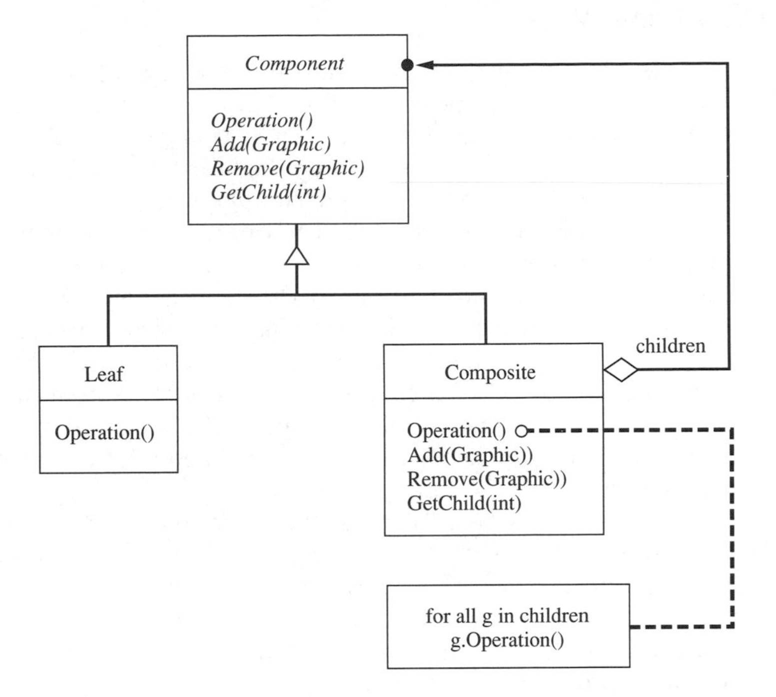

Figure 6.60 Composite Pattern Structure

(because attempt to apply them to Leaf components is detected as a compile-time error) but it is also less transparent (because Leaf and Composite objects cannot be treated as uniformly as might be desired). Placing the methods in the Component base class yields the opposite trade-off. A compromise strategy introduces a method "Composite (`getComposite`)" in the Component base class. This method is defined in the Leaf derived class to return a "null" pointer and defined in the Composite derived class to return its "this" pointer. This strategy minimizes the loss of transparency, because all base class methods apply equally to both Leaf and Composite objects, whereas it retains a large measure of safety by leaving to the Client the responsibility to differentiation between objects of the two derived classes.

The *sample code* section gives C++ code for an example of a part-whole problem. This most detailed level of presentation helps to give a concrete representation of the pattern that can be compiled and used for experimentation.

The *known uses* section lists three application domains (user interface toolkits, a compiler, and financial portfolios) where the pattern has been observed.

Finally, four *related patterns* are noted, including the Iterator pattern that can be used to traverse composite structures.

6.11.3 Summary

A design pattern is a means of fostering reuse of design knowledge and experience rather than the reuse of a specific implementation. A design pattern falls between a general design heuristic and actual code: it is less general (more limited) than a design heuristic or guideline, which might express, for example, that a class interface should be a coherent and complete set of methods for an abstraction. Although heuristics are intended to apply to the broadest range of cases, a design pattern is intended to capture in more detail a single structure or abstraction. At the same time, a design pattern is more general than an implemented class hierarchy or framework. Hierarchies and frameworks are limited in their reuse potential to a single programming language, a single (or small range) of situations, and perhaps even a single operating system or run-time environment. A design pattern, however, has none of these limitations. A design pattern is sufficiently focused to be useful, but general enough to be applicable in a range of applications.

The ultimate value of design patterns will only be realized by an organized, extensive collection of patterns that encompasses generic design problems as well as problems specific to particular applications domains. One might imagine a collection of patterns for real-time systems, distributed/concurrent/parallel applications, and other important application areas. The collection of patterns in *Design Patterns* is an important beginning.

CHAPTER 7

Building User Interfaces in Java

7.1 Introduction

In Java 1.2, The Java Foundation Classes (JFC) contains five libraries, one of which will be examined in detail in this chapter. The five libraries in the JFC are shown in Figure 7.1. Two of the libraries are used for the creation of GUIs: the AWT and its newer extension, the Swing library, that is the focus of this chapter. The other three libraries provide facilities for transferring information between Java interfaces and native applications through a drag-and-drop mechanism, providing accessibility to the user interface from devices such as braille keyboards or audible text readers, and creating customized two dimensional fonts, shapes, and colorings.

Although the AWT and Swing both provide classes for constructing GUIs they differ in one major way: the AWT relies on the host platform to draw and manage the actual user interface elements, or "widgets," whereas Swing contains its own mechanisms for drawing and managing them in a basic drawing region (a window) provided by the host platform. To illustrate this difference, consider how a user interface button would be handled in AWT and Swing. An object of the AWT Button class is associated with a "peer" represents the host platform's widget for a button. Operations on the AWT Button object, such as setting the button's label, are conveyed to the "peer" object that actually performs the action in the visible user interface. When the user pushes the button, the "peer" object notifies the AWT Button object of this event. In constract, an object of the Swing JButton class contains all of the code to draw its representation in the user interface and is notified directly of events that occur within its boundaries by the Swing event handling mechanism.The implications of the major difference between the AWT and Swing are summarized in Table 7.1 and discussed further below.

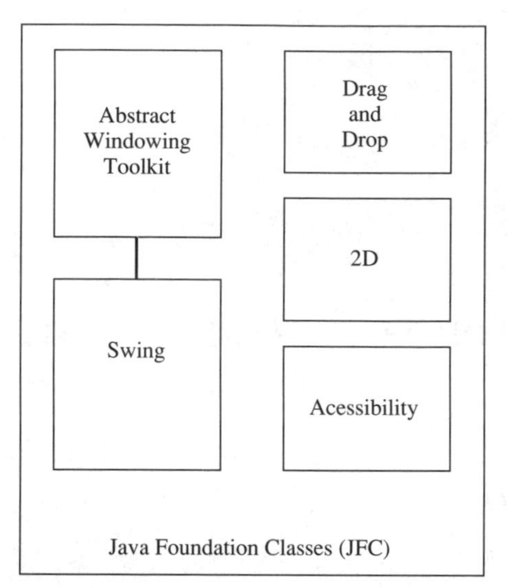

Figure 7.1 The JFC Classes

Table 7.1 AWT Vs. Swing

Characteristic	AWT	Swing
Look and Feel	Platform dependent	Platform independent
Customizable Look and Feel	No	Yes
Overhead	Heavyweight	Lightweight
Features	Common subset	Open-ended

The most obvious difference between Swing and the AWT is in the appearance of the user interface widgets, or termed the "look and feel" qualities of the user interface. The AWT depends on the host platform to supply "peer" objects for each widget. Thus, user interface components on a Windows platform have the look and feel of similar components in native Windows applications. The same program run on a Solaris platform has the look and feel of Solaris's widget set. The advantage of the AWT approach is that Java applications have the same look and feel as other native applications; the consistency with native applications is appealing to users of a single host platform. The disadvantage of AWT's approach is that the same application on different platform does not have the same look and feel, thus jeopardizing the full advantages of Java's write once, run anywhere philosophy. With Swing, however, the look and feel is platform independent because the drawing and functionality of each user interface compo-

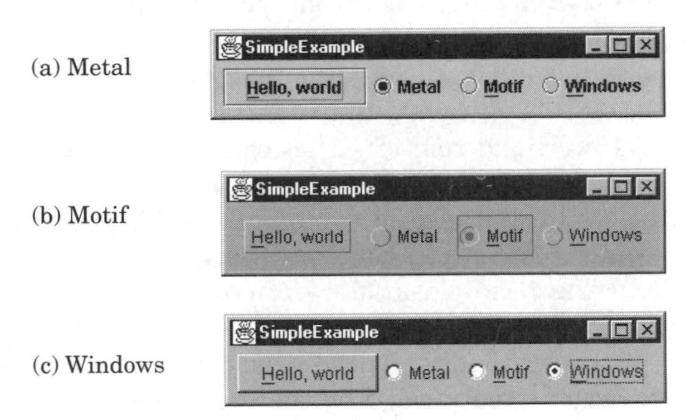

Figure 7.2 The Three Standard Swing Look and Feel Styles

nent is completely controlled by the Swing classes. Thus, a Swing-based application can have the same look and feel on any platform. In addition, the AWT look and feel cannot be customized because it is determined by the host platform whereas in Swing the look and feel can be customized by the application developer. Swing provides three ready-made look and feel customizations: a generic multi-platform style referred to as the "metal" style, one for a Motif style, and one for a Windows style. These three styles are illustrated in Figure 7.2, which shows how a several user interface components would appear in each of the three styles. Furthermore, it is possible for application developers to create their own look and feel for specialized applications.

Swing and AWT also differ in the overhead associated with creating and maintaining the user interface. The overhead associated with AWT components is often referred to as "heavyweight" because of the cost associated with maintaining the "peer" objects. Swing components are referred to as "lightweight" because they do not have the cost of the "peer" objects. Because of this lower overhead, Swing applications are generally viewed as being more economical of system resources and more efficient. The final difference between Swing and the AWT is that the feature set provided by AWT components is limited to what is available on all common host platforms. This "least common denominator" requirement restricts the kinds of user interface components that AWT can provide and the functionality of these components. Swing, however, is open-ended. The Swing feature set is considerably more extensive than that provided by the AWT and it can be further expanded by individual developers or the community of developers without limitations imposed by any single platform.

As other Java libraries, the Swing components are organized as a collection of packages, each typically containing one or more interfaces and one or more class hierarchies. It is also common that the elements in one package may refer to classes or interfaces define in another package. To become a proficient user of Swing, two packages must be understood. One package contains the basic classes of Swing and is named javax.swing. The second package, named javas.event, contains interfaces and classes related to handling events that are generated by actions such as the user moving or clicking the mouse, pressing buttons, selecting from a menu, or manipulating other interactive elements in the user interface.

Inheritance plays a critical role in structuring the classes in JFC. Understanding how inheritance is used is important in learning how to use the full power of these libraries. Inheritance is useful to the library implementors, of course, because it avoids duplicating code and data in derived classes that is instead inherited from the base class. More importantly, the libraries heavily exploit polymorphism because a number of important classes manipulate objects from a wide variety of classes using only their base class methods that, through dynamic binding, are actually performed by the derived class methods. General purpose structures in the Java libraries depend on this mechanism. Finally, programmers using the libraries take advantage of the extensibility properties of the inheritance hierarchy. As will be seen, developing a user interface in Java involves extending a class in the Java libraries to add application-specific methods that override the default methods defined in the library base class. For example, the outer structure of a user interface is typically constructed by by deriving a class from the class representing a top-level window (Swing's JFrame class). The extension of the JFrame class constains the components of the application's user interface.

This chapter is organized into two basic parts. The first part, from Sections 7.2 through 7.5, presents the fundamental ideas and classes of the JFC. This presentation explains the *structural* aspects of a user interface and illustrates them through two simple applications, one for *graphical drawing* and one for *text editing*. The first part of this chapter also explains how actions are added to a user interface through *events handling*. Event handling is illustrated by *extending the two simple applications*. The second part of this chapter, from Section 7.6 through 7.15, presents variations of the simple applications to illustrate other user interface controls (*menus*, *checkboxes*, *lists*, *dialogs*, *scrollbars*, and *textfields*), *fonts*, *images*, how to extend the Component hierarchy to define your own *custom* user interface elements, and details about *layout managers* that control the placement of elements in the user interface.

Exercises

1. Examine applications on two different platforms (e.g., Windows and Solaris) and identify several differences in the appearance of similar components (e.g., buttons or menus).
2. Examine applications on two different platforms (e.g., Windows and Solaris) and identify differences in the operation of one or more similar components (e.g., a file selection dialogue).

3. Examine applications on two different platforms (e.g., Windows and Solaris) and identify one or more widgets on one platform that do not have a counterpart on the other.
4. Identify a type of application where AWT's platform dependence is useful from a user's perspective.
5. Identify a type of application where Swing's platform independence is useful from a user's perspective.

7.2 Structure of a User Interface

The Swing library is an extension of the AWT. Swing classes inherit from AWT classes as shown by the partial class hierarchy in Figure 7.3. All classes in Java inherit from the Object class. The Component, Container, and Graphics classes are key classes in the AWT library. The Container class is a specialized Component that holds and manages other Components. Because a Container is itself a Component, it is possible to define a hierarchical structure of Container objects in which some Container objects hold and manage other Container objects. This hierarchical structuring allows a complex user interface to be constructed in an incremental and manageable manner because portions of the user interface can be grouped together in a Container object, this object and other Components or Container objects can be grouped in another Container objects, and so on. Two specific kinds of Containers in the AWT are Panels, which do not themselves have a visible appearance in the user's display, and a Window, which does. A Frame is a specialized Window that may contain a menu bar. A Dialog is a specialized kind of Win-

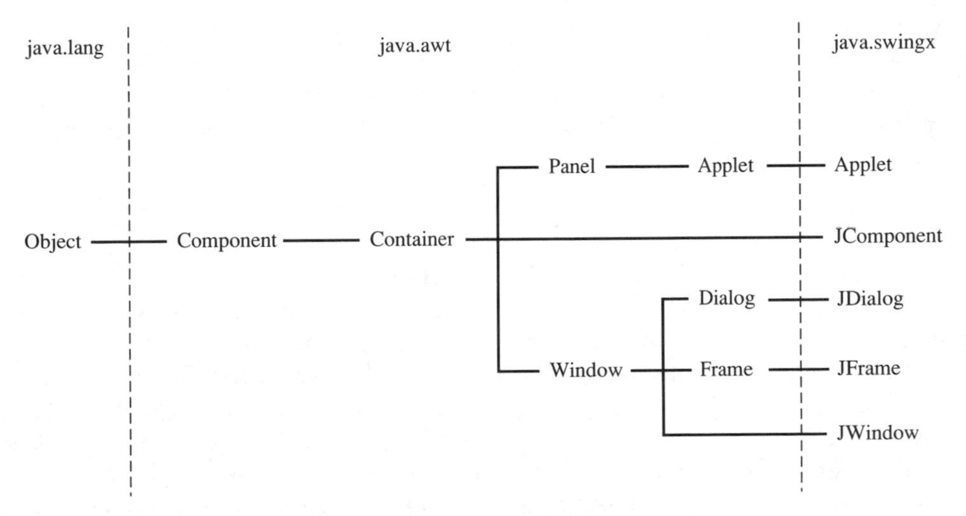

Figure 7.3 The AWT and Swing Class Hierarchies

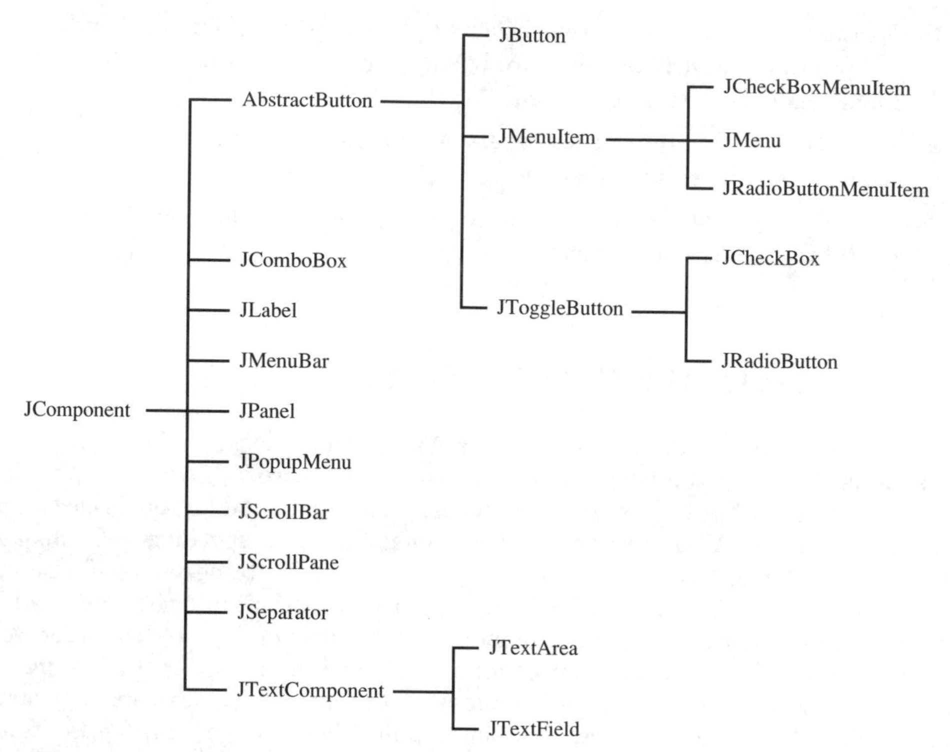

Figure 7.4 Swing Class Hierarchy

dow that can preclude any other actions in the user interface until the Dialog has been completed. Dialogs are used to present the user with critical questions whose answers are needed before the system can procede (such as a password dialog) or to warn the user of irreversible actions (such as terminating an application). As shown in Figure 7.3, some Swing classes directly extend their AWT counterparts. Examples of this are JApplet, JDialog, JFrame, and JWindow. Many of the Swing components are derived from the JComponent class. As suggested by these names, the names of most Swing classes begin with "J".

The principal classes in the Swing class hierarchy that extend the JComponent class are shown in Figure 7.4. As can be seen by examining the names of these classes, Swing supports a wide variety of commonly used user interface components. The AbstractButton class is the root class of a subhierarchy whose classes implement selectable user interface components; for example, buttons that can be pushed or menu items that can be chosen. The JTextComponent class defines the general properties of text-oriented user interface components in Swing. One extension defines a single line field of editable text whereas another extension defines a multiple-line editable area. Another user interface control that is defined by direct extensions of the JComponent class is the JComboBox that allows selection of one from among many alternatives. Organization of other

- (Container: a holder and manager of AWT or Swing Components
    - Window: a Container associated with an area in the user's display
        - Frame: a bordered Window that can have a MenuBar
            - JFrame: a lightweight Frame
        - Dialog: a Window
    - Panel: a Container that is itself not visible
        - Applet: a Container that displays itself in a browserJComponent
            - JApplet: a lightweight Applet
        - JComponent:
        - AbstractButton:
            - JButton: a labelled interactive control that can be "pushed"
            - JMenuItem: a selectable element of a menu
                - JMenu: a list of menu items
                - JCheckBoxMenuItem: menu item that is "on" or "off"
                - JRadioButtomMenuItem: mutually exclusive menu items
            - JToggleButton: a labeled interactive control with state
                - JCheckBox: a control that is "on" or "off"
                - JRadioButton: mutually exclusive buttons
        - JMenuBar: an ordered collection of menus
        - JPanel: a container used to group other components
        - JComboBox: a one-of-many selection
        - JLabel: a fixed, uneditable text string
        - JScrollbar: a control for selecting a single value by a sliding indicator
        - JScrollPane: adds vertical and horizontal scrolling to any Component
        - JTextComponent:
            - JTextArea: multiple-line editable text
            - JTextField: a single line of editable text
        - JPopupMenu: a menu that appears when triggered

Figure 7.5 Summary Selected AWT and Swing Classes (the indentation relects the inheritance hierarchy)

components is provided by the JPanel class that is a general grouping mechanism, JMenuBar and JPopupMenu that are used to arrange menus and menu items, respectively. Scrolling is provided by the JScrollBar class and the JScrollPane classes. The JLabel class allows titles or labelling to be associated with other components. Menu items can be divided visually by the JSeparator class. A brief summary of these Swing components is given in Figure 7.5. The components described here are only the basic elements of the Swing library. The complete Swing library includes many more components for constructing complex user interfaces.

The AWT and Swing class hierarchies uses the power of inheritance in three ways. First, the inheritance avoids duplicating methods and data in derived classes by generalizing them into a base class. This use of generalization is illustrated by the Component and JComponent classes that contains all the attributes and behavior common to many user interface elements. For example, any user interface element has a position attribute determining where it appears in the interface and behavior that changes its position. Another class that uses generalization in this way is the Container class, which defines all the common properties of classes that manage some number of other Components. Each such container has a mechanism to store the set of Components within the Container and size method that report the current number of contained Components. The effects of polymorphism is the second way in which the AWT class hierarchy uses the power of inheritance. The Container class illustrates the role of polymorphism because its methods are defined in terms of the Component base class and not in terms of the derived classes. For example, the Container class has an add method defined as:

```
public void add (Component component);
```

Because the `add` method's parameter is a Component, any object of a class derived from Component can be passed as the actual parameter. For example, because a JPanel is a specialization of Container it is possible to add a JButton object to a JPanel object as follows:

```
JPanel controls = new JPanel();
JButton quitButton = new JButton(...);
controls.add(quitButton);
```

In this example, the `quitButton` object is implicitly type cast to its base class type, namely Component. Any other object of a class derived from Component can be added to a JPanel, or any other Container, in a similar way. The third effect of inheritance is that the AWT class hierarchy is extensible in two ways. A developer may introduce a new type of user interface element by defining a new class that is derived from the JComponent class. For example, a new control might be needed in an application that allows a user to select up to two choice from a set of alternatives. The existing Java controls allow one of many or several of many alternatives, but not two of many. This new control would inherit all of the basic machinery provided in the JComponent class and objects of the new class could be added to a Container in the same way that an object any of the existing Component class. The second aspect of extensibility is that Swing classes are commonly subclassed to provide application-specific behavior. For example, a user interface is typically constructed by defining an application specific extension of the JFrame class.

7.2.1 Key Relationships

The Component and Container classes have important relationships with other classes that are defined in the AWT and Swing libraries but are not part of the Component hierarchy. Understanding these relationships helps to develop proficiency in using the Swing classes. Several important relationships are shown in Figure 7.6. These relationships are the key elements that affect the component's

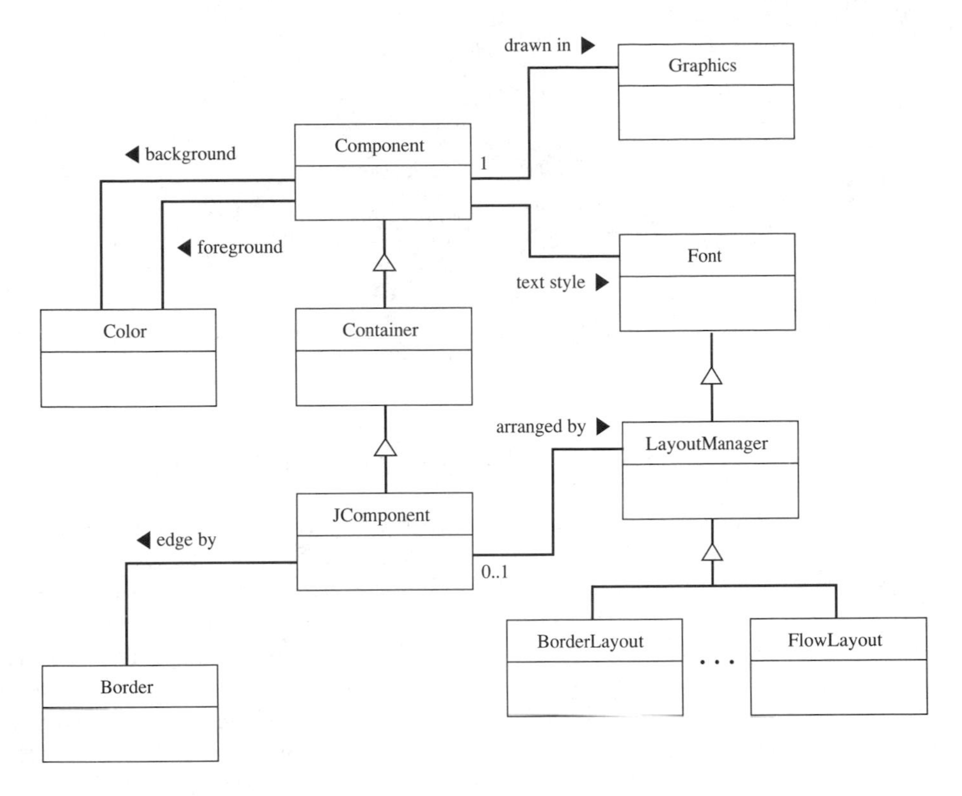

Figure 7.6 Relationships Involving Component and Container

appearance, how Swing manages the redrawing of components in the user interface, and how the layout (i.e., the spatial arrangement of the components) of the user interface is determined.

Appearance of a Component

Four of the properties affecting the visual appearance of a component are its foreground color, background color, font, and border. These properties are illustrated by a button component shown in Figure 7.7. In this example, the background color of the button is yellow and the foreground color is red. In general, the background color is the color given to the underlying drawing surface on which the foreground elements (such as the text on the button) are drawn; the foreground elements are drawn in the foreground color. The component's current font is used to represent any text that appears in the foreground. It is evident that a font could be associated with a JTextField or a JTextArea because these components display text. However, a font can also be associated with an JComponent. For a JButton, the text in the label of the JButton is written using its current font. In the button shown in Figure 7.7, an italic font is used as seen by the

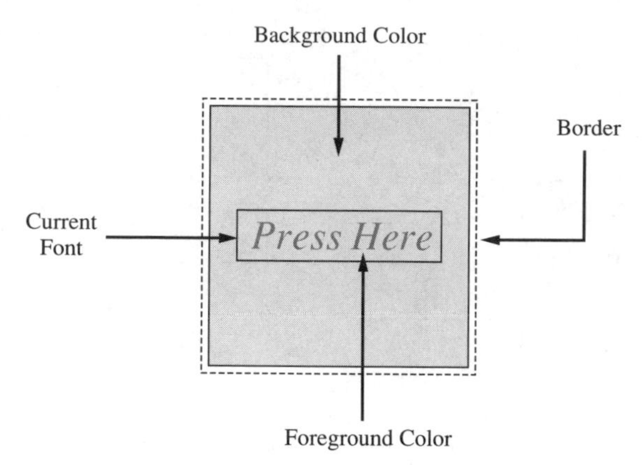

Figure 7.7 Attributes that Affect the Appearance of a Component

slope of the characters in the text "Press Here". The thin box drawn around the text is a result of the metal style used in this example. The border of a component helps to visually distinguish the boundaries of the component's representation in the user interface. This is clearly important for controls such as a button where the user must click within the boundaries of the button to have the effect of activating the control. In other cases, the border simply provides a useful visual separation of the component from other elements adjacent to it in the user interface. For example, the border around a drawing area can be used in this way. In Figure 7.7, the border is drawn in blue to distinguish it from the button itself.

The properties affecting a components appearance can be set and tested by method in either the Component or the JComponent classes. A component's color and font attributes are examined or altered through set and get methods defined in the Component class as shown in Figure 7.8. Some details of the Color and Font classes are also explained below. The background color attribute is used if the component is "opaque" but the background color is ignored if the component is "transparent." An opaque component completely fills its drawing area with the background color, completely hiding any underlying material over which it may be superimposed. A transparent component allows any of its unpainted area to expose any such underlying material. The `setOpaque` method allows this attribute to be set; the property can be tested by the `isOpaque` method. The Border attribute of a component is defined by the `setBorder` method in the JComponent class as shown in Figure 7.8. The figure also shows that other attributes of a component, such as its size and shape, can be controlled through methods in the JComponent class. Other component attributes are presented in the description of individual components as needed. When an attribute is changed, it will take effect the next time that the component is redrawn in the user interface. The mechanism controlling the redrawing of the user interface and its components is explained below.

```
public abstract class Component
{
   //...
   public Color getBackground()
   public Color getForeground()
   public Font getFont()

   public void setBackground(Color c)
   public void setForeground(Color c)
   public void setFont(Font f)

   //...
}

public abstract class JComponent extends Container
{

  //...

  public boolean isOpaque()
  public void setOpaque(boolean b)

  public void setBorder(Border border)
  public Dimension getMaximumSize()
  public Dimension getMinimumSize()
  public Dimension getSize()

  public void setMaximumSize(Dimension d)
  public void setMinimumSize(Dimension d)
  public void setSize(Dimension d)
}
```

Figure 7.8 Attribute Methods in the Component Class

The Color Class

The Color class provides a simple means of defining an object that represents a color to be used in the user interface. Colors objects are used in many contexts including specifying the color with which text is drawn, the color that fills an opaque component's areas, and the color used to fill closed graphical shapes. A standard set of colors are provided by the constant names defined in the Color class as shown in Figure 7.9. Thus, in any context where a Color object is required it is possible to use, for example, `Color.red`. Arbitrary colors can be created by using the basic methods of the Color class also shown in Figure 7.9. Each color can be defined by specifying the constituent amounts of the three colors red, green, and blue. The mixture of these colors in the specified amounts produces the resulting color. The red, green, and blue components can be given values in the range of 0 to 255. The accessor methods return the intensity of the corresponding component.

```
public class Color
{

  public static final Color black;
  public static final Color blue;
  public static final Color cyan;
  public static final Color darkGray;
  public static final Color gray;
  public static final Color green
  public static final Color lightGray;
  public static final Color magenta;
  public static final Color orange;
  public static final Color pink;
  public static final Color red;
  public static final Color white;
  public static final Color yellow;

  public Color(int red, int green, int blue)
  //...

  public int getRed()
  public int getGreen()
  public int getBlue()

}
```

Figure 7.9 The Color Class

The Font Class

A font is a consistent and distinctive style for presenting the symbols of an alphabet, usually the alphabetic characters of a written natural language. A large variety of fonts have been created over several centuries for use in the print media and more recently for use in digitally rendered documents. Fonts may be used to convey impressions such as formality, simplicity, elegance, antiquity, or humor. The design of a font may also take into account such factors as legibility, compactness, or emphasis. A quick scan of a newspaper, magazine, or web page easily illustrates that there are many fonts and a single document often includes several fonts.

The Font class defines a font by three properties referred to as family, style and size. The family is a string name corresponding to a font with a particular appearance. The defined families are: "Serif", "SansSerif", "Monospace", "Dialog", and "DialogInput". Examples of these fonts are shown in Figure 7.10. A portion of the code used to produce these fonts is:

```
...new Font("Serif",       Font.PLAIN, 16)...
...new Font("SanSerif",    Font.PLAIN, 16)...
...new Font("Monospaced", Font.PLAIN, 16)...
...new Font("Dialog",      Font.PLAIN, 16)...
...new Font("DialogInput",Font.PLAIN, 16)...
```

This is Serif font.

This is SanSerif font.

`This is Monospaced font.`

This is Dialog font.

`This is DialogInput font.`

Figure 7.10 Examples of Java Fonts

This is Serif/plain/16 font.

This is Serif/italic/16 font.

This is Serif/bold/16 font.

This is Serif/italic+bold/16 font.

This is Serif/plain/20 font.

This is Serif/plain/24 font.

Figure 7.11 Examples of Java Fonts

The second and third parameters in this code are explained next.

The style and size properties of a font allow for variation in the apperance of characters drawn in a given family. The style property of a font allows for a choice among four alternatives that are defined by named constants in the Font class: `Font.PLAIN`, `Font.ITALIC`, `Font.BOLD`, and `Font.ITALIC + Font.BOLD`. The last of the style choices listed is an expression that denotes a combination of the two properties **bold** and *italics*. The size property determines how large or small the letters appear. Examples of the Serif font with different styles and sizes are shown in Figure 7.11. A portion of the code used to generate the text in this figure is:

```
...new Font("Serif", Font.PLAIN, 16)...
...new Font("Serif", Font.ITALIC,16)...
...new Font("Serif", Font.BOLD, 16)...
...new Font("Serif", Font.ITALIC+Font.BOLD, 16)...
...new Font("Serif", Font.PLAIN, 20)...
...new Font("Serif", Font.PLAIN, 24)...
```

Of course, the style and size attributes can be set with the other families as well.

```
public class FontArea extends JComponent
{
  Font font;
  String text;

  public FontArea (Font font, String fontName)
  { this.font = font;
    this.text = "This is " + fontName + " font. ";
  }

  public void paint(Graphics g)
  {
    g.setFont(font);
    g.drawString(text, 20,20);
  }
}

public class FontDemoFrame extends JFrame implements WindowListener
{

  public FontDemoFrame()
  {
    this.setLocation(100,100);
    this.setSize(300,300);
    this.addWindowListener(this);
    Container content = this.getContentPane();
    //...

    content.add(new FontArea(new Font("Serif", Font.PLAIN, 16),
                                  "Serif/plain/16"));
    content.add(new FontArea(new Font("Serif", Font.ITALIC,16),
                                  "Serif/italic/16"));
    content.add(new FontArea(new Font("Serif", Font.BOLD,  16),
                                  "Serif/bold/16"));
    content.add(new FontArea(new Font("Serif", Font.ITALIC+Font.BOLD,
16),
                                  "Serif/italic+bold/16"));
    content.add(new FontArea(new Font("Serif", Font.PLAIN, 20),
                                  "Serif/plain/20"));
    content.add(new FontArea(new Font("Serif", Font.PLAIN, 24),
                                  "Serif/plain/24"));

  }

  //...

}
```

Figure 7.12 Setting the Font in a JComponent Object

A font can be associated with any component using the `setFont` method. The essential code to set the font in a JComponent object is shown in Figure 7.12. The class FontArea is a specialized JComponent designed to display a single line of text in a given font. The font is given as a constructor argument along with a string that is used to form the full line of text printed in the Canvas area. The `paint` method simply sets the font in the Graphics object using the `set-`

Font method and uses the drawString method to display the line of text. The line of text will be drawn using the Graphic object's "current" font. The FontDemoFrame class simply creates a number of FontAreas, each given a different font and a string descriptive of that font.

The Border Classes

The boundaries of a component can be indicated visually by establishing a border that surrounds the component. Swing provides a number of predefined border styles that are shown for a button object in Figure 7.13. The LineBorder creates a line of specified thickness at the edges of the component. The border color in this figure is set to blue to accent the border. Notice that a thin box is drawn around the text drawn on the button. The BevelBorder and SoftBevelBorder contain a slanted edge that gives the impression of a raised or a lowered surface area depending on the shading. The colors gray and black are used to accent the borders of these two buttons. Notice that the soft beveled border has a thinner edge and slightly different corners than the bevel border. An EtchedBorder is defined by a pair of thin lines surrounding the component. The shading or coloring of the two lines can also give the impression of a raised or lowered surface. The TitleBorder decorates another border style with a specified text label. The text can be placed in a variety of predefined positions inside or outside of the border. The figure shows a title added to a line border. In the figure, the title is placed at the default position. The title may also appear either inside, on, or outside the border at a variety of positions. The MatteBorder fills the area around the component with either a specified color (as shown in the figure) or an icon that is repeated in a wallpaper fashion. Not shown in the figure are two other border classes. The CompoundBorder allows the developer to create a tailored border that is a combination of two other borders. Because one, or both, of the combined borders can itself be a CompoundBorder, it is possible to create arbitrarily complex border combinations. The EmptyBorder simply places an amount of empty space around a component. The EmptyBorder can be used in conjunction with the CompoundBorder to create a space between two other border styles. The simple constructors for each of the border styles is summarized in Table 7.2.

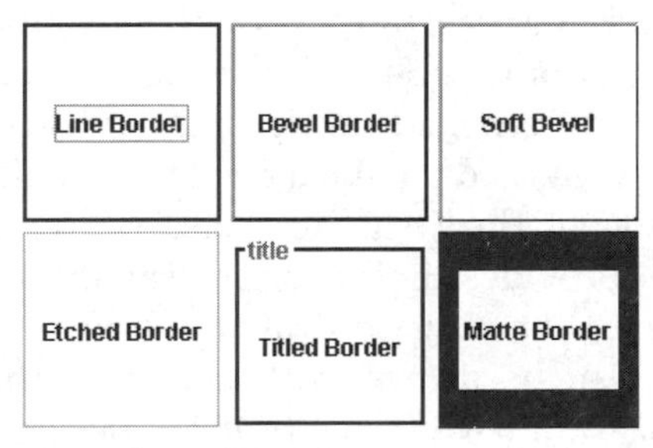

Figure 7.13 Examples of Borders

Table 7.2 Summary of Borders

Border Style	Constructor
Bevel	`BevelBorder(int type)` Type is RAISED or LOWERED.
Soft bevel	`SoftBevelBorder(int type)` type is RAISED or LOWERED.
Empty	`EmptyBorder(int top, int left, int bottom, int right)` Values specify the pixel widths on each side.
Etched	`EtchedBorder()`
Line	`LineBorder(Color color)`

Matte	`MatteBorder(Icon matteIcon)`
	`MatteBorder(int top, int left, int bottom, int right, Color color)`
	The value of matteIcom specifies the image to use. The second constructor specifies the pixel width on each side that are filled with the given color.

Titled	`TitledBorder(Border border, String title)` The border is the basic border object to which the given title is added in a default position.
Compound	`CompoundBorder(Border outside, Border inside)`

Redrawing of Components

Each component is responsible for (re)drawing its visible representation when objects of its class are displayed in the user interface. Predefined Swing classes generally contain the programming to draw themselves in the user interface. For example, the JButton class defines how a JButton object is represented in the user interface. For application-specific extensions of the JComponent class, it is the class developer's responsibility to define the (re)drawing behavior. Swing provides a general framework for objects to draw their visible representation. This framework consists of a Graphics object that is used to draw the object's visible representation and a set of methods that drive the drawing process. The Graphics class contains all of the methods in Java for drawing bit-mapped graphics and text. A partial description of the Graphics class's interface is given in Figure 7.14. The Graphics class provides methods for drawing basic shapes (line, oval/circle, rectangle, polygon) that may be drawn simply as an outline or may be solid. A rectangle may also be drawn with a simple three-dimensional effect drawn so as to appear to be above (raised) or below the surface. The Graphics class contains many other methods that deal with selecting the Color for the

```
public abstract class Graphics extends Object
{
   //basic graphics and text

   public abstract void drawLine(int x1, int y1, int x2, int y2);
   public abstract void drawOval(int x, int y, int width, int height);
   public abstract void drawRect(int x, int y, int width, int height);
   public abstract void drawString(String str, int x, int y);

   // filled (solid) graphics
   public abstract void fillRect(int x, int y, int width, int height);
   // similar methods for arcs, oval, and polygons

   // simple 3D rectangle
   public abstract void draw3DRect(int x, int y, int width, int height,
                                   boolean raised);
   // ...
}
```

Figure 7.14 Partial Interface of the Graphics Class

drawing operations, the font for drawing Strings, drawing Images, and others. Notice that the methods in the Graphics class are declared as abstract because the actual object used for drawing is defined in a class derived from Graphics. Because Graphics is an abstract class, it is not possible to directly create objects of this class. Instead, the Java run-time environment will create an object of a class derived from Graphics that implements the Graphics methods for the platform or device being used. This object is made available to Component and its derived classes by the methods associated with the (re)drawing behavior defined in the Component class.

The (re)drawing process is managed by a repaint manager that maintains a list of rectangular areas on the screen that must be redrawn. The repaint manager processes the list as rapidly as possible and order the list to avoid unnecessary work (e.g., redrawing areas that are overlayed by other areas also to be redrawn. The repaint manager redraws a component by calling the `paint` method defined in the JComponent class. The `paint` method has a Graphics object (technically, as described above, an object of a class derived from Graphics) as its single parameter. The Graphics object is created by the underlying run-time environment that initiates the redrawing process by calling the `paint` method. A class derived from JComponent may override the `paint` method to draw the representation appropriate for that specialized type of component. The paint method invokes three subordinate methods, `paintComponent`, `paintBorder`, and `paintChildren`, that are invoked in this order. Instead of overriding the `paint` method it is easier and safer to override one of more of these subordinate methods.

Examples of situations where portions of the user interface need to be redrawn include the following. A window of the application needs to be redrawn: if the user moves a window that was overlapping the application's window or if the user resizes the window. When a window is resized the components to draw

```
public class Component
{  //...
   public void repaint()
}

public class Containter extends Component
{ //...
}

public class JComponent extends Container
{
   //...
   public void paint(Graphics g)
   public void paintBorder(Graphics g)
   public void paintComponent Graphics g)
   public void paintChildren Graphics g)

   public void repaint(long tm, int x, int y, int width, int height)
   public void repaint(Rectangle r)
}
```

Figure 7.15 Redrawing Methods in the JComponent Class

themselves closer together; if the size of the window is made smaller or draw themselves farther apart if the window was enlarged. It is also possible for the application itself to require that the user interface be redrawn in situations where the structure of the user interface changes (e.g., a button is removed in certain application states where its action is not appropriate) or where a graphics components needs to be updated (e.g., the program draws a new shape in a drawing area). The application can give work to the repaint manager by invoking one of the `repaint` methods defined in the JComponent class or the Component class (see Figure 7.15). Note that the argument of type long in the first `repaint` method is required, but not used. The `repaint` method with no arguments causes all of a component to be refreshed whereas the `repaint` methods with arguments specify a selected portion of the component that must be refreshed.

The Layout of the Interface

The specialized classes derived from Container, particularly JPanel and JFrame, are responsible for determining how the components that they contain are physically arranged in the user interface. For example, if three JButton objects are added to a JPanel, the JPanel must determine such things as how much space to leave between adjacent buttons, whether the buttons are arranged left-to-right, top-to-bottom, or some other way, and how much each button should be stretched or compressed to occupy the available space. Determining the layout of the user interface may occur numerous times during an application's execution because the user may resize the windows being displayed by the application, requiring a new layout to be computed.

Because there are numerous strategies for organizing the layout of a container's components, a separate interface is defined that is implemented by

Table 7.3 Summary of Layout Managers

Layount Class	Layout Pattern
FlowLayout	Arrange components left-to-right, top-to-bottom
BorderLayout	Arrange components at the top, bottom, sides, and center
GridLayout	Arrange components at positions in a mesh or two-dimensional array
CardLayout	Presents one of several "cards," each containing its own layout of components
GridBagLayout	A "grid" with rows and columns of varying size
BoxLayout	Arrange components in a horizontal row or vertical column
OverlayLayout	Arrangement of components in possibly overlapping positions

classes embodying a particular strategy. This interface is named LayoutManger in the original AWT. The container is insensitive to which layout strategy is used; it maintains a reference to the layout object by using a reference of type Layout-Manger. The layout manager for a container object is established by using the method defined as

```
public void setLayout(LayoutManager mgr)
```

that creates an association between the container object and an object that implements the LayoutManager interface.

Two of the several layout manager classes in Java are shown in Figure 7.15: BorderLayout and FlowLayout. Briefly, the BorderLayout places its components in one of five areas referred to as "North," "South," "East," "West," and "Center." The term "Border" in BorderLayout comes from the use of the compass direction terminology to refer to the borders of the area being arranged. A FlowLayout organizes its components in a left-to-right, top-down manner begining in the upper left-hand part of the region. The components "flow" across and down the region. A brief summary of various LayoutManagers is given in Table 7.3. Many of layout managers are explored in detail in a later section of this chapter. The last two LayoutMangers listed in Table 7.3 are managers introduced in Java 1.2.

The following code segment illustrates how Container-type objects are created and assigned a particular LayoutManager:

```
JPanel controls = new JPanel();
BorderLayout border = new BorderLayout();
controls.setLayout(border);
//...
JFrame display = new JFrame(...);
display.setLayout(new FlowLayout());
```

In the first part of the code segment a JPanel container is created and a BorderLayout manager is associated with it. In the second part of the code segment a JFrame container is created and a FlowLayout is associated with it. The first part shows that the LayoutManager can be eplicitly assigned to a variable whereas in the second part the LayoutManager is created and passed as an argument of the `setLayout` method as an anonymous object. Passing the LayoutManager as an anonymous object is the more usual practice because the code creating the LayoutManager often has no need itself to manipulate the LayoutManager other than to pas it to a container-type object.

Exercises

1. How many different kinds of fonts can you identify in the user interface of some application (e.g., a word processing system) that you use?
2. How many different kinds of borders can you identify in the user interface of some application (e.g., a word processing system) that you use?
3. How many different kinds of background colors can you identify in the user interface of some application (e.g., a word processing system) that you use?
4. Examine the user interface of a relatively complex application and identify how a border layout scheme might be used to organize the spatial arrangement of some groups of components.
5. Examine the user interface of a relatively complex application and identify how a grid layout scheme might be used to organize the spatial arrangement of some groups of components.

7.3 Two Simple Applications

Two simple applications are used in this chapter to illustrate the JFC classes and concepts. The first application is a simple *drawing tool*; it allows the user to draw and move a single, fixed-sized rectangle. The second application is a simple *text editing tool*; it allows the user to type, cut, and paste text in a window. These simple applications are typical of more sophisticated drawing and editing tools. Other sections in this chapter and the exercises show how to elaborate these simple tools.

For simplicity, the interfaces constructed in this section will be incomplete; they will have the desired structure but they lack the programming to respond to the user's actions. In fact, the window displayed by the application cannot be closed nor can the application be terminated except by aborting the program using the CNTRL-C key combination in a command window. The concepts and classes needed to program a response to the user's actions will be added in the next section.

7.3.1 The DrawTool Application

The user interface of the simple drawing tool consists of a bit-mapped drawing region in which a single rectangle of a fixed size can be drawn in one of three colors (red, green, or blue). The bit-mapped drawing region has a yellow background color. The appearance of this application is shown in Figure 7.16. The figure shows a rectangle drawn with a red border. The color of the rectangle's border is determined by the selection control that has three items: Red, Green, and Blue. In the figure, the selection control shows that the curent color is Red. A button is provided that allows the user to clear the drawing region. The label on the face of the button is "Clear Canvas". When completed, the DrawTool will allow the single rectangle in the bit-mapped drawing area to be repositioned in the drawing area by dragging the mouse when the cursor is within the boundaries of the rectangle.

The simple drawing tool is constructed from the following classes:

DrawTool: the class that contains the main program,

DrawFrame: an extension of the JFrame class that present the user interface of the drawing tool,

DrawCanvas: an extension of the JComponent class that knows whether and in what color a single rectangle is drawn,

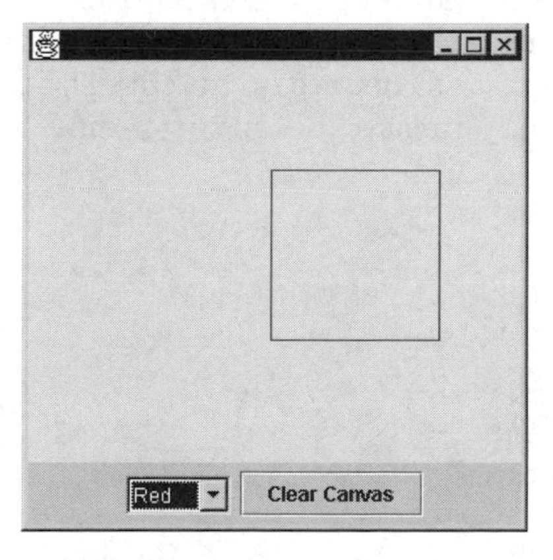

Figure 7.16 The DrawTool Application

ClearButton: an extension of the JButton class that will clear the DrawCanvas, and

Rectangle: a class that maintains the curent location of the rectangle and knows how to draw the rectangle into a supplied Graphics object.

These classes are presented and explained in two levels of completeness. Below, the structural aspects of the class are defined and implemented. At this level, the DrawTool system will have the right user interface but will not respond to the user's actions (e.g., clicking in the drawing area). In later sections, the mechanisms for detecting and responding to actions in the user interface are studied and the DrawTool system will be completed.

Step 1: The main Program: The DrawTool program is implemented as a stand-alone Java program. A stand-alone program is executed directly from the command line and may receive command-line arguments. A stand-alone program—like everything else in Java—is defined by a class that, like all other classes in Java, is in a file whose name is the same as the name of the class. The drawing tool is defined by a class named DrawTool, shown in Figure 7.17. This class is contained in the file DrawTool.java that is compiled to produce a corresponding .class file. In the JDK environment the drawing tool is executed by invoking the Java interpreter on the compiled DrawTool.class file as:

```
prompt java DrawTool
```

In development environment (such as J++) the interpreter is invoked through the development environment's user interface. In either case, the Java interpreter initiates the execution of the stand-alone program.

The execution of a stand-alone Java program begins in a method named "main" that must be declared exactly as shown in the DrawTool class in Figure 7.17. The `main` method is declared public so that it is visible outside of the class in which it is declared. The `static` qualifier on the `main` method is necessary because the Java interpreter will not create an object of the class containing the `main` method, it will simply invoke the `main` method directly passing to this

```
import DrawFrame;

public class DrawTool
{
  private static DrawFrame drawFrame;

  public static void main(String [] args)
  { drawFrame = new DrawFrame();
    drawFrame.show();
  }
}
```

Figure 7.17 The Main Program of DrawTool

```
import DrawFrame;

public class DrawTool
{
  private DrawFrame drawFrame;
  private static DrawTool application;

  public DrawTool()
  { drawFrame = new DrawFrame();
    drawFrame.show();
  }

  public static void main(String [] args)
  { application = new DrawTool();
  }
}
```

Figure 7.18 An Alternative Main Program

method any command line arguments. The `main` method has a `void` return type and has a single argument, an array of Strings, that will contain the command-line arguments, if any. There are no command-line arguments in this version of the DrawTool application. The `main` method of the DrawTool class is very simple—it creates a new DrawFrame object, the DrawFrame class defines the user interface for the drawing tool. The `main` method also uses the DrawFrame's `show` method to make the drawing tool's window visible on the user's display. The drawing tool application can be terminated by closing its window. Two important facts must be kept in mind when writing a stand-alone program. First, because the Java interpreter does not create a DrawTool object, the constructor of the DrawTool class will not be executed prior to the `main` method. Second, because the `main` method is declared as `static`, it may not access directly non-`static` private data in its class. This explains why the drawFrame variable in the DrawTool class is also declared as `static`.

An alternative way of defining a stand-alone program is shown in Figure 7.18 where the `main` method creates an object of the class in which the main method is defined (DrawTool in this example). The creation of this object causes the class's constructor to be executed. The advantage of this style is that the constructor plays its usual initialization role. Notice that the instance variable `application` is defined as a `static` variable so that it can be accessed by the `main` method. In some cases the alternative style is useful because it allows multiple instances of the DrawTool to be dynamically created using a natural syntax. In the original DrawTool class, a single new instance of a DrawTool could be created by:

```
DrawTool tool = DrawTool.main(arglist);
```

which has both an awkward syntax and requires passing an array of strings (arglist) even if this serves no practical purpose. Using the alternative version of the DrawTool class, a complex drawing system could create two DrawTool objects by:

```
DrawTool tool1 = new DrawTool();
DrawTool tool2 = new DrawTool();
```

which would not be possible in the original definition of the DrawTool because: (1) the original DrawTool class did not contain a constructor that would create the needed DrawFrame object, and (2) the DrawFrame object was referenced by a single `static` variable; attempting to create two DrawFrame objects would be problematic.

Step 2: The DrawFrame Class: The structure of the drawing application's user interface is defined in the DrawFrame class as shown in Figure 7.19. The DrawFrame extends the JFrame class defined in the `javax.swing` package. A JFrame object represents an independent, top-level window in the user inter-

```
import java.awt.*;
import java.awt.event.*;
import javax.swing.*;
import DrawCanvas;
import ClearButton;

public class DrawFrame extends JFrame
{
  public DrawFrame()
  { // Step 1: define appearance of the DrawFrame
    this.setLocation(100,100);
    this.setSize(300,300);

    // Step 2: create the parts of the user interface
    JComboBox colorChoice = new JComboBox();
    colorChoice.addItem("Red");
    colorChoice.addItem("Green");
    colorChoice.addItem("Blue");
    colorChoice.setSelectedItem("Blue");

    ClearButton clearButton = new ClearButton();

    DrawCanvas canvas = new DrawCanvas(clearButton);
    // Step 3: arrange the parts of the user interface
    JPanel panel = new JPanel();
    panel.setLayout(new FlowLayout());
    panel.add(colorChoice);
    panel.add(clearButton);

    Container content = this.getContentPane();
    content.setLayout(new BorderLayout());
    content.add(canvas, BorderLayout.CENTER);
    content.add(panel, BorderLayout.SOUTH);
  }
}
```

Figure 7.19 The DrawFrame Class

face. A JFrame has a border, an optional menu bar, and possibly other decoration or controls. The DrawFrame class's constructor has three basic steps as noted by the boldface comments in the code. The first step defines the location and shape of the window using the inherited methods setLocation and setSize, respectively. The second step defines the three principal elements of the user interface: a selection control to choose the drawing color, a button to clear the drawing area, and the drawing area itself. The third step specifies how the three principal elements are arranged in the user interface; an auxiliary JPanel object and the two types of layout managers, the FlowLayout and the BorderLayout, are used to define the arrangement. The second and third steps are explained in more detail below.

Three elements created in the second step of the DrawFrame's constructor are a JComboBox, a ClearButton that extends the JButton class, and a DrawCanvas that extends the JComponent class. The JComboBox, Button, and JComponent classes are defined in the `javax.swing` package. The ClearButton and the DrawCanvas classes are described below. As implied by their names, the ClearButton object is a control that, when pushed by the user, clears the drawing area; the DrawCanvas is a bit-mapped drawing area.

A JComboBox control, also known as a dropdown list or an option menu, shows which one of its several alternatives is currently selected and has an arrowhead shape at its right end that can be used to display its entire list of alternatives. The list of alternatives will be displayed when the user presses down the mouse button while the cursuor is on the arrowhead. By holding the mouse button down, the user can move the cursor over the alternatives and each alternative will be highlighted when the cursor is over it. When the mouse button is released the list of alternatives is closed and the last highlighted alternative becomes the new value for the JComboBox. A JComboBox is created without any arguments. Simple String values are used to define the alternatives using the `addItem` method. The items in the dropdown list are displayed vertically in the order in which they are added. The `setSelectedItem` method allows the program to choose the currently selected item. In this example, when the program is run, the initial choice seen by the user is "Blue". The currently selected value can be obtained by the `getSelectedItem` method.

The third step of the DrawFrame's constructor defines how the user interface elements are arranged within its boundaries. A JPanel object is created that groups together the JComboBox and the ClearButton. A JPanel is a container used to organize other components but which itself is not visible in the user interface. In the DrawFrame constructor, the JPanel object is associated with a FlowLayout so that its components will be arranged left-to-right and top-to-bottom. The JPanel's `add` method is used to enter the JComboBox and the ClearButton objects into the JPanel. Finally, the DrawFrame sets its own layout to be managed by a BorderLayout. Recall that JFrame is also a type of container and has an associated layout manager. The DrawCanvas object is entered into the "Center" position of the BorderLayout whereas the JPanel containing the JComboBox and the ClearButton is entered into the "South" position. The use of one or more JPanel's and a mixture of layout managers is typical in the arrangement of user interfaces.

Step 3: The DrawCanvas Class: The DrawCanvas class extends the JComponent class as shown in Figure 7.20. The JComponent provides a basic bit-mapped drawing area on which text and graphics may be presented in the user interface. Several inherited methods are used in the DrawCanvas class. The `setBackground` method defines the background color of the JComponent. The `paint` method defines what information (text and graphics) is displayed in the JComponent's area. The `paint` method is passed a Graphics object whose methods are used to draw the required text and graphics. The shape of the JComponent is found by the `getSize` method that returns a Dimension object. The Dimension object has two public fields, `height` and `width`, that are measured in pixels.

The DrawCanvas maintains the state information necessary to represent the contents of the drawing area. Its state variables define the Rectangle, if any,

```
import java.awt.*;
import java.awt.event.*;
import javax.swing.*;
import Rectangle;
import ClearButton;

public class DrawCanvas extends JComponent
{
  private Rectangle rectangle;
  private ClearButton clearButton;
  private Color currentColor;

  public DrawCanvas(ClearButton clearButton)
  { this.clearButton = clearButton;
    rectangle = null;
    currentColor = Color.red;
    this.setBackground(Color.yellow);
  }

  public void setColor(Color color)
  { currentColor = color;
  }

  public void paint(Graphics g)
  { g.setColor(getBackground());
    Dimension size = getSize();
    g.fillRect(0, 0, size.width, size.height);

    if (rectangle != null)
    { g.setColor(color);
      rectangle.draw(g);
    }
  }
}
```

Figure 7.20 The DrawCanvas Class

```
import java.awt.*;
import javax.swing.*;
import DrawCanvas;

public class ClearButton extends JButton
{
  public ClearButton()
  { super("Clear Canvas");          // sets label for button
  }
}
```

Figure 7.21 The ClearButton Class

to be drawn, the current color with which the Rectangle will be drawn, and the ClearButton that is used to clear the drawing area. The constructor of the DrawCanvas initializes its state variables and sets its own background color using the named constant "yellow" defined in the Color class. The current drawing color is initialized to the color red. The DrawCanvas includes a method `setColor` that allows the drawing color to be changed. The `paint` method of the DrawCanvas defines how the object will redraw itself when asked to do so by the run-time system. The `paint` method takes no action if it is called when no rectangle object is defined; otherwise the `paint` method sets the drawing color in the Graphics object using the `currentColor` object, and asks the Rectangle object to draw itself in the Graphics object.

Step 4: The ClearButton Class: The ClearButton class is an extension of the JButton class as shown in Figure 7.21. The JButton constructor defines the text string that appears on the face of the button in the user interface. In this example, the String "Clear Canvas" will appear on the button. All of the other functionality needed for the ClearButton is inherited from the JButton class.

Step 5: The Rectangle Class: The Rectangle class maintains the coordinates of where within the DrawCanvas area the rectangle should be drawn. The Rectangle class is shown in Figure 7.22. The `moveTo` method allows the coordinates of the rectangle to be changed. Using the Graphics object passed to it, the `draw` method draws a fixed-size rectangle using the Graphics class's `drawRect` method.

As noted above, the DrawTool application as developed thus far is structurally complete because it has all of the desired user interface components, but it is functionally incomplete because it does not respond to any of the users actions. The exercises below experiment with the structural aspects of this simple applications. The next section describes how applications can be programmed to react to events that are generated by the user.

```
import java.awt.*;

public class Rectangle
{
  private int x;
  private int y;

  public Rectangle(int x, int y)
  { this.x = x;
    this.y = y;
  }

  public void moveTo(int x, int y)
  { this.x = x;
    this.y = y;
  }

  public void draw(Graphics g)
  { g.drawRect(x,y, 100,100);
  }
}
```

Figure 7.22 The Rectangle Class

7.3.2 The EditTool Application

Manipulating text information is one of the basic ways by which people interact with computerized systems. The operations of entering and editing text is a necessary aspect of program development environments, document preparation and management tools, web page editors, search engines, and many other commonplace and useful systems. Typical editing operations include selecting text, cutting selected text, and pasting previously cut text.

A simple application, EditTool, is used to illustrate how text manipulation is supported in the JFC. As shown in Figure 7.23, the EditTool has an area containing text with an area containing three controls below it. The leftmost control allows the user to choose the size of the font used in the main text area. The current value is set to a 16-point font. The other choices are 12 and 20 point. The rightmost two controls are buttons whose labels suggest their use for cutting and pasting text. The EditTool's text area has both horizontal and vertical scrollbars. The text area contains a caret that is currently positioned in the fifth line in front of the word “development”. The caret is shown here as a solid vertical bar. In the actual user interface, the caret blinks to improve its visibility within the text. The position of the caret determines where typed characters will be inserted. The text area also has an “I-beam” shaped cursor. The cursor can be used to reposition the caret by moving the cursor to the desired position and clicking. The cursor can also be used to select a portion of the text by dragging the mouse with the mouse button depressed.

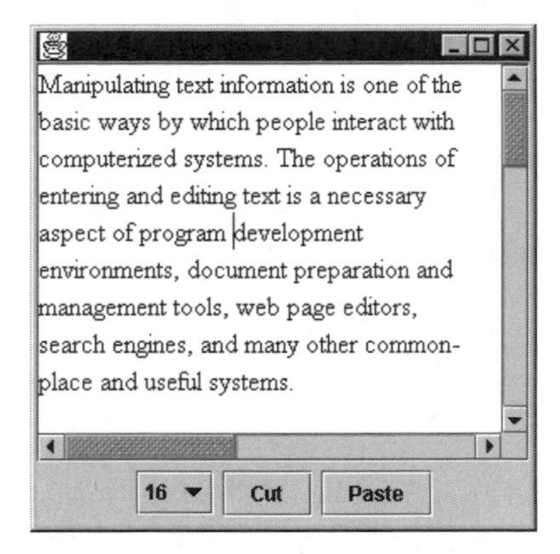

Figure 7.23 The EditTool User Interface

The simple editing tool is constructed from the following classes:

EditTool: the class that contains the main program,

EditFrame: an extension of the JFrame class that presents the user interface of the editing tool, and

EditArea: a text area with methods to cut a selected part of the text, and to paste at a selected position the text, if any, that was last cut from the area.

As with the DrawTool application, the structural aspects of these classes are defined and implemented here. In later sections, the mechanisms for detecting and responding to actions in the user interface (changing the size of the font and cutting or pasting text) are presented.

Step 1: The main Program: As shown in Figure 7.24, the EditTool class contains a single method, `main`, whose signature follows the Java conventions for defining the starting point of a stand-alone application. The `main` method simply creates a new EditFrame object and uses the EditFrame's `show` method to make the EditFrame visible to the user. The EditFrame class defines the structure of the user interface for the EditTool application. Remember that the EditTool class must be contained in a file named EditTool.java. The other aspects of this main program are the same as those for the DrawTool main program explained *above*.

Step 2: The EditFrame Class: The second part of the EditTool application is the EditFrame class that is shown in Figure 7.25. After setting parameters for its own shape and location, the EditFrame creates an EditArea object with 40 rows and 60 columns of visible text. The setFontSize method of the Edit

```
import EditFrame;

public class EditTool
{
  private static EditFrame editFrame;

  public static void main(String [] args)
  { editFrame = new EditFrame();
    editFrame.show();
  }
}
```

Figure 7.24 The EditTool Class

Area class is used to set the current size of the font to a 16-point font. Scrollbars are added around the EditArea by means of a JScrollPane constructed with the EditArea as it parameter. The JScrollPane adds horizontal and vertical scrolling controls around any component as shown in Figure 7.23. The horizontal scroll control is at the bottom of the EditArea and the vertical scroll control is at the right of the EditArea. Next, two JButtons labelled "Cut" and "Paste" are created. The control to choose the text font is then created. Finally, the EditArea and the three controls are arranged in the user interface using the JPanel, FlowLayout, and BorderLayout classes as was done in the DrawTool applications.

Step 3: The EditArea Class: The JTextArea class provides the basic mechanisms for editing text. A JTextArea consists of a rectangular area measured in rows and columns, and a visible, movable caret. The number of rows and the columns can be set when the JTextArea is constructed and they may be changed under program control. The caret denotes the position within the TextArea of where the next character entered from the keyboard will be placed. The caret can be moved by mouse actions (clicking at the desired position), by the keyboard arrow keys, or by the program.

A portion of the functionality available in the JTextArea class is inherited from the JTextComponent base class from which the JTextField is also derived. The JTextField class represents a single line of editable text whereas the JTextArea represents multiple lines of editable text. A JTextField is usually used for entering options, names, or other simple parameters whereas the JTextArea is used for displaying and editing larger, multiple-line passages of text such as file, notes, electronic mail, and so on. The JTextComponent class is an abstract class that is a base class for all other text-oriented classes in the JFC. Some of the methods of the JTextArea and JTextComponent class are shown in Figure 7.26. The JTextComponent class provides a number of set and get methods for the current position of the edit caret, the positions that start and end the selected (highlighted) text. The entire text can be retrieved as a single string or changed to a given string by the `getText` and `setText` methods, respectively. The `getSelectedText` method returns as a string the currently selected (highlighted) text. Because it deals with text information, the dimensions of the JTextArea are measured in rows and columns rather than pixels. Finally, additional methods

```
public class EditFrame extends JFrame
{

  private EditArea editArea;

  public EditFrame()
  { Container content = this.getContentPane();
    content.setLayout(new BorderLayout());
    this.setLocation(100,100);
    this.setSize(300,300);

    editArea = new EditArea(40,60);
    editArea.setFontSize(16);
    JScrollPane editAreaScroller = new JScrollPane(editArea);

    JButton cutButton = new JButton("Cut");
    JButton pasteButton = new JButton("Paste");

    JComboBox sizeChoice = new JComboBox();
    sizeChoice.addItem("12");
    sizeChoice.addItem("16");
    sizeChoice.addItem("20");
    sizeChoice.setSelectedItem("16");

    JPanel controls = new JPanel();
    controls.setLayout(new FlowLayout());
    controls.add(sizeChoice);
    controls.add(cutButton);
    controls.add(pasteButton);

    content.add(editAreaScroller, BorderLayout.CENTER);
    content.add(controls, BorderLayout.SOUTH);
  }
}
```

Figure 7.25 The EditFrame Class

are provided for appending text to the end of the text in the JTextArea (`append`), inserting text at a given position (`insert`), or replacing a specified part of the curent text with another string (`replaceRange`).

Though the JTextArea is constructed in rows and columns, a position within the JTextArea is denoted by a single integer that corresponds to the number of characters in the text preceding that position where the end of a line is treated as a non-visible character. Thus, position does not denote a character, but a place between two adjacent characters (or the place before the first or after the last character) in the text. For example, the position before the first character is position 0 (zero), the position after the first character is position 1, and so on. If the first line of the TextArea has 10 characters then the position before the first character of the second line is position 11 because the end of the first line is counted as one character.

The EditArea class, shown in Figure 7.27, extends the JTextArea by adding two new methods for manipulating the text, `cut` and `paste`, and one new method, `setFontSize`, for selecting the size of the current font. The `cut`

```
public class JTextComponent extends JComponent
{
   public int getCaretPosition();
   public String getSelectedText();
   public int getSelectionStart();
   public int getSelectionEnd();
   public String getText();
   //...
   public void select(int start, int end);
   //...
   public void setCaretPosition();
   public void setSelectionStart(int start);
   public void setSelectionEnd(int end);
   public void setText(String text);
   //...
}

public class JTextArea extends JTextComponent
{

   //...
   public TextArea (int row, int columns);
   public TextArea (String text, int row, int columns, int
scrollbars);
   //...
   public void append(String text);
   public void insert(String text, int where);
   public void replaceRange(String text, int start, int end);
   //...
```

Figure 7.26 Important Methods in the TextArea and TextComponent Classes

method uses the inherited `getSelectedText` method to retrieve whatever text is currently selected in the text area. This text is stored as the value of the EditArea's `clipboard`. The inherited `getSelectionStart` and `getSelectionEnd` methods are used to obtain the positions that delimit the selected text. The delimited range of text is then removed by replacing it with a null string using the inherited `replaceRange` method. The `paste` method finds the position of the caret in the text area using the inherited `getCaretPosition` method. The `clipboard` text is inserted at the current caret position using the `insert` method. The `setFontSize` method creates a new Font object denoting a plain, Serif font of the size indicated by the method's parameter. Recall that the `setFont` method is inherited from the JComponent class.

The simplicity of the EditArea class derives from the powerful functionality provided by the JTextArea class and from the EditArea's limited responsibilities. An EditArea, for example, has no user interface capability other than those inherited from the JTextArea class. Limiting the EditArea's responsibilities makes it more resuable because the class does not embody design decisions that are not essential. In this way, an EditArea can be reused with a variety of user

```
public class EditArea extends JTextArea
{
  private String clipboard = "";

  public EditArea(int rows, int columns)
  { super(rows, columns);
  }

  public void cut()
  { clipboard = this.getSelectedText();
    int start = this.getSelectionStart();
    int end   = this.getSelectionEnd();
    this.replaceRange("", start, end);
  }

  public void paste()
  { int position = this.getCaretPosition();
    this.insert(clipboard, position);
  }

  public void setFontSize(int size)
  { this.setFont(new Font("Serif", Font.PLAIN, size));
  }
}
```

Figure 7.27 The EditArea Class

interfaces because the decisions about the structure of the user interface are not preempted by the EditArea itself.

Exercises

1. Compile, execute, and test the DrawTool application.
2. Revise the DrawTool application by defining a ColorChoice class that extends JComboBox. The ColorChoice class should encapsulate the details of the constructing and managing the selection of the drawing color.
3. Revise the DrawTool application so that the button for clearing the drawing area appears to the left of the selection for choosing the drawing color.
4. Revise the DrawTool application so that controls for clearing the drawing area and choosing the drawing color appear at the top of the drawing area.
5. Revise the DrawTool application so that the control for selecting the drawing color appears above the drawing area and the button for clearing the drawing area appears at the bottom.

6. Revise the DrawTool application so that the control for selecting the drawing color appears at the left of the drawing area and the button for clearing the drawing area appears at the right of the canvas.
7. Compile, execute, and test the EditTool application.
8. Revise the EditTool application by adding a third button labelled "copy". This button should appear as the rightmost control in the EditTool user interface.
9. Revise the EditTool application by adding a second EditArea in which the cut or copied text might be viewed.
10. Revise the EditTool application by adding a second choice control that would allow the user to specify one of the following font families: Serif, SanSerif, Monospaced, Dialog, and DialogInput. The new choice control should appear as the leftmost control in the EditTool's user interface.
11. Revise the EditTool application by adding two new choice controls: one choice controls allows selection of a font family as in the previous exercise and the second choice control allows selection from among the following font styles: Plain, Italic, and Bold. The two new controls should appear as the leftmost controls in the EditTool's user interface.

7.4 Event Handling Concepts

7.4.1 The Java Event Model

An event is a condition or action that is observed by a system but occurs outside the system's control. A system that reacts to events is termed an "event-driven system". Commonplace event-driven systems are smoke detectors and an automobile's cruise control. The smoke detector is designed to recognize conditions that are indicative of smoke commonly associated with a fire and react to this condition by sounding an alarm. The cruise control is designed to recognize when the driver has pressed the brake pedal and react to this action by returning the speed adjustment to manual control. As illustrated by these simple examples, events are anticipated but unplanned; the fact that the event will occur is known but the circumstances or timing of when it will occur are usually unconstrained. The smoke detector cannot plan for when the smoke will occur and the cruise control cannot know in advance when the driver will use the brake. In the context of Swing, events arise from actions in the user interface. Examples of Swing events are those caused by the user selecting an item from a menu, pushing a button, or moving the mouse. Like the events in the smoke detector and cruise

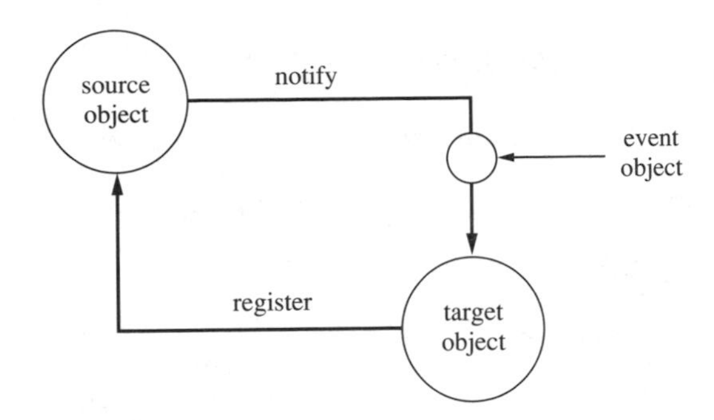

Figure 7.28 Elements of the Java Event Model

control, Swing events occur outside of the program's control; they can be anticipated but not planned. A JButton object displayed in the user interface cannot be programmed to know exactly when it will be pressed by the user nor can the system be built to anticipate that the shift key will be down at a certain point in time.

The model used by Swing to detect and react to events is comprised of three elements:

1. The source object: a component in which the event "occurs" and that maintains an association to a set of one or more objects "listening" for the event.
2. The listener object: an object of a class that implements a prescribed interface and that is programmed to react to the occurrence of the event.
3. An event object: an object that contains information describing a particular event passed from the source to the listener when the event occurs.

These three elements are shown in Figure 7.28. In addition to creating the source and listener objects, a program must arrange for the listener to be made known to, or registered with, the source object. Each source object maintains a list of registered listeners and provides a method for adding a listener object to this list. A listener object will be notified of those events occuring in a source object only after the listener is registered with the source object. In many cases, the listener objects are registered with their source objects when the objects are first created so that the listener may receive notifications of all events that happen in the source object. Once registered with the source object, the listener continues to receive notification of all events; it is not necessary to register again with the source object after each event. If a listener no longer needs to listen for

Table 7.4 Components and Their Event Types

Event Type	Component	Description
ActionEvent	JButton JCheckBox JComboBox JMenuItem JRadioButton	Clicking on, selecting, or choosing
ChangeEvent	JSlider	Adjusting the position of a movable element
ItemEvent	JComboBox JCheckBox JRadioButton JRadioButtonMenuItem JCheckBoxMenuItem	Selecting a item from among a set of alternatives
KeyEvent MouseEvent	JComponent and its derived classes	Manipulating the mouse or the key-board
CaretEvent	JTextArea JTextField	Selecting or editing text
WindowEvent	Window (and its derived classes) especially JFrame	Opening, closing, iconifying, etc. a window

events from a particular source object, the listener may remove itself from the list of listeners using a method provided by the source object.

An example of a source object is an object of the JButton class. A JButton object generates an ActionEvent when the user presses the user interface button (by clicking within the boundaries of the button's display). For a user-defined class to listen for the event of a button being pushed, the class must implement the ActionListener interface that is defined in the AWT. An object of this user-defined class would register itself (or would be registered) as a listener for the object of the Button class using the `addActionListener` method. Finally, when a user-interface button is pushed, an ActionEvent object is passed from the source to the listener. The ActionEvent object contains data that describes in which button the event occurred and other descriptive information about the event.

Java Event Types

The most commonly used events and the Swing components that generate these events are summarized in Table 7.4. A brief description of each type of event is also given. This table is not an exhaustive list of either Swing components or their events; it is meant only to give a useful and representative sample that is sufficient for many simple applications. A complete listing of all Swing events would be lengthy because Swing components fire events when any of their significant properties are changed. In many cases, these PropertyChangeEvents and ChangeEvents reflect detailed actions in the user interface that are not of concern to the application. For example, when a JButton object in the user interface is pushed it generates the following sequence of events:

```
ChangeEvent - the button is "armed" when the cursor is over the button
ChangeEvent - the button is "pressed" when the mouse button is depressed
ActionEvent - the button is released while the cursor is still over the button
ChangeEvent - the button is no longer "armed"
```

Most applications are interested only in the single ActionEvent that represents the user's complete action of pushing the button. The more detailed ChangeEvents are usually ignored in these applications. However, other applications could take advantage of the detailed events to provide more sophisticated management of the user interface. For example, when a button is "armed" its appearance may be altered to show that it is the currently selected control and that it is available to be pushed in the current system state.

It is interesting to notice that several different components generate the same type of event. For example, a JComboBox and a JButton both generate ActionEvents. This property can sometimes be exploited to create a flexible design because a listener object can listen for an ActionEvent without needing to know, or be dependent upon, the exact type of the component that generated the event. Thus, it might be possible to change the user interface so that a JComboBox is used instead of a JButton without the listener object being in any way affected by this substitution.

The classes that define the event objects are organized into a class hierarchy whose base class, EventObject class, maintains a reference to the object that generated the event. This reference is set by the EventObject's constructor and can be retrieved by the `getSource` method. Through inheritance, every event object has associated with it a source object. The AWTEvent class adds to the source object inherited from the EventObject class an "`id`"—an integer value returned by the `getID` method that identifies the specific kind of event that occurred. Classes derived from AWTEvent define named constants for the `"id"` value. For example, the ActionEvent class defines the named constant `ACTION_PERFORMED` that will be returned by the `getID` method. The event represented by classes derived from ComponentEvent can occur in any component. These events include gaining or losing the focus (having the cursor placed within its border), mouse or keyboard actions (both of which are treated as an InputEvent), opening or closing a window, adding a Component to or removing a Component from a Container, and events related to repainting components.

A consistent set of naming conventions makes the programming of Java events easier. In the naming convention, the name of each listener interface is derived from the name of the corresponding event type. For the event type *xEvent*, the listener interface is defined as:

```
public abstract interface xEventListener
{
   // listener methods
   public void methodName( xEvent eventObject);
}
```

Although the names of the methods defined in the interface vary among events depending on the nature of the event, each listener method has as a parameter an event object of the type corresponding to the listener interface. Also in the naming convention, a component that generates an *xEvent* event provides two methods whose signatures are:

```
public void addxEventListener( xEventListener listener);
public void removexEventListener( xEventListener listener);
```

The listener object given as a parameter in these methods is added or removed from the list of registered listeners maintained by the component.

The naming conventions are illustrated by the JButton class. Because this class generates an ActionEvent (see Table 7.4), there is a listener interface defined as:

```
public abstract interface ActionEventListener
{
   // ActionEvent listener methods
}
```

and a JButton object will respond to two methods named:

```
public void addActionEventListener( ActionEventListener listener);
public void removeActionEventListener( ActionEventListener listener);
```

These two methods will also be implemented in other classes that generate ActionEvents.

Listener Interfaces

Each event type has a corresponding listener interface all of whose methods must be implemented by a listener object. The methods for each interface are shown in Table 7.5. Some event types, such as the ActionListener, have a single method in their listener interface. When related, but different, events are grouped together in a single event type, the listener interface has a method corresponding to each of the specific events. The methods' names suggests the particular event that is the basis for that method's name. For example, the WindowEvent type is a related collection of events that can occur to a window; the names of the methods, such as `windowClosed` and `windowOpened`, suggest the particular kind of WindowEvent is the basis of each method's name. In one case, mouse events, the events are divided among two event types, MouseEvent and MouseMotionEvent, and two different interfaces, MouseListener and MouseMotionListener.

Table 7.5 Listener Interface Methods

Listener Interface	Methods
ActionListener	actionPerformed
ChangeListener	stateChanged
FocusListener	focusGained, focusLost
ItemListener	itemStateChanged
KeyListener	keyPressed, keyReleased, keyTyped
CaretListener	caretUpdate
MouseListener	mouseClicked, mouseEntered mouseExited, mousePressed mouseReleased
MouseMotionListener	mouseDragged, mouseMoved
WindowListener	windowClosed, windowClosing windowDeactivated, windowDeiconified windowIconified, windowOpened

As with all interfaces, a class implementing a listener interface must implement all of the methods defined in the interface even if it only some of the methods are relevant to the listener. A method implementation whose body has no code can be used, of course, in those cases where a method must be implemented but is not relevant. An alternative solution, called adapters, is discussed below.

Patterns of Event Handling

There are three relationships, or patterns, that can be established between the source object and a listener object: reactor, monitor, and delegator. These relationships, shown in Figures 7.29 through 7.31, define the association between the source object, which generates an event, the listener object, which is notified of the occurrence of the event, and a handler object, which performs the actions responding to the event.

A reactor pattern defines a single object with a self-contained, responsive ability: the object itself is programmed to deal with its own events. As illustrated in Figure 7.29, the single object combines the three roles of source, listener, and handler. The term "reactor" suggests that an object is autonomous and reactive; it does not need the support of other external objects to manage events that occur within it. In the DrawTool application, the DrawFrame will be defined as a reactor. When the user clicks on the "close window" icon, the DrawFrame itself will generate, recognize, and respond to this event. The response will be to terminate the program.

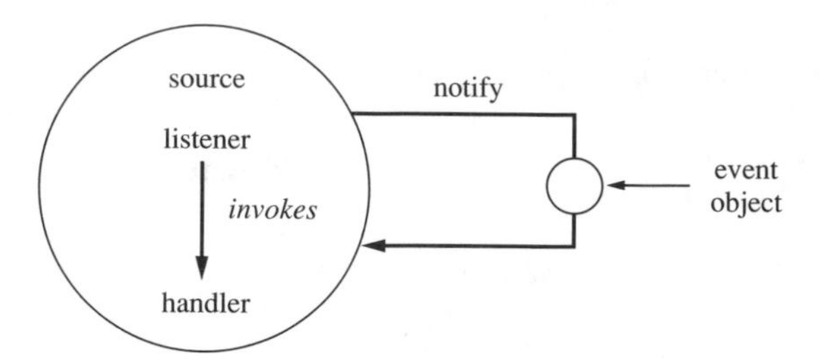

Figure 7.29 The Reactor Pattern

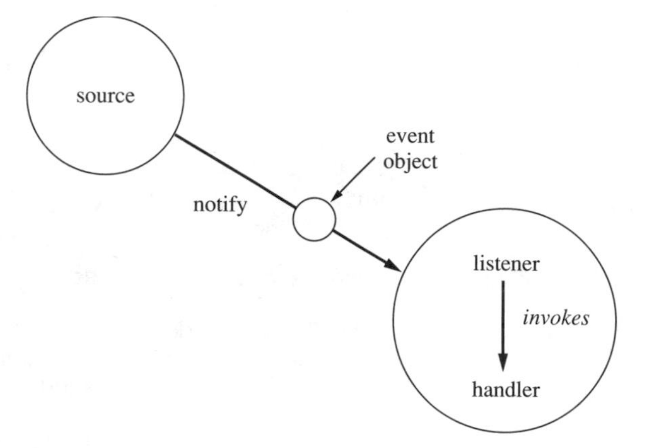

Figure 7.30 The Monitor Pattern

A monitor pattern, illustrated in Figure 7.30, is probably the most commonly used form. In this case is the listener object also plays the role of the handler object. The term "monitor" is used in this case because the listener/handler object has the responsibility of monitoring and adjusting to changes in the source object. In the DrawTool application, the DrawCanvas object will be used to monitor the "Clear Canvas" button; listening for an event that means the button has been pushed and reacting by clearing the drawing area. It is possible for a single listener object to be registered with multiple source objects at the same time. The monitor pattern might be used to have a single listener monitoring and reacting to the events from several sources. For example, in a user interface with several buttons a single listening object might be registered with each of the buttons, providing a single listener programmed to handle the events generated by any of the buttons.

A delegator pattern is one in which the listener object uses the services of other objects to respond to the events generated by the source object. This pattern is illustrated in Figure 7.31. In this pattern the roles of the source, listener, and handler are played by different objects. The term "delegator" is used to convey the idea that the listener object is an intermediary that facilitates the

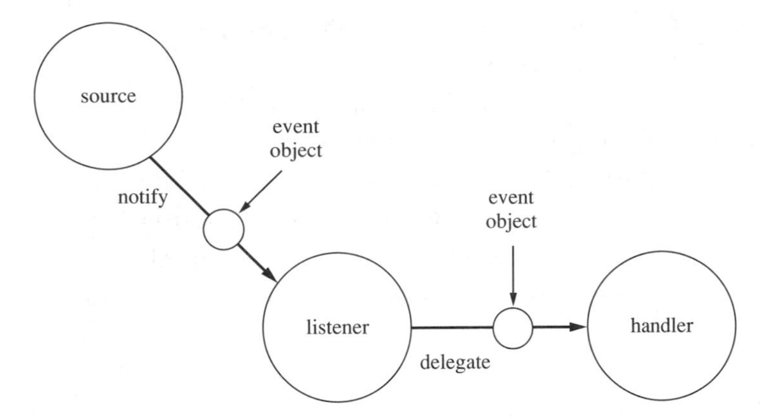

Figure 7.31 The Delegator Pattern

response to the events; it delegates to the handler object(s) the responsibility for responding to an event that occurs in the source object. A delegator relationship is particularly effective in either of two situations. First, a delegator can be used where a sequence of actions must be taken that involve two or more parts of the application. The delegator is able to coordinate the sequencing of these actions. Second, a delegator can be used where it is desired to insulate the handler object from the details of the user interface. In this situation, the handler object provides the necessary methods to respond to the event but the handler is insulated from any knowledge (or dependence upon) the particular user interface strategies used to cause these events. In the DrawTool application, a delegator will be created to deal with the color selection. By using a delegator, the DrawFrame will not be sensitive to changes in the user interface mechanism that is used to select the drawing color. The delegator pattern is the most flexible of the event handling patterns because it partitions the responsibilities of event handling more finely than the other patterns do. This partitioning allows the event-handling structure to be configured and adapted in a variety of ways. It is possible, for example, to have a listener delegate the response to different handlers at different times depending on the state of the system or to dynamically replace on handler with a different one.

Exercises

1. Identify a situation where an event source (e.g, a button or other control) would have several objects registered as listeners for its events.

2. Identify a situation where an object whould be registered as a listener for several different event sources.

3. Identify a situation where an object would dynamically remove itself as a listener from an event source.
4. Identify a situation where an object would dynamically add itself as a listener to an event source.
5. What are two items of information might be contained in an event object that was generated as a result of pushing a button?
6. What are two items of information that might be contained in an event object that was generated as a result of selecting an item from a menu?
7. Which of the three event-handling patterns best conforms to the notion of encapsulation?
8. Which of the three event-handling patterns offers the most flexibility?
9. Which event-handling pattern is best used in a situation where the same response can be triggered by different events in the user interface? Justify your selection.
10. Which event-handling pattern is best used in a situation where the response to a given event in the user interface changes dynamically during the course of the application?

7.5 Handling Events in Simple Applications

The techniques for responding to events are illustrated by extending the DrawTool and EditTool applications. These two applications, developed in Section 7.3, were structurally complete but did not respond to any of the events generated by user's actions. In this section, the event-handling code is added to both applications so that they are able to respond to the events caused by movement of the mouse, selection or pressing of control elements, and window-related events such as closing the window.

7.5.1. Handling Events in DrawTool

The simple DrawTool application is extended so that it can respond to four types of events:

1. WindowEvent: closing the DrawTool window and terminating the application
2. MouseEvent: responding to mouse clicking and dragging by drawing and moving a rectangle in the drawing area

3. ActionEvent: clearing the drawing area in response to the "Clear Canvas" button being pressed

4. ItemEvent: changing the drawing color when the user selects an alternative from the JComboBox component

These event are among the most commonly occurring ones and include events that are generated by many of the Swing components. The major events not touched on in this section are events related to text processing (KeyEvent and CaretEvent) and the events generated by the Slider (ChangeEvent). These events will be illustrated in other sections of this chapter.

The events in the DrawTool application will be handled using each of the three event-handling patterns. The WindowEvent and MouseEvent will be handled by a reactor pattern; the DrawFrame will listen for and respond to the events related to its own closing and the DrawCanvas will listen for and respond to the mouse events that occur within its drawing area. The ActionEvent will be handled by a monitor pattern; the DrawCanvas will listen for and react to the event of the "Clear Canvas" button being pressed. Finally, the delegator pattern will be used to handle the ItemEvents that are generated by the Choice component. A new class, ColorDelegator, will be defined that listens for the ItemEvents and responds to the event by using the `setColor` method in the DrawCanvas class.

The event-handling code will be incorporated into the DrawTool application in incremental steps. First, the DrawFrame will be expanded to allow it to listen for its own WindowEvent. Second, the DrawCanvas will be expanded to allow it to listen to its own mouse events and to monitor the events generated by the "Clear Canvas" button. Third, the ColorDelegator class will be defined and added to the DrawTool system. The third step involves a minor addition to the DrawFrame class: constructing the ColorDelegator. At the end of these steps the first version of the DrawTool application will be complete. This example will be used in subsequent sections to illustrate other Swing components and their operation.

Step 1: Handling Window Events in the DrawFrame Class: The DrawFrame class is enhanced to deal with its own WindowEvents using the *reactor* event-handling pattern in which the DrawFrame plays all three roles of source, listener, and handler. The DrawFrame will terminate the application when the user closes the user interface window associated with the DrawFrame. The revised DrawFrame class is shown in Figure 7.32.

To play the role of the listener, the DrawFrame class must implement the WindowListener interface that, by the *naming conventions*, is the listener interface corresponding to the WindowEvent event type and register itself as a listener with the source object. The DrawFrame class includes in its declaration the clause "`implements WindowListener`" to signal that it will implement the stated interface. To implement the WindowListener interface, the DrawFrame class must implement all of the seven methods defined by this interface. Because

```
public class DrawFrame extends JFrame implements WindowListener
{
  public DrawFrame()
  {
    // other constructor code as before

    this.addWindowListener(this);

  }
  public void windowClosing      (WindowEvent event)
  { System.exit(0);
  }

  public void windowActivated   (WindowEvent event) {}
  public void windowClosed      (WindowEvent event) {}
  public void windowDeactivated (WindowEvent event) {}
  public void windowDeiconified (WindowEvent event) {}
  public void windowIconified   (WindowEvent event) {}
  public void windowOpened      (WindowEvent event) {}

}
```

Figure 7.32 Event Handling in the DrawFrame Class

the DrawFrame is both the source of the events and the listener for those events, the DrawFrame constructor includes the line of code

```
this.addWindowListener(this);
```

that registers the DrawFrame object as its own listener.

To play the role of the handler, the DrawFrame class must completely deal with the relevant WindowEvents. Of these seven methods defined in the WindowListener interface, only the `windowClosing` method has any code associated with it in the DrawFrame class. The `windowClosing` method simply terminates the application using the `System.exit` method. Because the DrawFrame completely deals with the WindowEvents, it is also playing the handler role.

Step 2: Handling Mouse and Button Events in the DrawCanvas Class: The DrawCanvas class is enhanced so that it deals with its own mouse events using the *reactor* pattern of event handling and also deals with the events generated by the ClearButton using the *monitor* pattern. The DrawCanvas plays the roles of source, listener, and handler for the mouse events and also plays the listener and handler roles for the button events. This class shows that it is possible for a single object to listen for several different types of events and to use different patterns of event handling in dealing with these events. There are two sources of events relevant to the DrawCanvas class. The JButton class is a source of ActionEvents, and the JComponent class, from which DrawCanvas inherits, is a source of MouseEvents and MouseMotionEvents. The revised DrawCanvas class is shown in Figure 7.33.

Because the DrawCanvas listens for different event types it must implement several interfaces, one interface for each event type, and register itself as a listener with those objects that generate the events. By the *naming conventions*, the listener interfaces for the event types are ActionListener (for the ActionEvents generated by the ClearButton) and MouseListener and MouseMotionListener (for the MouseEvents and MouseMotionEvents generated by JComponent). To complete its role as a listener for these events, the DrawCanvas must register itself with the objects that are the sources of these events. Because the DrawCanvas is the source of the mouse events, it uses the reactor pattern to register itself as a listener for its own events using the code:

```
this.addMouseListener(this);
this.addMouseMotionListener(this);
```

and the code:

```
clearButton.addActionListener(this);
```

to register itself as a listener for the event generated by the ClearButton object.

The DrawCanvas reacts to mouse events by drawing or moving a rectangle. The `mousePressed` method is called when the user presses the mouse button when the cursor is inside of the DrawCanvas's drawing area. The `mousePressed` method constructs a new Rectangle whose upper left-corner coordinates are obtained from the MouseEvent object passed to the `mousePressed` method as a parameter. The coordinates in the MouseEvent object are the coordinates of where the mouse event occurred (the cordinates of the cursor when the mouse button was pushed). The coordinates are obtained from the MouseEvent object using the `getX` and `getY` accessor methods. The other MouseListener methods have empty code bodies because they must be implemented to satisfy the MouseListener interface but have no effect in this application. The `mouseDragged` method is called when the user drags the mouse (moves the mouse while holding down the mouse button) within the drawing area. If there is a rectangle object, it is moved to the coordinates of the mouse drag event. The other methods of the MouseListener interface and the MouseMotionListener interface are defined with no code bodies because they do not play a role in the operation of the DrawCanvas.

The ClearButton class, also shown in Figure 7.33, along with the `actionPerformed` method in the DrawCanvas class, illustrate how ActionEvents are handled using the monitor pattern. An ActionEvent may have associated with it a String that is referred to as the "action command." The value of this String can be set and retrieved by the program using the `setActionCommand` and `getActionCommand` methods. The value of this String is used to convey the action that the listening or handling object should perform in response to the ActionEvent. Because the JButton class generates an ActionEvent, it has a `setActionCommand` method that defines the String associated with the ActionEvents that it generates. The ClearButton constructor sets its action command to the String "clear." The `actionPerformed` method, the only method defined in the Action-

```
import java.awt.*;
import java.awt.event.*;
import javax.swing.*;
import Rectangle;
import ClearButton;
public class DrawCanvas extends JComponent implements ActionListener,
                                                      MouseListener,
                                                      MouseMotionListener
{
  private Rectangle rectangle;
  private ClearButton clearButton;
  public DrawCanvas(ClearButton clearButton)
  { // same as before
    rectangle = null;

    this.clearButton = clearButton;
    clearButton.addActionListener(this);
    this.addMouseListener(this);
    this.addMouseMotionListener(this);
  }

  public void setColor(Color color)
  { // same as before
    repaint();
  }
  public void paint(Graphics g)
  { // same as before
  }
  // methods to implements the MouseListener interface
  public void mousePressed(MouseEvent event)
  { rectangle = new Rectangle(event.getX(), event.getY());
    repaint();
  }
  public void mouseEntered (MouseEvent event) {}
  public void mouseExited  (MouseEvent event) {}
  public void mouseClicked (MouseEvent event) {}
  public void mouseReleased(MouseEvent event) {}
  // methods to implement the MouseMotionListener interface
  public void mouseDragged(MouseEvent event)
  { if (rectangle != null)
    { rectangle.moveTo(event.getX(), event.getY());
      repaint();
    }
  }
  public void mouseMoved(MouseEvent event) {}
  // method to implement the ActionListener interface
  public void actionPerformed(ActionEvent event)
  { if (event.getActionCommand().equals(clearButton.etActionCommand()))
    { rectangle = null;
      repaint();
    }
  }
}
// in file ClearButton.java (given here for reference)
public class ClearButton extends JButton
{
  public ClearButton()
  { super("Clear Canvas");            // sets label for button
    this.setActionCommand("clear");
  }

}
```

Figure 7.33 Event Handling in the DrawFrame Class

Listener interface, retrieves the action command from the ActionEvent generated by the ClearButton and tests to see if this command string is the same as the action command from the ClearButton. This test is more complicated than what is strictly required in the simple DrawTool application because there is only one button in the user interface and it is clear without testing the action command what should be done when an ActionEvent occurs. However, this more complicated test is shown here to illustrate the action command and the testing of this command that is typical in more complex applications that contain numerous ActionEvents.

The DrawCanvas updates its on-screen representation by using the `repaint` method. The `repaint` method is called in each method that changes the state of the DrawCanvas in such a way that its visual display should be updated: in `mousePressed` when a new Rectangle is created and should be displayed, in `mouseDragged` when the position of the Rectangle object is changed, in `actionPerformed` when the drawing area should be cleared, and in `setColor` when the drawing color is changed by the user through the JComboBox component. Recall, that invoking `repaint` is a request for the run-time system, at some convenient time in the near future, to call the `paint` method, allowing the DrawCanvas to update its visual representation.

Step 3: Handling the Item Selection Events in the ColorDelegator Class: The ColorDelegator class uses the *delegator* pattern to handle the ItemEvents generated by the JComboBox component that allows the user to select among three different drawing colors: Red, Green, and Blue. The ColorDelegator class is shown in Figure 7.34. The constructor for the ColorDelegator is passed the DrawCanvas whose drawing color it will update using the `setColor` method of the DrawCanvas. In the constructor the reference to the DrawCanvas is retained as a private variable. As shown in the bottom part of Figure 7.34, the ColorDelegator is registered as a listener of the JComboBox component by the DrawFrame constructor that creates both the Choice component and the ColorDelegator object.

The ColorDelegator implements the ItemListener interface's single method, `itemStateChanged`, whose parameter, an ItemEvent, carries the String that was selected by the user from among the JComboBox component's list of alternatives. The String is extracted from the ItemEvent using the `getItem` method and tested against the three possible values. Depending on the String's value, one of the three predefined colors, `Color.red`, `Color.green`, or `Color.blue` is assigned to the variable `newColor`. The DrawCanvas' setColor method is used to delegate to the DrawCanvas the responsibility of changing its drawing color and its appearance in the user interface.

```
import java.awt.*;
import java.awt.event.*;
import DrawCanvas;

public class ColorDelegator implements ItemListener
{
  private DrawCanvas drawingArea;

  public ColorDelegator (DrawCanvas canvas)
  { drawingArea = canvas;
  }

  public void itemStateChanged(ItemEvent event)
  { String colorName = (String)event.getItem();

    Color newColor;
    if      (colorName.equals("Red"))   newColor = Color.red;
    else if (colorName.equals("Green")) newColor = Color.green;
    else                                newColor = Color.blue;

    drawingArea.setColor(newColor);
  }
}

// addition to the DrawFrame class to create the ColorDelgator
public class DrawFrame extends JFrame implements WindowListener
{
  private ColorDelegator choiceHandler;
  public DrawFrame()
  { //...

    JComboBox colorChoice = new JComboBox();
    //...
    ClearButton clearButton = new ClearButton();
    DrawCanvas canvas = new DrawCanvas(clearButton);
    choiceHandler = new ColorDelegator(canvas);
    colorChoice.addItemListener(choiceHandler);
    //...
  }
  //...
}
```

Figure 7.34 Handling the Choice Events

7.5.2. Handling Events in EditTool

The EditTool application is extended so that it can respond to three types of events:

1. WindowEvent: closing the EditTool window and terminating the application
2. ActionEvent: cutting and pasting text in response to the "cut" or "paste" buttons being pressed
3. ItemEvent: changing the font size when the user selects an alternative from the JComboBox component

As was done in the DrawTool application, the event-handling code will be incorporated into the EditTool application in incremental steps. First, the EditFrame class will be expanded to allow it to listen for its own WindowEvents. Second, the EditArea will be expanded to monitor the events generated by the font size JCombBox. Third, the EditCommands class will be defined and added to the EditTool system. The action events generated by the "cut" and "paste" buttons will be delegated to the an EditCommands object. At the end of these steps the first version of the EditTool application will be complete. This example will be used in subsequent sections to illustrate other Swing components and their operation.

Step 1: Handling Window Events in the EditFrame Class: The EditFrame class is modified using the reactor pattern so that an EditFrame object will listen for and react to window-related events that occur in the EditFrame. The additional code added to the EditFrame is shown in Figure 7.35. The definition of the class includes the "implements WindowListener" clause to signify that the class will implement the required methods of a listener for window events. The required methods are shown near the botton of the EditFrame code in the figure. Of these methods, only the `windowClosing` method contains any code. This method simply terminates the application. Because the reactor pattern is used, the EditFrame object is both the source of the window-related events and the object that responds to these events. Therefore, in the EditFrame constructor, the EditFrame object registers itself (a valid WindowListener) as a window listener for events that it itself generates. This is all of the code necessary to handle the window-related events. With these extensions, the EditTool application can be terminated by simply closing the window.

```
public class EditFrame extends JFrame implements WindowListener
{

  public EditFrame()
  {

    //...
    this.addWindowListener(this);
  }

  public void windowClosing      (WindowEvent event)
  { System.exit(0);
  }

  public void windowActivated   (WindowEvent event) {}
  public void windowClosed      (WindowEvent event) {}
  public void windowDeactivated (WindowEvent event) {}
  public void windowDeiconified (WindowEvent event) {}
  public void windowIconified   (WindowEvent event) {}
  public void windowOpened      (WindowEvent event) {}
}
```

Figure 7.35 Handling Window Events in the EditFrame Class

```
public class EditFrame extends JFrame implements WindowListener
{

  private EditArea editArea;

  public EditFrame()
  {

    //...
    editArea = new EditArea(40,60);
    EditCommands delegator = new EditCommands(editArea);

    JButton cutButton = new JButton("Cut");
    cutButton.setActionCommand("cut");
    cutButton.addActionListener(delegator);

    JButton pasteButton = new JButton("Paste");
    pasteButton.setActionCommand("paste");
    pasteButton.addActionListener(delegator);

  }

  //...
}

public class EditCommands implements ActionListener
{
  private EditArea editArea;

  public EditCommands (EditArea area)
  { editArea = area;
  }

  public void actionPerformed(ActionEvent event)
  { if(event.getActionCommand().equals("cut"))
      { editArea.cut();
      }
    if (event.getActionCommand().equals("paste"))
       { editArea.paste();
       }
  }

}
```

Figure 7.36 Handling Button Events in the EditTool Application

Step 2: Handling the "cut" and "paste" Button Events: A delegator pattern is used to handle the events generated by the "cut" and "paste" buttons in the EditTool's user interface. The modifications needed to implement this pattern are shown in Figure 7.36. The delegation structure is created by the constructor of the EditFrame class. An EditCommands object is constructed to receive and dispatch the action events generated by the two buttons. The EditCommands objects is added as an ActionListener to each of the two buttons. Each button is given an action "command" so that the EditCommands object can distinguish which of the two buttons caused the action event that it receives.

Assigning the action command and adding the EditCommands object as a listener is shown by the boldface code in Figure 7.36.

The EditCommands class is also shown in Figure 7.36. This class implements the ActionListener interface so that it can be registered as a listener for the action events generated by the "cut" and "paste" buttons. The single method required by this interface is the `actionPerformed` method. In the EditCommands class, this method simply gets the action command from the action event and compares it to the action commands associated with the two buttons, calling the `cut` or `paste` method in the EditArea object with which it is associated. The EditArea class was described in Section 7.3 and is extended below.

Step 3: Handling Font Size Changes in the EditTool: A monitor pattern is used to respond to the events generated by the choice control. In this case, the EditArea is extended as shown in Figure 7.37 to be able to monitor the events that occur as a result of the user making a selection of a font size in the JComboBox control. Some additional code is added to the EditFrame class to register the EditArea as a listener for the JComboBox object. This code is shown in boldface in Figure 7.37. As also shown in the figure, the EditArea class implements the ItemListener interface that requires a single method, `itemState-`

```
public class EditFrame extends JFrame implements WindowListener
{
  private EditArea editArea;

  public EditFrame()
  {
    editArea = new EditArea(40,60);
    //...
    JComboBox sizeChoice = new JComboBox();
    sizeChoice.addItemListener(editArea);

    //...
  }
}

public class EditArea extends JTextArea implements ItemListener
{
  //...

  public void setFontSize(int size)
  { this.setFont(new Font("Serif", Font.PLAIN, size));
  }

  public void itemStateChanged(ItemEvent event)
  { String fontSize = (String)event.getItem();
    try {int size = Integer.valueOf(fontSize).intValue();
         this.setFontSize(size);
    } catch (NumberFormatException nfe) {}
  }

}
```

Figure 7.37 Changing the Font Size in the EditTool Application

`Changed`. In the EditTool, the JComboBox offers the user a choice among the three font sizes of 12, 16, and 20 points. In the `itemStateChanged` method, the current choice is retrieved from the item event and converted to an int value. The `setFontSize` method is then used to change the current font size in the EditArea.

Exercises

1. Revise the DrawTool application so that the events generated by the JComboBox are treated as Action events rather than Item events.
2. Revise the DrawTool application so that the events generated by the JComboBox are handled by a monitor pattern.
3. Revise the DrawTool application so that the action events generated by the buttons are handled by a delegator pattern.
4. Revise the DrawTool application so that all events (window events, action events, and item events) are handled by a single object to which all events are delegated.
5. Revise the EditTool by adding the ability to copy the currently selected text. The copied text can be inserted elsewhere by the existing EditTool ability to paste text into the TextArea.
6. Revise the EditTool so that clicking highlights the entire line of text containing the caret.
7. Revise the EditTool so that clicking highlight the entire sentence containing the caret. A sentence ends with the first period after the caret and begins with the first character after the end of the previous sentence or the beginning of the entire text if it is the first sentence.
8. Extend the EditTool by adding a second EditArea in which the contents of the primary EditArea's clipboard are displayed. An additional button labelled "Clear" visually associated with the new EditArea cause all of its text to be erased. Notice that this extension allows text to be cut from the primary EditArea, edited in the clipboard EditArea, and the edited text pasted back into the primary EditArea.
9. Modify the EditTool application so that the action events generated by the buttons are handled using a monitor pattern.
10. Modify the EditTool application so that the item events generated by the choice control are handled by a delegator pattern.

11. Revise the EditTool application so that all events (window events, action events, and item events) are handled by a single object to which all events are delegated.

12. Revise the EditTool application so that the user interface has two buttons labelled "Larger" and "Smaller" that cause the size of the font in use to increase and decrease, respectively, by 2 points each time the button is pressed. Establish reasonable upper and lower limints on the size. When a size limit is reached, the button that would cause the size to go beyond that limit is ignored until the size is no longer at the limit.

13. Revise the EditTool application so that instead of allowing the user to select different sizes of the same family and style of font it allows the user to selecte a different family of the same size and style.

14. Revise the EditTool application so that the user is allowed to select the family and size of the font independently through two sets of buttons, one set of buttons for the family choice and one set for the size choice.

15. Revise the EditTool application so that the user is presented with three JComboBoxes in the same user interface: one selects the font family, one selects the font style, and one selects the font size.

7.6 Menus

7.6.1 General Concepts

There are two types of menus, *pulldown menus* and *popup menus*, that differ in where they can appear and how they are activated but are the same in how their items are selected and in the type of events that they generate. Either type of menu, when activated, becomes visible and displays a set of items, among which at most one item may be selected; after the selection is made, the menu is no longer visible and an event is generated informing any listeners of the selection that was made. The menu differs from both a JComboBox and JCheckBoxes in that the menu is only visible when it has been activated, whereas a JComboBox and JCheckBoxes are always visible in the user interface. A menu is similar to a JComboBox in that only one alternative may be selected at a time.

An ActionEvent is generated by the selection of an item in a popup or pulldown menu. A listener object is registered with each individual menu item, not with the menu as a whole. When the item is selected, an ActionEvent describing the item is sent to that item's listeners. The listener object does not need to be aware of the type of menu that contained the menu item; the listener simply knows that it receives an ActionEvent corresponding to the selection of an item from a menu. Each item may have associated with it an "action command"—a simple String value whose meaning is interpreted by the listener. Usually, the action command denotes an "action" or a "command" that the listener should carry out. The action command string can be obtained from the ActionEvent object that is passed to the listener.

Multi-level menus, also called cascading or hierarchical menus, can be created in either popup or pulldown menus. A multi-level menu is one in which one or more of the menu's items is itself a complete menu. Because any item of any menu can be another complete menu, a general tree-structured hierarchy of menu choice can be created. Such a menu structure is desirable when there are a large number of total menu items, too many to present usefully in a single menu, which can be organized into sets of items with a common theme. Starting at the top-level menu, the user is able to navigate through the levels more easily than if the many items were presented in a single-level menu.

A *check-box menu item* combines the state-oriented characteristics of a JCheckBox with the organizing and accessing characteristics of a menu item. Such a menu item is state-oriented in that the user is presented with a menu item that can be check or unchecked to indicate whether a particular option or property should apply (when checked) or not apply (when unchecked). A given menu can contain any combination or regular menu items and check-box menu items.

Separators can be used to help provide a visual organization to lengthy menus. The separator is a simple horizontal line between adjacent menu items. This visual cue can be used effectively to indicate logical groupings of menu items and assist the user in understanding the structure of a possibly complex menu.

Pulldown Menus

A pulldown menu is represented visually by a name attached to a menu bar that typically appears at the top of a JFrame. The menu bar displays the names of one or more pulldown menus. The pulldown menu is activated and used in one of two ways. The first way is to press and hold the mouse button down until the selection is made, in which case the selection is the highlighted menu item when the button is released. The second way is to click (press and release) the mouse button while the cursor is over the name of the menu in the menu bar. In this case the menu is expanded and the menu items are highlighted as before as the cursor is moved over the menu items. To select a menu item, the user clicks (presses and releases) the mouse button while the desired menu item is highlighted.

The DrawTool application will be modified to use two pulldown menus. The first pulldown menu, named Color, is used to select the drawing color, whereas the second pulldown menu, named Commands, contains two commands that (1) clear the display, replacing the button used for this purpose in the previous interfaces, and (2) quit the application, adding to the previous method of quitting the

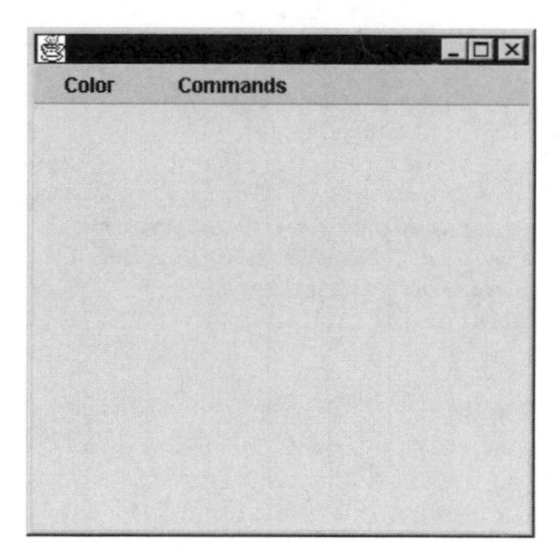

Figure 7.38 DrawTool Interface with Menus

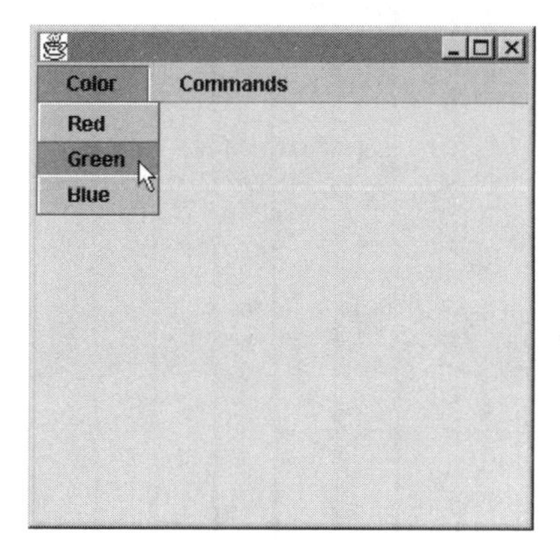

Figure 7.39 DrawTool Interface with Menus

application by using the close window icon. The DrawTool user interface with the two menus is shown in Figure 7.38. Notice that the application now contains a menu bar towards the top of the frame. On the menu bar there are two menu names: Color and Commands.

The Color menu is shown in its expanded state in Figure 7.39. As shown, the Color menu offers the choice among the three alternative colors, Red, Green, and Blue. The Green color is highlighted to indicate that this alternative is the current one indicated by the location of the cursor within the menu.

An Example of Using Pulldown Menus

The two pulldown menus, named Colors and Commands, for the DrawTool application as pictured above are constructed in the DrawFrame class as shown by the code in bold in Figure 7.40. Notice that the DrawFrame class implements the ActionListener interface so that it can serve as a listener for the "Quit" selection in the "Commands" menu.

```
public class DrawFrame extends JFrame implements WindowListener,
                                                 ActionListener
{
  private ColorDelegator colorHandler;

    private void addItem(JMenu menu, String colorName,
                         ActionListener listener)
  { JMenuItem nextItem = new JMenuItem(colorName);
    nextItem.setActionCommand(colorName);
    nextItem.addActionListener(listener);
    menu.add(nextItem);
  }

  public DrawFrame()
  { Container content = this.getContentPane();
    content.setLayout(new BorderLayout());
    this.setLocation(100,100);
    this.setSize(300,300);
    this.addWindowListener(this);

    DrawCanvas canvas = new DrawCanvas();
    colorHandler = new ColorDelegator(canvas);

    JMenu colorMenu = new JMenu("Color");
    addItem(colorMenu, "Red"   , colorHandler);
    addItem(colorMenu, "Green", colorHandler);
    addItem(colorMenu, "Blue"   , colorHandler);

    JMenu commandMenu = new JMenu("Commands");
    addItem(commandMenu, "Clear", canvas);
    addItem(commandMenu, "Quit" , this);

    JMenuBar menuBar = new JMenuBar();
    menuBar.add(colorMenu);
    menuBar.add(commandMenu);
    this.setJMenuBar(menuBar);

    content.add(canvas, BorderLayout.CENTER);
  }

  // WindowListner methods as before

  public void actionPerformed(ActionEvent event)
  { if (event.getActionCommand().equals("Quit"))
    { System.exit(0);
    }
  }

}
```

Figure 7.40 Constructing the Pulldown Menus in the DrawTool Application

To simplify the construction of the two menus a private convenience method, `addItem` is defined. This method takes three parameters: the JMenu to which an item will be added, the String name of the item to be added, and an ActionListener that will be registered as a listener for the item. In this method, a

```
public class ColorDelegator implements ActionListener
{
  private DrawCanvas drawingArea;

  public ColorDelegator (DrawCanvas canvas)
  { drawingArea = canvas;
  }

  public void actionPerformed(ActionEvent event)
  { String colorName = event.getActionCommand();

    Color newColor;
    if      (colorName.equals("Red"))   newColor = Color.red;
    else if (colorName.equals("Green")) newColor = Color.green;
    else                                newColor = Color.blue;

    drawingArea.setColor(newColor);
  }

}
```

Figure 7.41 ColorDelegator Class Used With Pulldown Menus

new JMenuItem, nextItem, is constructed whose name and action command are both set from the itemName parameter. The listener parameter is registered with nextItem. Finally, the new JMenuItem is added to the JMenu.

The Color and Commands menus are created in the DrawFrame constructor using the addItem convenience method. The Color menu is constructed first. Notice that the JMenu constructor argument gives the name of the JMenu as it will appear on the JFrame's menu bar. The addItem convenience function is used to add three items to the Color menu, one item for each of the three colors. The ColorDelegator object is given as the listener for each of the these three menu items. The Commands menu is constructed in a similar way with the DrawingCanvas object being given as the listener for the "Clear" command and the DrawFrame itself (denoted by the this variable) as the listener for the "Quit" command. The last step in building the menu structure is to construct a JMenuBar object, add JMenus to the JMenuBar, and associate the JMenuBar with the current JFrame object using the JFrame class's setJMenuBar method.

The last addition to the DrawFrame class is the actionPerformed method that is necessary in order to implement the ActionListener interface. This method extracts the action command from the ActionEvent object and tests if it is equal to the String "Quit". If this test is true, the application is terminated.

The ColorDelegator class, shown in Figure 7.41, is defined so that it can serve as an ActionListener. Recall that in the DrawFrame constructor a ColorDelegator was created and assigned as the listener for each item in the Color menu. When an item in the Color menu is selected, an ActionEvent object is constructed and the actionPerformed method of the ColorDelegator object will be invoked passing to it the ActionEvent object. The action command is extracted

```
public class DrawCanvas extends JComponent implements ActionListener,
                                                      MouseListener,
                                                      MouseMotionListener
{
  private Rectangle rectangle;
  private Color currentColor;

  // other methods as before

  // MouseListener and MouseMotionListener Methods as before

  public void actionPerformed(ActionEvent event)
  { if (event.getActionCommand().equals("Clear"))
    { rectangle = null;
      repaint();
    }
  }

}
```

Figure 7.42 DrawCanvas Used With Pulldown Menus

from the ActionEvent object and its value is used to define a Color value. This Color value is used to update the DrawingCanvas's drawing color.

The DrawCanvas class is revised so that it can serve as an ActionListener. The revision is shown in Figure 7.42. Recall that in the DrawFrame constructor, the DrawCanvas is registered as a listener for the "Clear" item in the Commands menu. When the user selects the "Clear" item, an ActionEvent object is created and passed to the ActionPerformed method of the item's listener, in this case the DrawCanvas class. The DrawCanvas extracts the action command from the ActionEvent object and tests if this string equals "Clear". If the test is true, the DrawCanvas sets its Rectangle reference to null and, by invoking `repaint`, requests that the user interface—and, hence, the DrawCanvas itself—be redrawn. When the DrawCanvas redraws itself, there will be no Rectangle to draw and thus the drawing area will be cleared.

Popup Menus

A popup menu can be activated under program control by any component, such as a JCanvas or a JApplet, and the menu will appear at a location determined by the activating component. A component that manages a popup menu has some event, termed a "trigger", that it listens for and in response to which it activates the popup menu. Selections are made from a popup window in the same way as with a pulldown menu. The popup menu behaves like a modal window in that it retains the focus of control in the user interface—the menu must be dismissed before the user interface will respond to any other user action. The menu is dismissed by making a selection from the menu or clicking outside of the menu area. Figure 7.43 shows a popup menu that appears in the drawing area of the DrawTool application.

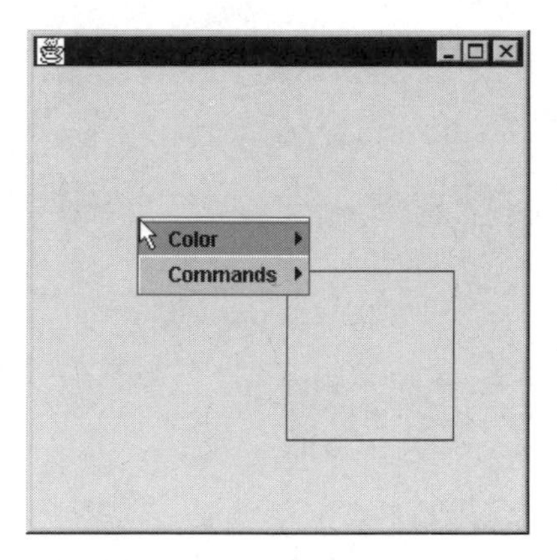

Figure 7.43 A PopupMenu in the DrawTool Example

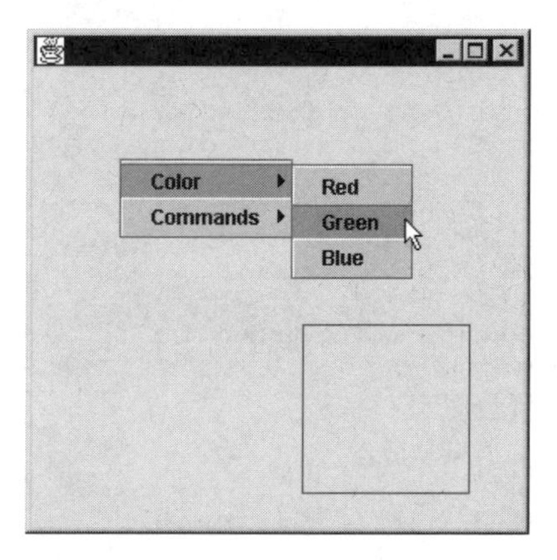

Figure 7.44 The Expanded PopupMenu

The popup menu has two entries as in the pulldown menu example above. The triangular icon at the left margin of each of the two menu entries indicates they are menus that can be exposed by moving the cursor over one of the entries. The contents of the expanded menu named Color is shown in Figure 7.44. This expanded menu presents three alternatives, one for each of the choices of color.

An Example of Using Popup Menus

The similarity between pulldown menus and popup menus is seen in the constructor of the DrawFrame class, shown in Figure 7.45, that creates a popup menu for the DrawTool application. Notice that the construction of the two menus—one for choosing colors and one for selecting a command—are exactly the same as in the pulldown menu case. The difference is that instead of creating a JMenuBar, a JPopupMenu is created to which the two menus are added. Because the popup menu will be triggered by a MouseEvent in the drawing area, the popup menu is passed to the DrawingCanvas using the `addPopupMenu` that

```
public class DrawFrame extends JFrame implements WindowListener,
                                                  ActionListener
{
  private ColorDelegator colorHandler;

  private void addItem(JMenu menu, String colorName,
                       ActionListener listener)
  { // same as with pulldown menus
  }

  public DrawFrame()
  { Container content = this.getContentPane();
    content.setLayout(new BorderLayout());
    this.setLocation(100,100);
    this.setSize(300,300);
    this.addWindowListener(this);

    DrawCanvas canvas = new DrawCanvas();
    colorHandler = new ColorDelegator(canvas);

    JMenu colorMenu = new JMenu("Color");
    addItem(colorMenu, "Red"  , colorHandler);
    addItem(colorMenu, "Green", colorHandler);
    addItem(colorMenu, "Blue" , colorHandler);

    JMenu commandMenu = new JMenu("Commands");
    addItem(commandMenu, "Clear", canvas);
    addItem(commandMenu, "Quit" , this);

    JPopupMenu popupMenu = new JPopupMenu();
    popupMenu.add(colorMenu);
    popupMenu.add(commandMenu);

    canvas.addPopupMenu(popupMenu);

    content.add(canvas, BorderLayout.CENTER);
  }

  // WindowListener methods

  public void actionPerformed(ActionEvent event)
  { if (event.getActionCommand().equals("Quit"))
    { System.exit(0);
    }
  }

}
```

Figure 7.45 Creating a Popup Menu

is defined in the DrawingCanvas for this purpose. Notice that the `actionPerformed` method in the DrawFrame class remains unchanged, reflecting the fact that the listener does not need to be concerned about whether the item is contained in a pulldown or a popup menu.

The DrawCanvas class is modified so that it can manage the popup menu created and passed to it by the DrawFrame class. The modified DrawFrame

```
import java.awt.*;
import javax.swing.*;
import java.awt.event.*;
import Rectangle;

public class DrawCanvas extends JComponent implements ActionListener,
                                                    MouseListener,
                                                    MouseMotionListener

{
  private Rectangle rectangle;
  private Color currentColor;
  JPopupMenu popup;

  public DrawCanvas()
  { // as before
  }

  public void addPopupMenu(JPopupMenu popup)
  { this.popup = popup;
    this.add(popup);
  }

  // other methods as before

  public void mousePressed(MouseEvent event)
  { if (event.isShiftDown())
     popup.show(this, event.getX(), event.getY());
    else
    { rectangle = new Rectangle(event.getX(), event.getY());
      repaint();
    }
  }

  // other MouseEvent and MouseMotionEvent methods

  public void actionPerformed(ActionEvent event)
  { if (event.getActionCommand().equals("Clear"))
    { rectangle = null;
      repaint();
    }
  }

}
```

Figure 7.46 Managing the PopupMenu

class is shown in Figure 7.46. Notice that the DrawCanvas implements the ActionListener interface so that it can act as a listener for the "Clear" item in the Commands menu. Recall that the DrawFrame constructor registered the DrawCanvas as a listener for this item. The `addPopupMenu` is introduced so that the DrawCanvas can be passed the JPopupMenu constructed in the DrawFrame class. In addition to keeping a reference to this JPopupMenu, the JPopupMenu object must be made known to the component that will trigger its activation. The method to add a JPopupMenu is inherited from the Component class (thus, any component can trigger a JPopupMenu).

In the DrawTool application a particular mouse event is used to trigger the JPopupMenu as shown in the `mousePressed` method. To trigger the JPopupMenu, the user must move the cursor to within the boundaries of the DrawCanvas, and simultaneously press the mouse button while holding down the shift key (a shift-click). The method `isShiftDown` applied to a MouseEvent object is used to test whether the shift key was down when the mouse button was pressed. The decision to use the shift-click mouse event as the menu trigger is purely arbitrary, any other event for which the DrawCanvas could be a listener would serve as well. Other mouse event triggers might test for control-shift, alt-shift, or meta-shift combinations using the methods `isControlDown`, `isAltDown`, and `isMetaDown`.

The JPopupMenu is activated by using its `show` method whose three parameters collectively specify where in the user interface the JPopupMenu should appear. The last two parameters are the x and y coordinates of the upper left-hand corner of the menu, and the first parameter is the component used to interpret the coordinates. In this example, the x and y coordinates are obtained from the MouseEvent object using the `getX` and `getY` methods, respectively, and these coordinates are interpreted with respect to the coordinate system defined by the DrawCanvas itself (denoted by the `this` variable as the first parameter).

Due to the similarity between the pulldown and popup menus, the ColorDelegator class is the same in both version of the DrawTool application. Thus, it is relatively easy to change the menu structure without significantly disturbing the structure of the application that listens for and responds to the events generated by the items in the menu.

Multi-Level Menus

An example of using multi-level menus for the DrawTool application is shown in Figure 7.47 to provide a structured choice among a number of different drawing colors. This figure shows that the main level Color menu offers three submenus, Reds, Blues, and Others, that the user is able to recognize as submenus because of the right-pointing triangule icon at the right edge of the menu. When the cursor is moved over the submenu item, the submenu item is highlighted and the submenu is expanded. In the figure, the Blues submenu is shown expanded. The Blues submenu contains three menu items, two of which (Blue and Cyan) are simple menu items and the last of which, Grays, is another submenu. The Grays submenu contains three simple menu items.

The structure of the Swing class hierarchy facilitiates the easy construction of multi-level menus. The JMenuItem class is a base class from which the JMenu class is derived. This relationship is similar to the one between a Component and a Container in which Container is derived from Component. In the case of the menu classes, the inheritance relationship means that the `add` method of the Menu class can be defined as

```
public void add(JMenuItem item);
```

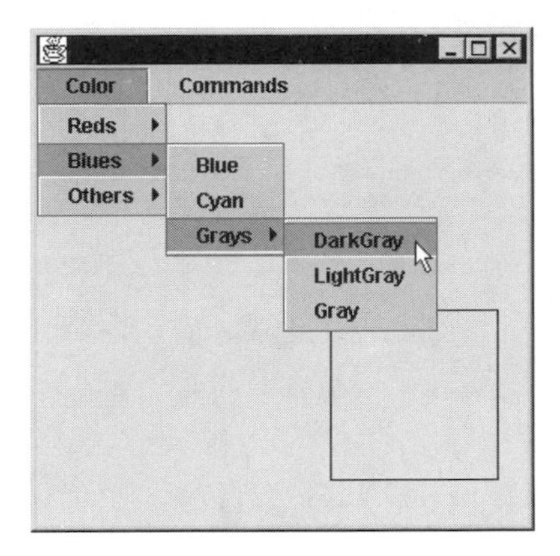

Figure 7.47 Multi-Level Menus in the DrawTool Application

This declaration allows the parameter of the `add` method to be either a simple JMenuItem, such as the Blue and Cyan item in the DrawTool example, or another (sub)Menu, such as the Reds, Blue, and Others. A JMenu can be passed as a parameter to the `add` method because the JMenu parameter can be type cast to a JMenuItem, thus satisfying the type requirements of the `add` method.

The multi-level menus shown above for the DrawTool application are created by the constructor of the DrawFrame class as shown in Figure 7.48. The DrawFrame constructor creates six menus, the first five of which are named Color, Reds, Blues, Grays, and Others. The sixth menu is the Commands menu. Each of these individual menus is created without any multi-level attributes. The four lines of boldface code create the multi-level aspect of the Color menu. The first line adds the Grays menu as an item of the Blues menu, creating the deepest level of the multi-level menu structure. The next three lines add the Reds, Blues, and Grays menus as submenus of the Color menu, creating the first level of the multi-level menu.

The only other change needed in the DrawTool application is a straightforward extension of the ColorDelegator class to recognize the menu items that were added to the Color menu. This extension is shown in Figure 7.49. The extension is straightforward because it is only necessary to incorporate additional `else-if` clauses to deal with the recognition of the individual menu items. Nine such clauses are added to the ColorDelegator class as shown by the boldface code. There is no need to deal with or be aware of the multi-level structure of the menus in the ColorDelegator class. All that the ColorDelegator class knows is that a given menu item has been selected; it is not aware of the menu structure in which this item has embedded. This flexibility is useful because it allows the menu structure of an application to be changed without requiring significant changes in other parts of the application

```
public class DrawFrame extends JFrame implements WindowListener,
                                                 ActionListener
{
  private ColorDelegator colorHandler;

  private void addItem(JMenu menu, String colorName,
                       ActionListener listener)
  { // as before
  }

  public DrawFrame()
  { Container content = this.getContentPane();
    content.setLayout(new BorderLayout());
    this.setLocation(100,100);
    this.setSize(300,300);
    this.addWindowListener(this);

    DrawCanvas canvas = new DrawCanvas();
    colorHandler = new ColorDelegator(canvas);

    JMenu colorMenu = new JMenu("Color");

    JMenu redMenu = new JMenu("Reds");
    addItem(redMenu, "Red",     colorHandler);
    addItem(redMenu, "Pink",    colorHandler);
    addItem(redMenu, "Magenta", colorHandler);
    addItem(redMenu, "Orange",  colorHandler);

    JMenu blueMenu = new JMenu("Blues");
    addItem(blueMenu, "Blue",      colorHandler);
    addItem(blueMenu, "Cyan",      colorHandler);

    JMenu grayMenu = new JMenu("Grays");
    addItem(grayMenu, "DarkGray",  colorHandler);
    addItem(grayMenu, "LightGray", colorHandler);
    addItem(grayMenu, "Gray",      colorHandler);

    JMenu otherMenu = new JMenu("Others");
    addItem(otherMenu, "Green", colorHandler);
    addItem(otherMenu, "White", colorHandler);
    addItem(otherMenu, "Black", colorHandler);

    blueMenu.add(grayMenu);
    colorMenu.add(redMenu);
    colorMenu.add(blueMenu);
    colorMenu.add(otherMenu);

    JMenu commandMenu = new JMenu("Commands");
    addItem(commandMenu, "Clear", canvas);
    addItem(commandMenu, "Quit" , this);

    JMenuBar menuBar = new JMenuBar();
    menuBar.add(colorMenu);
    menuBar.add(commandMenu);
    this.setJMenuBar(menuBar);

    content.add(canvas, BorderLayout.CENTER);
  }

  // WindowEvent methods as before

  // ActionEvent method as before
}
```

Figure 7.48 Constructing Multi-Level Menus

```
public class ColorDelegator implements ActionListener
{
  private DrawCanvas drawingArea;

  public ColorDelegator (DrawCanvas canvas)
  { drawingArea = canvas;
  }

  public void actionPerformed(ActionEvent event)
  { String colorName = event.getActionCommand();

    Color newColor = null;
    if      (colorName.equals("Red"))       newColor = Color.red;
    else if (colorName.equals("Pink"))      newColor = Color.pink;
    else if (colorName.equals("Magenta"))   newColor = Color.magenta;
    else if (colorName.equals("Orange"))    newColor = Color.orange;
    else if (colorName.equals("Blue"))      newColor = Color.blue;
    else if (colorName.equals("Cyan"))      newColor = Color.cyan;
    else if (colorName.equals("DarkGray"))  newColor = Color.darkGray;
    else if (colorName.equals("LightGray")) newColor = Color.lightGray;
    else if (colorName.equals("Gray"))      newColor = Color.gray;
    else if (colorName.equals("Green"))     newColor = Color.green;
    else if (colorName.equals("White"))     newColor = Color.white;
    else if (colorName.equals("Black"))     newColor = Color.black;

    drawingArea.setColor(newColor);
  }

}
```

Figure 7.49 Recognizing Added MenuItems in the ColorDelegator Class

Exercises

1. Modify the DrawTool code using the JPopupMenu to eliminate the `addPopupMenu` method by passing the JPopupMenu created in the DrawFrame as a constructor argument of the DrawCanvas.

2. When the user makes a selection from a popup menu the `show` method returns to its caller and the listener's `actionPerformed` method is called. By instrumenting (i.e., inserting output or other statement in the code) the DrawCanvas class, conduct an experiment to determine if the following hypothesis is true: the `actionPerformed` method is always invoked before the `show` method returns to the caller.

3. Revise the DrawTool application so that the user interface has a single pulldown menu labelled Action that has two menu items labelled Color and Commands. The Color menu item is itself a menu that has

three menu items labelled Reds, Blues, and Others, similar to the interface shown in Figure 7.47. The Commands menu item is itself a menu that contains two entries, one for the cut command and one for the past command.

4. Revise the DrawTool application so that a popup menu can be used to select among one of four actions: move right, more left, move up, and move down. These actions move the rectangle in the drawing area a fixed distance (e.g., 20 units) in the direction indicated.
5. Revise the EditTool application so that the user changes the size of the font used in the editing area by using a pulldown menu labelled Size. The user interface also contains the original buttons for cutting and pasting text.
6. Revise the EditTool application so that it has a menu bar containing two pulldown menus, one menu named Font for selecting the font family and one menu named Size for selecting the size of font. The user interface also contains the original buttons for cutting and pasting text.
7. Revise the EditTool application so that it has a menu bar containing three pulldown menus, labelled Font, Size, and Style that are used to select the font's family, size, and style attributes (italics, bold, etc.), respectively.
8. Revise the EditTool application so that it uses multi-level pulldown menus in the following way. The menu bar contains a single menu labelled Action. The Action menu has two menu items labelled Text and Commands. The Text menu item is itself a menu that has three menu items labelled Font, Size, and Style; each of these is a menu for selecting the family, size, and style attributes. The Commands menu item is itself a menu that contains two entries, one for the cut command and one for the past command.
9. Revise the EditTool application so that the user changes the size of the font used in the editing area by using a popup menu. The user interface also contains the original buttons for cutting and pasting text.
10. Revise the EditTool application so that it has a popup menu containing two menus, one menu named Font for selecting the font family and one menu named Size for selecting the size of font. The user interface also contains the original buttons for cutting and pasting text.
11. Revise the EditTool application so that it has a popup menu containing three menu items labelled Font, Size, and Style that are used to select the font's family, size, and style attributes (italics, bold, etc.), respectively.

12. Revise the EditTool application so that it uses multi-level popup menu in the following way. The popup menu has two menu items labelled Text and Commands. The Text menu item is itself a menu that has three menu items labelled Font, Size, and Style; each of these is a menu for selecting the family, size, and style attributes. The Commands menu item is itself a menu that contains two entries, one for the cut command and one for the past command.

7.7 Checkboxes

7.7.1 Introduction

In this section, the DrawTool application is used to illustrate the use of Swing JCheckboxes that can be used in one of two ways:

JCheckboxes: choosing from among a set of alternatives all of which are visible. The chosen alternative is indicated by a visual annotation (e.g., a filled circle, or a check symbol in a rectangular box, depending on the look and feel chosen). The choice can be constrained so that no more than one is chosen at a time through the use of a ButtonGroup.

JCheckboxMenuItems: including in a pulldown or popup menu entries that appear and act like Checkboxes. When used in a menu the ButtonGroup feature is not available.

Check Boxes

A checkbox is a user interface control that is always in one of two states: selected or unselected. Typically, the state of a checkbox indicates to the application whether a particular option or property has been chosen by the user and should or should not apply in subsequent processing. The default (initial) value of the checkbox may be either checked or unchecked. The user interface checkbox is modelled after the device used on surveys or questionnaires where a circle is filled in or a box is marked with an "X" or a check mark to indicate if a statement is true. Similarly, a visual cue is given in the user interface to indicate whether a checkbox is or is not currently selected. The visual cue may take the form of a filled circle, a checked box, or a diamond-shape that is elevated or depressed. Figure 7.50 shows the appearance of the DrawTool interface using checkboxes for the color selection. Notice that the "Red" checkbox is currently selected.

Checkboxes may be used individually or in groups. When used individually, the checkbox provides a binary choice: the option indicated by the checkbox does or does not apply. For example, in the Netscape browser the user may check a box

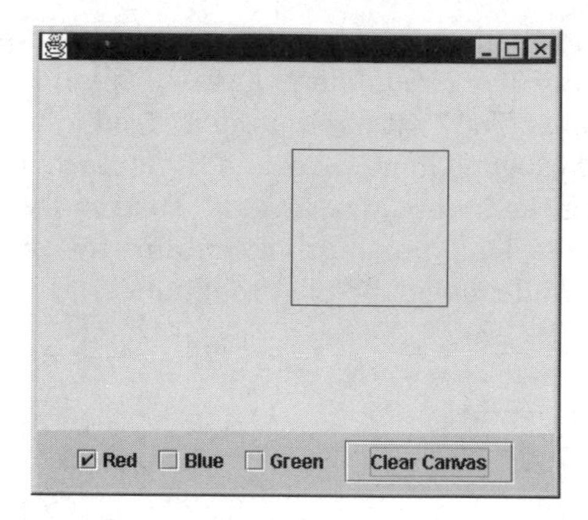

Figure 7.50 DrawTool Interface with Checkboxes

to indicate whether links in the document should be underlined. This is a binary choice. When used in a group, the set of checkboxes provides a many-among-many choice: all of the checkboxes that have been selected apply. For example, many document formatting systems allow the user to specify the properties of the current font—bold, italics, underlined—through a set of checkboxes. The user may check none, one, two, or all of the checkboxes depending on which set of properties are desired. In this example, the user might check both the bold and underlined checkboxes to specify that combination of properties for the current font. The default (initial) value of each individual checkbox may be either checked or unchecked.

When used in groups, the selection among the checkboxes in the group can be restricted to a one-of-many choice when the alternatives are mutual exclusive. For example, a document formatting system may offer the user a set of three checkboxes to indicate if the current text should be left justified, right justified, or centered. Clearly, the choice among these alternatives is mutually exclusive—the text cannot be both centered and left justified, or both right and left justified at the same time. When used in a mutually exclusive group, a set of checkboxes is often referred to as "radio buttons" because the manual station selector buttons on earlier radios enforced a similar mutually exclusive choice. Each of the buttons can be set to a particular radio channel; selecting one channel automatically deselects the previously selected channel because the radio can only be tuned to one channel at a time. A convenience class in Java, ButtonGroup, is used to form a mutually exclusive group of checkboxes. Each checkbox in the group is constructed and manipulated as an individual element by the program. The ButtonGroup itself insures the mutually exclusive selection property.

A JCheckbox object generates an ItemEvent whenever its state changes and a JCheckbox's listener must implement the ItemListener interface. The *table* of listener interfaces (Table 7.5) shows that the ItemListener interface has a single method, `itemStateChanged`. The ButtonGroup does not affect the events generated by the group of checkboxes that it contains. Each individual checkbox generates an event when its state is changed by the user. The ButtonGroup silently maintains the mutual exclusion among the checkboxes.

JCheckboxes and a ButtonGroup are used in the DrawTool application to provide a mutually exlusive choice among the drawing colors. The construction of the JCheckboxes and the ButtonGroup is shown in the DrawFrame constructor in Figure 7.51. The significant code in this constructor is shown in bold. In the first block of code, the ButtonGroup object is created along with three JCheckboxes. The boolean (second) argument on each JCheckbox indicates the initial state of the JCheckbox. In this example, the JCheckbox corresponding to the the color red is initially selected (true) and the JCheckboxes for the other two colors are not selected (false). The third argument on each JCheckbox object indicates which ButtonGroup the JCheckbox should be added to as a member. In the second block of code, the event-handling relationships are established. A ColorDelegator object (`checkboxHandler`) is constructed and this object is registered as a listener with each of the three JCheckboxes. The ColorDelegator uses the delegator event handling pattern to listen for ItemEvents and invoke and appropriate method on the DrawCanvas object that is passed to the ColorDelegator's constructor. Notice that the listener object is added to the JCheckboxes and not to the ButtonGroup because the ButtonGroup does not generate the events, only the JCheckboxes do so. In the third block of code each of the individual JCheckbox objects are added to a JPanel. Because the JPanel is governed by a FlowLayout manager, the JCheckboxes will be arranged in a left-to-right manner. Notice again, that it is the individual JCheckboxes that are added to the Panel, not the ButtonGroup.

The ColorDelegator class in the DrawTool application reflects how the event model adds flexibility to a system's design because the listeners need not be concerned about the exact type of the object generating the event. The ColorDelegator implements the ItemListener interface and is concerned only with processing ItemEvents regardless of the source of these events. The ColorDelegator code, repeated in Figure 7.52 for reference, is used unchanged in the original DrawTool example where it processed ItemEvents from a JComboBox component and in the current DrawTool example where it processes ItemEvents from a set of JCheckbox components. The same ColorDelegator could also be used with a JCheckboxMenuItem that also generates ItemEvents.

Checkbox Menu Items

Menus may also contain items that have the persistent state of a JCheckbox. These special menu items are defined in the JCheckboxMenuItem class. Like a JCheckbox, these menu items represent a condition or preference that is enabled or disabled. The CheckboxMenuItem objects are like other menu item objects in that they can be added to a popup or pulldown menu.

```
import java.awt.*;
import java.awt.event.*;
import javax.swing.*;
import javax.swing.ButtonGroup;
import DrawCanvas;
import ClearButton;
import ColorDelegator;

public class DrawFrame extends JFrame implements WindowListener
{
  private ColorDelegator checkboxHandler;

  public DrawFrame()
  { Container content = this.getContentPane();
    content.setLayout(new BorderLayout());
    this.setLocation(100,100);
    this.setSize(300,300);
    this.addWindowListener(this);

    ButtonGroup colorGroup = new ButtonGroup();
    JCheckBox redCheckBox   = new JCheckBox("Red",   true );
    JCheckBox blueCheckBox  = new JCheckBox("Blue",  false);
    JCheckBox greenCheckBox = new JCheckBox("Green", false);
    colorGroup.add(redCheckBox);
    colorGroup.add(blueCheckBox);
    colorGroup.add(greenCheckBox);

    ClearButton clearButton = new ClearButton();

    DrawCanvas canvas = new DrawCanvas(clearButton);

    checkboxHandler = new ColorDelegator(canvas);
    redCheckBox.addItemListener(checkboxHandler);
    blueCheckBox.addItemListener(checkboxHandler);
    greenCheckBox.addItemListener(checkboxHandler);

    JPanel panel = new JPanel();
    panel.setLayout(new FlowLayout());
    panel.add(redCheckBox);
    panel.add(blueCheckBox);
    panel.add(greenCheckBox);
    panel.add(clearButton);

    content.add(canvas, BorderLayout.CENTER);
    content.add(panel, BorderLayout.SOUTH);
  }

  // implement WindowListener methods as before

}
```

Figure 7.51 Constructing a ButtonGroup and Checkboxes

```
public class ColorDelegator implements ItemListener
{
  private DrawCanvas drawingArea;

  public ColorDelegator (DrawCanvas canvas)
  { drawingArea = canvas;
  }

  public void itemStateChanged(ItemEvent event)
  { String colorName = (String)event.getItem();

    Color newColor;
    if      (colorName.equals("Red"))   newColor = Color.red;
    else if (colorName.equals("Green")) newColor = Color.green;
    else                                newColor = Color.blue;

    drawingArea.setColor(newColor);
  }

}
```

Figure 7.52 Reusing the ColorDelegator to Handle Checkbox Events

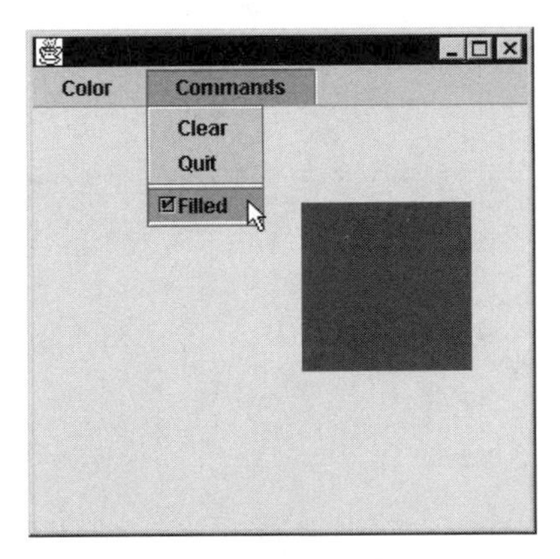

Figure 7.53 Checkbox MenuItem Appearance

In the DrawTool application, a new option will be introduced to illustrate the use and operation of CheckboxMenuItems. The new option determines whether the Rectangle will be drawn filled or unfilled. The previous examples of the DrawTool application used only an unfilled rectangle. A filled rectangle and the appearance of a JCheckboxMenuItem are shown in Figure 7.53. The Commands menu's last item is a JCheckboxMenuItem named Filled, which is pictured in the "checked", or selected, state as denoted by the check symbol in front of the item. The current state of the JCheckboxMenuItem is indicated in the user interface by the presence or absence of the "check" mark. The state of a JCheckboxMenuItem can be queried by the program using the `getState` method of the JCheckboxMenuItem which returns a boolean value.

```
public class DrawFrame extends JFrame implements WindowListener,
                                                 ActionListener
{
  private ColorDelegator colorHandler;

  private void addItem(JMenu menu, String colorName,
                       ActionListener listener)
  { JMenuItem nextItem = new JMenuItem(colorName);
    nextItem.setActionCommand(colorName);
    nextItem.addActionListener(listener);
    menu.add(nextItem);
  }

  public DrawFrame()
  { //...

    DrawCanvas canvas = new DrawCanvas();
    colorHandler = new ColorDelegator(canvas);

    JMenu colorMenu = new JMenu("Color");
    // construct Color Menu

    JMenu commandMenu = new JMenu("Commands");
    addItem(commandMenu, "Clear", canvas);
    addItem(commandMenu, "Quit" , this);

    commandMenu.addSeparator();

    JCheckBoxMenuItem filledItem = new JCheckBoxMenuItem("Filled");
    filledItem.addItemListener(canvas);
    commandMenu.add(filledItem);

    JMenuBar menuBar = new JMenuBar();
    menuBar.add(colorMenu);
    menuBar.add(commandMenu);
    this.setMenuBar(menuBar);

    content.add(canvas, BorderLayout.CENTER);
  }

  // WindowListner methods

}
```

Figure 7.54 Adding a CheckboxMenuItem

The Command menu uses a menu separator to indicate logical groups of menu items. In this case, the separator divides the two action-oriented items (clear the display and quit the application) from the option-oriented menu item (whether the rectangle is filled).

The code to create a menu containing a separator and a JCheckboxMenu-Item is shown in the DrawFrame constructor in Figure 7.54. Adding a separator simply involves using the `addSeparator` method. The Command menu adds the two action-oriented items, Clear and Quit, and then inserts the separator. Like other menu items, a JCheckboxMenuItem is constructed with a String value

```
public class DrawCanvas extends JComponent implements ItemListener,
                                                      ActionListener,
                                                      MouseListener,
                                                      MouseMotionListener
{
  private Rectangle rectangle;
  private Color currentColor;

  //...

  // MouseListener and MouseMotionListener methods

  // ActionListener method

  public void itemStateChanged(ItemEvent event)
  { JCheckBoxMenuItem item = (JCheckBoxMenuItem)event.getSource();
    Rectangle.setFilled(item.getState());
    repaint();
  }

}
```

Figure 7.55 Handling ItemEvents from the JCheckBoxMenuItem

that is the name that appears in the menu and is added to the menu using the JMenu's `add` method. Unlike other JMenuItems, but like a JCheckbox, the JCheckboxMenuItem generates an ItemEvent when its state is changed. In the DrawTool code, the DrawCanvas is added as a listener for the ItemEvents generated by the Filled JCheckboxMenuItem.

The DrawCanvas class is modified to implement the ItemListener interface so that it can listen for the ItemEvents that are generated by changes in state of the Filled menu item. The `itemStateChanged` method is defined in the DrawCanvas to satisfy the requirements of the ItemListener interface. In this method, the source of the ItemEvent is extracted from the ItemEvent object. Because the `getSource` method returns its value as a type Object, this value is type cast to a JCheckboxMenuItem.This type cast is safe because in the structure of this program the only source of ItemEvents is the JCheckboxMenuItem in the Commands menu. The `getState` method is used to determine the current state of the JCheckboxMenuItem—a true state means that the item is now checked and a false state means that the item is now not checked. The boolean value returned by the `getState` method is passed to a new method added to the Rectangle class to reflect whether the Rectangle should be drawn as filled (true) or unfilled (false). Notice that the method is applied to the Rectangle class name and not to a Rectangle object. This is necessary beause it is possible for the user to set the filled/unfilled option before creating any Rectangle objects. The filled/unfilled property is a "class property" and not an "object property," class properties are defined in Java by static variables and methods as shown in the Rectangle class in Figure 7.55.

```
import java.awt.*;

public class Rectangle
{
  private static boolean filled = false;

  private int x;
  private int y;

  //...

  public static void setFilled(boolean state)
  { filled = state;
  }

  public void draw(Graphics g)
  { if (filled)
         g.fillRect(x,y,100,100);
    else
         g.drawRect(x,y, 100,100);
  }
}
```

Figure 7.56 The Modified Rectangle Class

The modified Rectangle class contains a new class property represented by the boolean state variable `filled` and an new method, `setFilled`, to change this property. The `filled` variable is defined as a private variable so that it can be directly accessed only by objects of the Rectangle class. The `filled` variable is also declared as a static variable to reflect that it is a class property—a value shared by all objects of the Rectangle class. The `setFilled` method simply changes the `filled` value to whatever boolean state is indicated by the method's parameter. Finally, the `draw` method uses the value of `filled` to determine whether to draw the rectangle as unfilled, using `drawRect`, or filled, using `fillRect` (Figure 7.56).

Exercises

1. Modify the EditTool application so that JCheckboxes and a Button-Group are used to allow the user to select the size of the current font from among three choices.

2. Modify the EditTool application so that JCheckboxes and a Button-Group are used to allow the user to select the family of the current font from among three choices.

3. Modify the EditTool application so that JCheckboxMenuItems are used to allow the user to select in a menu the bold and italics options

for the current font. Notice that these options may be selected individually or both may be selected at the same time.

4. Modify the EditTool application so that JCheckboxMenuItems are used to allow the user to select the size of the current font from among three choices. Be sure that your application allows only one of the three choices to be in effect at a time and that the user interface correctly shows which size is currently in effect.
5. Modify the EditTool application so that JCheckboxMenuItems are used to allow the user to select the family of the current font from among three choices. Be sure that your application allows only one of the three choices to be in effect at a time and that the user interface correctly shows which size is currently in effect.
6. Modify the DrawTool version that uses JCheckboxMenuItems by adding two additional JCheckboxMenuItems named "Wide" and "Tall". When neither of these items is selected the rectangle is drawn as a 100 by 100 rectangle. When "Wide" is selected alone the rectangle is drawn as a 200 by 100 rectangle. When "Tall" is selected alone the rectangle is drawn as a 100 by 200 rectangle. When both items are selected, the size of the rectangle is 200 by 200.

7.8 Lists

A Swing list allows the user to select one or more entries from a scrollable linear list. A list is useful in those cases where the number of list entries is large enough that it is not convenient to display all of them at one time. The list display allows a specified number of items to be viewed at one time, other being made visible as the list is scrolled. The list is scrolled by a moveable control in the right margin of the list. Moving the control toward the top of its vertical track displays those items toward the front of the list and moving the control toward the bottom displays items toward the end of the list. An item in the display portion of the list is selected by clicking on it. The currently selected item in a list is highlighted. If a list permits it, a contiguous set of list items may be simultaneously selected. All of the items in a selected contiguous set are highlighted.

The DrawTool application is modified to use a list whose entries are the names of colors used in drawing the rectangle. Figure 7.57 shows the appearance of the list control. The list is shown at the bottom of the drawing area, to the left of the Clear button. The list is constructed so that four list entries can be seen at the same time. The list's movable controls are arranged verticaly in the right margin of the list. When clicked, the upward-and downward-pointing arrowheads at the top and bottom of the control move the visual portion of the list for-

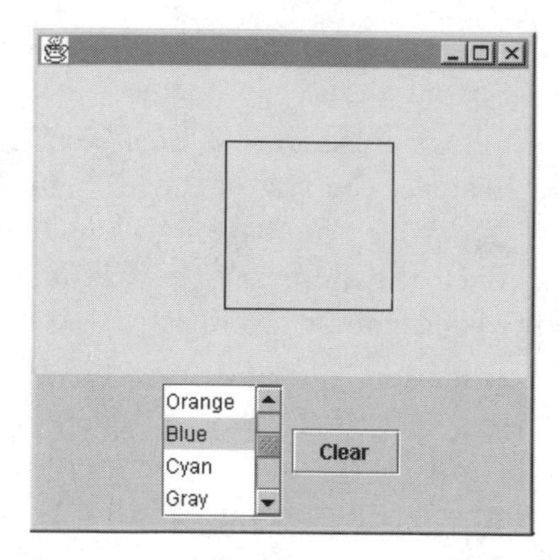

Figure 7.57 A List in the DrawTool Application

ward or backward, respectively, by one entry. The sliding part of the control, which is the small box located between the two arrowheads, can be dragged upward or downward to move the visual portion of the list by larger amounts. The areas between the sliding part and the arrowhead can also be clicked to move the list. As shown in Figure 7.57, the currently selected color is Blue.

The code for creating a list and establishing a listener for its events is given in the DrawFrame class shown in Figure 7.58. The code related to the list is shown in boldface. First, the list constructor argument is an array of strings. These strings are the entires that appear in the list. Their order of appearance in the list is the same as their subscript ordering in the array. The number of list elements visible at any one time is specified by the `setVisibleRowCount` method. In this example, only four items at a time are visible. The `setSelectionMode` method is used to indicate whether one or multiple entries may be selected at one time. The named constant `SINGLE_SELECTION` defined in the ListSelectionModel class is used in this example because only one color at a time should be selected as it is not possible to draw the rectangle in more than one color at a time. The code in Figure 7.58 also shows that the ColorDelegator is registered with the List `colorList` as an ActionListener.

The ColorDelegator, shown in Figure 7.59, implements the listener for the events generated by the list defined in Figure 7.58. This class defines a `valueChanged` method to satisfy the requirement of the ListSelection interface. The critical code in this method is shown in boldface in Figure 7.59. The steps in the `valueChanged` method are as follows. The method retrieves from the ListSelectionEvent the JList object that is the source of the event. The currently selected value of the JList is then obtained from the JList and converted to a String that is compared against all of the list's entries. The matching comparison defines the value of the variable `newColor` that is subsequently passed to the DrawingArea by the `setColor` method.

```
public class DrawFrame extends JFrame implements WindowListener
{
  private ColorDelegator colorHandler;

  public DrawFrame()
  { Container content = this.getContentPane();
    content.setLayout(new BorderLayout());
    this.setLocation(100,100);
    this.setSize(300,300);
    this.addWindowListener(this);

    DrawCanvas canvas = new DrawCanvas();
    colorHandler = new ColorDelegator(canvas);

    String[] colors = {
      "Red"",
      "Pink"",
      "Magenta",
      "Orange",
      "Blue",
      "Cyan",
      "Gray",
      "LightGray",
      "DarkGray",
      "Green",
      "White",
      "Black"};
    JList colorList = new JList(colors);
    colorList.setVisibleRowCount(4);
    colorList.setSelectionMode(ListSelectionModel.SINGLE_SELECTION);

    colorList.addListSelectionListener(colorHandler); // add listener

    JButton clearButton = new JButton("Clear");
    clearButton.addActionListener(canvas);

    JPanel controls = new JPanel();
    controls.setLayout(new FlowLayout());

    controls.add(colorList);
    controls.add(clearButton);

    content.add(canvas, BorderLayout.CENTER);
    content.add(controls, BorderLayout.SOUTH);

  }

  // WindowListener methods
}
```

Figure 7.58 Creating a List and Its Listener

```
import java.awt.*;
import javax.swing.*;
import javax.swing.event.*;
import DrawCanvas;

public class ColorDelegator implements ListSelectionListener
{
  private DrawCanvas drawingArea;

  public ColorDelegator (DrawCanvas canvas)
  { drawingArea = canvas;
  }

  public void valueChanged(ListSelectionEvent event)
  { Object value = ((JList)event.getSource()).getSelectedValue();
    if (value != null) {
      String colorName = value.toString();

      Color newColor = null;
      if      (colorName.equals("Red"))       newColor = Color.red;
      else if (colorName.equals("Pink"))      newColor = Color.pink;
      else if (colorName.equals("Magenta"))   newColor = Color.magenta;
      //.. other cases
    }
    drawingArea.setColor(newColor);
  }
}
```

Figure 7.59 Listening for ListSelectionEvents from a List

Exercises

1. Revise the DrawTool application by adding another list for selecting the background color. The list should show only two colors at any one time.

2. Revise the DrawTool application so that the rectangle can be moved by a user interface designed as follows. Two lists allow the user to specify a direction (up, down, left, right) and an amount (5, 10, 15, etc., up to 100) in pixels. When a "move" button is pushed, the rectangle is moved according to the currently selected values of the two lists.

3. Revise the DrawTool application so that the "clear" and "quit" commands are selected from a list and an "execute" button that performs the currently selected command. The list should show only the currently selected command.

4. Revise the EditTool application so that a list is used to select the family for the current font.

5. Revise the EditTool application so that a list is used to select the size for the current font.

7.9 Dialogues

A dialogue is a structured interaction through which an application provides information to or solicits information from the user. A dialogue is structured in the sense that there is a pattern to the interaction that guides its progress. Dialogues familiar to most computer users include login dialogues through which username and password are obtained by a system; file selection dialogues where the user is able to select the file to be used by an application for some purpose; error reporting dialogues that convey information about an abnormal event to the user and possibly allows the user to select among various remedies; information or help dialogues used by a system to provide guidance or suggestions to the user; and confirmation dialogues where the system asks the user to acknowledge that the effects of an irreversible operation are understood and truly intended. Some of these forms will be illustrated by the examples below.

A dialogue may be either modal or non-modal. A modal dialogue is one in which the dialogue must be completed before the application is free to take any other action. In some cases, a modal dialogue is required by the nature of the application. For example, an application that is going to read from a file needs the user to complete the file selection dialogue before the application can do anything else. In other cases, a modal dialogue is a design decision made to focus the user's attention. For example, a confirmation dialogue may be made modal if it asks the user to confirm that a large number of files will be deleted, insuring that the user must focus on the implications of an operation. Non-modal dialogues are used when the normal operation of the application can proceed in parallel with the dialogue. A non-modal help dialogue allows the user to see the help information displayed by the dialogue at the same time the user is performing the operation for which help was requested.

Dialogues are programmed in Swing using the JDialog class and the JOptionPane class. The JDialog class provides a general-purpose mechanism for constructing and managing a dialogue. The JOptionPane class provides a number of easier to use, predefined options for commonly occurring dialogues, such as a simple "yes-no" dialogue in which only one of two responses is solicited from the user. This section first examines the JDialog class as it is used to contruct a specialized dialogue for the DrawTool application. The end of the section gives a brief overview of the predefined dialogues that can be constructed using the JOptionPane class.

7.9.1 The JDialog Class

A general purpose dialogue in Swing is supported by the JDialog class, whose partial description is shown in Figure 7.60. This figure also shows the other classes from which JDialog inherits important properties or methods. The Dialog class, an AWT component, defines the title and modal properties of the dialogue and provides accessor methods to examine and change these properties. This class also contains the **show** method that exposes the dialogue to the user and suspends activity outside of the dialogue itself until the dialogue is completed. The Dialog class extends the Window class so that the user interface presented by the dialogue (sometimes called the "dialogue box") will appear as an independent window on the user's display. Because the Window class extends Container, the JDialog can be assigned a layout manager and components can be added to the Dialog's **contentPane** to create a user interface for the dialogue. Finally, because the Container class extends the Component class, the **setVisible** method is inherited by the JDialog class. This method is used to make the dia-

```
public class JDialog extends Dialog      // Swing component
{
   public JDialog()
   public JDialog (Frame parent)
   public JDialog (Frame parent, boolean modal)
   public JDialog (Frame parent, String title)
   public JDialog (Frame parent, String title, boolean modal)

   //...
}

public class Dialog extends Window       // AWT component
{
   // set and get methods for title, modal, resizeable attributes
   public void show()
}

public class Window extends Container
{
   public void pack()
   public void dispose()
   //...
}

public class Container extends Component
{
  // allows a layout manager to be associated with the dialog
}

public class Component
{
   public void setVisible(boolean onoff)
   //...
}
```

Figure 7.60 The JDialog Class

logue appear and disappear from the user's display. The JDialog constructors, except the first one, specifies a parent window with which the dialogue is associated so that if the parent window is destroyed the dialogue's window will also be destroyed. For the first constructor, an invisible parent window is created automatically. The constructor's other parameters specify the the text string, **`title`**, that will appear as the title of the dialogue window (usually at the top of the window), and the boolean **`modal`** value that determines whether the dialogue is modal (**`true`**) or non-modal (**`false`**). Two methods in the Window class are also important in dealing with dialogues. The **`pack`** method, inherited by a Dialog object from the Window class, must be called in order to initiate the action of the LayoutManager associated with the Dialog. The **`dispose`** method releases the resources associated with the window and should be called when the dialogue is completed. The use of these methods will be illustrated in the example code later in this section.

A Modal Dialogue

The DrawTool application is redesigned to use a modal dialogue for changing the drawing color. This design assumes that changing the drawing color is an infrequent operation. Thus, it is acceptable to remove the color selection controls from the main interface and "recall" those controls via the dialogue only when they are needed. In a complex user interface—one with tens of controls and hundreds of options Ñ dialogues are often used to structure the user interface so that only the more frequently used controls are always visible. The redesigned DrawTool user interface, shown in Figure 7.61, includes a button labelled "Change Color" that initiates the dialogue to select a new drawing color. This dialogue will be modal; the user must complete the dialogue before any other action in the DrawTool user interface are possible. The "Clear Canvas" button has the same use as previously.

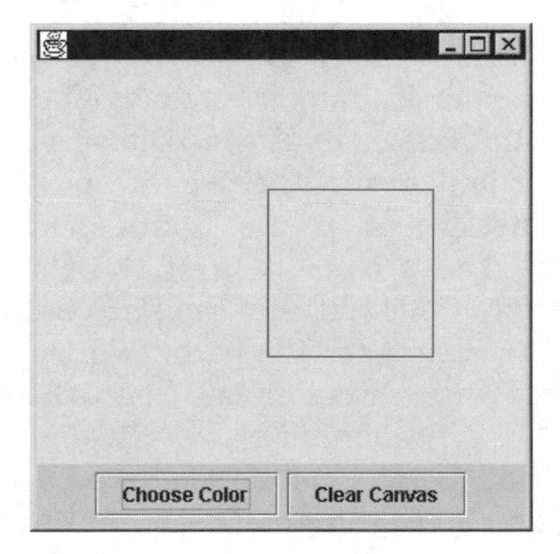

Figure 7.61 Redesigned DrawTool User Interface

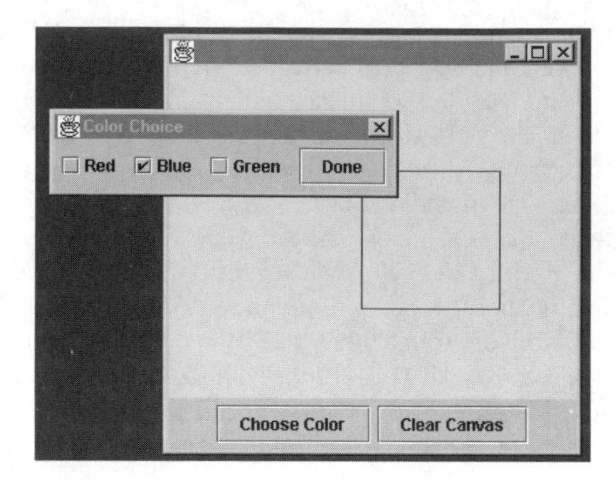

Figure 7.62 The Choose Color Dialog Box

The dialogue box that appears when the user must press the "Choose Color" button is shown in Figure 7.62. The dialogue box is a separate, independent window that can be moved around on the screen; it can be resized (unless it is explicitly constructed so that it cannot be resized) and it can be dismissed (note the dismiss control in the upper right-hand corner of the dialogue's window. Also notice that the top part of the dialogue's window has the title "Color Choice". This string is specified as the `title` of the window when the Dialog object is constructed. While the dialogue box is visible the user may select a new drawing color through the dialogue's supplied interface, in this case a set of CheckBoxes allowing only one choice at a time to be selected. To complete the dialogue, the user must press the "Done" button. The drawing color is only changed when the dialogue is completed by the user pressing the "Done" button. Thus, the user may check and uncheck the CheckBoxes many times, but only the CheckBox selected at the time the "Done" button is pushed has any effect on the drawing color. Of course, this could be designed differently (see the exercises).

The DrawTool dialogue is implemented by the ColorChoiceDialog class shown in Figure 7.63. This class extends the JDialog class because it is a specialization of JDialog and it implements the two interfaces necessary for it to serve as a listener for the JCheckBoxes' events (ItemListener) and the Done button's events (ActionListener). The private data of the class records the currently selected color (initialized to Color.red) and the DrawCanvas whose drawing color it can change. The constructor takes the parent window (this will be the DrawTool's main window) and the DrawCanvas. The JDialog constructor is called using the `super(....)`. In addition to the parent window, the JDialog constructor is given the title ("Color Choice"), and the boolean `true` value making the dialogue modal. After establishing a FlowLayout as the layout manager, the user interface of the color choice dialogue is constructed. Notice that the ColorChoiceDialog establishes itself as the listener for the JCheckBox events and the

```
public class ColorChoiceDialog extends JDialog implements ItemListener,
                                                          ActionListener

{
  private DrawCanvas drawingArea;
  private Color selectedColor;

  public ColorChoiceDialog(DrawFrame parent, DrawCanvas canvas)
  { super(parent, "Color Choice", true);
    drawingArea = canvas;
    selectedColor = Color.red;

    Container content = this.getContentPane();
    content.setLayout(new FlowLayout());

    ButtonGroup colorGroup = new ButtonGroup();
    JCheckBox redCheckBox   = new JCheckBox("Red",   true);
    JCheckBox blueCheckBox  = new JCheckBox("Blue",  false);
    JCheckBox greenCheckBox = new JCheckBox("Green", false);
    colorGroup.add(redCheckBox);
    colorGroup.add(blueCheckBox);
    colorGroup.add(greenCheckBox);

    redCheckBox.addItemListener(this);
    blueCheckBox.addItemListener(this);
    greenCheckBox.addItemListener(this);

    JButton selectionMade = new JButton("Done");
    selectionMade.addActionListener(this);

    content.add(redCheckBox);
    content.add(blueCheckBox);
    content.add(greenCheckBox);
    content.add(selectionMade);

    this.pack();
  }

  public void itemStateChanged(ItemEvent event)
  { String colorName = ((JCheckBox)event.getItem()).getText();

    if      (colorName.equals("Red"))   selectedColor = Color.red;
    else if (colorName.equals("Green")) selectedColor = Color.green;
    else                                selectedColor = Color.blue;

  }

  public void actionPerformed(ActionEvent event)
  { drawingArea.setColor(selectedColor);
    setVisible(false);
    dispose();
  }

}
```

Figure 7.63 The ColorChoiceDialog Class

events from the "Done" button. The three check boxes and the "Done" button are added to the dialogue's user interface. Finally, the `pack` method is called (recall

```
public class DrawFrame extends JFrame implements WindowListener,
                                                 ActionListener
{
  private DrawCanvas canvas;

  public DrawFrame()
  { //...

    ClearButton clearButton = new ClearButton();
    canvas = new DrawCanvas(clearButton);

    JButton choiceButton = new JButton("Choose Color");
    choiceButton.addActionListener(this);

    JPanel panel = new JPanel();
    panel.setLayout(new FlowLayout());
    panel.add(choiceButton);
    panel.add(clearButton);

    content.add(canvas, BorderLayout.CENTER);
    content.add(panel, BorderLayout.SOUTH);
  }

  public void actionPerformed (ActionEvent event)
  { ColorChoiceDialog dialog = new ColorChoiceDialog(this, canvas);
    dialog.show();
  }
}
```

Figure 7.64 Creating and Initiating the ColorChoiceDialog

that this method is inherited from the Window class) to initiate the action of the LayoutManger.

In the ColorChoiceDialog class, the events generated by the CheckBoxes are handled by the `itemStateChanged` method and the event generated by the "Done" Button is handled by the `actionPerformed` method. The itemState-Changed method simply converts the CheckBoxes string to the corresponding color and updates the class variable `selectedColor`. The `actionPerformed` method sets the drawing color of the DrawCanvas with which it is associated and then terminates the dialogue by making itself invisible (the `hide` method) and reclaiming the resources allocated for its window (the `dispose` method). Calling the `dispose` method signals that the dialogue is completed and that the Draw-Tool application can resume processing its own events.

The final changes in the DrawTool application are in the DrawFrame class. These changes are shown in Figure 7.64. The DrawFrame creates two buttons and a drawing area. Recall that the DrawCanvas listens for the event generated by the ClearButton. The DrawFrame registers itself as a listener for the Action-Events generated by the "Choose Color" button.When the "Choose Color" button is pushed, the `actionPerformed` method reacts by creating a new ColorChoice-Dialog and invoking the `show` method on the ColorChoiceDialog object. The `show` method, inherited from the Dialog class, makes the JDialog's window visible and blocks the invoker (the DrawFrame object) from proceeding until the dialogue is complete (i.e., until the Dialog window no longer exists). As was seen above, the ColorChoiceDialog will `dispose` of itself when the user presses the dialogue's "Done" button. Thus, after the "Done" button is pressed, the `actionPerformed` method will return and the DrawFrame can continue.

A Non-Modal Dialogue

A non-modal dialogue allows the user to interact with the main application while the dialogue is in progress. A non-modal dialogue allows the effects of the dialogue to be made visible in the application's interface while the dialogue takes place. This allows the user to observe the effects of options and settings, possibly changing them in light of their effect. In the DrawTool case, making the ColorChoiceDialog non-modal means that the user will be able to see the drawing color change immediately when a new color is selected during the dialogue. In some settings, it might be easier to think about non-modal dialogues as a pallette or toolbar rather than as dialogues. In the non-modal version of DrawTool, this point of view would consider the ColorChoiceDialog as a "color pallette" or "color toolbar." In these terms, the "dialogue" window is simply a detached part of the user interface that the user can show, hide, and move around on the screen as convient for the user.

The changes in the DrawTool code to use a non-modal dialogue are few. The changes to the ColorChoiceDialog are shown in Figure 7.65. The first change is

```
public class ColorChoiceDialog extends JDialog implements ItemListener,
                                                           ActionListener
{
  private DrawCanvas drawingArea;

  public ColorChoiceDialog(DrawFrame parent, DrawCanvas canvas)
  { super(parent, "Color Choice", false);

    //.. same as in modal case
  }

  public void itemStateChanged(ItemEvent event)
  { String colorName = ((JCheckBox)event.getItem()).getText();

    Color selectedColor = Color.red;

         if (colorName.equals("Green")) selectedColor = Color.green;
    else if (colorName.equals("Blue"))  selectedColor = Color.blue;

    drawingArea.setColor(selectedColor);
  }

  public void actionPerformed(ActionEvent event)
  { setVisible(false);
    dispose();
  }
}
```

Figure 7.65 A Non-Modal Dialgoue in the DrawTool Application

```
public class DrawFrame extends JFrame implements WindowListener,
                                                   ActionListener
{
  private DrawCanvas canvas;
  private boolean dialogVisible = false;

  //...

  public void actionPerformed (ActionEvent event)
  { if (!dialogVisible)
      { ColorChoiceDialog dialog = new ColorChoiceDialog(this, canvas);
        dialog.show();
        dialogVisible = true;
      }
  }

  public void dialogDone()
  { dialogVisible = false;
  }
  //...
}

public class ColorChoiceDialog extends JDialog implements ItemListener,
                                                           ActionListener
{
  private DrawCanvas drawingArea;
  private DrawFrame  drawFrame;

  public ColorChoiceDialog(DrawFrame parent, DrawCanvas canvas)
  { super(parent, "Color Choice", false);
    drawingArea = canvas;
    drawFrame = parent;

    //...
  }

  //...

  public void actionPerformed(ActionEvent event)
  { drawFrame.dialogDone();
    setVisible(false);
    dispose();
  }
}
```

Figure 7.66 Avoiding Duplicate ColorChangeDialog Windows

that the JDialog class constructor, using the `super(...)` notation, uses the `false` value as the last parameter, indicating that the dialogue is not modal. The second change is that in the `itemStateChanged` method, the selected color is immediately forwarded to the DrawCanvas by calling its `setColor` method. The invocation of the `setColor` method was previously done when the user terminated the dialogue by pressing the "Done" button. One things to note is that the appearance of the ColorChoiceDialog on the display has not changed, it still has the same three JCheckBoxes and the "Done" button. What has changed is the way the dialogue box works; it immediately reflects in the drawing area the selection made in the dialogue box.

One, perhaps unexpected, result of using the non-modal dialogue as structured above is that it is possible to have two or more ColorChoiceDialog windows visible and active at the same time. This can be caused simply by pressing the "Change Color" button in the DrawFrame window several times. Each time that the button is pressed another ColorChoiceDialog is created. Because the dialogues are non-modal, invoking the `show` method on each ColorChoiceDialog does not block the DrawTool application. In the DrawTool case this is harmless, though unintended. In other user interfaces it may be important to insure that the dialogue is in progress at most once. To insure that at most one ColorChoice-Dialog window is visible at any time, two small changes are needed in the Draw-Frame class and the ColorChoiceDialog class. The relevant code for both of these classes are shown together in Figure 7.66. In the DrawFrame class, a boolean variable, `dialogVisible`, is added so that the DrawFrame object is able to keep track of whether a dialogue has already been created. The DrawFrame only creates a new ColorChoiceDialog when one is not already visible (i.e., when `dialogVisible` is `false`) and changes `dialogVisible` to `true`. In addition, the DrawFrame must be informed when the dialogue is finished so that the `dailogVisible` variable can be reset to `false`. For this purpose, a new method, `dialogDone`, is added. An invocation of this method is placed in the termination code for the ColorChoiceDialog. To be able to invoke the dialogDone method, the ColorChoiceDialog object must retain a reference to the DrawFrame object that created it. This is also shown in the bold code in the ColorChoiceDialog class.

7.9.2 The JOptionPane Class

Many user interfaces require simple dialogues that have a common structure across many applications. To simplify the programming of these commonly occurring dialogues, the JOptionPane class defines a simplified way of constructing and using four dialogue types. These four dialogue types are summarized in Table 7.6. Simple examples of the first three of these types of dialogues are described below. The JOptionPane class contains a set of static methods by which each type of dialogue can be shown the user. The standard declaration of these static methods is:

```
public static result showTYPEDialog(parameters)
```

where *TYPE* is the type of the dialogue being created and *parameters* define optional information about the content and structure of the specified dialogue type. The parameters often include defined constants describing particular options of each dialogue. These constants are shown in the code example below. The *result* value returned by the method allows the program to determine what

Table 7.6 JOptionPane Dialogue Types

Input	Solicits input through a text field, list, or other means and also includes buttons for "OK" and "Cancel" to complete or dismiss the dialogue
Confirm	Asks the user a question usually confirming an action that will be taken and includes buttons such as "Yes" and "No"
Message	Displays a simple message to the user and includes an "OK" button to dismiss the dialogue
Option	Displays a list of buttons to the user by which a selection is made

information the user supplied to the dialogue. The result type is either void, if no input from the user is expected, a String, if the user typed in data, or an int, if a button or option was selected.

The confirm dialogue is the simplest of the four types. This type of dialogue shows a message to the user and provides buttons by which the user can confirm that a given action (usually with significant consequences) should be taken. For example, a confirm dialogue could be added to the DrawTool application to confirm that the user really wants to quit the application. This dialogue can be created as follows:

```
int result = JOptionPane.showConfirmDialog(parent, "Really Quit DrawTool?", "Quit Confirmation",
                                           JOptionPane.YES_NO_CANCEL_OPTION);
```

where the first parameter specifies the parent component with which this dialogue is associated, the next two strings define the question placed inside the dialogue window and the title of the window, and the final parameter defines which buttons the dialogue presents to the user for answering the question. In this case, the dialogue window will contain three buttons labelled "Yes", "No", and "Cancel". The result returned by the method indicates how the user responded to the dialogue. The possible replies are shown in Table 7.7.

A simple message dialogue is used to provide information to the user where no feedback from the user is needed. Such a dialogue can be created as follows:

```
JOptionPane.showMessageDialog(parent, "This is DrawTool", "About Dialog",
                              JOptionPane.PLAIN_MESSAGE);
```

where the first parameter specifies the parent component with which this dialogue is associated, the first string defines the information placed inside the dialogue window, the second string specifies the title of the window, and the final

Table 7.7 Returned Results from JOptionPane Dialogues

YES_OPTION	The user pressed the "Yes" button
NO_OPTION	The user pressed the "No" button
CANCEL_OPTION	The user pressed the "Cancel" button
OK_OPTION	The user pressed the "OK" button
CLOSED_OPTION	The user closed the dialogue's window without pressing any of the supplied buttons

Table 7.8 JOptionPane Dialogue Options

PLAIN_MESSAGE	Do not include any icon
WARNING_MESSAGE	Include a warning icon
QUESTION_MESSAGE	Include a question icon
INFORMATION_MESSAGE	Include an information icon
ERROR_MESSAGE	Include an error icon
WARNING_MESSAGE	Include a warning icon

parameter defines a type of message that can be interpreted by the user interface's prevailing look and feel. The `PLAIN_MESSAGE` parameter specifies that no icon should be used in the dialgoue window. The other options specify what type of look and feel dependent icon should appear in the window. The complete set of options that can be specified are listed in Table 7.8.

An input dialogue solicits simple text information from the user in the form of a list from which the user can select an item or a field in which the user can type. An input dialogue can be used in the DrawTool application to allow the user to select the drawing color. This input dialogue can be created as follows:

```
String result = JOptionPane(parent, "Select the drawing color:", "Color Selection"
                JOptionPane.QUESTION_MESSAGE, null, new Object[] {"red", "green",
                "blue"}, "red");
```

where the first four parameters are the same as in the earlier examples. The next to the last parameter defines an array of strings that are used to construct a list from which the user can select. The default value initially highlighted in this list is the last parameter. The dialogue also includes "OK" and "Cancel" buttons. The returned result conveys which list item was selected by the user.

Exercises

1. Change the modal DrawTool application so that the dismiss control on the Color Choice dialogue box is active. When the window is dismissed, the window should disappear but no change should be made to the drawing color.

2. Change the modal DrawTool application so that using the dismiss control and pressing the Done button have the same effect.

3. Change the modal DrawTool application so that the change in the drawing color is made as soon as a CheckBox is selected in the dialogue window.

4. Add another layer of dialogue to the modal DrawTool application. When the user presses the "Done" button in the ColorChoiceDialog window, a confirmation dialogue should take place in which another dialogue box appears with the question "Are you sure you want the drawing color changed to <color?" where <color is a string denoting the selected color. The confirmation dialogue has two buttons, "Yes" and "No". Pressing the "Yes" button allows the color choice dialogue to complete and the change in drawing color to be made. Pressing the "No" button returns the user to the color choice dialogue as if the "Done" button had not been pressed.

5. Change the modal DrawTool application by replacing the CheckBoxes by a different user interface control (e.g., a list, scrollbars, a textfield, or the custom components).

6. Change the non-modal DrawTool application so that the dismiss control on the Color Choice dialogue box is active and should have the same effect as pressing the "Done" button.

7. Add another layer of dialogue to the non-modal DrawTool application. When the user presses the "Done" button in the ColorChoiceDialog window, a *modal* confirmation dialogue should take place in which another dialogue box appears with the question "Are you sure you want to dismiss the ColorChoice window?" The confirmation dialogue has two buttons, "Yes" and "No". Pressing the "Yes" button allows the color choice dialogue to be dismissed. Pressing the "No" button returns the user to the color choice dialogue as if the "Done" button had not been pressed.

8. Change the non-modal DrawTool application by replacing the CheckBoxes by a different user interface control (e.g., a list, scrollbars, a textfield, or the custom components).
9. Modify the EditTool application so that a modal dialogue is used to select the current size of the font for text that appears in the text area.
10. Modify the EditTool application so that a non-modal dialogue is used to select the current size of the font for text that appears in the text area.
11. Modify the EditTool application so that different modal dialgoues are used to select the current size and the current family of the font for the text that appears in the text area.
12. Modify the EditTool application so that different non-modal dialgoues are used to select the current size and the current family of the font for the text that appears in the text area.
13. Modify the DrawTool application so that a JOptionPane confirm dialogue is used to confirm the change in drawing color.
14. Modify the DrawTool application so that a JOptionPane message dialogue is used to inform the user that the drawing area is about to be cleared. This dialogue is shown when the user presses the "Clear Canvas" button.
15. Modify the DrawTool application so that a JOptionPane input dialogue is used to obtain the new drawing color from the user.
16. Modify the EditTool application so that a JOptionPane confirm dialogue is used to confirm the change in font size or font family.
17. Modify the EditTool application so that a JOptionPane message dialogue is used to inform the user that the text area is about to be changed. This dialogue is shown when the user changes the font size or font family.
18. Modify the EditTool application so that a JOptionPane input dialogue is used to obtain the new font size from the user.

7.10 Scrollbars

A scrollbar, also known as a slider, provides a means of choosing a value that is, or can be mapped into, an integer within a specified range. In some cases, the scrollbar's value directly represents an application quantity. For example, in a 50-page document a document scrollbar may be used to select the number of the page to display. In other cases, the scrollbar represents a proportion. For exam-

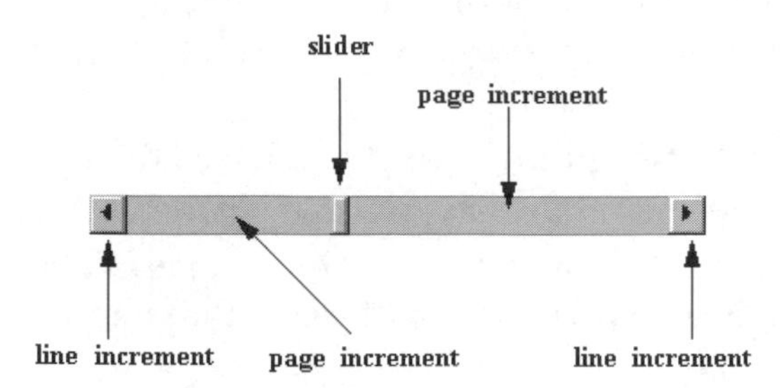

Figure 7.67 Structure of a Scrollbar

ple, when viewing a a large drawing area—an area whose vertical dimension cannot be fully displayed in the available display area—a scrollbar may be used to indicate which part of the drawing area should be displayed. If the scrollbar is near its minimum value, the portion of the drawing area toward its top is displayed, and if the scrollbar is near its maximum value, the portion toward the drawing area's bottom is displayed. The structure of a horizontal scrollbar is shown in Figure 7.67. The minimum and maximum values of the range is associated with the left and right edges, respectively, of the scrollbar. The structure of a vertical scrollbar is similar with the minimum value of the range at the top and the maximum value at the bottom.

The value of the scrollbar is altered by changing the position of the sliding indicator within the scrollbar. The sliding indicator is moved by dragging it, by clicking on either of the visible parts of the scale between the sliding indicator and either arrowhead, or by clicking on one of two arrowheads. Each way of moving the sliding indicator changes value of the scrollbar by an "increment" that is specified when the scrollbar is constructed. The terminology associated with the different increments reflects the original use of a scrollbar in paging through a large, continuous document divided into lines and pages of text. These increments are also referred to as block and unit increments instead of page and line increments, respectively. Clicking on one of the arrowheads changes the value of the scrollbar by the "line" or "unit" increment; clicking in the area between the sliding indicator and the arrowhead changes the value by the "page" or "block" increment. Dragging the sliding indicator changes the value proportionally to the distance that it is moved.

The JScrollBar class implements the `Adjustable` interface. This interface is intended to capture the common behavior of user interface controls which, like the JScrollBar, can be "adjusted" to yield a value within a range. The Adjustable interface defines methods for adding and removing listeners (`addAdjustmentListener`, `remove-AdjustmentListener`), and setting and getting the current increments (`getUnitIncrement`, `setUnitIncrement`, `getBlockIncrement`, `setBlockIncrement`), boundary values (`getMaximum`, `setMaximum`, `getMinimum`, `setMinimum`), and the current value (`getValue`, `setValue`).

A JScrollBar generates `AdjustmentEvents` that will be forwarded to any AdjustmentListener registered with the JScrollBar. An AdjustmentListener must implement a single method named `adjustmentValueChanged`. The AdjustmentEvent class provides a method, `getAdjustable`, that returns the Adjustable object whose value has been changed. This returned object can be manipulated using the methods of the `Adjustable` interface described above.

Two variations of the DrawTool application are used to illustrate the uses of a scrollbar. In the first variation, three horizontal scrollbars are used to select the red, green, and blue intensities of the current drawing color. Rather than selecting from a predetermined set of colors, the user is able to create a customized color. In the second variation, a vertical scrollbar is used to move the rectangle vertically in the drawing area, moving the scrollbar's slider up or down causes the rectangle to move up or down accordingly. One Swing component, the JScrollPane, has a built-in pair of scrollbars for controlling the horizontal and vertical panning of the JScrollPane across a larger area than is possible to view at one time in the JScrollPane itself. Thus, the JScrollPane provides a way of viewing a large area, that is to say a large image or drawing surface, in a smaller space on the display. Another variation of the DrawTool application is presented that uses the JScrollPane to provide a large drawing area, only a portion of which is visible in the JScrollPane at any one time.

7.10.1 Using ScrollBars for Value Selection

In the Java libraries, colors are defined in one of three ways, two of which are suitable for use with a scrollbar. The first way of defining a color is by the Red-Green-Blue (RGB) model where a triple of integers specifies the intensities of red, green, and blue that, when combined, produce the color. This model assumes that each intensity is given as either an integer value in the range of 0 to 255, inclusive, or as a floating point value in the range of 0.0 to 1.0, inclusive. The second way of defining a color is by the HSB model, so named because three floating point values are used to specify the color's hue, saturation, and brightness. The Color class provides methods to convert between the RGB and HSB representations of a given color. The RGB model is illustrated in the following example and the exercises at the end of this section work with the HSB model. The third way of specifying a color is by a set of named constants defined in the Color class (Color.black, Color.blue, Color.cyan, Color.darkGray, Color.Gray, Color.green, Color.lightGray, Color.magenta, Color.orange, Color.ink, Color.red, Color.white, and Color.yellow). Color objects, regardless of how they were defined, are equivalent in the sense that a method requiring a Color object need not know which way was used to define the object.

The DrawTool application is used to illustrate how scrollbars can be used to obtain a value in a fixed range. A set of three scrollbars are used, each one of which will represent the value of one of the RGB color values. By adjusting the scrollbars, the user is able to generate a customized color with which the rectan-

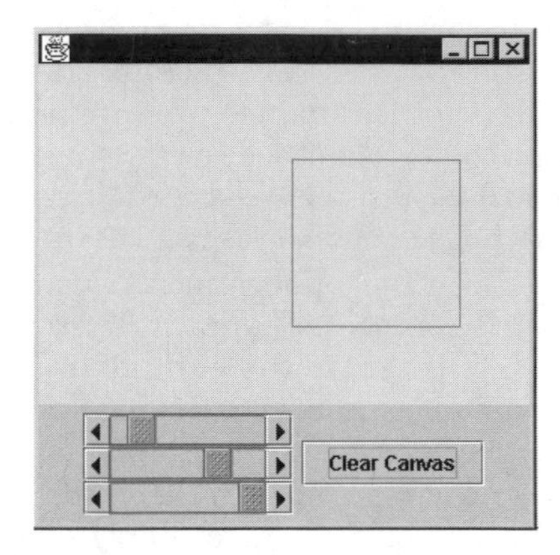

Figure 7.68 Using Scrollbars in the DrawTool Applications

gle will be drawn. Each time one of the scrollbars is adjusted, a new color will be generated and the rectangle is redrawn using that new color. The user interface for this version of the DrawTool application is shown in Figure 7.68. The interface is rudimentary the three scrollbars are not even labelled! An exercise at the end of this section will add these labels. From top to bottom, the three scrollbars indicate the amounts of red, green, and blue in the drawing color. As shown in the figure, the current color has little red (the slider in the top scrollbar is close to its minimum value position), a large amount of green (the slider in the middle scrollbar is beyond the halfway point towards its maximimum value position), and the maximim amount of blue (the slider in the bottom scrollbar is at its maximum value position).

A new class, ColorScrollbar, is defined that represents a scrollbar for selecting the intensity of a color. Three instances of this class are created in the DrawTool applications, one for each of three colors. The ColorScrollbar class, shown in Figure 7.69, extends the JScrollBar class by adding an attribute that records the name of the color represented by the JScrollBar. The value of this attribute is set by the constructor and can be queried by the `getColor` method. The ColorScrollBar constructor uses the `super(...)` notation to pass five integer arguments to the JScrollBar class constructor. The first argument specifies that the scrollbar is horizontal using the named constant defined in the JScrollBar class; the alternative is JScrollBar. VERTICAL that would create a vertical scrollbar. The second constructor argument gives the initial value of the scrollbar, namely 100. This initial value determines where the slider element of the scrollbar will be positioned originally and what value will be returned if the scrollbar is queried for its value before the user has made any change in the scrollbar's settings. The last two arguments, 0 and 255, specify the lower and upper values, respectively, of the scrollbar's range. The middle parameter, 10 in this example, gives the width of the slider element of the scrollbar, a larger value giving a wider slider element.

```
public class ColorScrollbar extends JScrollBar
{
  private String color;

  public ColorScrollbar(String colorName)
  { super(JScrollBar.HORIZONTAL, 100, 10, 0, 255);
    color = colorName;
  }

  public String getColor()
  { return color;
  }

  public Dimension getPreferredSize()
  { return new Dimension(125,20);
  }
}
```

Figure 7.69 The ColorScrollbar Class

The significance of this value is that it can affect the actual maximum or minimum value obtainable by the scrollbar. An implementation may use the left (or right or middle) of the slider to determine its actual position. If the left edge of the slider is used, then the maximum value that the scrollbar can achieve will be the value specified as its maximum minus the width of the slider element. In the example shown here, the scrollbar's value in such a case could not exceed 245 (255 - 10).

The ColorScrollbar class also illustrates how the the size of a user interface element can be determined by overriding the `getPreferredSize` method defined in the Component class. When a layout manager is arranging the components in a Container, it calls the component's `getPreferredSize` method to determine how much of its screen space to allocate for the component. This method returns an object of type Dimension whose two integer values are a width and a height. In the code example for ColorScrollbar, the `getPreferredSize` method specifies that each ColorScrollbar object will be allocated an area whose width is 125 pixels and whose height is 20 pixels. Because the `getPreferredSize` method is defined in the Component class, this technique can be used for any subclass of Component and is not limited to just the JScrollBar class.

Three ColorScrollbars are constructed and added to the DrawTool's interface as shown in the DrawFrame class below. The code relevant to the scrollbars is shown in bold. First, each ColorScrollbar is constructed with a String corresponding to the names of the one of the three colors (“Red”, “Green”, and “Blue”). Second, the ColorDelegator object is added as an AdjustmentListener for each of the three Scrollbars. The revised definition of the ColorDelegator class is shown below. Third, a JPanel is created to contain the three scrollbars and this Panel is assigned a GridLayout to manage its arrangment. A GridLayout arranges the components into rows and columns. In this example, there are three rows and 1 column, meaning that the three scrollbars will be arranged one above the other.

```
public class DrawFrame extends JFrame implements WindowListener
{
  private ColorDelegator colorDelegator;

  public DrawFrame()
  { //...

    ColorScrollbar redScrollbar   = new ColorScrollbar("Red");
    ColorScrollbar greenScrollbar = new ColorScrollbar("Green");
    ColorScrollbar blueScrollbar  = new ColorScrollbar("Blue");

    ClearButton clearButton = new ClearButton();

    DrawCanvas canvas = new DrawCanvas(clearButton);

    colorDelegator = new ColorDelegator(canvas);

    redScrollbar.addAdjustmentListener(colorDelegator);
    greenScrollbar.addAdjustmentListener(colorDelegator);
    blueScrollbar.addAdjustmentListener(colorDelegator);

    JPanel scrollBarPanel = new JPanel();
    scrollBarPanel.setLayout(new GridLayout(3,1));
    scrollBarPanel.add(redScrollbar);
    scrollBarPanel.add(greenScrollbar);
    scrollBarPanel.add(blueScrollbar);

    JPanel controls = new JPanel();
    controls.setLayout(new FlowLayout());
    controls.add(scrollBarPanel);
    controls.add(clearButton);

    content.add(canvas, BorderLayout.CENTER);
    content.add(controls, BorderLayout.SOUTH);
  }

  // WindowListener methods as before

}
```

Figure 7.70 Creating the ColorScrollbars

In general, a GridLayout can be constructed with any number of rows and columns. As elements are added to the Panel managed by a GridLayout, their placement begins with the first row and first column (the upper left-hand position) and proceeds column by column across the row, moving to the first column of the next row after filling the last column of the current row. In this example there is only one column, so the `redScrollbar` will be placed first, filling the first row, and then the `greenScrollbar` below it, filling the second row, and finally the `blueScrollbar` in the third row. Finally, along wth the ClearButton object the Panel (scrollbarPanel) containing the ColorScrollbars is added to the `controls` JPanel that is itself added to the DrawFrame (Figure 7.70).

The ColorDelegator class is revised (see Figure 7.71) so that it can respond to the adjustment events generated by the ColorScrollbars. Notice that the Col-

```
public class ColorDelegator implements AdjustmentListener
{
  private DrawCanvas drawingArea;
  private int redValue   = 100;
  private int greenValue = 100;
  private int blueValue  = 100;

  public ColorDelegator (DrawCanvas canvas)
  { drawingArea = canvas;
  }

  public void adjustmentValueChanged(AdjustmentEvent event)
  { ColorScrollbar colorBar = (ColorScrollbar)event.getAdjustable();
    String colorName = colorBar.getColor();
    int colorValue   = colorBar.getValue();

         if ( colorName.equals("Red"))   redValue   = colorValue;
    else if ( colorName.equals("Blue"))  blueValue  = colorValue;
    else if ( colorName.equals("Green")) greenValue = colorValue;

    drawingArea.setColor(new Color(redValue, greenValue, blueValue));
  }
}
```

Figure 7.71 Responding to Adjustment Events in the ColorDelegator

orDelegator class implements the AdjustmentListener interface that requires the definition of a method named `adjustmentValueChanged` whose single argument is an AdjustmentEvent. The AdjustmentEvent object provides a method `getAdjustable` that returns the object that is the source of the AdjustmentEvent. In this case, the source object can be correctly type cast to a ColorScrollbar. This type cast is necessary so that the `getColor` method can be used to determine the color corresponding to the adjusted scrollbar. Recall that this method returns one of the strings "Red", "Green", or "Blue". The `getValue` method is inherited from the JScrollBar class and returns the current value of the scrollbar. Given the name and current value of the adjusted color, the ColorDelegator updates one of its state variables accordingly. A new Color object is formed from the updated state variables and the DrawingCanvas object is informed of its new drawing color via its `setColor` method as in previous examples.

7.10.2 Using ScrollBars for Proportional Movement

A scrollbar's value may indicate a proportion rather than an absolute value. For example, when scrolling through a document the location of the sliding indicator may be though of more appropriately as specifying the proportional position within the document (at its midpoint, the indicator selects the text at the middle of the document) rather than the actual number of the line of text. In other words, at its midpoint in a scrolled text, the sliding indicator selects the middle

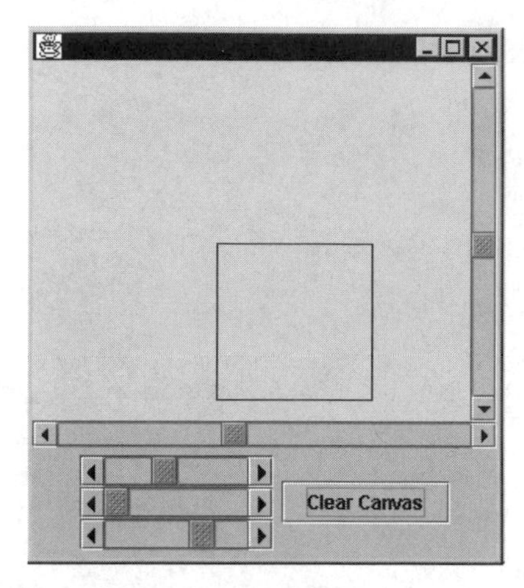

Figure 7.72 Proportional Scrollbars in the DrawTool Application

text regardless of how many actual lines of text are present in the document; the meaning of the position is given by its proportional position in the scrollbar's scale and not by its absolute value.

A revised version of the DrawTool program is developed that uses the value of a pair of scrollbar in a proportional manner. Together the two scrollbars indicate the position of the rectangle presented in the drawing area of the DrawTool application. One scrollbar indicates the relative position of the rectangle in the x-axis (the left-right position of the rectangle) and the other scrollbar indicates the relative position of the rectangle in the y-axis (the up-down position of the rectangle). When the sliding indicators of both scrollbars are at their middle position, the upper left-hand corner of the rectangle will be at the middle of the drawing area, regardless of the dimensions of the drawing area itself. The layout of the user interface for this version of the DrawTool is shown in Figure 7.72. As shown in the figure, the drawing area is bordered on the right and the bottom with two scrollbars. The right scrollbar is oriented vertically while the bottom scrollbar has a horizontal orientation. Because both of the sliders in the figure are near the middle of their respective scrollbars, the upper left-corner of the rectangle is near the center of the drawing area.

This version of the DrawTool program also illustrates how scrollbars can be manipulated under program control. To maintain the relationship between the position of the sliders and the location of the rectangle, it is necessary for the program (not the user) to adjust the sliders' position when the user drags the rectangle using the mouse. For example, if the user dragged the rectangle in Figure 7.72 straight up (down), then the slider in the vertical scrollbar should correspondingly move toward the top (bottom) of its scrollbar, and if the user dragged the rectangle in the figure to the left (right) then the slider in the horizontal scrollbar should correspondingly move toward the left (right), end of its scrollbar.

```
public class DrawFrame extends JFrame implements WindowListener
{
  private ColorDelegator colorDelegator;

  public DrawFrame()
  { Container content = this.getContentPane();
    content.setLayout(new BorderLayout());
    this.setLocation(100,100);
    this.setSize(300,300);
    this.addWindowListener(this);

    // ...

    JScrollBar xAxis = new JScrollBar(JScrollBar.HORIZONTAL, 50, 1, 0, 100);
    JScrollBar yAxis = new JScrollBar(JScrollBar.VERTICAL,   50, 1, 0, 100);

    DrawCanvas canvas = new DrawCanvas(clearButton, xAxis, yAxis);
    JPanel scrolledCanvas = new JPanel();
    scrolledCanvas.setLayout(new BorderLayout());
    scrolledCanvas.add(canvas, BorderLayout.CENTER);
    scrolledCanvas.add(yAxis, BorderLayout.EAST);
    scrolledCanvas.add(xAxis, BorderLayout.SOUTH);

    xAxis.addAdjustmentListener(canvas);
    yAxis.addAdjustmentListener(canvas);

    //...

    JPanel controls = new JPanel();
    // create panel for ColorScrollbars and Button

    content.add(scrolledCanvas, BorderLayout.CENTER);
    content.add(controls, BorderLayout.SOUTH);
  }

  //..WindowListener methods
}
```

Figure 7.73 Creating the ColorScrollbars

Thus, the user has two ways of moving the rectangle in the drawing area—one by dragging by the mouse and one by adjusting the scrollbars. However, the position of the scrollbars' sliders should always be consistent with the current position of the rectangle, regardless of how the rectangle is moved.

Creating the scrollbars that control the rectangle in the DrawingCanvas is straightforward as shown in the code below in Figure 7.73. The relevant code is shown in bold. The two scrollbars are created with different orientations, one vertical and one horizontal, though they have the same range, from 0 to 100, the same initial value, 50, and the same slider width, 1. These two scrollbars are passed to the DrawCanvas constructor (see below). The DrawCanvas and the two scrollbars are organized by a JPanel that uses a BorderLayout arrangement with the DrawCanvas being placed in the "Center" position, the vertical scrollbar to its left in the "East" position, and the horizontal scrollbar at the bottom in the "South" position.

Because of the way the BorderLayout manager operates, the lengths of the vertical and horizontal scrollbars will be set by the BorderLayout manager at run-time to the full height and width, respectively, of the JPanel itself. Thus, it is not necessary here to specify the dimensions of the Scrollbars themselves as was done for the three scrollbars that control the color intensities. To handle the events generated by the horizontal and vertical Scrollbars, the DrawCanvas is added as a listener for their Adjustment events. Finally, the JPanel containing the DrawCanvas and its two scrollbars is added to the DrawFrame.

The DrawCanvas class is modified so that it reacts to the JScrollBar events and adjusts programatically these scrollbars in response to mouse events that move the rectangle. The significant parts of the code are shown in bold in Figure 7.74. The DrawCanvas class implements the AdjustmentListener interface and the `adjustmentValueChanged` method is defined. The DrawCanvas defines two JScrollBar references, `xScrollbar` and `yScrollbar`, that are initialized by the class's constructor; these are the JScrollBars created in the DrawFrame class. Reacting to the JScrollBar events is done by the code in the `adjustmentValueChanged` method. This code determines the current location of the rectangle based on the settings of the two scrollbars. The coordinates of the rectangle are computed by treating the current value of each of the two scrollbars as a proportional amount; the value of the scrollbar (in the range of 0 to 100) is divided by 100. This proportion is multiplied by the current size (either height or width) of the DrawingCanvas (using the `getSize` method that returns a `Dimension` object whose public fields are `height` and `width`). The result of this multiplication is the location of the rectangle scaled to the dimensions of the DrawCanvas. Notice that the `adjustmentValueChanged` method ignores the AdjustmentEvent object that it is passed. For simplicity, this method determines both of the coordinates even though only one of them could possibly have changed.

Changing the settings of the scrollbars under program control is shown in the definition and use of the private `updateScrollbars` method. This method converts the current location (given by the x and y coordinates passed as parameters) of the rectangle into settings for the two Scrollbars. Each coordinate value is divided by the corresponding dimension of the DrawCanvas, producing a floating point value in the range of 0 to 1, and the result is multiplied by 100 to convert the value to the range of the scrollbar (0 to 100). Each time the rectangle is moved, the `updateScrollbars` method is called with the new coordinates of the rectangle. Thus, consistency is maintained between the location of the rectangle and position of the sliding control in the scrollbars.

```
public class DrawCanvas extends JComponent implements ActionListener,
                                                  MouseListener,
                                                  MouseMotionListener,
                                                  AdjustmentListener
{
  private Rectangle   rectangle;
  private Color       currentColor;
  private ClearButton clearButton;
  private JScrollBar xScrollbar;
  private JScrollBar yScrollbar;

  private void updateScrollbars(int x, int y)
  { xScrollbar.setValue( (int)( ((float)x /(float)getSize().width)*100.0 ));
    yScrollbar.setValue( (int)( ((float)y /(float)getSize().height)*100.0));
  }

  public DrawCanvas(ClearButton button, JScrollBar xaxis, JScrollBar yaxis)
  { xScrollbar = xaxis;
    yScrollbar = yaxis;
    //...
  }

  //...

  public void mousePressed(MouseEvent event)
  { int x = event.getX();
    int y = event.getY();
    rectangle = new Rectangle(x,y);
    updateScrollbars(x,y);
    repaint();
  }

  //...

  public void mouseDragged(MouseEvent event)

  { if (rectangle != null)
    { int x = event.getX();
      int y = event.getY();
      rectangle.moveTo(x,y);
      updateScrollbars(x,y);
      repaint();
    }
  }

  //...

  public void adjustmentValueChanged(AdjustmentEvent event)
  { int xLocation = (int) ( (float)(xScrollbar.getValue()/100.0)
                              * getSize().width );
    int yLocation = (int) ( (float)(yScrollbar.getValue()/100.0)
                              * getSize().height );
    rectangle = new Rectangle(xLocation, yLocation);
    repaint();
    xScrollbar.repaint();
    yScrollbar.repaint();
  }
}
```

Figure 7.74 Handling Scrollbars in the DrawCanvas Class

7.10.3 Using ScrollPanes

Because scrollbars are often used to provide a means of viewing a part of an area too large to be displayed as a whole, Swing includes a convenience class for this purpose, the JScrollPane class. A single Component can be added to the JScrollPane (using the JScrollPane's `add` method). In typical use, the dimensions of the Component added to the JScrollPane are larger than the dimensions of the JScrollPane itself. Thus, a JScrollPane object may be thought of as a viewport through which a partial view of a larger component is visible. The viewport may be moved to display different parts of the larger area by using the one or two scrollbars that are part of the JScrollPane object. As a simple analogy, imagine looking out of the window of an airplane in flight. The airplane's window is like the JScrollPane in that it gives you a view of the larger area over which you are

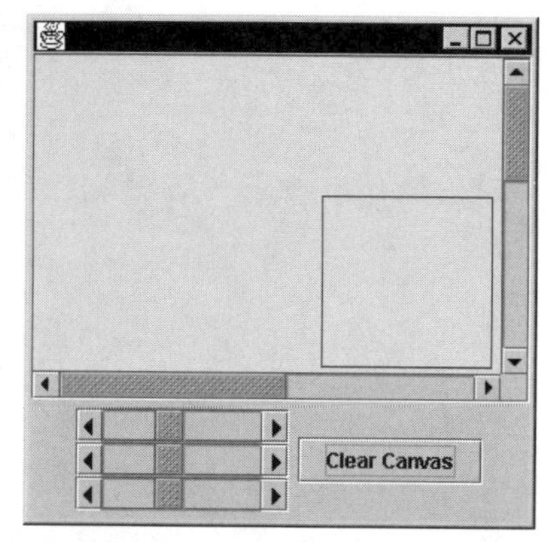

Figure 7.75 DrawTool with a ScrollPane (First Figure)

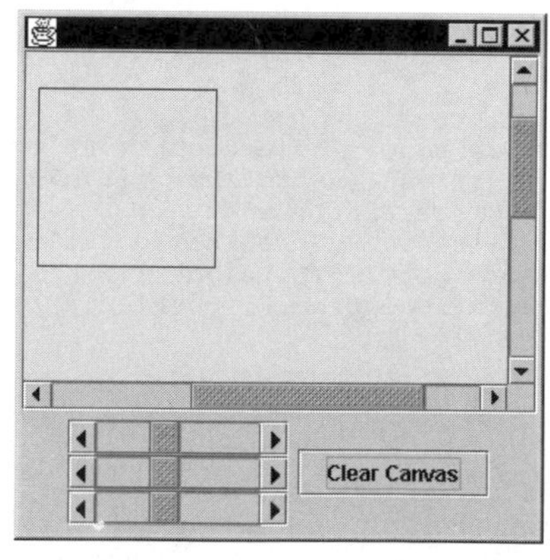

Figure 7.76 DrawTool with a ScrollPane (Second Figure)

```
public class DrawFrame extends JFrame implements WindowListener
{
  private ColorDelegator colorDelegator;

  public DrawFrame()
  { Container content = this.getContentPane();
    content.setLayout(new BorderLayout());
    this.setLocation(100,100);
    this.setSize(300,300);
    this.addWindowListener(this);

    //...


    ClearButton clearButton = new ClearButton();

    DrawCanvas canvas = new DrawCanvas(clearButton);

    //...

    canvas.setPreferredSize(new Dimension(500,500));
    JScrollPane scrollableCanvas = new JScrollPane(canvas);
    scrollableCanvas.setSize(300,300);

    //...

    this.add("Center", scrollableCanvas);
    this.add("South", controls);
  }

  //...

}
```

Figure 7.77 Using a ScrollPane

flying. The motion of the airplane is similar to the effect of adjusting the scrollbars—your viewing area changes. It is important to keep in mind that changes in what you see in the viewing area come from changing the portion of the landscape that is visible and not from changes in the landscape itself. The lakes, rivers, roads, and building remain fixed, only your view of them changes.

In the DrawTool application, a JScrollPane is used to create a large drawing area only a portion of which is visible at one time. A large version of the DrawCanvas component is added to the JScrollPane. The scrollbars can be used to change the currently viewable part of the DrawCanvas. It should be emphasized that the two scrollbars are part of the JScrollPane, they do not have to be separately created and managed. It is exactly the purpose of the JScrollPane to provide a convenient, prepackaged class that handles the scrolling-related aspects of the area being viewed. Figures 7.75 and 7.76 illustrate the operation of the JScrollPane in the DrawTool application. In the first figure, a rectangle has been drawn near the bottom right-hand corner of the currently visible part of the drawing area. The JScrollPane's two built-in scrollbars are shown at the right and bottom sides of the

JScrollPane. It is important to remember that in this version of DrawTool, the scrollbars are moving the viewing area and *not* the rectangle.

Figure 7.76 shows the result of adjusting both of the scrollbars. The rectangle remains in the same position in the drawing area, but the part of the drawing area that is visible has now changed. In the portion of the drawing area that is now visible, the rectangle appears toward the upper left-hand corner.

The code to create the DrawTool application using a JScrollPane is shown in Figure 7.77. The JScrollPane object, `scrollableCanvas`, is created and its size is set to be a 300 by 300 area. The size of the DrawCanvas object, `canvas`, is set to be a 500 by 500 area and this object is added to the JScrollPanel. The `scrollableCanvas` is later added to the DrawFrame object being constructed. This is all of the code necessary to create the JScrollPane. Furthermore, because the JScrollPane internally handles the events that might be generated by its own scrollbars, there is no more coding that has to be done to make use of the JScrollPane class. The simplicity of this code demonstrates the "convenience" aspect of the JScrollPane class.

Exercises

1. Modify the DrawTool program so that the RGB values are specified as floating point values. This means that you will have to convert the Scrollbar's integer value to a floating point value.
2. Modify the DrawTool program so that the three scrollbars are used to specify the hue, saturation, and brightness. A Color object is created in the HSB model as follows: `Color color = Color.getHSBColor(hue, saturation, brightness)` where the three parameters are floating point values.
3. Modify the DrawTool program so that each of the three scrollbars has a text label to its left that indicates which color each scrollbar adjusts. A text label is created by a Label object whose constructor takes a string that defines the text of the label. It will also be necessary to use a GridLayout that has three rows and two columns.
4. Modify the DrawTool program so that each of the three scrollbars has a text label to its right that indicates which color each scrollbar adjusts. A text label is created by a Label object whose constructor takes a string that defines the text of the label. It will also be necessary to use a GridLayout that has three rows and two columns.
5. Modify the DrawTool program so that the `adjustmentValueChanged` method only gets the value of the single Scrollbar that was changed.

6. Modify the EditTool program so that the current size of the font is selected by a scrollbar.

7.11 TextFields

Through a GUI, a user may communicate textual information to a Java program via a JTextField object. The JTextField object silently processes all of the keystrokes that occur within its region in the user interface including echoing characters that have been typed, backspacing to erase characters, scrolling characters if the user types more characters than can be accomodated in its width, and positioning the cursor within the current characters in response to cursor movement keys such as forward or backward arrow keys. The JTextField generates an event when the user types the enter (carriage return) key. In response to this event, the JTextField's listener(s) can process the text in the JTextField. The use of a JTextField to enter the name of a color in the DrawTool example is shown in Figure 7.78. This figure depicts a situation where the user has created a rectangle and then typed the color name "blue" in the textfield followed by the "enter" (or "return") key. In response, the DrawTool application has changed the color of the rectangle to the color blue. The user is allowed to enter the name of any of the predefined colors (e.g., the named constants in the Color class such as blue, black, red, magenta, etc.). If the user enters the name of an unrecognized color (e.g., azure), the DrawTool system will ignore the user's input.

Creating the JTextField is straightforward as shown in Figure 7.79. The JTextField constructor shown in bold specifies an initial string to appear in the JTextField (as a prompt to the user on how the textfield can be used) and the number of columns that the textfield can show at one time. In this case, the text-

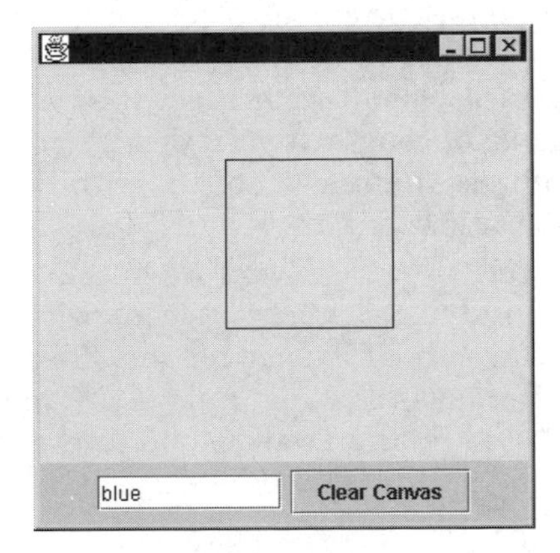

Figure 7.78 Using a TextField in the DrawTool Example

```
public class DrawFrame extends JFrame implements WindowListener
{
  private ColorDelegator colorHandler;

  public DrawFrame()
  { Container content = this.getContentPane();
    content.setLayout(new BorderLayout());
    this.setLocation(100,100);
    this.setSize(300,300);
    this.addWindowListener(this);

    DrawCanvas canvas = new DrawCanvas();
    colorHandler = new ColorDelegator(canvas);

    JTextField colorName = new JTextField("Enter Color", 10);
    colorName.addActionListener(colorHandler);

    ClearButton clearButton = new ClearButton();
    clearButton.addActionListener(canvas);

    JPanel controls = new JPanel();
    controls.setLayout(new FlowLayout());

    controls.add(colorName);
    controls.add(clearButton);

    content.add(canvas, BorderLayout.CENTER);
    content.add(controls, BorderLayout.SOUTH);

  }

  //...
}
```

Figure 7.79 Creating a Textfield in the DrawTool Application

field has 10 columns. If the user types more than 10 characters, the characters are automatically scrolled by the JTextField object so that additional characters can be added at the right end. The cursor placement and scrolling are processed by the JTextField object itself and do not generate events. Thus, a JTextField object can hold an arbitrarily long string regardless of how many columns the JTextField may have. It is, of course, a good design principle that the width of the JTextField should represent a reasonable fit with the typical strings entered by the user in normal operation.

A JTextField generates an ActionEvent when the “enter” (or “return") key is pressed. This is reflected in the DrawFrame's constructor code because the ColorDelegator is added as an ActionListener for the JTextField. The ColorDelegator code is shown later. Because the JTextField is a Component, it can be added to the user interface defined by the DrawFrame in the usual way. As shown in the DrawFrame’s constructor, the JTextField `colorName` is added to the user interface next to the ClearButton object.

To complete the relevant parts of the DrawTool application using the JTextField, the ColorDelegator is shown below. The ColorDelegator handles the

```
public class ColorDelegator implements ActionListener
{
  private DrawCanvas drawingArea;

  public ColorDelegator (DrawCanvas canvas)
  { drawingArea = canvas;
  }

  public void actionPerformed(ActionEvent event)
  { String colorName = event.getActionCommand();

    Color newColor = null;
    if      (colorName.equals("red"))       newColor = Color.red;
    else if (colorName.equals("pink"))      newColor = Color.pink;
    else if (colorName.equals("magenta"))   newColor = Color.magenta;
    else if (colorName.equals("orange"))    newColor = Color.orange;
    else if (colorName.equals("blue"))      newColor = Color.blue;
    else if (colorName.equals("cyan"))      newColor = Color.cyan;
    else if (colorName.equals("darkGray"))  newColor = Color.darkGray;
    else if (colorName.equals("lightGray")) newColor = Color.lightGray;
    else if (colorName.equals("gray"))      newColor = Color.gray;
    else if (colorName.equals("green"))     newColor = Color.green;
    else if (colorName.equals("white"))     newColor = Color.white;
    else if (colorName.equals("black"))     newColor = Color.black;

    if (newColor != null)
      drawingArea.setColor(newColor);
  }

}
```

Figure 7.80 The ColorDelegator Class Handling ActionEvents from the Textfield

ActionEvents that are generated by the JTextField. As noted above, the ColorDelegator is registered as an ActionListener for the JTextField object created in the DrawFrame constructor. Notice that the ColorDelegator class is declared to implement the ActionListener interface and it fulfills this declaration by providing the `actionPerformed` method. One fact to notice is that the "action command" for a JTextField is the string of text that was present in the JTextField when the ActionEvent was created. As shown in the ColorDelegator's `actionPerformed` method, the `getActionCommand` is used to obtain the text entered by the user. This text string is compared to all of the valid color names (those corresponding to the named constants defined in the Color class). If the text string entered by the user matches one of the color names, this color is passed to the DrawCanvas through the `setColor` method. If the text string entered by the user does not correspond to any of the known color names, the event is silently ignored (Figure 7.80).

Exercises

1. Control the color JTextField so that it can only be edited when the canvas is clear.
2. Modify the DrawTool appliction so that typing “clear” in the JTextField has the same effect as pressing the “Clear Canvas” button.
3. Modify the DrawTool application so that if the user enters an unknown color name in the JTextField, the contents of the JTextField is changed to the text string “Bad Color”.
4. Modify the DrawTool application so that it contains three JTextFields representing the intensities of the red, green, and blue components of a custom color.
5. Use a pair of JTextFields to enter the coordinates of the rectangle's upper left-hand corner. Be sure to keep the current location of the rectangle consistent with the values displayed in the JTextFields (i.e., if the rectangle is moved through mouse events, the JTextFields shold be updated by the program to reflect the current location of the rectangle).
6. Modify the EditTool application so that the current size of the text font can be entered by the user in a JTextField. If invalid text is entered in the textfield, it should be silently ignored.
7. Modify the EditTool application so that the current family of the text font can be entered by the user in a JTextField. If invalid text is entered in the textfield, it should be silently ignored.
8. Modify the EditTool application so that it contains two JTextFields, one for entering the size of the current font and one for entering the family of the current font. If invalid text is entered in one of the textfields, it should be silently ignored.

7.12 Images

Images are bit-mapped graphical representations that are stored in one of several standard file formats. Images are commonly produced by scanners that create an image file from a printed page, digital cameras, programs that capture screen snapshots, and from drawing or rendering programs. Such images are frequently found in web pages where they serve as decorative elements or as a means of presenting information in a visual form. Two of the most frequently encountered standard file formats are "gif" (Graphics Interchange Format) files and "jpeg" (Joint Photographics Expert Group) files. Swing provides facilities to handle both of these image formats. Programmers can directly handle the low-level issues of how images are loaded by an application using the Image class. Alternatively, many of these issues can be ignored by using the ImageIcon convenience class. This section first shows the details of how images are handled using the Image class. The ImageIcon class is described at the end of the section. Readers who are not interested in the lower-level details can skip directly to the part that describes the ImageIcon class.

7.12.1 Using the Image Class

There are three steps in handling an image, summarized in Table 7.9. First, an object of the Image class must be created so that it will hold the representation of the image. As part of this step the source of the image is identified, which in the most common case is the name of a file on the local machine or a machine that is accessible over the network. The Image object is not created by a `new` operation but is returned as a result of utility methods that are part of the run-time mechanism. Second, the transfer of the data from the image source—in our case a file—to the Image object must be initiated and monitored. The monitoring also involves recognizing when the data transfer is complete. Third, the image can be drawn, either partially or completely, using one of several methods defined in the Graphics class. It is possible to display that portion of an image that has been transferred; only at the completion of the transfer can the full image be displayed. It will be seen that the first and last of these steps are straightforward whereas the middle step can be more difficult to understand.

Initiating the image's data transfer and monitoring the progress or completion of this transfer are distinct actions in handling an image because the run-time mechanism is designed to transfer image data "asynchronously." This means that the operation to initiate the transfer does *not* wait for the transfer to complete before returning. Asynchronous loading is used because the time to load the image's data may be long if the image is large or complex and/or the net-

Table 7.9 Steps in Manipulating a Graphical Image

1. Creation:
    - Create an Image object
    - Specify the image's source
2. Data Transfer:
    - Initiate the data transfer from the source to the Image object
    - Monitor the data transfer and detect its completion
3. Display:
    - Drawing the full or partial image

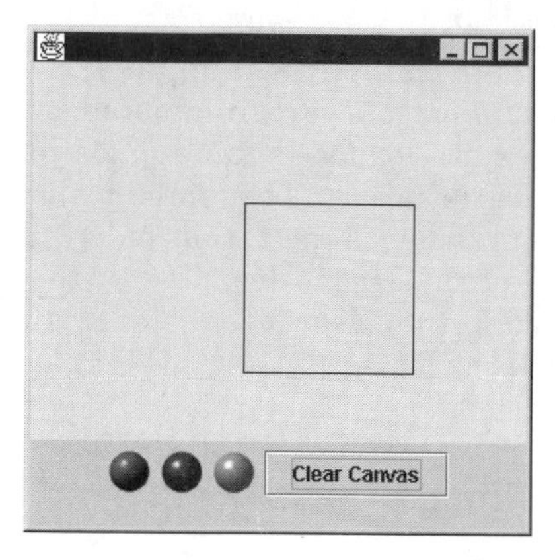

Figure 7.81 The DrawTool Interface with Three Images

work connection is slow. Users experienced with web browsers have undboutedly seen a similar effect when loading web pages that contain rich visual information. To prevent the user from waiting while all of the image data is loaded, the browser initiates the transfer and updates the display as more of the data is loaded. During the data transfer the web browser may display a default graphic in its place while allowing the user to view the other parts of the document. The user may even decide to follow a link to another page before the image is completely loaded. The run-time mechanism adopts these same techniques in its image handling.

To illustrate the steps in manipulating an image, the DrawTool application will be revised so that three images are used, each indicating a different color to use in drawing the rectangle. The revised interface is shown in Figure 7.81. In this interface the three images are shown at the left of the "Clear Canvas" button. The shading and lighting effects within each of the images gives the impression of a color sphere. Clicking on one of the spheres changes the drawing color to that of the sphere. In the figure, the user has clicked on the blue sphere because the rectangle is drawn in the blue color. The images as used here are for visual appeal; there is no functional difference between the user clicking on a blue sphere as opposed to selecting the item "blue" from a menu, list, or checkbox. However, the aesthetic value of using more visually attractive representations can be meaningful. Which would you rather see and use?

Creating and Drawing an Image

Creating and drawing the image, the first and third steps, are straightforward. These steps are shown in the ColorImage class given in Figure 7.82. Because each ColorImage object holds an image of one colored sphere, the DrawTool application needs three ColorImage objects. The ColorImage class extends the Canvas class, providing a place to draw the image, and also implements the MouseListener interface so that the ColorImage class can sense when the user

```
public class ColorImage extends JComponent implements MouseListener
{
  private Color color;
  private Image image;
  private DrawCanvas canvas;

  public ColorImage(String imageName, Color color, DrawCanvas canvas)
  { this.color = color;
    this.canvas = canvas;

    Toolkit toolkit = Toolkit.getDefaultToolkit();
    image = toolkit.getImage(imageName);
    //...
    this.addMouseListener(this);
  }

  public void paint(Graphics g)
  { g.drawImage(image, 0,0, image.getWidth(null), image.getHeight(null), null);
  }

  public Dimension getPreferredSize()
  { return new Dimension( image.getWidth(null), image.getHeight(null) );
  }

  public void mousePressed(MouseEvent event)
  { canvas.setColor(color);
  }

  //...
}
```

Figure 7.82 Creating and Drawing an Image

has clicked within the image. The constructor of the ColorImage class takes three arguments that denote the name of the file containing the image (this file must be a .gif or a .jpeg file), the Color that is to be associated with the image, and the DrawCanvas whose drawing color should be changed when the image is clicked on by the user. The code shown in bold in the constructor illustrates how an Image object is created and how the source of the Image object's data is specified in a stand-alone Java application such as DrawTool. The Toolkit class has a static method `getDefaultToolkit` that returns a Toolkit object containing a number of platform-specific methods, one of which is the `getImage` method. The getImage method takes the name of a file (that may be a pathname on the local machine or a complete URL for a network accessible file) and returns an Image object. It is important to remember that the `getImage` method does *not* initiate the data transfer, it merely identifies the soure of the data for the Image object. Skipping for the moment the second and third steps, the fourth step, drawing the image is shown in the `paint` method. The Graphics class has several overloaded `drawImage` methods one of which is used here. The form used here specifies the Image object, the coordinates of the upper left-hand corner of the image, the width and height of the image obtained by using accessor methods in the Image class, and a final parameter that is null in this case. The uses of the null values in this statement will be made clear below. The other methods in the ColorImage class return the preferred size of the Canvas (equal to the size of the image itself) and notify the DrawCanvas to change its drawing color when a mouse click is detected.

Loading the Image's Data

Initiating and monitoring the loading of an image uses either the MediaTracker class or the ImageObserver interface and, for the MediaTracker, may be used either in a blocking or a non-blocking mode. By using the MediaTracker in a blocking mode the application is forced to wait until the image is completely loaded before the application can proceed. The advantage of the blocking mode is that the application programming is simpler. However, the application may be awkward for the user in those cases where a sizable delay is encountered in loading the image. In the non-blocking mode, the application and the data transfer proceed independently. In the non-blocking case, the application must periodically assess the progress of the data transfer, possibly redrawing the image as more of its data is available, and must detect the completion of the data transfer. The advantage of the non-blocking mode is that the user is able to use the application while the image is loading. However, the application programming in this case is more difficult to construct. To illustrate the various techniques for loading the image data three versions of the DrawTool application will be presented. The critical methods used in these three variations are summarized in Table 7.10. The first of the three versions will use the blocking form of the MediaTracker, the second will use the non-blocking form of the MediaTracker, and the third will use the ImageObserver interface.

These versions illustrate three basic strategies that are found in many applications and are commonly termed blocking, polling, and notification. Blocking means that the requested operation must be completed before the invocation returns. Polling means that the invocation returns immediately and the invoker will periodically check to see if the operation is complete. Notification means that the invocation returns immediately and that the invoker will be informed periodically of the progress, or completion, of the operation. An everyday analogous sit-

Table 7.10 Methods Used in Image Loading

	Media Tracker	**ImageObserver**
Initiating data transfer	• Blocking: `waitForID` • Non-blocking: `statusID`	`drawImage`
Monitoring data transfer	`statusID` or `checkID`	`imageUpdate`

uation occurs when calling someone on the phone who is in the middle doing something. When they answer the phone you may elect to be put on hold until they can talk (the blocking strategy), say that you will call back later (the polling strategy), or ask them to call you back when they are free to talk (the notification strategy). Different circumstances of priority, control, and timing dictate which of these strategies is used in any given situation.

Waiting for the Image Loading Using the MediaTracker Class: The simplest way to program the loading of an image uses the MediaTracker's `waitForID` method as shown in Figure 7.83 in the constructor for the ColorImage class. The code in bold is the code that is needed to initiate the data transfer and wait until the data transfer is complete. The MediaTracker is constructed with an argument that denotes for which Component the tracking is being performed. Next, the desired Image object is made known to the MediaTracker by using the MediaTracker's `addImage` method that also takes an integer index by which the image may be referred to in subsequent calls to the MediaTracker. Several images may be added to the MediaTracker with the same index if they are to be treated as a group. The `waitForID` method initiates the data transfer for the images(s) whose index is given as a parameter and does not return until

```
public class ColorImage extends JComponent implements MouseListener
{
  private Color color;
  private Image image;
  private DrawCanvas canvas;

  public ColorImage(String imageName, Color color, DrawCanvas canvas)
  { this.color = color;
    this.canvas = canvas;

    Toolkit toolkit = Toolkit.getDefaultToolkit();
    image = toolkit.getImage(imageName);
    MediaTracker tracker = new MediaTracker(this);
    tracker.addImage(image, 0);
    try
    { tracker.waitForID(0);
    } catch (InterruptedException e) {}

    this.addMouseListener(this);
  }

  public void paint(Graphics g)
  { g.drawImage(image, 0,0, image.getWidth(null), image.getHeight(null), null);
  }

  //...

}
```

Figure 7.83 Loading an Image Using the MediaTracker's waitforID Method

the transfer is complete. In the event of an error during transfer, the `waitForID` method throws an InterruptedException exception back to the invoking code. For simplicity in this example, the exception is caught and ignored by the `try/catch` structure; without the try/catch structure the thrown exception would cause the application to abort. A more robust handling of this error condition is explored in the exercises. A normal completion of the `waitForID` method guarantees that the waited for image has been completely transferred.

Polling the Image Loading Using the MediaTracker Class: The polling strategy applied to image loading means that the application will periodically check how much of the image has been loaded. In some cases it might be preferable to update the user interface as more of the image is transfered, though the transfer is not yet complete. This case usually occurs when the image is large and it is useful to show the user however much of the image has been loaded at any given time. In other cases a default image, graphic, or text is shown to the user until the image has been completely loaded. This case occurs when the image does not make sense in a partially completed form. In the DrawTool variation that uses the polling strategy, the user is shown a colored text string in place of an incompletely loaded image. The appearance of the user interface when only one of the images has completed loading is shown in Figure 7.84. Notice that the red sphere image has been completely loaded and appears in the user interface whereas the blue and the green sphere images have not been completely loaded and are represented by the text strings whose colors match those of the missing spheres. The text string exhibits the same functionality as the colored sphere in the sense that the user can click on the color text string to change the drawing color in the same way that the drawing color can be changed by clicking on the sphere graphic. Alternatives other than a text string as a temporary visible element are considered in the exercises.

The `statusID` method of the MediaTracker class can be used to check the status of the image transfer that is taking place asynchronously. As shown by the boldface code in the ColorImage constructor given in Figure 7.85, the `statusID` method initiates but does *not* wait for the completion of the image data transfer. The `statusID` method asks the MediaTracker to report the status of the image(s) whose index matches that of the integer parameter and, optionally, to initiate the transfer of an image not already being transfered; the image transfer is initiated if the boolean argument is true but it is not initiated if the boolean argument is false. The returned result from the `statusID` method is ignored in the constructor code because it is clear at this point that the image has just begun loading and need not be checked further. The `paint` method uses the `statusID` method to assess the progress of the image transfer. The result of the status check is compared to the named constant value `MediaTracker.COMPLETE`; thus, the test will be true only when the image has been completely loaded. The other named constants defined by the MediaTracker are ABORTED, ERRORED, and LOADING that indicate, respectively, that the image transfer was aborted and will not be resumed, that an error was encountered during the

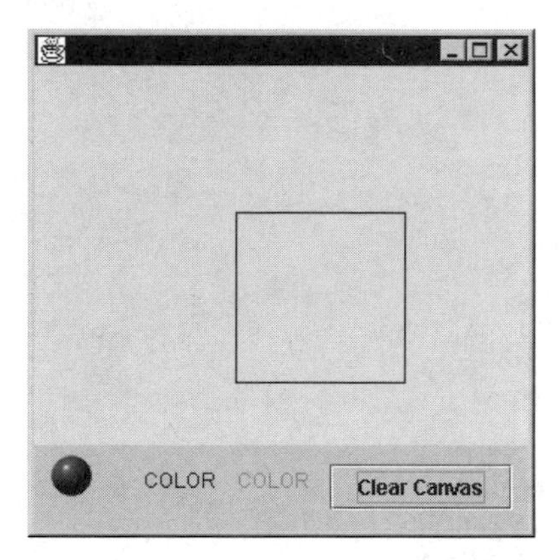

Figure 7.84 The DrawTool Interface With Partially Loaded Images

image transfer and that no further transfer will take place, and that the image transfer is still in progress. In the paint method, the image will be drawn in the user interface if the image has been completely loaded or the text string "COLOR" will be drawn in the user interface using the color associated with the ColorImage object.

An overloading of the `repaint` method is needed to insure continuous polling of the image transfer. As shown in the `paint` method given in Figure 7.85, the invocation `repaint(1000)` will cause the repaint cycle to begin again 1000 milliseconds in the future. Notice that the `repaint(1000)` invocation returns immediately; it does not wait for 1000 milliseconds, but instead it asks the run-time environment to schedule a repaint cycle for that amount of time in the future. During each repaint cycle, the paint method will be called and the status of the image transfer is reevaluated. The interval of 1000 milliseconds (one full second) is arbitrary. In practice, the interval is chosen to be much shorter but is deliberately made long so that the effect of the polling can be made visible. When the image loading is completed, the image is drawn instead of the text string and the `repaint` call is not made, thus ending the polling activity.

Notification of Image Loading Using the ImageObserver Interface: Using the ImageObserver interface to be notified of progress in an image's transfer involves two related issues: (1) how an observing component receives notifications of the progress of the loading of an image, and (2) how a component initiates the image loading and identifies that it is interested in monitoring the image's loading. These steps are related because the observing component must implement the ImageObserver interface and it is through the method of this interface that the progress is reported; the observing component is "called back" from time to time, each "callback" giving an update of progress. The definition of the ImageObserver, interface as shown in Figure 7.86, consists of a set of named constants, and a single method, `imageUpdate`. The named constants defined in the ImageObserver interface identify the conditions that are reported

```
public class ColorImage extends JComponent implements MouseListener
{
  private Color color;
  private Image image;
  private DrawCanvas canvas;
  private MediaTracker tracker;
  private int width = 50;
  private int height = 40;

  public ColorImage(String imageName, Color color, DrawCanvas canvas)
  { this.color = color;
    this.canvas = canvas;

    Toolkit toolkit = Toolkit.getDefaultToolkit();
    image = toolkit.getImage(imageName);
    tracker = new MediaTracker(this);
    tracker.addImage(image, 0);
    tracker.statusID(0,true);  // initiate image transfer

    this.addMouseListener(this);
  }

  public void paint(Graphics g)
  { if (tracker.statusID(0,false) == MediaTracker.COMPLETE)
    { g.drawImage(image, 0,0, image.getWidth(null),
                              image.getWidth(null), null);
    }
    else
      { g.setColor(color);
        g.drawString("COLOR",0,20);
        repaint(1000);  // try again in 1000 milliseconds
      }
  }

  //...
}
```

Figure 7.85 Polling the Image Transfer Using the MediaTracker

by the imageUpdate method. The conditions include inability to complete the loading (ABORT and ERROR), the amount of the image that has been loaded (SOMEBITS, FRAMEBITS, ALLBITS), and the attributes of the image that are known (HEIGHT, WIDTH, PROPERTIES). The values of the named constants are chosen so that they can be and-ed together into a single integer value.

The imageUpdate method is the means by which the Java run-time environment informs the observing component about the progress of the loading of an image. The first two parameters of the imageUpdate method specify the Image object whose progress is being reported and an integer value, infoflags, that is a bit-mask whose fields are defined by the named constants. The last four parameters (x, y, width, and height) are only relevant in a single case (the SOMEBITS case). Specific bits of the infoflags parameter can be tested as follows:

```
public abstract interface ImageObserver
{
   public static final int ABORT;         // loading aborted
   public static final int ALLBITS;       // all bits of image loaded
   pblic static final int ERROR;         // error in handling image
   public static final int FRAMEBITS;     // new frame of multi-frame image
available
   public static final int HEIGHT;        // true height of image known
   public static final int PROPERTIES;    // image properties known
   public static final int SOMEBITS;      // additional bits of the image loaded
   public static final int WIDTH;         // true width of image known
   public abstract boolean imageUpdate (Image image, int infoflags,
                                        int x, int y, int width, int height);
}
```

Figure 7.86 The ImageObserver Interface

```
if ( ((infoflags & ImageObserver.HEIGHT) !=0) && ((infoflags & ImageObserver.WIDTH) != 0)
   { ... // getHeight and getWidth methods return actual height and width of image
   }
```

that tests if both the height and width of the image are known. Recall that `&&` is the logical "and" operator whereas `&` is the bit-wise "and" operator. Finally, the imageUpdate method returns a boolean value. If the returned value is `true` the component continues to receive any additional updates for this image. If the returned value is `false` the component will not receive any further updates for this image.

The ImageObserver interface is implemented by the java.awt.Component class allowing derived classes to be treated as ImageObservers and also to override the imageUpdate method to provide a specialized form of observing behavior. This technique will be used in the ColorImage class that is derived from Component, indirectly via the Canvas class. Thus, a ColorImage object can be passed as a parameter where an ImageObserver is required and it can provide its own implementation of the `imageUpdate` method.

The implementation of the `imageUpdate` method in the ColorImage class is shown in the code in Figure 7.87. This method simply sets a private boolean variable, `imageLoaded`, to true when the `ALLBITS` condition indicates that the entire image has been loaded and calls repaint to insure that the user interface is updated to reflect the presence of the image. The use of the `imageLoaded` boolean variable and the paint method for the ColorImage class are shown below. When the `ALLBITS` condition is true, the `imageUpdate` method returns false to indicate that it no longer needs update notifications (because the image is now completely loaded). In other cases, the `imageUpdate` method returns true to signal that it wants to continue to receive update notifications (because the image has not yet been completely loaded).

```
public class ColorImage extends JComponent implements MouseListener
{
  private Color color;
  private Image image;
  private DrawCanvas canvas;
  private int width = 50;
  private int height = 40;
  private boolean imageLoaded = false;

  //...
  public boolean imageUpdate(Image img, int infoflags, int x, int y,
                             int width, int height)
  { if ((infoflags & ImageObserver.ALLBITS) != 0)
       {   imageLoaded = true;
           repaint();
           return false;
       }
    ele  return true;
  }


  //...
}
```

Figure 7.87 Image Transfer Using the ImageObserver

The loading of an image whose progress is reported through the ImageObserver is initiated when the first attempt is made to draw the image using the Graphics class's `drawImage` method. This creates a seeming dilemma because to load the image it must first be drawn, but to draw the image it must first be loaded. A common practice in this situation is to create a dummy Graphics object and draw the image to that Graphics object solely to trigger the loading of the image. This strategy is used in the `paint` method in the ColorImage class shown in Figure 7.88. The ColorImage's `paint` method takes two different actions depending on the value of the `imageLoaded` boolean variable. Recall that this variable was initialized to `false` and is set to `true` when the `imageUpdate` method is informed that the image has been completely loaded. If `imageLoaded` is `true`, the `paint` method simply draws the image knowing that the image's data has been loaded. However, at the beginning `imageLoaded` is `false`, in which case the `paint` method initiates the image's transfer by drawing the image in a graphics object obtained from a temporary image returned by the `createImage` method defined in the Component class. As noted above, this invocation of `drawImage` is sufficient to initiate the image's transfer. The last parameter of the drawImage method is critical: it specifies the identity of an ImageObserver to be notified as the image's loading progresses. The value passed here is `this` because the ColorImage is an ImageObserver (because it is derived from Component as explained above) and because it wants to know about the image's loading. Notice that after the image is loaded, the `drawImage` method (the one in the else clause) specifies null as the last argument, indicating that it

```
public class ColorImage extends JComponent implements MouseListener
{
  private Color color;
  private Image image;
  private DrawCanvas canvas;
  private int width = 50;
  private int height = 40;
  private boolean imageLoaded = false;

  public ColorImage(String imageName, Color color, DrawCanvas canvas)
  { this.color = color;
    this.canvas = canvas;

    Toolkit toolkit = Toolkit.getDefaultToolkit();
    image = toolkit.getImage(imageName);

    this.addMouseListener(this);
  }

  public void paint(Graphics g)
  { if (!imageLoaded)
      { Image tempImage = createImage(1,1);
        Graphics tempGraphics = tempImage.getGraphics();
        tempGraphics.drawImage(image, 0,0,this);

        g.setColor(color);
        g.drawString("COLOR",0,20);
      }

    else
      { width  = image.getWidth(null);
        height = image.getHeight(null);
        g.drawImage(image, 0,0, width, height, null);
      }
  }

  //...
}
```

Figure 7.88 Initiating the Image Transfer

is unnecessary to inform any ImageObserver of the image's loading (because the image is already loaded). Also notice that when the image is not yet loaded (in the then clause) the text string "COLOR" is drawn in the color corresponding to the ColorImage's intended color. Thus, the user has a visible representation of the color selection control in the user interface until the color sphere image is available.

7.12.2 Using the ImageIcon Class

The Swing ImageIcon class hides all of the details of initiating and tracking the loading of an image. The principal methods of the ImageIcon class are shown in Figure 7.89. The ImageIcon class uses the Image class and the MediaTracker

```
public class ImageIcon
{
   public ImageIcon (String filename)
   public ImageIcon (URL location)
   //...
}
```

Figure 7.89 The ImageIcon Class

class internally to store and load the image. The first two constructors of the ImageIcon class load an image from the local file system. The name of the file is given as the constructor argument. The ImageIcon class also allows an image to be loaded across the network. The second constructor takes as its input argument a URL where the image can be found. This URL is used to access the image's contents and load them over the network. With either constructor, the image is guaranteed to have been loaded when the constructor returns. This simplicity is also the drawback of the ImageIcon class because the application is blocked until the image is completely loaded and the ImageIcon object is completely constructed. Using the Image and MediaTracker classes allows the application more control of the loading processes so that the application can proceed while the image is being loaded. If the loading time is not significant then the ImageIcon class is certainly simpler to use. If the loading time is potentially long, then the added complexity of using the Image and MediaTracker classes may be justified to achieve better application responsiveness.

Exercises

1. In the DrawTool version that used the blocking strategy (i.e., the one with the waitForID method) add code to the catch clause so that a default image is used whenever the intended image cannot be loaded. Pass the loaded default image as a argument to the ColorImage's constructor.
2. In the polling version take out the statusID call in the constructor and explain the program's behavior.
3. In the polling version, take out the repaint (1000) call in the paint method and explain the program's behavior.
4. In the polling version, use a filled circle instead of a text string.
5. In the polling version, experiment with different values of the repaint interval.
6. Enhance the paint method of the ImageObserver version so that `ERROR` and `ABORT` conditions are detected and handled in a reasonable way.

7. Revise the DrawTool application so that the three images are defined by ImageIcons.
8. Revise the EditTool application so that the size of the current font is selected by pressing on an image that shows the word "font" drawn in the size that will be selected. Use a drawing program to make an image for this exercise. Use the ImageIcon class to load and display this image.

7.13 Layout Managers

The layout of a user interface refers to the placement of the individual user interface components (such as buttons, canvases, text areas) within the user interface's window(s). A layout is determined by assigning to each component a location (within a given window) and a size (height and width). A proper layout must insure that the regions assigned to different components do not overlap within a given window and that all of the components will fit within the boundary of the window. In addition, a good layout will insure that the placement of the component reflects their logical relationships; for example, a label for a choice and the choice component itself should be placed close together so that it is clear to the user which control the label describes. Some user interface components are sufficiently structured so that their layout is predetermined. For example, a pulldown menu always appears in a menubar at the top of the window and different menus are placed left-to-right across the menubar. Other user interface elements are less sructured; a button, for example, may appear almost anywhere in a user interface.

Manually designing the placement of components for a statically sized window may be tedious and error-prone, especially if there are a large number of user interface components. Because the underlying window systems typically allocate screen space in rectangular areas, each component—regardless of its actual shape—is allocated a rectangular area sufficient to hold its visible representation. To insure that two components do not overlap, it is necessary to check that the corners of one component's rectangular area do not lie inside of the area assigned to the other component or that the sides of the two components' rectangular areas do not intersect. Furthermore, because some components (such as a panel) are containers of other components (such as a set of buttons), the size of the container must be checked to insure that it is large enough to fully display the contained components. These checks involve computing the coordinates of the different corners and making a number of comparisons, all of which are very detailed and subject to oversights and mistakes.

Additional complexity arises when the layout must be dynamically reconfigured. It is a common feature of most windowing systems that the user is able to expand or contract the window that contains the user interface. This causes two major problems with respect to the layout. First, if the window is contracted the window may no longer have sufficient height and/or width to contain all of the components of the user interface at their original locations or with their original sizes. Each of the components must be dynamically repositioned and/or resized. Second, if the window is expanded, how should the additional space be used? Several possibilities exist: the individual elements can expanded in size to occupy the additional space; the individual elements can retain their size and simply move farther apart; some combination of growth and spacing can be used to try to maintain the proportions of the user interface. An awkward looking interface can result if the reconfiguration is not done in a reasonable way. If the components do not change their size or location, they simply become surrounded by a large margin of unused space and the user's intent of resizing the window is probably defeated. If individual components are simply made bigger, some components may grow to disproportionately large sizes (a huge dismiss button in a dialog window). If the components retain their original sizes but simply move farther apart, related components (a choice and the choice's label) simply drift apart and become visually disassociated. To maintain its desired "look," the reconfiguration may need to use a complex strategy that allows different components to grow by different amounts. Consider the simple DrawTool application that has a drawing area and some related controls. When the user enlarges the size of the DrawTool application's window, the presumed intent is to make the drawing area larger, not to make the button larger. In this case most of the new space should be used to expand the drawing area.

To aid the programmer with the placement and dynamic reconfiguration of components in the user interface, there is a set of layout managers that are briefly described in Table 7.11. A layout manager can be assigned to any type of Container (Window, JFrame, JPanel, Dialog, JApplet). A container's layout manager is responsible for determining the placement and size of the container''s components. Once assigned to a container, the layout manager is called automatically; the programmer never has to invoke the layout manager's methods directly.

The BorderLayout, FlowLayout, and GridLayout are simple to use, and when used in combination are often sufficient to obtain a usable layout. The GridBagLayout is quite complicated and is used only when finer control of the dynamic reconfiguration is required. Examples of each of the layout managers is given below along with a simple example showing the *combined use* of several layout managers.

Table 7.11 Layout Managers

Border Layout	Places the components at the margins (top, bottom, left, right) and the center. The margins are named by the compass points (North, South, East, West).
FlowLayout	Places the components in a left-to-right, top-to-bottom fashion
GridLayout	Places the components in a two dimensional grid. All grid elements are the same size. Components are placed in successive elements starting in the upper left-hand grid position and proceeding column by column and row by row.
CardLayout	Presents only one of its components at a time. The choice among components can be made by a name associated with each component or by navigation.
GridBagLayout	Similar to the GridLayout except that the grid elements are not necessarily of the same size. Each component can have an associated GridBagConstraint to controls its reconfiguration.
null	No layout manager is used. The programmer indirectly determines the layout by adjusting the size and placement of each component. Only useful for hand crafting statically sized interfaces.

7.13.1 BorderLayout

The code in Figure 7.90 shows the construction of an example interface that has five buttons arranged by a BorderLayout manager. Because the Frame class is derived from Container, the BorderFrame class inherits the setLayout method. In this code a new BorderLayout is constructed and assigned as the layout manager using the inherited setLayout method. The five buttons are constructed with labels, suggesting where they will appear in the user interface. These buttons are then added to the BorderFrame. The string values "North", "South", "East", "West", and "Center" are used by the BorderLayout to indicate the position of each element when it is added to the BorderFrame. Of course, only one component can be assigned to each of the BorderLayout's five positions. The string values naming each of the BorderLayout's positions are also defined as the named constants BorderLayout.NORTH, BorderLayout.SOUTH, BorderLayout.EAST, BorderLayout.WEST, and BorderLayout.CENTER.

```
public class BorderFrame extends JFrame implements WindowListener
{

  public BorderFrame()
  {
    //...
    Container content = this.getContentPane();
    content.setLayout(new BorderLayout());
    JButton button1 = new JButton("North");
    JButton button2 = new JButton("South");
    JButton button3 = new JButton("East");
    JButton button4 = new JButton("West");
    JButton button5 = new JButton("Center");
    content.add(button1, BorderLayout.NORTH);
    content.add(button2, BorderLayout.SOUTH);
    content.add(button3, BorderLayout.EAST);
    content.add(button4, BorderLayout.WEST);
    content.add(button5, BorderLayout.CENTER);

  }

  //...
}
```

Figure 7.90 Using a BorderLayout

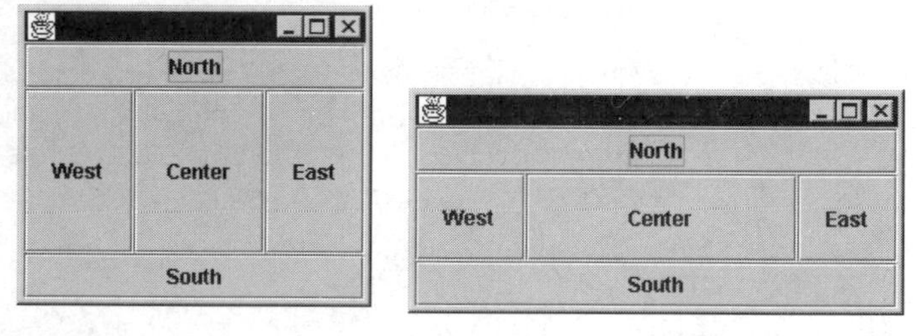

Figure 7.91 BorderLayout Examples

The appearance of the BorderFrame with two different resizings is shown in Figure 7.91. As can be seen in these figures, the components have been resized to take up all of the space; each component abuts with the adjacent components. The components at the margins are elongated horizontally (for the "North" and "South" components) or vertically (for the "East" and "West" components) to stretch across the entire border of the frame. The components at the "North" and "South" positions are assigned the minimum height necessary to display the component (in this case, the minimum height needed to draw the Button's label). Similarly, the components at the "East" and "West" positions are assigned the minimum width. The "Center" position in the BorderLayout is expanded horizontally and vertically to take up all unused space. Notice how this expansion affects the dimensions of the "Center" button in the examples pictured in Figure 7.91.

The BorderLayout provides a way to separate adjacent components by introducing "gaps" into the layout. Both a vertical gap and a horizontal gap can be defined. The BorderLayout's gaps can be defined either by arguments on the

(a) Using the constructor to define the gaps.

```
public class BorderFrame extends JFrame implements WindowListener
{

  public BorderFrame()
  {
    // set the horizontal gap to 10 pixels, vertical gap to 20 pixels
    content.setLayout(new BorderLayout(10, 20));
    //...
  }

  //...
```

(b) Using the set methods to define the gaps.

```
public class BorderFrame extends JFrame implements WindowListener
{

  public BorderFrame()
  { BorderLayout layout;
    layout = new BorderLayout();

    layout.setHgap(10);    // set the horizontal gap to 10 pixels

    layout.setVgap(20);    // set the vertical gap to 20 pixels

    content.setLayout(layout);
    //...

  }
  //...
}
```

Figure 7.92 Defining "gaps" in the BorderLayout

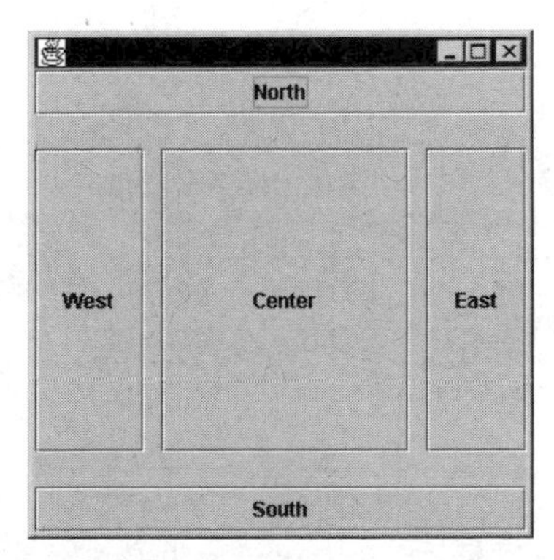

Figure 7.93 Gaps in the BorderLayout Example

BorderLayout constructor or by using set methods as shown in the code segments in Figure 7.92.

The effect of the horizontal and vertical gaps in the example layout are shown in Figure 7.93. Notice that the five buttons are now separated from each other. The vertical gap of 20 pixels separates the components at the top (North) and bottom (South) from the other components. The horizontal gap of 10 pixels separates the middle (Center) components from those at the right (East) and left (West) edges.

7.13.2 FlowLayout

The use of a FlowLayout is shown in the code example in Figure 7.94. In this code a new FlowLayout is constructed and assigned as the layout manager using the FlowFrame's inherited setLayout method. Five buttons are constructed and added to the FlowFrame. The order in which the components are added to the Frame is significant because the first component added will be the first component placed in the layout, followed by the second element to be added, and so on. Thus, in this example the button labelled "Button 1" will appear in the left-most, top-most position and the button labelled "Button 5" will appear in the right-most, bottom-most position.

The FlowLayout strategy is illustrated in Figure 7.95 that shows how the FlowLayout arranges the five buttons in two frames of different sizes. The only difference in these two interfaces is the width of the frame. In the left-hand part of the figure, the Frame is only wide enough to allow two of the buttons to be placed across the frame. Thus, the button labelled "Button 3" is placed lower in the Frame and below the button labelled "Button 1". In the right-hand part of the figure, the Frame's width has been extended so that three buttons can be placed across the frame. In this case, the first three buttons are placed in a row

```
public class FlowFrame extends JFrame implements WindowListener
{

  public FlowFrame()
  {
    //...
    Container content = this.getContentPane();
    content.setLayout(new FlowLayout());
    JButton button1 = new JButton("Button 1");
    JButton button2 = new JButton("Button 2");
    JButton button3 = new JButton("Button 3");
    JButton button4 = new JButton("Button 4");
    JButton button5 = new JButton("Button 5");
    content.add(button1);
    content.add(button2);
    content.add(button3);
    content.add(button4);
    content.add(button5);

  }
  //...
}
```

Figure 7.94 Using a FlowLayout

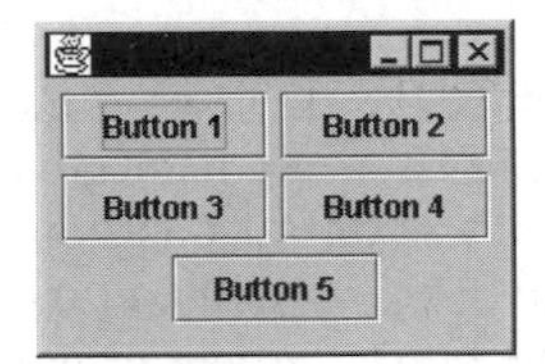

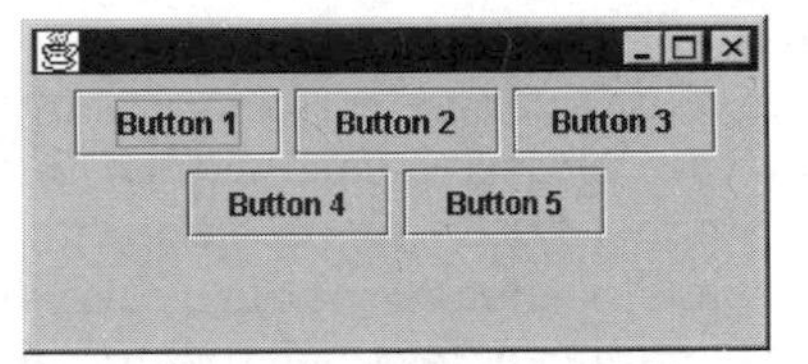

Figure 7.95 FlowLayout Examples

```
public class FlowLayout...
{
   //...
   public FlowLayout (int alignment);
   public FlowLayout (int alignment, int hgap, int vgap);
   //...
   public void setAlignment(int alignment);
   public void setHgap(int hgap);
   public void setVgap(int vgap);
   //...
}
```

Figure 7.96 Specifying Alignment and Spacing in the FlowLayout Class

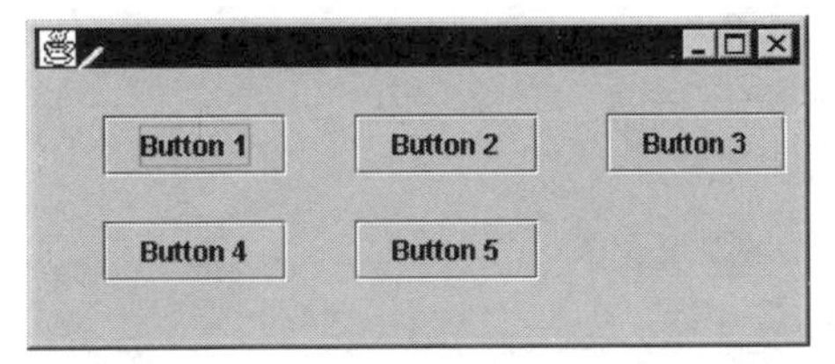

Figure 7.97 The Effect of Changing Gaps and Alignment in the FlowLayout

at the top of the frame and the remaining two buttons are placed in a row lower in the frame.

Notice in the two FlowLayout examples that the bottom row (containing either one button in the narrower frame or two buttons in the wider frame) is centered. Notice also that the adjacent components are separated by a horizontal or vertical gap. Both of these effects can be controlled by using overloaded constructors or set methods. A partial description of the FlowLayout class is given in Figure 7.96 that shows the overloaded constructors, the set methods, and the defined constants that are used in setting the alignment.

The effect of specifying a larger horizontal gap (20 pixels), a larger vertical gap (30 pixels), and an alignment of LEFT is shown in Figure 7.97. By comparison with the previous layout, notice that the buttons are spaced farther apart due to the larger gaps, and that the last row of buttons are left justified and not centered.

7.13.3 GridLayout

The GridLayout arranges its components in a regular two-dimensional grid. As components are added to the grid, the size of the grid positions are adjusted so that all components can be accomodated. However, all positions in the grid are the same size. This means that the each grid position will be large enough to hold the largest component even if that position holds only a much smaller component. Thus, the grid is regular in the sense that all of the rows and colums are aligned. The code to create a GridLayout to hold three buttons and their corresponding labels is shown in Figure 7.98. The constructor for the GridLayout can take two integer values that specify the number of rows and columns, respectively, in the grid. In the example below, there are three rows and two columns. As with the FlowLayout, the order in which the components are added is significant. The first component that is added is placed in the first row, first column—in other words, the upper left-hand grid position; subsequent components are placed in the following columns until the first row is filled, after which the next component is placed in the first column of the next row, and so on. In this example, each label-button pair fill a row (because each row has two columns).

The appearance of the user interface created by the GridLayout is shown in Figure 7.99. The regularity of the grid is most evident in both of the examples.

```
public class GridFrame extends JFrame implements WindowListener
{

  public GridFrame()
  {
    //...

    Container content = this.getContentPane();
    content.setLayout(new GridLayout(3,2)); // 3 rows, 2 columns

    JLabel  label1  = new JLabel("First Button");
    JButton button1 = new jButton("Button 1");

    JLabel  label2  = new JLabel("Second Button");
    JButton button2 = new JButton("Button 2");

    JLabel  label3  = new JLabel("Third Button");
    JButton button3 = new JButton("Button 3");

    content.add(label1);
    content.add(button1);
    content.add(label2);
    content.add(button2);
    content.add(label3);
    content.add(button3);

  }

  //...
}
```

Figure 7.98 Creating a GridLayout

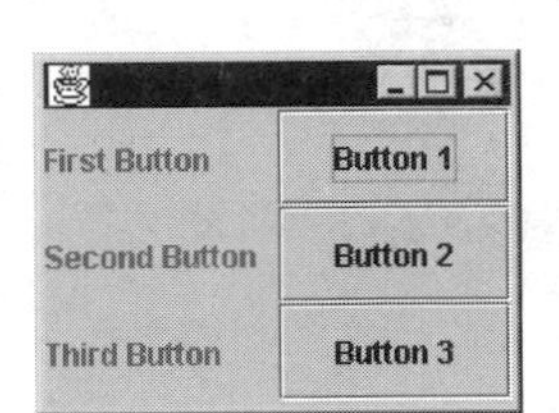

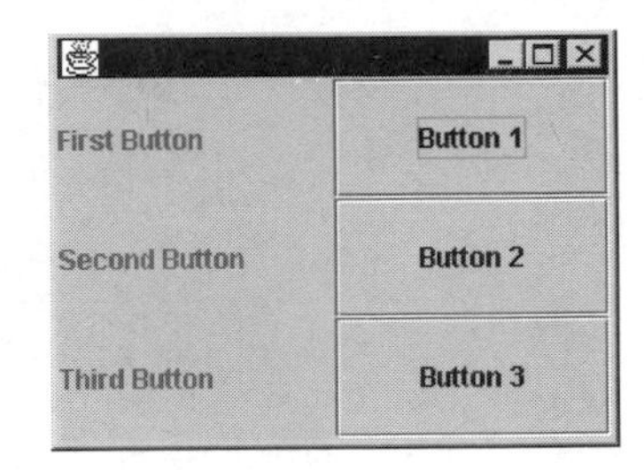

Figure 7.99 GridLayout Examples

```
public class GridFrame extends JFrame implements WindowListener
{
  public GridFrame()
  {
    //...
    GridLayout layout = new GridLayout(3,2);
    layout.setVgap(10);
    Container content = this.getContentPane();
    content.setLayout(layout);
    //...
  }

  //...
}
```

Figure 7.100 Specifying Vertical Gaps in the GridLayout

Notice also that as the size of the frame is increased the regularity and structure of the grid is maintained. As the frame exapands, the additional space is divided equally among the grid positions. This is most evident in the buttons that increased in both height and width. The regularity of the grid is in contrast to the FlowLayout where increasing the size of the frame might change the number of components in a given row. The equal size of the grid positions is also in contrast to the FlowLayout where each element may have a different size.

As with the other layout managers, vertical and horizontal separations can be specified for the GridLayout. Notice in the examples above that the top and bottom edges of immediately adjacent buttons are touching. To provide greater visual separation between the buttons, a vertical gap can be specified as shown in the code segment shown in Figure 7.100. Here a set method is used to specify the vertical gap. A similar set method is available to define a horizonatal gap. Alternatively, the gaps can be specified on an overloaded constructor.

The effect of the vertical spacing in the GridLayout is shown in Figure 7.101. Notice that by comparison with the previous layout shown in Figure 7.99, the buttons are now distinctly separated. Although it is less obvious, the fields containing the labels are also separated because the vertical spacing applies uniformly to all grid positions.

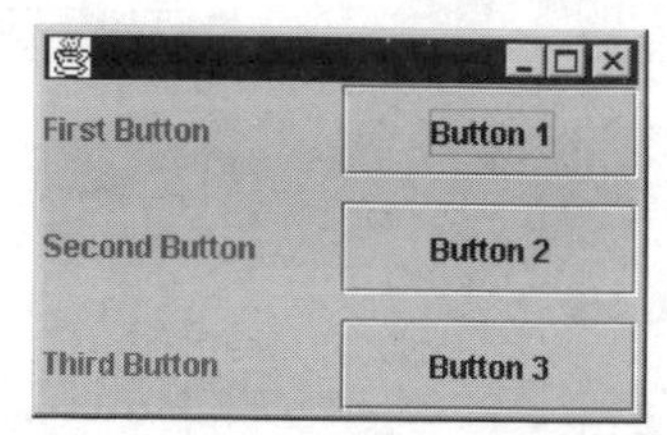

Figure 7.101 The Effect of Vertical Spacing in the GridLayout

7.13.4 CardLayout

The CardLayout provides a way of partitioning a complex user interface into smaller, self-contained units that can be displayed one at a time. In a complex interface it is often possible to divide the components into logical groups such that a set of related controls are placed in the same group and that it is unlikely that the user would need to use more than one group at a time. Each such group of components are placed in a single subinterface that is thought of as a "card." The complete user interface is represented by a collection of cards. The CardLayout presents one of the cards at a time. In addition to the individual cards, the interface also contains some controls for navigating to adjacent cards. Under program control, a card can be selected by a name that is associated with the card or by navigation forward or backward through the set of cards.

To illustrate the CardLayout, three sets of related controls will be organized as a group of cards with simple controls to navigate forward or backward among the cards. Figure 7.102 shows the sequence of related controls and the navigational controls. The initial interface (part a) shows the two navigational controls, the buttons labelled "Previous" and "Next" together with the first card, a set of three buttons below a label indicating the purpose of the buttons. Pressing the "Next" button causes the interface to that shown in part b of the figure. The two navigational buttons remain the same but the "card" portion of the user interfaces changes to another related set of controls. The second card contains another group of three buttons beneath a label. Pressing the "Previous" button when the second card is displayed causes the first card to be displayed. Pressing the "Next" button when the second card is displayed causes the third, and last, card to be displayed. The third card contains two buttons and a label.

Unlike the other layout managers, the programming aspects of a CardLayout require the program to directly interact with the CardLayout itself. With the other layout managers, it is only necessary to establish an association between the container and the layout manager; the layout manager will then operate transparently. However, a CardLayout manager must be explicitly told when to change from one "card" to the next. The methods necessary to manipulate the cards cannot be part of the container's interface because these methods do not apply to all layout managers. Therefore, the CardLayout class provides a set of methods, as shown in Figure 7.103, to manipulate the set of cards.

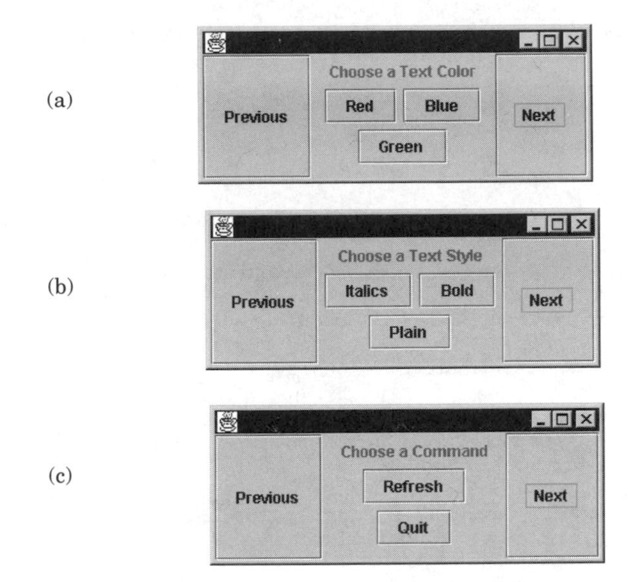

Figure 7.102 The Sequence of Controls in a CardLayout

```
public class CardLayout extends Object implements LayoutManager2 ...
{
   public void first(Container parent)
   public void last(Container parent)
   public void next(Container parent)
   public void previous(Containr parent)
   public void show(Container parent, String name)
}
```

Figure 7.103 The CardLayout Class

The methods of the CardLayout manager operate as follows. The CardLayout treats each component in a container as representing a "card." Thus, the programmer must insure that each component is itself a container that encapsulates all of the related controls for the card. The cards are ordered by the sequence in which they were added to the container. The `first` and `last` methods of the CardLayout class cause the first and last cards, respectively, to be displayed. The CardLayout manager maintains an index of which card in the sequence is currently displayed. The navigational methods, `next` and `previous`, make the currently displayed card the predecessor and successor, respectively, of the current card. The next and previous methods wrap around in the sense that the predecessor of the first card is the last card and the successor of the last card is the first card. Each of these methods takes the Container that holds the cards as a parameter. Each card can also be assigned a name when it is added to the Container using the Container's method:

```
public Component add(String name, Component comp);
```

```
public class CardFrame extends JFrame implements WindowListener,
                                                   ActionListener
{
  private JPanel cards = new JPanel();
  private CardLayout cardLayout = new CardLayout();

  public CardFrame()
  {
    //...

    Container content = this.getContentPane();
    content.setLayout(new BorderLayout());
    JButton previous = new JButton("Previous");
    previous.setActionCommand("previous");
    previous.addActionListener(this);

    JButton next = new JButton("  Next  ");
    next.setActionCommand("next");
    next.addActionListener(this);

    content.add(previous, BorderLayout.WEST);
    content.add(next, BorderLayout.EAST);

    // Create cards and add them to cards (see below)

    content.add(cards, BorderLayout.CENTER);

  }

  public void actionPerformed(ActionEvent evt)
  { if (evt.getActionCommand().equals("next"))
    { cardLayout.next(cards);
      return;
    }
    if(evt.getActionCommand().equals("previous"))
    { cardLayout.previous(cards);
      return;
    }
  }

  //...
}
```

Figure 7.104 Creating the Structure of the Card-Based Interface

This name is used by the CardLayout's `show` method to select one of the cards directly and explicitly.

The code to create the card-based interface shown above is presented in two parts. The first part of the CardFrame code, shown in Figure 7.104, creates the outer structure of the interface, including the two navigational buttons ("Next" and "Previous"), the container for the cards and its associated CardLayout object, and the methods for handling the events generated by the navigational buttons. The CardFrame class implements the ActionListener interface because it will respond to the event generated by the two buttons. The private data of the Card-Frame consists of a Panel object that acts as a Container to hold the cards, and a

```
public class CardFrame extends JFrame ...
{
  private JPanel cards = new JPanel();
  private CardLayout cardLayout = new CardLayout();

  public CardFrame()
  {
    //...

    JPanel card1 = new JPanel();
    card1.setLayout(new FlowLayout());
    card1.add(new JLabel("Choose a Text Color"));
    card1.add(new JButton("Red"));
    card1.add(new JButton("Blue"));
    card1.add(new JButton("Green"));

    JPanel card2 = new JPanel();
    card2.setLayout(new FlowLayout());
    card2.add(new JLabel("Choose a Text Style"));
    card2.add(new JButton("Italics"));
    card2.add(new JButton("Bold"));
    card2.add(new JButton("Plain"));

    JPanel card3 = new JPanel();
    card3.setLayout(new FlowLayout());
    card3.add(new JLabel("Choose a Command"));
    card3.add(new JButton("Refresh"));
    card3.add(new JButton("Quit"));

    cards.add(card1);
    cards.add(card2);
    cards.add(card3);
    cards.setLayout(cardLayout);

    //...
  }

  //...
}
```

Figure 7.105 Constructing the Cards

CardLayout object that acts as the layout manager for the cards. The CardFrame constructor creates two buttons, assigns action commands to each, and registers itself as a listener for the events of each button. These two buttons are added to the "East" and "West" positions of the CardFrame, which is itself managed by a BorderLayout manager. The container of the cards—the Panel object named `cards`—is assigned to the "Center" position in the CardFrame. The `actionPerformed` method is invoked whenever one of the two buttons is pushed. Because of the `actionPerformed` method, pushing the "Next" button causes the next method of the CardLayout manager to be invoked and pushing the "Previous" button causes the previous method of the CardLayout manger to be invoked.

The second part of the code to create the card-based interface constructs the individual cards. This code is shown in Figure 7.105. Because each card holds several components (Buttons and Labels), a Panel container is used for each card. The

Panel objects, `card1`, `card2`, and `card3`, are constructed and the appropriate components for each card are added to the card. The three cards are then added to the container `cards` that is managed by the CardLayout manager. This code also shows that the `cardLayout` object is defined as the layout manager for the `cards` container. The construction of the cards for a functional interface would also include the code to handle the events generated by each card.

7.13.5 GridBagLayout

The GridBagLayout is the most complex of the layout managers but the one that offers the most control over the appearance of a resizable interface. The complexity of the GridBagLayout is due to the fact that the programmer is responsible for specifying a number of properties that determine the placement and the sizing of each component when the interface is changed in size. These properties relate to:

- where is the component placed in the user interface with respect to other components,
- in what directions (horizontal, vertical) does the component stretch or compress,
- how much does the component stretch or compress in each direction relative to other components, and
- where is the component placed within its allocated area (top, bottom, left, right,etc.).

Because each of these properties can be specified separately for each component in the interface, the GridBagLayout permits the greatest control of the interface's appearance.

To illustrate the operation of the GridBagLayout, a simple interface for examining a list of URLs will be implemented. The interface is pictured in Figure 7.106. The interface consists of a labelled area that displays a URL, a labelled area containing a textual description of what can be found at the URL, and two buttons for navigating to the previous (Back button) and the following (Next button) entries in the list of URLs. If the interface is expanded by the user, the following constraints should be applied in rearranging the interface:

- The URL text field should only expand horizontally, not vertically.
- The URL label field should not expand vertically.
- The description label field should expand vertically and the label should be centered within the field.
- The description text area should expand both horizontally and vertically.
- The buttons should expand horizontally and vertically.
- The text area should expand much more rapidly than the buttons.

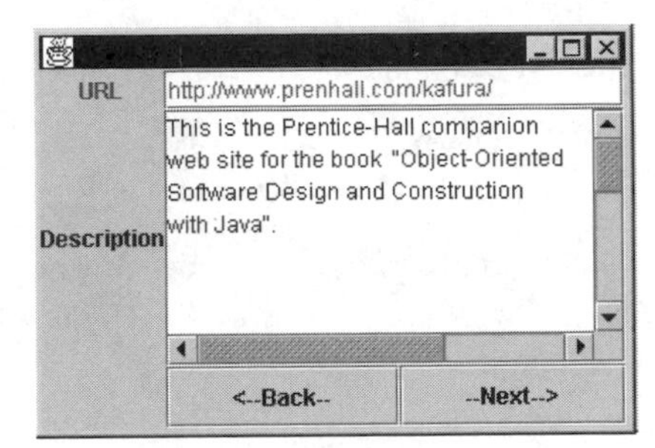

Figure 7.106 Example Interface for the GridBagLayout

Figure 7.107 Defining a Grid for the GridBagLayout

The same constraints should apply when the interface is compressed by the user. In simpler terms, these constraints imply that the text area should take up most of the available space created by an expansion while also keeping the other components proportionally sized and relatively positioned with respect to the text area.

The overall organization of the interface is determined by a grid that is drawn over a sketch of the desired layout. A drawing and its grid for the example interface is shown in Figure 7.107. The rows and columns that make up the grid are numbered starting from zero (0) with row 0 being the top row and column 0 being the left-most columns as shown in the diagram. Notice that the rows and columns can be of unequal size. For example, row 1 is larger than the other rows. Also notice that not all of grid positions need to contain a component. For example, there is no component in column 0 and row 2. The flexibility to have unequally-sized positions and to leave some grid positions empty are ways in which the GridBagLayout differs from the more rigid, but simple, *GridLayout*. The location of the components within the grid will be used to identify the place-

Table 7.12 Constraints in the GridLayout

Constraint	Description	GridBagConstraint field name(s)	Possible Values
Placement	The location in the grid of the upper left-hand corner of the component	gridx, gridy	Any non-negative integer value consistent with the grid structure
Size	The number of rows and columns spanned by the component	gridwidth, gridheight	Any non-negative integer value consistent with the grid structure
Growth	The directions in which the component may expand	fill	GridBagConstraint.HORIZONTAL GridBagConstraint.VERTICAL GridBagConstraint.BOTH GridBagConstraint.NONE

ment of the components in the interface. The grid lines in this figure coincides with the edges of components. Although this is a convenient scheme it is not strictly required; additional grid lines can be added to the figure. There must be sufficient grid lines to allow the position of each component to be given.

The constraints for each component are defined using the grid and an associated class, GridBagConstraints. The GridBagConstraints class provides a number of public integer data elements and various named constants. The basic constraints and the public data elements in the GridBagConstraints class are summarized in Table 7.12. Several other constraints are explained below. The placement constraints, `gridx` and `gridy`, specify where the component is located in the grid. The size contraints specify the width (in grid columns) and height (in grid rows) of the components. The growth constraint defines in which dimensions the component is allowed to expand or contract. As shown, four named constants are defined for this purpose. The proportion constraint is the most difficult of the constraints to adjust. This constraint determines how much a component expands or contracts relative to other components. In other words, when additional space becomes available the weights determine how this space is allocated among the components or, similarly, when the interface is reduced in size, the weight determine how much each component is reduced.

The constraints for the text area are as follows. The text area is located at the position gridx=1 and gridy=1 and has gridwith=2 (because it spans two columns) and gridheight=1. Because it is desired that the text area grow both horizontally and vertically, fill=GridBagConstraints.BOTH. Finally, the text area is

Table 7.13 Summary of Constraints for the Example Interface

Component	gridx	gridy	gridwidth	gridheight	fill	weightx	weighty
URL label	0	0	1	1	NONE	0	0
URL text field	1	0	2	1	HORIZ.	100	0
Description label	0	1	1	1	VERT.	0	100
Text area	1	1	2	2	BOTH	100	100
Back button	1	1	1	1	BOTH	100	5
Next button	2	2	1	1	BOTH	100	5

Note: HORIZ. denotes HORIZONTAL; VERT. denotes VERTICAL.

```
public class GridBagConstraints ...
{
  //named constants for fill constraint
    public static final int BOTH;
    public static final int NONE;
    public static final int HORIZONATAL;
    public static final int VERTICAL;

  // public fields for basic constraints
    public int gridx;
    public int gridy;
    public int gridwidth;
    public int gridheight;
    public int fill;
    public int weightx;
    public int weighty;
  //...
}
```

Figure 7.108 Partial Definition of the GridBagConstraints Class

assigned weightx=100 and weighty=100. These weights have no absolute meaning. Because the design constraints indicate that the text area should expand more rapidly than the two buttons, the weights for the text area are set larger than those for the buttons. By comparison the vertical weight for the buttons is set to 5. It is only the relative values of the weights for components that is significant. The constraints for each of the components in the simple interface are summarized in Table 7.13.

The GridBagConstraints class is used to encode the constraints for a component. A portion of the GridBagConstraints class is shown in Figure 7.108. The

GridBagLayout class defines a set of public integer fields, each of which corresponds to a constraint. There are no set or get methods for these fields; the fields themselves are directly accessible. The GridBagConstraint class also defines a set of named constants associated with some of the fields. The named constants shown below are those associated with the `fill` constraint.

Once the constraints for each component has been determined the coding of the layout is straightforward. A portion of the code for the sample interface is shown in Figure 7.109. This code has three major parts. The first part of this code creates a GridBagLayout object and a GridBagConstraints object. Only a single GridBagConstraint is needed because it can be reused for each component that is added to the interface. The GridBagLayout is established as the layout manager using the usual `setLayout` method. The second part of the code creates the components of the interface. There is nothing new in this part of the code. The third part of the code defines the constraints for and then adds each component to the user interface. The sequence of statements is highly repetitive for each component. For each component the fields of the GridBagConstraint object are assigned. For example, the statements:

```
constraints.gridx = 0;
constraints.gridy = 0;
```

assign the grid coordinates for the URL label component. The other contraint fields are assigned values in a similar way. The constraints defined by a GridBag-Constraint object are associated with a component by the GridBagLayout's `setConstraints` method. After the constraints are associated with a component, the component can be added to the container. For example, the code:

```
layout.setConstraints(urlLabel, constraints);
add(urlLabel);
```

associate the constraints encoded in the GridBagConstraint object named `constraints` with the `urlLabel` component and then adds the `urlLabel` object to the user interface. This pattern of associating the constraints with the component using the `setConstraints` method and then adding the component to the layout is repeated for each of the components.

Several additional constraints can be defined using the GridBagConstraint class that affect the size and positioning of the component within its assigned area. These additional constraints are summarized in Table 7.14. The padding constraint increases the size of the component beyond its minimum size. The two fields, `ipadx` and `ipady`, specify amounts to add to the width and height of the component. This constraint is used to insure that a component is given more space beyond that otherwise allocated by the layout manager. The margin constraint can be used to prevent contiguous components from touching by adding an addition border around the outside of the component. The margin constraint is specified by an Insets object. An Insets object can be created and initialized as follows:

Table 7.14 Additional Constraints

Constraint	Description	GridBag-Constraint Field	Possible Values
Padding	Additional space added to the component's minimum size	ipadx, ipady	integer values
Margin	The thickness of a border that surrounds the component	insets	an Insets object
Alignment	The positioning of the component within the area allocated to it	anchor	GridBagConstraints.EAST GridBagConstraints.WEST GridBagConstraints.SOUTH GridBagConstraints.NORTH GridBagConstraints.CENTER GridBagConstraints.NORTHEAST GridBagConstraints.NORTHWEST GridBagConstraints.SOUTHEAST GridBagConstraints.SOUTHWEST

```
Insets margins = new Insets(5, 10, 5, 10);
```

which specifies a 5 pixel border on the top (the first 5) and the botton (the second 5), and a 10-pixel border on the left (the first 10) and the right (the second 10). An alternative way to define the same Insets object is through public fields declared in the Insets class as follows:

```
Insets margins;
margins.top    =  5;
margins.left   = 10;
margins.bottom =  5;
margins.right  = 10
```

It does not matter in which way the Insets object is created.

The alignment constraint is used to determine where to place a component within an area that is larger than the component itself. In the example user interface, the text labels are of a fixed size, but the areas in which they are placed are generally much wider and taller than the text string of the label. The anchor field in the GridBagConstraints object allows one of nine (9) different alignments to be specified. The possible alignments are defined by the named constants shown in the table. The names of these constants suggest the nature of

```
public class GridBagFrame extends JFrame implements WindowListener
{

  public GridBagFrame()
  {
    //..
    // Part 1: create GridBagLayout and GridBagConstraints

    GridBagLayout layout = new GridBagLayout();
    GridBagConstraints constraints = new GridBagConstraints();
    Container content = this.getContentPane();
    content.setLayout(layout);

    // Part 2: create components
    JLabel urlLabel = new JLabel("URL");
    urlLabel.setForeground(Color.red);
    JTextField urlText = new JTextField();
    urlText.setForeground(Color.red);
    JLabel descriptionLabel = new JLabel("Description");
    descriptionLabel.setForeground(Color.blue);
    JTextArea descriptionText = new JTextArea(20,30);
    descriptionText.setForeground(Color.blue);
    JScrollPane descriptionTextScroller = new JScrollPane(descriptionText);
    JButton back = new JButton ("<--Back--");
    JButton next = new JButton("--Next--");

    //Part 3: add each component with its constraints
    // add URL Label
    constraints.gridx = 0;
    constraints.gridy = 0;
    constraints.gridwidth = 1;
    constraints.gridheight = 1;
    constraints.weightx = 0;
    constraints.weighty = 0;
    constraints.fill = GridBagConstraints.NONE;
    layout.setConstraints(urlLabel, constraints);
    content.add(urlLabel);

    // add URL TextField
    constraints.gridx = 1;
    constraints.gridy = 0;
    constraints.gridwidth = 2;
    constraints.gridheight = 1;
    constraints.weightx = 100;
    constraints.weighty = 0;
    constraints.fill = GridBagConstraints.HORIZONTAL;
    layout.setConstraints(urlText, constraints);
    content.add(urlText);

    // add Description label
    constraints.gridx = 0;
    constraints.gridy = 1;
    constraints.gridwidth = 1;
    constraints.gridheight = 1;
    constraints.weightx = 0;
    constraints.weighty = 100;
    constraints.fill = GridBagConstraints.VERTICAL;
    layout.setConstraints(descriptionLabel, constraints);
    content.add(descriptionLabel);
```

Figure 7.109 *(continued)*

```
        // add Description TextArea
        constraints.gridx = 1;
        constraints.gridy = 1;
        constraints.gridwidth = 2;
        constraints.gridheight = 1;
        constraints.weightx = 100;
        constraints.weighty = 100;
        constraints.fill = GridBagConstraints.BOTH;
        layout.setConstraints(descriptionTextScroller, constraints);
        content.add(descriptionTextScroller);

        // add Back button
        constraints.gridx = 1;
        constraints.gridy = 2;
        constraints.gridwidth = 1;
        constraints.gridheight = 1;
        constraints.weightx = 100;
        constraints.weighty = 5;
        constraints.fill = GridBagConstraints.BOTH;
        layout.setConstraints(back, constraints);
        content.add(back);

        // add Next button
        constraints.gridx = 2;
        constraints.gridy = 2;
        constraints.gridwidth = 1;
        constraints.gridheight = 1;
        constraints.weightx = 100;
        constraints.weighty = 5;
        constraints.fill = GridBagConstraints.BOTH;
        layout.setConstraints(next, constraints);
        content.add(next);

    }

    //...

    }
```

Figure 7.109 Using the GridBagLayout in the Example Interface

the alignment at a compass point or at the center of the area. The default alignment is at the center.

The effects of using the padding and margins can be seen by comparing the two versions of the sample user interface shown in Figure 7.110. The image on the left is the version of the interface in which the padding and margin constraints have not been set. In this version the two buttons are vertically compressed and the two buttons touch in the middle and there is little if any visible separation between the top edge of the button and the lower edge of the text area. The image on the right is the version of the interface in which the padding and margin constraints have both been set. In this version the padding constraint has added more of the available space to the buttons (causing the text area to shrink vertically) and the margin constraint has separated the buttons from each other and from the adjacent text area.

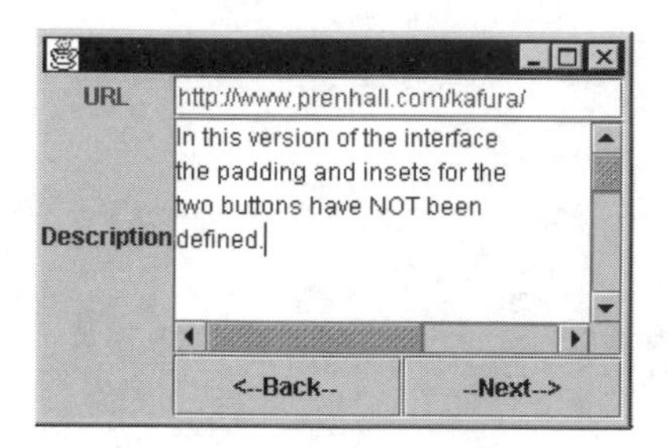

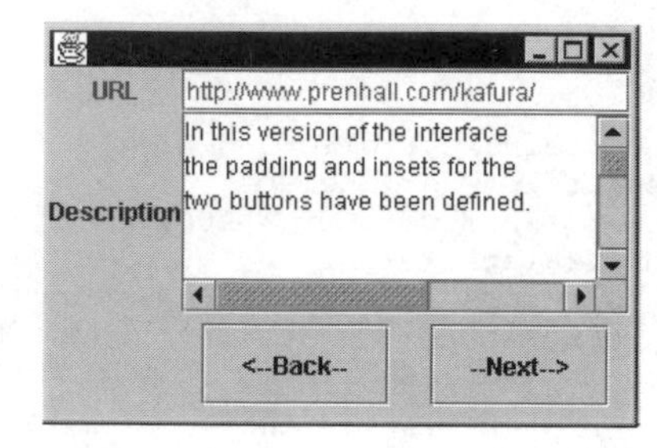

Figure 7.110 Effect of the Padding and Margin Constraints

```
public class GridBag2Frame extends JFrame implements WindowListener
{

  public GridBag2Frame()
  {
    //...

    GridBagLayout layout = new GridBagLayout();
    GridBagConstraints constraints = new GridBagConstraints();
    Container content = this.getContentPane();
    content.setLayout(layout)

    //...

    // add Back button
    constraints.gridx = 1;
    constraints.gridy = 2;
    constraints.gridwidth = 1;
    constraints.gridheight = 1;
    constraints.weightx = 100;
    constraints.weighty = 5;
    constraints.fill = GridBagConstraints.BOTH;
    constraints.ipadx = 10;
    constraints.ipady = 10;
    constraints.insets = new Insets(5,10,5,10);
    layout.setConstraints(back, constraints);
    content.add(back);

    // add Next button
    constraints.gridx = 2;
    constraints.gridy = 2;
    constraints.gridwidth = 1;
    constraints.gridheight = 1;
    constraints.weightx = 100;
    constraints.weighty = 5;
    constraints.fill = GridBagConstraints.BOTH;
    constraints.ipadx = 10;
    constraints.ipady = 10;
    constraints.insets = new Insets(5,10,5,10);
    layout.setConstraints(next, constraints);
    content.add(next);

  }
}
```

Figure 7.111 Defining the Padding and Margin Constraints

The code to create the padding and margin constraints is shown in Figure 7.11. Only the constraints for the buttons are shown. The additional constraints are shown in boldface. The constraints for the two buttons are the same. Each button has a padding of 10 pixels in the vertical direction and 10 pixels in the horizonal direction. Each button also has 5 pixels of inset at the top and bottom edges and 10 pixels of inset at the right and left edges.

7.13.6 Combining Several Layout Managers

Using several different layout managers for different parts of an interface is often necessary to obtain the desired layout in a simple way. As an example, consider the interface shown in Figure 7.112 for a variation of the simple drawing application. The drawing area, a Canvas, is the largest component and is approximately centered in the interface with the two control buttons arranged left-to-right below the drawing area. This spatial confguration should be maintained when the interface's window is resized. The BorderLayout alone is not sufficient because only one of the two buttons could be placed in the `South` position. The FlowLayout can not be used alone because as the window is expanded it might place one or both of the buttons to the right of the drawing area. The GridLayout is not sufficient because the components are not of the same size. The CardLayout is inappropriate because there is only a single interface. Although the GridBagLayout could be used, a simpler solution is possible by combining two layout managers.

The desired layout can be obtained by combining a BorderLayout and a FlowLayout. The BorderLayout is the top-level manager whose `Center` position is occupied by the drawing area and whose `South` position is occupied by a container that contains and manages the two controls (a Choice and a Button). The layout manager for the container is a FlowLayout to insure that the controls are organized left-to-right (except when the window is too small horizontally to present them both).

Figure 7.112 An Interface with Two Layout Managers

```
public class DrawFrame extends JFrame implements WindowListener
{
  public DrawFrame()
  { Container content = this.getContentPane();
    content.setLayout(new BorderLayout());
    //...

    JPanel canvas = new JPanel();
    canvas.setBackground(Color.yellow);

    JComboBox colorChoice = new JComboBox();
    colorChoice.addItem("Red");
    colorChoice.addItem("Green");
    colorChoice.addItem("Blue");
    colorChoice.setSelectedItem("Blue");

    JButton clearButton = new JButton("Clear Canvas");

    JPanel panel = new JPanel();
    panel.setLayout(new FlowLayout());
    panel.add(colorChoice);
    panel.add(clearButton);

    content.add(canvas, BorderLayout.CENTER);
    content.add(panel, BorderLayout.SOUTH);
  }

  //...
}
```

Figure 7.113 Using Multiple Layout Managers

The code using the two layout managers is shown in Figure 7.113. The relevant parts of the code are shown in boldface. A BorderLayout object is constructed and set as the layout manager for the DrawFrame. The Canvas and the two control objects, a Choice and a Button, are then constructed. A Panel object is created that will serve as the container for the two controls. Note that java.awt.Panel is derived from java.awt.Container. Because it is a container, the Panel object will have its own layout manager, separate and distinct from that of the DrawFrame. A FlowLayout object is constructed and set as the layout manager for the the Panel object. The Choice object and the Button object are then added to the Panel where they will be arranged by the Panel object's FlowLayout manager. Finally, the Canvas object is added to the `Center` position of the DrawFrame (recall that the DrawFrame has a BorderLayout manager) and the Panel object (containing the two controls) is added to the `South` position in the DrawFrame.

The most significant aspect of the code in the DrawFrame class is the relationship among hierarchically nested containers managed by different layout managers. The example has a simple, two-level hierarchy—the Panel container was added to the DrawFrame container—and each container has its own layout manager. The hierarchical organization can be carried out to as many levels as necessary to achieve the desired arrangement of components. The exercises suggest several variations to illustrate this point.

Exercises

1. Modify the BorderLayout example to remove one of the components at the margins (the North, South, East, or West) and observe whether unoccupied space is reserved for the missing component or whether the other components expand into that space.
2. Modify the BorderLayout example to remove the Center component. How does this affect the sizing of the other components.
3. Using only a BorderLayout, show how you would create a layout in which four buttons appear in a single column.
4. Using only a BorderLayout, show how you would create a layout in which four buttons appear in a single row.
5. Modify the FlowLayout example to add the buttons in a different order and observe the effect on the user interface.
6. Modify the FlowLayout example so that the last row of buttons is right justified.
7. Modify the FlowLayout example so that the buttons have label of very different sizes. For example, make one button with the label "A Very Long, Long Label" and another button with a single character for a label. Experiment with adding these buttons to the FlowLayout in different orders and observing the effect on the layout for frames of different size.
8. Modify the FlowLayout so that the buttons use *fonts* of different sizes. This will make the heights of the buttons different from each other. Experiment with adding these buttons the FlowLayout in different orders and observing the effect on the layout for frames of different sizes.
9. Modify the FlowLayout by using labels of different lengths and *fonts* of different sizes to create a set of buttons such that no two buttons have the same shape. Experiment with adding these buttons the FlowLayout in different orders and observing the effect on the layout for frames of different size.
10. Modify the GridLayout example so that the buttons are in a single row with the appropriate label above each button.

11. Modify the GridLayout example so that the buttons are in a single row with the appropriate label below each button.

12. Modify the GridLayout by using button labels of different lengths and *fonts* of different sizes to create a set of buttons such that no two buttons have the same shape. Experiment with adding these buttons the GridLayout and observing the effect on the layout for frames of different size.

13. Using only the GridLayout manager, create a user interface that has three buttons in a single column with the text "Push One Button" to the left of column of buttons.

14. Modify the CardLayout example by adding the existing cards to their container in a different order and observe the effect on the ordering of cards presented in the user interface.

15. Modify the CardLayout example so that it includes two additions navigational buttons, "First" and "Last", that cause the first and last cards, respectively, in the CardLayout to be displayed.

16. Modify the CardLayout example so that it includes another card. The new card contains the label "Choose a Background Color", below which are three buttons labelled "Red", "Green", and "Blue".

17. Modify the CardLayout example so that the "Next" and "Previous" buttons are part of each card rather than part of the outer structure of the user interface.

18. For the GridBagLayout example, add two additional horizontal and two additional vertical lines to the grid for the example interface shown above. The exact placement of these additional grid lines is not important. Using the revised grid, modify the code of the example interface. Experiment with resizing the original interface and the revised interface and note any discernible differences.

19. For the GridBagLayout example, change the weights in the example interface to use the values 20,1, and 0 rather than 100, 5, and 0. Is there any difference in the resizing behavior? What does this mean about the absolute versus relative values of the weights?

20. Modify the GridBagLayout example so that the text labels are both aligned to the right of their respective areas.

21. In the GridBagLayout example, increase the padding and margin values and observe the effect on the layout of the user interface.

22. Design, implement, and test the code for creating a user interface that has two drawing areas side-by-side. Each drawing area has two buttons labelled "Clear" and "Save" below the drawing area. Combine the use of three different layout managers.

23. Design, implement, and test the code for creating a user interface that has a single drawing area beneath of which is a control area managed by a CardLayout. The control area can either show two buttons labelled "Clear" and "Save" or three buttons labelled "Red", "Green", and "Blue". Combine the use of three different layout managers.

24. Design, implement, and test the code for creating a user interface that has a layout approximately that of the example used in the GridBag-Layout section above. What differences do you note between your solution that combines several layout managers and the solution using the GridBagLayout?

25. Design, implement, and test the code for creating a user interface that has a layout that consists of two parts. The left part has a large text area, below which are two buttons labelled "Cut" and "Paste". The right part has three "lines": the first line has the label "Foreground" and a Choice for selecting a color; the second line has the label "Background" and a Choice for selecting a color; the third line has a button labelled "Search" and a TextField for entering a search string. Use at least three different types of layout managers in solving this problem.

CHAPTER 8

Input/Output in Java

8.1 Introduction

8.1.1 The Complexity of I/O

Those features of a programming language that relate to i/o are usually among the more complex and difficult to learn. There are four reasons for this apparent, and often real, complexity. First, the input or output of data involves many issues, such as: must the data be accessed in sequential order or can the data be accessed in non-sequential order? if the data is only accessible in sequential order, can the program "look ahead" in the data? if the requested data is not available, does the program wait for the data or can it proceed with other tasks? can the data be read in large "chunks" or only one date element at a time? Although simple programs are usually not concerned with many, if any, of these issues and although more complicated programs may only deal with some of them, the programming language must provide mechanisms to deal with all of them.

Second, the i/o features of a language stand at the border between two very different domains. Within the program, the data exists in strongly typed, highly structured objects and structures whereas outside of the program the data exists in untyped, byte-oriented form. In memory, the data is represented for the convenience of the programmer whereas outside of the program it is represented for the convenience of the storage device. For example, when a database entry is output by a program to a file, the type and structure of the database entry is usually reduced to a string of bits or characters that encode the information in a serial form. When this information is read by the same or a different program, the input data must be parsed to recover its type and structure. This means that the programmer must do a substantial amount of work to output the data in a recoverable form and to reconstruct the data on input.

Third, the storage of data usually involves numerous, low-level details that are ripe for many programming mistakes. For example, if an integer value is stored in a field how is it justified in the field? Does it have a preceding sign? Can it have leading zeros? What is its base? Each basic data type raises its own set of similar questions. These issues are compounded in user-defined objects that have several basic data types to be read or written as a single unit.

Fourth, most I/O operations throw exceptions. In file I/O, for example, any output operation can potentially raise the exception that the operation cannot be completed because the disk is full. The statement to open a file can potentially raise the exception that the file could not be found. Most input operations can raise an exception that the expected format (type) of the data does not match that of the actual data present in the input stream. Because of these exceptions, the user's I/O code must contain numerous try/catch clauses. Furthermore, a carefully designed program must consider what remedial action to take when an error condition occurs and an exception is raised. Should the application simply be terminated? Can a default value be given? Should a warning dialog be initiated? Should the condition be written to a log file? All of these exceptional conditions and the questions of how to deal with each exception help to illustrate why I/O programming is complicated and difficult to program.

8.1.2 The Java I/O Model

One way of coping with the complexity of input/output is to understand the basic characteristics of the language's model of I/O. In Java, there are three principle characteristics of the I/O model: media, encoding, and access. The Java I/O library, named java.io, defines a set of classes that can be composed in regular patterns based on the characteristics of the input or output. These three characteristics are summarized in Figure 8.1. The media characteristic identifies what type of storage structure or device is used to receive or produce the data that is input or output. The storage structures include interactive devices, disk-based

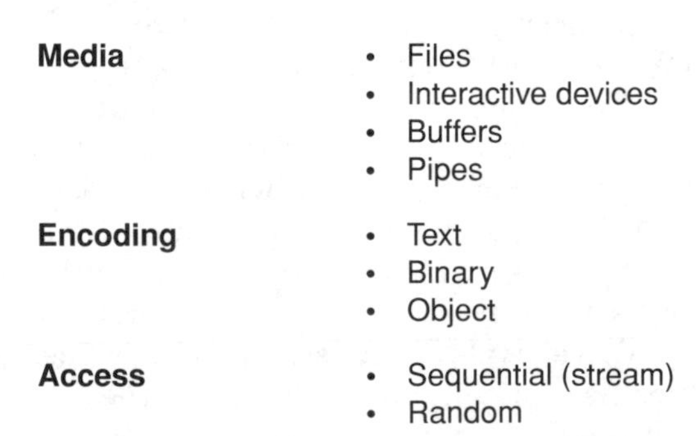

Media
• Files
• Interactive devices
• Buffers
• Pipes
Encoding
• Text
• Binary
• Object
Access
• Sequential (stream)
• Random

Figure 8.1 Characteristics of the I/O Model

files, memory-based buffers, and memory-based pipes. Most programmers have a great deal of experience with disk-based files. Memory-based buffers are sometimes needed in handling data that is supplied by a user to a graphical interface. If the interface contains a text field in which the user is allowed to type a textual form of some data (e.g., a postal address), this data is often placed in a buffer (an array of characters or a string) from which the data is then read and parsed. Memory-based pipes are used for communication between different concurrent tasks in a single application. Concurrent tasks are described in the Chapter 9.

The encoding characteristic determines the basic method used to represent the data in its stored (external) form. Three possible encodings are text, binary, and object. Text encoding simply means that the value of the data is represented externally in a readable string form. For example, the value of an integer, which is represented internally in binary form as `00100110`, would be stored externally as the sequence of text, characters `38`. Binary encoding means that the external representation is the same as the internal representation. Thus, the integer value represented internally in binary form as `00100110` would be stored externally as exactly the same sequence of bits on the external storage medium. Unlike-text encoded data, binary-encoded data cannot be read directly by people (or other programs that do not use exactly the same internal representation of the data). The object encoding is a powerful mechanism supported in Java that allows a complete object—of any size or complexity—to be output and input by a single command. The power and simplicity of this encoding is obtained at the price of incompatibility with non-Java systems. The object encoding can only be used by Java programs that agree on the class definitions of objects that they communicate among themselves.

The access characteristic determines whether the data can only be processed sequentially, often called stream data, or whether the data can be accessed non-sequentially, often called random access. Sometimes the nature of the media requires a certain type of access be used. For example, the keyboard device on which a user types cannot be treated as a random-access data source because the sequence of key strokes must be processed in the sequential order they were typed. Although disk-based files can be treated as either stream access or random access, many applications treat a file as a stream because it is sufficient and simpler.

8.1.3 The Pattern of Text and Binary Stream I/O Classes

Another way to reduce the complexity of the Java I/O classes is to understand the pattern that organizes the collection of Java's I/O classes. The pattern for text encoded stream I/O and binary encoded stream I/O is shown in Figure 8.2. In the middle of the figure are the various storage media (file, buffer, pipe) that serve as the data repositories. The classes for output, on the left, and for input, on the right, are arranged in several layers. It is important to notice that these

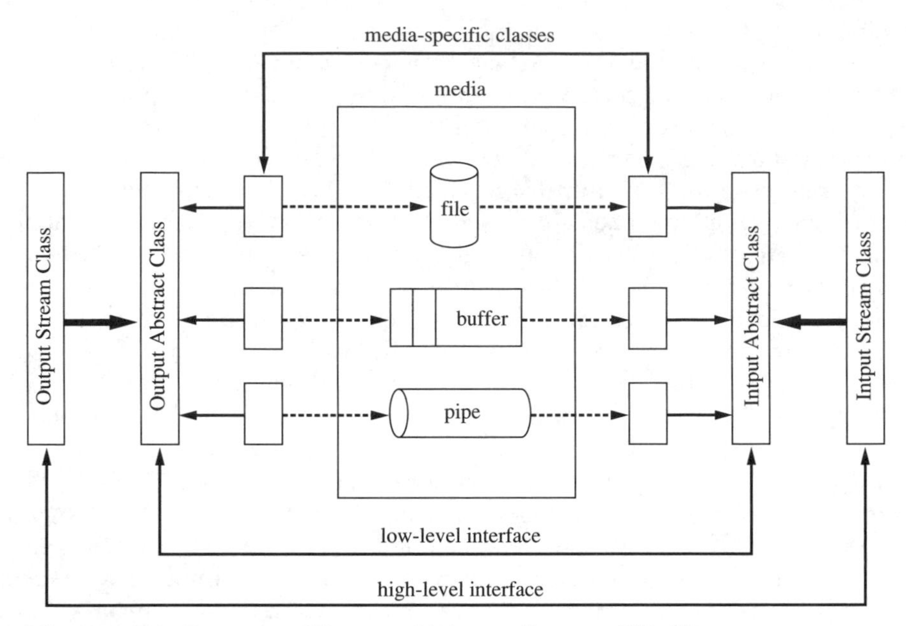

Figure 8.2 Pattern of Text and Binary Stream I/O Classes

layers are related by two distinct relationships. The thin arrows represent an inheritance relationship and the thick arrows represent composition, or association. The dotted arrows represent data flowing to or from a device. The general sense of this figure is that the actual data will flow from left-to-right through these classes being stored in one of the media types. For example, the topmost part of the figure means that data can be output to a file by using the interface of a high-level OutputStream class. This class deals with the data by using an abstract class to refer to an associated object that is an instance of a media specific (in this case, file media) class that actually outputs the data to the file.

As shown in Figure 8.2, the I/O classes provide both low-level and high-level interfaces. Each media type has a pair of associated Java classes that provide a low-level, byte-oriented interface for writing data to and reading data from that media. The interface of these classes is low-level and byte-oriented in the sense that only a single byte or an array of bytes can be written or read. These media-specific classes usually have constructors and other methods that are related to the distinct properties of the media type. The media-specific stream classes are specializations of abstract stream classes. These abstract classes are important elements in the Java I/O structure because, through polymorphism, they allow any of the media-specific classes to be treated as objects of the abstract class in a uniform and type-safe manner. Like the media-specific classes, the abstract classes also provide a low-level, byte-oriented interface. The high-level interface layer provides an interface oriented toward the built-in Java types. For each built-in Java type there is a corresponding facility provided by

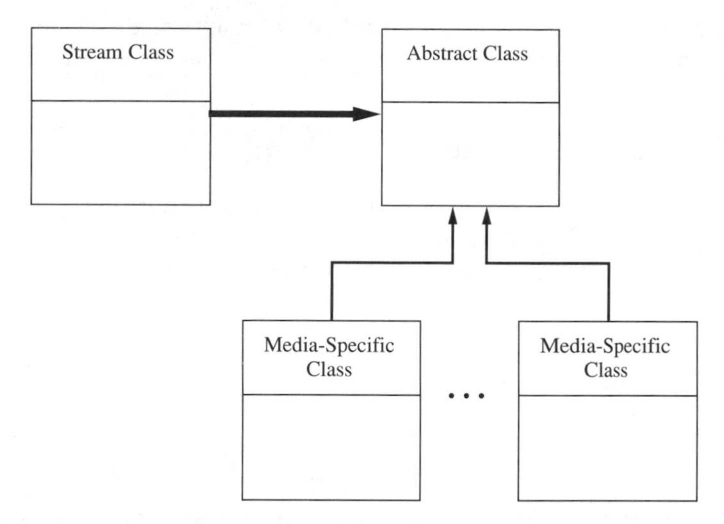

Figure 8.3 Class Diagram of Text/Binary Stream I/O Classes

the classes in the high-level interface layer allowing a value of the basic Java type to be output or input.

A class diagram view of the pattern among the I/O classes is shown in Figure 8.3. This figure shows even more clearly the role of the abstract stream classes. As shown in this figure, each stream class has an association with an object that the stream class identifies through the abstract class. The actual object is an instance of a media-specific class that extends the abstract class. This structure helps to reduce the complexity of the I/O classes because it allows the stream class to work with any media-specific class. Furthermore, all of the media-specific classes have the same interface, the one defined by the abstract class, making them more uniform and easier to understand. Finally, the structure shown in Figure 8.3 allows for separation of concerns: the stream class is concerned with dealing with the conversion of the data from the high-level to the low-level form whereas the media-specific classes are concerned with manipulating the storage unit to accept or produce the data.

A common coding pattern for using the I/O classes is shown in this code segment:

```
MediaSpecificClass media = new MediaSpecificClass(...);
StreamClass stream = new StreamClass( (AbstractClass)media );
stream.IOmethod(...);
```

where a media-specific object is first constructed to provide a low-level means of transporting data to or from a specific media. This media-specific object is then type-cast to its abstract class and used to construct a stream object. As part of this construction, the stream class maintains an association (keeps a reference to) the media-specific class. The I/O methods of the stream object are used to read or write the data.

8.1.4 The Book Example

Throughout this chapter a single, simple example based on a database of information about books will be used to illustrate the various forms of Java I/O. Each book in the database is represented by four pieces of information:

- title: a String
- author: a String
- year (of publication): an integer
- price: a double

The information about a book is captured by the Book class whose definition is shown in Figure 8.4. The private data of the class reflects the book abstraction given above. The two constructors are used to create either a book with given characteristics or a book with unknown characteristics. The `read` and `write` methods of this class will be rewritten for various combinations of media, encoding, and access. The arguments for the `read` and `write` methods will also vary with each different type of I/O considered. A `print` method is also provided in the Book class to aid in constructing and verifying the execution of the examples presented in later sections. In an actual application there would undoubtedly be more accessor/query methods as well as more information maintained about each book. However, the example is deliberately simplified to illustrate more specifically the facilities of Java I/O.

8.1.5 Chapter Organization

The presentation of the `java.io` library is organized around the characteristics outlined above as shown in Table 8.1. Across the different sections of this chapter, all of the three types of encoding are considered, as are both types of access methods. The last section, on filtering, is a technique that applies to all stream-oriented forms of input and output. Only the file and interactive media are considered, as these are the most common. The pipe media is covered as part of the chapter on concurrent programming with threads.

8.2 Binary I/O

8.2.1 The Java Classes

The collection of Java classes for binary encoded stream I/O follows Java's pattern of stream I/O classes. The specific classes for binary encoded stream I/O is

```
public class Book
{
   private String title;
   private String author;
   private int    year;
   private double price;

   public Book()
   { title  = "Unknown";
     author = "Unknown";
     year   = 0;
     price  = 0.0;
   }

   public Book(String title, String author, int year, double price)
   { this.title  = title;
     this.author = author;
     this.year   = year;
     this.price  = price;
   }

   public void read(...)  //depends on encoding/media/access
   { }

   public void write(...) //depends on encoding/media/access
   { }
   public void print() // displays the Book information on the
   {}                  // standard output (screen)
}
```

Figure 8.4 The Book Class

Table 8.1 Organization of Material on java.io

Section	Media	Encoding	Access
8.2	File	Binary	Stream
8.3	File, interactive	Text	Stream
8.4	File	Binary	Random
8.5	File	Object	Stream
8.6	Filtering		Stream

shown in Figure 8.5. As in the general pattern, the middle of the figure contains the various storage media (file, buffer, pipe). The media-specific classes write and read data to their respective medium in a binary encoded form. Recall that the thin arrows represent an inheritance relationship so, for example, `FileOutputStream` extends `OutputStream`. The thick arrows represent composition, or

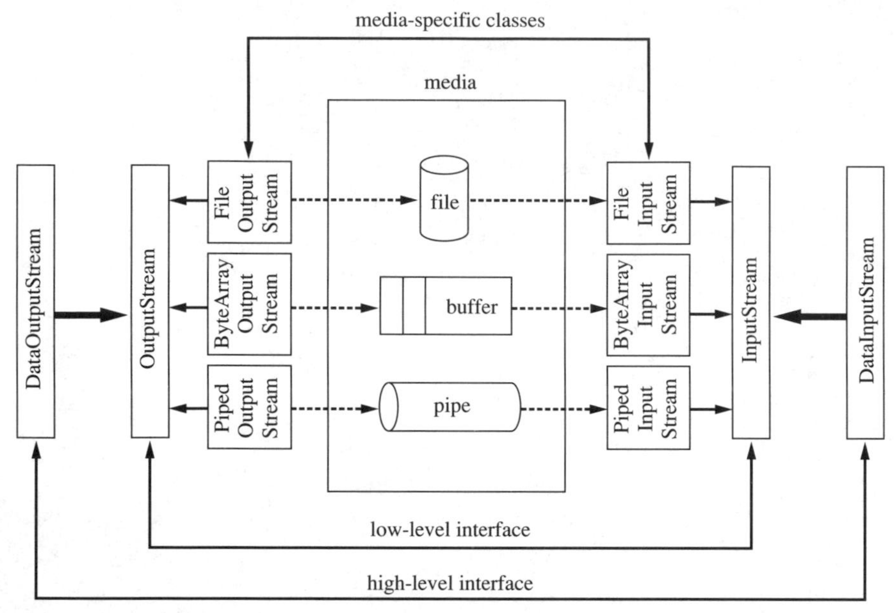

Figure 8.5 The Binary Encoding Classes for Java I/O

```
public class FileOutputStream extends OutputStream
{
   public FileOutputStream(String fileName) throws IOException;
   public FileOutputStream(String fileName,
                           boolean append) throws IOException;
   //...
   public void write(byte[] b) throws IOException;
   public void write(byte[] b, int off, int len) throws IOException;
   //...
}
```

Figure 8.6 FileOutputStream: A Media-Specific Class

association; for example, a `DataInputStream` object has a reference to an `InputStream` object. The dotted arrows represent data flowing to or from a device. The general sense of this figure is that the actual data will flow from left-to-right through these classes being stored in one of the media types.

Examples of the media-specific classes are the `FileOutputStream` and the `FileInputStream` classes for the file media. The `FileOutputStream` classes is shown in Figure 8.6. As is typical of the media-specific classes, the data-handling methods are low-level and byte-oriented in the sense that only a single byte or an array of bytes can be written or read in each operation. Also, note that the constructors for the class are specific to a file media, that is, the constructor arguments refer to the name of the file and whether the output data should be appended to the file. Finally, notice that all of the operations throw exceptions that must be handled in all of the code that uses these methods. Other media-

```
public abstract class OutputStream
{
   public void close() throws IOException;
   public void flush() throws IOException;
   public abstract void write(int b) throws IOException;
   public void write(byte[] b) throws IOException;
   public void write(byte[] b, int off, int len) throws IOException;
}
```

Figure 8.7 The OutputStream Class

specific classes that use binary encoding are `ByteArrayOutputStream` and `ByteArrayInputStream` that use an in-memory buffer, and `PipedOutputStream` and `PipedInputStream` that are intended for use among concurrent threads.

The abstract classes for the binary-encoded stream classes are named `OutputStream` and `InputStream`. Notice that the `FileOutputStream` class shown above extends the abstract class `OutputStream`. The `OutputStream` class is shown in Figure 8.7. Notice that the three `write` methods take as their arguments primitive byte or int types. The `close` method indicates that no further operations will be done on the data stream. This operation allows media such as a file to perform any useful or necessary operations to conclude its use. The `flush` method forces any data internally buffered in the output stream to be transferred to the medium. Such buffering can be explicitly arranged by the user for efficiency as explained later. All of the methods throw the `IOException` exception. Lastly, notice that the `OutputStream` class does not have a constructor because it is not intended that an object of the `OutputStream` class itself would be created. Instead, an object of one of the media-specific classes is constructed and type-cast to its base class, the `OutputStream` class.

The final part of the pattern of I/O classes are the DataOutputStream and DataInputStream classes that provide the higher-level interface oriented toward basic Java types. For each basic Java type there is a corresponding write method in the DataOutputStream class and a corresponding read method in the DataInputStream class. For example, the DataOutputStream class has a `writeInt` method and the DataInputStream has a `readInt` method. A partial description of the two stream classes is shown in Figure 8.8. Notice that all of the methods in these two classes are declared final so that, for safety, they cannot be changed in a derived class, and that, as with other I/O methods, they throw an exception.

One aspect of the DataInputStream and DataOutputSteam classes that requires some explanation is the treatment of String and character data. Internally, Java represents text-oriented data in a format defined by the international Unicode Consortium (see `http://unicode.org`). Each Unicode character is represented by two bytes, providing a sufficiently large character space to contain, according to the standard, the characters of "the principal written languages of the Americas, Europe, the Middle East, Africa, India, Asia, and Pacifica." The 16-bit Unicode encoding is double the length of the more limited

```
public class DataOutputStream ...
{
   public DataOutputStream(OutputStream out);
   //...
   public final void writeBoolean(boolean b) throws IOException;
   public final void writeChar(int c)        throws IOException;
   public final void writeDouble(double d)   throws IOException;
   public final void writeInt(int i)         throws IOException;
   public final void writeUTF(String s)      throws IOException;
   //...
}

public class DataInputStream ...
{
   public DataInputStream(InputStream in);
   //...
   public final boolean readBoolean() throws IOException;
   public final char    readChar()    throws IOException;
   public final double  readDouble()  throws IOException;
   public final int     readInt()     throws IOException;
   public final String  readUTF()     throws IOException;
   //...
}
```

Figure 8.8 The DataOutputStream and DataInputStream Class

but more commonly used 8-bit ASCII encoding. For practicality, Java provides a conversion between character data represented externally in 8-bit form to the Unicode 16-bit form. This conversion is defined by a Unicode transformation format, or UTF. This explains why the method names `writeUTF` and `readUTF` are used in DataOutputStream and the DataInputStream classes, respectively, for the method that write and read a String. It also explains why the parameter on the `writeChar` method in the DataOutputStream is defined by an `int` rather than a `char` type; because the character being written is internally represented by a 16-bit entity (equal in size to an `int`) whereas the `char` type is only 8 bits in length.

In addition to their higher-level interface, the DataOutputStream and DataInputStream classes provide flexibility because they can be composed with any OutputStream object and InputStream object, respectively, as shown by their constructors in Figure 8.8. The flexibility provided by these classes comes from the fact that the program component manipulating a DataOutputStream or a DataInputStream does not depend on knowledge of the specific media being used. For example, a FileOutputStream object can be used to construct a DataOutputStream. If a method takes a DataOutputStream object as its parameter, that method can manipulate the underlying media, in this case a file, without being concerned about the fact that the data is being written to a file. Without any change, the same method can be used to write data to a buffer or a pipe simply by passing to it a DataOutputStream object that has been constructed with a buffer or a pipe output stream. This effect is illustrated in the Book class example presented later in this section.

8.2.2 An Example

The Book example is used to illustrate how to write and read binary encoded data using a file. The example is presented in several steps. First, a file containing a single book entry is created by showing how to create the necessary output streams and then showing the code for the `write` method of the Book class. Second, the single entry is read from the file by showing how to create the necessary input streams and then showing the code for the `read` method of the `Book`.

The output streams needed to create a file containing a single `Book` entry are constructed as shown in the main program in Figure 8.9. The streams are created by the code shown in boldface in two steps. First, a media-specific FileOutputStream object is constructed; the constructor argument names the file to which the data will be written. Remember that the FileOutputStream itself provides only a low-level, byte-oriented interface. Thus, the FileOutputStream object, `bookFile`, is used to construct a DataOutputStream, `bookStream`, that has a higher-level interface because this will make the writing of the book entry simpler. A `Book` object is then constructed and its `print` method is used to display what entry will be written to the file. Finally, the file entry is written using the `write` method of the `Book` class that is explained below. Notice that the DataOutputStream object, `bookStream`, is passed as an argument to the `write` method so that the `Book` object knows on which stream it should write its data. Notice that an `IOException` must be dealt with because that exception is thrown by the FileOutputStream constructor. Exceptions that might occur are due to such conditions as an invalid file name, lack of disk space to create a file, or the user lacking sufficient privileges to create the file.

The code for the `write` method of the `Book` class is shown in Figure 8.10. This method takes a single parameter, a DataOutputStream object, named

```
import java.io.*;
import Book;

public class Write
{
  public static void main (String args[])
  {

    try
    {
       FileOutputStream bookFile     = new FileOutputStream("books");
       DataOutputStream bookStream   = new
DataOutputStream(bookFile);
       Book book = new Book("War and Peace", "Leo Tolstoy", 1800, 25.95);
       book.print();
       book.write(bookStream);
    } catch (IOException error) {}

  }
```

Figure 8.9 Creating the Output Streams

```
import java.io.*;

public class Book
{
  private String title;
  private String author;
  private int    year;
  private double price;

  //...

  public void write(DataOutputStream bookStream)
  {
    try
    {
      bookStream.writeUTF(title);
      bookStream.writeUTF(author);
      bookStream.writeInt(year);
      bookStream.writeDouble(price);

    } catch (IOException error) {}
  }

}
```

Figure 8.10 The `write` Method of the Book Class

`bookStream`. The `write` method is straightforward. Using the methods of the DataOutputStream class, each of the four data items of the `Book` class `title`, `author`, `year`, and `price` are written to the `bookStream`. The `title` and `author` are written to the `bookStream` using the `writeUTF` method. The `year` and `price` are written to the `bookStream` using the `writeInt` and `writeDouble` methods, respectively. Each of the four write methods can throw an `IOException`. These exceptions are dealt with by the `try/catch` construct. A real application would take some appropriate remedial action if such exceptions occurred; in this simple example, only the outline of the exception handling is shown.

The input streams needed to read the Book entry contained in a file are illustrated by the main program shown in Figure 8.11. The streams are created by the code shown in boldface in two steps. First, a media-specific FileInputStream is constructed whose constructor argument names the file from which the data will be read. Remember that the FileInputStream itself provides only a low-level, byte-oriented interface. Thus, the FileInputStream object, `bookFile`, is used to construct a DataInputStream, `bookStream`, that has a higher-level interface as this will make the reading of the book entry simpler. The file entry is read from the stream using the `read` method of the Book class that is explained below. Notice that the DataInputStream object, `bookStream`, is passed as an argument to the `read` method so that the Book object knows from which stream it should read its data. Finally, the Book object's `print` method is used to display what entry was read from the stream. Notice that an `IOException` must be

```
import java.io.*;
import Book;

public class Read
{
  public static void main (String args[])
  {
    Book book = new Book();

    try {
      FileInputStream bookFile    = new FileInputStream("books");
      DataInputStream bookStream = new DataInputStream(bookFile);
      book.read(bookStream);
      book.print();
    } catch (FileNotFoundException fnf) {}

  }
}
```

Figure 8.11 Creating the Input Streams

```
public class Book
{
  private String title;
  private String author;
  private int    year;
  private double price;

  //...

  public void read(DataInputStream bookStream)
  {
    try {
       title  = bookStream.readUTF();
       author = bookStream.readUTF();
       year   = bookStream.readInt();
       price  = bookStream.readDouble();
    } catch (IOException error) {}

  }

}
```

Figure 8.12 The `read` Method of the Book Class

dealt with because that exception is thrown by the FileInputStream constructor. Exceptions that might occur are due to such conditions as an invalid file name, a file with the given name not existing, or the user lacking sufficient privileges to read the file.

The code for the `read` method of the `Book` class is shown in Figure 8.12. This method takes a single parameter, a DataOutputStream object, named `bookStream`. The `read` method is straightforward. Using the methods of the DataInputStream class, each of the four data items of the `Book` class `title`, `author`, `year`, and `price` are read from the `bookStream`. The `title` and `author` are read from the `bookStream` using the `readUTF` method. The `year` and `price` are read from the `bookStream` using the `readInt` and `readDouble` methods, respectively. Each of the four read methods can throw an `IOException` that are dealt with by the `try/catch` construct. A real application would take some appropriate remedial action if such exceptions occurred; in this simple example, only the outline of the exception handling is shown.

Exercises

1. Compile and execute the example main programs that write and read a single Book entry to a file and verify that they work correctly on your system.

2. Use a common text display utility (such as `type` on Windows95 or `cat` on Unix systems) to verify that the file containing the Book entry is not in a human-readable text form.

3. Check the length of the file created by the Write class on your system. What can you infer by comparing the file's length with the data written to the file?

4. Construct simple GUIS for the two main programs. For example, the GUI for the main program in the `Write` class might have four text fields into which the book's attributes could be entered. For this exercise you should consider adding additional accessor and query methods to the Book class.

5. Revise the main program in the `Write` class so that the same book entry is written to two different files. Use the existing main program in the `Read` class to read both files.

6. Revise the `Write` class so that several different book entries can be written to the file and revise the `Read` class so that each entry in the file is read and displayed.

7. Create a new main program in a new class named `Append` that appends a single new book entry to a file of entries. Use the revised `Read` class created in the previous exercise to verify that the `Append` class works properly.

8. Write a new main program in a class named Buffer so that the book entry data is written to and read from a byte array buffer declared in the main program. Do not change the Book class. Explain why this exercise illustrates the flexibility afforded by the `DataOutputStream` and `DataInputStream` classes.

9. Decide on a reasonable action to take if the book data could not be written or read. Add appropriate code in the catch clauses of both the `Read`, `Write`, and `Book` classes. Test your code by running the programs with illegal files names and improperly formatted files.
10. In the main program in the `Write` class, put the try/catch construct around only the statement containing the `FileOutputStream` constructor. What problem does this cause? Fix this problem.

8.3 Text I/O

8.3.1 The Java Classes

The collection of Java classes related to text encoded stream I/O is shown in Figure 8.13. These classes follow the general pattern of stream I/O classes that has three layers. The classes in the first layer are media-specific classes that write data to or read data from a specific type of storage. The classes in this collection write data to and read from the storage in a human-readable text form. The second layer contains abstract classes that define the common interface of the media-specific classes. Because the media-specific classes extend the abstract

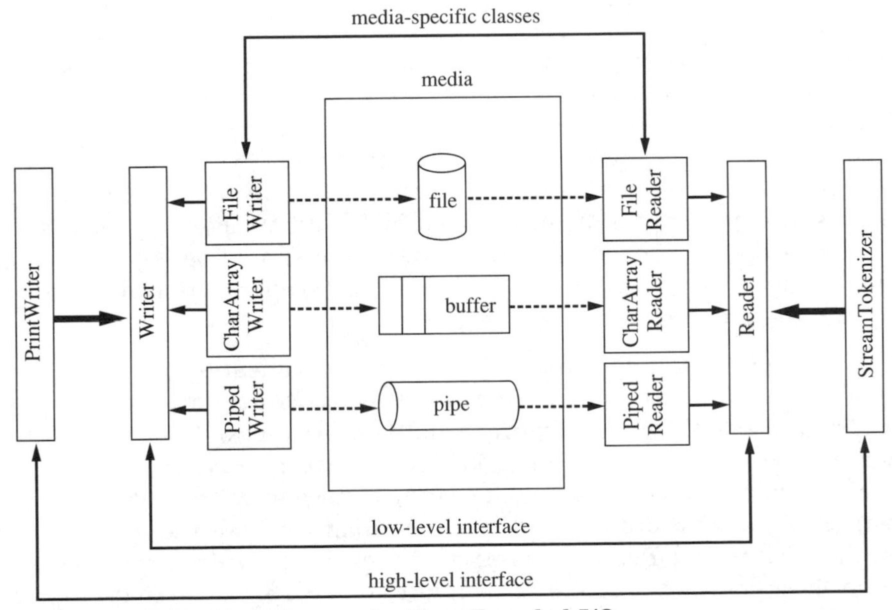

Figure 8.13 The Classes for Text Encoded I/O

```
public class FileWriter extends OutputStreamWriter
{
   public FileWriter(String fileName) throws IOException;
   public FileWriter(String fileName,
                     boolean append) throws IOException;
   //...
}

public class OutputStreamWriter extends Writer
{
   public void write(int c) throws IOException;
   public void write(char[] cbuf, int off, int len) throws IOException;
   //...
}
```

Figure 8.14 The FileWriter and OutputStreamWriter Classes

classes, any media-specific class can be type-cast to the abstract class type. The interface defined in the abstract classes contain only low-level operations that write or read data as single characters or groups of characters. A higher-level interface is provided by the third layer in the pattern. On the output side, methods in the third layer convert from the primitive Java types to a character string that is written to the storage medium using one of the media specific classes. On the input side, methods in the third layer provide a way to parse the character stream obtained from the storage medium and produce value for primitive Java types. Two different approaches to parsing a text input stream will be shown in this section.

The classes for writing text data to and reading text data from a file are used as an example of the media-specific classes. Output to a file is provided by a pair of classes, FileWriter and its base class OutputStreamWriter, and input from a file is provided by a similar pair of classes, FileReader and its base class InputStreamReader. The pair of classes for output is shown in Figure 8.14. The pair of classes for text input are similar. Note that the `write` methods takes as their arguments only the primitive `char` type. Also, note that the constructors for the class are specific to a file media, that is, the constructor arguments refer to the name of the file and whether the output data should be appended to the file. Finally, notice that all of the operations throw exceptions that must be handled in all of the code that uses these methods.

The media-specific text stream classes are specializations of the abstract classes Writer and Reader. An example of this specialization is the OutputStreamWriter class shown in Figure 8.15. The Writer and Reader abstract classes are important elements in the Java I/O structure because, through polymorphism, they allow any of the media-specific classes to be treated as objects of the abstract class in a uniform and type-safe manner. Like the media-specific classes, the Writer and Reader classes also provide a low-level, character-oriented interface. The Writer class is shown in Figure 8.16. Notice that the `write` methods take as their arguments primitive `int`, `char`, or `String` types. The

```
public abstract class Writer
{
   public void close() throws IOException;
   public void flush() throws IOException;
   public abstract void write(int c) throws IOException;
   public void write(char[] c) throws IOException;
   public void write(String str) throws IOException;
   //...

}
```

Figure 8.15 The Writer Class

```
public class PrintWriter ...
{
   public PrintWriter(Writer out);
   //...
   public void print(boolean b);
   public void print(int i);
   public void print(double d);
   public void print(String s);
   //...
   public void println(boolean b);
   public void println(int i);
   public void println(double d);
   public void println(String s);
   //...
}
```

Figure 8.16 The PrintWriter Class

`close` method indicates that no further operations will be done on the data stream. This operation allows media such as a file to perform any useful or nec - essary operations to conclude its use. The `flush` method forces any data internally buffered in the output stream to be transferred to the medium. Such buffering can be explicitly arranged by the user for efficiency as explained later. All of the methods throw the `IOException` exception. Lastly, notice that the Writer class does not have a public constructor because it is not intended that an object of the Writer class itself would be created. Instead, an object of one of the media-specific classes is constructed and type cast to its base class, the Writer class.

A higher-level interface for performing text formatted output is provide by the PrintWriter class. For each primitive Java type there is a pair of overloaded `write` methods. For example, the `int` type has the two methods `print` and `println`. The first of these methods adds to the output text stream a series of characters that represents the value of its integer argument. The second of these methods adds the same series of characters as the first method but also adds an end of line character. The difference between these methods is how the text appears when it is displayed by typical utilities such as "type" on Windows systems or "cat" on Unix systems. Three data items output using the `print` methods would appear on the same line whereas those same data items output using the `println` methods would appear on different lines. A partial description of the PrintWriter stream class is shown in Figure 8.16. Notice that the Print-Writer constructor takes as its argument a Writer object. Because Writer is an abstract class, this Writer object is actually a media-specific class that extends the Writer class.

Reading text from an input stream is more complicated and involves two steps. The first step is concerned with extracting "tokens" from the input stream. A token is a sequence of characters read from the input stream that presumably represents the representation of some value. A token is usually described by specifying sets of characters that delimit its beginning and its end. The second step converts the sequence of characters to the internal (binary) representation of a value of a given type. For example, if the input stream is:

```
2234 3.14159
```

then the first token to be extracted might be the string "2234" and the second token extracted might be the string "3.14159" assuming that any non-blank character begins a token and that a token is ended by a blank character or end of line. These two tokens could then be converted to the value of an `int` variable and a `double` value, respectively.

The Java classes provide two approaches for parsing a text input stream. The first approach uses a StreamTokenizer object. A StreamTokenizer partially combines the two steps of parsing an input stream. Not only does the StreamTokenizer extract the next token from the text stream to which it is attached, but it also recognizes and converts a `double` value to its internal representation. The details of the StreamTokenizer are presented in the example below. The second approach uses a combination of a BufferedReader object and a StringTokenizer object. The BufferedReader obtains successive strings that represent complete lines of input and the StringTokenizer is used to extract the tokens from each of these strings. A series of Java classes is used to convert the token strings into values. This approach is also illustrated in more detail in the example that follows.

8.3.2 An Example

The Book example is used to illustrate how to write and read a text encoded data stream contained in a file. The example is presented in several steps. First, a file containing a single book entry is created by showing how to create the necessary output streams and then showing the code for the `write` method of the Book class. Second, the single entry is read from the file by showing the code that creates the necessary input streams and the code for the `read` method of the `Book` class.

Writing to the File

The output streams needed to create a file containing a single `Book` entry are constructed as shown in the main program below. The streams are created by the code shown in boldface in two steps. First, a media-specific FileWriter is created whose constructor argument names the file to which the data will be written. Remember that the FileWriter itself provides only a low-level, byte-oriented interface. Thus, the FileWriter object, `bookFile`, is used to construct a PrintWriter object, `bookStream`, that has a higher-level interface; as this will simplify the writing of the book entry. A Book object is then constructed and its `print` method is used to display what entry will be written to the file. Next, the book entry is written to the file using the `write` method of the Book class that is explained below. The PrintWriter object, `bookStream`, is passed as an argument to the `write` method so that the `Book` object knows to which stream it should write its data. Finally, the output stream is closed. Notice that an `IOException` must be dealt with because that exception is thrown by the FileWriter constructor. Conditions that might cause such an exception are an invalid file name, lack of disk space to create a file, or the user lacking sufficient privileges to create a file (Figure 8.17).

The code for the `write` method of the `Book` class is shown in Figure 8.18. This method takes a single parameter, a PrintWriter object, named `bookStream`. The `write` method is straightforward. Using the methods of the PrintWriter class, each of the four data items of the `Book` class `title`, `author`, `year`, and `price` are written to the `bookStream` using the overloaded `println` and `print` methods of the `PrintWriter` class. The `title` and `author` are written on separate lines. The `year` and `price` are written on the same line with a separating blank character. Unlike the other I/O methods, the `print` an `println` methods do not generate exceptions.

```
public class Write
{
  public static void main (String args[])
  {
    FileWriter bookFile;
    PrintWriter bookStream = null;

    try
    {
         bookFile = new FileWriter("books");
         bookStream = new PrintWriter(bookFile);

    } catch (IOException error) {}

    Book book = new Book("War and Peace", "Leo Tolstoy", 1800, 25.50);
    book.print();
    book.write(bookStream);
    bookStream.close();
  }
}
```

Figure 8.17 Creating the Text Output Stream

```
import java.io.*;

public class Book
{
  private String title;
  private String author;
  private int    year;
  private double price;

  //...

  public void write(PrintWriter bookStream)
  {
     bookStream.println(title);
     bookStream.println(author);
     bookStream.print(year); bookStream.print(' ');
     bookStream.println(price);
  }

  //...
}
```

Figure 8.18 The `write` Method of the Book Class

```
public class Read
{
  public static void main (String args[])
  {
    Book book = new Book();
    FileReader bookFile = null;
    StreamTokenizer bookStream = null;

    try {
      bookFile   = new FileReader("books");
      bookStream = new StreamTokenizer(bookFile);
    } catch (FileNotFoundException fnf) {}

    book.read(bookStream);
    book.print();
    try
    { bookFile.close();
    } catch (IOException ioe) {}

  }
}
```

Figure 8.19 Creating the Text Input Stream

Reading From the File: StreamTokenizer Approach: The input structure needed to read the Book entry contained in a text file using a StreamTokenizer is shown in the main program presented in Figure 8.19. The structure is created by the code shown in boldface. A media-specific FileReader object is constructed. The constructor's argument names the file from which the data will be read. Notice that a `FileNotFoundException` must be dealt with because that exception is thrown by the FileReader constructor. Remember that the

```
public class StreamTokenizer
{
  public StreamTokenizer(Reader r);

  public static final int TT_EOF;
  public static final int TT_EOL;
  public static final int TT_NUMBER;
  public static final int TT_WORD;

  public double nval;
  public String sval;
  public int ttype;

  public void eolIsSigificant(boolean flag);
  public int nextToken() throws IOException;

  //...
}
```

Figure 8.20 The StreamTokenizer Class

FileReader itself provides only a low-level, byte-oriented interface. Therefore, a StreamTokenizer object is created to provide a higher-level interface for reading data from the file. The StreamTokenizer class is explained in more detail below. The file entry is read from the stream using the `read` method of the `Book` class that is also explained below. Notice that the StreamTokenizer object, `bookStream`, is passed as an argument to the `read` method so that the `Book` object knows from where it should read its data. Finally, the `Book` object's `print` method is used to display what entry was read from the stream. After the book entry has been read, the input stream is closed and the exception thrown by this operation is handled.

The StreamTokenizer class reads individual characters from a low-level input stream and produces a sequence of "tokens." The partial definition of the `StreamTokenizer` class is shown in Figure 8.20. The argument of the StreamTokenizer's constructor specifies the stream from which the tokenizer will obtain the stream of characters to parse. The constructor's argument is the abstract class Reader so that the tokenizer can work with any of the media-specific classes derived from Reader. Each time that the `nextToken` method is called, the StreamTokenizer reads and parses the characters from the input stream and assembles a token. As shown by the named constants, the StreamTokenizer recognizes four types of tokens in the input stream: a number (`TT_NUMBER`) that includes numeric values written with or without a decimal point, a word (`TT_WORD`) that is any text not recognized as a number, and two special tokens denoting the end of the current line of text (`TT_EOL`) and the end of the file (`TT_EOF`). The type of the current token is indicated by the public variable `ttype`. If the current token is a number (i.e., `ttype==TT_NUMBER`), the numeric value of the token is available as the value of the public variable `nval`. If the current token is a word (i.e., `ttype==TT_WORD`), the string value of the token is available as the value of the public variable `sval`. Only one of `nval` or `sval` will be defined for any token. If the token type is an end of line (i.e., ttype==TT_EOL) or end of file (i.e., ttype==TT_EOF), neither nval nor sval is defined. The method eolIsSignficant has a boolean value that indicates whether the token should recognize the end of line condition (i.e., flag==true) or to disregard the end of line condition (i.e., flag==false). Not shown are other methods of the StreamTokenizer that define which characters are to be considered parts of number, parts of words, parts of comments, or "white space" characters to be ignored.

The code for the read method of the Book class is shown in Figure 8.21. This method takes a single parameter, a StreamTokenizer object, named bookStream. The read method is relatively straightforward. The title and author values are read using the readLine private utility method that is described below. The year value is read in two steps. First, the tokenizer is advanced to its next token using the nextToken method. Due to the structure of the input data, the token just read should be the numeric value of the year. So, second, the tokenizer's nval field (a double type) is type cast to an int and assigned as the value of year. The price is read in a similar manner except that the type casting of the nva field is not needed as the price is a double type. If the file is malformed and the nval field is undefined, the type cast or the assignment can fail and throw a NumberFormatException exception. The read method catches these exceptions and assigns default values to the year and price.

The readLine method returns a single string that is the con-catenation of a sequence of words obtained from a StreamTokenizer. The words in the returned string are separated by a single blank character. This method is appropriate for reading titles that do not contain tokens that could be parsed as numeric values. For example, the title "The Year 2000 Problem" would not be read properly by this method because the token "2000" would be interpreted as a numeric token. This problem is corrected in the exercises below. Because the readLine method must detect the end of line condition, the eolIsSignificant method is called with a true value. The readLine method then reads the first token. If the first token is the end of line, then a string with no characters is returned. Otherwise, the line is set to the string token (sval) obtained from the tokenizer. The while loop continues to read tokens and concatenate them to the line with a separating blank character between adjacent words. When the end of the line is reached, the line is returned. If any exceptions occur during this processing, the string "Unknown" is returned.

Reading from the File: BufferedReader Approach

The second method of reading text information from a file uses a combination of two classes: the BufferedReader I/O class and the StringTokenizer utility class. The BufferedReader class is designed to buffer characters from an input stream and return them as complete lines of input. The StringTokenizer class is designed to parse a String into tokens. Each of the tokens returned by the StringTokenizer is itself a String. The relevant parts of the BufferedReader and

```
public class Book
{
  private String title;
  private String author;
  private int    year;
  private double price;

  //...

  public void read(StreamTokenizer bookStream)
  {
    title  = readLine(bookStream);
    author = readLine(bookStream);

    // read year
    try
    { bookStream.nextToken();
    } catch(IOException ioe) {}
    try
    { year = (int)(bookStream.nval);
    } catch (NumberFormatException error) {year = 0;};

    // read price
    try
    { bookStream.nextToken();
    } catch(IOException ioe) {}
    try
    { price = bookStream.nval;
    } catch (NumberFormatException error) {price = 0.0;};

  }

  private String readLine(StreamTokenizer tokenStream)
  {
    String line = new String("");

    tokenStream.eolIsSignificant(true);
    try
    {  tokenStream.nextToken();
       if(tokenStream.ttype == StreamTokenizer.TT_EOL) return line;
       line = new String(tokenStream.sval);
       tokenStream.nextToken();

       while (tokenStream.ttype != StreamTokenizer.TT_EOL)

       {  line  = line.concat(" " + tokenStream.sval);
          tokenStream.nextToken();
       }
    } catch(IOException ioe) {line = new String("Unknown");}

    return line;
  }
  //...
}
```

Figure 8.21 The `read` and `readLine` Methods of the Book Class

StringTokenizer classes are shown in Figure 8.22. The constructor for a Buff-ered-Reader object takes any object of a media-specific reader class that extends,

```
public class BufferedReader extends Reader
{
   public BufferedReader (Reader r);
   public String readLine() throw IOException;
   public void close() throws IOException;
   //...
}

public class StringTokenizer
{
   public StringTokenizer (String str);
   public String nextToken();
   //...
}
```

Figure 8.22 `BufferedReader` and `StringTokenizer` Classes

```
public class Integer
{
  public static Integer valueOf(String str) throw NumberFormatException;
  public int intValue();
  //...
}

public class Double
{ public static Double valueOf(String str) throw NumberFormatException;
  public double doubleValue();
  //...
}
```

Figure 8.23 The `Integer` and `Double` Classes

and can be type-cast to, the `Reader` class. The `readLine` method returns a complete line of text from the input stream. The `close` method indicates that no further reading will be done from the BufferedReader. A StringTokenizer object is constructed with a String that it will parse into tokens. The `nextToken` method returns the next token in the String. Each token is delimited by "white space" characters (e.g., blanks, tabs). Other methods in the StringTokenizer class allow the delimiting of a token to be controlled.

Strings obtained from a StringTokenizer that represent numeric values, such as the integer-valued `year` or the double-valued `price`, can be converted from text strings to their respective values using the Integer and Double classes in the java.lang package. The relevant parts of the Integer and Double classes are shown in Figure 8.23. Both classes contain a static `valueOf` method that takes a String and returns an object of the class whose value is obtained by parsing the string. These methods throw the `NumberFormatException` exception in the event that the String cannot be parsed. Both classes also contain conversion methods, `intValue` and `doubleValue`, that return an `int` from an `Integer` object and a `double` from a `Double` object, respectively. Be sure to note the difference between `int` and `double` that are primitive types and Integer and Double that are classes written in Java.

```
public class Read2
{
  public static void main (String args[])
  {
    Book book = new Book();
    FileReader bookFile = null;
    BufferedReader bookStream = null;

    try
    { bookFile = new FileReader("books");
      bookStream = new BufferedReader(bookFile);
    } catch (FileNotFoundException fnf) {}

    book.read(bookStream);
    book.print();

    try
    { bookStream.close();
    } catch (IOException ioe) {}
  }
}
```

Figure 8.24 Constructing the `BufferedReader` Stream for Text I/O

The streams needed in this approach are constructed as shown in Figure 8.24. The critical steps of the code, shown in boldface, create a media-specific FileReader object, `bookFile`, and use this object as the argument to construct the BufferedReader object, `bookStream`. The `FileNotFoundException` exception can be thrown by the FileReader constructor. After the streams are constructed, the Book object is asked to read its value from the `bookStream`. The Book object is then asked to display its value and the `BufferedStream` is closed.

The `read` method in the Book class is overridden to allow a `Book` object to read its value from a `BufferedReader` stream. The additional `read` method in the `Book` class is shown in Figure 8.25. The first section of the `read` method simply use the `readLine` method of the BufferedReader to obtain the values of the `title` and `author` fields. In each case, the value is set to "Unknown" if an exception occurs. The middle section of the `read` method creates a `StringTokenizer` using the third line of input from the `BufferedReader` stream; this line contains both the year and the price values. The final section of the `read` method uses the `StringTokenizer` to extract the String representing the year and price, respectively. For the year value, the token is obtained from the tokenizer using the `nextToken` method, the obtained token String is an argument to the static method `Integer.valueOf` that produces an `Integer` object whose `intValue` method is called to obtain a primitive `int` value that is assigned to `year`. The handling of the price token is similar except that it uses the `Double` class and the `doubleValue` method.

```
public class Book
{
  private String title;
  private String author;
  private int year;
  private double price;
  //...

  public void read(BufferedReader bookStream)
  {
    try
    { title = bookStream.readLine();
    } catch (IOException ioe) { title = "Unknown"; }

    try { author = bookStream.readLine();
    } catch (IOException ioe) { title = "Unknown"; }

    String yearpriceLine;
    try
    { yearpriceLine = bookStream.readLine();
    } catch (IOException ioe) { yearpriceLine = "";}

    StringTokenizer tokenizer = new StringTokenizer(yearpriceLine);

    try
    { year = Integer.valueOf(tokenizer.nextToken()).intValue();
    } catch (NumberFormatException nfe) { year = 0; }

    try
    { price = Double.valueOf(tokenizer.nextToken()).doubleValue();
    } catch (NumberFormatException nfe) { price = 0.0; }
  }

  //...
}
```

Figure 8.25 The `read` Method in the Book Class

8.3.3 Interactive I/O

Interactive text input from the keyboard and text output to the console display involves two predefined objects that represent the standard input stream and standard output stream. The declarations of these two objects in the java.lang.System class are shown in Figure 8.26. The PrintStream class is deprecated for general use, having been superseded by the PrintWriter class in later releases of Java, but it is retained because of its use in defining the standard output stream. The standard input stream object, `System.in`, is of the abstract class type InputStream so that the actual class of the standard input stream is hidden; the user really does not care how this class is implemented, only that it provide those methods defined in the InputStream base class.

The `PrintStream` class provides the same pairs of overloaded methods as the `PrintWriter` class. Some of these methods are shown in Figure 8.27 for ref-

```
public final class System
{
  //...
  public static final PrintStream out;
  public static final InputStream in;
  //...
}
```

Figure 8.26 Interactive Streams Declared in the System Class

```
public class PrintStream ...
{
   //...
   public void print(boolean b);
   public void print(int i);
   public void print(double d);
   public void print(String s);
   //...
   public void println(boolean b);
   public void println(int i);
   public void println(double d);
   public void println(String s);
   //...
}
```

Figure 8.27 The `PrintStream` Class

```
public class Book
{
  private String title;
  private String author;
  private int    year;
  private double price;

  //...

  public void write()
  {
     System.out.println(title);
     System.out.println(author);
     System.out.println(year);
     System.out.println(price);
  }
}
```

Figure 8.28 Writing Text to the Standard Output

erence. As with the `PrintWriter` class, the `print` method output a text representation of their argument values on the same line whereas the `println` method outputs the same text and then ends the current line of output.

The write method for the Book class that outputs its text to the console display is shown in Figure 8.28. This method is extremely simple. Each of the four data fields of a Book object are written on separate lines to the standard output

```
Public class ReadWrite
{
  public static void main (String args[])
  {
    Book book = new Book();
    InputStreamReader bookInfo = null;
    StreamTokenizer bookStream = null;

    bookInfo   = new InputStreamReader(System.in);
    bookStream = new StreamTokenizer(bookInfo);

    book.read(bookStream);
    book.write();
  }
}

public class ReadWrite2
{
  public static void main (String args[])
  {
    Book book = new Book();
    InputStreamReader bookInfo = null;
    BufferedReader bookStream = null;

    bookInfo   = new InputStreamReader(System.in);
    bookStream = new BufferedReader(bookInfo);

    book.read(bookStream);
    book.write();
  }
}
```

Figure 8.29 Text I/O Using the Standard Streams

stream. Because the `println` method is overloaded for each basic Java type, the same method name can be used in each case. The argument's type is sufficient to select the correct `println` method.

Because `System.in` is declared as an InputStream, the standard input stream can be used to construct other text stream objects such as a BufferedReader or a StreamTokenizer. The two main programs shown in Figure 8.29 illustrate how the already developed `read` methods of the `Book` class can be used in conjunction with the standard input stream. The first class, ReadWrite, illustrates how the standard input stream, `System.in`, is used to construct an InputStreamReader. This InputStreamReader is then used to construct a StreamTokenizer. The `read` method of the `Book` class developed above (see Figure 8.25) is then used, without change, to read the book information from the standard input stream. The fact that the `Book` class is unchanged is a reflection of the flexibility of the Java I/O classes. The second class, ReadWrite2, illustrates how an InputStreamReader constructed using `System.in` is used to construct a BufferedReader object. The overloaded `read` method developed above (see Figure 8.25) is used intact to extract from this BufferedReader the book information that is entered on the standard input stream.

Exercises

1. Compile and execute the example main programs that write and read a single Book entry in text form to a file and to the standard input and verify that they work correctly on your system.
2. Use a common text display utility (such as `type` on Windows95 or `cat` on Unix systems) to verify that the file containing the Book entry is in a human-readable text form.
3. Construct simple GUIs for the main programs that output text to a file. For example, the GUI for the main program in the `Write` class might have four text fields into which the book's attributes could be entered. For this exercise you should consider adding additional accessor and query methods to the Book class.
4. Revise the main program in the `Write` class so that the same book entry is written to two different files. Use the existing main program in the `Read` class to read both files.
5. Revise the `Write` class so that several different book entries can be written to the file and revise the `Read` class so that each entry in the file is read and displayed.
6. Create a new main program in a new class named `Append` that appends a single new book entry to a file of entries. Use the revised `Read` class created in the previous exercise to verify that the `Append` class works properly.
7. Write a new main program in a class named Buffer so that the book entry data is written to and read from a bye array buffer declared in the main program. Do not change the Book class. Explain why this exercise illustrates the flexibility afforded by the `DataOutputStream` and `DataInputStream` classes.
8. Decide on a reasonable action to take if the book data could not be written or read. Add appropriate code in the catch clauses of both the `Read`, `Write`, and `Book` classes. Test your code by running the programs with illegal files names, and improperly formatted files.
9. Extends the `readLine` method in the `Book` class so that it correctly handles titles that contain numeric values such as "The Year 2000 Problem".

10. Suppose that the format of the book information was changed so that the title and the author appeared on the same line of input. Modify one of the `Write` and `Read` classes to handle this format.

8.4 Random Access File I/O

8.4.1 Concepts

In contrast to stream access to a file in which the data must be processed in sequential order, random access allows the data to be processed in non-sequential order. The term "random" in this context means that the next data that is accessed need not have any relationship to the past history of accessed data. The unpredictable nature of the data access pattern usually arises because the data access is driven by factors outside of the control, planning, and arrangement of the processing system. For example, in a digital library it is not possible to predict which book would be accessed next because that depends on which patron issues the next request. In a telephone directory service, the directory entry accessed by the current customer has no relationship to those accessed by previous customers.

A file organized for random access has a controllable, logical pointer that indicates at what position in the file the next input or output operation will take place. The file's pointer is controllable in that the program can directly set the pointer to any valid position in the file. The pointer is "logical" in the sense that the pointer is usually expressed as an offset from the beginning of the file rather than in terms of such physical properties of a file as disk blocks, tracks, or sectors. In Java, as in many other application programmer interfaces for random access files, the operation to move the file's pointer is called `seek`. This name reflects the historical use of that term to describe the movement of a disk drive's arm to a new position on the disk.

The structure of a random access file is shown in Figure 8.30. The arrow is a symbolic representation of the file's logical pointer. Internally, the file is usually divided into fixed-length blocks of data often termed records. Conceptually, the file may be thought of as an array or vector of records where each record is identified by its index in the array or vector. If the fixed record length, *length*, is known, then it is a simple matter to determine the file pointer's value for record *i* by the expression *i*length*. While more complicated file structures allow the record lengths to vary, this case is not considered here.

While individual records are usually of a fixed size, the fields within the records may be either fixed or varying in size. Fields in record often have natural, fixed lengths. For example, when an `int` or a `double` is written in binary form they naturally are recorded in 2 and 8 bytes, respectively. The `year` and the `price` fields in the entry for a Book object are of this kind. However, other fields,

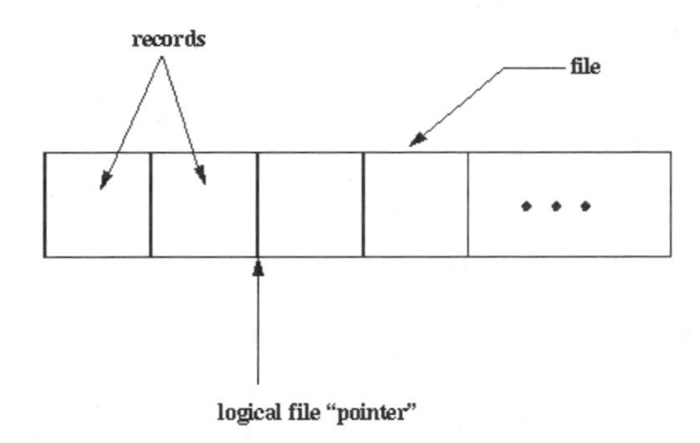

Figure 8.30 Structure of a Random Access File

such as the `title` and `author` fields in a Book entry have no natural, fixed length. The file designer has two choices if the entry contains variable length data. One choice is to force each field to be a fixed length. In the case of a Book entry this means that the title and author fields would be truncated or padded with blanks so that the Strings were always of a given size. A second choice is to allow each of the variable-length fields to be stored in its natural length so long as the record size as a whole remains within its fixed limit. With such varying fields it is necessary to add information to the record so that the beginning and the end of the varying-length fields can be determined. For example, when Java writes a String value in binary form it writes a two byte header for the string that is the number of bytes in the string. If the beginning of the String in the record is known, the end of the String can be determined. When the varying length fields are all small in size, the second strategy means that some of the available space for a record might not be used.

8.4.2 The RandomAccessFile Class

Java provides a single class, RandomAccessFile, that serves both for reading and writing a file using random access. The dual-purpose nature of this class is reflected in that it implements both the DataOutput and DataInput interfaces as shown in Figure 8.31. The DataOutput methods write basic Java types (`boolean`, `int`, `String`) to the file in a binary encoding while the DataInput methods read the binary encoded data and recover the values of these types. The constructor of a RandomAccessFile object takes two String arguments; the first Strings is the name of the file and the second String denotes whether the program will only read from the file (`mode=="r"`) or both read from and write to the file (`mode=="rw"`). The `getFilePointer` method returns the current position of the file's logical pointer. The `seek` method sets the logical pointer to the value of its argument. The current size of the file is returned by the `length` method. The

```
public class RandomAccessFile implements DataOutput, DataInput
{
   public RandomAccessFile(String file, String mode)throws IOException;

   public long getFilePointer() throws IOException;
   public void seek (long pos) throws IOException;
   public long length() throws IOException;

   // from DataInput
   public boolean readBoolean() throws IOException;
   public int readInt() throws IOException;
   public String readUTF() throws IOException;
   //...
   //from DataOutput
   public void writeBoolean(Boolean b) throws IOException;
   public void writeInt(int i) throws IOException;
   public void writeUTF(String s) throws IOException;
   //...
}
```

Figure 8.31 The RandomAccessFile Class

`length` method is useful to insure that the file pointer is not moved beyond the end of the file. Being consistent with the `DataOutput` and `DataInput` interfaces, all of the methods throw an IOException that the program must handle.

8.4.3 The Book Example

The example of book information is revised to use a random access file. The code to create the file is shown in Figure 8.32. The critical parts of the code are shown in boldface. The RandomAccessFile is created with the file name "books" and with a mode ("`rw`") allowing the program to both read from and write to the file. Although this program does not read from the file, the RandomAccessFile does not have a mode that allows only write access. The while loop writes a series of 10 Book objects each of which will be denoted by their loop index (0..9). The fields of each `Book` object are modified by the loop index so that the test cases can clearly demonstrate if the code is working properly. For example, the title of the third book, with an index of 2, is "Book Title 2". The `title` and `year` fields are similarly modified but the `price` field is the same in each record.

The Write class simulates a random writing pattern by creating the `random` array that specifies where each record will be written. This array is used when a Book object is written to the file to indicate at which position in the file that object should write its record. For example, the random array denotes that the first record, denoted by the loop index 0, will be written at `random[0]`, that is, at file record position 4. Similarly, the last record written, denoted by the loop index 9, will be written at random[9], that is, at file record position 6. Keep in mind that the random array is merely a convenience used in this sample program to represent a pattern of random access; realistic applications do not have, and do not need, a counterpart to the `random` array.

```
public class Write
{
  public static void main(String[] args)
  {
    int random[] = {4, 3, 8, 5, 0, 9, 2 , 7, 1, 6 };
    try
    { RandomAccessFile randomFile = new RandomAccessFile("books", "rw");

      for(int i = 0; i<10; i++)
      { Book book = new Book("Book Title "+i,
                             "Author Name "+i, 1800+i, 24.95);
        book.write(randomFile, random[i]);
      }
    } catch (IOException ioe) {}
  }
}
```

Figure 8.32 Writing the Random Access Book File

```
public class Read
{
  public static void main (String[] args)
  {  RandomAccessFile file = null;
     try
     { file = new RandomAccessFile("books", "r");
     } catch (IOException ioe) {}

     int random[] = {4, 3, 8, 5, 0, 9, 2 , 7, 1, 6 };

     Book book = new Book();
     for(int i=0; i<10; i++)
     { book.read(file, random[i]);
       book.print();
     }
  }
}
```

Figure 8.33 Reading the Random Access Book File

The random access file is read by the code in the Read class shown in Figure 8.33. This code is straightforward. Notice that the RandomAccessFile constructor specifies only a read-access mode ("`r`"). Also notice that the `random` array is used to read the entries in the same simulated pattern with which they were written. Thus, when the book entries are displayed, by `book.print()`, the entries will appear in their natural order, that is, the first record displayed will be the one whose title is "`Book Title 0`", the second will be the one whose title is "`Book Title 1`", etc.

The Book class is modified to read and write its data to a `RandomAccessFile`. Because the book information contains two variable-length values (the `title` and `author` Strings) a decision must be made on how the fixed length record for a Book entry will be written. The example presented here limits each String to twenty (20) characters. The limit of 20 is purely arbitrary and is not a

Field Name (Type)	Field Length (in bytes)
title (String)	22
author (String)	22
year (int)	2
price (double)	8
Total	**54**

Figure 8.34 Lengths of Fields in a Book Object

critical part of the example. What is important is that some limit be used to insure that the file's records are of a fixed length. The exercises explore an alternative decision on how to store the variable-length Strings. With this decision, the length of a Book record will be 54 bytes as shown in Figure 8.34. Each String is 22 bytes because the characters in the String are limited to 20 and each String is written with a 2 byte header that gives the length of the String. The String header is a standard part of the Java I/O mechanisms. Even though our design decision makes the String header predictable (and strictly speaking unnecessary for this example) it will be written by the low-level Java I/O code and must be accounted for. The fixed length fields, `year` and `price`, occupy 2 and 8 bytes, respectively.

The code for the revised Book class is shown in Figure 8.35. For clarity, the Book class defines a private constant, `BOOK_SIZE`, that is the length of the entry written to the file. The constructor enforces the rule that the `title` and `author` strings can each be at most 20 characters; longer strings are truncated. Both the `read` and `write` methods take a RandomAccessFile and a position within the file as parameters. The position is a logical index of the entry and not a file offset. Both methods computes the file offset by multiplying the logical index (`position`) by the length of each entry (`BOOK_SIZE`). The file's logical pointer is moved to the starting position for the entry by the `seek` method. The individual fields in each entry are then read or written using the methods of the RandomAccessFile class that input or output each of the primitive types.

```
import java.io.*;

public class Book
{
  private String title;
  private String author;
  private int    year;
  private double price;

  private static final int BOOK_SIZE = 54;

  //...

  public Book(String title, String author, int year, double price)
  { if (title.length()  20)
        this.title  = title.substring(0,19);
    else this.title = title;
    if (author.length()  20)
        this.author = author.substring(0,19);
    else this.author = author;
    this.year   = year;
    this.price  = price;
  }

  public void read(RandomAccessFile file, int position)
  {
    try
    {  file.seek(position * Book.BOOK_SIZE);
       title  = file.readUTF();
       author = file.readUTF();
       year   = file.readInt();
       price  = file.readDouble();
    } catch (IOException error) {}
  }

  public void write(RandomAccessFile file, int position)
  {
    try
    {
      file.seek(position * Book.BOOK_SIZE);
      file.writeUTF(title);
      file.writeUTF(author);
      file.writeInt(year);
      file.writeDouble(price);
    } catch (IOException error) {}
  }
  //...
}
```

Figure 8.35 The Book Class Using RandomAccessFile I/O

Exercises

1. In the main program in the Write class what is the loop index of the record that is written at the first record position in the file?
2. Use a text display utility (e.g., `type` in Windows or `cat` in unix) to verify that the random access file is not written in a readable text format.
3. Execute the programs in the Write and Read classes and verify that they operate as described above.
4. Modify the Read class so that the Book records are read in sequential order and verify that the records were written in the simulated random order specified by the `random` array.
5. Modify the main programs in the original Read and Write classes using the random array: {4, 3, 8, 10, 0, 9, 2 , 7, 1, 6 }. Run the programs to verify that they work. Compare the length of the file produced using the original `random` array to the length of the file produced using the new random array. Can you explain the difference? What does this imply about the nature of a random access file?
6. Modify the Book class so that the *sum* of the lengths of the title and author Strings is less than 40 characters. Run the programs in the Read and Write classes to verify that the modifications are correct. What advantage might this limit have over the original limit?
7. Modify the Book class so that the author and title strings are padded with trailing blanks if necessary to insure that each string is exactly 20 characters. Run the programs in the Read and Write classes to verify that the modifications are correct. What advantage might this technique have over the original design of the Book class?
8. Implement a class `Update` whose main program increases the `price` of all books by 10%.
9. Modify the Book class so that each Book object contains an `int` value, pages. Run the programs in the Read and Write classes to verify that the modifications are correct.
10. Design and implement a user interface for writing entries to the random access file. The interface should have ways for the user to specify the author, title, year, and price along with the desired position in the file.

11. Design and implement a user interface for reading entries to the random access file. The interface should have ways for the user to view the author, title, year, and price of a book whose position in the file the user has specified.

8.5 Object I/O

8.5.1 The Java Classes

As was noted in the introduction, much of the complexity of input and output comes from the fact that richly structured objects are reduced on output to a stream of bytes or characters and reconstituted on input from that stream of bytes and characters. Attendant with the transformation to and from a stream of bytes or characters are the difficulties of formatting and parsing (in text I/O), problems with representing variable length entities in a fixed-length record (in random access I/O), and the possibilities of exceptions (in all forms). Conceptually, of course, all of these problems and details are irrelevant to the purpose of the computation, which simply wants to write an object to a file and read that object from the file. Usually, this simplicity is constructed by the programmer by encapsulating all of the I/O details in a class as was done with the Book class in the previous sections.

Several object-oriented frameworks and some object-oriented languages, Java included, provide an I/O mechanism that is designed to write and read complete objects in a general purpose way. The terms persistence and serializability are frequently used to describe these I/O mechanisms. The term persistence is derived from the use of object I/O mechanisms to allow objects to exist, or persist, beyond the lifetime of the program that created them. The term serializability reflects the role of the I/O mechanism in transforming a structured object into a stream. (i.e. a series, of bytes that completely represents the class and all of its data values).

Java provides a powerful mechanisms for writing and reading objects through two classes named ObjectOutputStream and ObjectInputStream. As implied by their names, these two classes operate on a stream basis; objects are written to the stream one after another and read from the stream in that same order. The power of these classes is that, from the programmer's perspective, the stream contains objects, not bytes or characters or primitive types. What's more, the object I/O mechanism can be used to write and read objects of any user-defined class; it is not restricted to predefined classes or types. When an object is written to an object stream all of the data associated with that object is saved: both public and private attributes are saved; attributes that are primitive types are saved, as are attributes that are themselves other user-defined classes.

```
public class ObjectOutputStream
{
   public ObjectOutputStream (OutputStream out) throws IOException;
   //...
   public void writeObject(Object obj) throws IOException;
   //...
}

public class ObjectInputStream
{
   public ObjectInputStream(InputStream in) throws IOException,
                                              StreamCorruptedException;

   //...
   public Object readObject() throws IOException, ClassNotFoundException;
}
```

Figure 8.36 Object Stream I/O Classes

Although powerful, the Java object stream classes are easy to use. The simplicity of the two object I/O classes, defined in Figure 8.36, is evident in that only two methods in each class are needed for writing and reading objects. The constructors of these two classes take as their argument either a simple OutputStream or a simple InputStream. Typically, a media-specific stream is created for this purpose. In the example below, a FileOutputStream is created and used to construct an ObjectOutputStream so that objects can be written to the file and a FileInputStream is created and used to construct an ObjectInputStream so that objects can be read from the file. The key method in the ObjectOutputStream class is the `writeObject` method that takes as its single parameter an `Object`. Because *every* class in Java is derived, directly or indirectly, from the `Object` class, any class can be type cast as an `Object type` and passed to the `writeObject` method. Along with the actual data of the class, the Java object I/O mechanism writes sufficient additional information so that it will be able to reconstruct the object when the object's representation is read. The key method in the ObjectInputStream class is the `readObject` method that returns an `Object` extracted from the input stream. The signature of the `readObject` method must work for all possible objects, so the return type is the generic `Object` type. As shown in the example below, the object returned by `readObject` is type-cast to its specific type. This implies that the programmer must know the actual type of the object.

In addition to the familiar `IOException`, the ObjectInputStream class throws two other exceptions. The constructor throws the exception `StreamCorruptedException`. This exception signals that the object stream mechanism does not recognize the InputStream given to it as a stream that was produced by an ObjectOuputStream object. The `readObject` method throws the `ClassNotFoundException` exception. This exception indicates that the object read from the InputStream does not correspond to any class that is known to this program. Such an exception indicates that the system generating the object stream and

```
public abstract interface Serializable
{
  // no methods - a "marker" interface
}
```

Figure 8.37 The Serializable Interface

the system reading the object stream are not in agreement on the classes of the objects contained in the stream.

The only requirement imposed on a class whose objects are to be written and read using the object streams is that the class implement the `Serializable` interface. The Serializable interface, shown in Figure 8.37, has no methods. Such interfaces are sometimes referred to as "marker" interfaces because their role is simply to announce that the designer of the class implementing that interface, in this case the Book class, intends that certain actions, in this case object I/O, are permissible for this class. The object stream mechanism will check whether an object being written to a stream implements the Serializable interface. Only those classes that implement the Serializable interface will be written to the stream.

There are two conditions under which a class designer might deliberately choose not to allow the objects of that class to be serializable. Both of these conditions are related to the use of Java objects in highly distributed environments, such as the World Wide Web, where Serializable objects can be easily transported from machine to machine. The first condition concerns security. By not implementing the Serializable interface, a class containing sensitive data can afford a degree of security to the objects of that class because these objects will not be transportable. The second condition concerns functionality. When an object is serialized only the data of the class is written to the object stream, not its code. Thus, a program reading the object from the stream must already have the code for the object. In a distributed environment if there is uncertainty that a class's code might not be present on other machines then that class can prevent its objects from migrating by choosing not to implement the Serializable interface.

8.4.2 The Book File Example

The generality of the object stream mechanism allows the Book class to be simplified dramatically. As shown in Figure 8.38, the `read` and `write` methods have been removed from the Book class because the object stream mechanism will assume all of the responsibility for writing the object to an object stream and reading the object from an object stream. The only new feature in the Book class, shown in boldface, is the declaration that the Book class implements the Serializable interface.

The code to write a stream of Book objects is shown in Figure 8.39 to illustrate how easily the object stream classes can be used. As in previous examples, a collection of 10 anonymous books are written to a file named "books". The File-

```
public class Book implements Serializable
{
  private String title;
  private String author;
  private int    year;
  private double price;

  public Book()
  { //...
  }

  public Book(String title, String author, int year, double price)
  { //...
  }

  public void print()
  { //...
  }
}
```

Figure 8.38 The Book Class Used for Object Stream I/O

```
public class Write
{
  public static void main(String[] args)
  {
    try
    { FileOutputStream file = new FileOutputStream("books");
      ObjectOutputStream objectStream = new ObjectOutputStream(file);

      for(int i = 0; i<10; i++)
      { Book book = new Book("Author Name "+i,
                             "Book Title "+i, 1800+i, 24.95);
        objectStream.writeObject((Object)book);
      }
    } catch (Exception ioe) {}
  }
}
```

Figure 8.39 Writing Objects to an Object Stream

OutputStream object is constructed and passed as the constructor argument of the ObjectOutputStream. This creates an object stream that will write its object representations to the file. The critical part of this example is the line of code shown in boldface that writes each Book object to the object stream. In this line of code, a Book object is explicitly type cast to an Object, to match the signature of the `writeObject` method.

The stream of Book objects can be recovered through an ObjectInput-Stream. The Read class shown in Figure 8.40 reads each Book object from an object stream and displays each one to verify that the object has been completely and correctly recovered. The important line of code in this example is shown in boldface. This line of code reads an Object from the object stream and type-casts

```
public class Read
{
  public static void main (String[] args)
  {
    try
    { FileInputStream file = new FileInputStream("books");
      ObjectInputStream objectStream = new ObjectInputStream(file);

      for(int i = 0; i<10; i++)
      { Book book = (Book)objectStream.readObject();
        book.print();
      }
    } catch (Exception ioe) {}
  }
}
```

Figure 8.40 Reading Objects from an Object Stream

the generic Object to its actual type, an object of the Book class. This type-cast is correct because we know that the file contains a stream of `Book` objects. Because the object is now known to be a `Book` object, its `print` method can be used to display the values of the object to verify that it has been fully reconstituted from the object stream.

Exercises

1. Run the sample code distributed with this chapter to verify it works on your system.
2. Compare lengths of files for outputting the same information in text form and in object form. Attempt to explain the differences that you observe.
3. Revise the Book class and leave out the Serializable interface. Explain what happens?
4. Revise the Book class so that it contains as part of its private data an object of another class that you define (e.g., a class that represents the publisher or a store where it can be purchased). Change the object I/O examples given in this chapter to output objects of your revised class.
5. Write object of a non-Book class to a stream and try and read it with the Read class. Explain what happens.
6. An attribute of a class can be declared `transient`, meaning that its value should not be serialized even though the object itself is serialized. Add the following declaration to the Book class:

```
private transient int copies = 0;
```

along with methods to set and get the value of copies. Revise the **Write** and **Read** classes to test the effect of the transient modifier.

8.6 I/O Filtering

8.6.1 Concepts

Data being written or read by a program may be processed, or filtered, before the data is written to the output media or before the data is presented to the program. Although such filtering may be very application specific, several general-purpose filters and have been implemented as part of the Java libraries. The logical use of a filter is shown in Figure 8.41. As shown in this figure, data that is being output by the program passes through the output filter on its way to the output medium. Similarly, on input, the data from the input medium passes through the input filter before it reaches the program. The filtering is usually transparent to the program; the program receives a stream of input data or generates a stream of output data and is unaware of the value-added service provided by the intermediate filter.

Filters may take a variety of actions. In some cases, the data is simply examined before it is passed on unchanged. An example of this is "line number counting" filter that simply counts how many "end of line" characters have passed through it. In other cases, the data may be transformed. Filters that performs compression of encryption transform the data to implement the compression or encryption. A compression output filter produces less data than it was passed whereas the compression input filter will produce more data than it receives. A final case is one in which the data may be suppressed as a result of the filter. For example, an input stream may contain descriptive comments intended for the human administrator but not for the processing program. A filter can be designed to suppress the comment data when it is read by the program.

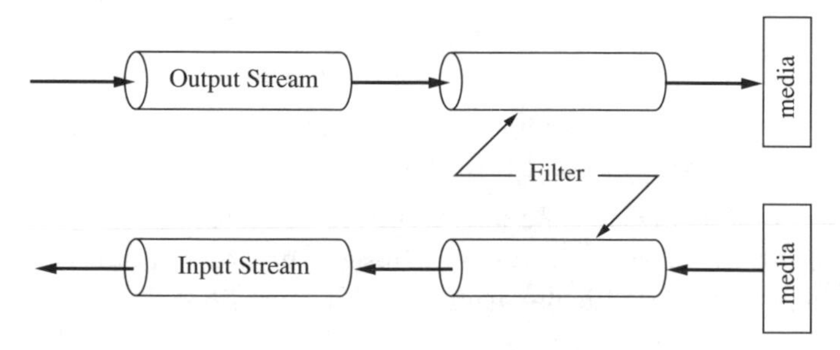

Figure 8.41 Role of Stream Filters

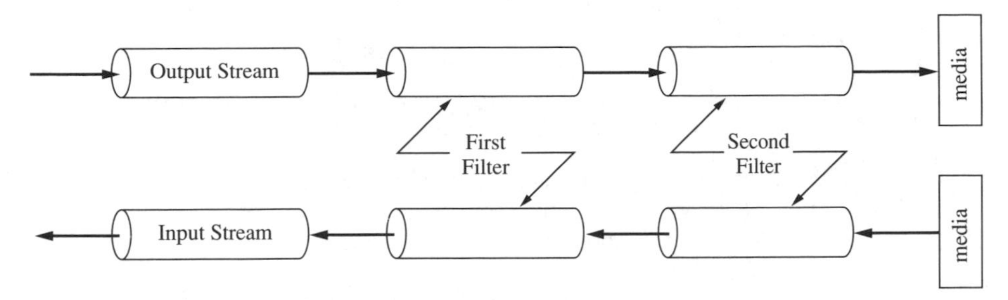

Figure 8.42 Composing Filters

Filters may be composed to concatenate their individual services. Figure 8.42 shows two filters interposed in sequence on both the input and output streams. Data that is presented to the output stream passes through the "First Filter" where is operations are applied to the data. The filtered data from the "First Filter" is passed to the "Second Filter" that performs its filtering actions before allowing the resulting data to reach the storage medium. On the input side, the data coming from the medium must pass through the "Second Filter" whose output data is passed to the "First Filter" whose output finally reaches the program reading from the input stream.

8.5.2 Java Classes

The Java I/O library provides a variety of generic filters for both binary streams and text streams. The Java filters can be composed in a number of useful ways. In addition, there are abstract base classes that can be extended to provide application-specific filters. A number of user-defined filters are proposed in the exercises at the end of this section.

Figure 8.43 summarizes the filtering classes and their purpose for binary streams. The services provided by these filtering classes include improved I/O efficiency through buffering, increased storage efficiency through compression, and enhanced utility through a "pushback" capability. The PushbackInputStream differs from the other filters in two ways: its capability applies only to an input stream and it is visible to the program because it adds an explicit operation to push the data back into the stream. The other filters are symmetric, providing their capabilities on both the output and input streams, and transparent to the program because these filters are inserted between the stream manipulated by the program and the output medium. All of the filtering classes extend one of the two base classes, FilterInputStream and FilterOutputStream. Additional user-defined filters can also be created by extending these base classes.

Class(es)	Purpose
`FilterInputStream` `FilterOutputStream`	Base classes from which other, or new user-defined, filters are derived.
`BufferedInputStream` `BufferedOutputStream`	Improves I/O efficiency by accumulating data in memory buffers so that fewer media-level operations are performed.
`PushBackInputStream`	Allows data already read to be "pushed back" into the stream as if it had not been read and may be read again.

`GZIPInputStream`
`GZIPOutputStream`
`ZipInputStream`
`ZipOutputStream`
	Provides data compression using the common *gzip* and *zip* formats.

Figure 8.43 Filter Classes for Binary Stream I/O

Class(es)	Purpose
`BufferedReader` `BufferedWriter`	Improves I/O efficiency by accumulating text data in memory buffers so that fewer media-level operations are performed.
`PushBackReader`	Allows text data already read to be "pushed back" into the stream as if it had not been read and may be read again.
`LineNumberReader`	Maintains a counter of the number of lines of data read from the input.

Figure 8.44 Filter Classes for Text Stream I/O

There are also a set of filter classes for text stream I/O. These classes are summarized in Figure 8.44. The BufferedReader and BufferedWriter classes are similar to their binary stream counterparts except that they provide their buffering capability for text streams. Similarly, the PushBackReader is like the PushBackInputStream. The LineNumberReader watches for, and counts, the number of end of line characters that have passed through the text data stream. Thus, the LineNumberReader filter is able to report the current line number of the text data being read. This filter is useful in associating output results, or error messages, with specific lines in the input text stream so that the user has more specific information on the data being referred to in the error message.

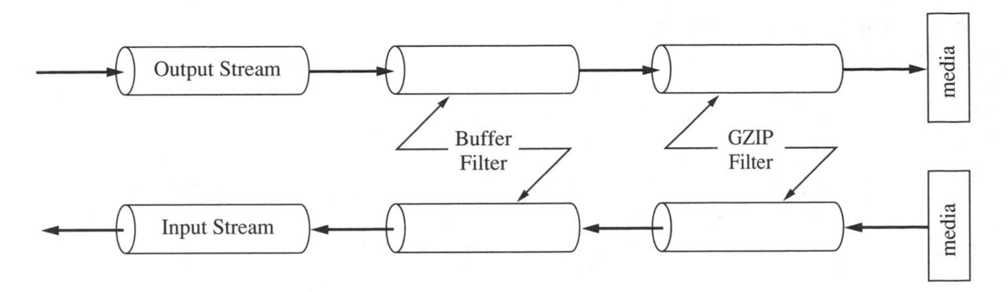

Figure 8.45 Composing Two Java Filters

The filter classes and the other I/O classes may be composed together. Not only does this feature allow the binary stream and text reader classes to be composed with the filters, but it also allows filters to be composed with each. This ability is suggested in Figure 8.45 which shows how the buffering and compressing filters might be used together. The details of this example is presented in the example section below. Conceptually, there is no difference between a "stream" and a "filter"; each accepts and produces data. The differences in terms reflect their purpose and role.

8.5.3 An Example

The file of books example is extended to illustrate how filters can be composed. The example follows the structure of the system referred to in Figure 8.46 in which a buffering and a compression filter are composed. Note first that a separate package, java.util.zip, contains the compression filter classes. The set of filters and streams are created and composed as shown by the boldface code in the main program given in Figure 8.47. The FileOutputStream and the ObjectOutputStream were presented earlier. What is new are the BufferedOutputStream and the GZIPOutputStream classes. The composition of the filters and the streams is simply done through their constructors. For example, the GZIPOutputFilter takes as its constructor argument an OutputStream to which it will send its compressed data; the FileOutputStream extends the OutputStream base class and is implicitly type-cast to that base class in this code. The GZIPOutputStream also extends the OutputStream class and its object is passed to the constructor of the BufferedOutputStream. Finally, the ObjectOuputStream is connected to the BufferedOutputStream in a similar way. An important aspect of this example is that the code in the main program that actually writes to the ObjectOutputStream is unchanged; the insertion of the filters is done transparently. This transparency is one of the major advantages of the filtering technique.

```
import java.io.*;
import java.util.zip.*;
import Book;

public class Write
{
  public static void main(String[] args)
  {
    try
    { FileOutputStream     file
                             = new FileOutputStream("books");
      GZIPOutputStream     zippedFile
                             = new GZIPOutputStream(file);
      BufferedOutputStream bufferedZippedFile
                             = new BufferedOutputStream(zippedFile);
      ObjectOutputStream   objectStream
                             = new ObjectOutputStream(bufferedZippedFile);

      for(int i = 0; i<10; i++)
      { Book book = new Book("Author Name "+i,
                             "Book Title "+i, 1800+i, 24.95);
        objectStream.writeObject((Object)book);
      }
    objectStream.close();
    } catch (Exception ioe) {}
  }
}
```

Figure 8.46 An Output Stream with Two Filters

```
import java.io.*;
import java.util.zip.*;
import Book;

public class Read
{
  public static void main (String[] args)
  {
    try
    { FileInputStream     file
                            = new FileInputStream("books");
      GZIPInputStream     zippedFile
                            = new GZIPInputStream(file);
      BufferedInputStream bufferedZippedFile
                            = new BufferedInputStream(zippedFile);
      ObjectInputStream   objectStream
                            = new ObjectInputStream(bufferedZippedFile);
      for(int i = 0; i<10; i++)
      { Book book = (Book)objectStream.readObject();
        book.print();
      }
    } catch (Exception ioe) {}
  }
}
```

Figure 8.47 An Input Stream with Two Filters

The code to create the corresponding composition of input streams is shown in Figure 8.47. The code related to the streams and filters is shown in boldface.

This code is symmetric to the code used to create the concatenated output streams and filters. In this case, a FileInputStream object is used to construct a GZIPInputStream. The FileInputStream class extends InputStream, the type of the argument expected by the GZIPInputStream constructor. Because the GZIP-InputStream itself extends the InputStream class, its object may be passed as the constructor argument of the BufferedInputStream. For similar reasons, the BufferedInputStream object can be used to construct the ObjectOutputStream.

Exercises

1. Execute the buffered/zipped Write and Read programs. Compare length of file produced by the Write program to the length of the file produced by unbuffered/unzipped object stream example.
2. Remove the `close` from the buffered/zipped example program. Execute the programs in the Write and Read classes. Explain and unusual effects that you observe.
3. Revise the Book, Read, and Write classes based on a binary stream so that the output and input streams use a a compression/decompression filter.
4. Revise the Book, Read, and Write classes based on a binary stream so that the output and input streams use a a compression/decompression filter composed with a buffered filter.
5. Revise the Book, Read, and Write classes based on a text stream so that the output and input streams use a a compression/decompression filter.
6. Revise the Book, Read, and Write classes based on a text stream so that the output and input streams use a a compression/decompression filter composed with a buffered filter.
7. Design, implement, and test a `CypherWriter` and a CypherReader class that extend `FilterReader` and `FilterWriter,` respectively. This pair of classes implement a simple substitution cypher. A simple substitution cypher consistently replaces a given character in the plain text by another character in the cypher text. For example, every "a" may be replaced by "d" on output and the reverse on input.
8. Test that your `CypherWriter` and `CypherReader` classes developed in the previous exercise are composable with other streams and filters by testing the cypher classes in composition with a `BufferedWriter` and a `BufferedReader`.

9. Design, implement, and test a `WordNumberReader` filter that extends `BufferedReader`. The `WordNumberReader` filter is similar to `LineNumberReader` filter except that the `WordNumberReader` counts the number of words read rather than the number of lines.

10. Test that your `WordNumberReader` class developed in the previous exercise is composable with other streams and filters by testing the word counting class in composition with a `LineNumberReader` filter.

11. Design, implement, and test a `NoCommentInputReader` that extends `FilterReader`. This filter removes from all comments from its input stream all comments. Comments begin with a pair of slash marks ("//") and terminate with the end of that line of input.

CHAPTER 9

Threads

9.1 Introduction

The central processing unit (CPU) of a computer is designed to perform one action at time. It is, of course, designed to perform these actions at an extremely rapid rate. The structure and execution of programs reflects this one-step-at-a-time point of view. The writers of code create programs by arranging a single sequence of statements that will be executed, some perhaps repetitively, to form the program's flow of control that moves from one statement to the next. Debugging commands that allow the program to be executed by single steps also show the single, sequential pattern of the program's execution.

Users, however, frequently want to perform many actions, or applications, all at the same time. It is not uncommon for a user to be formatting a document, sending or receiving electronic mail, executing a search through a web browser, and keeping their place in a game of Solitaire or Minesweeper. The ability to be executing more than once application at a time is often described as "multi-tasking" because the computer is engaged in performing multiple tasks simultaneously. The term "concurrency" is also used to describe this effect because the actions are, or at least appear to be, performed at the same time. An important aspect of the design of modern operating systems (like Unix and Windows 95) is how to provide multi-tasking or concurrency services.

A single application may also be programmed to perform several actions concurrently through one of three means. One way to implement concurrent programming is by adding multiple physical processors to the machine. Although this is the approach used in building very high-performance parallel processing systems, the cost of additional processors is often too high for use on desktop or workstation systems. A second way to implement concurrent programming is through "threads." Each thread is a separate computation. Just as a busy person (e.g., a short-order cook or a juggler) can manage multiple jobs by rapidly switching among them, the operating system rapidly switches among it threads, allocating some portion of the processor time to each thread. The third way to implement concurrent programming is in a distributed computing environment consisting of multiple systems connected via a communications network. A single "application" may have components executing on each of the networked computers in parallel. The distributed components interact with each other over the network and coordinate their activities by sending messages to each other.

Although Java does not have specific constructs for true parallel programming (exploiting multiple physical processors) it does support concurrent programming using threads and distributed computing. The study of Java's concurrent programming features is divided into three parts:

1. threads performing independent (asynchronous) actions,
2. threads performing synchronized actions, and
3. communication among threads on different networked computers.

Threads that perform independent actions are often used in simple simulations or animations. Each thread independently performs its actions without regard for other threads or their actions. The use of independent threads is illustrated by a simulation of a simple ecological model containing predators and prey that move about in a bounded environment. In this simulation, the predators and prey do not interact. Threads that engage in synchronized activities are used where the actions of one thread must be related to the actions of other threads. By analogy, an orchestra is a set of synchronized threads (instrumentalists) whose actions must be performed in proper relation with each other to achieve the desired effect. Interacting threads are illustrated by extending the ecology simulation to model the competition between the predators and the prey. Finally, the concurrent execution made possible in a distributed environment is examined. Java provides a library for using sockets, a commonplace data communications mechanisms. Sockets are used by familiar clients and servers. For example, web browsers communicate with HTTP servers through sockets. The ecological simulation is implemented using sockets so that a user on one machine can view and control the simulation running on another machine.

9.2 Independent Threads

9.2.1 The Thread Class

Objects of the `java.lang.Thread` class represent autonomous threads of control in an application. Like all other classes, many objects of the `Thread` class

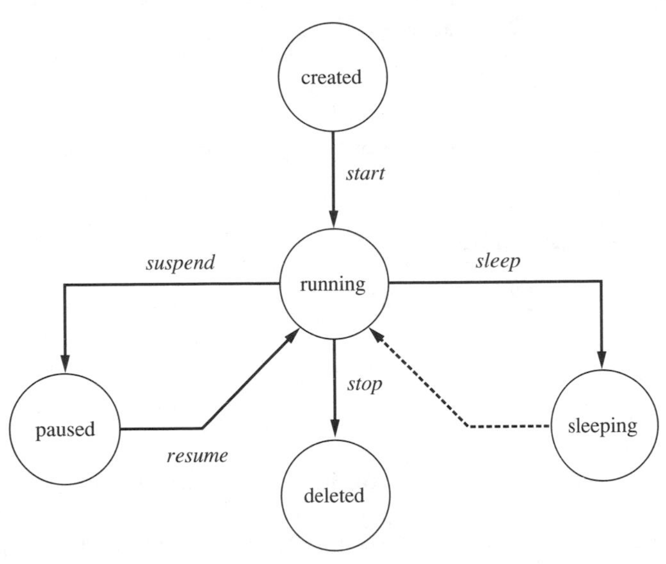

Figure 9.1 States of a Thread

can be created. Each `Thread` object corresponds to an independent thread of control that can be executing in the application. The methods of the `Thread` class provide operations that allow a new thread of control to be initiated and managed during the its lifetime.

Each thread has a structured life cycle that is defined by its progression through a series of specific states. The state-transition diagram for a thread engaged in an independent action is shown in Figure 9.1. In a state-transition diagram, the states are represented by circles and the directed arcs between states represent transitions. Both the states and the transitions are labelled to indicate the nature of the state and the action that causes the transition to occur. Additional states are needed to describe the life cycle of a thread that interacts with other threads; these states will be introduced later.

The meanings of the states and transitions in the figure are as follows. When a Thread object is created, the thread of control that it implements is in a "created" state. In this state the thread of control exists but is not yet performing any action. The "start" transition causes the thread to become active and enter the "running" state. From the running state, three transitions are possible. The "suspend" transition causes the thread to temporarily halt its activity. The "resume" transition moves the thread back into the running state where it continues it activity. When resumed, the thread continues exactly at the point where it suspended. The suspend and resume transitions allow a thread to be managed, halting and continuing under control of the application. The second transition from the running state is the "sleep" transition that moves the thread to the "sleeping" state. A sleeping thread remains in this state for a period of time specified by the transition. At the end of the specified period of time the thread is

```
public abstract interface Runnable
{
   public void run();
}

public class Thread implements Runnable
{
  public:
    public Thread();
    public Thread(Runnable target);
    ...
    public final  void start();
    public        void run();
    public final  void stop();
    public static void sleep(long millis)throws InterruptedException;
    public final  void suspend();
    public final  void resume();
}
```

Figure 9.2 The Thread Class and Runnable Interface

automatically moved back to the running state. The sleep transition is used by a thread to postpone its activity for a specific amount of time. Threads involved in animations often use the sleep transition to control the rate at which they perform the animation.

A partial definition of the `Thread` class and the related `Runnable` interface are shown in Figure 9.2. The methods of the Thread class have an obvious correspondence to the states and transition in the thread's life cycle. The `start` method cause the thread of control to initiate its execution. When started, the thread of control will execute the `run` method in an object whose class implements the Runnable interface. The two ways in which the `run` method can be defined are explained below. An executing thread is terminated by the `stop` method or if the thread returns from the `run` method. While executing, a thread can defer its execution for a specific interval of time through the `sleep` method. The argument of the `sleep` method is the interval of time measured in milliseconds. A sleeping thread may be awakened prematurely, in which case the `sleep` method throws the `InterruptedException`. Finally, the `suspend` and `resume` methods allow a thread to be halted and restarted.

The `run` method that is executed by a Thread object can be defined in one of two ways. These two ways are shown in diagram form in Figure 9.3. First, as shown in part (a) of the figure, the Thread class itself implements the `Runnable` interface. The `run` method implemented in the Thread class is only a placeholder method; it immediately returns without taking any actions. One way of providing a useful `run` method is to define an application-specific class that extends the Thread class and overrides the default `run` method with one that performs the actions required by the application. Second, as shown in part (b) of the figure, an association is established between a Thread object and an application-specific object of a class that implements the Runnable interface. The association is created through a Thread constructor that takes a Runnable

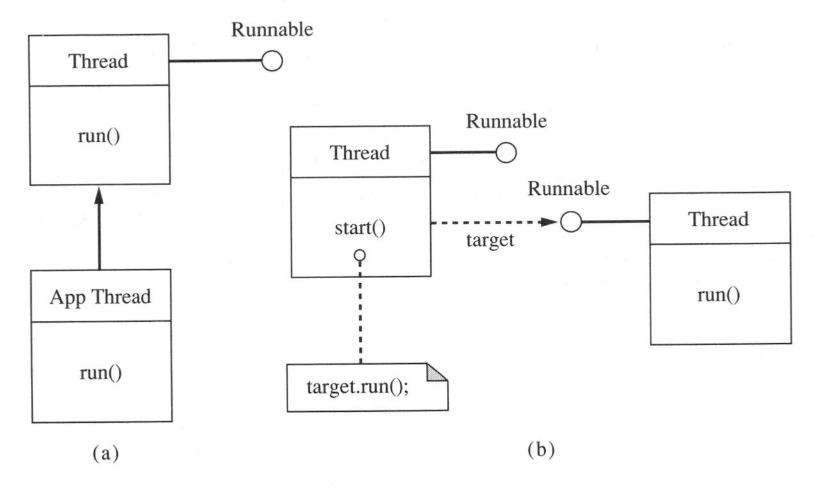

Figure 9.3 Defining the `run` Method for a Thread

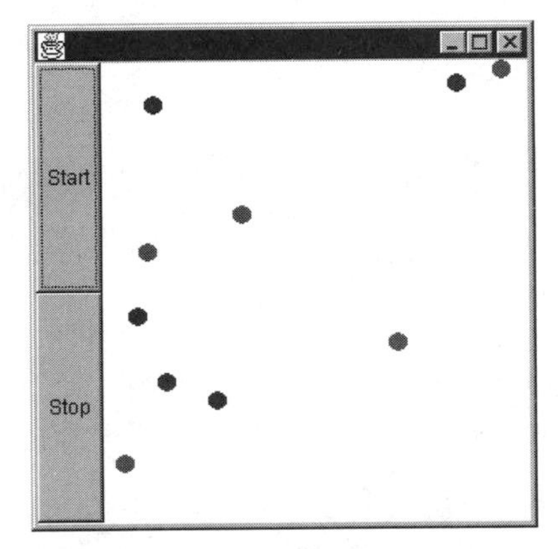

Figure 9.4 The Ecological Simulator

object, referred to as the "target", as an argument. When the `start` method of a Thread object constructed with a target is called, the thread of control will execute the `run` method of the target object rather than the default `run` method in the Thread class.

9.2.2 An Example

An animated simulation of a simple ecological model, named EcoSim1, illustrates the use of threads executing independent actions. The appearance of the simulation is show in Figure 9.4. The simulator's user interface has a drawing area in which the predators and the prey are represented by red and blue color

```
public class Predator extends Thread
{
  public Predator(EcoWorld env);
  public void run();
  public void paint(Graphics g);
}

public class Prey extends Thread
{
  public Prey(EcoWorld env);
  public void run();
  public void paint(Graphics g);
}

public class EcoWorld
{
  private Vector predators;
  private Vector prey;

  public EcoWorld();
  public void add(Predator predator);
  public void add(Prey prey);
  public void paint(Graphics g);
  public void start();
  public void stop();
  public void repaint();
}
```

Figure 9.5 Structure of the EcoSim1 Simulator

circles, respectively. The "Start" button initiates the simulation and the "Stop" button terminates the simulation. Once stopped, the simulation cannot be restarted. The exercises at the end of this section add other controls for pausing and resuming the simulation, and allows for restarting the simulation from the beginning. In this first version of the ecological simulation, the predators and prey do not interact with each other. Thus, only the movement of the predators and prey are accounted for in the simulation. A second version of the simulator, presented in the next section, illustrates how to structure the interaction between the predators and the prey by introducing additional concepts and operations on threads that support cooperation and coordination among threads.

The three principle components of the EcoSim1 simulator are shown in Figure 9.5. The Predator class and the Prey class model the creatures in the environment. Because the creatures are entities that operate independently in the real world, each creature is programmed as an independent thread of control. Hence, the Predator and Prey classes each extends Thread and implements an overriding run method that defines its actions. In addition, objects of the Predator and Prey classes know how to draw themselves into a Graphics object. The EcoWorld class models the environment in which the predators and prey live. The EcoWorld maintains two vectors, one for predators and one for prey. The `add` method allows another predator or another prey to be introduced into the environment. The `paint` method produces in a Graphics object a visualization of

```
public class Predator extends Thread
{
  private static final int SLEEP_TIME = 200;
  private static final int ROAM = 20;
  private static long seed = 654321;
  private EcoWorld environment;
  private int x;
  private int y;
  Random control;

  public Predator(EcoWorld env)
  { environment = env;
    control = new Random(seed);
    seed = control.nextInt();
    x = Math.abs(control.nextInt() % EcoWorld.WIDTH);
    y = Math.abs(control.nextInt() % EcoWorld.HEIGHT);
  }

  private void move()
  { x = x + control.nextInt() % Predator.ROAM;
    y = y + control.nextInt() % Predator.ROAM;
    if(x < 0) x = 0;
    else  if(x  EcoWorld.WIDTH ) x = EcoWorld.WIDTH;
    if(y < 0) y = 0;
    else if(y  EcoWorld.HEIGHT) y = EcoWorld.HEIGHT;
    environment.repaint();
  }

  public void run()
  { while(true)
    { move();
    try { sleep(SLEEP_TIME); }
    catch (InterruptedException ie ) {}
    }
  }

  public void paint(Graphics g)
  { g.setColor(Color.red);
    g.fillOval(x,y, 10,10);
  }
}
```

Figure 9.6 Extending Thread to Define the Predator Class

the current state of the simulation. The visualization is obtained by asking each of the predators and each of the prey to represent themselves in the Graphics object. The `start` and `stop` methods provide minimal control of the simulator; once the simulator is stopped, it cannot be restarted again. Finally, the `repaint` method indicates to the EcoWorld that its visualization should be updated in the near future to reflect possible changes in the state of the simulation.

The critical code for the Predator class and the Prey class are their `run` methods. Because these two classes are very similar, only the Predator class will be examined. As shown in Figure 9.6, the `run` method in the Predator class has a non-terminating iteration. On each iteration, the private `move` method is called

```
public class EcoWorld
{
  public final static int HEIGHT = 300;
  public final static int WIDTH = 300;
  private EcoDisplay display;
  private Vector predators;
  private Vector prey;

  public EcoWorld()
  { predators = new Vector();
    prey = new Vector();
    display = new EcoDisplay(this);
  }

  public void paint(Graphics g)
  { //...
  }

  public void add(Predator predator)
  { predators.addElement(predator);
  }
  public void add(Prey prey)
  { (this.prey).addElement(prey);
  }

  public void start()
  {for(int i=0; i < predators.size(); i++)
    { Predator predator = (Predator)predators.elementAt(i);
      predator.start();
    }
    for(int i=0; i < prey.size(); i++)
    { Prey aPrey = (Prey)prey.elementAt(i);
      aPrey.start();
    }
  }

  public void stop()
  {for(int i=0; i < predators.size(); i++)
    { Predator predator = (Predator)predators.elementAt(i);
      predator.stop();
    }
    for(int i=0; i < prey.size(); i++)
    { Prey aPrey = (Prey)prey.elementAt(i);
      aPrey.stop();
    }
  }

  public void repaint()
  { display.repaint();
  }
}
```

Figure 9.7 Managing Threads in the EcoWorld Class

to determine the predator's new (randomly chosen) nearby location. The `move` method calls the `repaint` method of the EcoWorld object that represents the predator's environment to inform the environment that its visualization should be updated. To provide a sense of animated motion, the predator must postpone its further execution for a brief period of time after adopting its new location. The `sleep` method, inherited from the Thread class, causes the Predator's thread to pause for the number of milliseconds specified by the named constant `SLEEP_TIME`. As the `sleep` method throws the `InterrupedException`, the `try-catch` structure is necessary even though no action is taken in the `catch` clause. Although the thread of one Predator is sleeping, other Predator and Prey threads will be scheduled for execution so that they can update their locations.

A portion of the EcoWorld class is examined to see how the Predator and Prey threads are started and stopped. The EcoWorld contains two vectors, one holding Prey objects and one holding Predator objects, that are initialized in the constructor. The overloaded `add` method allows a new Predator object or a new Prey object to be added to the EcoWorld by being inserted into the proper vector. The `start` and `stop` methods iterate through the contents of the two vectors and apply the `vstart` or `stop` method to each Predator and Prey object. The Predator and Prey classes inherit the `start` and `stop` methods defined in the Thread class. When the `start` method of a Predator or Prey is called, the thread of control begins executing the object's `run` method; this will be the `run` method defined in the Predator or Prey class that overrides the default `run` method in the Thread class (Figure 9.7).

Exercises

1. The `Thread` class also contains an `interrupt` method. Read the Java documentation to understand what this method does. Modify the state transition diagram to account for this method in the life cycle of a thread.
2. Change EcoSim1 by removing the start button and instead have the threads of control in Predators and Prey objects are started when they are added to the EcoWorld
3. Add buttons to Pause and Resume the EcoSim1 simulation.
4. After the simulation is stopped, allow it to be restarted.
5. Make class hierarchy so that Predator and Prey inherit from Creature.
6. Change the Predator and Prey classes so that each sleeps for a randomly chosen period of time in the range from 0 to 1000 milliseconds.
7. Define a class that models new type of predator, an aging predator, that moves more slowly as it grows older.
8. Redefine the Predator and Prey classes so that they do not extend the Thread class but implement the Runnable class instead.

9. Using the version of the Predator and Prey classes that implement the Runnable interface, allow the simulation to be restarted after being stopped.
10. Define, implement, and test a class that periodically chooses (randomly) to add either another Predator or another Prey to the environment.

9.3 Synchronized Threads

9.3.1 The Concept of Synchronization

Concurrent activities may compete or cooperate among themselves. Consider a real-world traffic intersection. Each car and its driver is a separate, independent activity; each has its own destination, route, and navigation. However, when different cars approach the same traffic intersection the independence of each car and driver must be moderated to avoid collisions. At the intersection, the cars are competing for use of the limited resource represented by the traffic intersection. Cars approaching the intersection must wait for the intersection to be clear before proceeding. In a different situation, cooperation is illustrated by the interaction of a customer and a clerk. The customer and the clerk each have their independent activities; the customer examines different items against a shopping list, compares prices, and decides whether and what to purchase whereas the clerk arranges the items on display, sets the price for each item, and maintains and inventory of merchandise. The otherwise independent activities of the customer and clerk become intertwined during a sale: the customer waits for the clerk to be available, the clerk then wait for the customer to identify the item to be purchased, and the customer and clerk then exchange the item and the payment.

Synchronization refers to the means by which interacting concurrent activities regulate their competition and guide their cooperation. In the case of the traffic intersection, the traffic light embodies the synchronization. Through its cyclic changes, the traffic light allows the fair use of the intersection by the cars competing for the right to use (i.e., pass through) the intersection. In the case of the customer and clerk, verbal communication ("May I help you?") and other observable events (the customer places a credit card on the counter) are used to achieve their cooperation.

Two forms of synchronization are "mutual exclusion" and "condition synchronization." Mutual exclusion requires that at most one activity at time be engaged in the synchronized action. For example, only one car a time can be engaged in the act of passing through the intersection. Mutual exclusion is often associated with the use of a shared, limited resource, such as the traffic interesection, and the mutual exclusion requirement is stated from the resource perspective as the rule that only one activity at a time can use the resource. Condition synchronization requires that a given condition hold (or a given system state be reached) before the synchronized action can be taken. For example, the customer cannot begin to purchase and item until the clerk is ready; the condition in this case is "clerk ready." Similarly, the clerk cannot give the item to the customer until the customer has offered the payment; the condition in this case might be "credit card or sufficient cash is on the counter."

Both mutual exclusion and condition synchronization involve potential waiting. If a mutually excluded action is in progress or a mutually excluded resource is in use, all other activities wishing to perform that action or use that resource must wait. Of course, if the action is not in progress or the resource is available, an activity need not wait before performing the action or using the resource. Similarly, in condition synchronization, the activity must wait for the required condition to hold before it can proceed with the synchronized action. Cars waiting their turn at an intersection and a customer waiting on clerk are manifestations of the need to delay one's progress to achieve a desired synchronization.

9.3.2 Thread States

Synchronization adds one additional state to the life cycle of a thread. In the state-transition diagram shown in Figure 9.8, this additional state is the waiting state. The pair of transitions labelled *wait* and *notify* move the thread between

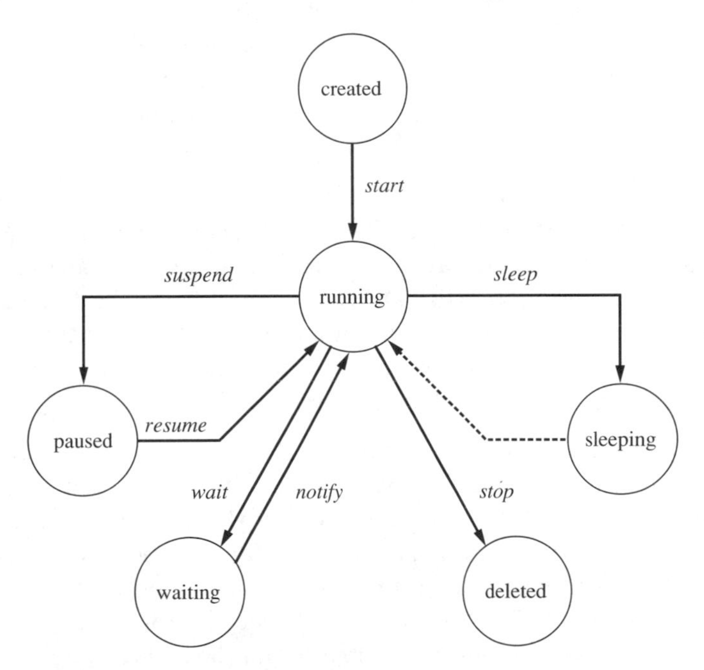

Figure 9.8 Additional Thread State

the running state and the waiting state. When a thread encounters a system state in which its further execution should be suspended, it follows the *wait* transition and enters the waiting state. In the waiting state, the thread's execution is postponed until the expected system state arrives. When some other thread changes the system state to the state that the waiting thread is waiting for, the waiting thread is notified of this change and, through the notify transition, reenters the running state and resumes its execution. The waiting state would be used by a car in the simulation of a traffic intersection as follows. When the thread simulating the car reached the intersection and found the traffic light was red, it would suspend its execution by entering the waiting state. When the thread simulating the traffic light changes its state to green, the traffic light would notify the car that the system state had changed to the one desired by the car. Due to the notification, the car thread would reenter the running state and resume its simulation.

The paused, sleeping, and waiting states all cause a thread to wait but they are used in different situations. The sleeping state is used when a thread wishes to suspend its own execution for a specific period of time regardless of the systems state when it sleeps or when it awakens. The waiting state is used when a thread wishes to suspends its own execution until a given system state has been reached regardless of the length of time needed for the system to reach that state. The paused state is used when some other thread wishes to suspend the execution of a target thread for reasons or durations that may be unknown to the target thread and are usually unrelated to the target thread's function. Pausing and resuming threads can be characterized as management operations. For example, in the ecology simulation the pause and resume operations are used to allow the user to manage the running of the simulator.

A thread may follow the *wait* transition either because of an explicit action or because of an implicit action. As explained below, Java and other languages provide an explicit method to cause a thread to enter the waiting state and an explicit method to notify the thread that it should reenter the running state. However, Java also provides certain constructs that implicitly may require a thread to enter the waiting state; in this case, an implicit notification will be given to thread when its execution can be resumed.

Java provides two synchronization facilities: an implicit means of achieving mutual exclusion and an explicit means of achieving condition synchronization. The synchronization facilities, like all other aspects of Java, are related to the object concept. The implicit mutual exclusion facility provides a simple way of insuring that specified methods of an object cannot be in execution at the same time by different threads. The explicit condition synchronization facility allows a thread to suspend its execution of an object's method until another thread, executing a method of that same object, notifies the waiting thread to continue.

Mutual Exclusion Using Synchronized Methods

A simple implicit way of achieving mutual exclusion for a single method is by declaring the method to be synchronized as illustrated by the TrafficIntersection class shown in Figure 9.9. This class might be used in a traffic simulation having the requirement that only one car enter the intersection at a time. Notice that the `enter` method has an additional modifier denoted by the `synchronized` keyword. The Java run-time environment will guarantee that once a thread begins executing a synchronized method no other thread will be allowed to begin executing this method until the executing thread has returned from the method. In the TrafficIntersection class, this means that only one thread at a time can ever be executing the `enter` method. To guarantee this mutual exclusion, the Java run-time environment will implicitly force a thread into the waiting state if it attempts to execute a synchronized method already being executed by another thread and will implicitly notify the waiting thread when it may continue its execution.

Mutual exclusion is applied to all and only those methods of a class declared as synchronized methods. The meaning of synchronized in this case is suggested by the `java.util.Vector` class shown in Figure 9.10. A `Vector` object has a capacity and a current size. The capacity is given when the object is constructed and is returned by the `capacity` method. The current size of the Vector is returned by the `size` method. The contents of the `Vector` are changed by the `addElement` and `removeElement` methods whereas the `elementAt` method returns the object at a given index. The `addElement`, `removeElement`, and `elementAt` methods are each declared to be synchronized methods, implying both individual and collective mutual exclusion. That is, no thread can begin executing any of these three methods if another thread is already

```
class TrafficIntersection
{
  //...
  public synchronized void enter(); // mutual exclusion
  //...
}
```

Figure 9.9 A Single Synchronized Method

```
public class Vector
{
  public Vector(int initialCapacity);
  //...
  public int capacity();
  public synchronized void addElement(Object obj);
  public synchronized Object elementAt(int index
  public synchronized boolean removeElement(Object obj);
  //...
}
```

Figure 9.10 Multiple Synchronized Methods in the Vector Class

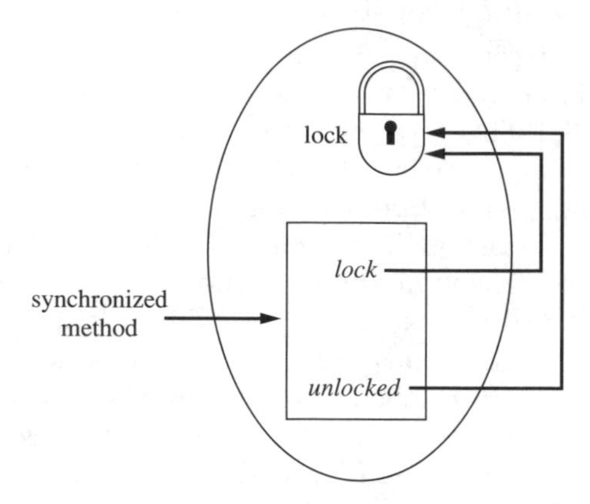

Figure 9.11 Java's Implementation of Synchronized Methods

executing any one of these three methods. Notice, however, that the `capacity` and `size` methods are not declared to be synchronized, so they can be executed by more than one thread at a time and without regard for whether other threads may be executing any of the synchronized methods.

The implementation used by the Java run-time environment to guarantee mutual exclusion for synchronized methods helps to understand the rules governing synchronized methods. As depicted in Figure 9.11, each Java object has a software "lock", represented by the padlock icon in the figure. The lock may be in only one of two states: locked and unlocked. The Java compiler generates code at the beginning of each synchronized method that tests the state of this lock and performs one of two actions: if the lock is unlocked, the state of the lock is changed to locked and the thread continues; if the lock is already in the locked state, the executing thread enters its *wait* state. The Java compiler also generates code that is executed immediately before a return from a synchronized method that performs one of two actions: if there are no waiting threads, change the state of the lock to unlocked; if there are waiting threads, notify one of them to continue leaving the lock in the locked state.

Mutual Exclusion in the Ecological Simulation

The ecological simulation is extended so that interactions among the predators and prey are achieved by the use of synchronized methods. In the original version of the simulation, the predators and prey were independent, moving randomly through the environment with no interaction. In the extended version the threads animating the prey are programmed to hunt, attempting to capture nearby prey. Mutual exclusion is needed in this case to prevent two predators from capturing the same prey.

The Predator class is modified to include as part of its behavior the hunting for nearby prey. The simple changes to accommodate this new behavior is shown in Figure 9.12. Boldface code is used to highlight the changes in the Predator

```
public class Predator extends Thread
{

  private EcoWorld environment;
  private int x;
  private int y;
  //..

  public static final int CAPTURE_ZONE = 70;

  public Predator(EcoWorld env)
  { environment = env;
    //..
  }

  private void move()
  { //...
  }

  public void run()
  { while(true)
    { move();
      hunt();
    try { sleep(SLEEP_TIME); }
    catch (InterruptedException ie ) {}
    }
  }
  private void hunt()
  { environment.huntPrey(this);
  }

  public Point location()
  { return new Point(x,y);
  }
}
```

Figure 9.12 Extending the Predator Class

class. The `run` method includes a call on a new method, `hunt`, which calls the `huntPrey` method in the `EcoWorld` class. To facilitate the `huntPrey` method's operation, the Predator class defines a public named constant, `CAPTURE_ZONE`, that specifies how close a predator must be to a prey to capture the prey. In addition, a `location` method returns a Point object giving the current coordinates of the predator.

When several Predator objects attempt to hunt for nearby Prey objects at the same time, synchronization is necessary to guarantee that two different Predator objects do not attempt to capture the same Prey object. The needed synchronization can be achieved by declaring the `huntPrey` method as a synchronized method as shown in Figure 9.13. Due to the `synchronized` modifier, only one Predator thread at a time will be able to execute the `huntPrey` method. Each hunting Predator thread scans the vector of prey and determines

```
public class EcoWorld
{
  //...
  private Vector predators;
  private Vector prey;

  public EcoWorld()
  { predators = new Vector();
    prey = new Vector();
    //...
  }

  //...

  private int distanceBetween(Prey prey, Predator predator)
  {
    double xdist, ydist;
    xdist = (double)(prey.location().x - predator.location().x);
    ydist = (double)(prey.location().y - predator.location().y);
    return (int)(Math.sqrt(xdist*xdist + ydist*ydist));
  }

  synchronized public void huntPrey(Predator aPredator)
  { for(int i=0; i < prey.size(); i++)
    { Prey aPrey = (Prey)prey.elementAt(i);
      if (distanceBetween(aPrey, aPredator) < Predator.CAPTURE_ZONE)
      { aPrey.stop();
        prey.removeElementAt(i);
        return;
      }
    }
  }
}
```

Figure 9.13 Synchronizing Interactions in the Ecological Simulation

whether the distance from itself to the prey is within its CAPTURE_ZONE. If a Prey object is found sufficiently close, the Prey thread is stopped and the Prey object is deleted from the environment by removing it from the vector of Prey objects.

Condition Synchronization Using `wait` and `notify`

Condition synchronization is required whenever simple mutual exclusion among methods is not sufficient to guarantee the desired interaction of concurrent threads. A careful study of the second version of the ecological simulation presented above reveals that the Prey threads are able to move while the Predator threads are searching through the vector of Prey objects. It is possible that a Prey object is within range of a Predator object when the search begins but the Prey move out of range while the search is in progress. It is reasonable to eliminate this possibility because in reality the predator does not have to search through a record of the prey; it directly and immediately senses the nearby prey. However, this desired synchronization cannot be achieved solely through syn-

```
public class SynchronizedObject
{
  private ... // variable defining the
              // state of the object

  private boolean condition()
  {// test the state of the object
   // and return true/false if the
   // object is/is not in the desired
   // condition
  }

  public synchronized void waitForCondition()
  {//...
     while (! condition() ) wait();
   //condition now true
   //...
  }

  public synchronized void changeCondition()
  { //.. change state of object
    notify();
    //...continue
  }
}
```

Figure 9.14 The Condition of Synchronization Pattern

chronized methods because the actions (the `move` method and the `findPrey` method) are in different classes and the synchronized property only applies to methods in the same class.

Condition synchronization is provided by `wait` and `notify` operations that must be used only in synchronized methods. Several variants of these two basic operations and the reason why they can only be used in synchronized methods are described below. The `wait` operation moves the executing thread from the running to the waiting state where it suspends its further progress in a queue of waiting threads associated with the object. A thread using the `wait` operation will remain blocked indefinitely until some other thread, executing in the same object, performs a `notify` operation. The notify operation has no effect if no thread is waiting at the time the notify is performed. A properly programmed object will use the `wait` and `notify` operations in such a way that threads progress in their execution only when the object is in a condition that makes it correct for them to do so. The Prey class will be reprogrammed below to illustrate how the `wait` and `notify` operations can be used to insure that a Prey object changes the position of its simulated prey only when the prey is not being hunted by a predator.

The typical pattern of using the `wait` and `notify` operations to provide condition synchronization is shown in the generic SynchronizedObject class given in Figure 9.14. This class defines private variables that define the "state" of the object. The number and types of these variables depends on the specific nature of the object and are not further identified in this example. The private method, `condition`, tests the state of the object and determines if a desired synchronization condition holds. Finally, the SynchronizedObject class defines two public methods, `waitForCondition` and `changeCondition`. When a thread executes the `waitForCondition` method the state of the object is tested for a desired condition using the private `condition` method. As long as the desired condition does not hold, the thread executes the `wait` method. It is important to remember that the `wait` operation moves the thread performing this operation to its waiting state, blocking its further progress and allowing other threads to execute. Each iteration of the loop in the `waitForCondition` method is completed each time that the thread executing this loop is returned to its running state by a notify operation. Thus, the iteration is not continuously executing in a "busy waiting" style; instead, the thread repetitively tests and waits until the condition holds. When a thread executes the `changeCondition` method it alters the state of the object and executes the `notify` method to inform any waiting threads that a condition for which they were waiting might now hold. The notifying thread does not need to know that the condition has been met; in fact, different threads may be waiting for different conditions.

A second scenario for the generic SynchronizedObject is one in which the `changeCondition` method is executed by one thread **before** the `waitForCondition` is executed by another thread. In this case, the first thread changes the state of the object to that expected by the other thread and performs the `notify` operation. The `notify` operation has no effect because there is no waiting thread at this time. When the `waitForCondition` method is executed by a different thread, the thread will find the object in an acceptable state (i.e.,the `condition` method returns `true`) and, appropriately, it does not execute the `wait` operation. This scenario and the previous one illustrate that the order of the method execution in a properly synchronized object is not important; maintaining the object's state correct is important.

Pictured in Figure 9.15 is a more detailed scenario of the `wait` and `notify` operations. The scenario has three steps shown by the numbered arrows. In step 1, a thread, *thread1*, is executing in the pictured object and performs a `wait` operation. The `wait` operation has two effects: first, it unlocks the object's mutual exclusion lock and, second, it enters *thread1* in a queue of waiting threads. After step 1 is completed, *thread1* is in its waiting state and the object's lock is unlocked, allowing another thread, *thread2*, to execute one of the object's methods. In step 2, *thread2* locks the object's mutual exclusion lock and executes the `notify` operation. The `notify` operation has two effects: first, it moves one of the threads in the object's queue from the waiting state to the running state (in our example, this would be *thread1*) and, second, it allows *thread2* to continue its execution of the object's method because *thread2* did not relinquish control of the object's lock. At some point *thread2* will complete the execution of the object's method and release the object's lock. In step 3, the notified thread, *thread1*, locks the object's mutual exclusion lock and resumes its execution of the

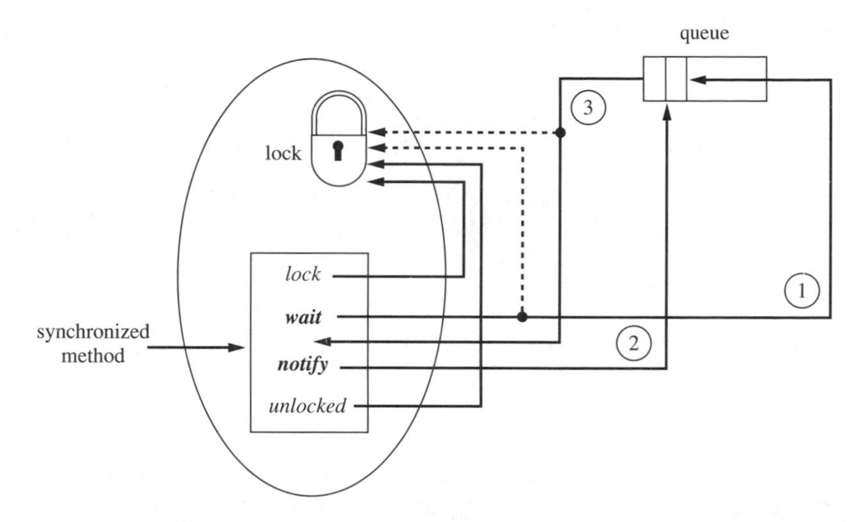

Figure 9.15 A Detailed Scenario of the Wait and Notify Operations

object's method immediately after the `wait` operation. As shown in the Synchronized-Object class above, an awakened thread typically retests the condition for which it is waiting. If the awakened thread finds that the object to be in the desired state it proceeds with the execution of the method, ultimately returning from the method after releasing the mutual exclusion lock. If the awakened threads finds that the object is not in the desired state it executes the `wait` operation again.

The detailed scenario motivates the rule that the wait and notify operation may be used only in synchronized methods. These operations involve changing a thread's state, adding or removing a thread from a queue, and possibly competing with other threads to test or retest the state of the object. Such actions can only be done safely and correctly in a state of mutual exclusion. If mutual exclusion did not apply it is possible that a waiting thread is changing its state to waiting at the same time that a notifying thread is changing its state to running, or two threads might attempt to enter themselves in the same position in the waiting queue. To prevent these and other similar problems, the wait and notify operations require that they can only be executed by a thread that has locked the object's mutual exclusion lock.

The `wait` method, the `notify` method, and their variants can be used in any class because these methods are defined in the java.lang. Object class as shown in the partial definition of this class presented in Figure 9.16. Recall that all classes are either implicitly or explicitly derived from the java.lang. Object class. In addition to the simple `wait` method explained above, two variants of the `wait` method allow the thread to bound its waiting time by specifying a time-out interval in either milliseconds or a combination of milliseconds and nanoseconds. Waiting with a time-out interval guarantees a thread that it will be allowed to

```
public class Object
{
  //...
  public void wait();
  public void wait(long milliseconds);
  public void wait(long milliseconds, int nanoseconds);

  public void notify();
  public void notifyAll();

  //...
}
```

Figure 9.16 The Condition Synchronization Methods Defined in the Object Class

continue its execution within the specified time interval. However, at the end of the time-out interval the waiting thread cannot be guaranteed that the condition on which it is waiting is valid. Usually, reaching the end of the time-out interval means that the waiting thread must take some alternative action because the awaited condition has not been found to hold within a "reasonable" amount of time. A common example of using the time-out interval is in the case of a thread timing out if a server does not respond for a lengthy time. This behavior is evident in web browsers that discontinue attempting to load a page from an unresponsive server.

In addition to the `notify` method explained above, there is a variant, `notifyAll`. The `notify` operation awakens one waiting thread whereas `notifyAll` awakens all of the threads on the object's waiting queue. The `notifyAll` is often used to construct a "barrier" form of synchronization. An example of barrier synchronization is the classic reader-writer problem. In the reader-writer problem, a shared database is accessed by several "reader" threads and several "writer" threads. One synchronization requirements is that no reader should be reading the database while a writer is updating the database. Readers attempting a read operation while writing is in progress use the `wait` operation to defer their execution until the writer finishes. When the writing thread completes it can use the `notifyAll` to awaken all blocked threads, allowing each reader thread among them to continue. A second synchronization requirement—that no two writers can be updating the database at the same time—involves only simple mutual exclusion.

Condition Synchronization in the Ecological Simulation

A modified Prey class in a third version (EcoSim3) of the ecological simulation uses condition synchronization to synchronize the movement of a prey with the hunting of a predator. The synchronization imposes two conditions: first, the Prey cannot move once the Predator begins to hunt it and second, the Predator must wait to hunt a Prey that is moving. Both of these conditions are taken into account in the revised code of the Prey class shown in Figure 9.17. Two boolean

```
public class Prey extends Thread
{
  //...

  private boolean beingHunted;
  private boolean moving;
  public Prey(EcoWorld env)
  { //...
    beingHunted = false;
    moving = false;
  }

  private synchronized void move()
  { try
    { while(beingHunted) wait();}
    catch(InterruptedException ie) {}
    moving = true;
    //...
    moving = false;
    notify();
  }

  public synchronized void hold()
  {
    try
    { if (moving) wait();
    } catch (InterruptedException ie){}
    beingHunted = true;
  }

  public synchronized void release ()
  {
    beingHunted = false;
    notify();
  }

  public  void run()
  { while(true)
    { try
      { move();
        sleep(SLEEP_TIME);
      }
      catch (InterruptedException ie )
    }
  }
  //...
}
```

Figure 9.17 The Prey Class in EcoSim3

variables are used to record the state of the Prey: `beingHunted` and `moving`. The `beingHunted` variable indicates whether or not the prey is currently being hunted by a predator. The `beingHunted` value is initialized to false, set to true by the `hold` method, and set to false by the `release` method. The `moving` variable indicates whether the Prey is in the process of moving to a new location. The moving value is initialized to false, set to true before changing its location in the move method, and set to false as the last step in the move method.

The move method is modified so that a Prey thread will defer its execution if the Prey object is being hunted. The first step in the move method causes the Prey thread to wait if the beingHunted value indicates that the prey is being hunted by a predator and is, therefore, not free to change its location. When the Prey thread is allowed to continue, it sets the moving variable to true—indicating that it is changing to a new location—until the move has been completed. A waiting Prey thread is allowed to continue as a by-product of the Prey object's release method being called. The release method changes the Prey object's state to indicate that the prey is free to move and uses the notify method to awaken a blocked Prey thread. A Predator thread executes the Prey object's hold method. If the Predator thread finds that the Prey object is moving (i.e., moving is true) it waits until the Prey is stationary. The Predator thread is awakened by the notify operation performed by the Prey thread when the Prey thread completes the move method. The awakened Predator thread then sets the beingHunted variable to true to prevent the Predator object's location from changing again until the Predator thread has completed its use of the Prey object. When the Predator thread is finished with the Prey object it calls the Prey object's release method that simply sets beingHunted back to false and performs a notify operation to awaken the Prey thread if its waiting to change the location of the Prey object.

The hold and release methods introduced in the modified Prey class are used to sychronizing the movement of the prey with the hunting of the predators. The revised EcoWorld class, shown in Figure 9.18, uses these methods in the huntPrey method. Notice that on each iteration of the loop the hold and release methods are used to synchronize the executing Predator thread with the thread of the Prey object being examined on that iteration. The use of the hold and release methods, together with the condition synchronization in the Prey class, guarantees the desired synchronization between the Predator and Prey threads.

9.3.3 ThreadGroups

Threads can be organized into groups to facilitate their management. When threads are placed into a group a single operation applied to the group is in turn applied to each thread in the group. The java.lang. ThreadGroups class implements the concept of a group of threads. Some of the operation defined by the ThreadGroup class are shown in Figure 9.19. Each ThreadGroup is given a name that serves to identify that group. The group's name is useful to distinguish among different groups when there are multiple groups. Various properties of the group can be obtained by query methods. A group's name is returned by the getName method. The activeCount and enumerate methods return the number of active threads in the group and an array of these threads, respectively. For

```
public class EcoWorld
{
  //...
  private Vector predators;
  private Vector prey;

  private int distanceBetween(Prey prey, Predator predator)
  {
   //...
  }

  synchronized public void huntPrey(Predator aPredator)
  { for(int i=0; i<prey.size(); i++)
    { Prey aPrey = (Prey)prey.elementAt(i);
      aPrey.hold();
      if (distanceBetween(aPrey, aPredator) < Predator.CAPTURE_ZONE)
      { aPrey.stop();
        prey.removeElementAt(i);
        return;
      }
      aPrey.release();
    }

  }
}
```

Figure 9.18 Using the Synchronized Prey Class Methods

```
public class ThreadGroup
{
  ThreadGroup(String name);
  public int activeCount();
  public int enumerate(Thread[] list);
  public final String getName();
  //...
  public final void resume();
  public final void stop();
  public final void suspend();
  //...
}
```

Figure 9.19 The `java.lang.ThreadGroup` Class

managing the entire group of threads the ThreadGroup class defines three management methods: `suspend`, `resume`, and `stop`. When invoked, each of these management methods are applied to all threads in the group. Somewhat surprisingly the ThreadGroup class does not provide a method that starts all the threads in a group. However, as shown in the EcoSim3 example given later, a list of threads in a group can be obtained by the enumerate method and the `start` method applied iteratively to each individual thread in this list.

An individual thread is added to a thread group when its Thread object is constructed and it remains in the group for its entire lifetime. Thus, the organization of threads into groups is static; threads cannot remove themselves

```
public class Thread
{
  public Thread(ThreadGroup group, String name);
  //...
  public final ThreadGroup getThreadGroup();
  //...
}
```

Figure 9.20 Thread Class Methods Related to Thread Groups

```
public class Predator extends Thread
{
  //...

  private static ThreadGroup predatorGroup = new ThreadGroup("Predators");
  private static int predatorNumber = 0;

  public Predator(EcoWorld env)
  { super(predatorGroup, "preadator"+predatorNumber);
    predatorNumber = predatorNumber + 1;
    //...
  }

  //...

  public static void stopAll()
  { predatorGroup.stop();
  }

  public static void startAll()
  { int size = predatorGroup.activeCount();
    Thread[] predators = new Thread[size];
    predatorGroup.enumerate(predators);
    for(int i=0; i<predators.length; i++)
       predators[i].start();
  }
}
```

Figure 9.21 Using a ThreadGroup in the Predator Class

from a group nor can they migrate among groups. Figure 9.20 shows two methods of the Thread class related to ThreadGroups. The Thread constructor shown here takes two arguments: the ThreadGroup of which the Thread will be a member, and a name for the String that can be used to identify the thread among all other threads in the group. The group of which the thread is a member is returned by the `getThreadGroup` method.

Two thread groups are used in the EcoSim3 system, one for Predator threads and one for Prey threads, to simplify the stopping and starting of threads. One of the exercises at the end of this section explores the use of thread groups to pause and resume. The two thread groups are defined and managed within the Predator and Prey classes. The parts of the Predator class related to the ThreadGroup is shown in Figure 9.21. The modifications to the Prey class are similar.

```
public class EcoWorld
{
  //...

  public void start()
  {
    Predator.startAll(); // start all Predator threads
    Prey.startAll();     // start all Prey threads
  }

  public void stop()
  { Predator.stopAll();  // stop all Predator threads
    Prey.stopAll();      // stop all Prey threads
  }
  //...
}
```

Figure 9.22 Changes in the EcoWorld Class

A single ThreadGroup object is constructed as a static member of the Predator class so that it can be shared by all Predator threads. A static integer is also defined that is used to construct unique names for each Predator thread. When a Predator object is constructed, the `super(...)` syntax is used to pass to the Thread class constructor the ThreadGroup object, which this Predator thread should be a member of and a distinguishing name for the thread. By incrementing the `predatorNumber` in the constructor, the distinguishing names have the form: "predator0", "predator1", "preadator2", and so on. The utility of the ThreadGroup is seen in the Predator class's `stopAll` method. By invoking the single `stop` method on the `predatorGroup`, all of the Predator threads will be stopped. The programming of the `startAll` method is slightly longer because, as noted above, the ThreadGroup class does not provide a method to start all of the threads in the group. The Predator class's `startAll` method first creates an uninitialized array whose length is equal to that of the number of active threads in the group. The array is initialized by the ThreadGroup's `enumerate` method. Iteratively, each individual thread in the initialized array is then started.

The thread groups used in the predator and Prey classes simplify the programming of other parts of the simulation. The revised EcoWorld class is shown in Figure 9.22. This class is responsible to responding to the user pressing the "Start" and "Stop" buttons. These responsibilities can now be satisfied by two lines of code each. The `start` method simply calls that `startAll` method in both the Predator class and the Prey class. Similarly, the `stop` method simply calss the `stopAl` method in both the Predator class and the Prey class.

Exercises

1. Is mutual exclusion simply a special case of condition synchronization. If not, what is the difference? If so, why bother to make the distinction?
2. Write a test program. Make the enter method in TrafficIntersection sleep for 5 seconds and print out different messages to follow the programs execution.
3. Do constructors ever have to be declared as synchronized? Justify your answer with an argument against or an example in favor of.
4. Modify the EcoSim2 so that a Predator will die if it does not capture a prey within a specified number of hunts.
5. Change implementation of EcoSim2 so that there are only two threads —one for all predators and one for all prey. Use only mutual exclusion.
6. Change implementation of EcoSim2 so that there are only two threads —one for all predators and one for all prey. Use condition synchronization.
7. In EcoSim3, remove the synchronized keyword from the Prey class's release method. Observe any run-time errors that occur. Describe the effect of these errors on the simulator and explain why these errors occur.
8. Change the condition synchronization in EcoSim3 so that **no** prey can move while the predators are hunting. The solution involves changes to both the Prey class and the EcoWorld class.
9. Using condition synchronization implement an unbounded buffer. Use a vector. Block if there are no elements.
10. Using condition synchronization implement a bounded buffer. Block if the buffer is full and if there are no elements.
11. Using condition synchronization write a solution to the readers-writers problem.
12. In the EcoSim3 system, why are the Predator class's startAll and stopAll methods declared as static methods?
13. Revise the ecological simulation that uses ThreadGroups so that only one threadgroup is used for all threads.
14. Extend the ecological simulation by adding to the user interface two buttons that allow the simulation to be paused or resumed. Use two ThreadGroups in this extension.

15. Extend the ecological simulation by adding to the user interface two buttons that allow the simulation to be paused or resumed. Use one ThreadGroup in this extension.
16. Add two threads, one that periodically create new Predators and one that periodically creates new Prey. Put these in a thread group that can be paused/resumed by buttons in the user interface.
17. Define, implement, and test a class that extends ThreadGroup that implements a `start` method that starts all the threads in the group. Modify EcoSim3 to use this class.

9.4 Distributed Concurrency

9.4.1 Concepts

In the distributed computing paradigm, programs on one machine are able to interact with programs on a different machine through an underlying data communications network. Distributed computing has been popularized by the World Wide Web, where web browsers obtain information from servers executing on machines around the world by using the physical networks that comprise the Internet as the vehicle for exchanging data. The communications network has little or no sense of the meaning of the data that it conveys, though it takes great care to deliver this data efficiently and reliably. The interacting programs exchange data using a communications protocol, a set of mutually agreed upon conventions and procedures that govern what data is exchanged and how it is exchanged.

Distributed computing is a powerful paradigm because it has several important advantages, such as improved reliability, easier administration, increased performance, and enhanced collaboration. The services and data of a distributed application are often replicated so that the application can continue to operate reliably even if a part of the system fails. If the services and data are fully replicated, the users might detect no loss of system functionality. If the services and data are only partially replicated, the system can continue to function in a reduced service mode. A system that includes numerous different organizations, perhaps even different governments, is easier to administer as a distributed entity. Each organization can structure, manage, and control its part of the system according to its own rules, laws, and preferences. The administrative advantage of a distributed system is clearly evident in the World Wide Web where even individuals have control over their personal web pages. The performance advantage of distributed systems lies in the ability to execute multiple programs at the same time on different machines. When a large computational problem can be subdivided into (at least relatively) independent subproblems,

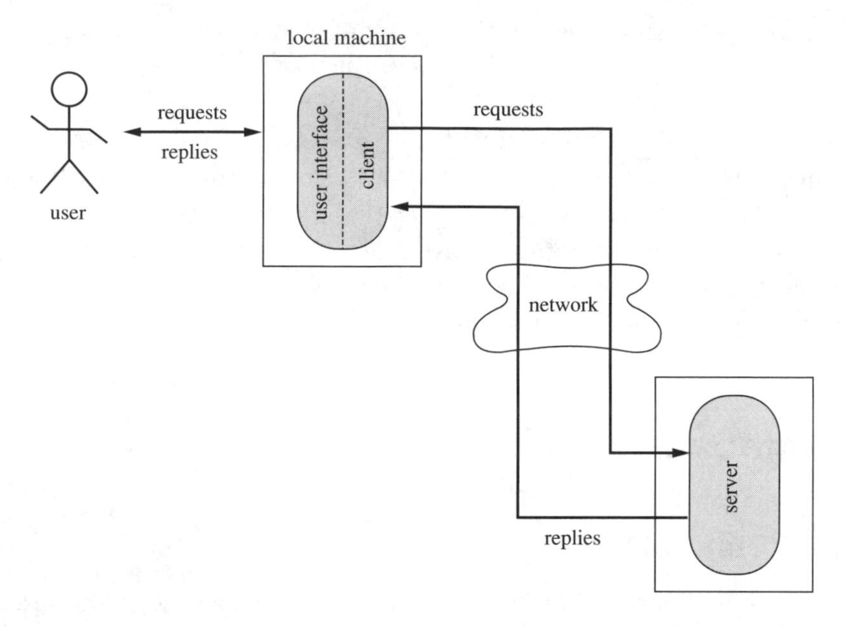

Figure 9.23 The Client-Server Model

the subproblems can be assigned to different machines for execution. The results from each machine may then be combined at a single site to obtain an overall answer. In some cases it is very easy to subdivide a problem. For example, 100 different aircraft designs can be evaluated by assigning one design evaluation problem to each of 100 different machines. These independent evaluations can then be combined to find the best of those 100 alternatives. This approach to high-speed computation is often termed the "network of workstations" or "meta-computing" approach. Finally, a distributed architecture enables the collaboration among people involved in solving a common problem. Increasingly, workers at geographically distant locations need to cooperate in solving a problem. Because much information is delivered through computer-based information systems, it is useful if the interaction, or collaboration, can also be computer-based. Collaborative systems are distributed systems through which individuals on different machines can observe and jointly manipulate shared information (programs, data, documents, visualizations, etc.).

An often-used organization for distributed applications is called the "client-server model." In this model, the "client" software and the "server" software communicate through a network connection, as shown in Figure 9.23, with the client software executing on the user's local machine and the server software executing on a remote machine. The client software implements a user interface and manages all of the direct interaction with the user. To the user, the client software appears to be the entire application: it accepts all inputs and produces all the

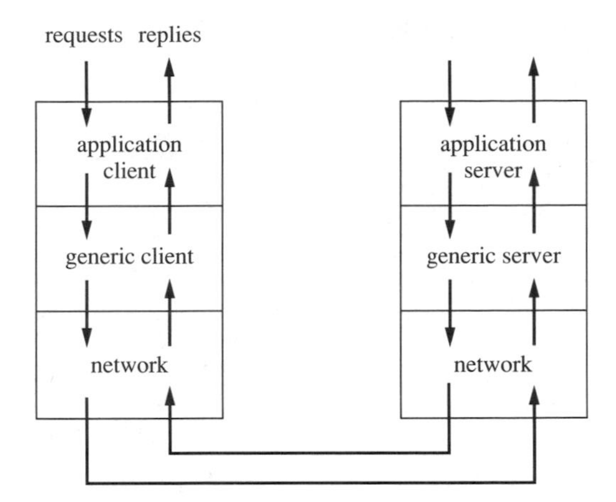

Figure 9.24 Simplified Layered Architecture

output. However, the client software forwards the user's requests to the server and presents to the user the replies received from the server. There are many ways to partition the processing between the client and the server. In some cases, the client simply forwards requests and replies as described above. In other cases, the client performs some of the application processing (e.g., filtering or sorting the server's replies based on a profile of the user known to the client but not to the server).

The architecture of an application using the client-server model usually has several layers. The layers divide the complexity of the entire application into manageable components and provide reuse across different applications. A simpified architecture with three layers is shown in Figure 9.24. A more realistic model often has seven or more layers. In general, each layer uses the services of the layer immediately below it (or the network hardware) to provide its own service to the layer immediately above it (or the user). Each layer has a set of responsibilities that define its role in the architecture. The network layer is responsible for reliably and efficiently delivering data from the client machine to the server machine through the data network. To fulfill its responsibilities the network layer has to deal with such issues as recovering from possible loss of data in the network, delivering received data to the proper layer at its site, ensuring the completeness and integrity of received data, and managing the flow of data so as not to overload the data's receiver. The generic client and generic server layers provides a suite of services that are usable across a broad range of specific applications. The generic layers are responsible for creating a naming system by which clients can identify a desired server in a high-level form, providing a directory system through with servers can register themselves and clients can locate them, and establishing and maintaining the connection between the client and the server even in the case of network failures. The application layers

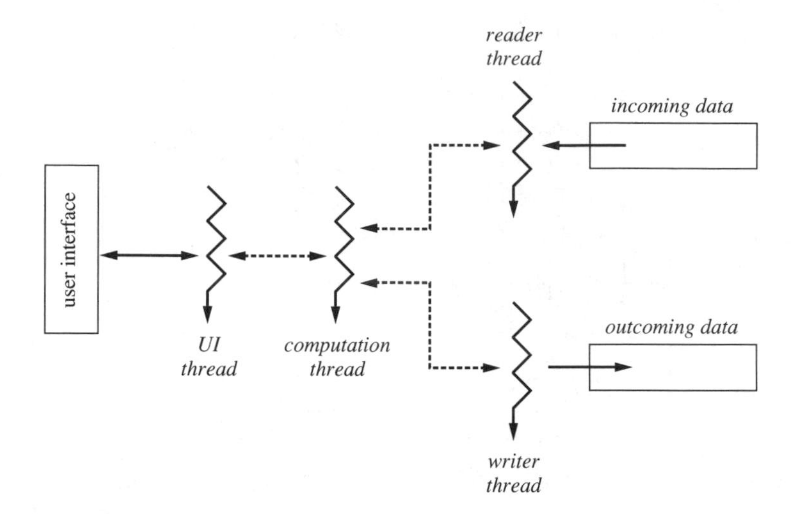

Figure 9.25 Using Threads in a Distributed Application

are responsible for defining and interpreting all of the application-specific data, implementing the required application functionality, and in the case of the application client layer presenting a user interface and managing the interaction with the user. As shown in the figure, a request flows down through the layers on the client side, across the communication network, and up the layers on the server side. The flow of a reply is in the reverse direction. This physical flow creates a logical connection between the application client layer and the application server layer.

Threads are often used in programming distributed applications. The application client layer must often manage multiple interacting activities at the same time. For example, the application client layer must react to the events generated by the user's manipulation of the user interface, update the user interface as needed to reflect the application's changing state, perform the applications basic computation, and send data to and/or receive data from one or more servers. These activities often take place on very different time scales. Data arrives at a much faster rate than user interface events and usually cannot be scheduled or predicted in advance. The application cannot control when the user will perform a given action and the arrival of data is unpredictable because of varying network delays. A separate thread is often used for each distinct activity. Synchronization among the threads is provided so that each thread's action are performed harmoniously with respect to the overall operation of the application. A typical case is shown in Figure 9.25 where four threads are used to structure the application client layer. One thread, the *UI thread*, is responsible for managing the user interface. Two threads, the *reader thread* and the *writer thread*, are used to manage the data communicated over the network to and from the server.

A fourth thread, the *computation thread*, performs the main work of the application. The dashes lines among the threads represent synchronization relationships. For example, the data generated by the *application thread* might be passed to the *writer thread* or data received by the *reader thread* might need to be delivered to the *computation thread*. This passing of data among threads requires the threads to be synchronized.

9.4.2 Sockets

The services provided by the network layer are often presented to an application in the form of an abstraction called a socket. A socket is a bidirectional conduit of data between two processes. Data written at one end of the socket may be read at the other end of the socket. Data may flow in opposite directions in the socket at the same time without interference. The logical structure of the socket is pictured in Figure 9.26. A socket provides reliable, sequenced, stream-oriented delivery of data. The delivery of data is reliable in that all data written to the socket is guaranteed to be delivered to the receiving end, barring a catastrophic, unrecoverable network failure. The socket's data delivery is sequenced in that the order of the data as it is written is preserved by the socket. A socket is a stream-oriented mechanism. Data may be read from the socket without regard for, and without knowledge of, how the data was inserted into the socket by the sender. For example, a receiver reading the 11-byte string "Hello World," cannot tell if these 11 bytes were written by a single write operation, by two write operations (one writing the 6-byte string "Hello" and a second writing the 5-byte string "World"), or by 11 write operations each writing a single byte.

The protocol used by a client and a server to interact through a socket involves three phases: connection, transfer, disconnection. The three phases and the operations involved in each phase are shown in Figure 9.27. The server begins the connection phase by performing an *accept* operation that announces its willingness to establish a connection with a client. The *accept* operation blocks the server until a connection has been established. The client's first step is to perform the *connect* operation that seeks to establish the connection. The

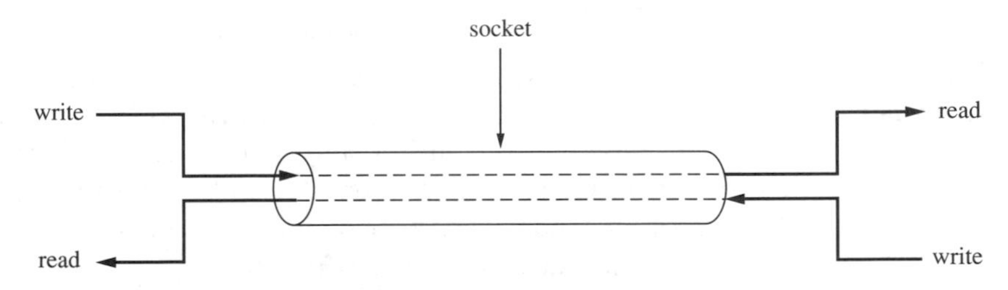

Figure 9.26 A Conceptual View of a Socket

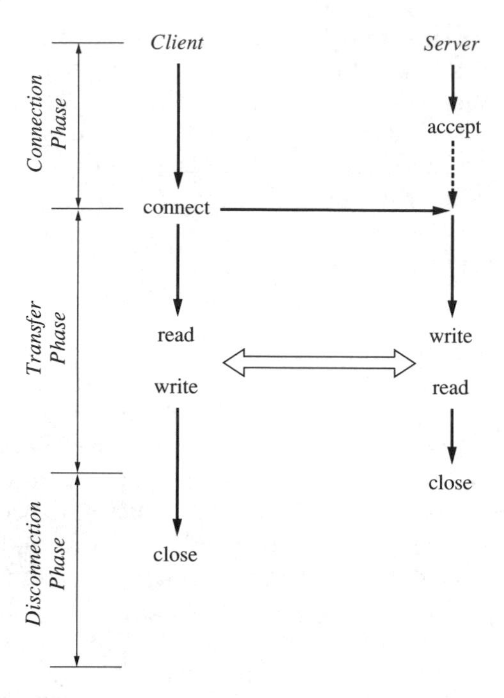

Figure 9.27 Socket Operations

server must perform its step first; the *connect* operation will fail if it is performed before the server has performed the *accept* operation. Once the connection is established the connection phase is completed and the transfer phase begins. In the transfer phase, the client and the server exchange data through the socket using *read* and *write* operations. The sequencing of these operations, the meaning of the data exchanged, and the length of the transfer phase is determined solely by the client and the server application code. The *read* operation on one end of the socket will block if there is no data available to read; it will unblock when data has been transmitted through the socket via a *write* operation performed at the other end. A *write* operation will block if a large amount of unread data has accumulated in the socket. Such blocking is used to guard against excessive buffer space being used at the receiving end of the socket. The *write* operation will unblock when a sufficient part of the accumulated data has been read. The transfer phase ends and the disconnection phase begins when one of the parties performs a *close* operation announcing that it will perform no further operations on the socket. Any data in the socket may still be read by the other party, but no further *write* operations are allowed. An end of file indication is returned when all of the data has been read. Which side performs the *close* operation first is a matter for the application designer.

During the connection phase, the client and server use a simple two-part names to identify the connection they wish to establish. This name is necessary

```
public class ServerSocket
{ //...
  public ServerSocket(int port) throws IOException;
  public Socket accept() throws IOException;
}

public class Socket
{
  //...
  public Socket(String host, int port)throws UnKnownHostException,
                                              IOException;
  public void close() throws IOException;
  public InputStream getInputStream() throws IOException;
  public OutputStream getOuputStream() throws IOException;
}
```

Figure 9.28 Socket Operations

because there are many clients and server, all operating simultaneously on a large network and the two-part name allows the network to know which client and which server should be connected. The two-part name of a socket connection is analogous to a phone number that also has a two-part name: a three-digit area code and a seven-digit number in the American telephone system. For two parties to talk, the called party must have the phone with a given area code and number and the caller must use that same area code and number. In the client-server case, the server announces to the network its two-part name in the *accept* operation; the client must use that same two-part name in performing the *connect* operation. The socket's two-part name consists of a hostname and a port number. The hostname is simply the network name of the machine on which the server is running (e.g., cs.vt.edu). The port number is an arbitrary positive integer value (e.g., 6598). User's port numbers should be chosen larger than 5000 to avoid accidental conflict with assigned port numbers less than 5000 used by standard servers (e.g., the ftp server and the http server). Servers on the same machine must also be given unique port numbers. An *accept* operation will fail if it uses a port number that is already in use on that machine.

The Java package `java.net` contains classes used in network programming including two classes for programming with sockets: Socket and ServerSocket. The principal methods of these two classes are summarized in Figure 9.28. The server uses the ServerSocket class whereas both the client and the server use the Socket class. The ServerSocket methods and the Socket constructor are used during the connection phase. The Socket class is used during the transfer and disconnection phases.

A connection between a server and client is established as follows. The ServerSocket constructor specifies the port number portion of the two-part name of the socket on which the server will listen for incoming connection requests. The hostname portion of the two-part name is the machine on which the server is executing. The ServerSocket constructor throws an IOException if an invalid port number has been specified. The `accept` method is used by the server to wait for a connection to be established. This method blocks the server until a client establishes a connection. The `accept` method returns a Socket object to the server that the server will use to communicate with the client whose connection has just been accepted. The Socket class is used by both the client and the server. The *connection* operation is performed when the client constructs a Socket object. The Socket constructor specifies the two-part name of the connection that the client wishes to establish. The connection will be established if and only if a server is listening on the specific host machine and at the specified port number. The Socket constructor throws exceptions if the specified host machine cannot be located or if the connection cannot be established.

Once a socket connection has been made between the client and the server, each side has a Socket object: the client's Socket object was obtained by using the Socket constructor and the server's Socket object was obtained as a returned result from the `accept` method. These two Socket objects are used during the transfer and disconnection phases. The Socket class does not directly provide read and write methods to transfer data through the socket. Instead, two methods are provided that return an InputStream from which data may be read from the socket and an OutputStream to which data may be written to the socket. The socket's InputStream and OutputStream may be combined with the other I/O classes to provide a higher level interface for transferring data in text, binary, or object form. The revised ecological simulator presented below gives one example of this combination. The disconnection phase is supported by the Socket class's `close` method. Once the `close` operation has been performed the Socket object cannot be used for further data transfer operations.

9.4.3 EcoSim Example

The ecological simulator will be revised as a simple client-server application whose overall architecture is shown in Figure 9.29. The architecture has three layers: the bottom-most layer is the network services provided by the socket implementation in the `java.net` package. The middle layer consists of the reader and writer components of the client and the server. These readers and writers are concerned with the passing of application data between the client and the server but are largely unaware of how this data was generated or how it will be used. The top layer contains the application logic and, on the client side, the user interface. This system uses threads in two ways. First, the ServerWorld component uses a thread to drive the simulation as in previous versions. Although not shown in the architecture, threads are also used in the classes that represent the predators and the prey on the server. Second, threads are used to manage the transfer of data from the server to the client. The `ServerReader` and the `ClientReader` components are both threaded. As explained above, these reader threads can block awaiting the arrival of data without blocking the other activities of the client or server.

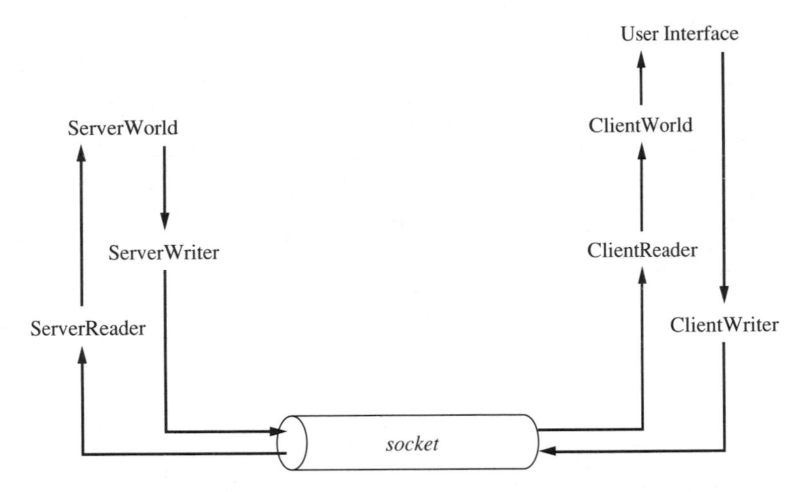

Figure 9.29 Structure of the Client-Server Ecological Simulator

The responsibilities of classes in the simulation are revised to conform to their role in the client-server architecture. In general, the server-side components are responsible for the computational aspects of the system whereas the client-side components are responsible for the user interface. For example, the single Predator and Prey classes are divided into client-side (ClientPredator, ClientPrey) and server-side (ServerPredator, ServerPrey) classes. The server-side classes are responsible for computing the state of and the interactions among the individual predator and prey objects. However, the server-side classes have no method for presenting this information in the user interface as that is strictly a client-side issue. Correspondingly, the client-side classes are responsible for presenting the predator and prey objects in the user interface, but they have no computational responsibilities.

Connection Phase: The connection phase of the client-server simulator involves two steps. First, the server is started on a given host. For this example it is assumed that the name of the host is `craig.vt.edu`. The command to execute the server specifies the port number of the socket that will be used to communicate with the client. If the port number is `6789`, the command would look like

```
java EcoSimServer 6789
```

Because the server is executing on craig.vt.edu, the complete two-part name of the socket is (`craig.vt.edu`, `6789`). After the server has been started, the client is executed using the command

```
java EcoSimClient craig.vt.edu 6789
```

```
public class EcoSimServer
{
  private static ServerWorld environment;

  public static void main(String args[])
  { int portNumber = Integer.parseInt(args[0]);
    environment = new ServerWorld(portNumber);

    // create initial predators and prey ...

    environment.start();
  }
}

public class ServerWorld extends Thread
{
  private ServerWriter serverWriter;
  private ServerReader serverReader;
  private int portNumber;
  private Socket client = null;
  //...

  public ServerWorld(String portNumber)
  { this.portNumber = portNumber;
    //...other initializations
  }

  public void run()
  { try
    { ServerSocket connection = new ServerSocket(portNumber);
      client = connection.accept();
    } catch (IOException ioe) {}

    serverWriter = new ServerWriter(client);
    serverReader = new ServerReader(this, client);

    serverReader.start();

    //...
  }
  //...
}
```

Figure 9.30 Server's Code for the Connection Phase

The client specifies the complete two-part name for the socket. For testing purposes it is often easier to run the server and the client on the same machine. On many systems, the name `localhost` can be used as the host name when running the client and the server on the same machine.

The connection code in the server is shown in Figure 9.30. As shown earlier, the server's command line argument is the port number represented as a String. The `main` method of the EcoSimServer class parses the command line argument and uses the resulting `int` value to construct a ServerWorld object. The Server-World object's constructor records the port number and performs other initializa-

```
public class EcoSimClient
{
  private static ClientWorld environment;
  public static void main(String args[])
  { String serverName = args[0];
    int portNumber = Integer.parseInt(args[1]);
    environment = new ClientWorld(serverName, portNumber);
  }
}

public class ClientWorld
{
  //...
  private ClientReader reader;
  private ClientWriter writer;

  public ClientWorld(String serverName, int portNumber)
  { //...
    try
    {  Socket server = new Socket(serverName , portNumber);
       reader = new ClientReader(this, server);
       writer = new ClientWriter(server);
    } catch (UnknownHostException uhe) {}
      catch (IOException ioe) {}
  }
  //...

}
```

Figure 9.31 Client's Code for the Connection Phase

tions. The `main` method's last step is to `start` the ServerWorld. Because the ServerWorld class extends Thread, the inherited `start` method will create a new thread that executes the `run` method of the ServerWorld. The first actions of the `run` method are to create a ServerSocket using the port number recorded earlier by ServerWorld's constructor and to perform an `accept` on this ServerSocket object. The `accept` will block until a client connects to the server. The client code is shown later. When the connection is established, the `accept` method returns to the server a Socket object that can be used to communicate with the client. This socket is used to construct the ServerWriter and ServerReader objects. The ServerReader is also a threaded object, so its thread is `started`. At this point the server is connected to the client and is ready to begin the transfer phase.

The client's code for the connection phase is shown in Figure 9.31. The `main` method of the EcoSimClient uses two command line argument that, as shown above, correspond to the host name and the port number of the socket to be created. The `main` method parses the second argument as an `int` value and uses the host name `String` and the `int` port number to construct a ClientWorld object. The constructor of the ClientWorld object uses the host name and port number information to create a Socket object. This Socket object construction performs the necessary steps to connect to the waiting server. After establishing the connection to the server, the Socket object is used to create a ClientWriter and a ClientReader; these two objects will use the socket connection to transfer data to and from the server.

At the end of the connection phase the client and the server each have created a socket object that represents its end of the data communications channel between them. The client and the server have each created a pair of reader and writer objects ready to transmit data across the channel. Both the client and the server are ready but passive at this point, waiting for the user to initiate the simulation by pressing the "Start" button in the user interface. When the user presses the "Start" button the transfer phase begins in which the simulation is computed by the server and displayed by the client.

Transfer Phase: The transfer phase operates in the following way. Commands enter by the user, using the "Start" and "Stop" buttons in the user interface, cause the user interface to send a string representing the command via the ClientWriter to the ServerReader; the ServerReader parses the received string and invokes an appropriate method in the ServerWorld object. When the ServerWorld receives a command to start, it begins periodically sending the current state of the simulation (the information about each predator and prey object) to the client using the ServerWrite and ClientReader components; the received predator and prey information is accumulated in vectors held by the ClientWorld object, which uses this information to update the user interface.

The transfer phase is initiated when the user presses the "Start" button. The client code reacts to these button push events by calling the `start` method or the `stop` method, respectively, in the ClientWorld. As shown in Figure 9.32, the ClientWorld invokes the methods `startServer` and `stopServer` in the ClientWriter object to notify the server of the action taken by the user. In the connection phase, the ClientWorld constructed the ClientWriter object with the Socket object that represents the data channel to the server as a constructor argument. The ClientWriter obtains an OutputStream from the socket using the `getOutputStream` method, and constructs a PrintStream with which it will write text formatted data to the server. The `startServer` and `stopServer` methods simply write the string "start" and "stop", respectively, to the PrintStream and flush the PrintStream to insure the timely delivery of the data to the server. In addition, when the "Start" button is pushed, the ClientWorld object starts the ClientReader object. The ClientReader object is a threaded object; its `start` method causes it to begin an independent thread of control that reads data from the server and passes it to the ClientWorld for display. The ClientReader will be examined in more detail below.

Data is read by the server's ServerReader object. This object will receive the "start" and "stop" text strings from the client. The ServerReader is shown in Figure 9.33. The ServerReader was constructed by the ServerWorld, having as one of it constructor arguments the Socket representing the data channel to the client. The ServerReader is a threaded object whose `run` method reads successive strings from the client. The input stream is constructed in three steps:

```
public class ClientWorld
{
  //...
  private ClientReader reader;
  private ClientWriter writer;
  public void start()
  { reader.start();
    writer.startServer();
  }
  public void stop()
  { writer.stopServer();
  }
  //...
}

public class ClientWriter
{ private PrintWriter outputStream;
  public ClientWriter(Socket server)
  { try
    { outputStream = new PrintWriter(server.getOutputStream());
    } catch (IOException ioe) {}
  }
  public void startServer()
  { outputStream.println("start");
    outputStream.flush();
  }
  public void stopServer()
  { outputStream.println("stop");
    outputStream.flush();
  }
}
```

Figure 9.32 Sending Commands Using the ClientWriter

1) obtaining an InputStream object from the Socket object, 2) constructing an InputStreamReader object using the InputStream object, and 3) constructing a StreamTokenizer using the InputStreamReader object. Once the StreamTokenizer is created, strings are read from the data channel using the `nextToken` method of the StreamTokenizer in the ServerReader's `readString` method. The `startSimulation` and `stopSimulation` methods of the ServerWorld object are invoked when the "start" and "stop" string, respectively, are read from the data channel. The important aspect of this code is the way in which a high-level interface is created for parsing the contents of the data passed to the server from the client.

The other half of the transfer phase involves sending simulation data from the server to client. Such data is written to the socket by a ServerWriter object and read from the socket by a ClientReader object. The code for a ServerWriter is shown in Figure 9.34. To write text formatted data to the socket, the ServerWriter creates a PrintStream object that is constructed using the OutputStream obtained from the socket using the `getOutputStream` method. In the ServerWriter's `write` method, the PrintStream is passed to each predator and prey object; each of these object will write their representation into

```
public class ServerReader extends Thread
{
  private ServerWorld environment;
  private Socket client;

  public ServerReader(ServerWorld env, Socket client)
  { environment = env;
    this.client = client;
  }

  private String readString(StreamTokenizer stream)
  { try
    { stream.nextToken();
    } catch (IOException ioe) {}
    return stream.sval;
  }

  public void run()
  { StreamTokenizer clientData = null;
    try
    { clientData = new StreamTokenizer(
                        new InputStreamReader(
                            client.getInputStream() ));
      clientData.eolIsSignificant(false);
    } catch (IOException ioe) {}

    String command = readString(clientData);
    while (! command.equals("stop"))
    { if (command.equals("start")) environment.startSimulation();
        command = readString(clientData);
    }
    environment.stopSimulation();
  }

}
```

Figure 9.33 Reading Commands Using the ServerReader

the data channel to the client using the PrintStream's methods. As an example, the `write` method of the ServerPredator class is also shown. This method receives the PrintWriter object that is connected to the socket and uses the `print` and `println` method of the PrintWriter to send to the client through the socket a representation of each predator and prey (a code differentiating predators from prey, and the x and y coordinates). After all of the predator and prey objects have been written to the Socket, the `END_UPDATE` code is sent to the client so that the client knows that all of the predators and prey have been sent. Another code, `END_DATA`, is sent to inform the client that no further data will be transmitted over the socket. This code is sent when the ServerWriter's close method is called by the ServerReader after the ServerReader receives a "stop" string from the client.

The final part of the transfer phase is the reading of the predator and prey data by the ClientReader. The ClientReader is similar to the ServerReader in two respects: they are both threaded objects so that they can block attempting to

```
public class ServerWriter
{
  private PrintWriter outputStream;
  private static final int END_UPDATE = 100;
  private static final int END_DATA   = 101;

  public ServerWriter(Socket client)
  {
    try
    { outputStream = new PrintWriter(client.getOutputStream());
    } catch (IOException ioe) {}
  }

  public void write(Vector predators, Vector prey)
  {
    for(int i=0; i<predators.size(); i++)
    { ServerPredator predator = (ServerPredator)predators.elementAt(i);
      predator.write(outputStream);
    }

    for(int i=0; i<prey.size(); i++)
    { ServerPrey aPrey = (ServerPrey)prey.elementAt(i);
     aPrey.write(outputStream);
    }

    outputStream.println(END_UPDATE);
    outputStream.flush();
  }

  public void close()
  { outputStream.println(END_DATA);
    outputStream.close();
  }

}

public class ServerPredator extends Thread
{
  //...
  private int x;
  private int y;
  //...

  public void write(PrintWriter writer)
  { writer.print(PREDATOR_CODE);
    writer.print("  ");
    writer.print(x);
    writer.print("  ");
    writer.println(y);
  }

  //...
}
```

Figure 9.34 Sending Simulation Data Using the ServerWriter

read data from the socket without interfering with the other activities of their respective sides, and they both uses the same techniques to create a higher-level

```
public class ClientReader extends Thread
{
  private ClientWorld environment;
  private static final int END_UPDATE    = 100;
  private static final int END_DATA      = 101;
  private Socket server;

  public ClientReader(ClientWorld env, Socket server)
  { environment = env;
    this.server = server;
  }

  private int readInt(StreamTokenizer stream)
  { try
    { stream.nextToken();
    } catch(IOException ioe) {}
    return (int)stream.nval;
  }

  public void run()
  { StreamTokenizer serverData = null;
    try
    { serverData = new StreamTokenizer(
                     new InputStreamReader(
                         server.getInputStream() ));
      serverData.eolIsSignificant(false);
    } catch (IOException ioe) {}

    int command = readInt(serverData);
      while (command != END_DATA)
      {  Vector predators = new Vector();
         Vector prey = new Vector();
        while (command != END_UPDATE)
        {  int x = readInt(serverData);
           int y = readInt(serverData);
           if(command == ClientPredator.PREDATOR_CODE)
              predators.addElement(new ClientPredator(x,y));
           if(command == ClientPrey.PREY_CODE)
              prey.addElement(new ClientPrey(x,y));
           command = readInt(serverData);
        }
        environment.update(predators, prey);
        command = readInt(serverData);
      }

     try
     { server.close();
     } catch (IOException ioe) {}
  }
}
```

Figure 9.35 Receiving Simulation Data in the ClientReader

interface for reading data from the socket. The main activity of the ClientReader is defined in its `run` method given in Figure 9.35. Recall that the thread in the ClientReader object was `start`'ed when the user pressed the "Start" button in the user interface (see the `start` method in the ClientWorld class that is called by the event handling method in the ClientFrame class). As shown in the boldface code, the ClientReader obtains an InputStream from the Socket object with which the ClientReader was constructed. This InputStream is used to construct a an InputStreamReader that is itself used to construct a StreamTokenizer for parsing the input data arriving in the socket connection. Using the StreamTokenizer, successive `int` values are read from the socket and interpreted in one of four ways: the `END_DATA` value causes the ClientReader to cease reading from the socket; the `END_UPDATE` value signifies that all of the predator and prey data has been read for a given simulation state and the accumulated predator and prey data is reported by calling the `update` method in the ClientWorld object; the `PREDATOR_CODE` value indicates that the x and y coordinate data in the input stream should be used to construct a `Predator` object that is added to the vector of received predators; the `PREY_CODE` value indicates that the x and y coordinate data in the input stream should be used to construct a Prey object that is added to the vector of received prey. The integer codes and the integer x and y coordinates are read using the `readInt` convenience method.

Disconnection Phase: The disconnection phase is begun when the user presses the "Stop" button in the user interface. The steps in the disconnection phase are pictured in Figure 9.36. The numbered arrows represent the sequence of steps to close both ends of the socket connection, thus disconnecting the client and the server. These step are:

1. The user pushes the "Stop" button in the user interface.
2. The event handling code in the ClientFrame calls the `stop` method in the ClientWorld.
3. The ClientWorld object invokes the `stopServer` method in the ClientWriter.
4. The ClientWriter object send the text string "stop" through the socket to the server.
5. The "stop" string is read by the `ServerReader` which calls the `stopSimulation` method in the ServerWorld.
6. The ServerWorld object invokes the `close` method in the ServerWriter.
7. The ServerWriter sends the `END_DATA` code to the client.

After sending the `END_DATA` code in step 7 the ServerWriter also closes the OutputStream, thus closing its end of the socket connection. When the ClientReader reads the `END_DATA` code, it closes its end of the socket connection. Because both ends of the socket connection have been closed, the connection between the client and the server has been terminated.

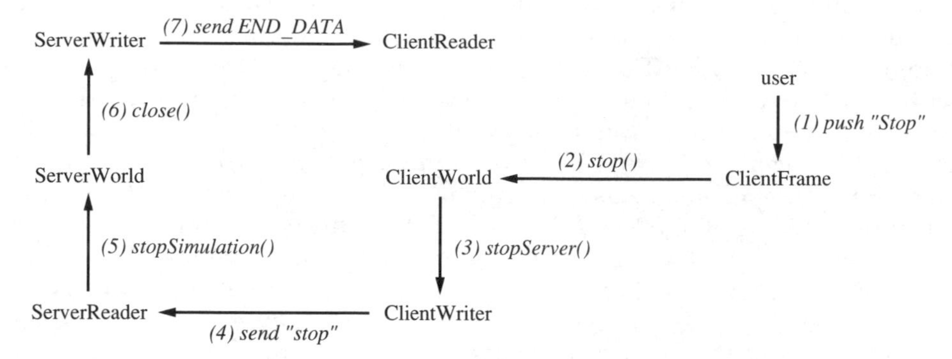

Figure 9.36 Steps in the Disconnection Phase

Exercises

1. Trace the sequence of events that happen during the connection phase and draw a number diagram similar to the one above (Steps in the Disconnection Phase).
2. Trace the sequence of events that happen when the server wants to update the client's view of the simulation and draw a number diagram similar to the one above (Steps in the Disconnection Phase).
3. Trace the sequence of events that happen during the disconnection phase and determine at what point the threads in the Predator and Prey objects are stopped.
4. Modify the EcoSim4 server so that up to two clients can connect to the server and see the same simulation. The simulation begins when the first client connects to the server. The second client to connect sees the simulation from whatever state the simulation happens to be in at the time that it connects to the server. The clients may disconnect in either order at any time. The server terminates when it has no more clients.
5. Modify EcoSim4 server so that up to two clients can connect to the server and see independent simulations. Each client sees a different simulation. The clients may disconnect in either order at any time. The server terminates when it has no more clients.
6. Modify the EcoSim4 client and server so that data conveyed in the socket is in binary format and not text format.

7. Modify the EcoSim4 client and server so that data is read from and written to the socket using and object I/O format.
8. Modify the EcoSim4 user interface that it contains a "Pause" button and a "Resume" button that cause the simulation to pause and resume, respectively. Modify the client and server as necessary to accommodate this addition.
9. Modify the EcoSim4 system so that up to two clients can connect to the server and see the same simulation (as in the first exercise) and the user interface of both clients have "Pause" and "Resume" buttons (as in the fourth exercise). When the simulation is running either client can pause the simulation for both clients. When paused, the simulation can be resumed by either client.
10. Modify the EcoSim4 system so that the server's predefined `ServerWorld.Heigth` and `ServerWorld.Width` values can be overridden by the user. Extend the user interface so that the user can select different height and width values that are transmitted to the server. You are free to require that these values be sent before the simulation is started.
11. Modify the EcoSim4 system so that new predators and new prey are introduced into the simulation by user's mouse clicks. For example, a mouse click means to create a new predator at the coordinates of the mouse cursor whereas a shift-click means to create a new prey at the coordinates of the mouse cursor. Modify the client and server components as needed to accommodate this extension.
12. Modify so that new predators and new prey are introduced into the simulation by a thread running in the client. This client thread sleeps for a period of time and then decides whether to introduce a new predator or a new prey and at what coordinates. Modify the client and server components as needed to accommodate this extension.

INDEX